Studies in Renaissance Literature

Volume 44

THE COLLECTED WORKS OF THOMAS KYD

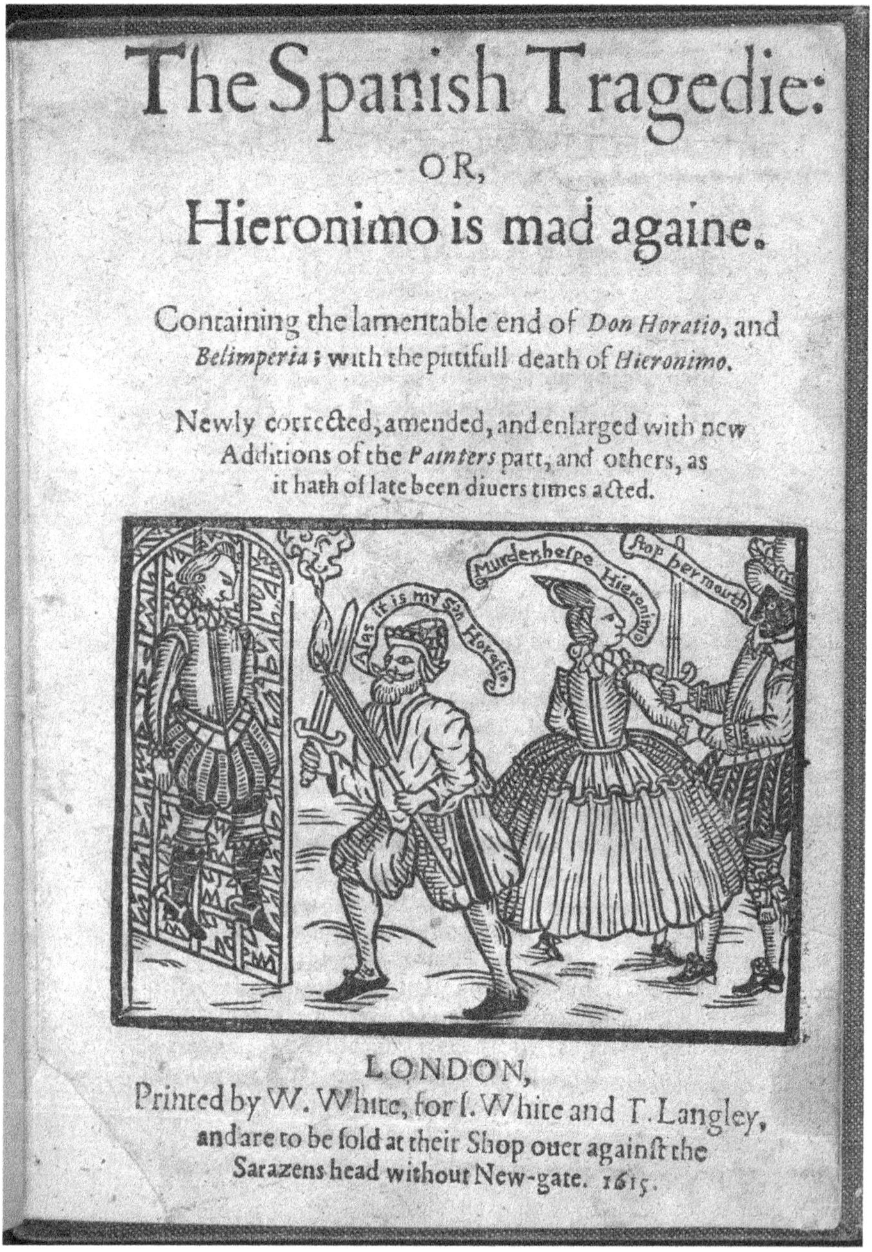

The Spanish Tragedie:
OR,
Hieronimo is mad againe.

Containing the lamentable end of *Don Horatio*, and *Belimperia*; with the pittifull death of *Hieronimo*.

Newly corrected, amended, and enlarged with new Additions of the *Painters* part, and others, as it hath of late been diuers times acted.

LONDON,
Printed by W. White, for I. White and T. Langley, and are to be sold at their Shop ouer against the Sarazens head without New-gate. 1615.

The Murder of Horatio, from the frontispiece of *The Spanish Tragedie: Or Heironimo is mad againe*, Thomas Kyd (1615), British Library C.117.b.36. Image in the Public Domain.

THE COLLECTED WORKS OF THOMAS KYD

Volume One

General Editor: Sir Brian Vickers

Associate Editor: Darren Freebury-Jones

D. S. BREWER

First published 2024
D. S. Brewer, Cambridge

ISBN 978-1-84384-694-9

D. S. Brewer is an imprint of Boydell & Brewer Ltd
PO Box 9, Woodbridge, Suffolk IP12 3DF, UK
and of Boydell & Brewer Inc.
668 Mt Hope Avenue, Rochester, NY 14620-2731, USA
website: www.boydellandbrewer.com

A catalogue record for this title is available
from the British Library

Dedicated to the memory of David Bevington (1931–2019)
Scholar and Shakespeare Editor extraordinary

CONTENTS

List of Illustrations ix

Preface xi

Abbreviations xv

Kyd and the London Theatre, *Brian Vickers* 1

Recognizing Kyd, *Brian Vickers* 39

Verses of Praise and Joy (1586), *ed. Daniel Starza Smith*

Introduction 53

Text 65

Textual Notes 69

Commentary 71

The Spanish Tragedy (1585–87), *ed. Brian Vickers*

Introduction 77

The Persons in the Play 110

Text 111

Textual Notes 210

Commentary 212

The Householder's Philosophy (1588), *ed. Domenico Lovascio*

Introduction 241

Text 259

Textual Notes 303

Commentary 305

Soliman and Perseda (1588–89), *ed. Matthew Dimmock*

Introduction 335

The Persons in the Play 354

Text 355

Textual Notes 434

Commentary 437

King Leir (1589), *ed. Eugene Giddens*

Introduction 467

The Persons in the Play 488

Text *with Authorship Commentary by Darren Freebury-Jones as Footnotes* 489

Textual Notes 586

Commentary 592

ILLUSTRATIONS

Frontispiece: The Murder of Horatio, from the frontispiece of *The Spanish Tragedie: Or Heironimo is mad againe*, Thomas Kyd (1615), British Library C.117.b.36. Image in the Public Domain.

1. Photo of the excavation of Rose Playhouse by the Museum of London Archaeology Unit, 1989. 30

2. Sketch of the ground plan of the Rose theatre, 1587 and 1592, by Walter Hodges, based on the 1989 excavations. Reproduced by permission of the Estate of C. W. Hodges. 31

PREFACE

The only previous attempt to collect Kyd's writings was made by Frederick S. Boas, a well-known historian of early modern drama.[1] Boas included three authentic works: *The Spanish Tragedy*, *Cornelia*, and *The Householder's Philosophy*. Boas rightly included *Soliman and Perseda*, urging its acceptance as genuine (pp. liv–lxi); this was just before Charles Crawford published his definitive attribution (1903). Boas was less judicious when he included the undistinguished prose pamphlet, *The Murder of John Brewen* (1592), which has no resemblance to Kyd. Boas accepted J. P. Collier's attribution on the basis of a signature, 'Tho. Kydd', in one copy: it has since been shown that this was another Collier forgery.[2] Boas forcefully rejected *The First Part of Ieronimo* as spurious (pp. xxix–xliv), but then printed it not as an appendix but in the text (pp. 295–337). Boas had followed up Sidney Lee's discovery of Kyd's first Letter to Puckering, and included a facsimile and a transcript. In an appendix, he included Kyd's *Verses of Praise and Joy* (pp. 339–42), but unkindly dismissed them as 'a specimen of Kyd's non-dramatic hack work' (p. xxv). Boas briefly discussed *Arden of Faversham*, finding it

> as a whole, too nakedly realistic, too free, as the Epilogue claims, from 'filed points' to be in his distinctive vein. Yet, in the cadence and diction of many passages, and in the combination of lyrically elaborate verse-structure with colloquial directness of speech, [it] recalls the manner of Kyd far more nearly than that of Shakespeare, to whom it has been often groundlessly attributed.
>
> (lxxxix–xc)

1 F. S. Boas (ed.), *The Works of Thomas Kyd* (Oxford, 1901). When Oxford University reprinted it unchanged in 1955, Boas added a perfunctory list of 'Corrections and Additions 1902–54' (pp. xxvii–cxxvi).

2 See R. M. Gorrell, 'John Payne Collier and "The Murder of John Brewen"', *MLN* 57 (1942), 441–4.

There are sensitive and perceptive comments in Boas's introduction, but the main weakness of his edition is its careless treatment of Kyd's text. The long critical review by W. W. Greg exposed an embarrassing number of errors.[3]

Kyd has been much more fortunate in editions of single works, such as the 'Revels Plays' editions of *The Spanish Tragedy* by Philip Edwards (1957) and of *Arden of Faversham* by M. L. Wine (1973), and the comparable edition of *The Spanish Tragedy* by Clara Calvo and Jesús Tronch (2013) for 'Arden Early Modern Drama'. While we acknowledge what we have learned from those editions, our aims are different. The priorities of this *Collected Works* are to provide textually accurate modern spelling versions, freshly derived from the original quarto editions, with full commentaries. We do not attempt the complete bibliographical collation that a single-text edition can offer, nor do we provide historical documentation of textual variants and stage directions. Our collations are limited to recording every substantive difference from the original editions, that is, changes in the meaning of the text. Since a main feature of this edition is its inclusion of newly attributed plays, for each of these an Authorship Commentary will be provided. These will document a selection of the most significant verbal matches between the new attributions and Kyd's accepted canon.

It only remains for me to thank all the people who have collaborated on this edition, starting with Boydell and Brewer. I was originally attracted to them partly because of their successful expansion to cover most of the humanities disciplines, partly because of their co-founder, my friend Derek Brewer. We both taught in the Cambridge English Faculty (in my case between 1964 and 1972), and were neighbours on Chesterton Road. Derek was the more senior but welcomed and encouraged his younger colleagues. He and his wife Elizabeth, a fellow medievalist, were a kind and generous couple and it gives me great pleasure to be associated with their memory in a new enterprise. I'm glad to know that Caroline Palmer, the current editorial director, worked very happily with Derek in her earlier career and regards him as her mentor. It has been a pleasure to work with her and Elizabeth McDonald, now the excellent commissioning editor for Studies in Renaissance Literature, who have the welcome but not universal characteristic attitude among publishers of being in a hurry to get a book published. I thank Nick Bingham, deputy head of production, for his efficiency, resourcefulness, and patience.

3 See *Modern Language Quarterly* 4 (1901), 186–90. Greg cited instances of 'a carelessness, not to say an utter indifference to accuracy, which it is impossible to pass over in silence' (187). See also J. Le Gay Brereton, 'Notes on the Text of Kydd', *Englische Studien* 37 (1907), 88–99.

I am extremely grateful to our team of editors, starting with the late David Bevington, an outstanding scholar and uncommonly generous colleague. David told me that he was happy to take on *1 Henry VI*, since it was the first Shakespeare play he edited, for Alfred Harbage's 'Pelican Shakespeare' in 1968. He was equally happy to add *Edward III*, a play he had never edited, showing his constant readiness to face new challenges. He completed this, his last assignment, just before his death and we dedicate the edition to his memory.

In Volume 1, I thank Daniel Starza Smith for editing Kyd's first publication, the *Verses of Praise and Joy* (1586), containing poems in both English and neo-Latin. Kyd demonstrated his linguistic skills again in his translation from Tasso, *The Householder's Philosophy* (1588), here edited by Domenico Lovascio. Matthew Dimmock has edited *Soliman and Perseda* (1588), and Eugene Giddens has been responsible for *King Leir* (1589). For the Authorship Commentary added to this, as to the other newly attributed plays, I have introduced a new method of documenting the phrasal matches with Kyd's accepted canon. When these are presented in a list printed after the play, I have noticed that few readers properly digest them. Here they will be shown as footnotes to the text as they occur, which will make them easier to take in and harder to ignore. Darren Freebury-Jones has kindly provided them for *King Leir*, as for *Arden of Faversham* and *Fair Em*. I owe Darren a special debt of gratitude: not only has he compiled these Authorship Commentaries, he has also edited *Arden of Faversham* and worked as my indefatigable Associate Editor. In this capacity he generously checked all of my contributions and has done the same for other editors. Each of us, however, is responsible for the texts published under our names.

Brian Vickers
11 April 2023

ABBREVIATIONS

AF	*Arden of Faversham*
ANQ	*American Notes and Queries*
BEPD	*A Bibliography of the English Printed Drama to the Restoration*
CELM	*The Catalogue of English Literary Manuscripts 1450–1700*
Corn.	*Cornelia*
E3	*Edward III*
EEBO	*Early English Books Online*
EMLS	*Early Modern Literary Studies*
EPT	*English Professional Theatre*
ES	*The Elizabethan Stage*
ESTC	*English Short Title Catalogue*
FE	*Fair Em*
1H6	*Henry VI Part One*
HD	*Henslowe's Diary*
HP	*The Householder's Philosophy*
KL	*King Leir*
LPD	*Lost Plays Database*
MLN	*Modern Language Notes*
MSR	*Malone Society Reprints*
N&Q	*Notes and Queries*
ODNB	*Oxford Dictionary of National Biography*
RD	*Renaissance Drama*
SP	*Soliman and Perseda*
Sp. T.	*The Spanish Tragedy*

SS	*Shakespeare Studies*
STC	*Short Title Catalogue*
TLS	*Times Literary Supplement*
VPJ	*Verses of Praise and Joy*

KYD AND THE LONDON THEATRE

Brian Vickers

As with many other Elizabethan writers, we know little about Thomas Kyd's life. On 6 November 1558, the parish register of St Mary Woolnoth recorded the baptism of 'Thomas, son of Francis Kidd, Citizen and Writer of the Courte Letter of London'. Kyd's father, Francis, rose to be Warden of the Company of Scriveners in 1580, the official body supervising 'a profitable and ancient trade'. Scriveners, officially known as 'Writers of the Court Letter', enjoyed 'a monopoly on engrossing charters, contracts, testaments, and official documents', functioning 'not only as notaries and copyists, but also as money lenders'.[1] The need for verbal accuracy in their profession made them insist that a scrivener's apprentice acquire a perfect knowledge of Latin grammar and be 'erudite in the books of genders, declensions, preterites and supines'. Francis Kyd had evidently had a grammar school education and ensured that his son had the same good start in life. Thomas must have received his first education at home, for when he entered the nearby Merchant Taylors' School on 26 October 1565, just before his seventh birthday, he was expected 'to know "the catechysm in English or Latyn" and be able to "read perfectly and write competently"'.

The curriculum of Merchant Taylors' envisaged six to eight years' intensive study of Latin grammar, as codified in the official 'King's grammar' of John Lily, reading a graded sequence of Latin authors (Cato, Terence, Virgil, Cicero's Letters, Sallust, Caesar, Horace's *Epistles*, Ovid's *Metamorphoses* and *Fasti*), and regularly composing Latin prose and verse, incorporating the figures of rhetoric. Although limited to Latin, the drilling in grammar, rhetoric, and classical prosody was so intense that it could hardly be matched in any modern university. Kyd published his Latin verse in his earliest work, *Verses of Prayse and Joye* (1586), celebrating Queen Elizabeth's escape from the Babington plot. *The Spanish Tragedy* includes several passages of Latin verse that Kyd wrote and also adapted to frame his quotations from classical Roman poets.

1 See Arthur Freeman, *Thomas Kyd: Facts and Problems* (Oxford, 1967).

In addition to a thorough acquisition of Latin, Kyd may have owed to Merchant Taylors' School his first exposure to drama. The headmaster Richard Mulcaster had been educated at Eton under Nicholas Udall, who had combined two Latin comedies (Plautus's *Miles Gloriosus* and Terence's *Eunuchus*) for his *Ralph Roister Doister*, the first English classical comedy (1567). Mulcaster emulated Udall by encouraging drama at Merchant Taylors', alongside music and games. The benefits of acting in Latin drama had been celebrated by humanist pedagogues throughout sixteenth-century Europe, but few schools can have brought their performances to such a high level as to be invited to act at court, which Mulcaster's boys did eight times between 1572 and 1583. His company also performed in the school hall in 1572–3 with an admission charge of one penny, 'the earliest record of a boy company playing before paying spectators'.[2]

There are no records of Kyd having been to either Oxford or Cambridge. After leaving school in about 1573 he may have worked for a while in his father's scriptorium, for the surviving examples of his handwriting show professional characteristics. One printed source (see below) associated Kyd with the Queen's Men in about 1585. Kyd may have written plays for that company, but none can be identified. In about 1588 Kyd was engaged by Lord Strange as a secretary, whose duties would include preparing legal documents and carrying out correspondence in English and Latin. He had a room in Strange's house and was able to continue writing plays.

The next stage in Kyd's life for which we have datable evidence is the period February to June 1592, when three of his plays were performed at the Rose theatre by Lord Strange's Men, a very successful season for Kyd (see below). His success was short-lived, however, for in April–May 1593 an outbreak of xenophobia in London resulted in a verse ultimatum calling for the murder of Protestant European refugees being posted on the walls of the Dutch church, signed 'Tamburlaine'. The authorities understood it as a declaration of authorship and ordered the arrest of Marlowe, at that time also in the employ of Lord Strange and sharing a room with Kyd. Unable to find Marlowe, the authorities arrested Kyd and seized his papers, which included 'vile hereticall Conceiptes denying the deity of Jhesus Criste our Saviour', which Kyd claimed belonged to Marlowe. To obtain more information they tortured Kyd, who wrote two letters to Sir John Puckering, Lord Keeper, protesting his innocence and describing Marlowe's well-documented atheism.[3]

2 Michael Shapiro, *Children of the Revels: The Boy Companies of Shakespeare's Time and their Plays* (New York, 1977), p. 14.

3 Freeman, *Thomas Kyd: Facts and Problems*, pp. 26–32.

Dismissed by Lord Strange, Kyd had to return to his parents' house, his professional and personal life ruined, and doubtless injured by torture. In the time remaining he was able to complete his translation of Garnier's *Cornélie*, which he dedicated to the Countess of Sussex in January 1594, probably in the hope of finding a future employer. He promised to send her his translation of Garnier's *Porcie*, but the parish register of St Mary Colchurch soon carried the entry: 'Thomas Kydd the sonne of ffrauncis Kydd was buryed the 15 day of August 1594.'

Kyd worked for London theatre companies from about 1585, as far as we can tell, to 1594, a period of great activity, if patchily documented. But enough evidence has survived for us to reconstruct several probable, and some possible, connections between his work and the theatrical context. These matters have been intensively studied by theatre historians for over a century, and much could be said about them. My aim here is to provide enough detail for us to appreciate the choices available to a dramatist in this period in terms of the acting companies, the theatres, and the preservation of his labours as either a manuscript or printed text. To set the scene I shall sketch in some relevant aspects of Elizabethan theatrical history, drawing on the classic synthesis by E. K. Chambers, but also on newer theatrical history, notably Glynne Wickham, Herbert Berry and William Ingram's volume in the series 'Theatre in Europe: a documentary history', dealing with the professional theatres in England between the Reformation and the Restoration.[4]

THE COMPANIES

Much of the surviving records from the administrative bodies during Elizabeth's reign – her government, the Lord Mayor, the Court of Aldermen, town and city councils across the land – concern attempts to control the public performance of plays, particularly during outbreaks of plague and at times of religious observance on Sundays, in Lent, and on other occasions (*EPT*, pp. 50–60, 77–89, 111–19). These attempted deterrents testify to the public demand for theatrical performances, to which the government responded in 1581 with the appointment of Edmund Tilney as Master of the Revels (*EPT*, pp. 69–73), giving him the power to license all plays, players, and playing places. One governmental regulation which had unlooked-for

[4] *English Professional Theatre, 1530–1660* (Cambridge, 2000). The three editors are each responsible for the following topics: 'Part one: documents of control, 1530–1660' (pp. 17–149) is by Glynne Wickham; 'Part two: players and playing' (pp. 151–284) is by William Ingram; 'Part three: playhouses, 1560–1660' (pp. 285–674) is by Herbert Berry. All the documents it contains are given in modern spelling. (Hereafter referred to as '*EPT*'.)

positive effects was the Act of 29 June 1572 for the Punishment of Vagabonds, which ruled that 'all Fencers, Bearwards, Common Playes in Enterludes & Minstrels, not belonging to any Baron of this Realm or towards any other honourable Personage of greater Degree', who 'wander abroad, and have not licence of two Justices of the Peace … shall be taken, adjudged and deemed Rogues, Vagabonds and Sturdy Beggars' (p. 62). The consequence of this Act may not have been anticipated by the authorities, for within the sixteenth century alone, as William Ingram estimates, 'the number of identifiable persons of rank or standing who were patrons of playing companies … approached 100; most prominent among them were the various members of the royal family' (p. 204). To have your own troupe of players was evidently a matter of considerable prestige, and in about 1572 a group of six actors already working for the Earl of Leicester petitioned him to be retained as 'your humble servants and daily orators your players', requesting 'your honour's licence to certify that we are your household servants when we shall have occasion to travel amongst our friends as we do usually once a year, and as other noblemen's players do and have done in times past …' (p. 205). In 1574 a royal patent was duly issued to those six actors, allowing them 'to use, exercise, and occupy the art and faculty of playing comedies, tragedies, interludes, stage plays, and such other like as they have already used and studied, or hereafter shall use and study …' (p. 206).

Forming a company was one thing; maintaining it was another. Many of these acting troupes enjoyed a brief period of success, performing regularly for a while before dissolving or moving on to create other formations. In his classic account of *The Elizabethan Stage*, E. K. Chambers listed eleven boy companies and twenty-four adult companies which plied their trade at some point during any year between 1558 and 1616.[5] As he recorded, 'It is improbable that there was any continuity as regards membership between the bodies of actors successively appearing, often after long intervals, under the names of Sussex or Hunsdon or Derby' (*ES*, 2:3). Some did manage to maintain a group, such as the company led by Lawrence and John Dutton, which served four masters between 1571 and 1583: first, Sir Robert Lane, then in turn, the Earls of Lincoln, Warwick, and Oxford (2:96–101). After the building of the first permanent theatres in 1576 there was a rapid growth in the number of adult companies maintained by the leading officers of state, such as that of the third Earl of Sussex, who became Lord Chamberlain in 1572 (2:92–6). A mark of a company's eminence was the invitation to perform at one of the two main court drama seasons, at Christmas and Shrovetide. A Privy Council order of 1578 limited the right

[5] See *The Elizabethan Stage*, 4 vols (Oxford, 1923), 2:1–260 (hereafter referred to as '*ES*').

to perform in the Christmas festivities to six companies, namely Leicester's men, Warwick's, Sussex's, Essex's, and the two boys' companies, the Children of the Chapel and St Paul's (2:4; 4:278). The Queen may have felt that members of her nobility were seizing the limelight, for on 10 March 1583 Edmund Tilney was ordered 'To choose out a companie of players for her majestie' from the leading groups, 'out of which companies there were twelve of the best chosen', who 'were sworn the queens servants and were allowed wages and liveries as grooms of the chamber' (2:104). The troupe, which included 'the famous clown Richard Tarlton and the tragedian John Bentley', in the words of one theatre historian, 'set new standards in performance' while enhancing 'royal status through association with a genuinely popular entertainment'.[6]

Some companies did not survive the death of their patron, as happened to Sussex's Men in 1583 (2:94), Leicester's in 1588 (2:91), Strange's in 1594 (2:126), and Essex's in 1601 (2:103). Others went into at least a temporary decline following the loss of a leading actor, as happened to the Queen's Men with the death of Tarlton in December 1588 (2:109). But their failure made room for other companies. Lord Howard, who had been deputy Lord Chamberlain in 1574–5 under the Earl of Sussex, succeeded to that post in December 1583, but soon achieved a greater honour, being appointed Lord High Admiral in July 1585, and serving in that office until 1619. The Admiral's Men, led by Edward Alleyn, were to become one of the leading theatre companies after the conclusion of the long plague in 1594, but in the fluid years of the late 1580s and early 1590s they had a loose association with Lord Strange's Men, patronised by the Earls of Derby. This family had maintained a troupe of players from the 1530s to the 1570s, reaching some eminence in the early 1580s, with invitations to perform at court on several occasions. They vanished from the records in 1583, however, perhaps due to their leading actors having been poached for the Queen's Men.[7] They were revived by Ferdinando Stanley, Lord Strange, forming themselves out of Leicester's Men, and performing at the Cross Keys Inn in Gracechurch Street in November 1589, a venue that became their winter quarters. They soon reached a degree of eminence, being invited to act at court in

6 John H. Astington, *English Court Theatre 1558–1642* (Cambridge, 1999), pp. 23, 109. For their dominance of court performances, see Astington's appendix listing all court performances, especially the period 1583–94 (pp. 231–4), where they appeared on 27 occasions.

7 Sally-Beth MacLean gives a scrupulously documented account of the family players' traditions in Lawrence Manley and Sally-Beth MacLean, *Lord Strange's Men and Their Plays* (New Haven, 2014), pp. 12–36, while Lawrence Manley continues the narrative in 'Lord Strange's Men in London, 1589–1593' (pp. 37–63). MacLean adds a detailed survey of 'Travels and Performance Venues' (pp. 247–79).

December 1590 and February 1591, being joined by Edward Alleyn of the Lord Admiral's Men, with three further court performances in 1592–3. Recently discovered documents show them performing at Henslowe's Rose theatre in the summer of 1590, where they later enjoyed two extended residences, from 19 February to 22 June 1592, and from 29 December 1592 to 1 February 1593. 'Involving an initial series of 105 consecutive performances of twenty-four different plays, old and new, and then a shorter series of twenty-nine performances, including three more new plays, for a total of twenty-seven plays in all', this was probably the longest tenure of one company of one playhouse, a rare period of stability in the fluid world of Elizabethan theatre.[8] Their takings varied between the packed house that attended '*harey the vj*' on 3 March to the low turn-out for *A Looking-Glass for London* on 7 March, which saw, respectively, 1,820 and 168 spectators in the galleries, but they were amongst the most profitable of the periods of playing recorded by Henslowe.[9] During these years Alleyn led Strange's Men while retaining his status as the Lord Admiral's servant, coming into his own once the latter company re-established itself in 1594, the year of Kyd's death.

Two other companies performed in London in the 1590s. The Earl of Pembroke's Men were not mentioned before 26 December 1592 and experienced difficulties in the summer of 1593, when they gave the first of two performances at court, but they must have been in existence for some time in order to achieve that eminence, performing alongside Lord Strange's Men.[10] In a much-quoted letter to his son-in-law Edward Alleyn, written on 28 September, Henslowe reported 'and as for my Lord of Pembroke's men which you desire to know where they be, they are all at home and have been this five or six weeks, for they cannot save their charges with travel, as I hear, and were fain to pawn their apparel for their charge'.[11] First, the troupe appeared on provincial tours eighteen times, sixteen of them '*after* June–July 1593, when they were supposedly forced to disband' (they evidently reclaimed their costumes from pawn). Secondly, analysis of their payments shows that 'Pembroke's Men enjoyed the second-highest average reward per visit, second only to the Queen's Men, before they disbanded upon the Earl's death in 1601'.[12] Indeed, all the evidence 'suggests that Pembroke's

8 Manley, ibid., p. 59.

9 Astington, op. cit., pp. 233–4.

10 See Manley and MacLean, *Lord Strange's Men*, p. 310.

11 R. A. Foakes and R. T. Rickert (eds), *Henslowe's Diary* (Cambridge, 1961), p. 280: I have expanded manuscript contractions.

12 Alan Somerset, 'Not Just Sir Oliver Owlet: From Patrons to Patronage of Early Modern Theatre', in Richard Dutton (ed.), *The Oxford Handbook of Early Modern Theatre* (Oxford, 2009), pp. 343–61 (345). Note, however, that for 'have been' or

was a remarkably successful and active company' (p. 347). One less resilient group was the company of Lord Hunsdon, Lord Chamberlain from 1585 to 1596, which gave a court performance on 6 January 1586, together with the Admiral's Men, but soon faded from record. A completely new Chamberlain's Men was formed in June 1594, when they shared a season for Henslowe with the new Admiral's company at Newington Butts before setting up on their own. These two companies dominated the London theatre scene for many years in that period of stability and success that Kyd did not live to see. In his brief career as a dramatist, five companies could have performed his plays, those patronized by the Earl of Leicester, the Queen, Lord Strange, the Lord Chamberlain, and the Lord High Admiral.

THE THEATRES

The range of theatre companies, bewildering in its diversity and fragility, is matched in more permanent form by the range of available performance spaces in London, further testimony to the remarkable appetite for the theatre in this period.[13] The first structure built as a regular professional theatre was the Red Lion in Whitechapel, scheduled for opening in July 1567 to perform a play called *The Story of Samson* (*EPT*, pp. 290–1). As Herbert Berry observes, 'within twenty years, professional actors were regularly at work in no fewer than ten other structures there', three of which involved large capital investment (p. 287). In all, 'twenty-three professional theatres ... were built in and around London during the seventy-five years from 1567 to 1642. Probably nothing of the kind had happened in any other city on earth' (p. 288). The growing desire to experience a flourishing secular theatre – the religious Guild plays were still being suppressed as late as 1576 (*EPT*, pp. 64–9) – led to four London inns doubling up as playhouses from about 1575 to 1596. These were the Bel Savage in Ludgate Hill, the Bull in Bishopsgate Street, the Cross Keys, and the Bull on the west side of Gracechurch Street, north of Lombard Street (where Kyd's family lived). In retrospect the inns may seem like interim solutions until the first purpose-built theatres were opened, but even after 1576 the major companies continued to use them. The Queen's Men acted at the Bull and the Bell during their first year, 1583; Lord Strange's Men performed at the Cross Keys in 1589,

'hauffe ben', in the transcription of R. A. Focker, Somerset reads 'hausse ben', reproducing the erroneous reading by E. K. Chambers in *ES*, 2:128.

13 See *ES*, 2:353–474. I take my documentation from Herbert Berry's wonderfully detailed survey in *EPT*, pp. 285–674.

defying the Lord Mayor's veto; and the Lord Chamberlain's wanted to act there in 1594 (pp. 295–305).[14]

The year 1576 is noted in theatrical history as that in which three new public playing spaces came into use. The least well documented is Newington Butts (*EPT*, pp. 320–9), probably because it was the least convenient, lying one mile south of the river, near the Elephant and Castle inn. The actor Jerome Savage (first recorded as performing at court in 1575 for the Earl of Warwick's new company) converted an existing building into a playhouse, and may have used it until 1580, when his company dissolved. Lord Strange's Men acted there in September 1593, after the Privy Council had closed the Rose theatre, and for the same reason Henslowe hired the playhouse in June 1594 for a short season in which the actors were 'the former Lord Strange's Men, who during the long closings from 22 June to 14 May 1594 had broken into two separate companies: the Lord Admiral's with Edward Alleyn and the Lord Chamberlain's with Richard Burbage. The two companies did not now reunite but took turns playing their own plays' (*EPT*, p. 328). They gave two performances of Marlowe's *The Jew of Malta*, two of Peele and Shakespeare's *Titus Andronicus*, and one of *Hamlet* (possibly by Kyd). This playing space closed later that year.

Much more is known about the Theatre, a name that, as George Puttenham reminded his readers, derived from the Greek *Théātron*, 'as much as to say a beholding place'.[15] This was a custom-built public playhouse in Shoreditch, situated a quarter of a mile outside the City boundary, largely due to a series of legal disputes between James Burbage ('a joiner turned actor') and his partners in the enterprise (*EPT*, pp. 330–87).[16] After a long stalemate Burbage's son Cuthbert hired a carpenter to dismantle the building at the end of December 1598, using the timbers to build the Globe theatre on a site in Southwark. With its large yard, tiring-house, and galleries, the Theatre was 'probably the archetypical Shakespearean public playhouse', and was used by every successful company: Leicester's, Warwick's, Oxford's, the Queen's, the Lord Admiral's, Lord Strange's (later Derby's Men), and the Chamberlain's (p. 332). Contemporary preachers disapprovingly described it as 'sumptuous' (p. 337) and 'gorgeous' (p. 339), and its name survived in

14 See also David Kathman, 'Inn-Yard Playhouses', in Dutton (ed.), *The Oxford Handbook of Early Modern Theatre*, pp. 153–67; and Lawrence Manley, 'Why did London inns function as theatres?', *Huntington Library Quarterly* 71:1 (2008): 181–97.

15 Puttenham, *The Arte of English Poesie*, ed. Gladys Doidge Willcock and Alice Walker (Cambridge, 1936, 1970), p. 37.

16 See also C. W. Wallace, *The First London Theatre* (Lincoln, NE, 1913); Herbert Berry, *Shakespeare's Playhouses* (New York, 1987); and William Ingram, *The Business of Playing: The Beginnings of the Adult Professional Theater in Elizabethan London* (Ithaca and London, 1992), pp. 182–218.

Lodge's famous comparison, 'Pale as the vizard of the ghost which cried so miserably at the Theatre, like an Oyster wife, "Hamlet, revenge"' (p. 367) – presumably the same play performed at Newington Butts in 1594 (possibly by Kyd).

In 1577, shortly after the Theatre's opening, an unknown entrepreneur built another public playhouse in Shoreditch, some 200 yards south of the Theatre, called the Curtain, of which few documents survive (*EPT*, pp. 405–18). During the period that concerns us here, up to Kyd's death in August 1594, 'no company is definitely known to have played there … though Lord Arundel's Men were probably there in 1584' (p. 406).

The last public playhouse built during Kyd's life was also the best documented, the first to be built on Bankside in Southwark, and Philip Henslowe's first theatre, the Rose (*EPT*, pp. 418–36). The playhouse opened in 1587, but no information survives about the companies that acted there. In early 1592 Henslowe enlarged the Rose so that it could hold more spectators, and at the same time he began keeping a record of the companies that acted there, listing his receipts from each performance. Starting on 19 February, with Lord Strange's Men, he noted the first takings: from *Friar Bacon* (by Greene), *Muly Molocco* (possibly Peele's *The Battle of Alcazar*), *Orlando Furioso* (Greene), *The Spanish Comedy Don Horatio* (Kyd?), *The Jew of Malta* (Marlowe), and so on. Kyd was still alive in the summer of 1594, when the Admiral's Men began their long and fruitful stay (until 1600). A further series of public theatres continued to be built in London, another ten between 1595 and 1623 (*EPT*, pp. 440–646), but Kyd did not live to see them.

The final element in this brief sketch of the London theatre world during Kyd's lifetime concerns the most ephemeral of all its artefacts, the scripts from which the actors performed. An unknown number of authors kept the theatre companies in business by writing plays for them, of which the vast majority have perished. William Ingram, following up a 1578 reference to there being '"eighte ordinarie places" of playing in the City', has estimated that, if eight companies performed 'for only nine months in the year and only four days each week, then those eight companies alone would have provided over twelve hundred performances each year for London playgoers'.[17] If we assume 'a dozen performances for each text', then 'the playing companies in these eight favored locations would have required a hundred or so different scripts each year'. Further, if we take into account 'the twenty-odd companies not playing in London' then 'something like two hundred plays a year' would have been needed (pp. 240–1). Companies must have regularly needed playwrights, but no documentation

[17] Ingram, *The Business of Playing*, p. 240.

of the negotiating process survives – with one exception, published by Mark Benbow in 1981.[18] In 1573 the brothers Lawrence and John Dutton, freemen of the Weavers' Company and stage players – who, as we have seen, successfully moved their acting company from patron to patron – sued one Rowland Broughton for breach of contract. The Duttons, together with Thomas Gough, a fellow actor (and barber-surgeon), had intended to set up a company of boy players, 'to play upon all Sundays and holidays in the year … being not prohibited', and to perform 'some one history, comedy, or tragedy whatsoever of the only device and making of the said Rowland Broughton'. The contract stipulated that during a term of 'two years and a half' Broughton should deliver 'eighteen several [separate] plays of the only devise of the said Rowland Broughton and never before played'. The stipulation that these compositions should be 'of the only device and making of the same Rowland Broughton' is further evidence (should it be needed) that the author was fully recognized as such during the sixteenth century, as in the medieval period, and indeed all the way back to classical antiquity.[19] It also shows the need, in this increasingly competitive world, for companies to obtain new playscripts, 'never before played'.

This single document apart, no evidence of the innumerable contracts between playwrights and theatre companies survives before December 1599, when Philip Henslowe began making records of the moneys he advanced to the Admiral's Men for the commission and supply of new plays.[20] Given that three new playing spaces were available in London after 1576, the demand for playbooks must have been greater; yet, as Ingram noted, 'for no single year in the ten years between 1576 and 1586 have more than five or six play texts survived, and the bulk of these are courtly or university plays' (p. 241). It is frustrating that fewer than a dozen plays from the public theatre survive from what must have been 'an astonishingly active period'. The situation changed with 'the sudden and gratifying appearance, in 1586 and 1587, of plays by the group collectively known as the University Wits', as Ingram put it, who seemed to realize for the first time 'the print worthiness of plays' (pp. 241–2). That is an account of a vital change in attitudes seen from the viewpoint of the professional theatre, and doubtless needs to be complemented by the simultaneous recognition by

18 See R. Mark Benbow, 'Dutton and Goffe versus Broughton: A Disputed Contract for Plays in the 1570s', *REED Newsletter* 2 (1981): 2, 3–9. My quotations come from the modernized text in *EPT*, pp. 234–5, expanding editorial supplements.

19 For a brief refutation of this modern misconception, see Brian Vickers, *Shakespeare, Co-Author* (Oxford, 2002), Appendix II: 'Abolishing the Author? Theory *versus* History', pp. 506–41.

20 See Grace Ioppolo, *Dramatists and their Manuscripts in the Age of Shakespeare, Jonson, Middleton and Heywood* (London, 2006).

the London stationers and printers that playbooks could constitute a small but commercially viable share of their output.[21]

So far, I have limited this sketch of the London theatre during Kyd's lifetime to the public playhouses, since there is no evidence that he ever worked for the boys' companies in the indoor theatres. But one other theatrical context needs to be considered. Despite Ingram's accolade, the 'University Wits' had been anticipated by members of 'the third university', as it was known, the Inns of Court, who managed to get their dramatic performances published in the 1560s. The great contribution of these university-educated authors was to introduce a new verse form into vernacular drama. As O. B. Hardison pointed out,

> One of the more interesting facts about English blank verse is that it was invented. The evidence suggests it was the result of a self-conscious effort by Henry Howard, earl of Surrey, around 1540, to create a vernacular English form equivalent to the dactylic hexameter of classical epic. It is thus a contribution to the efforts of English esoteric humanism to reproduce in the vernacular the great genres and effects of ancient literature. Surrey clearly derived much inspiration from Vergil, but he was also influenced by what he learned from Italian literature.[22]

Surrey's Italian models included poets who had published translations of the *Aeneid* into *versi sciolti*, unrhymed pentameters, especially Aristotle Zoppio's compilation of translations by various hands, of which 'Books 2 and 4 were published in 1539–40'.[23] Surrey translated Books 2 and 4 only, his version achieving wide circulation through Richard Tottel's *Songes and sonettes, written by Henry Haward late earle of Surrey and other* (1557; six editions by 1559, ten by 1584). Within a few years the Inns of Court dramatists adopted blank verse for their compositions. The 'gentlemen of the Inner Temple' acted a play called *Gorboduc* or *The Tragedy of Ferrex and Porrex* at their Christmas revels in 1561–2, and were invited to perform it again before the Queen on 18 January 1562. When published in 1565, the title page described it as *The Tragedie of Gorboduc, Where of three Actes were wrytten by Thomas Norton, and the two laste by Thomas Sackvyle*. That novelty was soon followed by *Jocasta: A Tragedie written in Greeke by Euripides, translated and digested into Acte by George Gascoyne, and*

21 See the excellent survey by Peter Blayney, 'The Publication of Playbooks', in J. D. Cox and D. S. Kastan (eds), *A New History of Early English Drama* (New York and London, 1997), pp. 383–422.

22 O. B. Hardison, Jr, *Prosody and Purpose in the English Renaissance* (Baltimore and London, 1989), p. 127.

23 Ibid., p. 130. Other exponents of *versi sciolti* who influenced Surrey probably included Luigi Alamanni and Giangiorgio Trissino.

Francis Kinwelmerse of Grayes Inne, and there by them presented 1566, and first published in Gascoigne's *A Hundreth sundrie Flowres* (1573). After an interval of some years, 1587 saw the publication of *The misfortunes of Arthur (Uther Pendragons Sonne) reduced into Tragicall notes by Thomas Hughes one of the societie of Grayes-Inne*, published in *Certaine Devises and shewes presented to her Majestie by the Gentlemen of Grayes-Inne at her Highnesse Court in Greenewich, the twenty-eighth day of Februarie in the thirtieth yeare of her Majesties most happy Raigne.*[24] All three plays are in blank verse, although *Gorboduc* includes some rhyming couplets, which may be 'relics of the old habit of rhyming,'[25] while both *Jocasta* and *The Misfortunes of Arthur* use rhyme for the choric odes. The modern reader, knowing how pliable it was to become, may find the iambic pentameter in these plays both irregular and monotonous, but the Inns of Court dramatists introduced a verse form which could range from the eloquently expressive to the conversational. As F. P. Wilson judged, 'nothing is more important in these years ... than the invention of blank verse and its transference to drama in *Gorboduc* and *Jocasta* ready for the hands of Kyd and Marlowe, an invention which was to rid the drama of the monstrous monotony of the fourteener.'[26]

From the surviving evidence, Thomas Kyd entered the London theatre world between 1585 and 1587, as near as can be judged, with *The Spanish Tragedy*, a play which confidently uses all the stylistic media available to the Elizabethan dramatist – blank verse, rhyme and prose – and daringly exploits theatrical resources. Of its first performances, we know neither the company's identity nor the place where it was first performed. The role of Hieronimo demands an actor of stature and energy, while the large cast needs a fully equipped performance space. Leicester's Men were still active in 1587–8, although they had lost some of their best players to the Queen's Men. They are recorded performing in London on about 25 January 1587, and toured extensively until 4 September 1588, a few days before Leicester died. A more likely troupe to have performed *The Spanish Tragedy* are the Queen's Men, who, as we have seen, were founded in March 1583 by royal command. Edmund Tilney, Master of the Revels, having been instructed 'to choose out a companie of players for her majestie', formed an unusually large company 'of twelve men and an undefined number of boys', an

24 All three Inns of Court plays are conveniently available in John W. Cunliffe (ed.), *Early English Classical Tragedies* (Oxford, 1912). Despite the title page's claim, *Jocasta* was based not on Euripides but on Lodovico Dolce's *Giocasta*, 'which in turn is an extensive adaptation of Euripides' *Phoenissae*': cf. G. W. Pigman III (ed.), *George Gascoigne: A Hundreth Sundrie Flowres* (Oxford, 2000), p. 508.

25 Cunliffe, *Early English Classical Tragedies*, p. 299 note.

26 F. P. Wilson, *The English Drama 1485–1585*, ed. G. K. Hunter (Oxford, 1969), pp. 142–3.

increase in scale which offered dramatists the chance to write '"large" plays requiring casts of fifteen or more speaking parts', with smaller roles being doubled.[27] Tilney took 'twelve of the best' actors, an early witness recorded, from the extant adult companies belonging to the Earls of Leicester, Sussex, Derby and others, so creating the Queen's Men,

> the best acting company in England ... an instant all-star troupe, which would hold the advantage on the calendar of holiday performances at court, would claim royal privileges for securing playing places in the inn yards of London and in the new purpose-built playhouses outside the city walls, and would receive higher rewards than their competitors as they toured the countryside.[28]

Our knowledge of Kyd's possible connection with the Queen's Men derives from Thomas Dekker's pamphlet, *A Knight's Conjuring* (1607). Dekker envisaged a scene in the Elysian fields, where a laurel grove shelters famous dead poets, one group including 'old *Chaucer*, reverend for prioritie', and '*Grave Spenser*'.

> In another companie sat learned *Watson*, industrious *Kyd*, ingenious *Atchlow*, and (tho hee had bene a Player, molded out of their pennes) yet because he had bene their *Lover*, and a Register to the Muses, Inimitable *Bentley*: these were likewise carowsing to one another at the holy well, some of them singing Pæans to *Apollo*, som of them *Hymnes* to the rest of the Goddes ... [29]

As T. W. Baldwin was the first to see, the implication of Dekker's grouping 'is that Kyd had written plays before 1585, probably for the Queen's Men'.[30] John Bentley (1553–85) was a well-known actor, a member of the Queen's Men from 1583–5, and friend of this trio of poets. The learned Thomas Watson (1557–92), equally fluent in Latin and English, translated Italian madrigals and wrote numerous sonnets. Kyd imitated one of them in *The Spanish Tragedy*.[31] Arthur Freeman was able to throw some light on Thomas Atchelow, whose name is variously spelled, 'Achelley' being the most likely

27 See *ES*, 2:104–15, and Andrew Gurr, *The Shakespearian Playing Companies* (Oxford, 1996), pp. 55–60.

28 Scott McMillin and Sally-Beth MacLean, *The Queen's Men and their Plays* (Cambridge, 1998), pp. xiii, 1–2.

29 Dekker, *A Knight's Conjuring Done in earnest: Discouered in Iest.* (London, 1607; *STC* 6508), sig. K8^v–L1^r. Cit. Freeman, *Thomas Kyd: Facts and Problems*, p. 13.

30 T. W. Baldwin, *On the Literary Genetics of Shakespeare's Plays 1592–1594* (Urbana, IL, 1959) (op. cit., n. 46), p. 178. See also Lukas Erne, *Beyond* The Spanish Tragedy: *A Study of the Works of Thomas Kyd* (Manchester, 2001), pp. 1–2, 163.

31 At 2.1.3–6, Lorenzo quotes lines from Watson's *Hekatompathia*, sonnet XLVII, to which Balthasar responds at ll. 9–10, quoting the two lines following. See Brian

version, and used in the *Short Title Catalogue* (*STC*). He published a diminutive prayer book, *The Key of Knowledge* (1571); a Hispanophobic narrative poem in 'poulter-meter' (1576); a prefatory poem in iambic pentameters to Thomas Watson's *Hekatompathia* (1582); and some verse fragments surviving in Robert Allott's anthology *England's Parnassus* (1600), the year in which Achelley died. The three poets had been already mentioned in the opportunistic compilation by Francis Meres, *Palladis Tamia* (1598), which included a treatise on 'Poetrie'. Meres twice referred to Kyd, first in a general list of notable English writers, where his name appears alongside Thomas Atchelow, Thomas Watson, Robert Greene, and George Peele. Secondly, in a list of 'our best [English poets] for Tragedie', Kyd is ranked with Marlowe, Watson, Peele, Shakespeare, Chapman, Jonson, and others.[32] As for John Bentley, he seems to have performed some works written by the others ('moulded out of their pennes'), which are now lost. The epithet 'industrious Kyd', coming from Dekker, who was involved in the composition of over eighty plays,[33] suggests a copious and accomplished dramatist, who might have produced a larger oeuvre than has survived.[34] He had certainly aligned himself with a major company.

Kyd's connection with this premier troupe indicates the high estimate that professional theatre men had formed of his abilities. Commenting on Dekker's testimony that Kyd was one of three authors who had written roles for the company's chief tragic actor, John Bentley, two historians of the company comment that

> Only Kyd is known to have written for the common stage among this group, and he is not known to have written for the Queen's Men. But 'known' is a rare quality when it comes to the authors of plays in the 1580s, even the titles of which have disappeared, with few exceptions. It is quite possible that the *Felix and Philiomena* or the *Phillyda and Corin* (both now lost) which the Queen's Men played at court in 1585 came

---

Vickers, 'Thomas Watson, Thomas Kyd, and Embedded Poetry', *Studies in Philology* 120:3 (2023): 557–601.

32 See Don Cameron Allen (ed.), *Francis Meres's Treatise "Poetrie"* (Urbana, IL, 1933; *University of Illinois Studies in Language and Literature*, vol. XVI), pp. 77, 78. Allen showed that Meres's treatise was a perfunctory imitation of a section in the *Officina*, a popular compendium of universal knowledge compiled by the humanist J. Ravisius Textor (1520; eight editions by 1595). Meres simply substituted English names for those of Greek, Latin, and neo-Latin authors.

33 Martin Wiggins, personal communication, 13 August 2023; an excerpt from *British Drama*, vol. 11 (forthcoming). He added: 'The only ones that look "bigger" at a glance on the page are Heywood and Jonson'.

34 Lukas Erne, *Beyond* The Spanish Tragedy, notes that '"industrious" also had the now obsolete meaning "showing intelligent or skilful work" (*OED*)' (p. 11, n. 8).

> from writers like Watson, Achlow, or Kyd, the three who are said to have moulded John Bentley with their pens.[35]

The Queen's Men play that McMillin and MacLean treat as foundational in studying the company's repertoire is *The True Chronicle History of King Leir*,[36] one of several plays based on English history, which the Queen's Men 'were the first professional company to undertake extensively' (p. 33). In the previous century two scholars ascribed *King Leir* to Kyd, and I have recently provided substantial new evidence for his authorship of this 'most famous Chronicle historye',[37] which Eugene Giddens has freshly edited for this volume.

The Queen's Men enjoyed only a brief period of eminence. As already noted, the company had been weakened by the deaths of several actors, culminating in 1588 with that of their leading player, Richard Tarlton, and seems to have gone into decline. In about 1588–9 (calculating back from the 'vi yeares' service that he counted in 1593), Kyd began working as a secretary (responsible for Latin correspondence and the preparation of official documents) for Ferdinando, fifth Earl of Derby. This would have given him privileged access to transfer his allegiance to Lord Strange's Men, the company in the service of the Earl. The only play for which his connection was formally recognized was the undated quarto (c. 1593), *A Pleasant Commodie of Faire Em … As it was sundrie times publiquely acted in the honourable citie of London, by the right honourable the Lord Strange his servants*,[38] but company connections were not universally recorded. Previous companies connected with the Derby family had been a mixture of actors and tumblers, but their Elizabethan formation was a formidable group of actors, many of whom were to have long and influential careers.[39] Their leading actor was Edward Alleyn, who retained his status as a member of the company patronized by Charles Howard, Lord Admiral, in a flexible amalgamation between the two companies which lasted from 1589–90 until 1594. In that year, a number of troupes collapsed during the plague

35 McMillin and MacLean, *The Queen's Men*, p. 29.

36 Ibid., pp. 94, 100–1, 107–8, 133–4, 137, 146–7, 161–2.

37 See Brian Vickers, 'Kyd's Authorship of *King Leir*', *Studies in Philology* 115 (2018): 433–71, and the Authorship Commentary supplied by Darren Freebury-Jones to Eugene Giddens's edition.

38 W. W. Greg, *A Bibliography of the English Printed Drama to the Restoration* (henceforth *BEPD*), 4 vols (London, 1939; 1970) #113; 1:192–3.

39 My account of Strange's Men is largely based on Chambers, *ES*, 2:118–27 and Gurr, 1996, pp. 259–77. See also Carol Chillington Rutter (ed.), *Documents of the Rose Playhouse*, rev. edn (Manchester, 1999), a valuable chronological arrangement of documentary evidence from Henslowe and other sources; Peter Thomson, *Shakespeare's Professional Career* (Cambridge, 1992), pp. 23–51.

that devastated London. The other members of Strange's Men mentioned in a Privy Council document of May 1593 included William Kemp, Thomas Pope, John Heminges, Augustine Phillipes, and George Brian. They enjoyed a 'remarkable success ... in the winter of 1591–2, during which they were called upon to give six performances at Court ... as against one each allotted to the Queen's, Sussex's, and Hertford's men'. On 19 February 1592 they acted for Philip Henslowe at the newly refurbished Rose theatre, where they 'played six days a week for a period of eighteen weeks, during which they only missed Good Friday and two other days', a total of 105 performances (*ES*, 2:121). Modern theatre historians agree about their eminence: one writes that the company reached 'the pinnacle of their national reputation in 1591–3' (Thomson, p. 41); another, that 'Lord Strange's Men had been formed and [were] working at a high level for several months before moving into the Rose', at which time 'they were London's most prestigious company' (Rutter, p. 50); a third, that by 1591 they 'had climbed to the peak of esteem' (Gurr, pp. 258–9). That Kyd should have worked in turn for the two leading London theatre companies shows the high standing he enjoyed among his peers.

THE LONDON THEATRE WORLD

Kyd's position as secretary to a noble lord placed him in an unusual position, having his plays performed in the public theatres but not as a colleague of the dramatists who earned their living there. As far as we know, Kyd had no university education, and it was his misfortune to fall foul of the two most vociferous of the 'University Wits', anxious to defend their status against interlopers, first Greene, then Nashe. Greene attacked *Fair Em* in an address 'to the Gentlemen Students of both Universities' prefixed to his moralizing fable, *Greenes farewell to Folly. Sent to Courtiers and Schollers as a president to warne them from the vaine delights that drawes youth on to repentance*. This pamphlet was entered in the Stationers' Register (S.R.) on 11 June 1587 to E. Aggas,[40] but the earliest known edition is the Quarto of 1592 (printed for T. Gubbin and N. Newton). Greg acutely observed that the term 'Martinize', which Greene uses in the dedication, dates the text to 1589 or later, since that was when the first Martin Marprelate tracts appeared; he concluded that *Fair Em* must have been staged between 1589 and 1591. Greene's diatribe against the play gains a new significance when we recognize that it was really directed against its author, Thomas Kyd.[41]

[40] Edward Arber, *A Transcript of the Registers of the Company of Stationers of London, 1554–1640*, 5 vols (London, 1875–94), 2:219.

[41] See the Introduction to my edition of *Fair Em* in Volume 2.

Having been mocked by Greene, Kyd received further attention that year from the copious and caustic pen of Thomas Nashe. We may take their joint displeasure as proving that Kyd had definitely made an impact in the London theatre. Greene criticized the author of *Fair Em* for two trivial solecisms, a common attitude among those dramatists who cherished a sense of scholarly superiority over their fellows.[42] Nashe went further, producing a lengthy put-down in his preface to Greene's romance, *Menaphon. Camillas alarum to slumbering Euphues, in his melancholie Cell at Silexedra* (entered S.R. 23 August 1589).[43] Nashe made fun of Kyd's use of Seneca, his translations from Italian and French, a supposed error concerning the classical underworld, and for daring 'to bodge up a blanke verse with ifs and ands', as if Kyd used those words to pad out his barren invention. But Nashe took the quotation out of context (the perennial method of facile polemic). It comes from *The Spanish Tragedy* (2.1.76–7) where Lorenzo is pressurizing Pedringano to reveal the name of Bel-Imperia's lover. When her servant tries to evade answering – 'If Madam Bel-Imperia be in love' – Lorenzo interrupts – 'What, villain, *if's* and *an's*?' – and threatens to kill him. Restoring the context destroys the witticism. Nashe described his outburst as having been written in a 'declamatorie vaine', suggesting that it was not to be taken entirely seriously, the *declamatio* being a rhetorical genre connected with mock praise and mock blame. Nashe's exuberant exercise in mockery at least establishes that *The Spanish Tragedy* was known in the London theatre long before Henslowe's first record of it being performed. Three years later Nashe collaborated with Kyd on the play that Henslowe called *harey the vi*, showing that he had been accepted as a professional dramatist.

Despite the mockery of Greene and Nashe, by 1592 Kyd's status in Lord Strange's company was assured, as can be seen if we return to Henslowe's records of their season in the spring and early summer of that year. Between 19 February and 23 June 1592, when an outbreak of plague closed the London theatres, they played six days a week for a period of eighteen weeks, apart from Good Friday and two other days, giving a total of 105 performances. When the theatres briefly reopened, from 29 December to the end of January 1593, Henslowe recorded a further twenty-nine performances.

[42] Compare Jonson's disapproving comments on Shakespeare's errors: 'His wit was in his own power; would the rule of it had been so too. Many times he fell into those things, could not escape laughter: as when he said in the person of Caesar, one speaking to him, "Caesar, thou dost me wrong"; he replied, "Caesar did never wrong, but with just cause"; and such like: which were ridiculous.' *Timber: or discoveries made upon men and matter*, in Brian Vickers (ed.), *English Renaissance Literary Criticism* (Oxford, 1999), pp. 561–2.

[43] For a discussion of Nashe's skirmishing see Brian Vickers, *Recovering Thomas Kyd: A Canon Restored* (Princeton, forthcoming).

During their first season at the Rose, Strange's Men performed twenty-three different plays, and added three more to their repertoire in the shorter second season. Inevitably, many of those have perished, including such evidently popular plays as *Sir John Mandeville* or *Henry of Cornwall*, which remained in their repertoire until the end. As we have seen, the plays of known authorship displayed the leading dramatists (Greene, Peele, Marlowe) appearing side by side. The co-authored play by Lodge and Greene, *A Looking Glass for London*, was performed four times, and a play of (as yet) unknown authorship, *A Knack to Know a Knave*, was played seven times.

Theatre historians document the activities of companies, their repertoires, and the venues at which they performed, but seldom consider the authors who provided the plays. An invisible demarcation line runs through contemporary scholarship, setting theatre historians on one side, literary historians on the other. Neither group has paid much attention to authorship attribution studies, an oversight which has perpetuated the occlusion of Thomas Kyd from the recognition he deserves as the leading playwright of Lord Strange's Men. Kyd's most famous play, 'Jeronymo', or *The Spanish Tragedy*, was given sixteen times in this season, and was often accompanied, either on the day preceding or following, by the piece that Henslowe variously named 'spanes comedye donne oracioe', 'the comodey of doneoracio', 'doneoracio', and 'the comodey of Jeronymo', given seven times. This play must have been by Kyd, it being inconceivable that any other dramatist would have been allowed to write a comedy for Strange's Men on (presumably) the pre-history of Horatio before the events depicted in *The Spanish Tragedy*. Two respected scholars have argued that parts of Kyd's 'comodey' survive in a short burlesque play, *The First Part of Ieronimo* (1605), performed by the Children of the Chapel.[44] The third play that came mostly from Kyd's pen, I shall argue, was *harey the vi*, performed on 3, 7, 11, and 28 March, 1592; 5, 13, and 21 April; 4, 7, 14, 19, and 25 May; 12 and 19 June. On 16 March, Henslowe noted simply receipts for *harey*, which could refer to another play in Strange's repertory, *harey of cornwell*. In the short winter season *harey the vj* was performed on 16 and 31 January 1593, in all a total of sixteen outings, with average receipts over £2.[45] Thus, of the 134 recorded performances by Strange's Men, thirty-nine, or more than a quarter, were of work by Kyd. If we add to this point his authorship of *Fair Em*, Kyd emerges as the foremost dramatist of Lord Strange's Men.

44 Andrew S. Cairncross (ed.), [*The Spanish Comedy, or*] *The First Part of Hieronimo and The Spanish Tragedy* [*or Hieronimo is Mad Again*] (London, 1967); Erne, *Beyond* The Spanish Tragedy, pp. 14–46.

45 *HD*, pp. 16–20.

Another important detail that theatre historians have missed concerning Kyd the playwright is the fact that he alone of the four known dramatists whose work was performed by Strange's Men served their patron in another capacity. He was employed by Strange from about 1588 to 1593, until the Dutch Libel affair caused his precipitate dismissal. Kyd's loyalty to his patron can be seen from the prominence that he and his co-author Nashe gave to the character of Talbot, a distinguished ancestor of Strange, who appears only in this play among the surviving corpus of Elizabethan drama. An additional fact, not often noted, is that Nashe had just as much reason to praise Lord Strange as Kyd, for in the summer of 1592 Strange became Nashe's patron. In *Pierce Pennilesse* (entered in the Stationers' Register on 8 August 1592), Nashe celebrated those 'patrons and Benefactors' whose 'exceeding bountie and liberalitie' provide writers with material support, singling out 'thou, most courteous Amyntas'.[46] McKerrow recorded that, long ago, 'Malone identified the Amintas of the present passage with Ferdinando Stanley ... who is alluded to under the same pastoral name in Spenser's *Colin Clout*, 1595', an identification with which F. P. Wilson concurred.[47] It is no coincidence that Kyd and Nashe should have elevated Talbot to such eminence, and added a complete list of all the titles which Lord Strange's ancestor had earned, including the obscure distinction, 'Lord Strange of Blackmere' (4.7.65). Nashe's authorship of Act 1 of *1 Henry VI* has been firmly settled,[48] and it will be further documented in Volume 2 of this edition, where detailed evidence will be provided for Kyd's authorship of Acts 2–5 of *1 Henry VI*, and Shakespeare's responsibility for three scenes (2.4, 4.2, 4.5), added at some stage after the Lord Chamberlain's Men acquired the play in 1594. The second volume of this edition will also produce strong evidence that Kyd and Shakespeare co-authored *Edward III* in 1593, with Shakespeare responsible for the King's adulterous wooing of the Countess of Salisbury (1.2–2.2) and the scene with Prince Edward and Audley on the eve of battle (4.4), while Kyd supplied the remainder of the play. Kyd's connection with Shakespeare, who edited one of his plays and co-authored another, must have been a major reason why Shakespeare agreed to write 'Additions' to *The Spanish Tragedy* in about 1599, appearing in print in the 1602 Quarto.

46 *The Works of Thomas Nashe*, ed. R. B. McKerrow, 5 vols, revised F. P. Wilson (Oxford, 1958), 1:243.

47 Nashe, *Works*, IV:151, and F. P. Wilson's *Supplement* to Vol. V, pp. 15–16. Wilson convincingly argued that Nashe also dedicated *The Choice of Valentines* to Lord Strange (V:141, n. 1).

48 See Brian Vickers, 'Incomplete Shakespeare: Or, Denying Co-authorship in *1 Henry VI*', *Shakespeare Quarterly* 58 (2007): 311–52, esp. 328–39, 343–5.

THE SPANISH TRAGEDY AND ITS TRAVAILS

Kyd died in late summer 1594, just as the London theatres were entering a long and fruitful creative period, with fewer closures due to plague and more stability among the companies. Where previous narratives conveyed a picture of theatre owners being engaged in continual quarrels and disputes, recent theatre historians, led by Roslyn Knutson, have emphasized the spirit of co-operation that existed between the companies, making a valid comparison with the London guilds, sharing a common profession while competing for customers.[49] Yet, to pursue that commercial analogy, it is equally clear that the companies were engaged in competition with each other, trying to match each other's successes by commissioning new plays and mounting revivals.[50] A condition of rivalry, as well as co-operation, may have accompanied *The Spanish Tragedy* in the theatre. The London theatres were closed due to the plague for two long periods, from 23 June to 29 December 1592, and from 1 February to 27 December 1593. During this hiatus some companies survived by touring, others were bankrupted. Strange's Men seem to have split up during the winter of 1593–4, following Strange's death, for when the Rose theatre reopened on 27 December it was with Sussex's Men.[51] By May 1594 part of the company had gone with Edward Alleyn to the Lord Admiral's Men, including Thomas Downton. The other part, comprising Richard Cowley, Augustine Phillips, Thomas Pope, George Bryan, John Heminges, and Will Kempe, joined the newly founded Chamberlain's Men. In some cases when a company broke up there was a clear division of the playbooks, but with *The Spanish Tragedy* it is possible that both companies claimed the right to perform Kyd's play, since it had not previously been claimed by any other company.

The play's remarkable popularity, with nearly 120 contemporary allusions, reflects its ubiquity in theatres of all kinds throughout this period. In 1975 D. F. Rowan noted that '*The Spanish Tragedy* was mounted on a wide variety of temporary and permanent stages over a period of at least fifty

49 Roslyn L. Knutson, *Playing Companies and Commerce in Shakespeare's Time* (Cambridge, 2001), pp. 21–47.

50 See Roslyn L. Knutson, 'Play Identifications: *The Wise Men of Westchester* and *John a Kent and John a Cumber*; *Longshanks* and *Edward I*', *Huntington Library Quarterly* 47 (1984): 1–11; 'Influence of the Repertory System on the Revival and Revision of *The Spanish Tragedy* and *Dr. Faustus*', *English Literary Renaissance* 18 (1988): 257–74; 'Toe to Toe across Maid Lane: Repertorial Competition at the Rose and Globe, 1599–1600', in P. Nelsen and J. Schlueter (eds), *Acts of Criticism: Performance Matters in Shakespeare and his Contemporaries* (Madison, NJ, 2006), pp. 21–37.

51 *HD*, pp. 20–1.

years.'[52] In addition to its stagings at the Rose from 1592 to 1597, Rowan observed,

> As a property of Strange's Men it could have been acted as well at the Cross Keys Inn, The Theatre and at Newington Butts. As an Admiral's play it was certainly acted at the Fortune, and again possibly at The Theatre and Newington Butts. There is some evidence – centred on Richard Burbage in the role of Hieronimo – to associate the play with the Chamberlain/ King's Men. If this evidence, suggesting multiple auspices for the play, be accepted, then the Curtain, the First Globe and possibly the Second Blackfriars can be added to the list. (pp. 113–14)

It was certainly acted on provincial tours; indeed Dekker reminded Jonson that he, too, had once had the starring role. In *Satiro-mastix, or The untrussing of the Humorous Poet* (1602), Captain Tucca, the principal satirist attacking Jonson (in the figure of Horace), taunts him: 'thou hast forgot how thou amblest (in leather pilch) by a play-wagon, in the high way, and took's't mad Jeronimoes part', also recalling 'when thou ranst mad for the death of Horatio'.[53]

A 'PROLIFERATION' OF *HIERONYMOS*?

Knutson has stated that actors in the 1570s and 1580s 'developed business guidelines for themselves, one of which was that a company should not acquire a script of another company and perform it as its own, even when that script had been published. When the protocol of ownership was abused, the violated company shamed the offender publicly, thus pressuring an adherence to normative practice'.[54] This may be true if the play

[52] D. F. Rowan, 'The Staging of *The Spanish Tragedy*', in G. R. Hibbard (ed.), *The Elizabethan Theatre V* (Hamden, CT, 1975), pp. 112–23, at p. 113.

[53] *Satiro-mastix*, 4.1.130–2 and 1.2.355–6, in Fredson Bowers (ed.), *The Dramatic Works of Thomas Dekker*, 4 vols (Cambridge, 1953–61), 1:351, 326. In his companion *Introductions, Notes, and Commentaries* to the Bowers edition, 4 vols (Cambridge, 1980, 2009), Cyrus Hoy notes the reference to 'Jonson's performance as Hieronimo … presumably both as a strolling player and at Paris Garden, in his acting days' (1:226).

[54] Knutson, *Playing Companies*, p. 42. She only cites one instance of this 'normative practice', 'the reaction of the King's Men to the acquisition of their play, "Jeronimo," by the Children of the Chapel at Blackfriars. As the Induction to *The Malcontent* makes clear, the King's Men justified their taking of the Blackfriars play as revenge for the theft of their own' (ibid.). For a full account of this episode see Lukas Erne, *Beyond* The Spanish Tragedy, who argues convincingly that the play mocked by the Children in their play, *The First Part of Jeronimo. With the Wars of Portugal, and the Death of Don Andrea* (1605), was *The Comedy of Don Horatio*, 'a forepiece to, or [constituting] a two-part play with *The Spanish Tragedy*' (pp. 14–46).

had been sold to a company, but there were exceptions, when an individual was the seller. As long ago as 1891, F. G. Fleay had traced the 'migration' of *Fair Em* to Sussex's Men by way of Alleyn, a member of Strange's Men in 1592.[55] Earlier in his career (1583), Alleyn purchased a handful of plays from Richard Jones, who was selling them on behalf of Worcester's Men, who were breaking up at that point.[56] Knutson herself drew attention to Alleyn's later activities as a trader in playbooks in his business dealings with the Admiral's Men.[57] On 22 August 1601, he sold them *Mahomet*, followed by *The Wise Man of West Chester* on 19 September and *Vortigern* on 20 November, each at the standard price of 40 shillings (£2). On 18 January 1602, Henslowe paid £6 for 'iii boockes wch wer played', namely *The French Doctor*, *The Massacre at Paris*, and *Crack Me this Nut*. On 8 August, he 'paid unto my sone EA' £4 for *Philip of Spain* and *Longshanks*, and on 2 October he paid £2 'unto my sonne EAlleyn at the Apoynment of the company for his Boocke of *Tamar Cham*'.[58]

In their book on Lord Strange's acting company, Sally-Beth MacLean and Lawrence Manley recorded how several plays 'passed through the hands of Alleyn or Henslowe back into the repertory of the rejuvenated Lord Admiral's Men, including *The Spanish Tragedy*, *The Jew of Malta*, *Tamar Cham*', and *The Massacre at Paris*.[59] MacLean and Manley noted that 'no edition of [*The Spanish Tragedy*] attributes it to any acting company' (p. 79), not even the 1602 Quarto, containing the 'Additions' that Shakespeare notionally wrote for the Chamberlain's Men, which describes itself as 'Newly corrected, amended, and enlarged with new additions of the Painters part and others, as it hath of late been divers times acted'.[60] Lacking the proprietorial statement by any company, it may have existed in what we would describe today as 'the public domain'. It is worth repeating MacLean and Manley's

55 See F. G. Fleay, *A Biographical Chronicle of the English Drama, 1559–1642*, 2 vols (London, 1891), 2:282.

56 I am grateful to Professor Susan Cerasano for some helpful discussions of Alleyn. As she commented, 'later in his career, Alleyn owned many plays that he sold to other companies with which he performed and/or managed. We could say that, in all of this, the plays were *travelling with Alleyn*. That is, they were plays in which he was performing, or had performed, and in which he had a major role. When he no longer needed, or wanted them, he sold them off. Consequently, the books seem to be moving erratically from company to company when, in reality, they would have been moving with the actor' (email, 8 August 2023).

57 See Knutson, *The Repertory of Shakespeare's Company 1594–1613* (Fayetteville, 1991), pp. 36, 49, 90.

58 For identification of these plays, see *HD*, pp. 180, 181, 184, 187, 204, 205, 217, and Neil Carson, *A Companion to Henslowe's Diary* (Cambridge, 1988).

59 *Lord Strange's Men*, p. 77, also pp. 86, 88, 381, n. 60.

60 Greg, *BEPD* #110 (d); 1:188–9.

conclusion that 'Like other plays in the repertory of Lord Strange's Men', which collapsed in 1593, '*The Spanish Tragedy* subsequently became a property of Henslowe or of the Lord Admiral's Men, who revived it in January 1596/97 and again, in collaboration with Pembroke's Men, in October 1597.'[61] In which case, they evidently went on using Kyd's original play.

In a recent essay, however, devoted to theatre history, among other topics, H. Schott Syme has argued that the Admiral's Men commissioned a revised version from some unknown dramatist.[62] Although he knows, and quotes from, the work of Knutson,[63] Maclean and Manley, Syme ignores their considered arguments and the evidence they cite. He bases his new claim on two details in Henslowe's *Diary*, the first of which he relegated to a footnote, as if to avoid attention:

> For convenience's sake, I will refer to the Strange's Men play as 'Jeronymo' (the most frequent spelling) and to the Admiral's Men as 'Joronymo' (the more frequent spelling in this second set of records). (p. 9, n. 27)

Scholars familiar with Henslowe's notoriously variable spelling may well think that to base any categorical distinction on such evidence is a mark of extreme self-confidence, or recklessness. For the record, in the 1592–3 season Henslowe spelled the title 'Jeronymo' fifteen times, 'Joronymo' four times. In the 1597 season Henslowe spelled 'Jeronymo' once, 'Joronymo' seven times, indeed more frequently. But he also referred to it as 'Joreneymo' and 'Joronemo' twice each. On such orthographic instability no serious argument can be based.

The second detail that Syme takes as supporting his thesis concerns the fact that Henslowe marked the first performance of this play in that season (29 January 1597) with the enigmatic term 'ne'.[64] Scholars have debated the meaning of this term for over a century, suggestions including 'new', for a new play, or 'ne' for a 'newly refurbished' performance, or one 'newly licensed'. Syme takes a new line altogether: 'Henslowe's "ne" marker' … [suggests] that this was not the old *Spanish Tragedy*, but a new play based on the Hieronimo character' (p. 9). But he fails to produce any evidence that such a play existed.

Syme's subsequent discussion of 'ne' (pp. 10–32) disputes the received explanations by Greg, Chambers, and many more recent scholars with a

61 Op. cit., p. 79.

62 See Syme, *Theatre History, Attribution Studies, and the Question of Evidence* (Cambridge, 2023).

63 See ibid., p. 91: 'Ros Knutson has seen, dissected, helped to reassemble, and prodded along more versions of this text than I dare admit. [It] would not exist without her or her work.'

64 *HD*, p. 55.

degree of detail that defies summary, and some special pleading (or, as he puts it, 'judicious speculation', p. 27). Having attempted to establish 'a sense of dwindling probability that "ne" meant anything other than "a newly licensed play," and that in every instance but the highly atypical "Alexander and Lodowick" that meant "a new play"', he claims that we should accept Henslowe's entry at face value. But this immediately raises other problems:

> If 'Joronymo' was in fact *The Spanish Tragedy*, we might wonder *why the Admiral's Men thought they had to revise it* ... The Admiral's Men evidently felt no need to revise other old plays with established track records: they reintroduced *Doctor Faustus* without revisions in the autumn of 1594, for instance, and kept staging the play, unrevised, twenty-three more times ... (p. 30; my italics)

The passage I have italicised is a blatant example of 'begging the question', or *petitio principii*, assuming the point that you are trying to prove – but he introduced it with 'if', and there is much virtue in 'if'. The fact that the company saw no reason to revise *Dr Faustus* might have caused Syme to doubt his thesis. He returns to Henslowe, however, trying to catch his opponents on the horns of a dilemma:

> Explaining away Henslowe's 'ne' makes 'Joronymo' highly idiosyncratic. Alternatively, the case was utterly conventional: a play marked 'ne' because when first performed, it had recently been commissioned and written. Either 'Joronymo' is the most unusual entry in the *Diary*, or it is not unusual at all. (p. 31)

Experienced readers will not accept this reduction of the issue to a simple binary question. There is more here than either or.

Syme regularly forces his arguments, especially those from analogy. Knutson introduced the idea of 'reportorial clusters', the existence of two or more plays on such subjects as Richard III, Henry V, Tamar Cham, and Hamlet,[65] to which Syme devotes much space (pp. 32–56). Of course, however many of these clusters are amassed, it does not prove that they included 'Hieronymo' plays. Syme observes that the story of Friar Bacon exists in a second version (*John of Bordeaux*) but speculates that there may have been 'three distinct plays', by the workings of 'polyreferentiality' (p. 41). He also observes that 'the fragmentary evidence allows for a proliferation of possible narratives', such as there being three versions of *The Spanish Tragedy* (p. 48). In that case incomplete evidence would allow infinite speculation, and knowledge would be seriously damaged. But one early meaning of 'proliferation' described the excessive unchecked growth

65 See Knutson, *Playing Companies and Commerce in Shakespeare's Time*, p. 58.

of a plant, resulting in its infertility. Fortunately, Syme can only proliferate speculative narratives, not material texts.

In his introduction Syme announced that Section 3 would discuss 'a complex of plays about Hieronimo, most of which are lost' (p. 11). Faced with the absence of texts, many scholars would recall Wittgenstein's principle, '*Wovon man nicht reden kann, darüber muss man schweigen*.'[66] But Syme flourishes in the freedom this absence gives him, devoting a third of his text to discussing 'The Hieronimo Complex' (pp. 56–87). Occasionally his argument gives way to optimistic assertion. Having quoted Richard Dutton's ruling that 'the Master of the Revels would not have licensed the same text for two companies [since] "Performing rights were specific and exclusive"', Syme states that 'it seems *overwhelmingly likely* that *the "specific and exclusive" license* the Admiral's Men *acquired in January 1597*, as the "ne" tag *probably confirms*, was for *their own Hieronimo script*' (p. 59). Every word that I have italicised is speculation. In any case the assertion is untrue that the company acquired a licence, since *The Spanish Tragedy* was never tied to any specific company. As I suggested earlier, its obscure origin in the 1580s may have placed it in the public domain. If it had been an Admiral's Men property, William White and Thomas Pavier would never have dared to publish the 1602 Quarto 'as it hath of late been diuers times acted', without specific acknowledgement to any company. If it had needed a licence in 1592, either Henslowe or Alleyn could have bought one, and would not have needed to pay the fee twice over. Also, as Susan Cerasano has reminded me,

> Henslowe occasionally mentions paying a fee for the licensing of a play, but never for 're-licensing' a play. It seems to me that the clear understanding is that if the Master of the Revels read and licensed a particular version of a play that some slight changes might be made to it, but that major alterations were strictly *verboten*. If this had not been the case then the entire process of licensing would have been undermined by companies that paid for one license and then went on to do whatever they wanted to change a text. It would have been totally unacceptable to the government, especially to one that was placing its faith in the ability to control what occurred on the stage (to some great extent) by requiring the license in the first place.[67]

Further, it would have been highly inconvenient if the scribe had had to produce a new Booke, copy out new parts, and for the actors to learn new lines. The situation in *Hamlet*, where the visiting players are asked to learn

66 *Tractatus logico-philosophicus* (1918), preface and conclusion (7): "What we cannot speak about we must pass over in silence."

67 Cerasano, email 8 August 2023.

a single insertion, can be taken as the norm. It has seldom been observed that the 320 lines, in five separate inserts, that Shakespeare seems to have written for the 1602 Quarto, billed as 'with new additions of the Painters part, and others' – some of which are additions, others substitutions of new material, or both – must have posed a major problem for the company to absorb.[68]

There is evidence of only two reworkings of *The Spanish Tragedy*, one commissioned, but not extant, the other extant but with no declaration of authorship or occasion. On 25 September 1601, Henslowe lent 'unto Bengemen Johnson upon his writtinge of his adicians in geronymo the some of 40 shillings' (£2). Further, on 22 June 1602, Henslowe 'Lent unto bengemy Johnsone ... in earnest of A Boocke called Richard crockbacke & for new adicyons for Jeronymo the some of £10'.[69] The larger sum includes an advance for a whole play, which might be for £2, leaving a substantial sum for the additions. Nothing further is known about either text, but the fact that Henslowe specified 'additions' may be due to him or Jonson having heard rumours of the imminent publication in 1602 of a new edition by a rival company. Some scholars have attributed these additional passages to Jonson, but a considerable amount of evidence, both external (several contemporary allusions linking the play with the Chamberlain's Men) and internal (nearly one hundred collocations uniquely shared with other of his plays and poems), suggests that Shakespeare was their author.[70] But this was still Kyd's play, not a complete reworking of it.

Syme seems oblivious to the limited evidence of substantive alterations. Any mention of the play or its main character could be proof of a new version. Dekker's jesting reference to Jonson playing Hieronimo on tour and at Paris Garden – the Swan theatre – provokes Syme to a long discussion of Pembroke's Men, culminating in the 'persuasive' proposition that 'the repertory of Pembroke's Men, like that of the Admiral's Men, contained

68 In their edition Clara Calvo and Jesus Tronch describe the first 'addition' (54 lines) showing Hieronimo already becoming 'deranged much earlier than in Q1' (p. 178); the second addition is an '11-line fragment' (p. 197), the third addition, a 47-line speech by Hieronimo dispraising sons, is 'awkwardly misplaced' (p. 233). The fourth and longest (167 lines), the celebrated scene with the painter, 'was probably meant to substitute for the whole of 3.13' (p. 245). The fifth (49 lines) is 'an addition-substitution' (p. 311).

69 *HD*, pp. 182, 203.

70 See Warren Stevenson, *Shakespeare's Additions to Thomas Kyd's 'The Spanish Tragedy': A Fresh Look at the Evidence Regarding the 1602 Additions* (Lewiston, NY, 2008); Brian Vickers, 'Identifying Shakespeare's Additions to *The Spanish Tragedy (1602)*: A New(er) Approach', *Shakespeare* 8 (2012): 13–43, and 'Shakespeare and the 1602 Additions to *The Spanish Tragedy*: A Method Vindicated', *Shakespeare* 13 (2017): 101–6.

their own treatment of the Hieronimo story' (pp. 66–75). A 'piece of scrap paper from the Revels' Office dating from between 1615 and 1621' lists 'The Tradgedy of Jeronimo' alongside several other plays being considered for performance at court during the Christmas season. For Syme, the document's failure to 'identify *which* Hieronimo play it means' (p. 64; author's italics) opens the door to various candidates, of which Syme prefers 'a play owned by the Palgrave's Men, written in 1597, rewritten by Jonson in 1601–2, and still in their repertory at the Fortune two decades later' (p. 65). Where is the evidence that such a play ever existed?

Having scattered around simulacra of Kyd's play like a latter-day sorcerer's apprentice, in the closing pages of his essay Syme adds a seventh author, perhaps the most insubstantial yet. In 1675 Edward Phillips, Milton's nephew, published an unreliable compilation, *Theatrum poetarum Anglicanorum: containing brief characters of the English poets*, in which he listed one William Smith as 'the author of a Tragedy entituled *Hieronymo* as also *The Hector of Germany*'. Syme objects that, while Smith did write the latter play, 'in the late 1580s he was living in Chester, writing works of antiquarian interest' (pp. 88–9). However, there was another 'W. Smith' to be considered, the minor playwright Wentworth Smith (b. 1571), whom Henslowe paid fifteen times between 1601 and 1603 as a co-author with Richard Hathway, John Day and others.[71] Little is known about him, but Syme assures us that 'he was certainly old enough to write a play for the Admiral's Men in 1597' – as were doubtless many other dramatists. Syme attempts to account for his absence from Henslowe's records before 1601:

> That his name does not appear in Henslowe's records for the first three years in which they contain payments to playwrights may not be significant. Some writers, including Jonson, disappear from the 'Diary' for years at a time. *The specifics of what we know about 'Joronymo'* might even explain Smith's absence: after all, the novice playwright who managed to turn a new Hieronimo play into a commercial mediocrity was perhaps not a prime candidate for immediate rehire. (p. 89; my italics)

That was a speculative argument – this essay abounds in *if*, *may*, *might*, *perhaps*, *could*, *might have been* – but I have italicised Syme's reference to so-called 'specifics' to show his ability to turn speculation into fact. He ends with an intended irony at his own expense: '"Wentworth Smith the Author of a Tragedy entitled *Hieronymo*" is little more than reckless speculation, but it is a possible answer to two puzzles', namely 'Who wrote a play about Hieronimo for the Admiral's Men in 1597?', and 'why did Edward Phillips' ascribe to 'a man called Smith' a play called *Hieronymo*? The phrase 'reckless

[71] See Chambers, *ES*, 3:393–4 and Carson, *A Companion to Henslowe's Diary*, Index, p. 147.

speculation' is dangerous in this context since some readers may not detect the self-irony.

It is hard to know what Syme hoped to achieve with this essay. In his Acknowledgements he relates that 'It began life as a blog post and then languished in a virtual drawer as an overlong article before being given a chance to reinvent itself' by the editors of this series. It announces its triple focus, 'Theatre History', 'Attribution Studies' (where?), and 'Evidence', but is deficient in each area. Good scholarship leaves a topic better understood, in a form that others can build on, but Syme leaves it in a state of confusion, a procession of speculations, suppressed information, forced arguments, and phantom texts. *The Spanish Tragedy* is not illuminated.

Coincidentally, Ben Jonson provides the final piece of evidence concerning Kyd's career in the London theatres. In his eulogy on Shakespeare, published in the First Folio (1623), Jonson places Kyd among other contemporaries outclassed by Shakespeare:

> For, if I thought my judgement were of yeeres,
> I should commit thee surely with thy peeres,
> And tell, how farre thou didst our Lyly out-shine,
> Or sporting Kyd, or Marlowes mighty line. (27–30)

Jonson's epithet 'sporting' may suggest that Kyd also wrote comedies; Dekker's epithet had been 'industrious', a term hardly merited by the canon of three plays which have come down to us. Both contemporary witnesses encourage the thought that Kyd's output may have been far greater. We know of many lost plays in Shakespeare's age from surviving records of their titles,[72] and it is not unlikely that the anonymously published plays of the period include as yet unrecognized work by Kyd.

One of the historic obstacles to forming a clear picture of Kyd's achievement as a dramatist has always been the smallness of his recognized oeuvre: two plays from the public theatre (*The Spanish Tragedy*, *Soliman and Perseda*) and one closet tragedy translated from the French are not much to go on. But that is not the whole story. My co-editors join me in enlarging his canon by ascribing to him sole authorship of three plays published anonymously: *Fair Em*, *King Leir*, and *Arden of Faversham*, and part authorship of *1 Henry VI* and *Edward III*. These claims will no doubt provoke some scepticism, not least because of the mastery of a wide range of genres that would be implied, from an Italianate revenge tragedy to a 'Turkish' revenge tragedy, a citizen tragedy, a romantic chronicle play, and two English history plays.

[72] See, e.g., Gertrude M. Sibley, *The Lost Plays and Masques, 1500–1642* (Ithaca, NY, 1933) and C. J. Sisson, *Lost Plays of Shakespeare's Age* (Cambridge, 1936). In 2009 Roslyn Knutson and David McInnis founded the excellent *Lost Plays Database*: see now https://lostplays.folger.edu.

However, Peele also produced six plays in widely different genres: a mythological pastoral, *The Arraignment of Paris* (1584); a Marlovian tragedy, *The Battle of Alcazar* (1588); two English history plays, *The Troublesome Reign of King John* (1589) and *Edward I* (1591); a biblical tragedy, *David and Bathsheba* (1590); and the unclassifiable *Old Wife's Tale* (1592). We are seldom encouraged to take Shakespeare's predecessors seriously, but it is time that scholars, ordinary readers, and theatre directors realized that Peele and Kyd were major innovators, playwrights of great flexibility, pioneers at a time when English drama was beginning to show its enormous possibilities.

AFTERWORD: THE ROSE THEATRE REDISCOVERED

On 24 March 1585 Philip Henslowe leased a plot of land about ninety-four feet square on the east corner of Maiden Lane (now Park Street) and Rose Alley, SE1. Two years later he hired John Griggs, a carpenter, to build the Rose Playhouse, which became the first of the Bankside theatres. It opened in 1587 with no recorded acting company and may have been used for other popular entertainment. It has recently been suggested that the original structure had no stage, being used for bear-baiting. Between February and April 1592 Henslowe spent well over £108 enlarging the Rose, partly to increase his audience but also to improve the building's theatrical functions. Although Henslowe recorded his expenditure on material and labour, he left no account of his alterations. Calculating the dimensions of Elizabethan theatres has always been problematic, with estimates based on rough and ready calculations from the few engravings that survive, or on the verbal reports of foreign travellers. It was not until excavations by English Heritage and the Museum of London archaeology departments uncovered the Rose's foundations in February 1989 that scholars were able to match a physical building with the inadequate pictorial record.[73] Architects and theatre historians found enough evidence to reconstruct both the 1587 structure and Henslowe's 1592 alterations. The first Rose was shown to be a rough polygon with fourteen sides, consisting of three tiers of roofed galleries (see the sketch by C. Walter Hodges, Fig. 2). The unexpected geometry of a fourteen-sided figure derived from Albrecht Dürer's 1520 publication of a

[73] For my description of these reconstructions, I have relied on Herbert Berry's account of 'The Rose', *EPT*, pp. 419–36; John Orrell and Andrew Gurr, 'What the Rose can tell us', *Antiquity* 63 (1989): 421–9; Andrew Gurr, *The Shakespeare Stage 1574–1642*, 3rd edn (Cambridge, 1992); Julian Bowsher, *The Rose Theatre, an Archaeological Discovery*, with a 'Postscript' by C. Walter Hodges (London, 1998); Jon Greenfield and Andrew Gurr, 'The Rose Theatre, London: The State of Knowledge and What We Still Need to Know', *Antiquity* 89 (2004): 330–40.

Fig. 1. Photo of the excavation of Rose Playhouse by the Museum of London Archaeology Unit, 1989.

method for dividing a circle into seven equal parts.[74] The building's diameter was seventy-two feet, making it smaller than some later theatres.

74 See Greenfield and Gurr, 'The Rose Theatre, London', pp. 334–5; Simon Blatherwick and Andrew Gurr, 'Shakespeare's Factory: Archeological Evaluations on the Site of the Globe Theatre at 1/15 Anchor Terrace, Southwark Bridge Road, Southwark', *Antiquity* 66 (1992): 315–33, a report on some trial work carried out by the Museum

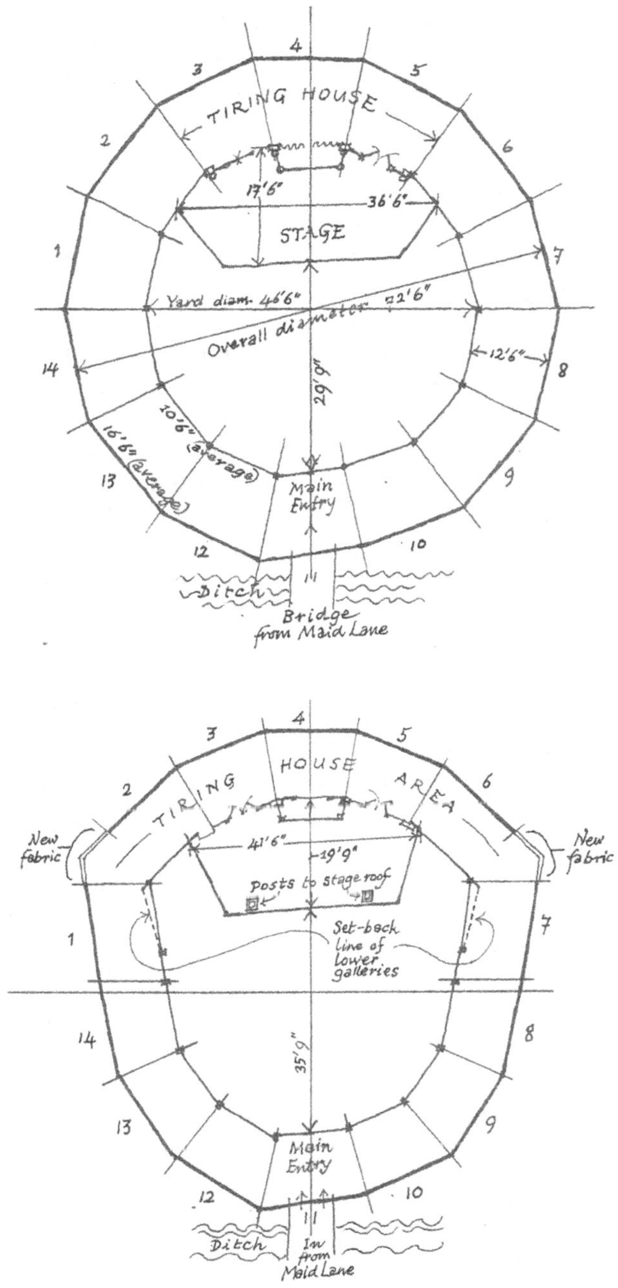

Fig. 2. Sketch of the ground plan of the Rose theatre, 1587 and 1592, by Walter Hodges, based on the 1989 excavations. Reproduced by permission of the Estate of C. W. Hodges.

In the 1592 alterations Henslowe slightly enlarged the theatre to the north, taking down the original outer wall, dismantling the wooden structure and rebuilding it on new foundations further north. The galleries were stretched by six or seven feet on either side of the stage, changing the original polygonal structure into an elongated, ovoid shape. It has been estimated that he increased the occupation of the galleries from 1,400 to 1,650 seated spectators and that of those standing in the yard from 606 to 775, giving a total of 2,425 spectators.[75] Henslowe improved the internal structure, changing the aspect of sight-lines from the galleries at the side of the stage. He also erected two columns at the front of the stage to support a roof over the stage, perhaps with machinery to lower props, and he enlarged the 'tiring house', the actors' changing rooms and other offices.

The detail of most interest to theatre and literary scholars is the size and shape of the stage. We know from the original building contracts that in 1587 the Red Lion's stage was thirty feet deep and forty feet across, while the Fortune's stage was twenty-seven-and-a-half feet deep and forty-three feet across. The Rose's was thirty-seven-and-a-half feet across at the rear, tapering to twenty-seven-and-a-half feet at the front, and fifteen-and-a-half feet deep. For the 1592 alterations Henslowe kept the taper of the stage (as far as we know, all other stages were rectangular) but increased the depth to seventeen feet. Compared to other stages, that of the Rose was smaller and significantly shallow in relation to its width. Yet these dimensions gave the Rose a certain advantage over other theatres. While it could not accommodate as many actors in crowd scenes or battles, the internal shallow stage meant that the actors would be standing nearer the audience. The tapering form also had a funnelling effect, projecting both sound and gesture towards the spectators. This closer contact must have given even greater impact to Edward Alleyn in such roles as Tamburlaine, Barabas, Titus Andronicus, Dr Faustus, Hieronimo, and John Talbot in *1 Henry VI*. Alleyn's acting style has been attacked, and defended.[76] I imagine that the

of London between 1989 and 1991 on the site of the Globe. The remains of the outer gallery wall 'prove that they formed a polygon' having twenty sides (p. 326).

75 R. A. Foakes gave slightly different figures in 'The Discovery of the Rose Theatre: Some Implications', *Shakespeare Survey* 43 (1991): 141–8.

76 See, e.g., the sympathetic estimate by William Armstrong, 'Shakespeare and the Acting of Edward Alleyn', *Shakespeare Survey* 7 (1954): 82–9, and the notably unsympathetic one by Andrew Gurr, 'Who Strutted and Bellowed?', *Shakespeare Survey* 16 (1963): 95–102. It is an easy, but unjustified, assumption that Shakespeare wrote Hamlet's advice to the players to comment on real contemporary actors rather than to criticize general faults that actors are prone to. It is a further error to assume that he intended to mock Alleyn. Gurr accused him of inventing 'the Red Bull style' of acting (p. 98). Yet that theatre has been undeservedly dismissed as crude

effect, together with the closer acoustic of a smaller, wood-built theatre, would have been of terrifying intensity. Two theatre historians have evoked the Rose's 'timber-framed structure of roofed galleries surrounding the yard where people stood around to hear Edward Alleyn roaring Marlowe's mighty lines'.[77]

The first excavations lasted from February to April 1989, uncovering only 10 per cent of the structure. Since then, the Rose Theatre Trust has been founded as a pressure group to launch further excavations of the eastern section of the site. It is exciting to think that the stage where Kyd enjoyed his greatest successes in 1592–3 can now be seen anew.

Staging at the Rose

Another method of defining the internal fittings of a theatre is to review the stage directions of plays known to have been performed there. Scott McMillin did this for the Rose theatre in the 1590s on the basis of 'more than three dozen published or manuscript plays',[78] including Kyd's *The Spanish Tragedy*, *King Leir*, and (co-authored) *1 Henry VI*; Marlowe's *Tamburlaine*, *The Massacre of Paris*, *Dr Faustus*, and *The Jew of Malta*; Peele's *David and Bathsheba*, perhaps *The Battle of Alcazar* (Henslowe records a 'Muly Molocco' and 'Mahomet'), and *Titus Andronicus* (co-authored with Shakespeare). A number of these plays depend on the theatre having a raised area for acting. They call for action to take place 'above' or 'aloft';[79] 'on the walls'.[80] In *The Spanish Tragedy* the ghost of Andrea and Revenge may sit in the gallery, from where they utter their comments on the play's action. Yet these scenes include Andrea's lengthy opening narration (90 lines) and the play's conclusion (40 lines), which would be awkwardly delivered from above. It would be better if they sat at the side of the stage. In the play, while Horatio and Bel-Imperia declare their love, as McMillin noted (p. 28), '"*Pedringano sheweth all to the Prince and Lorenzo, placing them in secret*" (760–1; Q lineation), from where they observe the action for 55 lines and Balthazar speak[s] from "*above*"' (773). McMillin failed to note the stage direction '*A letter falleth*' (1180), evidently from an upstairs window, but he recorded that Bel-Imperia subsequently appears '*at a window*' (1680), from where she

---

and sensational. See now Eva Griffith, *A Jacobean Company and its Playhouse: The Queen's Servants at the Red Bull Theatre (c.1605–1619)* (Cambridge, 2013).

77 Orrell and Gurr, 'What the Rose can tell us', p. 423.

78 S. McMillin, *The Elizabethan Theatre and the Book of Sir Thomas More* (Ithaca, NY, and London, 1987), ch. 6, 'Staging at the Rose' (pp. 113–34, at 115). McMillin's case for *Sir Thomas More* being an Elizabethan play has been qualified by subsequent research into its diction and style, suggesting a date of c. 1603.

79 See *Alc.*, *DB*; *Jew*; *Tit. A.*, *1H6*.

80 *DB*, *Tamb.*, *1H6*.

speaks a ten-line soliloquy. In his preparations of the inset play of *Soliman and Perseda*, Hieronimo asks the Duke of Castile to place the royal 'traine … into the gallerie' and then 'to throwe me downe the key' (2660–1). The stage direction duly follows: '*Enter Spanish King, Vice-Roy, the Duke of Castile, and their train*' (2681–3), from where, as McMillin puts it, 'they observe action below, with some interaction among themselves, for 165 lines' (p. 126). McMillin failed to note that the Spanish and Portuguese nobility are in effect trapped in the gallery, unwilling captives witnessing the murders of their children and hearing Hieronimo's lengthy account of the events that have provoked this multiple revenge (2764–2844). Having justified his – and Bel-Imperia's – actions, Hieronimo '*runs to hang himself*' (2845), and the Portuguese Viceroy belatedly realizes: 'We are betraide, my Balthazar is slaine, | Breake ope the doores, runne save Hieronimo' (2848–9). Kyd's use of the gallery space in the Rose is typically inventive. As McMillin deduces from DeWitt's drawing of the Swan theatre,

> The gallery seems to be a place for spectators or musicians, but one of its compartments could easily have been used for such small 'window' and 'wall' scenes … The one or two characters in the raised position usually speak to others on the platform below. No depth is required for the raised area in other words. Characters there are *held* in relation to others on the platform. (p. 126; my italics)

I have italicised the verb that describes the norm for characters in these raised acting areas: Kyd is the only one of the Rose playwrights to turn that feature into an integral part of the dramatic action.

The other stage action common to all the Rose playwrights is the use of what McMillin called 'a curtained enclosure' (p. 114), or discovery space. Most of the Rose plays making use of this feature used a curtain (pp. 130–2), as did Peele's *David and Bathsheba*, where a curtain is drawn and Bathsheba is discovered with her maid, bathing. In *2 Tamburlaine*, '*The arras is drawn and Zenocrate lies in her bed of state*', attended by servants. In *The Jew of Malta*, there is '*A cauldron discovered*', within which Barabas, '*boiling, speaks his last*'. In *The Spanish Tragedy*, Hieronimo '*knocks up the curtain*' (2647) to arrange a discovery space for the corpse of Horatio, and after the denouement of his play within a play, he '*Shewes his dead sonne*' (2780). But Kyd had used another form of discovery space, a 'special property', as Gurr calls it, such as 'a curtained "booth" set up on stage', a kind of 'discovery booth', which 'would have had to be attached to the tiring house in some way, at a door, so that the objects and players could be changed without the audience seeing'.[81] This category best fits Hieronimo's 'pleasant

[81] Gurr, *The Shakespearean Stage 1514–1642*, p. 149.

bower', as Bel-Imperia describes it: 'The Court were dangerous, that place is safe' (798–800). We see their next meeting, the scene set by Horatio:

> Come Bel-Imperia let us to the bower,
> And there in safetie pass a pleasant hower. (876–7; 2.4.4–5)

But Pedringano betrays them to Lorenzo and, alongside Balthazar and Serberine, they burst in when Lorenzo orders, 'Quickly dispatch my maisters', followed by the shocking stage directions: '*They hang him in the Arbor*' (917) and '*They stab him*' (920).

The arbour was probably a trellis-like structure, as shown in the 1602 Quarto. It was most likely a free-standing structure on the stage throughout,[82] for in her mania Isabella decides to 'revenge my selfe upon the place | Where thus they murdered my beloved Sonne'. '*She cuts downe the Arbour*'. Isabella doesn't merely cut it down, she curses it with great force:

> Down with these branches and these loathsome boughs
> Of this unfortunate and fatal pine.
> Down with them, Isabella, rend them up
> And burn the roots from whence the rest is sprung.
> I will not leave a root, a stalk, a tree,
> A bough, a branch, a blossom, nor a leaf,
> No, not an herb within this garden plot.
> Accursed complot of my misery,
> Fruitless for ever may this garden be. (4.2.6–15)

It is difficult to recall any other play in which the destruction of a stage property conveys such intensity of feeling. Isabella's act is futile in one sense, but also cathartic. The arbour represents a meeting place for love turned into a scene of death, a pollution of nature which Isabella must destroy before killing herself. It is a small gesture of defiance towards human perversion of a human code, an assertion of love and remembrance.

Kyd's final use of the Rose's stage resources is to 'knock up' a curtain, using a hammer and nails, to cover the space behind which a lifelike image of Horatio has been placed – presumably the same one that Hieronimo cut down after the murder (2.4.12). It may be a law of drama that whenever curtains are shown, a discovery must follow. (Compare Chekhov's famous advice to an author that if a pistol is seen hanging on a wall in Act 1, it must be used before the play ends.) The 'discovery' or display of his son's corpse gives Hieronimo the final chance to memorialize Horatio:

82 In their recent edition Calvo and Trench imagine it as a moveable structure: '[*An arbour set forth*]' at the beginning of 2.4 (p. 171) and '[*Arbour withdrawn*]' at the end (p. 184); similarly, at the beginning of 4.2: '[*Arbour set forth*]' (p. 294), but nothing at the end. This seems to me awkward, in theatrical terms.

See here my show, look on this spectacle.
Here lay any hope, and here my hope had end;
Here lay my heart, and here my heart was slain. (5.4.88–90)

Whatever resources the Rose could offer, Kyd made great use of them. We can celebrate the synergy between a playwright and his theatre.

BIBLIOGRAPHY

Allen, Don Cameron (ed.), *Francis Meres's Treatise "Poetrie"* (Urbana, IL, 1933; *University of Illinois Studies in Language and Literature*, vol. 16).

Armstrong, William, 'Shakespeare and the acting of Edward Alleyn', *Shakespeare Survey* 7 (1954): 82–9.

Astington, John H., *English Court Theatre 1558–1642* (Cambridge, 1999).

Baldwin, T. W., *On the Literary Genetics of Shakspere's Plays 1592–1594* (Urbana, IL, 1959).

Benbow, R. Mark, 'Dutton and Goffe versus Broughton: a disputed contract for plays in the 1570s', *REED Newsletter* 2 (1981): 2, 3–9.

Berry, Herbert, *Shakespeare's Playhouses* (New York, 1987).

Blayney, Peter, 'The publication of playbooks', in J. D. Cox and D. S. Kastan (eds), *A New History of Early English Drama* (New York, NY and London, 1997), pp. 383–422.

Bowers, Fredson (ed.), *The Dramatic Works of Thomas Dekker*, 4 vols (Cambridge, 1953–61).

Bowsher, Julian, *The Rose Theatre, an archaeological discovery*, with a 'Postscript' by C. Walter Hodges (London, 1998).

Cairncross, Andrew S. (ed.), [*The Spanish Comedy, or*] *The First Part of Hieronimo and The Spanish Tragedy* [*or Hieronimo is Mad Again*] (London, 1967).

Calvo, Clara and Jesús Tronch (eds), *The Spanish Tragedy* (London, 2013).

Carson, Neil, *A Companion to Henslowe's Diary* (Cambridge, 1988).

Chambers, E. K., *The Elizabethan Stage*, 4 vols (Oxford, 1923).

Chillington Rutter, Carol (ed.), *Documents of the Rose Playhouse*, rev. edn (Manchester, 1999).

Cunliffe, John W. (ed.), *Early English Classical Tragedies* (Oxford, 1912).

Dekker, Thomas, *A Knight's Conjuring Done in earnest: Discouered in Iest* (London, 1607; *STC* 6508).

Dutton, Richard (ed.), *The Oxford Handbook of Early Modern Theatre* (Oxford, 2009).

Erne, Lukas, *Beyond* The Spanish Tragedy: *A Study of the Works of Thomas Kyd* (Manchester, 2001).

Foakes, R. A., 'The discovery of the Rose Theatre: some implications', *Shakespeare Survey* 43 (1991): 141–8.

—— and R. T. Rickert (eds), *Henslowe's Diary* (Cambridge, 2002).

Freeman, Arthur, *Thomas Kyd. Facts and Problems* (Oxford, 1967).

Greenfield, Jon and Andrew Gurr, 'The Rose Theatre, London: the state of knowledge and what we still need to know', *Antiquity* 89 (2004): 330–40.

Greg, W. W. and F. S. Boas (eds), *The Spanish Tragedy with Additions 1602* (Oxford, 1925; *MSR*).

Griffith, Eva, *A Jacobean Company and its Playhouse: The Queen's Servants at the Red Bull Theatre (c.1605–1619)* (Cambridge, 2013).

Gurr, Andrew, 'Who strutted and bellowed?', *Shakespeare Survey* 16 (1963): 95–102.

—— *The Shakespeare Stage 1574–1642*, 3rd edn (Cambridge, 1992).

—— *The Shakespearian Playing Companies* (Oxford, 1996).

Hardison Jr, O. B., *Prosody and Purpose in the English Renaissance* (Baltimore, MD and London, 1989).

Hoy, Cyrus, *Introductions, Notes, and Commentaries … to the Bowers edition*, 4 vols (Cambridge, 1980, 2009).

Ingram, William, *The Business of Playing: The Beginnings of the Adult Professional Theater in Elizabethan London* (Ithaca, NY and London, 1992).

Ioppolo, Grace, *Dramatists and their Manuscripts in the Age of Shakespeare, Jonson, Middleton and Heywood* (London, 2006).

Kathman, David, 'Inn-yard playhouses', in Dutton, pp. 153–67.

Knutson, Roslyn L., *Playing companies and commerce in Shakespeare's time* (Cambridge, 2001).

—— 'Play identifications: *The Wise Men of Westchester* and *John a Kent and John a Cumber*; *Longshanks* and *Edward I*', *Huntington Library Quarterly* 47 (1984): 1–11.

—— 'Influence of the repertory system on the revival and revision of *The Spanish Tragedy* and *Dr. Faustus*', *English Literary Renaissance* 18 (1988): 257–74.

—— 'Toe to toe across Maid Lane: repertorial competition at the Rose and Globe, 1599–1600', in P. Nelsen and J. Schlueter (eds), *Acts of Criticism: Performance Matters in Shakespeare and his Contemporaries* (Madison, NJ, 2006), pp. 21–37.

McMillin, Scott, *The Elizabethan Theatre and the Book of Sir Thomas More* (Ithaca, NY and London, 1987).

—— and Sally-Beth MacLean, *The Queen's Men and their Plays* (Cambridge, 1998).

Manley, Lawrence, 'Why Did London Inns Function as Theatres?', *Huntington Library Quarterly* 71:1 (2008): 181–97.

—— and Sally-Beth MacLean, *Lord Strange's Men and Their Plays* (New Haven, CT and London, 2014).

Orrell, John and Andrew Gurr, 'What the Rose can tell us', *Antiquity* 63 (1989): 421–9.

Pigman III, G. W. (ed.), *George Gascoigne: A Hundreth Sundrie Flowres* (Oxford, 2000).

Puttenham, George, *The Arte of English Poesie*, ed. Gladys Doidge Willcock and Alice Walker (Cambridge, 1936, 1970).

Rowan, D. F., 'The staging of *The Spanish Tragedy*', in G. R. Hibbard (ed.), *The Elizabethan Theatre V* (Hamden, CT, 1975), pp. 112–23.

Shapiro, Michael, *Children of the Revels: The Boy Companies of Shakespeare's Time and their Plays* (New York, 1977).

Somerset, Alan, 'Not just Sir Oliver Owlet: from patrons to patronage of Early Modern theatre', in Dutton, pp. 343–61.

Thomson, Peter, *Shakespeare's Professional Career* (Cambridge, 1992).

Vickers, Brian (ed.), *English Renaissance Literary Criticism* (Oxford, 1999).

—— *Shakespeare, Co-Author* (Oxford, 2002), Appendix II: 'Abolishing the Author? Theory *versus* History', pp. 506–41.

—— 'Incomplete Shakespeare: or, denying co-authorship in *1 Henry VI*', *Shakespeare Quarterly* 58 (2007): 311–52.

—— 'Identifying Shakespeare's Additions to *The Spanish Tragedy (1602)*: a new(er) approach', *Shakespeare* 8 (2012): 13–43.

—— 'Shakespeare and the 1602 Additions to The Spanish Tragedy: a method vindicated', *Shakespeare* 13 (2017): 101–6.

—— 'Kyd's authorship of *King Leir*', *Studies in Philology* 115 (2018): 433–71.

—— 'Thomas Watson, Thomas Kyd, and Embedded Poetry', *Studies in Philology* 120:3 (2023): 557–601.

—— *Recovering Thomas Kyd: A Canon Restored* (Princeton, forthcoming).

Wallace, C. W., *The First London Theatre* (Lincoln, NE, 1913).

Wickham, Glynne, Herbert Berry and William Ingram (eds), *English Professional Theatre, 1530–1660* (Cambridge, 2000).

Wiggins, Martin, *British Drama, 1533–1642: a Catalogue*, 10 vols (Oxford, 2012 –).

Wilson, F. P., *The English Drama 1485–1585*, ed. G. K. Hunter (Oxford, 1969).

RECOGNIZING KYD

Brian Vickers

When I first started working on Thomas Kyd, some twenty years ago, I had no thought of enlarging his canon. My goal was to better understand his masterpiece, *The Spanish Tragedy* (written c. 1585, published 1592). I also studied the two other plays of accepted authorship, *Soliman and Perseda* (written c. 1588, published 1592), and *Cornelia*, translated from Garnier's *Cornélie* and published posthumously in 1594. Having a naturally inquisitive mind, I studied reference books and annual bibliographies to discover secondary literature on Kyd's life and works. As I worked through these sources, I noticed that other plays had been attributed over the years, some repeatedly, others only once or twice.

The play most often ascribed to him was *Arden of Faversham*, first made in 1903 by that knowledgeable scholar Charles Crawford, who in 1908 compiled by hand a *Concordance* to Kyd's three acknowledged plays.[1] Crawford had great expertise in identifying unattributed excerpts, as he showed in an exemplary edition of the 1600 verse anthology *England's Parnassus* (Oxford, 1913), in which he was able to identify over 3,000 of the quotations from anonymous poets and dramatists. His interleaved copy of another verse anthology, *Bodenham's Belvedére* (1600), identifying over 2,000 of the anthology's 4,400 quotations, has recently been published.[2] The fact that a scholar with these abilities ascribed *Arden of Faversham* to Kyd is of considerable significance. Crawford's pioneering identification was soon followed by the dissertation of Walter Miksch on 'The Authorship of *Arden of Faversham*', in which Miksch accepted Crawford's attribution

1 See Crawford, 'The Authorship of *Arden of Faversham*', *Jahrbuch der Deutschen Shakespeare Gesellschaft* 39 (1903): 74–86, reprinted in Crawford, *Collectanea*, First Series (Stratford-on-Avon, 1906), 101–30; quotations from the later version; and *A Concordance to the Works of Thomas Kyd*, in W. Bang (ed.), *Materialen zur Kunde des älteren englischen Dramas*, vol. XIX (Louvain, 1908).

2 See Lukas Erne and Devani Singh (eds), *Bel-vedére or The Garden of the Muses: An Early Modern Printed Commonplace Book* (Cambridge, 2020), and my assessment in *The Review of English Studies* 73 (2022): 593–6.

while adding many new matches between the play and Kyd. There were other contributions, English (H. Dugdale Sykes) and French (Felix Carrère),[3] until in 1948 the great Danish scholar Paul Rubow, in his study of 'Shakespeare and his contemporaries', settled the attribution by listing over a hundred verbal matches with Kyd.[4]

The documentation in that paragraph will surprise many modern readers, who only know the attribution made by MacDonald Jackson in numerous publications over the last fifty years, according to which Shakespeare wrote scene 8. Jackson dismissed Crawford, unfairly, and completely ignored Rubow, even though M. L. Wine, in his Revels edition of *Arden* – Jackson's preferred text – frequently cited Rubow in his commentary and included many of his identified Kyd matches in an appendix.[5] As Dr Johnson might have said, 'a scholar may ignore the evidence for a while, but others will rediscover it.' Jackson's arguments have been comprehensively refuted by myself and by Darren Freebury-Jones, who started later than me but finished earlier,[6] and we hope that the edition and accompanying documentation in Volume 2 will convince all non-partisan readers.

The other sole-authored plays that I add to Kyd's canon have a much smaller bibliography. *King Leir* was attributed to Kyd by another perceptive scholar writing before the second world war, William Wells, whose successes in attribution studies included identifying Middleton's hand in *Timon of Athens*.[7] For *Fair Em* I found a single hint in Rubow's book, which handsomely rewarded further research.[8]

3 For the scholarly tradition identifying Kyd's authorship of *Arden* see Brian Vickers, *Recovering Thomas Kyd: A canon restored* (Princeton, forthcoming), ch. 6.

4 See Paul V. Rubow, *Shakespeare og hans samtidige* (Copenhagen, 1948), pp. 108–44. Although the discussion is in Danish, all the quotations are in English, with full Act, scene, and line references. A reader with some knowledge of Kyd will have no difficulty in recognizing the matching passages. Since the original texts are found only in a few libraries, on my website, https://brianvickers.uk/databases/arden-of-faversham/, I have excerpted 50 matches from Crawford, 85 from Miksch, and 95 from Rubow.

5 See M. L. Wine (ed.), *The Tragedy of Master Arden of Faversham* (Manchester, 1973), pp. 141–7.

6 See Vickers, *Recovering Thomas Kyd*, ch. 8, and Darren Freebury-Jones, *Shakespeare's Tutor: The influence of Thomas Kyd* (Manchester, 2022), esp. pp. 49–51, 65–79, 83–8. I am happy to say that Freebury-Jones has confirmed and extended my argument, adding new evidence.

7 William Wells, 'The Authorship of "King Leir"', *Notes and Queries* 177 (16 December 1939): 434–8. On his Middleton attributions see Brian Vickers, *Shakespeare, Co-Author: A Historical Study of Five Collaborative Plays* (Oxford, 2002), pp. 264–7, 269–89.

8 See Rubow, pp. 132–3, and now the essay by Freebury-Jones, 'Possible Light on the Authorship of *Fair Em*', *Notes and Queries* 262 (2017): 252–4.

My aim, emerging from my study of the historical scholarship, is to justify my attribution to him of sole authorship of these three plays published anonymously: *King Leir* (written c. 1589, published 1605), *Arden of Faversham* (written c. 1590, published 1592), and *Fair Em* (written c. 1590, published c. 1593). My reason for attributing these three plays is rather unusual. Normally, attributions are based on small-scale resemblances between the text of an anonymously published play and one or more plays of known authorship. Such resemblances can be of parallel phrases occurring in two plays by the same author and nowhere else in the drama of the period. Other stylistic resemblances can include distinctive uses of blank verse or rhyme. But my attributions to Kyd were based on large-scale resemblances, as I had noted when I first announced my discoveries.[9] I noticed that all three plays include plot elements that are found in *The Spanish Tragedy* and *Soliman and Perseda*, namely murderous intrigues, the use of comedy in tragedy, and the presence of women ready to stab the man whom they – rightly or wrongly – accuse of having harmed them. Other Elizabethan dramatists may use one or other of these elements, but Kyd is the only one to use all three.

For the first, in *The Spanish Tragedy* there are three intrigues. Lorenzo hires accomplices to kill Horatio, so that his friend Balthazar may woo Horatio's beloved, Bel-Imperia. Secondly, in a subplot, set in the Portuguese court, the evil Villuppo gives false information to the Viceroy that his son has been killed in battle by Alexandro, who is arrested and condemned to death. But a true report arrives confirming that the son is still alive, so Alexandro is freed, and the evil courtier executed. Thirdly, in the main plot Hieronimo, the father of Horatio, joins with Bel-Imperia to avenge Horatio's murder. Hieronimo writes a play to be acted at the Spanish court on the story of Soliman and Perseda, in which all his enemies take part and are killed. Kyd returned to that story for his tragedy *Soliman and Perseda*, which uses one main intrigue. Erastus, having killed a man in a quarrel, flees from Rhodes to Constantinople, where the emperor Soliman accepts him as a friend. Perseda, Erastus's beloved, follows him to the Turkish court, where Soliman falls in love with her. Brusor, the emperor's bashaw, advises him to have Erastus killed, and they use Brusor's wife Lucina as a decoy to keep Perseda occupied. When Perseda discovers Lucina's betrayal she stabs her to death. In the final scene Perseda disguises herself in a man's armour to fight with Soliman. He kills her, but before dying she has her revenge on him with a poisoned kiss.

9 See Brian Vickers, 'Thomas Kyd, secret sharer', *Times Literary Supplement*, 18 April 2008, pp. 13–15.

In both tragedies Kyd introduces comic scenes in a tragic context. In *The Spanish Tragedy* Pedringano, one of the plotters hired by Lorenzo to kill Horatio, is brought to trial. Lorenzo has assured him that he will send his page with a pardon to be handed to the hangman on the scaffold. Left alone, the page tells the audience that Lorenzo has given him an empty box. Believing himself protected by the pardon, Pedringano insults the hangman outrageously in a very amusing manner, where the reader or theatregoer has difficulty stifling their laughter – until his hanging is simulated onstage. That is perhaps the first instance of black comedy in English drama. In *Soliman and Perseda* the cowardly braggart soldier Basilisco is a comic figure throughout, especially when Perseda asks him to kill Lucina, the woman who betrayed her husband. He takes a dagger, '*feels upon the point of it*', and objects: 'The point will mar her skin' (5.3.49–50). Our amusement is short-lived.

In both tragedies Kyd introduces vengeful women. It was a common belief in Renaissance society that women were too tender-hearted to carry out a murder. But in *The Spanish Tragedy* Kyd shows Bel-Imperia's determination to be revenged on the man who killed Horatio. Having been given the role of Perseda in Hieronimo's play-within-the-play, Bel-Imperia succeeds in stabbing Balthazar before unexpectedly killing herself. In *Soliman and Perseda* the heroine, frustrated by Basilisco's cowardice, says 'What, darest thou not? Give me the dagger then!', before stabbing Lucina (5.3.45–51). In the final scene Perseda receives her death stroke from Soliman, who had had her lover murdered, but kills him with a poisoned kiss.

All three of the plays I newly ascribe to Kyd have intrigue plots, two of them murderous. In *King Leir* Kyd follows the traditional story of the king dividing his kingdom between his three daughters but adds a plot by Leir to make the division dependent on his daughters' choice of husbands. Since Gonorill and Ragan already have royal suitors, Leir reveals to his courtiers his plan to force Cordella to marry the King of Ireland, although she 'vows | No liking to a monarch, unless love allows' (1.59–66). Unfortunately for his 'sudden stratagem', the corrupt courtier Skalliger reveals it to Gonorill and Ragan, who easily manipulate the ceremony and have Cordella banished. While that story has a happy ending, turning into a pastoral romance, the main intrigue in the play is the evil daughters' plot to have their father murdered. First Gonorill decides to 'intercept the Messenger' who travels between the two sisters and corrupt him (just as Lorenzo corrupted Pedringano) 'With sweet persuasions, and with sound rewards' (12.23–5), to murder Leir and his attendant, the good courtier Perillus. Ragan makes the same approach and the '*Messenger, or Murderer*', as a stage-direction describes him, accepts both bribes and promises to complete the contract (12.106; 15.50). Within his intrigue plots Kyd is free to vary the importance of the protagonists' roles. Here he shifts attention from the contract-giver to the hireling assassin who will carry out the hit, turning the Messenger into both a sinister and a comic figure, giving him more asides and soliloquies than any other character in his plays. In effect the Messenger provides a running commentary on his situation, full of black humour, enjoying his power to frighten his two victims, who we see through his eyes. He extracts more money from them, postponing their execution, until they manage to frighten him with fear of eternal damnation. Then he leaves them, unpunished, befitting the decorum of the play as it turns into a tragicomedy.

If Kyd innovated with the hireling assassin in *King Leir* he did so again with another recurrent feature of his plots, the role of vengeful woman. In his two tragedies both Bel-Imperia and Perseda acted that role with moral legitimacy, avenging the murder of their beloved partners on the men who had ordered their execution. (In Renaissance revenge plays both Christian morality and efficient legal systems are in abeyance.) But Gonorill and Ragan have no moral legitimacy in planning to murder Leir. Kyd had picked up this motive from a brief reference in William Warner's treatment of the Lear story in his poem *Albion's England* (1586) to a plot element that, with his interest in vengeful women, may have attracted Kyd to this story in the first place: 'Gonorill ... not only did attempt | Her father's death, but openly did hold him in contempt.' In his play she first orders Leir's murder, bribing the assassin. Ragan does the same, but Kyd gives her a far more violent nature. Not having seen or heard from the assassin she hired, Ragan widens her anger to take in the whole male sex:

> A shame on these white-livered slaves, say I,
> That with fair words so soon are overcome.
> O God, that I had been but made a man,
> Or that my strength were equal with my will! [10]
> These foolish men are nothing but mere pity
> And melt as butter doth against the sun.
> Why should they have preeminence over us
> Since we are creatures of more brave resolve? (25.13–20)

As throughout his playwriting career, Kyd put himself into the minds of his creations, imagining by what principles they motivate their actions.

He did this nowhere more successfully than with Alice Arden, who unites both roles of intriguer and vengeful woman. Her first speech when alone in scene 1, having just been informed that her husband will soon

[10] Cf. Beatrice's (misplaced) anger at Claudio for having rejected Hero: 'O that I were a man! ... O God, that I were a man! I would eat his heart in the marketplace ... O that I were a man for his sake! Or that I had any friend would be a man for my sake! But manhood is melted into cur'sies ...', *Much Ado about Nothing*, 4.1.303–19.

be going to London on business, is to wish his death so that she can enjoy her lover:

> Ere noon he means to take horse and away!
> Sweet news is this! Oh, that some airy spirit
> Would in the shape and likeness of a horse
> Gallop with Arden 'cross the ocean
> And throw him from his back into the waves!
> Sweet Mosby is the man that hath my heart;
> And he [Arden] usurps it, having nought but this:
> That I am tied to him by marriage.
> Love is a god and marriage is but words,
> And therefore Mosby's title is the best. (1.92–101)

There Kyd economically makes it clear that, like Gonorill and Ragan, in planning to murder her husband Alice has no moral legitimacy. Several times within the play Kyd makes her utter that death wish, right up to the murder that finally takes place in scene 14, line 229, when she echoes Perseda's command to Basilisco ('Give me the dagger then!') but in a much more gruesome context:

> *Alice* [*To Arden*] What, groans thou? [*To Mosby*] Nay, then, give me the weapon.
> [*To Arden*] Take this for hind'ring Mosby's love and mine.
> [*Alice stabs Arden and he dies.*] (14.229–30)

In other Kyd plays the intriguer has at the most one or two associates. In *Arden* Kyd follows his source, Holinshed's 1587 *Chronicles*, but enlarges the cast of characters. Apart from Arden and his loyal friend Franklin, almost everyone else in the play is an accomplice of the two main plotters, Alice and Mosby. In *Leir* Kyd experimented with the role of the assassin, turning him into an entertainer; in *Arden* he turns the would-be murderers into farcical blunderers. The two professional assassins, Black Will and Shakebag, are primarily sources of laughter. They have a succession of failures, starting with a scene where Arden has been walking a turn in St Paul's, a common rendezvous for business deals. But the churchyard was also lined with booksellers' stalls, and just as Will is preparing to 'run [Arden] through' with his sword, a printer's apprentice shuts up shop: '*Then he lets he down his window, and it breaks Black Will's head*', leading to this comic exchange:

> WILL Zounds, draw, Shakebag, draw! I am almost killed.
> PRENTICE We'll tame you, I warrant.
> WILL Zounds, I am tame enough already. (3.48–50)

Will's self-deflating reply shows the comic nature of his role, as the audience laughs both with and at him. Their subsequent failures include losing their prey in the fog, with Shakebag falling into a ditch; the murderers coming to blows over their respective abilities as a 'cutter'; and being defeated in a swordfight by Arden and Franklin, who are just normal citizens. As the failures stack up, we may think they will never succeed, but the gruesome murder is all the more shocking.

Kyd innovates further with the role of intriguer. In *The Spanish Tragedy* Lorenzo acts as the ruthless Machiavellian, hiring killers whom he intends to get rid of as soon as their contract is fulfilled. As he contemptuously puts it:

> They that for coin their souls endangered,
> To save my life, for coin shall venture theirs;
> And better 'tis that base companions die,
> Than by their life to hazard our good haps.
> Nor shall they live, for me to fear their faith:
> I'll trust myself, myself shall be my friend;
> For die they shall, slaves are ordained to no other end. (3.2.113–19)

In *Arden of Faversham*, as I observed, Alice and Mosby are the main plotters and we often see them together, discussing their plans and hopes of success. But Kyd shows Mosby alone, in a chilling soliloquy in which he reveals that, once Arden is dead, he intends to get rid of all his accomplices – Greene, Michael, the Painter:

> Then, Arden, perish thou by that decree,
> For Greene doth ear the land and weed thee up
> To make my harvest nothing but pure corn.
> And for his pains I'll heave him up awhile
> And, after, smother him to have his wax;
> Such bees as Greene must never live to sting.
> Then is there Michael and the painter too,
> Chief actors to Arden's overthrow …
> I'll cast a bone
> To make these curs pluck out each other's throat;
> And then am I sole ruler of mine own. (8.23–30, 36–8)

The ruthlessness, and the contempt for his accomplices ('curs'), are in the exact mould of Lorenzo's contempt for his 'base companions' and 'slaves'. But Mosby goes beyond Lorenzo, for his extinction list extends to Alice, the woman he has feigned to love and sworn to marry: 'I will cleanly rid my hands of her' (43). Knowing Mosby's plans to kill her may make theatregoers and readers feel sorry for Alice, whose desire to have a happier life will be extinguished by the man who has power over her. Yet at the same time we cannot approve her ruthlessness, especially the brutal way she stabs her dying husband. To create such a complex female character is an achievement for which Kyd deserves long withheld recognition.

The third of my newly attributed plays is the comedy *Fair Em*, which survives in a much abbreviated and damaged text, about half the length of a usual Elizabethan play. It contains neither vengeful women nor comedy in tragedy, but it includes intrigue in both plots. In the 'public' plot, involving historical figures (William the Conqueror, the Marquis of Lubeck), disguise is used for deceiving identity. In the 'private' plot, Em (short for 'Emma') is wooed by three men, two of whom she doesn't like. To deter one of them she pretends to be blind, to deter the other she pretends to be deaf. Her intrigues succeed as she finally gets the man she loves, who intuits that she is only feigning disability. The two plots are cleverly interwoven, and Kyd pokes fun at the two unwanted lovers, who utter identical formulaic speeches, as Perseda and Lucina do when they are separated from their lovers.

I have summarized that part of my attribution case based on major plot parallels between these three plays and Kyd's acknowledged work so that readers and theatregoers familiar with Elizabethan drama can get accustomed to this unusual feature.[11] For the new ascriptions I supplement those discussions with the small-scale approaches that usually form the basis of attributions. The most frequently used method in reading-based attribution is the identification of phrases that occur in both the anonymously published play and in a dramatist's acknowledged works. This method was used with great success by the series of scholars between 1903 and 1948 who identified Kyd's authorship of *Arden of Faversham*, citing hundreds of matches with his three plays and his prose work. Scholars with rival candidates (notably MacDonald Jackson) used to reject such evidence as 'subjective' and 'biased', even though their evidence was there for all to see. Since 2017 that is no longer possible, thanks to Pervez Rizvi's publication of a corpus of 527 plays published between 1552 and 1657 which he had programmed to identify every phrasal repetition in every play.[12] When the words are contiguous, linguists describe such repetitions as 'N-grams', where N is any number between 1 and 10. Rizvi discovered that the most effective lengths for attribution purposes are three-word phrases (trigrams) and four-word ones (tetragrams). When the phrase is interrupted by other words, that is known as a collocation, which Rizvi limits to a maximum of ten words intervening. N-gram matches are acceptable evidence when a phrase occurs in the target play and in other works by the same author,

11 In *Recovering Thomas Kyd*, I provide detailed treatment of these plot structures both for the accepted canon (*The Spanish Tragedy* and *Soliman and Perseda* in chapters 2 and 3) and the newly attributed plays (*King Leir*, *Arden of Faversham*, and *Fair Em* in chapters 5, 6, and 7). I also compare similarities of plot structure between the accepted and the newly attributed plays.

12 See Rizvi, https://www.shakespearestext.com/can/.

but the strongest evidence is provided when the match is unique, occurring only in two plays. Users of this database will find full explanations of the principles on which Rizvi has selected the most significant N-grams from the millions that he has identified. He also records several experiments that he has made, one of which, '*Arden of Faversham* and the Extended Kyd Canon', confirms my attribution to Kyd of *Arden of Faversham*, along with *Fair Em*. In this experiment *King Leir* was not as clearly profiled, due to the inevitable overlapping lexicon of rulers and subjects that it shares with other history plays. But analysis on its own terms leaves no doubt.

The unique matching phrases define an author's personal lexicon, and can be thought of as jigsaw pieces making up his 'phraseognomy', to use the convenient term invented by that pioneer in corpus linguistics, John Sinclair.[13] The usual way of presenting these matching phrases is by a list arranged in the order in which they occur in a play. This is a convenient form of presentation for the compiler, but experience has shown that few readers have the stamina, or patience, to inspect the whole evidence, so weakening its impact. In this edition, therefore, I have introduced a new way of presenting this evidence, as footnotes to the text at the point where they occur. Readers can hardly overlook such evidence, and this method has the added benefit of recording the dramatic context in which the phrasal match occurs, which can often be significant. The standard type of presentation is this (in which bold face indicates an exact match, underlining indicates a word having the same meaning or function):

> **What** dismal **outcry** calls **me from my** rest? *AF* 4.87
> **What outcries** pluck **me from my** naked bed? *Sp.T* 2.4.63

In our authorship commentaries on newly ascribed plays, the matching phrase from a play in the accepted canon will appear as a footnote at the appropriate point.

The other main attribution method involves measuring features of dramatists' verse styles. The pioneer study of prosody was P. W. Timberlake's dissertation on the incidence in Elizabethan drama of feminine endings,[14] that is, when a ten-syllable line receives an extra syllable, as in 'To be, or not to be, that is the ques`tion'. This feature had been successfully studied by Victorian scholars to identify the work of Fletcher and Massinger,[15] but

13 See his essay, 'Phraseognomy', in Sinclair, *Trust the Text: Language, corpus and discourse* (London, 2004), pp. 177–84, building on the notion of physiognomy as a defining feature of the human face.

14 See Timberlake, *The Feminine Ending in English Blank Verse: A Study of its Use by Early Writers in the Measure and its Development in the Drama up to the Year 1595* (Menasha, WI, 1931).

15 See Vickers, *Shakespeare, Co-Author*, pp. 47–53.

Timberlake supplied reliable statistics and established a sound historical basis. He showed that the 'University Wits' (Peele, Greene, Lodge, Marlowe) used a regular iambic line with a low incidence of feminine endings, ranging from 0.5 per cent to 3 (a statistic that removes any possibility of Marlowe as co-author of the *Henry VI* plays). His crucial finding for this study is that Kyd was the first dramatist to use feminine endings frequently, soon followed by Shakespeare. Timberlake's figures were for Kyd, *Soliman and Perseda* (1588): 10.2 per cent; *King Leir* (1589): 10.8; *Arden of Faversham* (1590): 6.2; *Fair Em* (1590): 6.5; *Cornelia* (1594): 9.5; and for Shakespeare, *2 Henry VI* (1591): 10.4; *3 Henry VI* (1591): 10.7.

The advent of the Russian school of metrics, which abandoned the classical quantitative system for one based on stress, either 'Strong' or 'Weak' (the regular iambic pentameter alternates the two: W S W S W S W S W S), allowed scholars to count the stress pattern for every line and establish percentages. In 1969 the Estonian scholar Ants Oras produced a study limited to pause patterns within the pentameter line, based on punctuation.[16] His results for *The Spanish Tragedy* and *King Leir* show great similarity. A much more comprehensive study was provided by Marina Tarlinskaja,[17] a pupil of the distinguished Russian prosodist M. L. Gavrilov. Her analysis of 'Kyd's versification' (87–116) endorses my attribution of *King Leir* and *Fair Em* to the Kyd canon. She originally gave the whole of *Arden of Faversham* to Kyd, but seems to have been influenced by the unreliable stylometric method of MacDonald Jackson that attributes scenes 4–8 to Shakespeare.[18] Other prosodic features of these scenes in her analysis, however, identify them as fully characteristic of Kyd.

When large-scale approaches, such as my studies of Kyd's three main plot-structures, are endorsed by those on a linguistic scale, instanced by phrase matches and prosodic measurements, an attribution can be regarded as highly probable. This edition will give readers every chance to evaluate my attributions.

My research also identified Kyd's part authorship of two history plays, *1 Henry VI* and *Edward III*, to which Shakespeare also contributed. For the first, I identify its origin in the play that Henslowe recorded as '*harey vi*', performed with great success by Lord Strange's Men at the Rose theatre

16 See Oras, *Pause Patterns in Elizabethan and Jacobean Drama: An Experiment in Prosody* (Gainesville, Fla., 1960).

17 See Tarlinskaja, *Shakespeare and the Versification of English Drama, 1561–1642* (Farnham and Burlington, VT, 2014).

18 For a full discussion of Jackson's methods, which are based on Caroline Spurgeon's discredited autobiographical approach to metaphor, see Vickers, *Recovering Thomas Kyd*, ch. 8.

on 3 March 1592 and on numerous occasions that season.[19] I agree with earlier scholars that Nashe wrote Act 1, but I attribute the remainder of the original text to Kyd.[20] I based the ascription partly on the many phrases that it shares with Kyd's other plays, and partly on resemblances in characterization and situation. Strange's Men disbanded in 1593 and their playbooks were divided between the Admiral's Men and the Lord Chamberlain's Men, Shakespeare's company. At some point in the mid-1590s Shakespeare added three scenes to the play: 2.4, giving a fictional account of the origin of the dispute between York and Lancaster, 4.2 and 4.5, showing Talbot, the play's hero and Strange's ancestor, fighting the French.

In *1 Henry VI* Shakespeare added to (and improved) an existing play by Kyd, but on *Edward III* evidence suggests that they were co-authors. Shakespeare dramatized the love plot, in which the king is infatuated with the Countess of Salisbury, while Kyd dealt with the political and war scenes.[21] I based my attribution partly on some theatrical elements shared with Kyd's other plays, together with many resemblances with his phraseology. Tarlinskaja's prosodic analyses endorsed my ascription of both plays, although she observed some smaller differences. These may well be due to the difference of genres, the use of Holinshed and Hall as source, and the 'givens' of historical events, all of which could have constrained Kyd's imagination.

This edition has an immediate and a long-term goal. The immediate one is to provide accurate modernized editions of Kyd's accepted plays and the ones I newly attribute to him. My long-term goal is to establish Kyd as a major dramatist, in his rightful place alongside Marlowe, Peele, Shakespeare, and Jonson. I hope that our collective labours will give both experienced and beginning students the excitement of a new discovery. Gary Taylor well described what my new Kyd attributions would mean for the study of Elizabethan drama:

> His certainty is enviable and hard to resist; his global claims are exciting. If Vickers is right, then he will, with a single hypothesis, have solved a whole series of important attribution problems and thereby reshaped our understanding of the rise of English commercial drama in the late 1580s and early 1590s. His claim would also make all five plays more interesting: it would relate them to each other and to the Kyd canon. It

19 See R. A. Foakes and R. T. Rickert (eds), *Henslowe's Diary* (Cambridge, 1961), pp. 16ff.

20 See Brian Vickers, 'Incomplete Shakespeare: Or, Denying Co-authorship in *1 Henry VI*', *Shakespeare Quarterly* 8 (2007): 310–52.

21 See Brian Vickers, 'The Two Authors of *Edward III*', *Shakespeare Survey* 67 (2014): 69–84, 'Kyd, *Edward III*, and "The Shock of the New"', *ANQ* 33:2 (2020): 172–88, and Brian Vickers, *Kyd, Shakespeare, and the History Play* (Princeton, forthcoming).

> would enable us to tell good new stories about five plays that are currently seldom discussed or taught at all.[22]

Now that readers have access to these painstaking scholarly editions of Kyd's collected works, I hope that any doubts about his authorship will be dispelled.

BIBLIOGRAPHY

Crawford, Charles, 'The Authorship of *Arden of Faversham*', *Jahrbuch der Deutschen Shakespeare Gesellschaft* 39 (1903): 74–86, reprinted in and quoted from Crawford, *Collectanea*, First Series (Stratford-on-Avon, 1906), 101–30.

—— *A Concordance to the Works of Thomas Kyd*, in W. Bang (ed.), *Materialen zur Kunde des älteren englischen Dramas*, vol. XIX (Louvain, 1908).

Erne, Lukas and Devani Singh (eds), *Bel-vedére or The Garden of the Muses: An Early Modern Printed Commonplace Book* (Cambridge, 2020).

Foakes, R. A. and R. T. Rickert (eds), *Henslowe's Diary* (Cambridge, 1961).

Freebury-Jones, Darren, 'Possible Light on the Authorship of *Fair Em*', *Notes and Queries* 262 (2017): 252–4.

—— *Shakespeare's Tutor: The influence of Thomas Kyd* (Manchester, 2022).

Oras, Ants, *Pause Patterns in Elizabethan and Jacobean Drama: An Experiment in Prosody* (Gainesville, Fla., 1960).

Rizvi, Pervez, https://www.shakespearestext.com/can/

Rubow, Paul V., *Shakespeare og hans samtidige* (Copenhagen, 1948). ('Shakespeare and his Fellows'.)

Tarlinskaja, Marina, *Shakespeare and the Versification of English Drama, 1561–1642* (Farnham and Burlington, VT, 2014).

Taylor, Gary, John V. Nance, and Keegan Cooper, 'Shakespeare and who? Aeschylus, *Edward III* and Thomas Kyd', *Shakespeare Survey 70* (2017): 146–53.

Timberlake, Philip, *The Feminine Ending in English Blank Verse: A Study of its Use by Early Writers in the Measure and its Development in the Drama up to the Year 1595* (Menasha, WI, 1931).

Vickers, Brian, *Shakespeare, Co-Author: A Historical Study of Five Collaborative Plays* (Oxford, 2002).

—— 'Incomplete Shakespeare: Or, Denying Co-authorship in *1 Henry VI*', *Shakespeare Quarterly* 8 (2007): 310–52.

—— 'Thomas Kyd, secret sharer', *Times Literary Supplement*, 18 April 2008, pp. 13–15.

—— 'The Two Authors of *Edward III*', *Shakespeare Survey* 67 (2014): 69–84.

—— 'Kyd, *Edward III*, and "The Shock of the New"', *ANQ* 33:2 (2020): 172–88.

—— *Recovering Thomas Kyd: A canon restored* (Princeton, forthcoming).

Wells, William, 'The Authorship of "King Leir"', *Notes and Queries* 177 (16 December 1939): 434–8.

Wine, M. L. (ed.), *The Tragedy of Master Arden of Faversham* (Manchester, 1973).

[22] See Gary Taylor, John V. Nance, and Keegan Cooper, 'Shakespeare and who? Aeschylus, *Edward III* and Thomas Kyd', *Shakespeare Survey* 70 (2017): 146–53 (147).

VERSES OF PRAISE AND JOY

Edited by Daniel Starza Smith

INTRODUCTION

Verses of Praise and Joy (*VPJ*) is a slim volume of poetry published in the immediate wake of the 1586 Babington Plot, a conspiracy to assassinate Elizabeth I and place her Catholic cousin Mary, Queen of Scots, on the throne in her stead. While the contents of *VPJ* certainly express joy at Elizabeth's delivery and praise her governance, they also pour scorn on the plotters and their ideological motives, and revel in their punishment. One of the verses in this volume is signed 'T.K.', and although no evidence unambiguously identifies him, circumstantial and linguistic evidence make Thomas Kyd the likely author. The text of the present edition reproduces the whole volume, including one poem certainly not by Kyd, a 'lamentation' by the Babington conspirator Chidiock Tichborne (c. 1558–86) written on the eve of his execution. Although various components of the printed volume circulated separately, the 1586 publication was evidently designed as a suite of texts to be read together, and there seems no reason to disagree with Boas's suggestion that 'T.K. was the writer of the whole tract' (Tichborne's poem excepted).[1]

CHIDIOCK TICHBORNE AND THE BABINGTON PLOT

The assassination plot has come to be named after one of its ringleaders, Anthony Babington (1561–86). But it was Tichborne who responded in verse to the plot's failure, setting up the poetical response of *VPJ*. Tichborne was born in Southampton to Roman Catholic parents, Peter Tichborne and Elizabeth, née Middleton. As a young man, he had travelled on the Continent without a licence and, with his father, had been interrogated about illegal 'popish relics' brought back from abroad.[2] In June 1586, just two

[1] Frederick S. Boas (ed.), *The Works of Thomas Kyd* (Oxford, 1901), p. xxvi. My thanks are due to Melanie Marshall, Mark Edwards, Robert S. Miola, Cathy Shrank, Clodagh Murphy, Murray Gove, Nadine Akkerman, and Henry Woudhuysen for their helpful comments on this work in various stages. Abbie Weinberg and Heather Wolfe at the Folger, Matthew Rowe at the Beinecke, and Scout Noffke at the Rauner, generously supplied me with digital images of manuscripts during the Covid pandemic of 2020–2.

[2] Alan Stewart, 'Chidiocke Tichborne', *The Encyclopedia of English Renaissance Literature* (2017), https://doi.org/10.1002/9781118297353.wbeerlt006.

months before the plot was exposed, the family had faced another accusation of 'popish practices'. In May 1586, Babington was visited by the Jesuit priest John Ballard, who told him of John Savage's plans to assassinate the Queen; the two men began to gather conspirators, including Tichborne. Letters to and from Mary were intercepted by Gilbert Gifford, a government plant among the conspirators, or by Thomas Barnes, then deciphered by Thomas Phelippes for Sir Francis Walsingham, resealed, and sent on to the intended addressees. In one of these letters, undated but perhaps written on 6 July, Babington wrote of freeing Mary from prison, killing Elizabeth, and restoring the Catholic English monarchy with the help of French Catholics and the Spanish; Mary's reply on 17 July, which Babington deciphered with Tichborne's help, encouraging further correspondence, proved her undoing.[3]

Ballard was arrested on 4 August 1586, spurring Babington to launch the assassination attempt in earnest and, in turn, prompting Walsingham's agents to move in and arrest all remaining conspirators. Under interrogation, Tichborne claimed he had intended to desert his fellows but had been thwarted by lameness. Ballard, Babington, Tichborne, and four others were mutilated and executed at St Giles-in-the-Fields on 20 September 1586; the other seven men were hanged the next day. As a display of the Queen's mercy, they were hanged until dead before their bodies were mutilated.[4] In his account of the execution, George Whetstone identified Tichborne as 'a goodly yong Gentleman' whose 'humilitie and mone, moued much compassion'. Acknowledging his crime, Tichborne nevertheless blamed Babington for engaging him in the conspiracy. On the scaffold, he 'compared his state to Adam, who said hee was placed in Paradice, and ther inioyed all the pleasures of the earth, he was onely forbidden to eate of the fruite of one tree: but for his transgression, he not onely procured wretchednesse and miserie vpon his owne heade, but vpon the heades of all his posteritie'.[5] Other writers, including Thomas Deloney, Raphael Holinshed, William Camden, and William Kemp, sought to understand Tichborne's treachery in prose, often treating him more sympathetically than his co-conspirators.[6]

3 For the claim that Tichborne helped Babington, see Ann Hoffman, *Lives of the Tudor Age, 1485–1603* (London, 1977), p. 436.

4 Penry Williams, 'Anthony Babington', *ODNB* (2004), https://doi.org/10.1093/ref:odnb/967.

5 George Whetstone, *The censure of a loyall subiect* (London, 1587; *STC* 25334), sigs. B4v-C1r, cited in Stewart.

6 Thomas Deloney, *A proper new ballad* (London, 1586; *STC* 6563.5); Raphael Holinshed, *The first and second volumes of Chronicles* (London, 1587; *STC* 13569), sig. MMMMMMMr–v (misnumbered pp. '1555–74'); William Camden, *Annales* (London, 1625; *STC* 4497), sig. T3v; William Kempe, *A dutiful inuective, against the*

TICHBORNE'S ELEGY

Supposedly written while awaiting his execution, Tichborne's elegy directly addresses his impending death. A poem of three six-line stanzas rhyming ababcc, in uniformly monosyllabic iambic pentameter, it draws heavily on antithesis. Tichborne laments that he is too young to die, using a series of self-negating images: a day ending before the sun has yet been seen; fruit falling from a tree before the leaves have turned brown; a thread cut before it has been spun. In its acknowledgement that his treason has cut his life short before it had truly begun, the 'affective force of the poem … serves the ruling political power', as Robert Miola argues, 'pitifully exemplifying the terrible consequences of rebellion'.[7] Yet, despite the clear sense of loss and painful curtailment, the speaker also discovers a paradoxical sense of completeness in death: 'And now I die, and now I was but made' (l. 42). While his earthly hopes as a nobleman have been ruined, he is 'made' in death as a martyr and the final couplet may convey a relatively peaceful resolution. The Catholic register of these martyrological sentiments is clear, and the poem has been identified as joining a recusant tradition both by modern editors (e.g. Louise Guiney, *Recusant Poets*, 1939, and Miola, *Early Modern Catholicism*, 2007) and by contemporary collectors (e.g. Lancashire Record Office, DDSC/19/11 and Harvard, MS Eng. 749).[8] Stewart has also pointed out similarities to the poem Sir Walter Ralegh addressed to his wife at his execution.[9]

Peter Beal lists forty-five manuscript copies (TiC2–46), with some variants of heading, text, and attribution, including nineteen not noted in Richard Hirsch's edition;[10] one copy supplies a title only. Some copies emphasize the claim that the poem was written while Tichborne awaited his execution. Stephen Powle, for example, notes that the poem was 'Written by him selfe .3. dayes before his exequution', adding, intriguingly, 'I haue the originall written with his owne hande' (Bodleian, MS Tanner 169, fol. 79r), although no holograph has been traced. In another manuscript Ralph Starkey, who copied the poem alongside Babington's letter begging clemency from the Queen and Tichborne's last letter to his wife, heads his text

moste haynous treasons of Ballard and Babington (London, 1587; *STC* 14925), sig. q2v.

7 Robert S. Miola, 'Text, Paratext, Context: The Scribal and Print Publications of Tichborne's Lament', unpublished article kindly shared with me by the author.

8 I am grateful to Professor Miola for these references.

9 Stewart, p. 4.

10 Richard S. M. Hirsch, 'The Works of Chidiock Tichborne', *English Literary Renaissance* 16 (1986): 303–18; 'The Text of "Tichborne's Lament" Reconsidered', *English Literary Renaissance* 17 (1987): 275–6.

'verses made by Chediock Tucheburne of him selfe in the Tower the nighte before hee suffered death who was Executed in Lincolnes Inne feilds for Treason' (BL, Harley MS 36, fol. 269v). Miola has pursued extensive further work to establish the poem's wide circulation in manuscript. Depending on the poems and prose pieces with which they surrounded the lament, manuscript compilers could present their copies of Tichborne's elegy as the words of a martyr or a traitor. As Stewart argues, contextual treatment in manuscript can make the poem read 'as the contrite realization of a justly condemned man who regrets the folly of his choices and his self-inflicted ruin'.[11] Miola expands on the potential readings generated by publication context:

> In manuscript and print publication the paratexts and contexts of Tichborne's Lament reconstruct the poem as moving religious witness, a statement of elegiac regret, a tragic soliloquy, a government document, a dolorous device of prophane poetry, a traitor's foolish outcry, an anonymous poetic posy, an aphorism, and, finally, into an edifying and delightful musical lyric. Correspondingly, they portray Tichborne himself as Catholic martyr, misled victim, tragic figure, generic traitor, sage advisor, Everyman, and finally as the picture of Nobody, a cipher whose very absence enables varying paratexts and contexts to create Anybody as the author.[12]

These considerations become particularly important when we turn to *VPJ*, since as a volume it situates the elegy inside a collection of verses, actively using context to shape the reading experience.

Hirsch has established the printing history of Tichborne's lament after 1586: it was reprinted in John Mundy, *Songs and Psalms* (London: T. Est [i.e. East], the assign of W. Byrd, 1594; *STC* 18284); Michael East, *Madrigales to 3, 4, and 5 parts apt for viols and voices* (London: T. Este [i.e. East], 1604; *STC* 7460); Henry Wotton, *Reliquiae Wottonianae* (London: R. Marriot, G. Bedel, and T. Garthwait, 1654), pp. 511–12; and Henry Huth, *Fugitive Poetical Tracts*, first series (London; n. p., 1875), no. 26. It has subsequently appeared in modern anthologies. The first two stanzas alone were reproduced in Richard Alison, *An Howres Recreation in Musicke* (London: J. Windet, the assign of W. Barley, 1606; *STC* 356); E. Arber, *An English Garner*, VI (London, 1886), p. 394; and A. H. Bullen, *Some Shorter Elizabethan Poems* (Westminster, 1903), p. 266.

11 Stewart.

12 Miola, 'Text, Paratext, Context'.

THE RIPOSTE TO TICHBORNE

Responding at speed to the plot's downfall, in late 1586 John Wolfe published a small quarto containing five pages of text plus a title page and two blank pages: the *Verses of prayse and ioye written vpon her Maiesties preseruation. Whereunto is annexed Tychbornes lamentation, written in the towre with his own hand, and an aunswere to the same* (*STC* 7605). The volume, a quarto (A^4) made of a single sheet, contains eight different textual components. Five of these components are verses, two of which are in Latin and accompanied by English translations; only two are attributed directly to authors.

1. the title page (sig. A1r; verso blank);
2. an unattributed 20-line poem beginning ''Mongst spiny cares', expressing praise of Elizabeth and joy at her escape from the assassination plot, unattributed (sig. A2r);
3. Tichborne's elegy for himself, beginning 'My prime of youth is but a frost of cares', said to have been composed in the Tower as he awaited execution (sig. A2v);
4. a parodic 'answer' to this elegy, beginning 'Thy prime of youth is frozen with thy faults', signed 'T.K.', and referred to as a 'hendecasyllabon' about Tichborne's 'swan song' (sig. A3r);
5. an unattributed 'hexasticon' in Latin, entitled *In nefariam Babingtoni caeterorumque coniurationem* (sig. A3v);
6. an unattributed English translation of the 'hexasticon' (sig. A3v);
7. an unattributed 'apostrophe' in Latin, entitled *Ad Serenissimam Reginam Elizabetham* (sig. A4r);
8. an English translation of the 'apostrophe', unattributed (sig. A4r; verso blank).

The title of the printed volume is repeated with slightly different wording in the head-title on sig. A2r.

None of these texts could have been composed before July 1586, when Tichborne was sent to the Tower, while his execution on 20 September establishes a latest date for his own elegy and an earliest date for the 'answer'. For *VPJ* to have been published in 1586, Kyd must have acquired Tichborne's poem and written his own response at speed. There is no entry in the Stationers' Register to establish Wolfe's right to the work, although several publishers had registered works on this topic by late August.[13] Kyd's own

[13] Around this time, Edward Allde paid 4d. for 'a newe ballad of Reioycinge for the Revealinge of the quenes enemyes' (24 August; *Stationers' Register Online*, 2513); Master Barker registered 'an order of prayer and thanckesgyvinge for the preservacon of her maiestie and the Realme from the Trayterous and bloudye practyses of the pope and his adherentes' (25 August; SRO2515); and Richard Jones announced 'a

'hendecasyllabon' survives in two manuscript copies, neither of them autographs. One is headed 'Answer', at Folger, MS V.a.161, pp. 13–14 (*CELM*, KyT 1).[14] The other, headed 'The Aunsweare to the same' (i.e., to Tichborne's poem, copied immediately before it) and beginning 'Thy theyme of youthe, is frozen with the faults', survives at Yale, Osborn MS fb 9, fol. 30v (*CELM*, KyT 2). The Yale manuscript adds two more stanzas, transcribed in the notes below at l. 64, of unknown authorship; these, as Stewart notes, emphasize that 'Treason leads inevitably to regret for a wasted life and a lamentable death.'[15] The Folger First Line Index lists no manuscript copies of the other poems in *VPJ*.

VPJ sets out to attack Tichborne's poem and, by extension, any sympathetic interpretation of his legacy. The first poem opens with overt allusions to the recent violent events ('spiny cares', l. 5), reassuringly presenting a queen who rises above topical peril with her 'rose-like royal peace' (l. 7), stabilizing her nation with 'godly love' (l. 12), and generating a unifying soundscape of public applause (l. 11). The reader is reminded that the monarch's security is identical with the 'Health of [the] country' and the prevention of 'harms' to the populace (l. 22); the thorns on a rose's stem are transcended by its glorious flowers. Only once these loyal statements have been made – and what patriot could argue with them? – do we encounter Tichborne's own lines.

The elegy is printed on the verso of a page, with Kyd's line-by-line riposte on the facing recto. The effect is both parodic and dialogic, as Kyd's speaker overturns Tichborne's statements one by one and collectively, mimicking his form by inverting or otherwise rephrasing each claim in order to undermine it. Kyd insistently points out ways in which Tichborne obscures his own role in his downfall. Tichborne's abstract 'frost of cares' (l. 27) is, Kyd makes clear, caused by 'thy faults' (l. 47); where Tichborne's 'fruit' has passively 'fallen' (l. 34), Kyd argues back that his downfall is the fruit of his 'faithless' actions (l. 54). In short: 'this … hath thy treason done' (l. 64). The imitation of Tichborne's form sets up the poems as a kind of visual dialogue, whether one poem is read after the other, or they are read alongside each other, line by line. As such, they enter a tradition of conversational

---

ioyfull songe made by a citizen of london in the behalf of all her maiesties subiectes touchinge the ioye for the takinge of the traitours' (27 August; SRO2516). A short while later, George Robinson paid 6d. to register 'a Shorte Discourse of the late pretendid treason againste the quenes maiestie and the states of the realme' (6 October; SRO2528). Giles Bergel and Ian Gadd, *Stationers' Register Online*, CREATe, University of Glasgow, https://stationersregister.online.

14 Cf. *HMC, 3rd report* (1872), Appendix, p. 253, and A. B. Grosart (ed.), *The Complete Poems of Richard Barnfield* (London, 1876), pp. 211–12.

15 Stewart.

verse, which often shows Catholics interrogated (and bested) by Protestant interlocutors.[16] Inevitably, Kyd's response has the last word.

The two short poems that follow each appear in Latin verses of six lines, followed by 12-line English translations in ballad metre (alternating eight-syllable and six-syllable lines). Both connect the failure of the plot to broader ideological battles. The first suggests that Babington's English plot was just one part of a co-ordinated European Catholic threat led by the Pope from his 'ruinous state' (l. 74), typified by seductive offers of riches and power. In this verse, the glories promised by the Pope's agents of corruption are justly transformed into corresponding punishments: lustful beds to shameful graves, sceptres to halters, crowns to the crows of the Tower, and the promise of the throne to the reality of the scaffold. The final poem returns to the praise of Elizabeth, an 'Apostrophe' (l. 87; i.e., direct address to the Queen) which also functions as a kind of prayer. The textual multiplicity on sigs A3v–A4r lends *VPJ* a sense of multi-vocality, as if capturing a chorus of celebration for Elizabeth's victory over the Babington Plot and its backers. It may also echo bibliographically the kinds of manuscript context in which Tichborne's own poem was circulating. As we have seen, the presence of Tichborne's elegy in manuscript collections of Catholic material encouraged readers to interpret his death as a martyrdom. By structuring *VPJ* as a collection of material beginning and ending with loyal praise for the Queen, Kyd and Wolfe crowd Tichborne's poem with antagonistic voices, leaving no room for sympathetic interpretation.

AUTHORSHIP

Previous researchers have not always been convinced that *VPJ* is by Kyd. Encountering a manuscript copy of the response to Tichborne transcribed alongside material by Richard Barnfield, Alexander Grosart edited it as Tichborne's in 1876. He found it 'historically interesting if harder and harsher than at this softened distance we can approve. The Author's patriotic love for the great Queen explains his passionate retort.'[17] In his 1901 edition of Kyd's works, Boas relegated *VPJ* to an appendix. He drew on it cautiously as potential evidence of Kyd's facility in Latin and pointed out that Francis Meres had celebrated Kyd as a poet.[18] As he noted, though, even a sympathetic reader of *VPJ* – which Boas dismissed as, at best, 'non-dramatic hack work' – could hardly think this the poetry that Meres considered comparable

16 Cathy Shrank, 'Answer Poetry and other Verse "Conversations"', in Catherine Bates (ed.), *A Companion to Renaissance Poetry* (Oxford, 2018), pp. 376–88.

17 A. B. Grosart (ed.), *The Complete Poems of Richard Barnfield* (London, 1876), pp. 211–12, xxiv.

18 Boas, pp. xix, xxv–xxvi.

to Tasso. More recently, Beal concluded in separate parts of the *Catalogue of English Literary Manuscripts* that *VPJ* is 'possibly but not certainly Kyd' and 'Probably not by Kyd', although he did not supply his rationale for these judgements.[19] Arthur Freeman thought Timothy Kendall to be 'the only other "T.K." of the period with printed poetry to his credit', dismissing him on grounds of style.[20] He concluded that Kyd could be identified as the author of the *Hendacasyllabon* and possibly the other poems 'For want of a better prospect', but that the proposition was 'no more than tentative'.

Robert Miola has suggested that 'T. K. is probably Thomas Knell rather than Thomas Kyd.' Thomas Knell the younger (1543/4–c. 1592) was a Church of England clergyman. A veteran pamphleteer – 'the Elizabethan equivalent of tabloid journalism', as Brett Usher suggests in his *ODNB* entry [21] – he is known to have responded in print to one previous state execution, that of John Felton in 1570.[22] His poem in *A piththy* [*sic*] *note to papists* is in Alexandrine couplets, and characterized by reported speech ('Oh iudge me not (quod *Felton* then)'), rhetorical questions ('To *Iesus Christe?* to him think yée?'), and frequent references to Felton himself; it bears little resemblance to the style of *VPJ*. Further counting in Knell's favour, though, is his *Answer to a Papisticall Byll* (1570) which, like *VPJ*, uses the dialogue form.[23] Reprinting 'the original offending piece in chunks in order to refute it', Knell sets out a conversation between a Catholic and his Protestant interlocutor.[24] Here, Knell's answers – in four-line stanzas alternating between tetrameter and trimeter – follow the language of the original much more closely, using word substitution and inversion to expose his antagonist's hypocrisy. To the Catholic's question 'What neede our women now take care', the Protestant responds 'What neede our men now to take care'; to the Catholic's 'The Devil when he would Christ attempt', he replies 'CHRIST, when the deuil did him tempt'.

Nevertheless, both of Knell's works were published a full sixteen years earlier than *VPJ*, and the *ESTC* attributes nothing to him after 1571. Kyd, on the other hand, was set to publish at least one significant work per year

19 Peter Beal, 'Thomas Kyd (1558–1594)', *CELM*, https://celm-ms.org.uk/introductions/KydThomas.html and https://celm-ms.org.uk/authors/kydthomas.html.

20 Arthur Freeman, *Thomas Kyd: Facts and Problems* (Oxford, 1967), p. 178.

21 Brett Usher, 'Thomas Knell', *ODNB*.

22 Thomas Knell, *A piththy note to papists all and some that joy in Feltons martirdome* (London, 1570; *STC* 15034).

23 Thomas Knell, *An answer to a papisticall byll, cast in the streetes of Northampton, and brought before the iudges at the last syses. 1570* (London: John Awdeley [i.e., Allde], 1570; *STC* 15030).

24 Shrank, 'Answer Poetry'.

for the next nine years. Furthermore, as Boas notes, around the time *VPJ* was published,

> the subject of conspiracies and murders in royal households, and the nemesis they involved, was occupying his mind, and was being worked up by him in plays which were to have a far-reaching influence upon dramatic history in England and abroad.[25]

Boas's politically sensitive reading of *VPJ* anticipates Freeman's objection that there is virtually 'no other indication of Kyd's involvement in the debilitating enterprise of Court-oriented compliment'.[26] While Freeman's words about courtiership describe some passages in this publication, they indicate a generic misidentification of *VPJ*, which has an overwhelmingly polemical purpose.

While the brevity of *VPJ* necessarily limits linguistic analysis, several verbal parallels have been observed. Boas draws attention to lines in the 'hendecasyllabon' which recall 'phrases of which Kyd is fond': 'thy hope, thy hap and all' (l. 50) may echo *The Spanish Tragedy*'s 'hopeless father of a hapless son' (5.4.83) and 'Hopeless to hide them in a hapless tomb?' (*Cornelia*, 1.1.214); 'Time trieth truth, and truth hath treason tripped' bears comparison to a couplet in *The Spanish Tragedy*, 'Time is the author both of truth and right, | And time will bring this treachery to light' (2.4.125–6); *VPJ*'s lucent metaphor 'thou shining lamp of th'earth' (l. 96) is also used in *The Spanish Tragedy*: 'Perseda, blissful lamp of excellence' (5.4.16). Boas notes that the uncommon word 'nipped' (l. 55) also occurs in *The Spanish Tragedy* (1.1.13); more recently, Vickers has pointed out another parallel, to *Arden of Faversham*, 8.5–6, in which Mosby complains that his sense of insecurity 'nips me as the bitter northeast wind | Doth check the tender blossoms in the spring'.[27] To these we can add two more uses from the extended canon. In *King Leir*, the king compares himself to a dying tree, 'Whose blossoms now are nipped with winter's frost' (3.28), while in *Edward III* a soldier's moral allegory features an improvident grasshopper who finds that winter 'hath nipped his careless head' (5.19).[28] The linguistic

25 Boas, p. xxvi.

26 Freeman, p. 178.

27 Brian Vickers, 'Is EEBO-TCP / LION suitable for attribution studies?', *Early Modern Literary Studies* 21:1 (2019): 1–34.

28 Interestingly, as Grosart noticed in his edition, the Yale scribe saw this word as 'impte' (i.e., 'imped'). The minims require an *m* rather than an *n*; the dot appears over the first minim; and there is precedent for a flourish on an initial *i* in the words 'in' and 'it' in subsequent lines. Grosart was evidently unaware of the printed text and, following the page-break in the manuscript, he reproduced the poem as two

and contextual evidence makes Kyd the most likely 'T.K.' known to be publishing verse in the 1580s.

COPIES COLLATED

The English Short Title Catalogue lists three copies of *VPJ* in research libraries, plus an unknown number in private collections. I have used the Dartmouth College copy (Rauner Special Collections Library, Rare Book PR1101 .V4 158) as my base text; it was formerly in the possession of Allerton Cushman Hickmott (1895–1977). This has been collated against imperfect copies at the Beinecke Library (Eliz 288) and the British Library (the copy digitized on *EEBO*). The British Library copy has been trimmed, causing loss to a couple of words; the Beinecke's copy lacks leaves 1 and 4, which are supplied in facsimile, and leaves 2 and 3 are damaged, causing some loss of text. All visible text is identical across the three exemplars, and I have not noted below variants caused by material damage.

BIBLIOGRAPHY

Manuscript sources

Cambridge, MA, United States of America
Harvard University, Houghton Library, MS Eng. 749
London, United Kingdom
British Library, Harley MS 36
New Haven, CT, United States of America
Yale University, Beinecke Library, Osborn MS fb 9
Oxford, United Kingdom
Bodleian Libraries, MS Tanner 169
Preston, United Kingdom
Lancashire Record Office, DDSC/19/11
Washington, DC, United States of America
Folger Shakespeare Library, MS V.a.161

Printed sources

Alison, Richard, *An Howres Recreation in Musicke* (London, 1606).
Arber, Edward, *An English Garner*, 7 vols (London, 1836–1912).
Beal, Peter, 'Thomas Kyd (1558–1594)', *CELM*, https://celm-ms.org.uk/introductions/KydThomas.html and https://celm-ms.org.uk/authors/kydthomas.html [accessed 20 August 2023].
Bergel, Giles and Ian Gadd (eds), *Stationers' Register Online*, CREATe, University of Glasgow, https://stationersregister.online [accessed 20 August 2023].

stanzas, beginning 'Thy prime' and 'Thine ill', thus obviating the need for the rhyme on 'nipped' and 'tripped'.

Boas, Frederick S. (ed.), *The Works of Thomas Kyd* (Oxford, 1901).
Bullen, A. H., *Some Shorter Elizabethan Poems* (Westminster, 1903).
Camden, William, *Annales* (London, 1625).
Campbell, Gordon, 'Chidiock Tichborne and T.K.'s *Hendecasyllabon*', *Notes & Queries* 232 (1987): 189.
Deloney, Thomas, *A proper new ballad* (London, 1586).
East, Michael, *Madrigales to 3, 4, and 5 parts apt for viols and voices* (London, 1604).
Freeman, Arthur, *Thomas Kyd: Facts and Problems* (Oxford, 1967).
Grosart, A. B., *The Complete Poems of Richard Barnfield* (London, 1876).
Guiney, Louise, *The Recusant Poets: with a Selection from their Work* (London, 1939).
Hirsch, Richard S. M., 'The Works of Chidiock Tichborne', *English Literary Renaissance* 16 (1986): 303–18.
—— 'The Text of "Tichborne's Lament" Reconsidered', *English Literary Renaissance* 17 (1987): 275–6.
Holinshed, Raphael, *The first and second volumes of Chronicles* (London, 1587).
Huth, Henry, *Fugitive Poetical Tracts*, first series (London, 1875).
K., T., *Verses of prayse and ioye written vpon her Maiesties preseruation. Whereunto is annexed Tychbornes lamentation, written in the towre with his own hand, and an aunswere to the same* (London, 1586).
Kempe, William, *A dutiful inuective, against the moste haynous treasons of Ballard and Babington* (London, 1587).
Knell, Thomas, *A piththy note to papists all and some that joy in Feltons martirdome* (London, 1570).
—— *An answer to a papisticall byll, cast in the streetes of Northampton, and brought before the iudges at the last syses. 1570* (London, 1570).
Miola, Robert S., *Early Modern Catholicism: An Anthology* of *Primary Sources* (Oxford, 2007).
—— 'Text, Paratext, Context: The Scribal and Print Publications of Tichborne's Lament', unpublished article.
Mundy, John, *Songs and Psalms* (London, 1594).
Shrank, Cathy, 'Answer Poetry and other Verse "Conversations"', in Catherine Bates (ed.), *A Companion to Renaissance Poetry* (London and New York, 2018).
Stewart, Alan, 'Chidiocke Tichborne', *The Encyclopedia of English Renaissance Literature*, https://doi.org/10.1002/9781118297353.wbeerlt006 (2017) [accessed 20 August 2023].
Third report of the Royal Commission on Historical Manuscripts presented to both Houses of Parliament by command of Her Majesty (London, 1872).
Usher, Brett, 'Thomas Knell the younger', *ODNB* (2008), https://doi.org/10.1093/ref:odnb/15708 [accessed 20 August 2023].
Vickers, Brian, 'Is EEBO-TCP / LION suitable for attribution studies?', *Early Modern Literary Studies* 22:1 (2019).
Whetstone, George, *The censure of a loyall subiect* (London, 1587).
Williams, Penry, 'Anthony Babington', *ODNB* (2004), https://doi.org/10.1093/ref:odnb/967.
Wotton, Henry, *Reliquiae Wottonianae* (London, 1654).

Verses

of Praise and Joy,

Written

upon her Majesty's preservation.

Whereunto is annexed Tychborne's lamen-

tation, written in the Tower with his

own hand, and an answer

to the same.

LONDON

Printed by John Wolfe

1586

VERSES OF PRAISE, AND JOY,

Written upon her Majesty, after the apprehension and execution of Babington, Tychborne, Salisbury, and the rest.

'Mongst spiny cares sprung up now at the last,
  Sprout higher than the haughtiest of their heads:
That with thy rose-like royal peace (O Prince)
  All other princes thou must overpeer.
Thee and thy realm oppressed, it happ'ly pleased
  Our highest God in safety to preserve.
For this, thy people publicly applaud,
  And everywhere aboundeth godly love.
Good fortune and an everlasting fame
  Attend on thee in all thine actions.
This makes thy friends, this makes thy foes admire,
  And daily hold thy name in reverence.
Honoured art, princely behaviour, zeal to good,
  And with thee rest a royal majesty.
These four fair gifts (O Prince, of right renown)
  Thy princely mind most princely entertains.
Live Sovereign Lady, live Elizabeth
  Health of thy country, help to all our harms.
Seld seen, thou Reign'st a maiden and a queen,
  Long may'st thou live, and heaven be thy home.

Tychborne's Elegy, written with his own hand in the Tower before his execution.

My prime of youth is but a frost of cares,
  My feast of joy is but a dish of pain:
My crop of corn is but a field of tares,
  And all my good is but vain hope of gain.
The day is past, and yet I saw no sun,
  And now I live, and now my life is done.

My tale was heard, and yet it was not told,
  My fruit is fallen, and yet my leaves are green:
My youth is spent, and yet I am not old,
  I saw the world, and yet I was not seen.
My thread is cut, and yet it is not spun,
  And now I live, and now my life is done.

I sought my death, and found it in my womb,
  I looked for life, and saw it was a shade:
I trod the earth, and knew it was my tomb,
  And now I die, and now I was but made.
My glass is full, and now my glass is run,
  And now I live, and now my life is done.

Hendecasyllabon T. K. in Cygneam Cantionem
Chidiochi Tychborne.

Thy prime of youth is frozen with thy faults,
  Thy feast of joy is finished with thy fall:
Thy crop of corn is tares availing naughts,
  Thy good God knows, thy hope, thy hap and all.
Short were thy days, and shadowed was thy sun
  T'obscure thy light unluckily begun.

Time trieth truth, and truth hath treason tripped,
  Thy faith bare fruit as thou had'st faithless been:
Thy ill-spent youth thine after-years hath nipped,
  And God that saw thee hath preserved our Queen.
  Her thread still holds, thine perished though unspun,
  And she shall live when traitors' lives are done.

Thou sought'st thy death, and found it in desert,
  Thou looked'st for life, yet lewdly forced it fade:
Thou trod'st the earth, and now on earth thou art
  As men may wish thou never had'st been made.
Thy glory and thy glass are timeless run,
  And this, O *Tychborne*, hath thy treason done.

In nefariam Babingtoni cæterorumque
coniurationem, Hexasticon.

Quid non Papa ruens spondet, modò iussa capessas?
  en diadema tibi, sceptráque, pactus Hymen.
Dissimilem votis mercedem nacta, sed ausis
  & sceleri retulit turba nefanda parem.
Successere regi regno, corvique coronæ,
  pro sceptro laqueus, pro thalamo tumulus.

The same in English.

The Pope to prop his ruinous state,
doth golden proffers make:
Crown, sceptre, royal marriage bed,
to those his part that take.
The traitorous crew late reaped reward,
not fitting their desire:
But as their purpose bloody was,
so shameful was their hire.
For chair of state, a stage of shame,
and crows for crowns they have:
Their sceptre to a halter changed,
their bed become their grave.

Ad Serenissimam Reginam Elizabetham, Apostrophe.

Regna, vive, vale, mundi, patriæ, atque tuorum,
splendida, sola, vigens, gloria, vita, salus.
In te speramus, per te spiramus ovantes:
det spirare tibi sæcula multa Deus.
Pro te dulce mori, nisi pro te vivere durum
at sine te mors est vivere, vita mori.

The same in English.

Reign, live, and blissful days enjoy,
thou shining lamp of th'earth:
The only life of country's state,
thy subjects' health and mirth.
On thee we ground our hope, through thee
we draw our breath with joy:
God grant thee long amongst us breathe,
God shield thee from annoy.
To die for thee were sweet, to live
were wretched but for thee.
Without thee, death a second life,
life double death should be.

TEXTUAL NOTES

Q = print
FSL = Folger, MS V.a.161, pp. 13–14
BY = Beinecke, Yale, Osborn MS fb 9, fol. 30v
Boas = Frederick S. Boas (ed.), *The Works of Thomas Kyd* (Oxford, 1901), pp. 340–1. Where Boas agrees with Q, only Q is cited.
Grosart = *The Complete Poems of Richard Barnfield*, ed. A. B. Grosart (London, 1876), pp. 211–12, an edition of FSL.

MAIN TEXT

5 sprung] *sprong* Q
7 rose-like] Q *(Roselike)*
8 overpeer.] *ouer-peere.* Q
11 publicly] *publikely* Q
19 renown)] renound) Q
20 entertains.] *Enterteignes.* Q
22 country,] *Countrey,* Q
23 Seld] *Seeld* Q
24 may'st] *maist* Q
25 *Tychborne's Elegy*, written] *Tychbornes Elegie, writen* Q; *Tichbornes Elegie Written* Boas
30 all] *al* Q
34 fallen,] *falne,* Q
37 thread] *thred* Q
40 looked] *lookt* Q
45–6 Hendecasyllabon … *Tychborne.*] Q; *Answer* FSL; *The Aunsweare to the same* BY
47 prime] Q, FSL; *theyme* BY
47 frozen] Q, FSL; *forzen* BY
47 [2]thy] Q, FSL; *the* BY
48 finished] *finisht* Q, FSL; *ffynishet* BY
48 thy fall:] Q; *thy fall.* FSL; *the fall* BY
49 is tares] Q, FSL; *are Teares* BY
49 naughts,] Q; *naughts* FSL; *nought* BY
51 shadowed] Q; *shadou* FSL; *shawdowed* BY

52 T'obscure] Q, FSL; *T' obscure* Boas; *To obscure* BY
53 tripped,] *tript,* Q; *tript;* Boas; *tript* FSL, BY
54 bare] Q, FSL; beare BY
54 had'st faithless] *hadst faithles* Q; *hadste faithlesse* FSL; *hadds faithfull* BY
55 Thy] Q; *Thine* FSL; *Thyne* BY
55 ill-spent] *ill spent* Q, FSL, BY
55 after-years] *after yeares* Q; *after years* FSL, BY
55 nipped,] *nipt,* Q; *nipt;* Boas; *nipt* BY; *impte* FSL, Grosart
56 And God that] Q; *and god yt* FSL; *and god that* BY
56 Queen] *Que<>* Q [text missing]; *Queene.* Boas; *Que\e/ne* FSL; *Queene* BY
57 thread] BY; *thred* Q; *thride* FSL
57 perished] *perisht* Q; *perish* FSL; *perisheth* BY
57 though unspun,] Q; *thowth vnspunne* FSL; *thy vnspunne thought \though vnspun/* BY
59 sought'st] *soughtst* Q, FSL; *soughts* BY
60 looked'st] *look'dst* Q; *lookst* FSL; *lookest* BY
60 forced] *forc'd* Q; *forcd* FSL; *forct* BY
61 trod'st] *trodst* Q, FSL; *trodes* BY
61 [1]earth,] Q; *y ea\r/th* FSL; *dearthe* BY
61 [2]earth] Q, BY; *y earth* FSL
62 thou] Q, BY; *yu* BY
62 never had'st been made,] *neuer hadst beene made* Q; *neuer hadst bin made.* FSL; *neuer had bene made* BY
63 run,] Q; *runne.* FSL; *runne* BY
64 And this, O *Tychborne,*] Q; *And this (O Tuchbourne);* FSL; *and thus O Tytchbourne* BY
64 hath thy treason done.] After these words, BY continues with two more stanzas not present in Q or FSL: 'Be could the [end] eie thou begann / haue mynde of [death] and feare to sinne / for death shall reape that first hath sowen / and first shall springe where death hath mowen // But whoe rhymes aboue ye meane / There is noe hope of staye / The higher vpp. ye sooner downe / And neerer his decaye /'
78 reaped] *reapt* Q
84 sceptre ... changed] *scepter ... changde* Q
97 country's] *countries* Q
101 grant] *graunt* Q

COMMENTARY

3–4 Babington … Salisbury Anthony Babington, Chidiock Tichborne, Sir Thomas Salisbury, John Ballard, Henry Donn, Robert Barnewell, and John Savage were all executed on 20 September 1586. A second group of conspirators – Jerome Bellamy, John Charnock, Robert Gage, Edward Habington, Edward Jones, Charles Tilney, and John Travers – were tried and executed separately.

5–8 'Mongst … over-peer The opening lines play on linguistic overlaps between the language of vegetation (thorns, sprouts, flowers) and those of height and backbones.

5 spiny a neologism: 'Having the characteristics of a thorn or thorns; resembling a thorn in form or qualities' (*OED*, 'spiny', adj. 1a). Alluding to both the Tudor symbolism of the rose and to Christ's crown of thorns.

5 at the last '(a) at the end, in the end, finally, ultimately; (also, at the last) at the end of one's life; (b) after a while, after a long time' (*OED*, P1.a.(a)(i)(a) and (b)).

6 Sprout Implying a new shoot from a plant, but also bearing of new growth more generally.

6 haughtiest retaining the etymological meaning 'highest' alongside obvious intimations of pride and being 'High in one's own estimation' (*OED*, 'haughty', adj., 1.a). Cf. Ps. 18:27: 'You save the humble but bring low those whose eyes are haughty.' Two syllables.

6 their heads i.e., of the metaphorical heads of the cares, or the real heads of the decapitated conspirators.

7 rose-like royal peace as the beauty of a rose transcends the ugliness of its thorns, the glory of royal peace must rise above thorny cares; as a compound, 'rose-like' dates to 1530.

8 overpeer 'To rise or appear above; to tower over; to have a higher position than; (figurative) to surpass, outdo' (*OED*, 'overpeer', *v.*1). The word is first recorded in Golding's 1565 translation of Ovid, where it refers to Phoebe's neck.

11 this i.e., God's preservation of queen and kingdom.

11 thy people publicly applaud Tichborne was the fifth conspirator to be executed and 'his speech as well as his demeanour moved many to compassion' (Secombe, *DNB*).

14 actions three syllables.

15[1] This i.e., good fortune.
15[2] this i.e., everlasting fame.
17 Honoured art An anapaest.
19 four fair gifts i.e., those described in ll. 17–18.
23 Seld i.e., seldom.
25 Elegy Miola observes that while contemporaries referred to the poem as Tichborne's 'Lament' or 'Elegy', both words are 'merely descriptions rather than titles *per se*'.
29 My … tares 'A reference to the parable of the wheat and the tares, Matthew 13:25-29' (Hirsch, 309). Tare, the seed of the vetch plant, is used more broadly in English translations of the Bible to signify 'an injurious weed among corn' (*OED*).
34 fallen fall'n.
39 I … womb 'In searching for the reason for his early death, Tichborne found it in his being born a Catholic' (Hirsch, 310).
43 glass 'hour-glass, but perhaps also a pun on looking-glass' (Hirsch, 310).
45–6 Hendecasyllabon … Tychborne 'Hendecasyllabon by T.K. on the swan song of Chidiock Tichborne.' According to Campbell (189), 'hendecasyllables should have eleven syllables to the line, and T.K.'s poem has only ten. It is of course possible that the author did not know what hendecasyllables are, but there is a more likely explanation. The -on suffix suggests that T.K. thought that the word was a Greek neuter noun (I assume that the o is short). *Hendeca* cannot refer to the number of syllables. I should like to suggest that it refers to the ancient Hendeka, the eleven Athenian officials in charge of executions. T.K.'s *hendecasyllabon* is presumably an "executioner's song", a poem composed from the viewpoint of those who had executed Tichborne and his fellow conspirators.'
54 bare i.e., bore.
64 treason done after these words, the Yale manuscript copy continues with two more stanzas not present in either other copy. See textual notes.
65–6 In … Hexasticon Literally: 'A hexastichon on Babington and the other infamous plotters.' A hexastichon or hexastich is a verse-form comprising six lines.
67–72 Quid … tumulus. Literally: 'What does the toppling Pope not promise, so long as you accept his commands? / Look, a crown for you, and sceptres, a marital bond. / The execrable crew has received a wage other than it hoped for / But commensurate with its temerity and its crime. / In place of dominion there is subjection and in place of a crown there are crows.' Although T.K.'s English translation gives 'crowns' in plural, *coronae* (l. 71) is dative singular here.
71 corvique corrected to the nominative plural (crows) from 'coruoque', a dative or ablative form which does not translate and is probably corrupt,

since a nominative is needed to match *successere* and *regi*. T.K.'s own translation supplies 'crows' as a plural (l. 83).

74–85 The ... grave Alternating lines of tetrameter and trimeter.

74 Pope Sixtus V (r. 1585–90).

76 Crown ... bed Not implying that the conspirators were offered papal gifts of marriage to royalty, but ironically to underscore the paucity of their true wages compared to the glory they had falsely been promised.

81 hire referring ironically to their execution as the payment due for their actions.

83 crows proverbially, because of their black feathers, portentous or evil birds. See Tilley, C844, C849–51.

84 halter i.e., a noose (*OED*, 'halter', *n.*[1], 2.a. and b).

86–7 Ad ... Apostrophe An apostrophe to the most serene majesty Elizabeth.

88–93 Regna ... mori Literally: 'Reign, live and prosper flourishing as the splendid and sole / glory, life and salvation of the world, your fatherland and your people. / In thee we hope, through thee we breathe in acclamation, / May God give you to draw breath for many ages. / To die for thee is sweet, to live were hard if not on thy account, / And without thee death is life and life is death.' Such language is commonplace in describing both Jesus and the Virgin Mary. *Pro te dulce mori* might be an allusion to Horace Odes 3.2, l. 13 (*Dulce et decorum est, pro patria mori*), especially since Elizabeth is earlier identified with the state.

95–106 Reign ... be. Alternating lines of tetrameter and trimeter.

98 annoy vexation.

THE SPANISH TRAGEDY

Edited by Brian Vickers

INTRODUCTION

DATE AND TEXT

The first of Kyd's plays to be published was his undisputed masterpiece, *The Spanish Tragedy*. Most scholars date it to a period before the Spanish Armada, variously 1583–4, 1583–7, 1585–7 and 1587.[1] Had it been written after 1588, they argue, it could hardly *not* have mentioned this famous victory in a drama that represents a war between Spain and Portugal, especially since Hieronimo presents a masque portraying three *English* warriors who allegedly defeated the Portuguese and Spanish forces (1.5.23–32).

In 1592 the first appearance of the text in print became the object of an extended dispute between two London stationers, Edward White and Abel Jeffes. Jeffes had got into trouble with the authorities in July, as the Court Book of the Stationers' Company recorded on 7 August, 'for that he contemptuously proceeded in printing a book without authority contrary to our Master his commaundement', and for violently refusing to 'deliver any of the Bookes' for official scrutiny.[2] Jeffes was 'committed to ward', remaining in prison until December. The book that Jeffes had been printing was *Arden of Faversham*, which had been legitimately entered to Edward White on 3 April 1592. White, in reply, seems to have taken the law into his own hands by printing *The Spanish Tragedy*, apparently from a more complete manuscript, according to the claim on the title page of the one surviving copy, now in the British Library:

> *The Spanish Tragedie, Containing the lamentable end of Don Horatio, and Bel-Imperia : with the pitifull death of olde Hieronimo. Newly corrected*

1 See T. W. Baldwin, 'On the Chronology of Thomas Kyd's Plays', *MLN* 40 (1925): 343–9, revised in Baldwin, *On the Literary Genetics of Shakespeare's Plays 1592–1594* (Urbana, IL, 1959), pp. 177–99; Joseph Schick (ed.), *The Spanish Tragedy* (London, 1898), pp. xxi–xxv; F. S. Boas (ed.), *The Works of Thomas Kyd* (Oxford, 1901), pp. xxviii–xxxi; Arthur Freeman, *Thomas Kyd: Facts and Problems* (Oxford, 1967), p. 77; Lukas Erne, *Beyond* The Spanish Tragedy: *A Study of the Works of Thomas Kyd* (Manchester, 2001), pp. 55–9; Martin Wiggins, *British Drama 1533–1642: A Catalogue*, 12 vols (Oxford, 2012 –), 2:369–75.

2 See W. W. Greg (ed.), *The Spanish Tragedy (1592)* (Oxford, 1949; *MSR*), pp. v–xi; Erne, pp. 51–67; and Clara Calvo and Jesús Tronch (eds), *The Spanish Tragedy* (London, 2013), pp. 85–8.

> *and amended of such grosse faults as passed in the first impression. At London. Printed by Edward Allde, for Edward White.*

The tit-for-tat nature of this dispute is shown by the fact that, on 6 October, while still in prison, 'Abell Jeffes Entred for his copie … a booke whiche is called the Spanishe tragedie of Don Horatio and Bellimpera.' On 18 December the Court of the Stationers' Company punished both men:

> Whereas Edward white and Abell Jeffes have eche of them offendyd. Viz Edw White in havinge printed[3] the spanish tragedie belonging to Abell Jeffes/ and Abell Jeffes in having printed the tragedie of arden of kent belonginge to Edw white: yt is agreed that all the books of eche ympression shalbe as confiscated and forfayted accordinge to th'ordonnances, disposed to th'use of the poore of the companye for that eche of them hath sev'ally [separately] transgressed the ordonnance in the seid impressions.

The offenders were also fined 'Ten shillinge a pece presently or betwene this and our Lady day next'. It is tantalizing to observe two plays by Kyd becoming the subject of dispute between London stationers in the summer of 1592, while lacking any clue as to how they came on to the market that year. It is also worth noting that Kyd's *Soliman and Perseda* was entered in the Stationers' Register on 20 November 1592 to Edward White, and published shortly afterwards, 'Printed by Edward Allde for Edward White', the old team.[4] White also secured the rights to print *King Leir* (which this edition attributes to Kyd), for he entered it in the Stationers' Register on 15 May 1594, not long before the dramatist's death in August of that year. The co-location of these four Kyd plays in the London publishing world at this time suggests some kind of co-ordinated movement by someone who had his interests at heart.

The complicated history of the rival claims of Jeffes and White to ownership of *The Spanish Tragedy* was greatly clarified by W. W. Greg, and it is worth repeating his reconstruction of its sequence, since it has implications not only for the play's textual history but for its theatrical history:

> subject to inevitable uncertainty of points of detail the history of the publication of *The Spanish Tragedy* would appear to have been as follows. In the spring, probably, of 1592 Jeffes somehow acquired a more or less corrupt

3 Greg noted that the term 'printed' here means 'published … for he did not own a press', and 'the edition he issued was in fact printed for him by Edward Allde' (pp. viii–ix).

4 R. B. McKerrow, in 'Edward Allde as a Typical Trade Printer', *The Library*, 4th ser., 10 (1929): 121–62, computed that between 1587 and 1621 Allde printed more than fifty books for Edward White, father and son.

> manuscript of the popular tragedy then revived, or about to be revived, on the London stage—possibly in circumstances that prompted him to avoid courting inquiry by an entrance in the Company's Register—and put it in print before becoming embroiled with the authorities towards the end of July. Meanwhile Edward White had obtained what is unquestionably an excellent version, perhaps supplied by the players with the express purpose of superseding the one already in print; and believing that Jeffes could be safely ignored, since he had neglected to register his own edition and was now in disgrace, he proceeded to produce an edition of his own. Jeffes, apprised of this, decided after all to protect his rights by an entrance in the Register, and did so on 6 October. Whether by then White's edition had actually appeared or not; we do not know, but it was certainly published before 18 December ... (pp. ix–x)

A further issue concerns the subsequent fate of the printed copies of both plays, which were to be confiscated 'to th'use of the poore of the companye'. Usually, such copies were seized by officers of the company and sold on to some needy booksellers, but Greg pointed out that a later entry in the wardens' accounts recorded the receipt of £3.10s from 'Edward White and Abel Jeffes for confiscated books'. Whether the company actually used that money for helping its poor cannot be established, but this transaction shows that both stationers were allowed to continue trading with these piratical editions, a point which affects the possibility of their having survived. In Greg's words,

> since in any case they were not destroyed, copies of the piracies stood about as good a chance of surviving as those of the lawful editions. In the case of *The Spanish Tragedy* Jeffes's original edition, legitimate but defective, wholly perished, whereas White's superior but piratical edition has survived in a single copy. In that of *Arden of Faversham*, on the contrary, it is White's original edition, containing a sound text, that has survived in three copies, and Jeffes's piracy, perhaps a mere reprint, that has perished. It is curious that in either case chance should have favoured White's editions, but it is fortunate for us, seeing that they presumably contained the more reliable texts. (pp. xi–xii)

In fact, Jeffes's original edition may not have 'wholly perished' but survived – at least in part – until the twentieth century. In 1909, the American drama scholar George P. Baker[5] published an essay strangely overlooked by Greg and all subsequent editors of *The Spanish Tragedy*, together with Kyd

[5] George Pierce Baker (1866–1935) published *The Development of Shakespeare as a Dramatist* (New York, 1907), and from 1905 onwards conducted a postgraduate course in playwriting at Harvard, called 'English 47': one of his students was Eugene O'Neill.

scholars. In it he recorded that some years previously he had bought at auction a copy of *The Spanish Tragedy*:

> When it came to me, I found it was printed almost half in Roman type and in black letter. As an inexperienced bibliophile I felt sure that some unscrupulous bookseller had foisted on the public a pieced copy. As at the time there was no bibliography complete enough to clear up the matter, I returned the book.[6]

Later, having access to 'the work of Greg and others', Baker learned that none of the surviving editions are in black letter, and he could only ruefully speculate how this chimera, this 'composite copy of *The Spanish Tragedy*', might have been created. Baker did not mention whether he collated this copy, but since it would be extremely unlikely that the division of the printed sheets would be identical in two independent editions, it was probably patched together with either a lacuna or an overlap between the two.[7] The motives that led early modern printers to choose one type font or the other are not altogether clear (there is some evidence that black letter was used for popular readership). Since the surviving copy of White's edition is in Roman type, we might infer that the edition by Jeffes must have been in black letter. However, the three surviving copies of White's piratical edition of *Arden of Faversham* are black letter, as are those of its second quarto (1599); not until the third quarto (1633) was it set in roman type.

As for the provenance of the manuscripts that the rival stationers possessed, the normal route to the publication of playbooks in this period begins with the author selling his play, and all reproduction rights, to the theatre company. The company hired a scribe to produce a fresh 'master' copy, which could be marked up by the actors preparing it for production, adding stage directions, producing the authorized 'Booke'.[8] The scribe would then copy out the individual actor's roles on separate rolls of paper, adding only one-line cues for the speeches preceding and following his own. Since the play was then the theatre company's property, they would only sell it to a printer/stationer at their own convenience, to promote a revival of the play two years or so after its premiere, or to raise money after a

6 Baker, 'Some bibliographic puzzles in Elizabethan quartos', *The Papers of the Bibliographical Society of America* 4 (1909): 9–20, at p. 9.

7 That the two texts could be joined in this way, doubtless with overlapping, gives the lie to H. Schott Syme's speculation that 'Jeffes, who had registered his rights in the play on 6 October 1602, owned a *different* text, which he may have printed first (although no copies survive) …' (p. 60; author's italics).

8 For all that was involved in this process see Paul Werstine, *Early Modern Playhouse Manuscripts and the Editing of Shakespeare* (Cambridge, 2012).

plague had closed the theatres.[9] When they did so, the printed copy usually carried their name, but not necessarily the author's. When *Tamburlaine the Great* was printed in 1590 it was as 'shewed upon Stages in the Citie of London By the right honorable the Lord Admyrall his servantes'.[10] All of John Lyly's plays reached print having been performed by either of the two boys' companies, the Children of the Chapel or that of St Paul's. But *The Spanish Tragedy* was ascribed to no theatre company, nor were *Soliman and Perseda* or *Arden of Faversham*, which suggests that an actor may have owned copies and sold them to a printer. They were not the only plays unassigned to a theatre company, but they were in a distinct minority.

The 1592 quarto has one other unusual, indeed unique feature, being the only play from the public theatres between 1578 and 1642 to be divided into four, not five Acts. The consequence is that Act 3 has fifteen scenes, extending to '1580 lines, nearly half the whole text'.[11] The play begins with a choric scene between the Ghost of Andrea and the allegorical figure of Revenge (*1592*, A3^r; 1.1 in modern editions).[12] They reappear at C2^r (1.5 in modern editions), at the end of which the quarto prints 'Actus Secundus', and at D4^r (2.6), followed by 'Actus Tertius'. They do not appear again until I2^r (3.15 in modern editions), at the end of which the quarto prints 'Actus Quartus' (I3^r). Greg found 'small doubt that ... the heading [for Act 3] is wanting merely owing to the absence, or possibly the accidental omission of a chorus at this point' and he dismissed the heading 'Actus Quartus' as 'probably little better than a misprint for "Actus Quintus"'.[13] A strong case for treating the play as a five-Act tragedy was made by Peter Biesterfeldt, who analyzed the 'strikingly regular relationship between long and short scenes in each Act' of *1592*, apart from Act 3, which occupies 45 per cent of the play.[14] Several other pieces of evidence confirm that Kyd cannot have intended a four-Act play. His next play, *Soliman and Perseda*, has the same structure as *The Spanish Tragedy*: the Chorus opens and closes the play and appears at the end of every Act, with no lacuna. T. W. Baldwin's massive survey of the literary tradition showed that five Acts was the norm, from

9 See, e.g., Lukas Erne, *Shakespeare as Literary Dramatist* (Cambridge, 2005).

10 See W. W. Greg, *BEPD*, 1:171.

11 W. W. Greg (ed.), *The Spanish Tragedy with additions 1602* (Oxford, 1925: *MSR*), p. xxii.

12 Greg (ed.), *The Spanish Tragedy (1592).*

13 Q1 1592, p. xxii. Cf. also Greg, *BEPD*, 1:187.

14 Biesterfeldt, *Die dramatische Technik Thomas Kyds: Studien zur inneren Struktur und szenische Form des Elisabethanischen Dramas* (Halle, 1936), pp. 76–87 (82–3). In his 1773 edition Hawkins was the first to divide Act 3. Oddly enough, both Boas and Schick rejected the alteration, claiming that Kyd had intended a four-Act play, citing Seneca's *Thebais* and *Octavia* as models; but they were unrepresentative.

the first commentators on Terence, Donatus and Servius to the seventeenth century and beyond, wherever Horace's *Ars poetica* was studied, with its laconic instruction: 'Let no play be either shorter or longer than five acts'.[15] Finally, I recently asked Professor Martin Mueller, a pioneer in the construction of literary databases (starting with the *Chicago Homer* in 2000), to check the number of references to Five Acts in *Early Print* (using TCP texts), which includes full titles and prefaces to over 52,000 books: they were unanimous. As he put it: 'Plays have Five Acts. Basta!'[16] In this edition I have divided Act 3 after scene 6, in which Hieronimo has taken part. In *1592* 3.7 begins with Hieronimo's soliloquy, 'Where shall I run to breathe abroad my woes', only seven lines after his exit. In my edition his soliloquy begins Act 4, where it has greater impact. I expect that readers unaware of this bibliographical anomaly will not notice anything unusual.

THE COURSE OF REVENGE

The Spanish Tragedy is Kyd's most complex, most carefully constructed play. Its subject matter is primarily revenge, its causes, and its consequences. The action is based on the lengths to which men and women will go to achieve their desires, at the cost of other people's suffering. In the compressed timescale of a play lasting around three hours we see patterns of action and reaction between agents and their victims, whose roles can be reversed. Any unjust or illicit act damaging the life or happiness of another person will have consequences for the agent. Only death can eliminate the possibility of retaliation. Since the complex course of revenge in this play is not clearly evident at a first reading, I now follow its unpredictable movements, which affect every stage of the action.

Kyd's play was the first of its kind, creating the genre of revenge tragedy that was to produce so many memorable plays, from *Hamlet* to plays by Marston, Middleton, Chapman, Webster, Fletcher, and Massinger. These plays have been admired by readers and theatregoers for centuries, yet they have been condemned by some modern literary historians for violating Christian doctrine. In the first full study, *Elizabethan Revenge Tragedy*, Fredson Bowers properly sketched in the condemnation of revenge in English law and in moral writings.[17] But he commendably showed that many Elizabethans regarded blood revenge for murder or flagrant injury as justifiable, when recourse to justice is unavailable. This exception

15 Baldwin, *William Shakespeare's Five-Act Structure* (Urbana, IL, 1947), pp. 1–543.

16 Mueller, email 28 August 2022. For a full listing see https://docs.google.com/spreadsheets/d/1QFhBk1TVYLJl7tsYZTtJqfYj6jiv3vABUrTumMHU8oI/edit#gid=0

17 Bowers, *Elizabethan Revenge Tragedy 1587–1642* (Princeton, NJ, 1940), pp. 3–61.

applied especially for some blood relations, notably that between father and son.[18] When Bowers discussed *The Spanish Tragedy*, however, his balanced historical judgment gave way to outright disapproval of Hieronimo. He argued that

> the carrying-out of the vendetta tradition … turns Hieronimo from a hero to an Italianate villain. So long as he is pitiful in his grief for Horatio and in search of his murderers, so long the English audience would give him full sympathy. When, at last spurred to action by complete knowledge, he rushes to the king for legal justice, he would still be the hero whose actions, according to the best Elizabethan ethics, were those of an honourable man. But when Lorenzo foils him in his attempt at legal redress and he consciously gives up an open revenge in favour of a secret, treacherous device, according to English standards he inevitably becomes a villain. Indeed, so transparently weak is his sophistry and so open-eyed his turning from God's to the devil's means in the soliloquy [beginning '*Vindicta mihi*'] that it is evident Kyd is deliberately veering his audience against Hieronimo. (pp. 76–7)

Bowers supported his claim by summarizing that soliloquy in unsympathetic terms:

> A quotation from Seneca then comes to his mind, and, swayed by the materialistic Senecan philosophy, he reflects that one crime opens the way for another, and he should repay wrong with wrong, for death ends both the resolute and the patient man and the end of destiny for each is merely the grave. Fortified by this un-Christian sophistry, he determines to anticipate Heaven's slow justice and to revenge for himself at his own appointed hour. (p. 77)

It is easy to invoke Christianity to condemn Hieronimo, but also pointless, for Kyd was not writing a play to justify God's moral system. His placing of the biblical verse in the opening line makes clear that Hieronimo's subsequent thought process rejects St Paul's ethics for the injunctions of classical Stoic philosophers and dramatists.

Unfortunately, Bowers was not alone in applying Christian ethics to evaluate a revenge play of the English Renaissance. Eleanor Prosser did so in great detail to *Hamlet*,[19] in the course of which she discussed *The Spanish Tragedy*. Prosser followed Bowers by seeing Hieronimo as gradually shifting his commitment from heaven to hell, finding it 'extremely doubtful that

18 Ibid., pp. 8, 15, 34–40.

19 Prosser, *Hamlet and Revenge* (Stanford, CA, and Oxford, 1967).

Kyd's audience viewed Hieronimo as justified'.[20] One way of avoiding problems concerning the revenge hero's motives is to portray them as mad, a rather desperate remedy.[21] Harry Keyishian introduced a more rewarding approach, placing revenge in the context of Renaissance psychology, and the experience of victimization. The victims of violence experience a loss of identity, a questioning of their own purpose in life:

> Through revenge they attempt, with varying degrees of justification and success, to restore their integrity – their sense of psychic wholeness – and stabilize their identities, often by restructuring them around their new roles as revengers (retaliating for wrongs done to themselves) or avengers (retaliating for the wrongs and sufferings of others).[22]

The Spanish Tragedy begins with a victim recounting his experience. The ghost of Don Andrea tells us that he was killed 'in the late conflict' between Spain and Portugal (1.1.15) and describes his descent into the classical underworld, where he passed examination by the judges Minos, Aeacus and Rhadamanth, who could not agree whether he should be placed among the lovers or warriors. They forwarded him to Pluto, the 'infernal king', to decide his fate. Andrea fortunately pleased Pluto's wife Proserpine, who allowed him to return to earth, accompanied by Revenge, to oversee the action of this play. Andrea failed to mention who had killed him, but Revenge does so, with an unexpected addition:

> Then know, Andrea, that thou art arrived
> Where thou shalt see the author of thy death,
> Don Balthazar, the Prince of Portugal.
> Deprived of life by Bel-Imperia. (1.1.86–9)

Rather than revealing all of his exposition in one chunk, Kyd preferred to release it in instalments. We next hear about the battle in which Andrea lost his life from the detailed account that the Spanish general gives to the King (1.2.23–84). Andrea, 'with his brave lanciers', made a breach in the enemy's defence, but Balthazar, 'the Portugals' young Prince', killed him. Then, 'insulting' over the corpse, Balthazar 'Breathed out proud vaunts, sounding for our reproach' (74), until 'Horatio, our young marshal's son', defeated

20 Prosser, pp. 44–52. Her survey of 'Revenge on the English stage, 1562–1607' concludes: 'we have considered thirteen plays that appeared before *Hamlet* or about the same time. Of these, nine indicate unmistakably that the audience condemned revenge' (p. 63).

21 Cf. Charles A. and Elaine S. Hallett, *The Revenger's Madness: A Study of Revenge Tragedy Motifs* (Lincoln, NE, 1980).

22 Harry Keyishian, *The Shapes of Revenge: Victimization, Vengeance and Vindictiveness in Shakespeare* (Amherst, NY, 2003), p. 2.

Balthazar and took him prisoner. We still do not know how Andrea died, and Kyd, in a third account of the battle, keeps us waiting for another two scenes, until Horatio explains to Bel-Imperia how her lover was killed (1.4.9–29). The Portuguese sent in

> a fresh supply of halberdiers
> Which paunched [disembowelled] his horse and dinged him to the ground.
> Then young Don Balthazar with ruthless rage,
> Taking advantage of his foe's distress,
> Did finish what his halberdiers begun,
> And left not till Andrea's life was done. (21–6)

By using armed infantry to unseat Andrea and deliver the death blow Balthazar violated the 'law of arms'.

This crucial detail reveals that Andrea's death was not a normal event in war. Taking advantage of numerical superiority, killing a defenceless man, then insulting over his corpse, sounds more like hunting down a hated enemy, perhaps a rival in love. Later in this scene Lorenzo, Bel-Imperia's brother, arrives, bringing Balthazar to meet her:

> *Lorenzo* But here the prince is come to visit you,
> *Bel-Imperia* That argues that he lives in liberty.
> *Balthazar* No madam, but in pleasing servitude.
> *Bel-Imperia* Your prison then belike is your conceit.
> *Balthazar* Ay, by conceit my freedom is enthralled. (79–83)

The dialogue shows such an instant rapport between them that they seem to know each other, picking up where they had left off. Balthazar describes himself as living 'in pleasing servitude', just as Andrea's ghost recalled his relationship with Bel-Imperia:

> For there, in prime and pride of all my years,
> By duteous service and deserving love
> In secret I possessed a worthy dame. (1.1.8–10)

That is the conventional language of a Petrarchan lover. But Balthazar's confidence in returning to that role is deluded, for we have just seen Bel-Imperia, in a soliloquy, express her disgust with him:

> For what was't else but murderous cowardice
> So many to oppress one valiant knight,
> Without respect of honour in the fight? (1.4.73–5)

Balthazar's cowardly murder of Andrea has a delayed consequence here, as Bel-Imperia sees Horatio in a new light, reasoning herself into taking him as a lover:

But how can love find harbour in my breast
Till I revenge the death of my beloved?
Yes, second love shall further my revenge.
I'll love Horatio, my Andrea's friend,
The more to spite the prince that wrought his end.
And where Don Balthazar, that slew my love,
Himself now pleads for favour at my hands,
He shall, in rigour of my just disdain,
Reap long repentance for his murderous deed. (1.4.64–72)

The audience watching a play, like a reader of the play text, has an enormous advantage over the personages represented. We see Bel-Imperia planning to use Horatio as a revenger, but she doesn't see the scenes that follow, in which her plan will be prevented. First, Balthazar complains to Lorenzo that she does not respond to his advances, and may perhaps love someone else (2.1.9–28). Lorenzo at once offers 'a stratagem' to find out if Bel-Imperia has some other interest by questioning Pedringano, her servant. With offers of reward and a threat of death, he makes the servant betray his mistress by revealing that she loves Horatio, not Balthazar (2.1.44–108). The news makes Balthazar both 'glad and sad', as he puts it:

Glad, that I know on whom to be revenged,
Sad, that she'll fly me if I take revenge.
Yet must I take revenge, or die myself,
For love resisted grows impatient. (2.1.116–19)

I began by observing that revenge plays show how far people are prepared to go in order to satisfy 'their desires'. As Francis Bacon wrote in his essay 'Of Revenge': 'There is no man doth a wrong for the wrong's sake; but thereby to purchase himself profit, or pleasure, or honour, or the like':[23] here several of those motives are in play. Balthazar murdered Andrea and vaunted over his corpse to punish a love rival. Now that Bel-Imperia has Horatio as a lover, who humiliated Balthazar by defeating him in single combat, he must be killed too. As for Bel-Imperia, a victim twice over, Balthazar still hopes to gain her love. As Lorenzo ends the scene: 'Let's go my lord, your staying stays revenge. | Do you but follow me and gain your love, | Her favour must be won by his remove' (2.1.134–6).

Two revenge plots are now in progress. Bel-Imperia, aided by Horatio, wants revenge on Balthazar. Unknown to them, Balthazar, aided by Lorenzo, plans to revenge himself on Horatio. In the scene following Kyd brings both groups in close proximity by making brilliant use of the flexible

[23] See Brian Vickers (ed.), *Francis Bacon, The Major English Works* (Oxford, 1996), p. 347.

conventions of the Elizabethan theatre. On the main stage Bel-Imperia and Horatio declare their love, unaware that Balthazar and Lorenzo not only overhear them from their position in the gallery overlooking the stage but counterpoint their dedication to love by uttering threats of death which verge on a dialogue in which one side cannot overhear the other. (I mark the speeches of the eavesdroppers with an asterisk.)

> *Bel-Imperia* But whereon dost thou chiefly meditate?
> *Horatio* On dangers past, and pleasures to ensue.
> **Balthazar* On pleasures past, and dangers to ensue.
> *Bel-Imperia* What dangers, and what pleasures dost thou mean?
> *Horatio* Dangers of war, and pleasures of our love.
> **Lorenzo* Dangers of death, but pleasures none at all. (2.2.25–31)

Two scenes later we see the lovers continuing their dialogue, beginning with speeches of four lines each (2.4.17–24), then of two lines, alternating with the greater urgency of single lines, with the overhearers' replies following fast:

> *Horatio* But gracious madam, then appoint the field,
> Where trial of this war shall first be made.
> **Balthazar* Ambitious villain, how his boldness grows. (39–41)

This is the pattern we saw when Bel-Imperia and Balthazar met up at the beginning of the Act. Suddenly their enemies enter, seize Horatio, hang him in the arbour and stab him, carrying Bel-Imperia off with them, all in a dozen lines. This is the speediest, most brutal murder yet performed on the London stage, and it still leaves modern audiences in shock. It is immediately followed by the entrance of Hieronimo in his night-shirt, who cuts down the body and identifies it as that of his son.

My interest, as I mentioned earlier, is in the causes and the consequences of revenge. For Balthazar the motive for murdering Andrea was to destroy a rival for the love of Bel-Imperia, the same motive that he repeated for Horatio. On any scale of human values, murder for one's own sexual pleasure is a trivial motive for a serious crime. The death of Horatio gives Hieronimo a worthwhile cause for revenge that many cultures would endorse. Yet at the same time its consequences for him and his wife are immense. They are the victims of the greatest loss that parents can bear, and Kyd keeps their sufferings before us until the last moments of the play. No other revenge tragedy focuses so intensely on the victims' suffering, the way it convulses their lives in the experience of loss. Hieronimo's first speech after cutting down the body is one of many questions – 'Who hath slain my son?' (2.4.80) – which remain unanswered. His confusion and anger gradually die down, leaving the agonised feeling of loss:

Ay me most wretched, that have lost my joy,
In leesing my Horatio, my sweet boy! (94–5)

'What world of grief', is Isabella's first reaction. She can barely accept the reality of what has happened: 'Then is he gone?' And is my son gone too?' (2.4.104). Father and mother pay the last rites to their son's corpse:

Hieronimo Fair worthy son, not conquered but betrayed:
I'll kiss thee now, for words with tears are stayed.

Isabella And I'll close up the glasses of his sight,
For once these eyes were only my delight. (109–12)

The consequences they draw from the catastrophe are different. Hieronimo immediately thinks of revenge: 'To know the author were some ease of grief, | For in revenge my heart would find relief' (102–3), and swears a solemn oath, given more emphasis by the repetition of the structure and the symmetrical placing of the key terms:

Seest thou this handkercher besmeared with blood?
It shall not from me *till I take revenge!*
Seest thou those wounds that yet are bleeding fresh?
I'll not entomb them *till I have revenged!* (118–21)

Isabella, however, at this point expresses conventional beliefs in a theodicy:

The heavens are just, murder cannot be hid.
Time is the author both of truth and right,
And time will bring this treachery to light. (124–6)

Those are the two poles that will dominate much of their behaviour in Acts 3 and 4, in both rational and demented states.

When Kyd next shows Hieronimo it is for a soliloquy expressing a grief that has shaken his whole existence:

Oh eyes, no eyes, but fountains fraught with tears;
Oh life, no life, but lively form of death:
Oh world, no world, but mass of public wrongs,
Confused and filled with murder and misdeeds. (3.2.1–4)

Confrontation with this chaos makes him challenge the certitude that Isabella cherishes in the 'sacred heavens':

If this incomparable murder thus
Of mine, but now no more my son,
Shall unrevealed and unrevengèd pass,
How should we term your dealings to be just,
If you unjustly deal with those that in your justice trust? (3.2.7–11)

The 'direful visions' of 'ugly fiends' that disturb his sleeping and waking hours drive him 'to seek the murderer' (12–21) but he has no thought of revenge. That suddenly arrives, from an unexpected source, in a letter from Bel-Imperia, whom her brother Lorenzo imprisoned in their house immediately after the murder. Having no ink, she has written it in blood, with an urgent message:

> 'Me hath my hapless brother hid from thee.
> Revenge thyself on Balthazar and him!
> For these were they that murderèd thy son.
> Hieronimo, revenge Horatio's death,
> And better fare than Bel-Imperia doth.' (27–31)

In some easily conceived fictions this information might be enough to set Hieronimo off on a revengeful murder spree. But Kyd makes Hieronimo stop and question 'this unexpected miracle'. What possible cause could make Lorenzo and Balthazar kill Horatio? Moreover, even if they had done so, what motive could Bel-Imperia have to accuse her brother? Unable to see any logical explanation for these events, he chooses caution: '– Hieronimo beware, thou art betrayed, | And to entrap thy life this train is laid. | Advise thee therefore, be not credulous: | This is devisèd to endanger thee' (37–40). It could be a trap to make him accuse Lorenzo, with dangerous consequences. To avenge Horatio's death Hieronimo must preserve his own life, so he resolves to try 'by circumstances' to confirm the truth of Bel-Imperia's accusations.[24]

While this decision might seem like an unwelcome postponement of revenge, Kyd has carefully prepared a parallel plot-strand to show the dangers of believing accusations without checking them. In the Portuguese court one Villuppo, a malicious nobleman, accuses another of having killed Balthazar on the battlefield. The ruler believes him and the innocent victim Alexandro is sentenced to death. Two scenes later news arrives from Spain that Balthazar is still alive: Villuppo replaces Alexandro at the stake.

Hieronimo uses a roundabout stratagem by enquiring after Bel-Imperia, but he nonetheless arouses the suspicions of her brother. Lorenzo wrongly concludes that Serberine, one of his servants, must have revealed her imprisonment, so he instantly hires Pedringano to meet Serberine in a public park and shoot him. He then alerts the watchman in that area to a likely disturbance and they catch and imprison Pedringano. In a clever closing move, Lorenzo gives his page a box said to contain a pardon for Pedringano to be given to the hangman, while assuring the scapegoat that

24 'Circumstances' are the conditions under which any event takes place. Derived from Greek philosophy, they were used as a teaching aid in classical legal rhetoric. See the commentary note to 4.7.44.

he, Lorenzo, will look after him. The page disobeys Lorenzo's order not to open the box and, finding it empty, describes the stratagem as 'a piece of gentlemanlike knavery' and 'a scurvy jest'. His discovery prepares the audience for a brilliant comic scene in which Pedringano, believing that he will be pardoned, exercises his wits in abusing the hangman. Kyd arouses our laughter at this, perhaps the first piece of black comedy on the English stage, but stops it again when Pedringano is 'turned off' the scaffold, apparently hanged before our eyes.

Lorenzo has congratulated himself on his 'policy' of using one instrument to eliminate the other while remaining unseen and unsuspected: 'He runs to kill whom I have holp to catch, | And no man knows it was my reaching fatch' (3.4.42–3). Both 'policy' and 'reaching' became key terms in the vocabulary of other Machiavels based on Lorenzo's Italianate skills. Yet he has forgotten one of the maxims found in *The Prince*: 'men must be flattered withal or quite crushed.'[25] With his clever device of feigning to give Pedringano a pardon, Lorenzo failed to realize that, while awaiting execution, his servant would have enough time to write a letter reminding Lorenzo of all the jobs he'd carried out for him, from murdering Horatio to killing Serberine.

When the hangman brings Pedringano's letter to Hieronimo, it provides independent proof of Bel-Imperia's veracity:

> Now see I what I durst not then suspect,
> That Bel-Imperia's letter was not feigned,
> Nor feigned she, though falsely they have wronged
> Both her, myself, Horatio, and themselves. (4.1.49–52).

He expresses his anger and disgust at Lorenzo and Balthazar, yet suddenly breaks off:

> – But wherefore waste I mine unfruitful words,
> When nought but blood will satisfy my woes?
> I will go plain me to my lord the king,
> And cry aloud for justice through the court,
> Wearing the flints with these my withered feet,
> And either purchase justice by entreats,
> Or tire them all with my revenging threats. (67–73)

25 *The Prince*, ch. 3. Many readers must have wondered how Machiavelli, a widely read humanist with great knowledge of classical history, could have recommended such ruthless behaviour. One clarification was provided by L. A. Burd in his great edition of *Il Principe*, who showed that Machiavelli adapted Aristotle's account of Greek tyrants' behaviour to shape his advice to the Renaissance prince. See L. Arthur Burd (ed.), *Il Principe* (Oxford, 1891, 1968), pp. 289–90.

At this point Hieronimo sees these as alternatives, but his intentions are disturbed by two unexpected events. We see Isabella rejecting medicines that her maid has brought, since 'none of them will purge the heart' of all the grief that has accumulated there. Then, as the stage direction puts it, '*She runs lunatic*' (4.2.5), asking 'Horatio, Oh where's Horatio?' and rebuking her maidservant:

> Why did I not give you gowns and goodly things,
> Bought you a whistle and a whipstalk too,
> To be revengèd on their villainies? (4.2.10–12)

Isabella has a mother's vision of Horatio in heaven, 'Dancing about his newly healed wounds', but that pleasing fantasy gives way to desperate questions:

> But say, where shall I find the men, the murderers
> That slew Horatio? Whither shall I run
> To find them out that murderèd my son? (23–5)

Hieronimo soon follows Isabella into madness. When a Portuguese visitor enquires as to Lorenzo's whereabouts Hieronimo gives him crazy directions to take 'a path upon your left-hand side' leading from 'a guilty conscience' to the underworld, where murderers have built their habitation:

> There in a brazen cauldron, fixed by Jove
> In his fell wrath upon a sulphur flame:
> Yourselves shall find Lorenzo bathing him
> In boiling lead and blood of innocents. (4.5.26–9)

The Portuguese laugh at this manic vision but conclude: 'Doubtless this man is passing lunatic' (32).

Kyd, having brought Hieronimo to this point, presses on with a sequence of unbalanced behaviour. First, he enters with a dagger and a noose, the stock attributes in the Elizabethan theatre for a suicide. The soliloquy that follows starts with him envisaging the King hearing his suit but at once deviates from human justice into a vision of hell, with its 'fiery tower' and a judge sitting 'Upon a seat of steel and molten brass', adjacent to the fiery lake Phlegethlon. He hesitates over which weapon to use, the noose or the dagger, but realizes that if he kills himself no one will 'revenge Horatio's murder' (4.6.15–19). '*He flings away the dagger and halter*', the stage direction instructs, but '*takes them up again*' as he sees the King approaching. Now he reverts to his first idea, appealing to the King: 'Justice! Oh, justice to Hieronimo!' (27). But the King is accompanied by Lorenzo, the man he would want to accuse, who drives him back. Hieronimo withdraws but returns a few moments later, calling for 'Justice! Oh, justice, justice, gentle King!' (62). Blocked again, he reverts to his alternative plan, to 'ferry over to th'Elysian plains | And bring my son to show his deadly wounds' (71–2). As

Calvo and Tronch observe, 'For the first time, Hieronimo publicly reveals that Horatio is dead'.[26] Yet at once he thinks of another plan, 'I'll go marshal up the fiends in hell, | To be avengèd on you all for this' (76–7).

At this point Kyd changes direction. We have seen Hieronimo fruitlessly hoping to receive justice from a King who doesn't even know that Horatio has been murdered. Lorenzo assures the King that Hieronimo was 'covetous' of his son and has become 'Distract, and in a manner lunatic' because he wanted to have for himself the ransom due to Horatio (86–8). In this whole sequence Hieronimo, the victim of an evil counsellor, has been mentally unstable, switching from one plan to another, blocked each way. Now Kyd gives him a long soliloquy (4.7.1–44) in which he reflects on the choices open to him. First, he quotes the biblical phrase '*Vindicta mihi!*', summarizing its assurance that 'heaven will [not] suffer murder unrepaid'. Then, Hieronimo switches to reviewing alternative courses of action via quotations from Seneca's tragedies, starting with *Agamemnon* and Clytemnestra's often-quoted maxim that 'for crimes the safest path is always through crimes'. Next he cites *Troades* for the conversation in which Andromache, widow of Hector, tries to protect her son Astyanax from the vengeful Greeks by placing him in his father's 'holy burial place', with the bleak alternative: 'If fate helps the wretched, you have a refuge; if fate denies you life you have a tomb.' Kyd presents Hieronimo arguing rationally, juxtaposing choices and their consequences, with logical objectives and deductions. The pagan world wins: 'And to conclude, I will revenge his death!' But he is already planning 'a secret, yet a certain' means, cloaked under 'kindship', a pretence of kindness.

At this point Kyd could have proceeded directly to the 'play within the play' and its spectacular revenge. But he chose to write a completely unexpected scene, the most imaginative, most powerful scene in English tragedy before Shakespeare's mature plays, and ranking with them. At the end of his '*Vindicta mihi*' speech a group of petitioners appears, diverting Hieronimo away from revenge for Horatio to his public office as a magistrate and advocate. Three of them have standard legal complaints (unpaid debt, a court case, the violation of a lease) but his attention is caught by the fourth, an old man (described as *Senex* in the quarto), 'With mournful eyes and hands to heaven upreared' (4.7.68). Hieronimo reads out his petition, 'The humble supplication | Of Don Bazulto for his murdered son', and his mind is violently forced back to his own matter:

> No sir, it was my murdered son,
> Oh my son, my son! Oh my son Horatio!

[26] Calvo and Tronch (eds), *The Spanish Tragedy*, p. 243.

> But mine, or thine, Bazulto, be content.
> Here, take my handkercher and wipe thine eyes. (79–82)

Wanting to offer a handkerchief from his pocket, instead he takes out 'a bloody napkin':

> Oh no, not this! Horatio, this was thine,
> And when I dyed it in thy dearest blood
> This was a token 'twixt thy soul and me
> That of thy death revengèd I should be. (85–8)

In what may be the first 'mirror scene' in Elizabethan tragedy Hieronimo sees in Bazulto 'The lively portrait of my dying self'.

The first effect of this mirror image is to remind him of his unfulfilled duty of revenge:

> Then sham'st thou not, Hieronimo, to neglect
> The sweet revenge of thy Horatio?
> Though on this earth justice will not be found,
> I'll down to hell. (105–8)

He fantasizes that he has gained Proserpine's permission to have

> Revenge on them that murderèd my son.
> Then will I rent and tear them thus and thus,
> Shivering their limbs in pieces with my teeth. (120–2)

But his revenge is pathetic and comic, tearing with his teeth the petitioners' costly official documents. In a farcical conclusion to this episode, Hieronimo runs off, pursued by the complainants. Kyd marks this rupture in the action with a striking stage direction:

> *Exeunt all but the old man. Bazulto remains till Hieronimo enters again, who, staring him in the face, speaks.* (129.0)

Bazulto stands alone on stage, a rare isolation of a character in the Elizabethan theatre, as we wait for Hieronimo's return. Now Kyd takes the father's madness into a new level of confused recognition:

> And art thou come, Horatio, from the depth,
> To ask for justice in this upper earth?
> To tell thy father thou art unrevenged ... (130–2)

I can never reread this scene without feeling shivers down my spine, as we enter into the mind of a deranged person, who can utter grammatically coherent sentences that refer to a completely distorted view of reality. It is like being inside a hallucination, as Hieronimo's mental vision substitutes one face for another. (The cinema would need to have been invented to do justice to this sequence.) With admirable economy Kyd uses Bazulto to register the deranged man's confusion: 'Alas, my lord, whence springs this troubled speech?' (141). By now Hieronimo has achieved a complete rupture between observation and recognition. He sees the signs of age on Bazulto's face but is incapable of reasoning that this man is not his son:

> Sweet boy, how art thou changed in death's black shade!
> Had Proserpine no pity on thy youth,
> But suffered thy fair crimson-coloured spring
> With withered winter to be blasted thus? (143–6)

Kyd charts Hieronimo's confused reasoning stage by stage, as he notes one paradoxical effect of age: 'Horatio, thou art older than thy father' (147), as if it were the answer to a riddle. He then blames 'ruthless fate' for having the power to change a person's appearance, at which Bazulto breaks in again on his distorted perception: 'I am not your young son.' This reminder triggers Hieronimo's obsession with hell and its judges, whom he imagines are waiting to rebuke him for not seeking revenge for Horatio's death. Bazulto interrupts his delusion again, this time bringing Hieronimo back to reality:

> I am a grievèd man and not a ghost,
> That came for justice for my murdered son.
>
> *Hieronimo* Ay, now I know thee, now thou nam'st my son:
> Thou art the lively image of my grief. (156–9)

Finally, he can separate the two images of men having suffered the same loss. This remarkable recreation of the visual and psychological deformation created by extreme grief looks ahead to the madness of King Lear, with which it deserves to be ranked.

After the intensity of this scene, theatregoers and readers are returned to the negotiations that have been proceeding for the wedding of Bel-Imperia to Balthazar (4.6.32–56, 102–10, 4.8.8–39). After the arrangements have been made the Duke of Castile remains with his son Lorenzo, whom he rebukes for having publicly slighted Hieronimo. Castile sends for the latter and a reconciliation takes place (4.8.121–67). Kyd uses the flexibility of Elizabethan drama to give Hieronimo an aside to the audience to show his real self, beneath the *persona* he has adopted:

> What new device have they devisèd, trow?
> *Pocas palabras*, mild as the lamb,
> Is't I will be revenged? No, I am not the man. (118–20)

When father and son have gone Kyd gives Hieronimo the final words:

> Your lordship's to command. – Pah! keep your way.
> *Chi mi fa piu carezze che non suole,*
> *Tradito mi ha, o trader mi vuole.* (169–71)

Previously, it was the Machiavel Lorenzo who ended a scene (a position of some power in drama) with an Italian maxim:

> *Et quel che voglio io, nessun lo sa.*
> *Intendo io; quel mi basterà.* (3.4.83–4)

Now Hieronimo takes over that role.

Having settled several plot lines Kyd needs to focus on the goal to which the whole play has been moving since Horatio's murder, the father's duty of revenge. He does so first in the longest scene between the two choric figures (4.9). Andrea's ghost repeatedly urges Revenge to awake, but Revenge denies the charge, explaining that he is still keeping watch on human affairs. To illustrate his dedication, Revenge brings on a dumb show in which Hymen, the Greek goddess of marriage, quenches 'nuptial torches' with blood, signifying to Andrea that the 'infernal powers ... will not tolerate a lover's woe'. Kyd's introduction of a dumb show at this point shows his creative use of visual resources.[27] It also has a more mundane purpose, allowing the actors a brief rest.

The action resumes with Kyd picking up an important plot strand in which Bel-Imperia had vowed to revenge herself on Horatio's murderers (1.4.45–75) and had written the crucial letter (3.2.25–31). Now she appears in person to deliver a swingeing rebuke to the 'unkind father' who had neglected his duty towards his son (5.1.1–29), ending with the vow that

> Shouldst thou neglect the love thou shouldst retain,
> And give it over and devise no more,
> Myself should send their hateful souls to hell
> That wrought his downfall with extremest death! (26–9)

Bel-Imperia's admirable dedication to Horatio makes her the first woman in Elizabethan tragedy ready to take on the traditional male duty of revenge. Hieronimo recalls her letter, apologizes for his 'fear and care in not believing it' (39), and informs her that he 'will ere long determine of their deaths | That causeless thus have murderèd my son' (44–5). He asks for her help in 'whatsoever I devise' for 'the plots already in mine head' (49–51), finally gaining her as an accomplice.

So far I have been tracing the causes and consequences of revenge in this play, from the murder of Horatio and the related murders that Lorenzo arranged to safeguard his position. Hieronimo intended revenge once he knew who were responsible. Bel-Imperia's letter identified them, but his prudence in not believing her unsupported word made it impossible to act

27 See Dieter Mehl, *The Elizabethan Dumb Show: The History of a Dramatic Convention* (London, 1965), pp. 68–71.

until Pedringano's intercepted letter to Lorenzo confirmed it (4.1.32–40). Any possibility that he might proceed to his revenge was then blocked by the remarkable confrontation with Bazulto (4.7.67–172), where his stored-up grief led to a mental breakdown. His interview with Bel-Imperia renews his resolve and gives him a helper. I have traced the interconnection between these events, passing by other matters, to show the coherence with which Kyd sustained the driving engine of his plot. The revenges now take place with some unexpected developments, but Kyd's orchestration of the sequence of shocks in the play-within-the-play is so clear and so vivid that commentary is unnecessary. The scene just needs to be experienced.

The following, final scene, however, may need some discussion. In it, Andrea's ghost and Revenge sum up the sequence of events, from 'Horatio murdered in his father's bower' to 'good Hieronimo slain by himself' (5.5.3–11). In our experience of the play Andrea has been onstage in the present, throughout the performance, but now he plans his return to the underworld to request assistance in completing the distribution of help and harm:

> Now will I beg at lovely Proserpine,
> That by the virtue of her Princely doom
> I may consort my friends in pleasing sort,
> And on my foes work just and sharp revenge. (13–16)

He announces his intention to look after his friends Horatio, Bel-Imperia and Hieronimo, then asks Revenge how he should deal with his enemies:

> *Revenge* This hand shall hale them down to deepest hell,
> Where none but Furies, bugs, and tortures dwell.
>
> *Andrea* Then, sweet Revenge, do this at my request,
> Let me be judge, and doom them to unrest. (27–30)

He proposes five punishments taken from classical mythology, each fitting the crime. Cyprian should release 'poor Tityus from the vultures' gripe'; Lorenzo should be placed 'on Ixion's wheel'; Balthazar should be hung 'about Chimera's neck', that composite creature of lion, snake and goat, snorting out 'terrible flames of bright fire', according to Homer. Serberine should replace Sisyphus in endlessly rolling a huge marble block uphill, while 'False Pedringano, for his treachery', should spend eternity in the 'endless flames' of 'boiling Acheron'. Revenge is given the closing lines (45–8).

For those in tune with the legitimacy of revenge, as Kyd presents it, this is a satisfying conclusion. For those who approach the play with the mindset of Christianity it is wholly unjustified. But other cultures, at other periods, accepted revenge as a legitimate reaction. As Mary Blundell has shown,

> Greek popular thought is pervaded by the assumption that one should help one's friends and harm one's enemies. These fundamental principles surface continually from Homer onwards and survive well into the Roman period, and indeed *to the present day, especially in international relations*. They are firmly based on observation of human nature, which yields the conclusion that most human beings do in fact desire to help their friends and harm their enemies, and derive satisfaction from such behaviour. Thus Xenophon's Socrates can count benefiting friends and defeating enemies as one of the things which brings 'greatest pleasures'.[28]

In his *Rhetoric* Aristotle linked the dyad (Help Friends/Harm Enemies) among 'the things that are good', especially an action 'useful to ourselves or our friends or hurtful to our enemies; this is true even if the action entails loss, provided the loss is outweighed by the solid advantage'.[29] Similar statements can be found in Isocrates and Plato, despite their divergent attitudes to the relationship between philosophy and rhetoric.

Blundell points out that 'the complementary principles Help Friends and Harm Enemies appear most characteristically not as a commandment but as an expression of desire or approval' (p. 28). But the Greeks were highly conscious of taking as a principle of justice the *talio*, 'the injury inflicted in return', or 'the reciprocation of an equivalent evil' (p. 54). As she observes:

> A court of law can in theory provide a disinterested arbiter with the authority to decide when such harms are right and just. Punishment – a harm inflicted by society in the name of justice – is thus distinguished from the personal retaliation of revenge … Revenge is prompted by the subjective feelings of the injured party, whereas punishment is, in theory, determined impersonally by society or its representative: 'To go to the judge is to go to justice, for the judge is supposed to be like justice incarnate.'[30]

(The reality in many situations, as Hieronimo discovers, is that justice cannot be found.) Despite that theoretical distinction, Blundell observes, 'revenge and justice are not so easily distinguished in practice. In Greek culture they remained persistently linked' (pp. 54–5). One final point from Blundell's discussion is relevant to Kyd's play:

28 Mary Whitlock Blundell, *Helping Friends and Harming Enemies: A Study in Sophocles and Greek Ethics* (Cambridge, 1989), p. 26; my emphasis.

29 Aristotle, *Rhetoric* 1.6 (1363 a 19–21, 33 f) and 2.22 (1399 b 36f).

30 Blundell, p. 54, citing Aristotle, *Nicomachean Ethics*, 5.4 (1132 a 20–2), in her translation. In W. D. Ross's translation, revised by J. O. Urmison, the phrase reads 'for the nature of the judge is to be a sort of animate justice'. See Jonathan Barnes (ed.), *The Complete Works of Aristotle: The Revised Oxford Translation*, 2 vols (Princeton, NJ, 1984), 2:1786.

> When Harm Enemies in the form of personal revenge is applauded, it is often in terms of manly honour. 'To have revenge on one's enemies and not to make terms is finer (more *kalos*). For to retaliate is just, and what is just is *kalos*, and not to be defeated is a sign of manliness'[31] … Failure to exact revenge may correspondingly be a matter for reproach, whether in Homer,[32] or in the fourth century, when an orator can claim that 'everyone' urged him to take revenge, reproaching him as 'most unmanly' not to do so. (p. 55)

Following Hieronimo's rejection of the divine claim – '*Vindicta mihi*' – Kyd ignores, with perfect propriety, New Testament ethics, and adopts the morality of the Greeks, the Romans, and many other cultures. To them there would be nothing inappropriate in the final utterance of Kyd's Revenge:

> Then haste we down to meet thy friends and foes,
> To place thy friends in ease, the rest in woes. (5.5.46–7)

RHETORIC AND STRUCTURES OF FEELING

As a dramatist, Kyd innovated in several ways. He was the first to write a revenge tragedy and the first to give a female character a driving role in revenge, accorded the same right to use violence as a man. He was the first to make a play-within-the play an integral part of the action. Although other dramatists had introduced dumb shows, Dieter Mehl recognized original features in the two that Kyd wrote for *The Spanish Tragedy*. The first one, devised by Hieronimo to entertain the Spanish and Portuguese guests, is no longer an entertainment 'apart from the main play … but is worked into a scene of normal dialogue, and therefore increasing its dramatic effect'. The second is unrehearsed, 'suddenly conjured up by Revenge', presenting a mime in which Hymen quenches with blood some 'nuptial torches' lighted for a wedding (4.9.24). It 'foreshadows the denouement in an allegorical manner' but is 'skilfully built into a scene and could not be detached from the play'.[33]

Kyd also innovated by introducing into Elizabethan drama the figures and tropes of classical rhetoric. As a student at Merchant Taylors' School, which modelled its curriculum on that of St Paul's, Kyd would have begun studying rhetoric in the upper school.[34] His teacher would have probably used the popular classical treatise long attributed to Cicero, the anonymous

31 Aristotle, *Rhetoric*, 1.9 (1367 a 20–3); *Nicomachean Ethics*, 5.5 (1132 b 21–35 a 5).

32 Homer, *Odyssey* 24.433–6, *Demosthenes* 59.12.

33 See Mehl, *The Elizabethan Dumb Show*, pp. 63–71.

34 See T. W. Baldwin, *William Shakspere's Small Latine & Lesse Greeke*, 2 vols (Urban, IL, 1944), 1:395–402.

Rhetorica ad Herennium, which concludes its account of Roman courtroom rhetoric with a concise list of forty-five 'Figures of Diction' and nineteen 'Figures of Thought'.[35] Many teachers supplemented the classical texts with one of the Renaissance compilations, such as that produced by the Ravensburg schoolmaster Joannes Susenbrotus, *Epitome troporum ac schematum* (1540). It is natural, but wrong, to assume that books printed in Latin were published in continental Europe: this handy compilation was published in London twelve times between 1562 and 1635, evidence of its popularity in grammar schools from St Paul's and Eton to Rivington and Stratford.[36] Several English authors of rhetoric books drew their definitions and illustrative quotations from it, including Wilson, Peacham and Puttenham.

Kyd grew up in a culture permeated by rhetoric, which had recently experienced a surge in the publication of books in English intended for a literate public. The pioneer was Thomas Wilson, in *The Arte of Rhetorique, for the use of all such as are studious of Eloquence, set forthe in Englishe* (1553, 1560), followed by Henry Peacham, *The Garden of Eloquence, Conteyning the Figures of Grammar and Rhetoric* (1577), which took its examples from Latin poetry and the Bible. Abraham Fraunce, *The Arcadian Rhetorike* (1588), took many of his examples from Sidney's *Arcadia*, the exclusive source for the brief but perceptive treatise by John Hoskyns, *Directions for Speech and Style* (c. 1599), only published in modern times.[37]

The two most important treatises were George Puttenham, *The Arte of English Poesie* (1589), and the enlarged edition of Peacham's *Garden of Eloquence* (1593), carrying the new subtitle: 'By which the singular partes of man's mind are most aptly expressed, and the sundrie affections of his heart most effectuallie uttered.' The significance of that addition lies in the characteristic focus of English Renaissance rhetoric on *movere*, arousing the audience's feelings and affecting its judgment.[38] As Puttenham argued, the effective 'use of words' can produce 'no little alteration in man':

35 See [Anon.] *Ad C. Herennium, De Ratione Dicendi*, ed. and tr. Harry Caplan (London and Cambridge, MA, 1954; Loeb Classical Library), pp. 275–411.

36 See Lawrence D. Green and James J. Murphy, *Renaissance Rhetoric Short-Title Catalogue*, 2nd edn (Aldershot and Burlington, VT, 2006), pp. 421–2, and Baldwin, Index, 2:768.

37 The manuscript in the British Library (MS Harl. 4604) has been edited twice: by Louise Brown Osborn, in *The Life, Letters, and Writings of John Hoskyns 1566–1638* (New Haven, CT, 1937; Hamden, CT, 1973), and by Hoyt H. Hudson, *Directions for Speech and Style* (Princeton, NJ, 1935), cited here.

38 In the 'affective triad', as defined by Cicero and disseminated by Horace's influential *Ars Poetica*, *movere* was the third goal that a speaker or writer had to address, the others being *delectare* and *docere*. On the dominance of *movere* in the Renaissance see Brian Vickers, *In Defence of Rhetoric* (Oxford, 1988), pp. 276–86.

> For to say truly, what else is man but his mind? Which, whosoever have skill to compass and make yielding and flexible, what may he not command the body to perform? He, therefore, that hath vanquished the mind of man hath made the greatest and most glorious conquest. But the mind of man is not assailable unless it is by sensible approaches … [perceptible to the senses][39]

Modern readers sometimes regard the figures and tropes as ornamental, or as pure display, but for the Elizabethan rhetoricians they were completely functional, the tools used to arouse the emotions. To quote Puttenham again: 'a figure is ever used to a purpose, either of beauty or efficacy' (p. 257), joining the aesthetic and the pragmatic – that is, the power to produce effects. Rhetoric was celebrated as an *ars* or *technē*, a practical discipline that could be taught, but it was based on nature. Since early times its historians have claimed that it systematized verbal effects used in natural language by untrained speakers. As anyone will have noticed, speakers wishing to emphasize an important point or to convey heightened feelings will naturally use repetition. English Renaissance rhetoricians noticed the psychological rationale for verbal repetition occasionally mentioned in the classical handbooks, and (as I have argued) gave it increased importance.[40] In his *Apology for Poetry* (c. 1582) Sir Philip Sidney characterized the famous opening of Cicero's first speech against Catiline in psychological terms, commenting (and punning) on the figure *conduplicatio*, or *plokē*, which Puttenham called 'the doubler':

> Tully, when he was to drive out Catiline, as it were with a thunderbolt of eloquence, often used the figure of repetition, *Vivit. Vivit? Imo vero etiam in senatum venit, &c.* Indeed, inflamed with a well-grounded rage, he would have his words (as it were) double out of his mouth, and so do that artificially which we see men do in choler naturally. (p. 386)

(The term 'artificially' here carries the dominant Renaissance meaning, 'artfully', or 'fashioned by art'.) In discussing the general category of figures which repeat a word in differing ways, Puttenham advised that 'your figure that worketh by iteration or repetition of one word or clause doth much

39 Unless otherwise indicated, subsequent quotations will be taken from Brian Vickers (ed.), *English Renaissance Literary Criticism* (Oxford, 1999), which contains substantial excerpts from the English rhetoric books: Thomas Wilson (pp. 73–124), George Puttenham (pp. 190–296), and John Hoskyns (pp. 398–427). Page references will be included in the text; here, p. 253.

40 See Brian Vickers, *Classical Rhetoric in English Poetry* (London and New York, 1970; 2nd edn, Carbondale, IL, 1989), ch. 3, 'The Functions of Rhetorical Figures' (pp. 83–121), an account enlarged and diversified in Vickers, *In Defence of Rhetoric*, ch. 6, 'The Expressive Function of Rhetorical Figures', pp. 294–339.

alter and affect the ear and also the mind of the hearer, and is therefore counted a very brave figure' (p. 254) – where 'brave' means 'excellent' or 'splendid'. Hoskyns extended this psychological analysis of repetition, observing that 'as no man is sick in thought upon one thing but for vehemency or distress, so in speech there is no repetition without importance' (p. 405). Of the figure *anaphora*, which repeats the same word at the beginning of a sequence of clauses, sentences, or verse lines, Hoskyns wrote that it 'beats upon one thing to cause the quicker feeling in the audience' (p. 406) – where 'quicker' means 'more lively'. Hoskyns emphasized that the writer or speaker must select appropriate verbal devices, in tune with his communicative intent. Rhetoric is simultaneously mimetic, representing human states of thought and feeling, and pragmatic, arousing such states in its audience. So he insisted that figures should be tied to sense and structure: 'let discretion [a choice that observes decorum] be the greatest and general figure of figures.' Hoskyns advised would-be writers always to consider the context and communicative intent: 'In these two sorts of amplifying you may insert all figures *as the passion of the matter shall serve*' (p. 411; my italics), that is, according to the emotions involved.

Kyd had absorbed the full range of rhetorical devices and used them to express the feelings that animated his characters, especially Hieronimo, who is a prime example of a man 'sick in thought upon one thing', whose 'vehemency' of utterance indeed arises from 'distress'. Two of the most frequently used figures of repetition are *plokē*, repeating a word with no other words intervening, and *epizeuxis*, immediate repetition. Hieronimo uses both in his anguished exclamations:

> Justice! O justice, O my son, my son,
> My son, whom nought can ransom or redeem! (4.6.64–5)

> No sir, it was my murdered son,
> Oh my son, my son! Oh my son Horatio! (4.7.79–80)

Kyd gives Hieronimo *plokē* to express the waste of his son's death:

> O poor Horatio, what hadst thou misdone
> To leese thy *life* ere *life* was new begun? (2.4.90–1)

On other occasions Kyd prefers to let Hieronimo use the verbal energy of *polyptoton*, repeating a word stem while varying its ending, the repetition gaining more force by the repeated word being bent into a new shape. This figure is a fitting frame to express Hieronimo's plan to avenge Horatio's death by 'a secret but a certain mean' [means] that will depend on subterfuge:

> Thus therefore will I *rest* me in *unrest*,
> Dissembling *quiet* in *unquietness*. (4.7.29–30)

It also fits his new suspicion of his enemies' plotting, as in his aside before meeting Castile and Lorenzo:

> What new *device* have they *devisèd*, trow? (4.8.118)

It is equally fitting to reassure Bel-Imperia that her suspicions he has neglected to revenge Horatio's murder are misplaced:

> Nor *think* I, *thoughtless*, *think* upon a mean
> To let his death be unrevenged at full. (4.1.40–1)

Most movingly, it expresses the survival of the past into the present, as he recalls to the audience of his play the permanent memory of Horatio's murder:

> He shrieks, I *heard*, and yet methinks I *hear*. (4.4.107)

Kyd uses many other rhetorical figures to express Hieronimo's feelings in the situations with which he is confronted, but he also creates larger rhetorical structures with a confidence that none of his contemporaries could match. We see Hieronimo's agonized reaction to discovering Horatio's corpse, sharing his grief with Isabella, and delivering an impromptu dirge before they carry away his body (2.4.65–143). The next time we see him he delivers a formal lament, a fifty-two-line soliloquy beginning:

> Oh eyes, no eyes, but fountains fraught with tears;
> Oh life, no life, but lively form of death:
> Oh world, no world, but mass of public wrongs,
> Confused and filled with murder and misdeeds.
> Oh sacred heavens! If this unhallowed deed,
> If this inhuman and barbarous attempt,
> If this incomparable murder thus
> Of mine, but now no more my son,
> Shall unrevealed and unrevengèd pass,
> How should we term your dealings to be just,
> If you unjustly deal with those that in your justice trust? (3.2.1–11)

I have underlined the key words by which – as Jonas Barish put it – Kyd packed 'three successive apostrophes into three successive lines and, stressing the correspondences between them, achieves an effect of swollen passion breaking loose'.[41] The chief figure he used is *correctio*, or *epan-*

[41] J. Barish, '*The Spanish Tragedy*, or The Pleasures and Perils of Rhetoric', in J. R. Brown and B. Harris (eds), *Elizabethan Theatre* (London, 1966; Stratford-upon-Avon Studies 9), pp. 58–85. Unfortunately, Barish made a false start by declaring that the purpose of rhetorical figures was 'simply to please, "to avoid societie, and cause delight, to refresh with pleasure"', quoting Wilson's *Art of Rhetoric* (p. 59). He

orthosis, by which a speaker recalls a word just uttered and substitutes another more suitable. Renaissance rhetoricians saw it as a form of amplifying an utterance's emotional impact. Hoskyns connected it with a greater weight of meaning and feeling: '*Correctio*, having used a word of sufficient force, yet pretending [intending] a greater vehemence of meaning, refuseth it and supplies the place with a greater' (p. 413). Kyd structures the speech by using several rhetorical figures that 'effectually amplifie' Hieronimo's feelings. In the line 'O life, no life, but lively form of death', *polyptoton*, which varies the form of words derived from the same root – 'life', 'lively' – leads on to 'death', a terminal *antithesis*. By giving the utterance such a clear structure, using *anaphora* (four clauses begin 'O', three begin 'If this'), *parison* (word corresponding to word: 'O *x*, no *x*, but *y*'; 'if this *x* …, if this *y*, … if this *z*'), and *isocolon* (a sequence of clauses or sentences of the same length), Kyd sets up a 'frame of order' which brings out more clearly the moral chaos that Hieronimo has discovered.[42] His bitter appeal to the 'sacred heavens', should Horatio's murderer not be found and punished, uses *polyptoton* on 'just' through three stages of increasing sarcasm, capped with a rhyme that highlights the commodity on which heavenly and earthly functioning rely, 'trust':

> How should we term your dealings to be *just*,
> If you *unjustly* deal with those that in your *justice* trust?

For that bitter question Kyd uses an unexpected longer line of fourteen syllables, highlighting the extra words, 'in your justice trust'. These rhetorical figures are channels of feeling, pressed into the most effective form.

The second part of this section is more loosely organized, reviewing other fixed points in Hieronimo's disturbed cosmos. 'The <u>night</u>' brings no rest, for 'direful visions wake my vexed soul' (12–15). 'The ugly fiends do sally forth of <u>hell</u>', bringing 'fierce inflamèd thoughts' (16–18). Finally, 'The

failed to realize that *delectare* (to please, or keep the listener's interest) was the first and least important part of the affective triad, completed by *docere* (to teach, or convey the speaker's message) and, most important, *movere* (to move the hearers' feelings and bring about persuasion). Despite this error, Barish was a perceptive reader who understood the affective role of the figures and gave an excellent account of Kyd's use of rhetoric in this play.

42 Barish finely observed that 'Kyd proceeds climactically, through circles of widening significance: eyes, life, world, heavens – organ, organism, social milieu, cosmos. The theme is the progressive perversion of all order and health into disease and disorder through the murder of Horatio. Each of the first three members of the series represents a realm felt to be deranged by the murder. In the case of the final realm, the heavens, the question is left open – left, indeed, for the heavens themselves to answer.' (pp. 76–7) There, you feel, a modern reader has really understood what an Elizabethan dramatist was doing with language four centuries ago.

cloudy day my discontents records', and all these forces 'drive me forth to seek the murderer' (19–21). I have underlined the key words in this passage, as in the first, to indicate the overarching rhetorical structure, which Kyd draws to our attention by summing up the main terms of the speech:

> Eyes, life, world, heavens, hell, night and day,
> See, search, show, send, some man, some mean, that may– (22–3)

For the first line of that couplet Kyd used the figure *synathroesmus*, for which Puttenham suggested the English names 'the collector' or 'the recapitulator' (pp. 273–4), summing up the main terms. For the second line he added a poetic, rather than a rhetorical, figure by pairing the terms with an appropriate verb ('eyes see …'). This is an instance of 'correlative or reporting verse', popular in the sixteenth century, by which (as a contemporary defined it) 'all the words have reference to each other respectively and match in exact order'. The closing couplet binds the speech together into a single rhetorical structure but, as Jonas Barish pointed out, Kyd integrated the highly formal rhetoric into a living design, Hieronimo's speech being the utterance of a father shattered by his son's murder and seeking retribution:

> What is remarkable is that Kyd has worked out the schematism of the speech with a high degree of precision – no rhetorical treatise of the day would have had to apologise for offering it in illustration of the figures it uses – yet with enough flexibility in detail, especially prosodic detail, to make it convincing as an expression of Hieronimo's grief. What Elizabethan audiences found exciting and memorable in the language of *The Spanish Tragedy* was precisely such moments of high artifice as these.[43]

In addition, I suggest, Kyd mitigated the sense of imposed order by leaving the final sentence incomplete, ending with a modal verb 'may – '. (This is the rhetorical figure *aposiopesis*, breaking off an utterance prematurely, leaving it incomplete. Rhetoricians described many uses to which it can be put, while Shakespeare added a few that they had not considered.)[44] In his final couplet Hieronimo had correlated 'heavens' with 'send, some man, some mean, that may' ['assist me to discover Horatio's murderer', or something similar]. At this point Kyd pulled off a *coup de théâtre* with some inventive stage business:

[43] Barish, p. 77.

[44] See Vickers, *In Defence of Rhetoric*, pp. 317–18, with a sketch by Rubens, illustrating the famous incomplete speech of Zeus as he interrupts himself to quell a storm: '*Quos ego–!*' 'Whom I–! But better it is to calm the troubled waves' (*Aeneid* 1:135), also pp. 328, 335–9.

A letter falls [*to the floor.*]

What's here? A letter? Tush, it is not so,
A letter written to Hieronimo! [*Opens it*] *Red ink*
'For want of ink receive this bloody writ. (3.2.23.0–26)

The letter, written in her blood, is from the imprisoned Bel-Imperia, identifying Lorenzo and Balthazar as the murderers. The placing of it, just after that highly structured speech, shows – if anyone had doubted it – Kyd's skill at integrating the rhetoric of feeling seamlessly into his drama.

There are many other occasions in *The Spanish Tragedy* where Kyd successfully used rhetorical devices to express Hieronimo's state of mind, especially the effect of suffering. An appropriate place to end this brief survey is the climax of the inset play of 'Soliman and Perseda', during which Hieronimo finally achieves his revenge by killing Lorenzo, and Bel-Imperia achieves her revenge by killing the co-murderer Balthazar, before killing herself. The royal spectators, imagining this to be all 'in play', applaud the actors and ask, 'what follows for Hieronimo?'. In reply, Hieronimo begins a long speech (seventy-nine lines) which discloses that the deaths were real, not pretended, and that the performance they have just witnessed concerned nature rather than art:

No, Princes, know I am Hieronimo,
The hopeless father of a hapless son,
Whose tongue is tuned to tell his latest tale,
Not to excuse gross errors in the play.
I see your looks urge instance of these words,
Behold the reason urging me to this. (5.4.82–7)

Ever sensitive to the links between form and meaning, Kyd echoes the melancholy sounds of 'No' and 'know', 'hopeless' and 'hapless', and slows down the actor's utterance by alliterating five times on the letter '*t*', to sound which the tongue must touch the soft palate to pronounce each word distinctly: 'whose *t*ongue is *t*un'd *t*o *t*ell his la*t*est [= last, final] *t*ale.' From *lexis* Hieronimo then moves to *opsis*, displaying Horatio's corpse, hidden behind a stage curtain, which the royal spectators regard with shock. At this point other revengers might gloat over their triumph, but Kyd's conception of Hieronimo the loving father makes him communicate his most important feeling, an unending sense of loss:

[*Draws the curtain and*] *shows his dead son.*

See here my show, look on this spectacle:
Here lay my hope, and here my hope hath end;
Here lay my heart, and here my heart was slain;
Here lay my treasure, here my treasure lost;

Here lay my bliss, and here my bliss bereft.
But hope, heart, treasure, joy, and bliss:
All fled, failed, died, yea, all decayed with this. (88–94)

Kyd uses syntactical symmetry, reinforcing the *anaphora* on 'here' with *parison*, word corresponding to word ('Here lay my … here my …'), and *isolocon*, equal length of clause. These two figures, often used together, set up a double movement, horizontal and vertical. Four consecutive lines repeat a substantive expressing the father's love for his son: 'my hope', 'my heart', 'my treasure', 'my bliss'. Each clause culminates in a verb describing the finality with which that love was snuffed out: 'hath end', 'was slain', 'lost', 'bereft'. As the eye moves down the page, we notice that the terms are arranged in a sequence of growing importance (the figure *auxesis*), 'hope', 'heart', 'treasure', 'bliss'. Finally, all four substantives are 'collected' or recapitulated in one line, followed by four verbs which are not identical with those originally used (impossible, in terms of grammar), but express the same idea:

But hope, heart, treasure, joy and bliss,
All fled, failed, died, yea, all decayed with this.

In other instances that we have considered, rhetorical figures channel excitement, or anger: here they communicate a tremendous sense of loss. Those four verbs, tautologous from a grammarian's viewpoint, reiterate Hieronimo's unassuageable feelings of regret, finality, devastation. As Jonas Barish commented, 'the disclosure of Horatio's mutilated body provides a more devastating climax, a silent spectacle of woe … The patterned litany, with its insistent anaphora on the adverb "here", pins us relentlessly to this moment in time and this point in space. It enforces repeatedly on us the reality of the visible, palpable fact' (p. 82). In the end Hieronimo's memorial of his son is more important to him than revenge.

BIBLIOGRAPHY

Baker, George Pierce, 'Some bibliographic puzzles in Elizabethan Quartos', *Papers of the Bibliographical Society of America* 4 (1909): 9–20.
Baldwin, T. W., 'On the Chronology of Thomas Kyd's Plays', *MLN* 40 (1925): 343–9.
—— *William Shakspere's Five-Act Structure* (Urbana, IL, 1947).
—— *On the Literary Genetics of Shakspere's Plays 1592–1594* (Urbana, IL, 1959).
Biesterfeldt, Peter, *Die dramatische Technik Thomas Kyds. Studien zur inneren Struktur und szenische Form des Elisabethanischen Dramas* (Halle, 1936).
Boas, F. S. (ed.), *The Works of Thomas Kyd* (Oxford, 1901).
Bowers, F. T., *Elizabethan Revenge Tragedy 1587–1642* (Princeton, NJ, 1940).
Burd, L. Arthur (ed.), Machiavelli, *Il Principe* (Oxford, 1891, 1968).
Calvo, Clara and Jesús Tronch (eds), *The Spanish Tragedy* (London, 2013).

Erne, Lukas, *Beyond* The Spanish Tragedy*: A Study of the Works of Thomas Kyd* (Manchester, 2001).
Freeman, Arthur, *Thomas Kyd: Facts and Problems* (Oxford, 1967).
Greg, W. W. (ed.), *The Spanish Tragedy with additions 1602* (Oxford, 1925: *MSR*).
—— (ed.), *The Spanish Tragedy (1592)* (Oxford, 1949; *MSR*).
—— *A Bibliography of the English Printed Drama to the Restoration. Vol. I: Stationers' Records; Plays to 1616* (London, 1939, 1970).
Hallett, Charles A. and Elaine S., *The Revenger's Madness: A Study of Revenge Tragedy Motifs* (Lincoln, NE, 1980).
Keyishian, Harry, *The Shapes of Revenge: Victimization, Vengeance and Vindictiveness in Shakespeare* (Amherst, NY, 2003).
McKerrow, R. B., 'Edward Allde as a Typical Trade Printer', *The Library*, 4th ser., 10 (1929): 121–62.
Mehl, Dieter, *The Elizabethan Dumb Show: The History of a Dramatic Convention* (London, 1965).
Prosser, Eleanor, *Hamlet and Revenge* (Stanford, CA and Oxford, 1967).
Schick, Joseph (ed.), *The Spanish Tragedy* (London, 1898).
Syme, H. Schott, *Theatre History, Attribution Studies, and the Question of Evidence* (Cambridge, 2023).
Wiggins, Martin, *British Drama 1533–1642: A Catalogue*, 12 vols (Oxford, 2012–).

THE

SPANISH TRAGEDY,

Containing the lamentable

end of *Don Horatio*, and *Bel-Imperia*:
with the pitiful death of
old *Hieronimo*.

Newly corrected and amended of such gross faults as passed in the first impression.

AT LONDON
Printed by *Edward Allde*, for
Edward White.

THE PERSONS IN THE PLAY

Ghost of ANDREA, a Spanish nobleman } Chorus
REVENGE }
KING OF SPAIN
CYPRIAN, DUKE OF CASTILE, his brother
LORENZO, the duke's son
BEL-IMPERIA, Lorenzo's sister
VICEROY OF PORTUGAL
BALTHAZAR, his son
DON PEDRO, the Viceroy's brother
HIERONIMO, Marshal of Spain
ISABELLA, his wife
HORATIO, their son
Spanish General
Deputy
DON BAZULTO ('Senex'), an old man
Three citizens
Portuguese ambassador
ALEXANDRO } noblemen at the Portuguese court
VILLUPPO }
Two Portuguese
PEDRINGANO, Bel-Imperia's servant
CHRISTOPHIL, Bel-Imperia's custodian
Lorenzo's page
SERBERINE, Balthazar's servant
Isabella's maid
Messenger
Hangman
Three kings and three knights in the first dumbshow
Hymen and two torch-bearers in the second
BAZARDO, a painter
PEDRO and JACQUES, Hieronimo's servants
Army. Banquet. Royal suites. Noblemen. Halberdiers. Officers. Three watchmen. Trumpets. Servants etc.

ACTUS PRIMUS.
[1.1]

Enter the ghost of Andrea, and with him Revenge.

ANDREA
When this eternal substance of my soul
Did live imprisoned in my wanton flesh,
Each in their function serving other's need,
I was a courtier in the Spanish court.
My name was Don Andrea, my descent
Though not ignoble, yet inferior far
To gracious fortunes of my tender youth,
For there, in prime and pride of all my years,
By duteous service and deserving love
In secret I possessed a worthy dame,
Which hight sweet Bel-Imperia by name.
But in the harvest of my summer joys
Death's winter nipped the blossoms of my bliss,
Forcing divorce betwixt my love and me.
For in the late conflict with Portugal
My valour drew me into danger's mouth,
Till life to death made passage through my wounds.
When I was slain, my soul descended straight
To pass the flowing stream of Acheron.
But churlish Charon, only boatman there,
Said that my rites of burial not performed,
I might not sit amongst his passengers.
Ere Sol had slept three nights in Thetis' lap,
And slaked his smoking chariot in her flood.
By Don Horatio, our Knight Marshal's son,
My funerals and obsequies were done.
Then was the ferryman of hell content
To pass me over to the slimy strand
That leads to fell Avernus' ugly waves.
There, pleasing Cerberus with honeyed speech,
I passed the perils of the foremost porch.
Not far from hence, amidst ten thousand souls,
Sat Minos, Aeacus, and Rhadamanth,
To whom no sooner began I make approach,

To crave a passport for my wandering ghost,
But Minos' engraven leaves of lottery,
Drew forth the manner of my life and death.
'This Knight', quoth he, 'both lived and died in love,
And for his love tried fortune of the wars,
And by war's fortune lost both love and life.'
'Why then,' said Aeacus, 'convey him hence,
To walk with lovers in our fields of love,
And spend the course of everlasting time
Under green myrtle trees and cypress shades.'
'No, no,' said Rhadamanth, 'it were not well
With loving souls to place a martialist.
He died in war, and must to martial fields,
Where wounded Hector lives in lasting pain,
And Achilles' myrmidons do scour the plain.
Then Minos, mildest censor of the three,
Made this device to end the difference.
'Send him,' quoth he, 'to our infernal King,
To doom him as best seems his majesty.'
To this effect my passport straight was drawn.
In keeping on my way to Pluto's court,
Through dreadful shades of ever-glooming night:
I saw more sights than thousand tongues can tell,
Or pens can write, or mortal hearts can think.
Three ways there were: that on the right-hand side,
Was ready way unto the foresaid fields,
Where lovers live and bloody martialists,
But either sort contained within his bounds.
The left-hand path, declining fearfully,
Was ready downfall to the deepest hell,
Where bloody Furies shakes their whips of steel,
And poor Ixion turns an endless wheel;
Where usurers are choked with melting gold,
And wantons are embraced with ugly snakes,
And murderers groan with never-killing wounds,
And perjured wights scalded in boiling lead,
And all foul sins with torments overwhelmed.
Twixt these two ways, I rode the middle path,
Which brought me to the fair Elysian green,
In midst whereof there stands a stately tower,
The walls of brass, the gates of adamant.
Here, finding Pluto with his Proserpine,

I showed my passport humbled on my knee:
Whereat fair Proserpine began to smile,
And begged that only she might give my doom.
Pluto was pleased and sealed it with a kiss.
Forthwith, Revenge, she rounded thee in th' ear,
And bade thee lead me through the gates of Horn,
Where dreams have passage in the silent night.
No sooner had she spoke but we were here,
I wot not how, in twinkling of an eye.

REVENGE
Then know, Andrea, that thou art arrived
Where thou shalt see the author of thy death,
Don Balthazar, the Prince of Portugal.
Deprived of life by Bel-Imperia.
Here sit we down to see the mystery,
And serve for Chorus in this tragedy.

[1.2]

Enter Spanish King, General, Duke of Castile, [*and*] *Hieronimo.*

KING
Now say Lord General, how fares our camp?

GENERAL
All well my sovereign liege, except some few
That are deceased by fortune of the war.

KING
But what portends thy cheerful countenance
And posting to our presence thus in haste?
Speak man, hath fortune given us victory?

GENERAL
Victory my liege, and that with little loss.

KING
Our Portuguese will pay us tribute then?

GENERAL
Tribute and wonted homage therewithal.

KING
Then blessed be heaven, and guider of the heavens,
From whose fair influence such justice flows.

CASTILE
O multum dilecte Deo, tibi militat aether,
Et conjuratae curvato poplite gentes
Succumbunt: recti soror est victoria juris.

KING
Thanks to my loving brother of Castile.
But General, unfold in brief discourse
Your form of battle and your war's success.
That adding all the pleasure of thy news
Unto the height of former happiness,
With deeper wage and greater dignity
We may reward thy blissful chivalry.

GENERAL
Where Spain and Portugal do jointly knit
Their frontiers, leaning on each other's bound,
There met our armies in their proud array,
Both furnished well, both full of hope and fear:
Both menacing alike with daring shows,
Both vaunting sundry colours of device,
Both cheerly sounding trumpets, drums and fifes,
Both raising dreadful clamours to the sky
That valleys, hills, and rivers made rebound,
And heaven itself was frighted with the sound.
Our battles both were pitched in squadron form,
Each corner strongly fenced with wings of shot,
But ere we joined and came to push of pike,
I brought a squadron of our readiest shot
From out our rearward to begin the fight;
They brought another wing to encounter us.
Meanwhile our ordnance played on either side,
And captains strove to have their valours tried.
Don Pedro, their chief horsemen's colonel,
Did with his cornet bravely make attempt
To break the order of our battle ranks.
But Don Rogero, worthy man of war,
Marched forth against him with our musketeers
And stopped the malice of his fell approach.
While they maintain hot skirmish to and fro
Both battles join and fall to handy blows,
Their violent shot resembling th'ocean's rage,
When roaring loud and with a swelling tide

It beats upon the rampiers of huge rocks
And gapes to swallow neighbour-bounding lands.
Now while Bellona rages here and there,
Thick storms of bullets rain like winter's hail
And shivered lances dark the troubled air.
Pede pes et cuspide cuspis,
Arma sonant armis, vir petiturque viro.
On every side drop captains to the ground,
And soldiers, some ill-maimed, some slain outright:
Here falls a body sundered from his head,
There legs and arms lie bleeding on the grass,
Mingled with weapons and unbowelled steeds,
That scattering overspread the purple plain.
In all this turmoil, three long hours and more,
The victory to neither part inclined,
Till Don Andrea with his brave lanciers,
In their main battle made so great a breach
That, half dismayed, the multitude retired.
But Balthazar, the Portugals' young Prince,
Brought rescue and encouraged them to stay:
Here-hence the fight was eagerly renewed
And in that conflict was Andrea slain –
Brave man at arms, but weak to Balthazar.
Yet while the Prince, insulting over him,
Breathed out proud vaunts, sounding to our reproach,
Friendship and hardy valour joined in one,
Pricked forth Horatio, our Knight Marshal's son,
To challenge forth that Prince in single fight.
Not long between these twain the fight endured,
But straight the Prince was beaten from his horse
And forced to yield him prisoner to his foe.
When he was taken, all the rest they fled,
And our carbines pursued them to the death,
Till Phoebus waning to the western deep
Our trumpeters were charged to sound retreat.

KING
Thanks, good Lord General, for these good news,
And for some argument of more to come,
Take this and wear it for thy sovereign's sake.

Gives him his chain.

But tell me now, hast thou confirmed a peace?

GENERAL
No peace, my liege, but peace conditional,
That if with homage tribute be well paid
The fury of your forces will be stayed;
And to this peace their Viceroy hath subscribed,

Gives the King a paper.

And made a solemn vow that during life
His tribute shall be truly paid to Spain.

KING
These words, these deeds, become thy person well.
But now Knight Marshal, frolic with thy King,
For 'tis thy son that wins this battle's prize.

HIERONIMO
Long may he live to serve my sovereign liege,
And soon decay, unless he serve my liege.

KING
Not thou nor he shall die without reward.

A tucket afar off.

What means the warning of this trumpet's sound?

GENERAL
This tells me that your grace's men of war,
Such as war's fortune hath reserved from death,
Come marching on towards your royal seat
To show themselves before your majesty,
For so I gave in charge at my depart.
Whereby by demonstration shall appear,
That all (except three hundred or few more)
Are safe returned and by their foes enriched.

The army enters, Balthazar between Lorenzo and Horatio captive.

KING
A gladsome sight, I long to see them here.

They enter and pass by.

Was that the warlike Prince of Portugal,
That by our nephew was in triumph led?

GENERAL
It was my liege, the Prince of Portugal.

KING
But what was he that, on the other side,
Held him by th'arm as partner of the prize?

HIERONIMO
That was my son, my gracious sovereign,
Of whom, though from his tender infancy
My loving thoughts did never hope but well.
He never pleased his father's eyes till now,
Nor filled my heart with overcloying joys.

KING
Go, let them march once more about these walls,
That staying them we may confer and talk
With our brave prisoner and his double guard.
Hieronimo, it greatly pleases us
That in our victory thou have a share,
By virtue of thy worthy son's exploit.

Enter [the army] again.

Bring hither the young Prince of Portugal.
The rest march on, but ere they be dismissed,
We will bestow on every soldier
Two ducats, and on every leader ten,
That they may know our largess welcomes them.

Exeunt all [the army] but Balthazar, Lorenzo, Horatio.

Welcome Don Balthazar, welcome nephew,
And thou Horatio, thou art welcome too.
Young Prince, although thy father's hard misdeeds
In keeping back the tribute that he owes
Deserve but evil measure at our hands,
Yet shalt thou know that Spain is honourable.

BALTHAZAR
The trespass that my father made in peace
Is now controlled by fortune of the wars:
And cards once dealt, it boots not ask why so.
His men are slain, a weakening to his realm,
His colours seized, a blot unto his name,
His son distressed, a cor'sive to his heart:
These punishments may clear his late offence.

KING
Ay, Balthazar, if he observe this truce
Our peace will grow the stronger for these wars.
Meanwhile live thou, though not in liberty,
Yet free from bearing any servile yoke.
For in our hearing thy deserts were great,
And in our sight thyself art gracious.

BALTHAZAR
And I shall study to deserve this grace.

KING
But tell me, for their holding makes me doubt,
To which of these twain art thou prisoner.

LORENZO
To me, my liege.

HORATIO
To me, my sovereign.

LORENZO
This hand first took his courser by the reins.

HORATIO
But first my lance did put him from his horse.

LORENZO
I seized his weapon and enjoyed it first.

HORATIO
But first I forced him lay his weapons down,

KING
Let go his arm upon our privilege!
[*Lorenzo and Horatio*] *let him go.*

Say worthy Prince, to whether didst thou yield?

BALTHAZAR [*indicating Lorenzo, then Horatio*]
To him in courtesy, to this perforce:
He spake me fair, this other gave me strokes;
He promised life, this other threatened death;
He won my love, this other conquered me;
And truth to say, I yield myself to both.

HIERONIMO
But that I know your grace for just and wise,

And might seem partial in this difference,
Enforced by nature and by law of arms,
My tongue should plead for young Horatio's right.
He hunted well that was a lion's death,
Not he that in a garment wore his skin:
So hares may pull dead lions by the beard.

KING
Content thee marshal, thou shalt have no wrong,
And for thy sake thy son shall want no right.
Will both abide the censure of my doom?

LORENZO
I crave no better than your grace awards.

HORATIO
Nor I, although I set beside my right.

KING
Then by my judgement thus your strife shall end:
You both deserve, and both shall have reward.
Nephew, thou took'st his weapon and his horse:
His weapons and his horse are thy reward.
Horatio, thou didst force him first to yield:
His ransom therefore is thy valour's fee.
Appoint the sum as you shall both agree.
But nephew, thou shalt have the Prince in guard,
For thine estate best fitteth such a guest.
Horatio's house were small for all his train,
Yet in regard thy substance passeth his,
And that just guerdon may befall desert,
To him we yield the armour of the Prince.
How likes Don Balthazar of this device?

BALTHAZAR
Right well my liege, if this proviso were,
That Don Horatio bear us company,
Whom I admire and love for chivalry.

KING
Horatio, leave him not that loves thee so,
Now let us hence to see our soldiers paid,
And feast our prisoner as our friendly guest.

Exeunt.

[1.3]

Enter Viceroy, Alexandro, Villuppo [*with Attendants*]

VICEROY
Is our Ambassador dispatched for Spain?

ALEXANDRO
Two days, my liege, are passed since his depart.

VICEROY
And tribute payment gone along with him?

ALEXANDRO
Ay, my good lord.

VICEROY
Then rest we here a while, in our unrest.
And feed our sorrows with some inward sighs,
For deepest cares break never into tears.
But wherefore sit I in a regal throne?
This better fits a wretch's endless moan.

Falls to the ground.

Yet this is higher than my fortune's reach
And therefore better than my state deserves.
Ay, ay, this earth, image of melancholy,
Seeks him whom fates adjudge to misery:
Here let me lie, now am I at the lowest.
    Qui jacet in terra non habet unde cadat.
In me consumpsit vires fortuna nocendo:
    Nil superest ut iam possit obesse magis.
Yes, Fortune may bereave me of my crown:
Here take it now, let Fortune do her worst,
She will not rob me of this sable weed.
Oh no, she envies none but pleasant things,
Such is the folly of despiteful chance!
Fortune is blind and sees not my deserts,
So is she deaf and hears not my laments:
And could she hear, yet is she wilful mad,
And therefore will not pity my distress.
Suppose that she could pity me, what then?
What help can be expected at her hands,
Whose foot is standing on a rolling stone,
And mind more mutable than fickle winds?
Why wail I then, where's hope of no redress?
Oh yes, complaining makes my grief seem less.

My late ambition hath distained my faith,
My breach of faith occasioned bloody wars,
Those bloody wars have spent my treasure,
And with my treasure my people's blood,
And with their blood, my joy and best beloved,
My best beloved, my sweet and only son.
O wherefore went I not to war myself?
The cause was mine, I might have died for both.
My years were mellow, his but young and green,
My death were natural, but his was forced.

ALEXANDRO
No doubt, my liege, but still the Prince survives.

VICEROY
'Survives'! Ay, where?

ALEXANDRO
In Spain, a prisoner by mischance of war.

VICEROY
Then they have slain him for his father's fault.

ALEXANDRO
That were a breach to common law of arms.

VICEROY
They reck no laws that meditate revenge.

ALEXANDRO
His ransom's worth will stay from foul revenge.

VICEROY
No, if he lived the news would soon be here.

ALEXANDRO
Nay, evil news fly faster still than good.

VICEROY
Tell me no more of news, for he is dead.

VILLUPPO
My sovereign, pardon the author of ill news,
And I'll bewray the fortune of thy son.

VICEROY
Speak on, I'll guerdon thee whatever it be.
Mine ear is ready to receive ill news,

My heart grown hard 'gainst mischief's battery,
Stand up I say, and tell thy tale at large.

VILLUPPO
Then hear that truth which these mine eyes have seen.
When both the armies were in battle joined,
Don Balthazar, amidst the thickest troops,
To win renown did wondrous feats of arms:
Amongst the rest I saw him hand to hand
In single fight with their Lord General.
Till Alexandro, that here counterfeits
Under the colour of a duteous friend,
Discharged his pistol at the Prince's back,
As though he would have slain their general.
But therewithal Don Balthazar fell down,
And when he fell, then we began to fly,
But had he lived, the day had sure been ours.

ALEXANDRO
O wicked forgery! O traitorous miscreant!

VICEROY
Hold thou thy peace! But now Villuppo, say,
Where then became the carcass of my son?

VILLUPPO
I saw them drag it to the Spanish tents.

VICEROY
Ay, ay, my nightly dreams have told me this:
[*to Alexandro*] Thou false, unkind, unthankful, traitorous beast!
Wherein had Balthazar offended thee
That thou shouldst thus betray him to our foes?
Was it Spanish gold that bleared so thine eyes,
That thou couldst see no part of our deserts?
Perchance because thou art Terceira's lord
Thou hadst some hope to wear this diadem,
If first my son and then myself were slain.
But thy ambitious thought shall break thy neck.
Ay, this was it that made thee spill his blood,
Takes the crown and put it on again.
But I'll now wear it till thy blood be spilt.

ALEXANDRO
Vouchsafe, dread sovereign, to hear me speak!

VICEROY
Away with him, his sight is second hell!

[*Exit Alexandro, guarded.*]

Keep him till we determine of his death.
If Balthazar be dead, he shall not live.
Villuppo, follow us for thy reward.

Exit Viceroy.

VILLUPPO
Thus have I, with an envious forgèd tale,
Deceived the King, betrayed mine enemy,
And hope for guerdon of my villainy.

Exit.

[1.4]

Enter Horatio and Bel-Imperia.

BEL-IMPERIA
Signior Horatio, this is the place and hour,
Wherein I must entreat thee to relate
The circumstance of Don Andrea's death,
Who, living, was my garland's sweetest flower,
And in his death hath buried my delights.

HORATIO
For love of him, and service to yourself,
I nill refuse this heavy doleful charge.
Yet tears and sighs, I fear, will hinder me.
When both our armies were enjoined in fight
Your worthy chevalier amidst the thickest,
For glorious cause still aiming at the fairest,
Was at the last by young Don Balthazar
Encountered hand to hand. Their fight was long,
Their hearts were great, their clamours menacing,
Their strength alike, their strokes both dangerous.
But wrathful Nemesis, that wicked power,
Envying at Andrea's praise and worth,
Cut short his life to end his praise and worth.
She, she herself disguised in armour's mask,
As Pallas was before proud Pergamus,
Brought in a fresh supply of halberdiers,

Which paunched his horse and dinged him to the ground.
Then young Don Balthazar with ruthless rage,
Taking advantage of his foe's distress,
Did finish what his halberdiers begun,
And left not till Andrea's life was done.
Then, though too late incensed with just remorse,
I with my band set forth against the Prince,
And brought him prisoner from his halberdiers.

BEL-IMPERIA
Would thou hadst slain him that so slew my love!
But then, was Don Andrea's carcass lost?

HORATIO
No, that was it for which I chiefly strove,
Nor stepped I back till I recovered him.
I took him up and wound him in mine arms,
And wielding him unto my private tent,
There laid him down and dewed him with my tears,
And sighed and sorrowed as became a friend.
But neither friendly sorrow, sighs nor tears,
Could win pale death from his usurpèd right.
Yet this I did, and less I could not do.
I saw him honoured with due funeral.
This scarf I plucked from off his lifeless arm,
And wear it in remembrance of my friend.

BEL-IMPERIA
I know the scarf, would he had kept it still,
For had he lived he would have kept it still,
And worn it for his Bel-Imperia's sake:
For 'twas my favour at his last depart.
But now wear thou it both for him and me,
For after him thou hast deserved it best.
But for thy kindness in his life and death,
Be sure while Bel-Imperia's life endures,
She will be Don Horatio's thankful friend.

HORATIO
And, madam, Don Horatio will not slack
Humbly to serve fair Bel-Imperia.
But now, if your good liking stand thereto,
I'll crave your pardon to go seek the Prince,
For so the Duke your father gave me charge.

Exit.

BEL-IMPERIA
Ay, go Horatio, leave me here alone,
For solitude best fits my cheerless mood.
Yet what avails to wail Andrea's death,
From whence Horatio proves my second love?
Had he not loved Andrea as he did,
He could not sit in Bel-Imperia's thoughts.
But how can love find harbour in my breast
Till I revenge the death of my beloved?
Yes, second love shall further my revenge.
I'll love Horatio, my Andrea's friend,
The more to spite the Prince that wrought his end.
And where Don Balthazar, that slew my love,
Himself now pleads for favour at my hands,
He shall, in rigour of my just disdain,
Reap long repentance for his murderous deed.
For what was't else but murderous cowardice
So many to oppress one valiant knight,
Without respect of honour in the fight?
And here he comes that murdered my delight.

Enter Lorenzo and Balthazar.

LORENZO
Sister, what means this melancholy walk?

BEL-IMPERIA
That for a while I wish no company.

LORENZO
But here the Prince is come to visit you,

BEL-IMPERIA
That argues that he lives in liberty.

BALTHAZAR
No madam, but in pleasing servitude.

BEL-IMPERIA
Your prison then belike is your conceit.

BALTHAZAR
Ay, by conceit my freedom is enthralled.

BEL-IMPERIA
Then with conceit enlarge yourself again.

BALTHAZAR
What if conceit have laid my heart to gage?

BEL-IMPERIA
Pay that you borrowed and recover it.

BALTHAZAR
I die if it return from whence it lies.

BEL-IMPERIA
A heartless man and live? A miracle!

BALTHAZAR
Ay, lady, love can work such miracles.

LORENZO
Tush, tush, my lord! Let go these ambages,
And in plain terms acquaint her with your love.

BEL-IMPERIA
What boots complaint when there's no remedy?

BALTHAZAR
Yes, to your gracious self must I complain,
In whose fair answer lies my remedy,
On whose perfection all my thoughts attend,
On whose aspect mine eyes find beauty's bower,
In whose translucent breast my heart is lodged.

BEL-IMPERIA
Alas my lord, these are but words of course,
And but device to drive me from this place.
She, in going in, lets fall her glove, which Horatio, coming out, takes up.

HORATIO
Madam, your glove.

BEL-IMPERIA
Thanks, good Horatio, take it for thy pains.

BALTHAZAR
Signior Horatio stooped in happy time.

HORATIO
I reaped more grace than I deserved or hoped.

LORENZO [*to Balthazar*]
My lord, be not dismayed for what is past,
You know that women oft are humorous.
These clouds will overblow with little wind.
Let me alone, I'll scatter them myself.
Meanwhile let us devise to spend the time
In some delightful sports and revelling.

HORATIO
The King, my lords, is coming hither straight,
To feast the Portugal Ambassador,
Things were in readiness before I came.

BALTHAZAR
Then here it fits us to attend the King,
To welcome hither our Ambassador
And learn my father and my country's health.

Enter [*Servants*] *with the banquet, trumpets, the King and Ambassador* [*Castile, and Nobles*]

KING
See, lord Ambassador, how Spain entreats
Their prisoner Balthazar, thy Viceroy's son:
We pleasure more in kindness than in wars.

AMBASSADOR
Sad is our King, and Portugal laments,
Supposing that Don Balthazar is slain.

BALTHAZAR
So am I, slain by beauty's tyranny.
[*to the Ambassador*] You see, my lord, how Balthazar is slain:
I frolic with the Duke of Castile's son,
Wrapped every hour in pleasures of the court
And graced with favours of his majesty.

KING
Put off your greetings till our feast be done,
[*Sits.*] Now come and sit with us and taste our cheer.
[*The Ambassador and others*] *sit to the banquet.*
Sit down young Prince, you are our second guest.
Brother, sit down, and nephew take your place.
Signior Horatio, wait thou upon our cup,
For well thou hast deserved to be honoured.
Now, lordings, fall to: Spain is Portugal,

And Portugal is Spain, we both are friends,
Tribute is paid, and we enjoy our right.
But where is old Hieronimo, our Marshal?
He promised us, in honour of our guest,
To grace our banquet with some pompous jest.

Enter Hieronimo with a drum, three Knights, each [hangs up] his scutcheon. Then he fetches three Kings; [the Knights] take their crowns and them captive.

Hieronimo, this mask contents mine eye,
Although I sound not well the mystery.

HIERONIMO
The first armed Knight that hung his scutcheon up,
He takes the scutcheon and gives it to the King.
Was English Robert, Earl of Gloucester,
Who, when King Stephen bore sway in Albion,
Arrived with five and twenty thousand men
In Portugal, and by success of war
Enforced the King, then but a Saracen,
To bear the yoke of English monarchy.

KING
My lord of Portugal, by this you see
That which may comfort both your King and you,
And make your late discomfort seem the less.
But say Hieronimo, what was the next?

HIERONIMO
The second Knight that hung his scutcheon up,
He does as he did before.
Was Edmund, Earl of Kent in Albion
When English Richard wore the diadem.
He came likewise and razed Lisbon walls,
And took the King of Portugal in fight.
For which, and other suchlike service done,
He after was created Duke of York.

KING
This is another special argument,
That Portugal may deign to bear our yoke
When it by little England hath been yoked.
But now Hieronimo what were the last?

HIERONIMO
The third and last, not least in our account,
Doing as before.
Was, as the rest, a valiant Englishman,
Brave John of Gaunt, the Duke of Lancaster,
As by his scutcheon plainly may appear.
He with a puissant army came to Spain
And took our King of Castile prisoner.

AMBASSADOR
This is an argument for our Viceroy,
That Spain may not insult for her success,
Since English warriors likewise conquered Spain
And made them bow their knees to Albion.

KING
Hieronimo, I drink to thee for this device,
Which hath pleased both the Ambassador and me.
Pledge me Hieronimo, if thou love thy King.
[*Hieronimo*] *takes the cup of Horatio.*
[*to the Ambassador*] My lord, I fear we sit but overlong.
Unless our dainties were more delicate.
But welcome are you to the best we have.
Now let us in, that you may be dispatched,
I think our council is already set.

Exeunt omnes.

[1.5]

[*Ghost and Revenge come forward*]

ANDREA
Come we for this from depth of underground,
To see him feast that gave me my death's wound?
These pleasant sights are sorrow to my soul,
Nothing but league, and love and banqueting!

REVENGE
Be still Andrea. Ere we go from hence
I'll turn their friendship into fell despite,
Their love to mortal hate, their day to night,
Their hope into despair, their peace to war,
Their joys to pain, their bliss to misery. [*Ghost and Revenge remain*]

* * * * *

[2.1]

Enter Lorenzo and Balthazar.

LORENZO
My lord, though Bel-Imperia seem thus coy,
Let reason hold you in your wonted joy.
In time the savage bull sustains the yoke,
In time all haggard hawks will stoop to lure,
In time small wedges cleave the hardest oak,
In time the flint is piercèd with softest shower,
And she in time will fall from her disdain
And rue the sufferance of your friendly pain.

BALTHAZAR
No, she is wilder and more hard withal,
Than beast, or bird, or tree, or stony wall.
But wherefore blot I Bel-Imperia's name?
It is my fault, not she that merits blame.
My feature is not to content her sight,
My words are rude and work her no delight.
The lines I send her are but harsh and ill,
Such as do drop from Pan and Marsyas' quill.
My presents are not of sufficient cost,
And being worthless, all my labour's lost.
Yet might she love me for my valiancy,
Ay, but that's slandered by captivity.
Yet might she love me to content her sire,
Ay, but her reason masters his desire.
Yet might she love me as her brother's friend,
Ay, but her hopes aim at some other end.
Yet might she love me to uprear her state,
Ay, but perhaps she hopes some nobler mate.
Yet might she love me as her beauteous thrall,
Ay, but I fear she cannot love at all.

LORENZO
My lord, for my sake leave these ecstasies
And doubt not but we'll find some remedy,
Some cause there is that lets you not be loved.
First that must needs be known and then removed.
What if my sister love some other Knight?

BALTHAZAR
My summer's day will turn to winter's night.

LORENZO
I have already found a stratagem,
To sound the bottom of this doubtful theme.
My lord, for once you shall be ruled by me,
Hinder me not whate'er you hear or see.
By force or fair means will I cast about
To find the truth of all this question out.
Ho, Pedringano!

PEDRINGANO [*within*]
Signior?

LORENZO
Vien qui presto!

Enter Pedringano.

PEDRINGANO
Hath your lordship any service to command me?

LORENZO
Ay, Pedringano, service of import,
And not to spend the time in trifling words
Thus stands the case. It is not long, thou know'st,
Since I did shield thee from my father's wrath
For thy conveyance in Andrea's love,
For which thou wert adjudged to punishment:
I stood betwixt thee and thy punishment.
And since, thou know'st how I have favoured thee.
Now to these favours will I add reward,
Not with fair words, but store of golden coin,
And lands and living joined with dignities,
If thou but satisfy my just demand.
Tell truth, and have me for thy lasting friend.

PEDRINGANO
Whatever it be your lordship shall demand
My bounden duty bids me tell the truth,
[*aside*] If case it lie in me to tell the truth.

LORENZO
Then, Pedringano, this is my demand,
Whom loves my sister Bel-Imperia?
For she reposes all her trust in thee.
Speak man, and gain both friendship and reward:
I mean, whom loves she in Andrea's place?

PEDRINGANO
Alas my lord, since Don Andrea's death
I have no credit with her as before,
And therefore know not if she love or no.

LORENZO
Nay if thou dally then I am thy foe, [*Draws his sword.*]
And fear shall force what friendship cannot win.
Thy death shall bury what thy life conceals,
Thou diest for more esteeming her than me.

PEDRINGANO
Oh stay, my lord!

LORENZO
Yet speak the truth and I will guerdon thee
And shield thee from whatever can ensue.
And will conceal whatever proceeds from thee;
But if thou dally once again, thou diest.

PEDRINGANO
If Madam Bel-Imperia be in love –

LORENZO
What, villain, *if's* and *an's*? (*Offers to kill him.*)

PEDRINGANO [*kneels*]
O stay my lord, she loves Horatio.

Balthazar starts back.

LORENZO
What, Don Horatio, our Knight Marshal's son?

PEDRINGANO
Even him my lord.

LORENZO
Now say but how know'st thou he is her love
And thou shalt find me kind and liberal.
Stand up I say, and fearless tell the truth.

PEDRINGANO [*stands up*]
She sent him letters which myself perused,
Full fraught with lines and arguments of love,
Preferring him before Prince Balthazar.

LORENZO
Swear on this cross, that what thou say'st is true,

And that thou wilt conceal what thou hast told.

PEDRINGANO
I swear to both by him that made us all.

LORENZO
In hope thine oath is true, here's thy reward.
[*Gives him money*]
But if I prove thee perjured and unjust,
This very sword whereon thou took'st thine oath
Shall be the worker of thy tragedy.

PEDRINGANO
What I have said is true, and shall for me
Be still concealed from Bel-Imperia.
Besides, your honour's liberality
Deserves my duteous service, even till death.

LORENZO
Let this be all that thou shalt do for me:
Be watchful when and where these lovers meet,
And give me notice in some secret sort.
PEDRINGANO
I will my lord.

LORENZO
Then shalt thou find that I am liberal.
Thou know'st that I can more advance thy state
Than she, be therefore wise and fail me not.
Go and attend her as thy custom is,
Lest absence make her think thou dost amiss.

Exit Pedringano.

Why so: *tam armis quam ingenio*:
Where words prevail not, violence prevails.
But gold doth more than either of them both.
How likes Prince Balthazar this stratagem?

BALTHAZAR
Both well, and ill. It makes me glad and sad:
Glad, that I know the hinderer of my love,
Sad, that I fear she hates me whom I love.
Glad, that I know on whom to be revenged,
Sad, that she'll fly me if I take revenge.
Yet must I take revenge, or die myself,

For love resisted grows impatient.
I think Horatio be my destined plague:
First, in his hand he brandishèd a sword,
And with that sword he fiercely wagèd war,
And in that war he gave me dangerous wounds,
And by those wounds he forcèd me to yield,
And by my yielding I became his slave.
Now in his mouth he carries pleasing words,
Which pleasing words do harbour sweet conceits,
Which sweet conceits are limed with sly deceits,
Which sly deceits smooth Bel-Imperia's ears,
And through her ears dive down into her heart,
And in her heart set him where I should stand.
Thus hath he ta'en my body by his force,
And now by sleight would captivate my soul:
But in his fall I'll tempt the Destinies,
And either lose my life, or win my love.

LORENZO
Let's go my lord, your staying stays revenge.
Do you but follow me and gain your love,
Her favour must be won by his remove. *Exeunt.*

[2.2]

Enter Horatio and Bel-Imperia.

HORATIO
Now madam, since by favour of your love
Our hidden smoke is turned to open flame,
And that with looks and words we feed our thoughts
Two chief contents, where more cannot be had,
Thus, in the midst of love's fair blandishments
Why show you sign of inward languishments?

[*Entering above*] *Pedringano shows all to the Prince and Lorenzo, placing them in secret.*

BEL-IMPERIA
My heart (sweet friend) is like a ship at sea:
She wishes port, where riding all at ease,
She may repair what stormy times have worn,
And leaning on the shore may sing with joy
That pleasure follows pain, and bliss annoy.
Possession of thy love is th'only port

Wherein my heart, with fears and hopes long tossed,
Each hour doth wish and long to make resort,
There to repair the joys that it hath lost.
And sitting safe, to sing in Cupid's choir
That sweetest bliss is crown of love's desire.

Balthazar and Lorenzo above.

(BALTHAZAR
(O sleep mine eyes, see not my love profaned,
(Be deaf my ears, hear not my discontent,
(Die heart, another 'joys what thou deserv'st.

(LORENZO
(Watch still mine eyes, to see this love disjoined,
(Hear still mine ears, to hear them both lament,
(Live, heart, to joy at fond Horatio's fall.

BEL-IMPERIA
Why stands Horatio speechless all this while?

HORATIO
The less I speak, the more I meditate.

BEL-IMPERIA
But whereon dost thou chiefly meditate?

HORATIO
On dangers past, and pleasures to ensue.

(BALTHAZAR
(On pleasures past, and dangers to ensue.

BEL-IMPERIA
What dangers, and what pleasures dost thou mean?

HORATIO
Dangers of war, and pleasures of our love.

(LORENZO
(Dangers of death, but pleasures none at all.

BEL-IMPERIA
Let dangers go, thy war shall be with me,
But such a war as breaks no bond of peace.
Speak thou fair words, I'll cross them with fair words,
Send thou sweet looks, I'll meet them with sweet looks,
Write loving lines, I'll answer loving lines,
Give me a kiss, I'll countercheck thy kiss,

Be this our warring peace, or peaceful war.

HORATIO
But gracious madam, then appoint the field,
Where trial of this war shall first be made.

(BALTHAZAR
Ambitious villain, how his boldness grows!

BEL-IMPERIA
Then be thy father's pleasant bower the field,
Where first we vowed a mutual amity.
The court were dangerous, that place is safe.
Our hour shall be when Vesper begins to rise,
That summons home distressful travellers.
There none shall hear us but the harmless birds.
Haply the gentle nightingale
Shall carol us asleep ere we be ware,
And, singing with the prickle at her breast,
Tell our delight and mirthful dalliance.
Till then each hour will seem a year and more.

HORATIO
But honey sweet, and honourable love.
Return we now into your father's sight,
Dangerous suspicion waits on our delight.

(LORENZO
(Ay, danger mixed with jealous despite
(Shall send thy soul into eternal night.

Exeunt.

[2.3]

Enter King of Spain, Portuguese Ambassador, Don Cyprian, [the Duke of Castile] and others

KING
Brother of Castile, to the Prince's love
What says your daughter Bel-Imperia?

CYPRIAN
Although she coy it as becomes her kind
And yet dissemble that she loves the Prince,
I doubt not I, but she will stoop in time.
And were she froward, which she will not be,

Yet herein shall she follow my advice,
Which is to love him or forgo my love.

KING
Then, lord Ambassador of Portugal,
Advise thy King to make this marriage up,
For strengthening of our late-confirmed league:
I know no better means to make us friends.
Her dowry shall be large and liberal,
Besides that, she is daughter and half-heir
Unto our brother here, Don Cyprian,
And shall enjoy the moiety of his land.
I'll grace her marriage with an uncle's gift,
And this it is: in case the match go forward,
The tribute which you pay shall be released,
And if by Balthazar she have a son
He shall enjoy the Kingdom after us.

AMBASSADOR
I'll make the motion to my sovereign liege,
And work it if my counsel may prevail.

KING
Do so my lord, and if he give consent,
I hope his presence here will honour us
In celebration of the nuptial day,
And let himself determine of the time.

AMBASSADOR
Will it please your grace command me aught beside?

KING
Commend me to the King, and so farewell.
But where's Prince Balthazar, to take his leave?

AMBASSADOR
That is performed already, my good lord.

KING
Amongst the rest of what you have in charge
The Prince's ransom must not be forgot.
That's none of mine, but his that took him prisoner,
And well his forwardness deserves reward:
It was Horatio, our Knight Marshal's son.

AMBASSADOR
Between us there's a price already pitched,
And shall be sent with all convenient speed.

KING
Then once again farewell my lord.

AMBASSADOR
Farewell my lord of Castile and the rest.

Exit

KING
Now brother, you must take some little pains
To win fair Bel-Imperia from her will:
Young virgins must be rulèd by their friends.
The Prince is amiable and loves her well.
If she neglect him and forgo his love
She both will wrong her own estate and ours:
Therefore, whiles I do entertain the Prince,
With greatest pleasure that our court affords
Endeavour you to win your daughter's thoughts,
If she give back, all this will come to naught.

Exeunt.

[2.4]

Enter Horatio, Bel-Imperia, and Pedringano.

HORATIO
Now that the night begins with sable wings
To overcloud the brightness of the sun,
And that in darkness pleasures may be done.
Come Bel-Imperia, let us to the bower
And there in safety pass a pleasant hour.

BEL-IMPERIA
I follow thee my love and will not back,
Although my fainting heart controls my soul.

HORATIO
Why, make you doubt of Pedringano's faith?

BEL-IMPERIA
No, he is as trusty as my second self.
Go Pedringano, watch without the gate
And let us know if any make approach.

PEDRINGANO
[*Aside.*] Instead of watching, I'll deserve more gold.
By fetching Don Lorenzo to this match.

Exit.

HORATIO
What means my love?

BEL-IMPERIA
I know not what myself:
And yet my heart foretells me some mischance.

HORATIO
Sweet say not so, fair fortune is our friend,
And heavens have shut up day to pleasure us.
The stars, thou seest, hold back their twinkling shine,
And Luna hides herself to pleasure us.

BEL-IMPERIA
Thou hast prevailed, I'll conquer my misdoubt,
And in thy love and counsel drown my fear.
I fear no more, love now is all my thoughts,
Why sit we not? for pleasure asketh ease.

HORATIO
The more thou sit'st within these leafy bowers
The more will Flora deck it with her flowers.

BEL-IMPERIA
Ay, but if Flora spy Horatio here
Her jealous eye will think I sit too near.

HORATIO
Hark, madam, how the birds record by night
For joy that Bel-Imperia sits in sight.

BEL-IMPERIA
No, Cupid counterfeits the nightingale
To frame sweet music to Horatio's tale.

HORATIO
If Cupid sing, then Venus is not far –
Ay, thou art Venus, or some fairer star!

BEL-IMPERIA
If I be Venus, thou must needs be Mars,
And where Mars reigneth there must needs be wars.

HORATIO
Then thus begin our wars: put forth thy hand,
That it may combat with my ruder hand.

BEL-IMPERIA
Set forth thy foot to try the push of mine.

HORATIO
But first my looks shall combat against thine.

BEL-IMPERIA
Then ward thyself, I dart this kiss at thee.

[*Kisses him.*]

HORATIO
Thus I retort the dart thou threw'st at me.

[*Kisses her.*]

BEL-IMPERIA
Nay then, to gain the glory of the field
My twining arms shall yoke and make thee yield.

[*They embrace.*]

HORATIO
Nay then, my arms are large and strong withal:
Thus elms by vines are compassed till they fall.

BEL-IMPERIA
O let me go, for in my troubled eyes,
Now may'st thou read that life in passion dies.

HORATIO
O stay a while and I will die with thee,
So shalt thou yield, and yet have conquered me.

BEL-IMPERIA
Who's there? Pedringano? We are betrayed!

Enter Lorenzo, Balthazar, Serberine, [*and*] *Pedringano, disguised.*

LORENZO
[*to Balthazar*] My lord, away with her, take her aside,
[*to Horatio*] O sir, forbear, your valour is already tried.
[*to Serberine and Pedringano*] Quickly dispatch, my masters!

They hang him in the arbour.

HORATIO
What, will you murder me?

LORENZO
Ay, thus, and thus, these are the fruits of love.

They stab him.

BEL-IMPERIA
O save his life and let me die for him!
O save him, brother, save him Balthazar!
I loved Horatio but he loved not me.

BALTHAZAR
But Balthazar loves Bel-Imperia.

LORENZO
Although his life were still ambitious proud,
Yet is he at the highest now he is dead.

BEL-IMPERIA
Murder! Murder! Help, Hieronimo, help!

LORENZO
Come stop her mouth, away with her.

Exeunt [leaving Horatio's body.]
Enter Hieronimo in his shirt [with a sword and a torch]

HIERONIMO
What outcries pluck me from my naked bed
And chill my throbbing heart with trembling fear,
Which never danger yet could daunt before?
Who calls Hieronimo? Speak, here I am!
I did not slumber, therefore 'twas no dream –
No, no, it was some woman cried for help,
And here within this garden did she cry
And in this garden must I rescue her.
But stay, what murderous spectacle is this?
A man hanged up and all the murderers gone,
And in my bower, to lay the guilt on me –
This place was made for pleasure not for death.

He cuts him down.

Those garments that he wears I oft have seen,
Alas, it is Horatio my sweet son!
Oh no, but he that whilom was my son.
Oh, was it thou that call'dst me from my bed?
O speak, if any spark of life remain!
I am thy father, who hath slain my son?
What savage monster, not of human kind,

Hath here been glutted with thy harmless blood?
And left thy bloody corpse dishonoured here,
For me amidst this dark and deathful shades
To drown thee with an ocean of my tears?
O heavens, why made you night to cover sin?
By day this deed of darkness had not been.
O earth, why didst thou not in time devour
The vild profaner of this sacred bower?
O poor Horatio, what hadst thou misdone
To leese thy life ere life was new begun?
O wicked butcher, whatsoe'er thou wert,
How could thou strangle virtue and desert?
Ay me most wretched, that have lost my joy,
In leesing my Horatio, my sweet boy!

Enter Isabella.

ISABELLA
My husband's absence makes my heart to throb –
Hieronimo!

HIERONIMO
Here Isabella, help me to lament,
For sighs are stopped, and all my tears are spent.

ISABELLA
What world of grief – my son Horatio!
O where's the author of this endless woe?

HIERONIMO
To know the author were some ease of grief,
For in revenge my heart would find relief.

ISABELLA
Then is he gone? and is my son gone too?
O gush out, tears, fountains and floods of tears,
Blow sighs and raise an everlasting storm!
For outrage fits our cursed wretchedness.

HIERONIMO
Sweet, lovely Rose, ill-plucked before thy time,
Fair worthy son, not conquered but betrayed:
I'll kiss thee now, for words with tears are stayed.

ISABELLA
And I'll close up the glasses of his sight,

For once these eyes were only my delight.

HIERONIMO
Seest thou this handkercher besmeared with blood?
It shall not from me till I take revenge!
Seest thou those wounds that yet are bleeding fresh?
I'll not entomb them till I have revenged!
Then will I joy amidst my discontent,
Till then my sorrow never shall be spent.

ISABELLA
The heavens are just, murder cannot be hid.
Time is the author both of truth and right,
And time will bring this treachery to light.

HIERONIMO
Meanwhile, good Isabella, cease thy plaints,
Or at the least dissemble them a while:
So shall we sooner find the practice out
And learn by whom all this was brought about.
Come Isabel, now let us take him up,

They take him up.

And bear him in from out this cursèd place,
I'll say his dirge, singing fits not this case.

Hieronimo sets his breast unto his sword.

O aliquis mihi quas pulchrum ver educet herbas
Misceat, et nostro detur medicina dolori;
Aut, si qui faciunt animis oblivia succos
Praebeat, ipse metam magnum quaecunque per orbem
Gramina Sol pulchras effert in luminis oras.
Ipse bibam quicquid meditatur saga veneni,
Quicquid et irarum Circeia naenia nectit.
Omnia perpetiar, letum quoque, dum semel omnis
Noster in extincto moriatur pectore sensus:
Ergo tuos oculos nunquam, mea vita, videbo.
Et tua perpetuus sepeliuit lumina somnus:
Emoriar tecum. Sic, sic iuvat ire sub umbras,
Attamen absistam properato cedere letho,
Ne mortem vindicta tuam tam nulla sequatur.

Here he throws [*the sword*] *from him*
and [*with Isabella*] *bears the body away.*

[2.5]

ANDREA
Brought'st thou me hither to increase my pain?
I looked that Balthazar should have been slain.
But 'tis my friend Horatio that is slain,
And they abuse fair Bel-Imperia,
On whom I doted more than all the world,
Because she loved me more than all the world.

REVENGE
Thou talk'st of harvest when the corn is green.
The end is crown of every work well done:
The sickle comes not till the corn be ripe.
Be still, and ere I lead thee from this place,
I'll show thee Balthazar in heavy case.

* * * * *

[3.1]

Enter Viceroy of Portugal, nobles, [*and Villuppo*].

VICEROY
Infortunate condition of Kings,
Seated amidst so many helpless doubts!
First we are placed upon extremest height,
And oft supplanted with exceeding heat,
But ever subject to the wheel of Chance.
And at our highest never joy we so
As we both doubt and dread our overthrow.
So striveth not the waves with sundry winds
As fortune toileth in the affairs of kings,
That would be feared, yet fear to be beloved,
Sith fear, or love, to kings is flattery
For instance, lordings, look upon your King,
By hate deprivèd of his dearest son,
The only hope of our successive line.

FIRST NOBLE
I had not thought that Alexandro's heart
Had been envenomed with such extreme hate.
But now I see that words have several works,
And there's no credit in the countenance.

VILLUPPO
No; for, my lord, had you beheld the train

That feignèd love had coloured in his looks,
When he in camp consorted Balthazar:
Far more inconstant had you thought the sun,
That hourly coasts the centre of the earth,
Then Alexandro's purpose to the Prince.

VICEROY
No more Villuppo, thou hast said enough,
And with thy words thou slay'st our wounded thoughts.
Nor shall I longer dally with the world,
Procrastinating Alexandro's death.
Go some of you and fetch the traitor forth,
That as he is condemnèd he may die.

Enter Alexandro with a nobleman and halberdiers.

SECOND NOBLE
In such extremes will nought but patience serve.

ALEXANDRO
But in extremes, what patience shall I use?
Nor discontents it me to leave the world,
With whom there nothing can prevail but wrong.

NOBLE
Yet hope the best.

ALEXANDRO
'Tis heaven is my hope.
As for the earth, it is too much infect,
To yield me hope of any of her mould.

VICEROY
Why linger ye? Bring forth that daring fiend,
And let him die for his accursed deed!

ALEXANDRO
Not that I fear the extremity of death,
For nobles cannot stoop to servile fear.
Do I, O King, thus discontented live.
– But this, O this torments my labouring soul,
That thus I die suspected of a sin
Whereof, as heavens have known my secret thoughts,
So am I free from this suggestion.

VICEROY
No more I say! To the tortures! When?

Bind him, and burn his body in those flames!
They bind him to the stake.
That shall prefigure those unquenchèd fires,
Of Phlegethon prepared for his soul!

ALEXANDRO
My guiltless death will be avenged on thee,
On thee, Villuppo, that hath maliced thus,
Or for thy meed hast falsely me accused.

VILLUPPO
Nay Alexandro, if thou menace me,
I'll lend a hand to send thee to the lake,
Where those thy words shall perish with thy works,
Injurious traitor, monstrous homicide!

Enter Ambassador.

AMBASSADOR
Stay, hold a while!
And here, with pardon of his majesty,
Lay hands upon Villuppo.

VICEROY
Ambassador,
What news hath urged this sudden entrance?

AMBASSADOR
Know, sovereign lord, that Balthazar doth live.

VICEROY
What sayest thou? Liveth Balthazar our son?

AMBASSADOR
Your highness' son, Lord Balthazar, doth live;
And, well entreated in the court of Spain,
Humbly commends him to your majesty.
These eyes beheld, and these my followers,
With these, the letters of the King's commends.
Gives him letters.
Are happy witnesses of his highness' health.
The King looks on the letters, and proceeds.

VICEROY [*Reads.*]
'Thy son doth live, your tribute is received,
Thy peace is made, and we are satisfied.
The rest resolve upon as things proposed,

For both our honours and thy benefit.'

AMBASSADOR
These are his highness' farther articles.

He gives him more letters.

VICEROY
Accursed wretch, to intimate these ills
Against the life and reputation
Of noble Alexandro! – Come my lord, unbind him.
Let him unbind thee that is bound to death,
To make a quittal for thy discontent.

They unbind him.

ALEXANDRO
Dread lord, in kindness you could do no less,
Upon report of such a damnèd fact.
But thus we see, our innocence hath saved
The hopeless life which thou, Villuppo, sought
By thy suggestions to have massacred.

VICEROY
Say, false Villuppo! Wherefore didst thou thus
Falsely betray Lord Alexandro's life?
Him whom thou knowest that no unkindness else,
But even the slaughter of our dearest son,
Could once have moved us to have misconceived?

ALEXANDRO
Say treacherous Villuppo, tell the King,
Wherein hath Alexandro used thee ill?

VILLUPPO
Rent with remembrance of so foul a deed
My guilty soul submits me to thy doom.
For, not for Alexandro's injuries,
But for reward, and hope to be preferred,
Thus have I shamelessly hazarded his life.

VICEROY
Which, villain, shall be ransomed with thy death,
And not so mean a torment as we here
Devised for him, who thou said'st slew our son:
But with the bitterest torments and extremes
That may be yet invented for thine end:

Alexandro seems to entreat.

Entreat me not, go, take the traitor hence!

Exit Villuppo [with Halberdiers]

And Alexandro, let us honour thee
With public notice of thy loyalty.
To end those things articulated here
By our great lord, the mighty King of Spain,
We with our council will deliberate.
Come, Alexandro, keep us company.

Exeunt.

[3.2]

Enter Hieronimo.

HIERONIMO
Oh eyes, no eyes, but fountains fraught with tears;
Oh life, no life, but lively form of death:
Oh world, no world, but mass of public wrongs,
Confused and filled with murder and misdeeds.
Oh sacred heavens! If this unhallowed deed,
If this inhuman and barbarous attempt,
If this incomparable murder thus
Of mine, but now no more my son,
Shall unrevealed and unrevengèd pass,
How should we term your dealings to be just,
If you unjustly deal with those that in your justice trust?
The night, sad secretary to my moans,
With direful visions wake my vexed soul,
And with the wounds of my distressful son
Solicit me for notice of his death.
The ugly fiends do sally forth of hell,
And frame my steps to unfrequented paths,
And fear my heart with fierce inflamèd thoughts.
The cloudy day my discontents records,
Early begins to register my dreams
And drive me forth to seek the murderer.
Eyes, life, world, heavens, hell, night and day,
See, search, show, send, some man, some mean, that may –
A letter falls [to the floor.]
What's here? A letter? Tush, it is not so,
A letter written to Hieronimo! *[Opens it]* *Red ink.*
'For want of ink receive this bloody writ.
Me hath my hapless brother hid from thee.

Revenge thyself on Balthazar and him!
For these were they that murderèd thy son.
Hieronimo, revenge Horatio's death,
And better fare than Bel-Imperia doth.'
What means this unexpected miracle?
My son slain by Lorenzo and the Prince!
What cause had they Horatio to malign?
Or what might move thee, Bel-Imperia,
To accuse thy brother, had he been the mean?
– Hieronimo beware, thou art betrayed,
And to entrap thy life this train is laid.
Advise thee therefore, be not credulous:
This is devisèd to endanger thee,
That thou by this Lorenzo shouldst accuse,
And he, for thy dishonour done, should draw
Thy life in question and thy name in hate.
Dear was the life of my beloved son,
And of his death behoves me be revenged.
Then hazard not thine own, Hieronimo,
But live t'effect thy resolution!
I therefore will by circumstances try
What I can gather to confirm this writ,
And, hearkening near the Duke of Castile's house,
Close if I can with Bel-Imperia,
To listen more, but nothing to bewray.

Enter Pedringano.

HIERONIMO
Now, Pedringano.

PEDRINGANO
Now, Hieronimo.

HIERONIMO
Where's thy lady?

PEDRINGANO
I know not; here's my lord.

Enter Lorenzo.

LORENZO
How now, who's this, Hieronimo?

HIERONIMO
My lord.

PEDRINGANO [*to Lorenzo*]
He asketh for my Lady Bel-Imperia.

LORENZO
What to do, Hieronimo? The Duke my father hath
Upon some disgrace awhile removed her hence,
But if it be aught I may inform her of,
Tell me Hieronimo, and I'll let her know it.

HIERONIMO
Nay, nay my lord, I thank you, it shall not need.
I had a suit unto her, but too late,
And her disgrace makes me unfortunate.

LORENZO
Why so, Hieronimo? use me.

HIERONIMO
Oh no, my lord, I dare not, it must not be.
I humbly thank your lordship.

LORENZO
Why then, farewell.

HIERONIMO [*aside*]
My grief no heart, my thoughts no tongue can tell.

Exit.

LORENZO
Come hither Pedringano, seest thou this?

PEDRINGANO
My lord, I see it, and suspect it too.

LORENZO
This is that damnèd villain Serberine,
That hath, I fear, revealèd Horatio's death.

PEDRINGANO
My lord, he could not, 'twas so lately done,
And since, he hath not left my company.

LORENZO
Admit he have not, his condition's such
As fear or flattering words may make him false.

I know his humour, and therewith repent
That e'er I used him in this enterprise.
But Pedringano, to prevent the worst,
And 'cause I know thee secret as my soul,
Here for thy further satisfaction take thou this.

Gives him more gold.

And hearken to me, thus it is devised.
This night thou must – and prithee so resolve –
Meet Serberine at Saint Luigi's Park.
Thou knowest 'tis here, hard by behind the house;
There take thy stand, and see thou strike him sure,
For die he must if we do mean to live.

PEDRINGANO
But how shall Serberine be there, my lord?

LORENZO
Let me alone. – I'll send to him to meet
The Prince and me, where thou must do this deed.

PEDRINGANO
It shall be done, my lord, it shall be done,
And I'll go arm myself to meet him there.

LORENZO
When things shall alter, as I hope they will,
Then shalt thou mount for this, thou knowest my mind.

Exit Pedringano.

Chi l'è? Jeron!

Enter Page.

PAGE
My lord?

LORENZO
Go, sirrah, to Serberine,
And bid him forthwith meet the Prince and me
At Saint Luigi's park, behind the house.
This evening, boy!

PAGE
I go, my lord.

LORENZO
But sirrah, let the hour be eight o'clock.

Bid him not fail.

PAGE

I fly, my lord.

Exit.

LORENZO [*to himself*]
Now to confirm the complot thou hast cast,
Of all these practices. I'll spread the watch,
Upon precise commandment from the King,
Strongly to guard the place where Pedringano
This night shall murder hapless Serberine.
Thus must we work that will avoid distrust,
Thus must we practise to prevent mishap,
And thus one ill, another must expulse.
This sly enquiry of Hieronimo
For Bel-Imperia breeds suspicion,
And this suspicion bodes a further ill.
As for myself, I know my secret fault,
And so do they, but I have dealt for them.
They that for coin their souls endangerèd
To save my life, for coin shall venture theirs:
And better 'tis that base companions die,
Than by their life to hazard our good haps.
Nor shall they live for me to fear their faith.
I'll trust myself, myself shall be my friend,
For die they shall, slaves are ordained to no other end.

Exit.

[3.3]

Enter Pedringano with a pistol.

PEDRINGANO
Now Pedringano, bid thy pistol hold,
And hold on, Fortune! Once more favour me,
Give but success to mine attempting spirit,
And let me shift for taking of mine aim!
Here is the gold, this is the gold proposed:
It is no dream that I adventure for,
But Pedringano is possessed thereof.
And he that would not strain his conscience
For him that thus his liberal purse hath stretched,
Unworthy such a favour may he fail,

And, wishing, want when such as I prevail.
As for the fear of apprehension,
I know, if need should be, my noble lord
Will stand between me and ensuing harms.
Besides, this place is free from all suspect.
Here therefore will I stay and take my stand.

Enter the watch.

FIRST WATCHMAN
I wonder much to what intent it is
That we are thus expressly charged to watch?

SECOND WATCHMAN
'Tis by commandment in the King's own name.

THIRD WATCHMAN
But we were never wont to watch and ward
So near the Duke his brother's house before.

SECOND WATCHMAN
Content yourself, stand close, there's somewhat in it.

Enter Serberine.

SERBERINE [*to himself*]
Here Serberine, attend and stay thy pace,
For here did Don Lorenzo's page appoint
That thou by his command shouldst meet with him.
How fit a place, if one were so disposed,
Methinks this corner is to close with one.

PEDRINGANO [*aside*]
Here comes the bird that I must seize upon,
Now, Pedringano, or never, play the man!

SERBERINE [*to himself*]
I wonder that his lordship stays so long,
Or wherefore should he send for me so late?

PEDRINGANO
For this Serberine, and thou shalt have it!
Shoots the dag. [*Serberine falls.*]
So, there he lies, my promise is performed.
The Watch. [*come forth*]

FIRST WATCHMAN
Hark, gentlemen, this is a pistol shot.

SECOND WATCHMAN
And here's one slain; stay the murderer!

PEDRINGANO
Now by the sorrows of the souls in hell,
He strives with the Watch.
Who first lays hand on me, I'll be his priest.

THIRD WATCHMAN
Sirrah, confess, and therein play the priest.
Why hast thou thus unkindly killed the man?

PEDRINGANO
Why, because he walked abroad so late.

THIRD WATCHMAN
Come sir, you had been better kept your bed
Than have committed this misdeed so late.

SECOND WATCHMAN
Come to the Marshal's with the murderer.

FIRST WATCHMAN
On to Hieronimo's! Help me here
To bring the murdered body with us too.

PEDRINGANO
Hieronimo? – Carry me before whom you will.
Whate'er he be, I'll answer him and you,
And do your worst, for I defy you all.

Exeunt [*with Serberine's body*].

[3.4]

Enter Lorenzo and Balthazar.

BALTHAZAR
How now my lord, what makes you rise so soon?

LORENZO
Fear of preventing our mishaps too late.

BALTHAZAR
What mischief is it that we not mistrust?

LORENZO
Our greatest ills we least mistrust, my lord,
And inexpected harms do hurt us most.

BALTHAZAR
Why, tell me Don Lorenzo, tell me man,
If aught concerns our honour and your own?

LORENZO
Nor you nor me my lord, but both in one.
For I suspect, and the presumption's great,
That by those base confederates in our fault
Touching the death of Don Horatio,
We are betrayed to old Hieronimo.

BALTHAZAR
Betrayed, Lorenzo? Tush, it cannot be.

LORENZO
A guilty conscience urgèd with the thought
Of former evils, easily cannot err.
I am persuaded – and dissuade me not –
That all's revealèd to Hieronimo.
And therefore know that I have cast it thus –

[*Enter Page*]

But here's the page. How now, what news with thee?

PAGE
My lord, Serberine is slain.

BALTHAZAR
Who? Serberine, my man?

PAGE
Your Highness' man, my lord.

LORENZO
Speak page, who murdered him?

PAGE
He that is apprehended for the fact.

LORENZO
Who?

PAGE
Pedringano.

BALTHAZAR
Is Serberine slain that loved his lord so well?
Injurious villain, murderer of his friend!

LORENZO
Hath Pedringano murdered Serberine?
My lord, let me entreat you to take the pains
To exasperate, and hasten his revenge
With your complaints unto my lord the King.
This their dissension breeds a greater doubt.

BALTHAZAR
Assure thee, Don Lorenzo, he shall die,
Or else his highness hardly shall deny.
Meanwhile, I'll haste the Marshal sessions,
For die he shall for this his damnèd deed.

Exit Balthazar.

LORENZO
Why so, this fits our former policy,
And thus experience bids the wise to deal.
I lay the plot, he prosecutes the point,
I set the trap, he breaks the worthless twigs,
And sees not that wherewith the bird was limed.
Thus hopeful men, that mean to hold their own,
Must look like fowlers to their dearest friends.
He runs to kill whom I have holp to catch,
And no man knows it was my reaching fatch.
'Tis hard to trust unto a multitude,
Or anyone, in mine opinion,
When men themselves their secrets will reveal.

Enter a messenger with a letter.

LORENZO
Boy!

PAGE
My lord.

LORENZO
What's he?

MESSENGER
I have a letter to your lordship.

LORENZO
From whence?

MESSENGER
From Pedringano that's imprisonèd.
[*Gives Lorenzo the letter.*]

LORENZO
So, he is in prison then?

MESSENGER
Ay, my good lord.

LORENZO
What would he with us? [*Reads the letter*]
He writes us here
To stand good lord and help him in distress.
Tell him I have his letters, know his mind,
And what we may, let him assure him of.
Fellow, be gone: my boy shall follow thee.

Exit messenger.

[*aside*] This works like wax, yet once more try thy wits,
Boy, go convey this purse to Pedringano,
[*Gives him a purse*]
Thou know'st the prison, closely give it him,
And be advised that none be there about.
Bid him be merry still, but secret;
And though the Marshal-sessions be today,
Bid him not doubt of his delivery.
Tell him his pardon is already signed,
And thereon bid him boldly be resolved.
For were he ready to be turnèd off –
As 'tis my will the uttermost be tried –
Thou with his pardon shalt attend him still,
Show him this box, tell him his pardon's in it,
But open't not, an' if thou lovest thy life.
But let him wisely keep his hopes unknown;
He shall not want while Don Lorenzo lives.
Away!

PAGE
I go my lord, I run.

LORENZO
But sirrah, see that this be cleanly done.

Exit Page.

Now stands our fortune on a tickle point,
And now or never ends Lorenzo's doubts.
One only thing is uneffected yet,
And that's to fee the executioner.
But to what end? I list not trust the air
With utterance of our pretence therein,
For fear the privy whispering of the wind
Convey our words amongst unfriendly ears,
That lie too open to advantages.
Et quel che voglio io, nessun lo sa.
Intendo io; quel mi basterà.

Exit.

[3.5]

Enter boy with the box.

PAGE

My master hath forbidden me to look in this box, and by my troth 'tis likely, if he had not warned me, I should not have had so much idle time, for we men's-kind in our minority are like women in their uncertainty: that they are most forbidden, they will soonest attempt – so I now. [*Opens the box.*] By my bare honesty, here's nothing but the bare empty box! Were it not sin against secrecy, I would say it were a piece of gentlemanlike knavery. I must go to Pedringano, and tell him his pardon is in this box, nay, I would have sworn it, had I not seen the contrary. I cannot choose but smile to think how the villain will flout the gallows, scorn the audience, and descant on the hangman, and all presuming of his pardon from hence. Will't not be an odd jest, for me to stand and grace every jest he makes, pointing my finger at this box: as who would say, 'Mock on, here's thy warrant'? Is it not a scurvy jest, that a man should jest himself to death? Alas poor Pedringano, I am in a sort sorry for thee, but if I should be hanged with thee, I cannot weep. *Exit.*

[3.6]

Enter Hieronimo and the deputy.

HIERONIMO

Thus must we toil in other men's extremes,
That know not how to remedy our own,

And do them justice, when unjustly, we,
For all our wrongs can compass no redress.
But shall I never live to see the day
That I may come (by justice of the heavens)
To know the cause that may my cares allay?
This toils my body, this consumeth age,
That only I to all men just must be,
And neither gods nor men be just to me.

DEPUTY
Worthy Hieronimo, your office asks
A care to punish such as do transgress.

HIERONIMO
So is it my duty to regard his death,
Who when he lived deserved my dearest blood:
– But come, for that we came for; let's begin,
For here lies that which bids me to be gone.

Enter Officers [including the Hangman, setting up the gallows], Page, and Pedringano, with a letter in his hand, bound [and guarded].

DEPUTY
Bring forth the prisoner, for the court is set.

PEDRINGANO [*to the Page*]
Gramercy boy, but it was time to come,
For I had written to my lord anew
A nearer matter that concerneth him,
For fear his lordship had forgotten me.
But sith he hath remembered me so well –
Come, come, come on, when shall we to this gear?

HIERONIMO
Stand forth thou monster, murderer of men,
And here for satisfaction of the world
Confess thy folly and repent thy fault,
For there's thy place of execution.

PEDRINGANO
This is short work! Well, to your marshalship
First I confess, nor fear I death therefore,
I am the man, 'twas I slew Serberine.
But sir, then you think this shall be the place,
Where we shall satisfy you for this gear?

DEPUTY
Ay, Pedringano.

PEDRINGANO
Now I think not so.

HIERONIMO
Peace impudent, for thou shalt find it so!
For blood with blood shall, while I sit as judge,
Be satisfied and the law discharged.
And though myself cannot receive the like,
Yet will I see that others have their right.
Dispatch, the fault's approvèd and confessed,
And by our law he is condemned to die.

HANGMAN
Come on sir, are you ready?

PEDRINGANO
To do what, my fine officious knave?

HANGMAN
To go to this gear.

PEDRINGANO
O sir, you are too forward, thou wouldst fain furnish me with a halter, to disfurnish me of my habit. So I should go out of this gear, my raiment, into that gear, the rope. – But hangman, now I spy your knavery, I'll not change without boot, that's flat.

HANGMAN
Come sir.

PEDRINGANO
So then, I must up?

HANGMAN
No remedy.

PEDRINGANO
Yes, but there shall be for my coming down.

HANGMAN
Indeed, here's a remedy for that.

[*Points to the noose*]

PEDRINGANO
How? Be turned off?

HANGMAN
Ay truly; come, are you ready? I pray sir dispatch, the day goes away.

PEDRINGANO
What, do you hang by the hour? If you do, I may chance to break your old custom.

HANGMAN
Faith, you have reason, for I am like to break your young neck.

PEDRINGANO
Dost thou mock me, hangman? Pray God I be not preserved to break your knave's pate for this.

HANGMAN
Alas sir, you are a foot too low to reach it, and I hope you will never grow so high while I am in the office.

PEDRINGANO
Sirrah, dost see yonder boy with the box in his hand?

HANGMAN
What, he that points to it with his finger?

PEDRINGANO
Ay, that companion.

HANGMAN
I know him not, but what of him?

PEDRINGANO
Dost thou think to live till his old doublet will make thee a new truss?

HANGMAN
Ay, and many a fair year after, to truss up many an honester man than either thou or he.

PEDRINGANO
What hath he in his box, as thou thinkst?

HANGMAN
Faith I cannot tell, nor I care not greatly. Methinks you should rather hearken to your soul's health.

PEDRINGANO
Why, sirrah hangman? I take it that that is good for the body, is

likewise good for the soul; and it may be, in that box is balm for both.

HANGMAN
Well, thou art even the merriest piece of man's flesh that ere groaned at my office door.

PEDRINGANO

Is your roguery become an office with a knave's name?

HANGMAN
Ay, and that shall all they witness that see you seal it with a thief's name.

PEDRINGANO
I prithee request this good company to pray with me.

HANGMAN
Ay, marry sir, this is a good motion: my masters, you see here's a good fellow.

PEDRINGANO
Nay, nay, now I remember me, let them alone till some other time, for now I have no great need.

HIERONIMO
I have not seen a wretch so impudent.
O monstrous times, where murder's set so light,
And where the soul, that should be shrined in heaven,
Solely delights in interdicted things,
Still wandering in the thorny passages,
That intercepts itself of happiness.
Murder, O bloody monster! God forbid
A fault so foul should escape unpunished.
Dispatch, and see this execution done,
This makes me to remember thee, my son.

Exit.

[*Hangman prepares the execution.*]

PEDRINGANO
Nay soft, no haste.

DEPUTY
Why, wherefore stay you, have you hope of life?

PEDRINGANO
Why, ay.

HANGMAN
As how?

PEDRINGANO
Why, rascal, by my pardon from the King.

HANGMAN
Stand you on that? then you shall off with this.

He turns him off.

DEPUTY
So executioner, convey him hence,
But let his body be unburied.
Let not the earth be chokd or infect.
With that which heaven contemns and men neglect.

Exeunt.

* * * * *

[4.1]

Enter Hieronimo.

HIERONIMO
Where shall I run to breathe abroad my woes,
My woes, whose weight hath wearièd the earth?
Or mine exclaims, that have surcharged the air
With ceaseless plaints for my deceased son?
The blustering winds, conspiring with my words,
At my lament have moved the leafless trees,
Disrobed the meadows of their flowered green,
Made mountains marsh with spring-tides of my tears,
And broken through the brazen gates of hell.
Yet still tormented is my tortured soul
With broken sighs and restless passions,
That wingèd mount, and, hovering in the air,
Beat at the windows of the brightest heavens,
Soliciting for justice and revenge.
But they are placed in those imperial heights
Where, countermured with walls of diamond,
I find the place impregnable, and they
Resist my woes, and give my words no way.

Enter Hangman with a letter.

HANGMAN
O lord sir, God bless you sir, the man sir, Petergade, sir, he that was so full of merry conceits –

HIERONIMO
Well, what of him?

HANGMAN
O lord sir, he went the wrong way! The fellow had a fair commission to the contrary. Sir, here is his passport, I pray you sir, we have done him wrong.

HIERONIMO
I warrant thee, give it me.
[*Takes the letter*]

HANGMAN
You will stand between the gallows and me?

HIERONIMO
Ay, ay.

HANGMAN
I thank your lord-worship.

Exit Hangman.

HIERONIMO
And yet, though somewhat nearer me concerns,
I will, to ease the grief that I sustain,
Take truce with sorrow while I read on this. [*Reads.*]
'My lord, I writ as mine extremes required,
That you would labour my delivery.
If you neglect, my life is desperate,
And in my death I shall reveal the truth.
You know, my lord, I slew him for your sake,
And was confederate with the Prince and you.
Won by rewards and hopeful promises,
I holp to murder Don Horatio too.'
Holp he to murder mine Horatio?
And actors in th'accursed tragedy
Wast thou, Lorenzo, Balthazar and thou,
Of whom my son, my son deserved so well?
What have I heard, what have mine eyes beheld?
O sacred heavens, may it come to pass,
That such a monstrous and detested deed,
So closely smothered, and so long concealed,

Shall thus by this be vengèd or revealed?
Now see I what I durst not then suspect,
That Bel-Imperia's letter was not feigned,
Nor feigned she, though falsely they have wronged
Both her, myself, Horatio, and themselves.
Now may I make compare 'twixt hers and this,
Of every accident I ne'er could find
Till now, and now I feelingly perceive,
They did what heaven unpunished would not leave.
O false Lorenzo, are these thy flattering looks?
Is this the honour that thou didst my son?
And Balthazar, bane to thy soul and me,
Was this the ransom he reserved thee for?
Woe to the cause of these constrainèd wars,
Woe to thy baseness and captivity,
Woe to thy birth, thy body, and thy soul,
Thy cursed father, and thy conquered self!
And banned with bitter execrations be
The day and place where he did pity thee!
– But wherefore waste I mine unfruitful words,
When nought but blood will satisfy my woes?
I will go plain me to my lord the King,
And cry aloud for justice through the court,
Wearing the flints with these my withered feet,
And either purchase justice by entreats,
Or tire them all with my revenging threats.

Exit.

[4.2]

Enter Isabella and her maid.

ISABELLA
So that you say this herb will purge the eye,
And this the head?
Ah, but none of them will purge the heart:
No, there's no medicine left for my disease,
Nor any physic to recure the dead.
She runs lunatic.
Horatio, Oh where's Horatio?

MAID
Good Madam, affright not thus yourself,
With outrage for your son Horatio.

He sleeps in quiet in the Elysian fields.

ISABELLA
Why did I not give you gowns and goodly things,
Bought you a whistle and a whipstalk too,
To be revengèd on their villainies?

MAID
Madam, these humours do torment my soul.

ISABELLA
'My soul'? Poor soul, thou talks of things
Thou knowst not what. My soul hath silver wings,
That mounts me up unto the highest heavens,
To heaven! Ay, there sits my Horatio,
Backed with a troop of fiery cherubins,
Dancing about his newly healèd wounds,
Singing sweet hymns and chanting heavenly notes,
Rare harmony to greet his innocence,
That lived, ay died, a mirror in our days.
But say, where shall I find the men, the murderers
That slew Horatio? Whither shall I run
To find them out that murderèd my son?

Exeunt.

[4.3]

Bel-Imperia at a window.

BEL-IMPERIA
What means this outrage that is offered me?
Why am I thus sequestered from the court?
No notice? Shall I not know the cause
Of this my secret and suspicious ills?
Accursèd brother, unkind murderer,
Why bends thou thus thy mind to martyr me?
Hieronimo, why writ I of thy wrongs,
Or why art thou so slack in thy revenge?
Andrea, O Andrea, that thou sawest
Me for thy friend Horatio handled thus,
And him for me thus causeless murdered!
Well, force perforce, I must constrain myself
To patience, and apply me to the time
Till heaven, as I have hoped, shall set me free.

Enter Christophil.

CHRISTOPHIL
Come Madam Bel-Imperia, this may not be.

Exeunt.

[4.4]

Enter Lorenzo, Balthazar, and the Page.

LORENZO
Boy, talk no further, thus far things go well.
Thou art assurèd that thou sawest him dead?

PAGE
Or else, my lord, I live not.

LORENZO
That's enough.
As for his resolution in his end,
Leave that to him with whom he sojourns now.
Here, take my ring, and give it Christophil,
And bid him let my sister be enlarged,
And bring her hither straight.

Exit Page.

This that I did was for a policy
To smooth and keep the murder secret,
Which, as a nine days' wonder, being o'erblown,
My gentle sister will I now enlarge.

BALTHAZAR
And time, Lorenzo, for my lord the Duke,
You heard, enquirèd for her yesternight.

LORENZO
Why, and my lord, I hope you heard me say
Sufficient reason why she kept away.
But that's all one. My lord, you love her?

BALTHAZAR
Ay.

LORENZO
Then in your love beware, deal cunningly,
Salve all suspicions, only soothe me up.
And if she hap to stand on terms with us,
As for her sweetheart, and concealment so,

Jest with her gently: under feignèd jest
Are things concealed that else would breed unrest.
– But here she comes.

Enter Bel-Imperia.

LORENZO
Now, sister –

BEL-IMPERIA
Sister? No,
Thou art no brother, but an enemy;
Else wouldst thou not have used thy sister so:
First, to affright me with thy weapons drawn,
And with extremes abuse my company;
And then to hurry me, like whirlwind's rage,
Amidst a crew of thy confederates,
And clap me up where none might come at me,
Nor I at any to reveal my wrongs.
What madding fury did possess thy wits?
Or wherein is't that I offended thee?

LORENZO
Advise you better, Bel-Imperia,
For I have done you no disparagement,
Unless, by more discretion than deserved,
I sought to save your honour and mine own.

BEL-IMPERIA
Mine honour! Why Lorenzo, wherein is it,
That I neglect my reputation so,
As you, or any, need to rescue it?

LORENZO
His highness and my father were resolved,
To come confer with old Hieronimo,
Concerning certain matters of estate,
That by the Viceroy was determinèd.

BEL-IMPERIA
And wherein was mine honour touched in that?

BALTHAZAR
Have patience Bel-Imperia, hear the rest.

LORENZO
Me next in sight as messenger they sent,

To give him notice that they were so nigh.
Now when I came, consorted with the Prince,
And unexpected in an arbour there
Found Bel-Imperia with Horatio –

BEL-IMPERIA
How then?

LORENZO
Why then, remembering that old disgrace
Which you for Don Andrea had endured,
And now were likely longer to sustain
By being found so meanly accompanied:
Thought rather, for I knew no readier mean,
To thrust Horatio forth my father's way.

BALTHAZAR
And carry you obscurely somewhere else,
Lest that his highness should have found you there.

BEL-IMPERIA
Even so, my lord? And you are witness,
That this is true which he entreateth of?
You (gentle brother) forged this for my sake,
And you, my lord, were made his instrument:
A work of worth, worthy the noting too!
But what's the cause that you concealed me since?

LORENZO
Your melancholy, sister, since the news
Of your first favourite Don Andrea's death,
My father's old wrath hath exasperate.

BALTHAZAR
And better was it for you being in disgrace,
To absent yourself and give his fury place.

BEL-IMPERIA
But why had I no notice of his ire?

LORENZO
That were to add more fuel to your fire
Who burnt like Etna for Andrea's loss.

BEL-IMPERIA
Hath not my father then enquired for me?

LORENZO
Sister he hath, and thus excused I thee.

He whispers in her ear.

But Bel-Imperia, see the gentle Prince,
Look on thy love, behold young Balthazar.
Whose passions by thy presence are increased,
And in whose melancholy thou mayst see
Thy hate, his love: thy flight, his following thee.

BEL-IMPERIA
Brother, you are become an orator,
I know not, I, by what experience
Too politic for me, past all compare,
Since last I saw you. But content yourself,
The Prince is meditating higher things.

BALTHAZAR
'Tis of thy beauty then that conquers Kings:
Of those thy tresses, Ariadne's twines,
Where with my liberty thou hast surprised;
Of that thine ivory front, my sorrow's map,
Wherein I see no haven to rest my hope.

BEL-IMPERIA
To love, and fear, and both at once, my lord,
In my conceit, are things of more import
Than women's wits are to be busied with.

BALTHAZAR
'Tis I that love.

BEL-IMPERIA
Whom?

BALTHAZAR
Bel-Imperia.

BEL-IMPERIA
But I that fear.

BALTHAZAR
Whom?

BEL-IMPERIA
Bel-Imperia.

LORENZO
Fear yourself?

BEL-IMPERIA
Ay, brother.

LORENZO
How?

BEL-IMPERIA
As those,
That what they love are loath and fear to lose.

BALTHAZAR
Then, fair, let Balthazar your keeper be,

BEL-IMPERIA
No, Balthazar doth fear as well as we.
Et tremulo metui pavidum iunxere timorem,
Et vanum stolidae proditionis opus.

Exit.

LORENZO
Nay, an' you argue things so cunningly
We'll go continue this discourse at court.

BALTHAZAR
Led by the lodestar of her heavenly looks,
Wends poor oppressèd Balthazar,
As o'er the mountains walks the wanderer,
Incertain to effect his pilgrimage.

Exeunt.

[4.5]

Enter two Portuguese, and Hieronimo meets them.

FIRST PORTUGUESE
By your leave, sir.

HIERONIMO
Good leave have you, nay, I pray you go,
For I'll leave you, if you can leave me, so.

SECOND PORTUGUESE
Pray you, which is the next way to my lord the Duke's?

HIERONIMO
The next way from me.

FIRST PORTUGUESE
To his house, we mean.

HIERONIMO
O hard by, 'tis yon house that you see.

SECOND PORTUGUESE
You could not tell us if his son were there?

HIERONIMO
Who, my lord Lorenzo?

FIRST PORTUGUESE
Ay sir.

He goes in at one door and comes out at another.

HIERONIMO
Oh forbear,
For other talk for us far fitter were.
But if you be importunate to know
The way to him, and where to find him out,
Then list to me and I'll resolve your doubt.
There is a path upon your left-hand side
That leadeth from a guilty conscience
Unto a forest of distrust and fear,
A darksome place and dangerous to pass,
There shall you meet with melancholy thoughts,
Whose baleful humours, if you but uphold,
It will conduct you to Despair and Death:
Whose rocky cliffs, when you have once beheld
Within a hugy dale of lasting night
That, kindled with the world's iniquities,
Doth cast up filthy and detested fumes.
Not far from thence where murderers have built
A habitation for their cursèd souls:
There in a brazen cauldron, fixed by Jove
In his fell wrath upon a sulphur flame:
Yourselves shall find Lorenzo bathing him
In boiling lead and blood of innocents.

FIRST PORTUGUESE
Ha, ha, ha!

HIERONIMO
Ha, ha, ha!
Why ha, ha, ha! Farewell, good! Ha, ha, ha!

Exit.

SECOND PORTUGUESE
Doubtless this man is passing lunatic,
Or imperfection of his age doth make him dote.
Come, let's away to seek my lord the Duke.

Exeunt.

[4.6]

Enter Hieronimo with a poniard in one hand, and a rope in the other.

HIERONIMO
Now sir, perhaps I come and see the King,
The King sees me, and fain would hear my suit.
Why, is not this a strange and seld-seen thing
That standers-by with toys should strike me mute?
Go to – I see their shifts, and say no more.
Hieronimo, 'tis time for thee to trudge.
Down by the dale that flows with purple gore
Standeth a fiery tower; there sits a judge
Upon a seat of steel and molten brass:
And 'twixt his teeth he holds a firebrand
That leads unto the lake where hell doth stand.
– Away Hieronimo, to him be gone!
He'll do thee justice for Horatio's death.
[*Points at the poniard*]
Turn down this path, thou shalt be with him straight;
[*Points at the rope*]
Or this, and then thou need'st not take thy breath.
This way, or that way? – Soft and fair, not so:
For if I hang or kill myself, let's know
Who will revenge Horatio's murder then?
No, no, fie no: pardon me, I'll none of that.
He flings away the dagger and halter.
This way I'll take, and this way comes the King,
He takes them up again.
And here I'll have a fling at him, that's flat.
And, Balthazar, I'll be with thee to bring,

And thee, Lorenzo! Here's the King – nay, stay,
And here, ay here – there goes the hare away!

Enter King, Ambassador, Castile, and Lorenzo.

KING
Now show, Ambassador, what our Viceroy saith.
Hath he received the articles we sent?

HIERONIMO
Justice! Oh, justice to Hieronimo!

LORENZO
Back, seest thou not the King is busy?

HIERONIMO
Oh, is he so?

KING
Who is he that interrupts our business?

HIERONIMO
Not I.
[*aside*] Hieronimo beware, go by, go by.

[*Withdraws*]

AMBASSADOR
Renownèd King, he hath received and read
Thy kingly proffers, and thy promised league,
And, as a man extremely overjoyed
To hear his son so princely entertained,
Whose death he had so solemnly bewailed,
This for thy further satisfaction
And kingly love, he kindly lets thee know:
First, for the marriage of his princely son
With Bel-Imperia, thy beloved niece,
The news are more delightful to his soul
Than myrrh or incense to the offended heavens.
In person, therefore, will he come himself
To see the marriage rites solemnized,
And in the presence of the court of Spain,
To knit a sure inexecrable band
Of kingly love and everlasting league,
Betwixt the crowns of Spain and Portugal.
There will he give his crown to Balthazar,
And make a queen of Bel-Imperia.

KING
Brother, how like you this our Viceroy's love?

CASTILE
No doubt my lord, it is an argument
Of honourable care to keep his friend,
And wondrous zeal to Balthazar his son.
Nor am I least indebted to his grace,
That bends his liking to my daughter thus.

AMBASSADOR
Now last (dread lord) here hath his highness sent,
Although he send not that his son return,
His ransom due to Don Horatio.
[Gives the King gold.]

HIERONIMO
Horatio, who calls Horatio?

KING
And well remembered, thank his majesty.
Here, see it given to Horatio.

HIERONIMO
Justice! O justice, justice, gentle King!

KING
Who is that? Hieronimo?

HIERONIMO
Justice! O justice, O my son, my son,
My son, whom nought can ransom or redeem!

LORENZO
Hieronimo, you are not well advised.

HIERONIMO
Away Lorenzo, hinder me no more
For thou hast made me bankrupt of my bliss.
Give me my son! You shall not ransom him.
Away! I'll rip the bowels of the earth,
He digs with his dagger.
And ferry over to the Elysian plains,
And bring my son to show his deadly wounds.
Stand from about me!
I'll make a pickaxe of my poniard,
And here surrender up my Marshalship:

For I'll go marshal up the fiends in hell,
To be avengèd on you all for this.

KING
What means this outrage? Will none of you restrain his fury?

HIERONIMO
Nay soft and fair: you shall not need to strive,
Needs must he go that all the devils drive.

Exit.

KING
What accident hath happed Hieronimo?
I have not seen him to demean him so.

LORENZO
My gracious lord, he is – with extreme pride,
Conceived of young Horatio his son,
And covetous of having to himself
The ransom of the young Prince Balthazar –
Distract, and in a manner lunatic.

KING
Believe me, nephew, we are sorry for it,
This is the love that fathers bear their sons.
But gentle brother, go give to him this gold,
[*Gives Castile the gold*]
The Prince's ransom, let him have his due,
For what he hath Horatio shall not want:
Haply Hieronimo hath need thereof.

LORENZO
But if he be thus helplessly distract,
'Tis requisite his office be resigned,
And given to one of more discretion.

KING
We shall increase his melancholy so.
'Tis best that we see further in it first,
Till when ourself will not exempt the place.
And brother, now bring in the Ambassador,
That he may be a witness of the match
Twixt Balthazar and Bel-Imperia,
And that we may prefix a certain time
Wherein the marriage shall be solemnized,

That we may have thy lord the Viceroy here.

AMBASSADOR
Therein your highness highly shall content
His majesty, that longs to hear from hence.

KING
On then, and hear you, Lord Ambassador.

Exeunt.

[4.7]

Enter Hieronimo with a book in his hand.

HIERONIMO
'*Vindicta mihi!*'
Ay, heaven will be revenged of every ill,
Nor will they suffer murder unrepaid.
Then stay Hieronimo, attend their will,
For mortal men may not appoint their time.
Per scelus semper tutum est sceleribus iter.
Strike, and strike home, where wrong is offered thee,
For evils unto ills conductors be,
And death's the worst of resolution.
For he that thinks with patience to contend
To quiet life, his life shall easily end.
Fata si miseros juvant, habes salutem:
Fata si vitam negant, habes sepulchrum.
'If destiny thy miseries do ease,
Then hast thou health, and happy shalt thou be.
If destiny deny thee life, Hieronimo,
Yet shalt thou be assured of a tomb:
If neither, yet let this thy comfort be,
Heaven covereth him that hath no burial.'
And to conclude, I will revenge his death!
But how? Not as the vulgar wits of men,
With open, but inevitable ills,
As by a secret, yet a certain mean,
Which under kindship will be cloakèd best.
Wise men will take their opportunity,
Closely and safely fitting things to time.
But in extremes, advantage hath no time,
And therefore all times fit not for revenge.
Thus, therefore will I rest me in unrest,

Dissembling quiet in unquietness,
Not seeming that I know their villainies,
That my simplicity may make them think
That ignorantly I will let all slip.
For ignorance, I wot, and well they know,
Remedium malorum iners est.
Nor aught avails it me to menace them,
Who as a wintry storm upon a plain
Will bear me down with their nobility.
No, no, Hieronimo, thou must enjoin
Thine eyes to observation, and thy tongue
To milder speeches than thy spirit affords;
Thy heart to patience, and thy hands to rest;
Thy cap to courtesy, and thy knee to bow,
Till to revenge thou know when, where, and how.

A noise within.

How now, what noise, what coil is that you keep?

Enter a servant.

SERVANT
Here are a sort of poor petitioners
That are importunate, and it shall please you sir,
That you should plead their cases to the King.

HIERONIMO
That I should plead their several actions?
Why let them enter and let me see them.

Enter three citizens and [*Bazulto*], *an old man.*

FIRST CITIZEN
So I tell you this, for learning and for law
There is not any advocate in Spain
That can prevail, or will take half the pain,
That he will, in pursuit of equity.

HIERONIMO
Come near you men that thus importune me,
[*Aside.*] Now must I bear a face of gravity,
For thus I used, before my Marshalship,
To plead in causes as Corregidor.
– Come on sirs, what's the matter?

SECOND CITIZEN
Sir, an action.

HIERONIMO
Of battery?

FIRST CITIZEN
Mine of debt.

HIERONIMO
Give place.

SECOND CITIZEN
No sir, mine is an action of the case.

THIRD CITIZEN
Mine an *ejectione firmae* by a lease.

HIERONIMO
Content you sirs, are you determinèd
That I should plead your several actions?

FIRST CITIZEN
Ay sir, and here's my declaration.

SECOND CITIZEN
And here is my bond.

THIRD CITIZEN
And here is my lease.

They give him papers.

HIERONIMO
But wherefore stands yon silly man so mute,
With mournful eyes and hands to heaven upreared?
Come hither, father, let me know thy cause.

BAZULTO
O worthy sir, my cause but slightly known,
May move the hearts of warlike Myrmidons
And melt the Corsic rocks with ruthful tears.

HIERONIMO
Say father, tell me, what's thy suit?

BAZULTO
No sir, could my woes
Give way unto my most distressful words
Then should I not in paper, as you see,
With ink bewray what blood began in me.

HIERONIMO
What's here? 'The humble supplication
Of Don Bazulto for his murdered son.'

BAZULTO
Ay, sir.

HIERONIMO
No sir, it was my murdered son,
Oh my son, my son! Oh my son Horatio!
But mine, or thine, Bazulto, be content.
Here, take my handkercher and wipe thine eyes,
Whiles wretched I in thy mishaps may see
The lively portrait of my dying self.
He draws out a bloody napkin.
Oh no, not this! Horatio, this was thine,
And when I dyed it in thy dearest blood
This was a token 'twixt thy soul and me
That of thy death revengèd I should be.
[*He draws out more objects.*]
But here, take this, and this – what, my purse? –
Ay this and that, and all of them are thine,
For all as one are our extremities.

FIRST CITIZEN
Oh, see the kindness of Hieronimo!

SECOND CITIZEN
This gentleness shows him a gentleman.

HIERONIMO
See, see, oh see thy shame, Hieronimo,
See here a loving father to his son!
Behold the sorrows and the sad laments
That he delivereth for his son's decease.
If love's effects so strives in lesser things,
If love enforce such moods in meaner wits,
If love express such power in poor estates:
– Hieronimo, whenas a raging sea,
Tossed with the wind and tide, o'erturneth then
The upper billows, course of waves to keep,
Whilst lesser waters labour in the deep –
Then sham'st thou not, Hieronimo, to neglect
The sweet revenge of thy Horatio?
Though on this earth justice will not be found,

I'll down to hell and in this passion
Knock at the dismal gates of Pluto's court,
Getting by force, as once Alcides did,
A troop of Furies and tormenting hags
To torture Don Lorenzo and the rest!
Yet, lest the triple-headed porter should
Deny my passage to the slimy strand,
The Thracian poet thou shalt counterfeit.
Come on, old father, be my Orpheus,
And if thou canst no notes upon the harp
Then sound the burden of thy sore heart's grief,
Till we do gain that Proserpine may grant
Revenge on them that murderèd my son.
Then will I rent and tear them thus and thus,
Shivering their limbs in pieces with my teeth.

Tears the papers.

FIRST CITIZEN
O sir, my declaration!

Exit Hieronimo and they after.

SECOND CITIZEN
Save my bond!

Enter Hieronimo.

THIRD CITIZEN
Alas my lease! It cost me
Ten pound, and you, my lord, have torn the same.

HIERONIMO
That cannot be, I gave it never a wound.
Show me one drop of blood fall from the same:
How is it possible I should slay it then?
Tush no; run after, catch me if you can!

Exeunt all but Bazulto.

Bazulto remains until Hieronimo enters again, who, staring him in the face, speaks.

HIERONIMO
And art thou come, Horatio, from the depth,
To ask for justice in this upper earth?
To tell thy father thou art unrevenged,
To wring more tears from Isabella's eyes,

Whose lights are dimmed with overlong laments?
Go back my son, complain to Aeacus,
For here's no justice; gentle boy, be gone,
For justice is exilèd from the earth.
Hieronimo will bear thee company.
Thy mother cries on righteous Rhadamanth
For just revenge against the murderers.

BAZULTO
Alas my lord, whence springs this troubled speech?

HIERONIMO
But let me look on my Horatio.
Sweet boy, how art thou changed in death's black shade!
Had Proserpine no pity on thy youth,
But suffered thy fair, crimson-coloured spring
With withered winter to be blasted thus?
Horatio, thou art older than thy father:
Ah ruthless fate, that favour thus transforms!

BAZULTO
Ah my good lord, I am not your young son.

HIERONIMO
What, not my son? Thou, then, a fury art,
Sent from the empty Kingdom of black night,
To summon me to make appearance
Before grim Minos and just Rhadamanth,
To plague Hieronimo, that is remiss
And seeks not vengeance for Horatio's death.

BAZULTO
I am a grievèd man and not a ghost,
That came for justice for my murdered son.

HIERONIMO
Ay, now I know thee, now thou nam'st my son:
Thou art the lively image of my grief.
Within thy face my sorrows I may see,
Thy eyes are gummed with tears, thy cheeks are wan,
Thy forehead troubled, and thy mutt'ring lips
Murmur sad words, abruptly broken off
By force of windy sighs thy spirit breathes.
And all this sorrow rises for thy son,
And selfsame sorrow feel I for my son.

Come in old man, thou shalt to Isabel,
Lean on my arm: I thee, thou me shalt stay,
And thou, and I, and she will sing a song,
Three parts in one, but all of discords framed.
– Talk not of cords, but let us now be gone,
For with a cord Horatio was slain.

Exeunt.

[4.8]

Enter [at one door the Spanish contingent] King of Spain, the Duke of Castile, Lorenzo, Balthazar and Bel-Imperia [with servants; enter at another door the Portuguese] Viceroy and Don Pedro.

KING
Go brother, it is the Duke of Castile's cause,
Salute the Viceroy in our name.

CASTILE
I go.

VICEROY
Go forth, Don Pedro for thy nephew's sake,
And greet the Duke of Castile.

PEDRO
It shall be so.

KING
And now to meet these Portuguese,
For as we now are, so sometimes were these,
Kings and commanders of the western Indies.
Welcome, brave Viceroy, to the court of Spain,
And welcome all his honourable train.
'Tis not unknown to us for why you come,
Or have so kingly crossed the seas.
Sufficeth it, in this we note the troth,
And more than common love you lend to us.
So is it that mine honourable niece
(For it beseems us now that it be known)
Already is betrothed to Balthazar,
And by appointment and our condescent
Tomorrow are they to be marrièd.
To this intent we entertain thyself,

Thy followers, their pleasure, and our peace.
Speak men of Portugal, shall it be so?
If ay, say so: if not, say flatly no.

VICEROY
Renowned King, I come not as thou think'st,
With doubtful followers, unresolvèd men,
But such as have upon thine articles
Confirmed thy motion and contented me.
Know sovereign, I come to solemnize
The marriage of thy beloved niece,
Fair Bel-Imperia, with my Balthazar –
With thee my son, whom sith I live to see
Here take my crown, I give it her and thee.
And let me live a solitary life,
In ceaseless prayers,
To think how strangely heav'n hath thee preserved.
[He weeps.]

KING
See brother, see, how nature strives in him!
– Come worthy Viceroy, and accompany
Thy friend with thine extremities:
A place more private fits this Princely mood.

VICEROY
Or here or where your highness thinks it good.

Exeunt all but Castile and Lorenzo.

CASTILE
Nay stay, Lorenzo, let me talk with you.
Seest thou this entertainment of these Kings?

LORENZO
I do my lord, and joy to see the same.

CASTILE
And knowest thou why this meeting is?

LORENZO
For her, my lord, whom Balthazar doth love,
And to confirm their promised marriage.

CASTILE
She is thy sister?

LORENZO
Who, Bel-Imperia?
Ay, my gracious lord, and this is the day
That I have longed so happily to see.

CASTILE
Thou wouldst be loath that any fault of thine
Should intercept her in her happiness?

LORENZO
Heavens will not let Lorenzo err so much.

CASTILE
Why then Lorenzo, listen to my words.
It is suspected, and reported too,
That thou, Lorenzo, wrong'st Hieronimo,
And in his suits towards his majesty
Still keep'st him back, and seeks to cross his suit.

LORENZO
That I, my lord –?

CASTILE
I tell thee son, myself have heard it said,
When to my sorrow I have been ashamed
To answer for thee, though thou art my son.
Lorenzo, know'st thou not the common love
And kindness that Hieronimo hath won
By his deserts within the court of Spain?
Or seest thou not the King my brother's care
In his behalf, and to procure his health?
Lorenzo, shouldst thou thwart his passions
And he exclaim against thee to the King,
What honour were it in this assembly,
Or what a scandal were't among the Kings
To hear Hieronimo exclaim on thee!
Tell me, and look thou tell me truly too,
Whence grows the ground of this report in court?

LORENZO
My lord, it lies not in Lorenzo's power
To stop the vulgar, liberal of their tongues.
A small advantage makes a water-breach,
And no man lives that long contenteth all.

CASTILE
Myself have seen thee busy to keep back
Him and his supplications from the King.

LORENZO
Yourself, my lord, hath seen his passions,
That ill beseemed the presence of a King.
And for I pitied him in his distress,
I held him thence with kind and courteous words,
As free from malice to Hieronimo
As to my soul, my lord.

CASTILE
Hieronimo, my son, mistakes thee then?

LORENZO
My gracious father, believe me so he doth.
But what's a silly man distract in mind
To think upon the murder of his son?
Alas, how easy is it for him to err.
But for his satisfaction and the world's
'Twere good, my lord, that Hieronimo and I
Were reconciled, if he misconster me.

CASTILE
Lorenzo, thou hast said, it shall be so.
Go one of you and call Hieronimo.

[*Exit servant.*]
Enter Balthazar and Bel-Imperia.

BALTHAZAR
Come Bel-Imperia, Balthazar's content,
My sorrow's ease and sovereign of my bliss,
Sith heaven hath ordained thee to be mine
Disperse those clouds and melancholy looks,
And clear them up with those thy sun-bright eyes,
Wherein my hope and heaven's fair beauty lies.

BEL-IMPERIA
My looks, my lord, are fitting for my love,
Which, new begun, can show no brighter yet.

BALTHAZAR
New-kindled flames should burn as morning sun.

BEL-IMPERIA
But not too fast, lest heat and all be done.
I see my lord, my father.

BALTHAZAR
Truce, my love,
I will go salute him.

CASTILE
Welcome Balthazar,
Welcome brave Prince, the pledge of Castile's peace,
And welcome Bel-Imperia. How now, girl?
Why com'st thou sadly to salute us thus?
Content thyself for I am satisfied:
It is not now as when Andrea lived,
We have forgotten and forgiven that,
And thou art gracèd with a happier love.
But Balthazar, here comes Hieronimo,
I'll have a word with him.

Enter Hieronimo and a servant.

HIERONIMO
And where's the Duke?

SERVANT
Yonder.

HIERONIMO
Even so.
[*Aside.*] What new device have they devisèd, trow?
Pocas palabras, mild as the lamb
Is't I will be revenged? No, I am not the man.

CASTILE
Welcome Hieronimo.

LORENZO
Welcome Hieronimo.

BALTHAZAR
Welcome Hieronimo.

HIERONIMO
My lords, I thank you for Horatio.

CASTILE
Hieronimo, the reason that I sent

To speak with you, is this.

HIERONIMO

What, so short?
Then I'll be gone, I thank you for't.

[*Offers to go*]

CASTILE

Nay, stay Hieronimo! Go call him, son.

LORENZO

Hieronimo, my father craves a word with you.

HIERONIMO

With me sir? Why, my lord, I thought you had done.

LORENZO

[*Aside.*] No, would he had.

CASTILE

Hieronimo, I hear
You find yourself aggrievèd at my son
Because you have not access unto the King,
And say 'tis he that intercepts your suits.

HIERONIMO

Why, is not this a miserable thing, my lord?

CASTILE

Hieronimo, I hope you have no cause,
And would be loath that one of your deserts
Should once have reason to suspect my son,
Considering how I think of you myself.

HIERONIMO

Your son Lorenzo? Whom, my noble lord?
The hope of Spain, mine honourable friend?
Grant me the combat of them if they dare:

Draws out his sword.

I'll meet him face to face to tell me so.
These be the scandalous reports of such
As love not me, and hate my lord too much.
Should I suspect Lorenzo would prevent
Or cross my suit, that loved my son so well?
My lord, I am ashamed it should be said.

LORENZO

Hieronimo, I never gave you cause.

HIERONIMO
My good lord, I know you did not.

CASTILE
There then pause,
And for the satisfaction of the world,
Hieronimo, frequent my homely house,
The Duke of Castile, Cyprian's ancient seat,
And when thou wilt, use me, my son, and it.
But here, before Prince Balthazar and me,
Embrace each other, and be perfect friends.
[*They embrace.*]

HIERONIMO
Ay, marry my lord, and shall:
'Friends', quoth he? See, I'll be friends with you all.
[*To Lorenzo*] Specially with you, my lovely lord,
For divers causes it is fit for us
That we be friends. The world is suspicious,
And men may think what we imagine not.

BALTHAZAR
Why, this is friendly done, Hieronimo.

LORENZO
And thus, I hope, old grudges are forgot.

HIERONIMO
What else? It were a shame it should not be so.

CASTILE
Come on Hieronimo, at my request,
Let us entreat your company today.

Exeunt [*all but Hieronimo.*]

HIERONIMO
Your lordship's to command. – Pah! keep your way.
Mi!
Chi mi fa piu carezze che non sole,
Tradito mi ha, o tradir mi vole.

Exit.

[4.9]

Enter ghost [of Andrea] and Revenge.

ANDREA
Awake, Erichtho! Cerberus, awake!
Solicit Pluto, gentle Proserpine,
To combat Acheron and Erebus in hell.
For ne'er by Styx and Phlegethon
Oe'r-ferried Charon to the fiery lakes,
Such fearful sights as poor Andrea sees!
Revenge, awake!

REVENGE
Awake? For why?

ANDREA
Awake, Revenge, for thou art ill-advised
To sleep. Awake! What, thou art warned to watch!

REVENGE
Content thyself, and do not trouble me.

ANDREA
Awake, Revenge, if love, as love hath had,
Have yet the power or prevalence in hell!
Hieronimo with Lorenzo is joined in league
And intercepts our passage to revenge.
Awake, Revenge, or we are woe-begone!

REVENGE
Thus worldlings ground what they have dreamed upon.
Content thyself, Andrea; though I sleep
Yet is my mood soliciting their souls.
Sufficeth thee that poor Hieronimo
Cannot forget his son Horatio.
Nor dies Revenge although he sleep awhile,
For in unquiet, quietness is feigned:
And slumb'ring is a common worldly wile.
Behold, Andrea, for an instance how
Revenge hath slept, and then imagine thou
What 'tis to be subject to destiny.

Enter a dumb show.

ANDREA
Awake Revenge, reveal this mystery.

REVENGE
The two first, the nuptial torches bear,
As brightly burning as the mid-day's sun.
But after them doth Hymen hie as fast,
Clothèd in sable and a saffron robe,
And blows them out, and quenches them with blood,
As discontent that things continue so.

ANDREA
Sufficeth me, thy meaning's understood,
And thanks to thee and those infernal powers
That will not tolerate a lover's woe.
Rest thee, for I will sit to see the rest.

REVENGE
Then argue not, for thou hast thy request.

Exeunt.

* * * * *

[5.1]

Enter Bel-Imperia and Hieronimo.

BEL-IMPERIA
Is this the love thou bear'st Horatio?
Is this the kindness that thou counterfeits?
Are these the fruits of thine incessant tears?
Hieronimo, are these thy passions,
Thy protestations, and thy deep laments,
That thou wert wont to weary men withal?
O unkind father, O deceitful world,
With what excuses canst thou show thyself,
With what dishonour, and the hate of men,
From this dishonour and the hate of men?
Thus to neglect the loss and life of him,
Whom both my letters, and thine own belief,
Assures thee to be causeless slaughterèd.
Hieronimo, for shame Hieronimo!
Be not a history to after times
Of such ingratitude unto thy son!
Unhappy mothers of such children then!
But monstrous fathers, to forget so soon
The death of those whom they with care and cost

Have tendered so, thus careless should be lost!
Myself, a stranger in respect of thee,
So loved his life, as still I wish their deaths,
Nor shall his death be unrevenged by me,
Although I bear it out for fashion's sake.
For here I swear in sight of heaven and earth,
Shouldst thou neglect the love thou shouldst retain,
And give it over and devise no more,
Myself should send their hateful souls to hell
That wrought his downfall with extremest death!

HIERONIMO
But may it be that Bel-Imperia
Vows such revenge as she hath deigned to say?
Why then, I see that heaven applies our drift,
And all the saints do sit soliciting
For vengeance on those cursed murderers!
Madam 'tis true, and now I find it so,
I found a letter written in your name,
And in that letter, how Horatio died.
Pardon, O pardon Bel-Imperia,
My fear and care in not believing it,
Nor think I, thoughtless, think upon a mean
To let his death be unrevenged at full.
And here I vow (so you but give consent
And will conceal my resolution)
I will ere long determine of their deaths,
That causeless thus have murderèd my son.

BEL-IMPERIA
Hieronimo, I will consent, conceal,
And aught that may effect for thine avail,
Join with thee to revenge Horatio's death.

HIERONIMO
On then, whatsoever I devise,
Let me entreat you grace my practices;
For why, the plot's already in mine head,
– Here they are.

Enter Balthazar and Lorenzo.

BALTHAZAR
How now, Hieronimo?
What, courting Bel-Imperia?

HIERONIMO
Ay my lord,
Such courting as, I promise you
She hath my heart but you, my lord, have hers.

LORENZO
But now Hieronimo, or never,
We are to entreat your help.

HIERONIMO
My help?
Why, my good lords, assure yourselves of me,
For you have given me cause,
Ay, by my faith have you.

BALTHAZAR
It pleasèd you,
At the entertainment of the Ambassador,
To grace the King so much as with a show.
Now, were your study so well furnishèd,
As for the passing of the first night's sport,
To entertain my father with the like
Or any such-like pleasing motion,
Assure yourself, it would content them well.

HIERONIMO
Is this all?

BALTHAZAR
Ay, this is all.

HIERONIMO
Why then, I'll fit you, say no more!
When I was young, I gave my mind,
And plied myself to fruitless poetry,
Which, though it profit the professor naught,
Yet is it passing pleasing to the world.

LORENZO
And how for that?

HIERONIMO
Marry, my good lord, thus –
And yet, methinks you are too quick with us –
When in Toledo there I studied
It was my chance to write a tragedy.
See here my lords,

He shows them a book.

Which long forgot, I found this other day,
Now, would your lordships favour me so much
As but to grace me with your acting it –
I mean each one of you to play a part.
Assure you, it will prove most passing strange,
And wondrous plausible to that assembly.

BALTHAZAR
What, would you have us play a tragedy?

HIERONIMO
Why, Nero thought it no disparagement,
And Kings and emperors have ta'en delight
To make experience of their wits in plays!

LORENZO
Nay, be not angry, good Hieronimo,
The Prince but asked a question.

BALTHAZAR
In faith Hieronimo, an' you be in earnest
I'll make one.

LORENZO
And I another.

HIERONIMO
Now my good lord, could you entreat,
Your sister Bel-Imperia to make one –
For what's a play without a woman in it?

BEL-IMPERIA
Little entreaty shall serve me, Hieronomo,
For I must needs be employed in your play.

HIERONIMO
Why, this is well! I tell you, lordings,
It was determinèd to have been acted
By gentlemen, and scholars too,
Such as could tell what to speak.

BALTHAZAR
And now it shall be played by Princes and courtiers,
Such as can tell how to speak.
If, as it is our country manner,
You will but let us know the argument.

HIERONIMO
That shall I roundly. The Chronicles of Spain
Record this written of a Knight of Rhodes,
He was betrothed, and wedded at the length
To one Perseda, an Italian dame,
Whose beauty ravished all that her beheld,
Especially the soul of Soliman,
Who at the marriage was the chiefest guest.
By sundry means sought Soliman to win
Perseda's love and could not gain the same.
Then 'gan he break his passions to a friend,
One of his Bashaws whom he held full dear.
Her had this Bashaw long solicited,
And saw she was not otherwise to be won
But by her husband's death, this Knight of Rhodes,
Whom presently by treachery he slew.
She, stirred with an exceeding hate therefor,
As cause of this slew Soliman.
And to escape the Bashaw's tyranny,
Did stab herself; and this the tragedy.

LORENZO
O excellent!

BEL-IMPERIA
But say, Hieronimo,
What then became of him that was the Bashaw?

HIERONIMO
Marry thus: moved with remorse of his misdeeds,
Ran to a mountain top and hung himself.

BALTHAZAR
But which of us is to perform that part?

HIERONIMO
Oh that will I, my lords, make no doubt of it:
I'll play the murderer, I warrant you,
For I already have conceited that.

BALTHAZAR
And what shall I?

HIERONIMO
Great Soliman, the Turkish emperor.

LORENZO
And I?

HIERONIMO
Erastus, the Knight of Rhodes.

BEL-IMPERIA
And I?

HIERONIMO
Perseda, chaste and resolute.
And here, my lords, are several abstracts drawn
For each of you to note your parts,
And act it as occasion's offered you.

Gives a paper to Balthazar.

You must provide a Turkish cap,
A black mustachio, and a falchion.

Gives another to Lorenzo.

You with a cross like to a Knight of Rhodes.

He gives Bel-Imperia another.

And madam, you must attire yourself
Like Phoebe, Flora, or the huntress,
Which to your discretion shall seem best.
And as for me, my lords, I'll look to one,
And with the ransom that the Viceroy sent
So furnish and perform this tragedy
As all the world shall say, Hieronimo,
Was liberal in gracing of it so.

BALTHAZAR
Hieronimo, methinks a comedy were better.

HIERONIMO
A comedy? Fie! Comedies are fit for common wits;
But to present a Kingly troop withal,
Give me a stately written tragedy,
Tragedia cothurnata, fitting Kings,
Containing matter, and not common things.
My lords, all this must be performed
As fitting for the first night's revelling.
The Italian tragedians were so sharp of wit
That, in one hour's meditation,
They would perform anything in action.

LORENZO
And well it may, for I have seen the like
In Paris, amongst the French tragedians.

HIERONIMO
In Paris? Mass, and well rememberèd!
There's one thing more that rests for us to do.

BALTHAZAR
What's that, Hieronimo? Forget not anything.

HIERONIMO
Each one of us must act his part
In unknown languages,
That it may breed the more variety.
As you my lord in Latin, I in Greek,
You in Italian, and, for because I know
That Bel-Imperia hath practisèd the French,
In courtly French shall all her phrases be.

BEL-IMPERIA
You mean to try my cunning then, Hieronimo?

BALTHAZAR
But this will be a mere confusion,
And hardly shall we all be understood.

HIERONIMO
It must be so, for the conclusion
Shall prove the invention and all was good.
And I myself, in an oration
And with a strange and wondrous show besides,
That I will have there behind a curtain,
Assure yourself shall make the matter known.
And all shall be concluded in one scene,
For there's no pleasure taken in tediousness.

BALTHAZAR [*aside to Lorenzo*]
How like you this?

LORENZO [*aside to Balthazar*]
Why thus, my lord:
We must resolve to soothe his humours up.

BALTHAZAR
On then Hieronimo, farewell till soon!

HIERONIMO
You'll ply this gear?

LORENZO
I warrant you.

Exeunt all but Hieronimo.

HIERONIMO
Why, so:
Now shall I see the fall of Babylon,
Wrought by the heavens in this confusion.
And if the world like not this tragedy,
Hard is the hap of old Hieronimo.

Exit.

[5.2]

[*Arbour set forth.*] *Enter Isabella with a weapon.*

ISABELLA
Tell me no more! O monstrous homicides!
Since neither piety nor pity moves
The King to justice or compassion,
I will revenge myself upon this place
Where thus they murdered my beloved son.
She cuts down the arbour.
Down with these branches, and these loathsome boughs
Of this unfortunate and fatal pine.
Down with them Isabella, rent them up,
And burn the roots from whence the rest is sprung!
I will not leave a root, a stalk, a tree,
A bough, a branch, a blossom, nor a leaf,
No, not an herb within this garden plot –
Accursed complot of my misery!
Fruitless for ever may this garden be,
Barren the earth, and blissless whosoever
Imagines not to keep it unmanured!
An eastern wind commixed with noisome airs
Shall blast the plants and the young saplings.
The earth with serpents shall be pesterèd,
And passengers for fear to be infect
Shall stand aloof, and looking at it, tell:
'There, murdered, died the son of Isabel.'
Ay, here he died, and here I him embrace.

See where his ghost solicits, with his wounds,
Revenge on her that should revenge his death!
Hieronimo, make haste to see thy son,
For sorrow and despair hath cited me
To hear Horatio plead with Rhadamanth.
Make haste, Hieronimo, to hold excused
Thy negligence in pursuit of their deaths,
Whose hateful wrath bereaved him of his breath!
Ah nay, thou dost delay their deaths,
Forgives the murderers of thy noble son,
And none but I bestir me – to no end.
And as I curse this tree from further fruit,
So shall my womb be cursèd for his sake!
And with this weapon will I wound the breast,

She stabs herself.

The hapless breast that gave Horatio suck. *[Dies.]*

[5.3]

Enter Hieronimo, he knocks up the curtain.
Enter the Duke of Castile.

CASTILE
How now Hieronimo, where's your fellows,
That you take all this pain?

HIERONIMO
O sir, it is for the author's credit
To look that all things may go well.
But good my lord, let me entreat your grace
To give the King the copy of the play:
This is the argument of what we show.

Gives him [the summary.]

CASTILE
I will, Hieronimo.

HIERONIMO
One thing more, my good lord.

CASTILE
What's that?

HIERONIMO
Let me entreat your grace,
That when the train are passed into the gallery

You would vouchsafe to throw me down the key.

CASTILE
I will, Hieronimo.

Exit

HIERONIMO
What, are you ready, Balthazar?
Bring a chair and a cushion for the King.

Enter Balthazar with a chair [a cushion, a title-board and a beard]

Well done Balthazar. Hang up the title:
Our scene is 'Rhodes'. – What, is your beard on?

BALTHAZAR
Half on, the other is in my hand.

HIERONIMO
Dispatch for shame, are you so long?

Exit Balthazar.

Bethink thyself, Hieronimo!
Recall thy wits, recount thy former wrongs
Thou hast received by murder of thy son,
And lastly, not least, how Isabel,
Once his mother and thy dearest wife:
All woe-begone for him, hath slain herself.
Behoves thee then, Hieronimo, to be revenged!
The plot is laid of dire revenge:
On then, Hieronimo, pursue revenge,
For nothing wants but acting of revenge.

Exit Hieronimo.

[5.4]

Enter Spanish King, Viceroy, the Duke of Castile, [*Don Pedro*] *and their train.*

KING
Now Viceroy, shall we see the tragedy
Of Soliman the Turkish emperor,
Performed of pleasure by your son the Prince,
My nephew Don Lorenzo, and my niece?

VICEROY
Who, Bel-Imperia?

KING
Ay, and Hieronimo our Marshal,
At whose request they deign to do't themselves.
These be our pastimes in the court of Spain.
Here brother, you shall be the bookkeeper:
This is the argument of that they show.

He gives him a book.

<Gentlemen, this play of Hieronimo in sundry languages was thought good to be set down in English more largely for the easier understanding to every public reader.>

Enter Balthazar [as Soliman], Bel-Imperia [as Perseda], and Hieronimo [as Bashaw].

BALTHAZAR
Bashaw, that Rhodes is ours, yield heavens the honour,
And holy Mahomet, our sacred prophet.
And be thou graced with every excellence
That Soliman can give, or thou desire.
But thy desert in conquering Rhodes is less
Than in reserving this fair Christian nymph,
Perseda, blissful lamp of excellence,
Whose eyes compel, like powerful adamant,
The warlike heart of Soliman to wait.

KING
See Viceroy, that is Balthazar your son
That represents the Emperor Soliman.
How well he acts his amorous passion!

VICEROY
Ay, Bel-Imperia hath taught him that.

CASTILE
That's because his mind runs all on Bel-Imperia.

HIERONIMO
Whatever joy earth yields betide your majesty –

BALTHAZAR
Earth yields no joy without Perseda's love –

HIERONIMO
Let then Perseda on your grace attend.

BALTHAZAR
She shall not wait on me, but I on her.
Drawn by the influence of her lights, I yield.
But let my friend, the Rhodian knight, come forth,
Erasto, dearer than my life to me,
That he may see Perseda, my beloved.

Enter [*Lorenzo as*] *Erasto.*

KING
Here comes Lorenzo; look upon the plot,
And tell me, brother, what part plays he?

BEL-IMPERIA
Ah my Erasto, welcome to Perseda.

LORENZO
Thrice happy is Erasto that thou livest,
Rhodes' loss is nothing to Erasto's joy.
Sith his Perseda lives, his life survives.

BALTHAZAR [*aside to Hieronimo*]
Ah Bashaw, here is love between Erasto
And fair Perseda, sovereign of my soul

HIERONIMO [*aside to Balthazar*]
Remove Erasto, mighty Soliman,
And then Perseda will be quickly won.

[*They continue to confer aside*]

BALTHAZAR
Erasto is my friend, and while he lives
Perseda never will remove her love.

HIERONIMO
Let not Erasto live, to grieve great Soliman.

BALTHAZAR
Dear is Erasto in our Princely eye.

HIERONIMO
But if he be your rival, let him die.

BALTHAZAR
Why let him die, so love commandeth me:
Yet grieve I that Erasto should so die.

HIERONIMO [*Approaches Lorenzo*]
Erasto, Soliman saluteth thee,

And lets thee wit by me his highness' will,
Which is, thou shouldst be thus employed.

Stabs him.

BEL-IMPERIA
Ay me,
Erasto! See, Soliman, Erasto's slain!

BALTHAZAR
Yet liveth Soliman to comfort thee.
Fair queen of beauty, let not favour die,
But with a gracious eye behold his grief,
That with Perseda's beauty is increased,
If by Perseda's grief be not released.

BEL-IMPERIA
Tyrant, desist soliciting vain suits.
Relentless are mine ears to thy laments,
As this thy butcher is pitiless and base,
Which seized on my Erasto, harmless knight.
Yet by thy power thou thinkest to command,
And to thy power Perseda doth obey.
But were she able, thus she would revenge
Thy treacheries on thee, ignoble Prince:

Stabs him.

And on herself she would be thus revenged!

Stabs herself.

KING
Well said, old Marshal, this was bravely done!

HIERONIMO
But Bel-Imperia plays Perseda well.

VICEROY
Were this in earnest, Bel-Imperia,
You would be better to my son than so.

KING
But now what follows for Hieronimo?

HIERONIMO
Marry, this follows for Hieronimo –
Here break we off our sundry languages,
And thus conclude I in our vulgar tongue.
Haply you think, but bootless are your thoughts,
That this is fabulously counterfeit,

And that we do as all tragedians do.
To die today (for fashioning our scene)
The death of Ajax, or some Roman peer,
And in a minute starting up again,
Revive to please tomorrow's audience.
No, Princes, know I am Hieronimo,
The hopeless father of a hapless son,
Whose tongue is tuned to tell his latest tale,
Not to excuse gross errors in the play.
I see your looks urge instance of these words,
Behold the reason urging me to this:
[*Draws the curtain and*] *shows his dead son.*
See here my show, look on this spectacle:
Here lay my hope, and here my hope hath end;
Here lay my heart, and here my heart was slain;
Here lay my treasure, here my treasure lost;
Here lay my bliss, and here my bliss bereft.
But hope, heart, treasure, joy, and bliss:
All fled, failed, died, yea, all decayed with this.
From forth these wounds came breath that gave me life,
They murdered me that made these fatal marks.
The cause was love, whence grew this mortal hate:
The hate, Lorenzo and young Balthazar,
The love, my son to Bel-Imperia.
But night, the coverer of accursèd crimes,
With pitchy silence hushed these traitors' harms
And lent them leave. For they had sorted leisure
To take advantage in my garden plot
Upon my son, my dear Horatio.
There, merciless, they butchered up my boy,
In black dark night, to pale dim cruel death.
He shrieks, I heard, and yet methinks I hear
His dismal outcry echo in the air!
With soonest speed I hasted to the noise,
Where, hanging on a tree, I found my son,
Through-girt with wounds, and slaughtered, as you see.
And grieved I, think you, at this spectacle?
Speak, Portuguese, whose loss resembles mine:
If thou canst weep upon thy Balthazar
'Tis like I wailed for my Horatio.
[*to Castile*] And you, my lord whose reconcilèd son
Marched in a net, and thought himself unseen,

And rated me for brainsick lunacy
With 'God amend that mad Hieronimo!'–
How can you brook our play's catastrophe?
And here behold this bloody handkercher,
[*Draws out a bloody napkin*]
Which at Horatio's death I, weeping, dipped
Within the river of his bleeding wounds.
It as propitious, see I have reserved,
And never hath it left my bloody heart,
Soliciting remembrance of my vow.
With these, O these accursèd murderers,
Which now performed, my heart is satisfied.
And to this end the Bashaw I became,
That might revenge me on Lorenzo's life;
Who therefore was appointed to the part,
And was to represent the Knight of Rhodes.
That I might kill him more conveniently.
So, Viceroy, was this Balthazar, thy son,
That Soliman, which Bel-Imperia
In person of Perseda murdered,
Solely appointed to that tragic part
That she might slay him that offended her.
Poor Bel-Imperia missed her part in this,
For though the story saith she should have died,
Yet I of kindness, and of care to her
Did otherwise determine of her end.
But love of him whom they did hate too much,
Did urge her resolution to be such.
And Princes, now behold Hieronimo,
Author and actor in this tragedy:
[*holding a rope in his hand*]
Bearing his latest fortune in his fist,
And will as resolute conclude his part
As any of the actors gone before.
And gentles, thus I end my play:
Urge no more words, I have no more to say.
He runs to hang himself.

KING
O hearken, Viceroy! Hold, Hieronimo!
Brother, my nephew and thy son are slain!

VICEROY
We are betrayed! My Balthazar is slain!
Break open the doors, run, save Hieronimo!
[*Attendants break in, and hold Hieronimo.*]
Hieronimo, do but inform the King of these events,
Upon mine honour thou shalt have no harm.

HIERONIMO
Viceroy, I will not trust thee with my life,
Which I this day have offered to my son.
Accursèd wretch, why stayest thou him that was resolved to die?

KING
Speak, traitor: damnèd, bloody murderer, speak!
For now I have thee I will make thee speak.
Why hast thou done this undeserving deed?

VICEROY
Why hast thou murderèd my Balthazar?

CASTILE
Why hast thou butchered both my children thus?

HIERONIMO
O good words!
As dear to me was my Horatio,
As yours, or yours, or yours, my lord to you.
My guiltless son was by Lorenzo slain,
And by Lorenzo and that Balthazar,
Am I at last revengèd thoroughly.
Upon whose souls may heavens be yet avenged
With greater far than these afflictions!

CASTILE
But who were thy confederates in this?

VICEROY
That was thy daughter Bel-Imperia,
For by her hand my Balthazar was slain:
I saw her stab him.

KING
Why speakst thou not?

HIERONIMO
What lesser liberty can Kings afford
Than harmless silence? Then afford it me:

Sufficeth I may not, nor I will not tell thee.

KING
Fetch forth the tortures!
Traitor as thou art, I'll make thee tell.

HIERONIMO
Indeed
Thou mayst torment me, as his wretched son
Hath done in murdering my Horatio.
But never shalt thou force me to reveal
The thing which I have vowed inviolate.
And therefore, in despite of all thy threats,
Pleased with their deaths, and eased with their revenge:
First take my tongue, and afterwards my heart!

He bites out his tongue.

KING
O monstrous resolution of a wretch!
See, Viceroy, he hath bitten forth his tongue!
Rather than to reveal what we required.

CASTILE
Yet can he write.

KING
And if in this he satisfy us not,
We will devise th'extremest kind of death
That ever was invented for a wretch.

Then he makes signs for a knife to mend his pen.

CASTILE
Oh, he would have a knife to mend his pen.

VICEROY
Here, and advise thee that thou write the troth.

Hieronimo with a knife stabs the Duke of Castile and himself [*to death*].

KING
Look to my brother! Save Hieronimo!

KING
What age hath ever heard such monstrous deeds?
My brother, and the whole succeeding hope
That Spain expected after my decease!
Go bear his body hence, that we may mourn

The loss of our belovèd brother's death,
That he may be entombed whate'er befall.
I am the next, the nearest, last of all.

VICEROY
And thou, Don Pedro, do the like for us,
Take up our hapless son, untimely slain.
Set me with him, and he with woeful me
Upon the mainmast of a ship unmanned,
And let the wind and tide haul me along
To Scylla's barking and untamèd gulf,
Or to the loathsome pool of Acheron,
To weep my want for my sweet Balthazar;
Spain hath no refuge for a Portuguese.

The trumpets sound a dead march, the King of Spain mourning after his brother's body, and the King of Portugal bearing the body of his son. [*Exeunt.*]

[5.5]

Enter Ghost and Revenge.

ANDREA
Ay, now my hopes have end in their effects,
When blood and sorrow finish my desires:
Horatio murdered in his father's bower;
Vild Serberine by Pedringano slain;
False Pedringano hanged by quaint device;
Fair Isabella by herself misdone;
Prince Balthazar by Bel-Imperia stabbed;
The Duke of Castile and his wicked son
Both done to death by old Hieronimo;
My Bel-Imperia fallen as Dido fell;
And good Hieronimo slain by himself.
Ay, these were spectacles to please my soul!
Now will I beg at lovely Proserpine,
That by the virtue of her Princely doom
I may consort my friends in pleasing sort,
And on my foes work just and sharp revenge.
I'll lead my friend Horatio through those fields
Where never-dying wars are still inured.
I'll lead fair Isabella to that train
Where pity weeps but never feeleth pain.
I'll lead my Bel-Imperia to those joys

That vestal virgins, and fair queens possess.
I'll lead Hieronimo where Orpheus plays,
Adding sweet pleasure to eternal days.
But say, Revenge, for thou must help or none,
Against the rest how shall my hate be shown?

REVENGE
This hand shall hale them down to deepest hell,
Where none but Furies, bugs, and tortures dwell.

ANDREA
Then, sweet Revenge, do this at my request,
Let me be judge, and doom them to unrest.
Let loose poor Tityus from the vultures' gripe,
And let Don Cyprian supply his room.
Place Don Lorenzo on Ixion's wheel,
And let the lover's endless pains surcease –
Juno forgets old wrath and grants him ease.
Hang Balthazar about Chimera's neck,
And let him there bewail his bloody love,
Repining at our joys that are above.
Let Serberine go roll the fatal stone,
And take from Sisyphus his endless moan.
False Pedringano, for his treachery,
Let him be dragged through boiling Acheron,
And there live, dying still in endless flames,
Blaspheming gods and all their holy names!

REVENGE
Then haste we down to meet thy friends and foes,
To place thy friends in ease, the rest in woes.
For here, though death hath end their misery,
I'll there begin their endless tragedy.

Exeunt.

FINIS

TEXTUAL NOTES

For a detailed description of the eleven Quarto editions from 1592 to 1633, and modern editions from Dodsley 1744 to his own 1898 pocket edition for Gollancz's 'Temple Dramatists' series, see Josef Schick (ed.), *Thomas Kyd's Spanish Tragedy, I. Kritischer Text und Apparat* (Berlin, 1901), pp. X–LXXXXI. In defining his 'text-critical principles' (LXXXXI–CIII) Schick makes many astute observations on prosody and lineation. In their recent edition (London, 2013; pp. 85–112), Clara Calvo and Jesús Tronch give a concise survey of the textual tradition up to the present day, including the 'Additions' printed in Q4 (1602) often attributed to Shakespeare.

1.1

36 Minos' engraven] CALVO-TRONCH; *Minos in graven* Q1

1.2

53 rain] COLLIER; *ran* Q1
102 the] SCHICK 1898; *this* Q1
179 set] *conj* EDWARDS; *sit* Q1

1.3

29 in] DODSLEY; not in Q1

1.4

35 wielding] SCHICK 1898; *welding* Q1
146 English] BEVINGTON; *the English* Q1
174 thy] SCHICK 1898; *the* Q1

2.2

9 may] Q4; *mad* Q1
33 war] DODSLEY; *warring* Q1

3.1

92 Wherein] HAZLITT; *Or wherein* Q1

3.2

98 *Chi l'è?* Jeron!] CRAIK; *Che le Ieron* Q1

3.4
77 fee] *conj* EDWARDS; *see* Q1

4.2
22 That lived] Q2; *That died* Q1

4.4
75 Etna for] Q2; *Etna and* Q1

4.5
23 fumes,] *conj* MULRYNE; *fumes.* Q1

4.6
80 that all the] HAZLITT; *that the* Q1

4.7
52 There is] HAWKINS; *There's* Q1
156 fate] DODSLEY; *Father* Q1

4.8
105 show no] Q2; *show* Q1
177–9 *Mi!... vole.*] As in CALVO-TRONCH; Q1 garbles this passage

4.9
5 O'er-ferried Charon] SCHICK 1898; *Nor ferried Charon* Q1
10 To sleep. Awake!] Q10; *Th sleepe, away,* Q1

5.4
24 majesty –] this edition; *majesty.* Q1
25 love –] this edition; *love.* Q1

COMMENTARY

Act 1, scene 1

0 SD Both characters enter on the main stage; at the end of the scene, they move up to the gallery above the stage, where they sit for the remainder of the play.

2 wanton lascivious: see line 10 on his clandestine affair with Bel-Imperia.

8 prime and pride the most flourishing state of life.

10 secret Necessarily so, due to the gap in social rank. Her father is the Duke of Castile, who in a later scene declares that he has 'forgotten and forgiven' her previous liaison with Andrea, a mere courtier (3.14.112).

11 Which hight who was called.

15 late conflict recent; there were several conflicts between Spain and Portugal in the 1580s.

18–83 For the ghost's account of his journey to and from the underworld Kyd draws on Virgil's description of Aeneas's descent to Hades, *Aeneid* 6.295–713. References are to the Loeb Classical Library edition: *Virgil, Eclogues, Georgics, Aeneid* 1–6, tr. H. R. Fairclough, revd F. P. Goold (Cambridge, MA and London, 1999).

19 Acheron one of the five rivers in the lower world, 'thick with mire and of fathomless flood' (*Aen.* 6.295).

20 churlish Charon the ferryman who conveyed the souls of those properly buried across the rivers in Hades. Virgil describes him as 'terrible in his squalor … on whose chin lies a mass of unkempt, hoary hair' (6.298–301).

23 Sol … Thetis in Roman mythology the sun god and a sea divinity; **three nights** the time Andrea's ghost had to wait before Horatio had performed the necessary burial rituals.

25 Knight Marshal an official of the English royal household who acted as judge in disputes between the monarch's servants.

28 strand shore.

29 fell terrible; **Avernus** a lake that provided the entrance to the lower world.

30 pleasing … honeyed speech having charmed Cerberus, the three-headed dog guarding the entrance.

33 Minos, Aeacus, and Rhadamanth judges of the dead in the classical underworld. 'Minos, presiding, shakes the urn' (*Aen.* 6.432).

35 crave a passport request permission to pass.

36 engraven leaves of lottery 'records of allotted life' (Gibson). I prefer Calvo and Tronch's treatment of Q's 'ambiguous ... space between "in" and "graven" ... We interpret Q's reading as one word ... Thus, the subject of "*Drew forth*" is not Minos but the *leaves* themselves, which "displayed" or "delineated" the manner of Andrea's life and death' (p. 124).

38–53 Kyd engineers a dispute ('difference') between the judges that allows him to define Andrea as both a lover and a warrior ('Martialist', born under the influence of Mars).

42 fields of love region of the lower world where lovers are grouped, 'those whom stern Love has consumed with cruel wasting' (*Aen.* 6.440 ff).

44 myrtle trees ... cypress the symbols of love and mourning.

47 martial fields a neutral region, neither Elysium nor Tartarus, 'where the renowned in war dwell apart' (*Aen.* 6.475–8).

49 Achilles' Myrmidons a tribe of savage soldiers serving Achilles, the killer of Hector.

53 doom pronounce judgment on.

55 Pluto the Roman name for Hades, ruler of the underworld.

59 Three ways In *Aen.* 6.540–3 the Sybil describes two ways, one for virtuous people, to Elysium, the other for the punished, leading to Tartarus. Hieronimo describes the latter more fully later (3.11.13–29). Erne (p. 72) rightly sees that Kyd deliberately added a third path so that Andrea's ghost should see the dreadful punishments that the evil suffer (63–71), while allowing them to reach Elysium. There Andrea charms Proserpine (Persephone) who intercedes with Pluto to let him pass on. The punishments for the evil will recur in the closing scene.

82 gates of Horn Virgil (following Homer, *Odyssey* 19.562–7) describes 'two gates of sleep', one made of *cornea* (horn), which 'offers a ready exit to true shades', the other of polished ivory, which leads to 'delusive dreams' issuing from the world below.

88–9 Balthazar ... | Deprived of life by Bel-Imperia Elizabethan society, reluctant to think that women were capable of physical violence, would have been shocked by this prediction.

90 sit we down Presumably an alternative solution, to have Andrea's ghost and Revenge sitting on the stage rather than ascending to the gallery.

1.2

1 camp army.

12–14 O ... juris As Schick noted (1898, p. 135), Kyd adapted a passage from Claudian, *Panegyric on the Third Consulship of the Emperor Honorius (A.D. 396)*, 96–8: 'O [prince] greatly beloved by God, heaven fights on your side, and the conspiring peoples, on bended knee, fall down: victory is the sister of just right' (tr. Calvo and Tronch, 129). There are several other examples of Kyd following the fashion in Renaissance neo-Latin poetry of writing a passage of Latin verse into which the poet 'embeds' quotations from other works which are appropriate to the immediate dramatic context. Well-educated readers could appreciate both the poet's originality and his skill in adaptation. See Brian Vickers, 'Thomas Watson, Thomas Kyd, and Embedded Poetry', *Studies in Philology* 120:3 (Summer, 2023): 557–601.

20 wage reward.

21 chivalry military skill.

22–84 Such lengthy accounts of battles were popular set pieces in Elizabethan drama. As Boas pointed out, at 52–4 and 57–63, Kyd borrowed some details from Garnier's *Cornélie*, a long messenger speech describing the Battle of Thapsus. Kyd's translation, *Cornelia*, was published posthumously in 1594, but he was evidently acquainted with the play much earlier. He echoed these accounts again in *Edward III.*

27 vaunting ... device proudly displaying heraldic banners.

30 made rebound echoed.

33 battles ... squadron both battalions were arranged in square formation; **wings of shot** armed soldiers guarding the flanks.

34 push of pike close-quarter fighting.

38 ordnance played the artillery discharged their fire.

41 cornet troop of cavalry.

47 handy hand-to-hand.

50 rampiers ramparts.

52 Bellona Roman goddess of war.

54 shivered shattered, splintered.

55–6 Pede pes ... viro A cento of passages from Virgil, Statius and Curtius: 'Foot against foot, pike against pike, arms thundering on arms, and man attacked by man.' The Latin text uses four instances of the rhetorical figure *polyptoton*, repeating a word stem while varying its ending.

59 sundered separated.

61 unbowelled disembowelled.

67 dismayed routed.

70 Here-hence 'from this point forward' (*OED adv.*).

82 carbines 'mounted musketeers' (*OED*).

83 Phoebus ... deep A conventional account of the setting sun.

86 argument proof, token.

96 frolic rejoice.

100 tucket trumpet flourish.

103 reserved preserved.

107 demonstration visible proof.

135 tribute ... owes Tribute money is a form of tax paid by a vassal country to its superior. The Portuguese refusal to pay it had caused the war.

138 trespass crime.
139 controlled rebuked, held in check.
142 colours the flags or ensigns carried by the crack troops.
143 cor'sive corrosive.
144 clear acquit, discharge.
155 courser large battle horse.
162 strokes blows.
167 partial biased.
171 garment Referring to 'the Fourth Fable of Avian (in Caxton) concerning the ass who sports himself in a lion's skin which he has found' (Edwards). Cf. Caxton, *The fables of Esope in Englysshe ... Whereunto is added the fables of Avyan* (London, c. 1555; *STC* 179.5). Avianus (fifth century A.D.), a Roman fabulist whose main source was the Greek poet Babrius, enjoyed popularity in medieval schools.
177 set ... right forego my entitlement.
185 guard custody.
187 train attendants and servants.
188 passeth surpasses, exceeds.
192 proviso condition.

1.3
0 Location: The Portuguese court, with a throne
0 SD *Villuppo* According to Joseph Schick, in his 1898 edition, p. 140, '*Viluppo* ... means *confusion, entanglement.* We have an Italian play with the title *Il Viluppo*, by Girolamo Parabosco.' *The Cambridge Italian Dictionary*, ed. Barbara Reynolds (Cambridge, 1962), endorses those meanings, but adds: '*Villuppone* great confusion; † intriguer' [obsolete].
7 cares ... tears Cf. Seneca, *Phaedra* 607: '*Curae leves loquuntur, ingentes stupent*': 'light cares can speak; huge cares are dumbfounded.' There are many versions of this idea in Elizabethan drama.
15 Qui jacet in terra non habet unde cadat From Alanus de Insulis's collection of proverbs: 'If one lies on the ground, one can fall no further' (Edwards). Cf. Bunyan, *Pilgrim's Progress*: 'He that is down need fear no fall.'
16 In me ... nocendo Adapted from Seneca, *Agamemnon* 698: 'Fortune has used up all her resources.'
17 Nil ... magis 'there is nothing left that can harm me more' (Edwards). Kyd's own composition, unifying the two preceding allusions into an elegiac couplet, in which the first line is in dactylic hexameter, the second in dactylic pentameter.
20 sable weed black garment, signifying mourning.
29 rolling stone the traditional image for fortune's instability.

33–9 Kyd uses the rhetorical figure *anadiplosis*, in which a word (usually the last) of one line is repeated (usually to begin) the line following: 'ambition ... faith, faith ... wars, wars ... treasure, treasure ... blood, blood ... beloved, beloved ... son', ending on the most important word.

33 distained defiled, sullied.

35–6 treasure ... treasure Trisyllabic.

48 reck heed.

54 bewray reveal.

55 guerdon reward.

57 battery battered by blows.

59–70 Kyd provides two true narratives of the battle from the Spanish General (1.2.65–80) and Horatio (1.4.9–29, 32–43) in order to highlight this false account ('forgery', 72).

82 Terceira's lord ruler of an island in the Azores. The Viceroy suspects Alexandro of planning to supplant him.

1.4

0 Location: The Spanish court

7 nill will not.

16 Nemesis Greek goddess who was thought to punish both criminals and outstandingly fortunate people.

20 Pallas ... Pergamus the Greek goddess of wisdom supported the Greeks in the Trojan war (Pergamus: a citadel in Troy).

22 paunched stabbed in the belly; **dinged** knocked down.

27 remorse pity, compassion.

35 wielding carrying with effort.

44–5 The consecutive lines end with the same phrase (*would ... still*), an instance of the rhetorical figure *epistrophe*, used by Kyd many times in this play and elsewhere.

60–72 A dynamic soliloquy, in which Bel-Imperia resolves to adopt Horatio as a lover to help her gain revenge on Balthazar. It was unusual in early Elizabethan drama for a woman to plan revenge, but Kyd conceives Bel-Imperia as having the strength and determination of a man.

82 conceit Balthazar's love is imagined, not real.

90 ambages roundabout utterances.

99 SD *lets fall her glove* Bel-Imperia provocatively favours Horatio.

105 humorous capricious, variable.

116 SD *banquet* light meal, easily portable.

137 pompous stately; **SD *scutcheon*** shield with coat of arms.

138–74 Hieronimo presents a dumbshow of three famous victories by English soldiers in Spain and Portugal. Many of the details are unhistorical.

178 dispatched allowed to return home once a peace treaty has been agreed.

1.5
6 fell despite violent desire to harm.

2.1 Location: either the Duke of Castile's castle or Lorenzo's palace.
1 coy unresponsive.
3–10 In time … stony wall Attempting to encourage Balthazar's patience, Lorenzo quotes from Sonnet 47 in Thomas Watson's *Hekatompathia* (1582). But Balthazar caps those lines with Watson's concluding rejection of hope. Although unacknowledged, Watson's source was a passage in Ovid's *Ars Amatoria*, 1.467–78. See Brian Vickers, 'Thomas Watson, Thomas Kyd, and the Re-Use of Ovid', *Notes and Queries* 266:1 (March 2021): 99–100.
4 haggard untamed; **stoop to lure** During a hawk's training their master would recall the bird to feed from the 'lure' or bait.
16 Pan and Marsyas The god Pan and the peasant Marsyas each challenged the god Apollo to a musical contest: both lost and were punished.
19–28 Kyd gives Balthazar a carefully patterned rhetorical sequence of rhyming couplets in which each utterance is denied by the one following, conveying his inability to reach a decision.
29 ecstasies unreasoning passions.
36 doubtful theme unresolved argument.
41 Vien qui presto 'Come here quickly'. Italian is the language of the Machiavellian intriguer: cf. also Lorenzo's words ending 3.4.
47 conveyance clandestine or underhand service.
48–9 punishment … punishment the figure *epistrophe*; again at 57–8.
58 If case i.e., 'In case I am able to tell the truth.'
67 dally trifle, play with.
77 if's and an's indeterminate answers.
85 Full fraught richly laden.
87 cross his sword-hilt, in the shape of Christ's cross.
107 tam armis quam ingenio 'as much by force as by guile'. A cynical reworking of the phrase *tam Marti quam Mercurio*, 'as much for war as for eloquence', the motto of George Gascoigne, subsequently adopted by Raleigh.
111–33 Both well, and ill Kyd gives Balthazar another carefully structured speech with little forward momentum, the style showing the character.
126 limed made into traps, like the sticky lime spread on branches to catch birds.

2.2
4 contents sources of satisfaction.
7 friend also 'lover'.

7–17 Unusually for a woman in Elizabethan drama, Bel-Imperia takes the initiative with this declaration of love, carefully formulated over eight lines. Kyd frames it with two couplets ('joy', 'annoy', 'choir', 'desire') surrounding a quatrain ('port', 'fussed', 'resort', 'lost'). The answering three-line speeches of Balthazar and Lorenzo, the one suffering, the other plotting revenge, form a sestet, the last six lines of a Petrarchan sonnet with partial rhymes ('discontent', 'lament'). The effect is simultaneously one of concord and discord.

18–23, 28, 31, 41, 56–7 I have used round brackets to mark the comments by the eavesdroppers Balthazar and Lorenzo, inaudible to the lovers.

23 fond foolish.

41 villain in the original sense of 'low-born man'.

45 Vesper the evening star.

48–50 nightingale A tradition held that the nightingale sang with its breast against a thorn, kept awake by the pain.

56 jealous Trisyllabic.

54–8 The scene ends with four lines using the same rhyme, one happy couplet from Horatio ('sight', 'delight'), the other sinister from Lorenzo ('despite', 'night'). For readers and theatregoers, the lovers' anticipation of happiness has already been blotted out.

2.3

3 coy behaves coyly ('coy' as a verb is unusual).

5 stoop become obedient, as the hawk does when trained.

6 froward obstinate, difficult.

15 Cyprian Duke Cyprian, brother to the King of Spain, is variously addressed as the Duke of Castile, 'Castile', 'Duke'.

16 moiety half.

23 work it ensure that the proposal is accepted.

35 forwardness zeal, enterprise.

37 pitched settled in advance.

42 will wilfulness.

43 friends relatives. In Elizabethan marriage arrangements family relations played a major part.

50 give back 'turn away from us'.

2.4.

2.4.0. SD *An arbour set forth* The arbour is represented on the title page of Q7 (1615) as an arched trellis decorated with leaves and branches. It must be sturdy enough to sustain Horatio's body.

1 sable black.

3 pleasures Renaissance moralists often conceived pleasure (*hēdonē*, *voluptas*) negatively as an indulgence in the appetites, the opposite to virtue and self-control.

7 controls her feelings overpower her judgment or moral sense: see 19–20.

13 match contest, game; well-matched power.

17, 19 Both lines end with 'to pleasure us' (*epistrophe*).

19 Luna the Latin for 'moon'.

23 ease *otium*. Renaissance moralists often equated the concept of leisure with idleness. Cf. Brian Vickers, 'Leisure and idleness in the Renaissance: the ambivalence of otium', *Renaissance Studies* 4 (1990): 1–37, 107–54.

24–9 The lovers speak in rhymed couplets, with one exception: 36 and 37 end with 'hand' (*epistrophe*).

31 frame fashion, compose.

32–43 Venus … Mars Kyd uses the traditional concept of love as a kind of warfare, following the famous line by Ovid: '*Militat omnis amans, et habet suo castra Cupido*', *Amores*, 1.9.1: 'Every lover is a soldier, and Cupid has a camp of his own.'

37 ruder both 'rougher' and 'of a lower social class'.

40 ward defend.

43 My twining arms shall … make thee yield Again Bel-Imperia takes the initiative.

45–7 Kyd darkens the mood in preparation for the sudden murder. First Horatio inverts the traditional relationship between the vine as supporting the elm (an emblem of friendship) to destroying it. Then Bel-Imperia describes the brief life and death of passion, as moralists warned. Horatio's allusion to 'die' in the sense of having an orgasm is juxtaposed with his real death.

51–2 The lovers have spoken in couplets since line 24, now Kyd gives Lorenzo a terminal couplet (rhyming 'aside … tried').

54 fruits result, consequence: invoking both the moralists' disparagement of sexual pleasure and perhaps the death of Horatio, hanging from the tree-like trellis.

59 at the highest A characteristically cold-blooded pun by Lorenzo.

63 SD *shirt* night-shirt; **naked bed** The adjective is transferred to the bed from the speaker: Hieronimo has hurriedly pulled on his night-shirt.

74 pleasure … death Kyd echoes the lovers' language with an added level of irony.

77 whilom formerly.

84 this … shades In Elizabethan English this mixture of single and plural forms was accepted.

89 vild Elizabethan spelling of 'vile'.

91 leese lose.

99 stopped blocked.
102 were would be.
107 outrage mad behaviour.
108 ill-plucked prematurely.
111 glasses of his sight Closing the dead person's eyes was a mark of respect.
118 handkercher handkerchief.
121 entomb bury. Hieronimo preserves Horatio's corpse until the final scene.
125 time ... truth the well-known phrase '*Veritas filia temporis*'.
128 dissemble conceal.
129 practice treachery.
132 dirge mourning song.
133.0 SD *sets his breast unto his sword* a solemn gesture of devotion, the sword's hilt forming a cross.
134–47

'If only somebody would mix a brew for me
From certain herbs that the fair springtime nourishes,
And physic be provided for what pains me; or
If they'd show me what extracts work forgetfulness
In souls; then I myself would cull the grassy fields
Where'er in the great sphere the Sun delivers them
To the fair shores of light. I'd drink whatever drug
The sorceress concocts, whatever madnesses
The spell of Circe weaves. I would endure it all,
Death too – provided only that my consciousness
Died altogether in the quenched breast, once for all.
So, my dear, my life, I will never meet your gaze.
And an eternal sleep has sepulchred your eyes;
I'll die with you. It suits me thus to go below,
Thus, to the shades – but I won't rush to yield to death,
Lest your death should be followed, then, by no revenge.'

I am extremely grateful to Dr Nick Moschovakis for allowing me to quote both his Latin text and his verse translation (into iambic hexameters) from his forthcoming essay, 'A dirge for Horatio: New light on a neo-Latin speech in *The Spanish Tragedy*'. Dr Moschovakis made the exciting discovery of Kyd's source in the first fourteen lines of 'Orion', a pastoral elegy on his dead wife by the pastor Johannes Fabricius Montanus (1527–66). First printed in his *Poemata* (Zurich, 1556), the poem achieved wider circulation in an anthology edited by Aegidius Periander, *Hortus Amorum secundus floribus illustrium Germanorum poetarum consitus* (Frankfurt-am-Main, 1567), copies of which exist in the British Library, the Cambridge University Library, and the Bodleian. In the 1592 quarto the Latin text is extremely corrupt, and although editors beginning with Thomas Hawkins in 1773 have corrected most errors, some cruxes remain. In *1592* line 2 of the Latin text contained the puzzling phrase *annum oblimia* (the latter not a Latin word). Moschovakis has retrieved from 'Orion' the correct reading, *animis oblivia*, which he translated as 'forgetfulness in souls'. In 1959 Edwards read *animis*, the conjecture of a Latinist colleague, but in 2013 Calvo–Tronch preferred Hawkins's 1793 emendation *annorum*, which they translated as 'oblivion of years', a puzzling solution. The 1592 quarto contained a double portion of confusion in line 7 with the phrase *irraui euecaeca* (1592, sig. D3ᵛ), where the second word is in no language. In his critical edition (1900) Joseph Schick emended *irraui* to *herbarum* and the non-word to read *vi caeca*, 'with blind power'. He was followed by all Kyd editors up to Calvo–Tronch, who translated 'whatever herbs her funeral song combines with her sightless power', another puzzling solution. Fortunately for posterity, Moschovakis retrieved from 'Orion' the true readings, *irarum Circeia*, in the line '*Quicquid et irarum Circeia naenia nectit*': 'whatever madnesses | The spell of Circe weaves.' As he points out, 'the subject is Circe's magic, often moralized in pre-modern Europe as a passionate temptation to defy divine reason. When Hieronimo says he would gladly succumb to Circe's madding spell, he seeks an un-Christian remedy for his pain. This theme builds in the next lines, where he proposes to die—if only suicide could be counted on to bring a total end to human consciousness, and so to put him out of his misery.' Kyd also combines phrases from Tibullus, Virgil, and Ovid, which he 'embedded' in his own Latin verse, a common practice in Renaissance neo-Latin poetry: see 1.2 12–14 note.

2.5

2–3, 5–6 Kyd twice gives Andrea's ghost an *epistrophe* to embody his disappointment at not having achieved revenge.

3.1

1–11 Boas noted that Kyd adapts a passage from Seneca's *Agamemnon* (57–73).

1 condition Four syllables.

4 heat passion, anger; **supplanted** deposed, overthrown.

10 feared … beloved cf. Machiavelli, *The Prince*, ch. 17: 'Of cruelty and clemency, and whether it is better to be loved or feared.'

11 sith since.

14 successive line line of royal succession.

17 several works separate, different outcomes.

18 no credit … countenance The familiar injunction *Frontis nulla fides* (Juvenal, *Sat*. 2.8): 'There's no art | To find the mind's construction in the face' (*Macbeth* 1.4.12–13).

19 train treachery, lure to a trap; **coloured** disguised.
21 consorted accompanied.
22–3 Far more inconstant ... earth Kyd borrowed these two lines from Garnier's *Cornélie*, 345–6, which appear in his later translation as 'Thus as the heav'ns, by whom our hopes are guided, | Do coast the earth with an eternal course' (2.1.128–9). (Edwards).
31 extremes dangerous situations, 'last moments of life' (*OED*).
36 infect infected with corruption.
40 daring defiant.
47 suggestion false accusation.
50 Phlegethon a river of fire in the underworld.
52 maliced uttered malicious slander.
53 meed gain.
55 lake Acheron, into which Phlegethon flows.
75 intimate suggest; **ills** wicked acts.
79 quittal repayment, acquittal.
81 fact evil deed, crime.
92 Rent torn.
95 preferred promoted.
105 articulated listed in the articles.

3.2

1–11 no eyes ... tears Kyd adopts a highly emotional style, since Renaissance rhetoric taught that appropriate devices could convey the speaker's feelings and arouse those of the theatregoer or reader. Hieronimo begins with *epanarthosis*, recalling a word or phrase in order to substitute a more expressive one: 'eyes' are 'fountains filled with tears'; 'life' is replaced with 'lively [or 'living'] form of death', where *polyptoton* creates emphasis by repeating a word's root ('life ... lively'), and *antithesis* shows what such a 'life' is for the survivors: 'death'. Alliteration adds emphasis ('mass ... murder and misdeeds'). Kyd also uses *anaphora*, beginning a succession of phrases or lines with the same words ('If this ...') building up to the painful self-correction 'of mine, but now no more *my* son', the loss made more emphatic by the monosyllables. This seven-line sentence was launched by the *apostrophe*, 'O sacred heavens!' and is completed with the question challenging Christian notions of divine justice, when a supposedly *just* being deals *unjustly* (the figure *polyptoton*). Kyd underlines the seriousness of the question by enlarging Hieronimo's climactic line from ten syllables to fourteen.
5 unhallowed unholy.
12–21 The second part of Hieronimo's speech shifts from outrage at injustice to the search for those guilty of Horatio's murder. The combination

of night, in which he dreams of his dead son's wounded body, and a sense of diabolic forces disturbing his mind, urge him on – if only he knew who the murderers were.

15 Solicit seek my attention.

17 frame direct.

20 register tot up, take stock of.

22–3 Eyes … day Kyd 'collects' the key term of Hieronimo's speech (lines 1–3, 5, 12, 16, 19), adding verbs matching the nouns of the preceding line, so forming the overarching rhetorical figure that Puttenham named in his *Arte of English Poetry* as *synathroesmus*, or 'the Collector', which lists various items and then recapitulates them. The line uses alliteration six times, building up to a climax, 'some mean, that may –', left incomplete. This is the figure *aposiopesis*, which breaks off a sentence due to incomplete knowledge, a vacuum fortunately filled by Bel-Imperia's letter.

24 Tush exclamation of disbelief.

27 hapless without 'hap' or good fortune.

34 malign hate, recant.

38 train a lure designed to trap him.

45 behoves … revenged Hieronimo regards revenge as a moral obligation.

48 circumstances external conditions affecting an action, especially as indicating criminality (*OED*).

51 Close come into contact.

52 bewray reveal.

58 disgrace bad behaviour.

62 suit petition.

72 lately recently.

76 humour character, personality.

78 prevent anticipate, block.

93 mount be promoted, be hanged.

95 Chi l'è? 'Who's there?' Lorenzo calls for his servant, Jeron.

100 complot conspiracy; **thou** Lorenzo is addressing himself.

101 practices tricks, schemes; **spread** distribute, set out.

107 ill evil act; **expulse** expel.

111 fault misdeed.

115 companions fellows (contemptuous).

116 haps fortune

117 fear their faith be concerned about their loyalty.

3.3

0 SD *pistol* a heavy handgun (cf. '*dag*', 32 SD): 'the earliest documented instance among surviving Elizabethan play texts' of this prop (Calvo-Tronch).

1 Now Pedringano self-address.
4 shift manage things, prosper.
5 proposed that Lorenzo offered as a gift.
8 strain his conscience have ethical objections.
9 liberal purse Lorenzo's generosity.
11 want lack.
12 apprehension arrest (five syllables).
20 watch and ward the watchman's duty.
23 Here, Serberine self-address; **stay thy pace** 'halt your steps' (Bevington).
27 close come to grips with.
35 stay stop.
39 unkindly cruelly.

3.4

2 preventing anticipating.
3 mischief harm.
10 fault crime. Lorenzo earlier referred to his 'secret fault' (3.2.118).
14–15 guilty … err Lorenzo claims that his guilty conscience and previous crimes qualify him to know what Hieronimo suspects. Cf. 'It takes a thief to catch a thief.'
22 fact crime
28 exasperate irritate; **his revenge** on Pedringano.
30 dissension between Serberine and Pedringano.
35 fits confirms; **former policy** the stratagem he had devised.
37 prosecutes the point pursues the objective.
39 limed birds were caught with birdlime, a sticky substance smeared on the branches of a tree or bush.
40 hold their own realize their ambition.
41 fowlers bird-catchers.
42 He The accomplice that Lorenzo has engaged; **holp** helped.
43 reaching carefully planned; **fatch** plot, stratagem.
52 stand … distress protect him from punishment.
56 works … wax is easily shaped; **try thy wits** self-address.
58 closely secretly.
61 Marshal-sessions legal process presided over by the Lord Marshal.
65 turned off the scaffold, hanged.
74 tickle tricky, risky.
78 list not do not want to.
80 privy private, sacred.
82 advantages looking for opportunities to gain.
83–4 Et … basterà 'Nobody knows what I want. I do, and that's enough for me'; source unknown. Domenico Lovascio comments: 'I believe it is

Kyd's invention, as corroborated by the fact that this is iambic pentameter, a metre not normally used in Italian poetry. There's a similar line in Marston ('*Così, così mi converrà morir*').' Personal communication, 7 August 2023.

3.5

3 idle time to wonder what's in the box.

3–4 men's kind … minority adolescent boys.

4 uncertainty changeableness, which makes them disobedient.

8 gentlemanlike knavery An oxymoron, uniting two semantic opposites.

12 flout mock; **audience** public hangings regularly attracted bystanders; **descant** criticize.

14 grace honour.

3.6

1 extremes extreme situations, hardships.

4 compass get, achieve.

8 consumeth age corrodes my life.

16 For here 'in his heart or his head, which he touches' (Edwards).

16.0 SD *Enter officers* These include the hangman, who may carry a rope and a ladder, stool or box to form the raised surface from which the criminal will be '*turned off*' (SD 105.0). Cf. John H. Astington, 'Gallows scenes on the Elizabethan stage', *Theatre Notebook* 37 (1983): 3–9.

17 set sitting, in session.

20 nearer more personal, private.

22 sith since.

27 there's either the apparatus, or the hanging. Pedringano expects to receive his pardon once the 'business' has been set up, and is impatient for it to start.

32 gear deed or action.

35 blood with blood cf. Genesis 9:6.

39 dispatch hurry, get on with it; **approved** proved.

42 officious knave an oxymoron.

45 halter a rope with a noose; **disfurnish … habit** One of the hangman's perks was to receive the criminal's clothes (habits).

48 boot compensation.

68 truss Pedringano uses the word for a close-fitting body garment.

69 truss up The hangman means 'string up'.

73 hearken pay attention to.

83 motion proposal, as if for a meeting. The hangman begins a speech but Pedringano cuts him off.

90 interdicted forbidden, as in the ten commandments.

92 intercepts itself 'cuts itself off from' (Tydeman).
102 Stand you rely on, also 'to have a sound footing'. The hangman has the last pun.

4.1
1 breathe … woes utter my miseries. Kyd builds the speech around 'woes' (ll.1, 2, 18) and 'words' (5, 18), varied with 'exclaims' and 'plaints'. The terms recur at 67–8.
6 moved … trees 'stripped the trees of their leaves' (Bevington), with a pun on *movere*, to move the feelings, one of rhetoric's aims.
11 passions sufferings; trisyllabic.
13 windows Kyd gives Hieronimo a complete metaphor of the heavens forming a house.
15 empyreal the highest celestial region.
16 countermured having an outer wall for additional defence.
17 impregnable it resists attack and keeps out sound.
20 Petergade The hangman confuses Pedringano's name.
32–40 Somewhat unusually, Kyd chooses verse for the letter, so that it fits the serious tone and substance of Hieronimo's speech.
33 labour my delivery get me released.
40 holp helped.
45 sacred heavens Hieronimo questioned 'sacred heavens' and the 'just dealings' attributed to them earlier (3.2.5–11).
49 durst dared.
53 hers Bel-Imperia's letter.
54 accident incident, happening.
59 bane poison.
60 reserved preserved.
61 constrainèd forced, violent.
65 banned cursed.
66 he did pity Horatio, in preserving Balthazar's life.
69 plain complain.

4.2
1 purge cleanse.
5 physic medicine; **recure** restore to health.
8 outrage mad, violent behaviour or speech (*OED*).
10–12 In her lunatic fit Isabella confuses children's toys ('whistle' and 'whipstock', the handle of a whip) with weapons.
13 humours moods, distorted feelings.
14–22 Philip Edwards, in his edition of *The Spanish Tragedy*, showed that Kyd adapted several passages from Thomas Watson's own translation of *Meliboeus* (his 1590 Latin elegy on Walsingham), the longest being for

Isabella's scene. See Edwards (ed. cit.), xxvi and Appendix D, 'Watson's Elegy on Walsingham' (pp. 143–4). Some critics have rejected the *Meliboeus* parallels since its publication date is later than Kyd's presumed composition of the play. As a personal friend, Kyd read much of Watson's poetry in manuscript before publication, and could well have known *Meliboeus* in the late 1580s, when he was writing this play. See Vickers, 'Embedded Poetry.'

22 **died, ay died** The rhetorical figure *epizeuxis*, repeating a word, was used to express intense feelings.

4.3

2 **sequestered** kept apart, secluded.

3 **notice** information.

4 **ills** harms done to her.

9 **that thou sawest** I wish you saw: 'dramatic irony, considering that Andrea's ghost is presumably onstage' (Calvo-Tronch).

4.4

7 **him** the devil; **enlarged** set free.

8 **policy** stratagem. In Elizabethan drama this word became synonymous with ruthless Machiavellian plotting.

19 **Salve** smooth over; **soothe me up** support what I say.

28 **company** companion; **abuse** wrong, hurt. 'Lorenzo's jaunty and laconic allusion to Horatio's murder and Bel-Imperia's secret detention is highly characteristic' (Boas).

37 **discretion** judgment.

44 **estate** state.

45 **determined** decided, settled.

46 **touched** affected.

48 **next in sight** person standing nearby.

50 **consorted with** accompanied by.

54 **disgrace** Bel-Imperia's sexual relationship with Andrea.

57 **meanly** of a lower class.

63 **entreateth of** discusses.

64 **forged** devised, fabricated ('forgery').

66 **worth, worthy** By varying the ending (*polyptoton*) Kyd creates a scornful emphasis.

70 **exasperate** intensified, made worse.

85 **politic** cunning, devious.

89 **tresses ... twines** Balthazar compares Bel-Imperia's hair to the 'twines' or thread with which Ariadne helped her lover Theseus escape from the Minotaur's labyrinth. The comparison is only partly relevant and may

be a deliberate choice by Kyd to mock Balthazar, the self-dramatizing Petrarchan lover.

91 ivory front smooth white forehead; a stage in the blazon, the conventional description of a woman's beauty, from top to toe; **Sorrow's image** the typically self-pitying attitude of the conventional lover.

102–3 Et tremulo … opus 'They joined dismayed dread to quaking fear, a futile deed of sottish betrayal.' As Bevington comments: 'Another medley of classical sayings, suggesting here perhaps the futility of uniting Bel-Imperia's fear of loss with Balthazar's fear of rejection.'

106 Led by the lodestar Balthazar begins with high praise for Bel-Imperia as his guiding star but ends with a self-pitying description of himself: Kyd mocks the diction of conventional love-poetry.

4.5

4 next nearest.

6 hard by close by.

8 SD *He goes in at one door and comes out at another* can refer either to Hieronimo (probably) or the First Portuguese. See Alan C. Dessen and Leslie Thomson, *A Dictionary of Stage Directions in English Drama 1580–1642* (Cambridge, 1999), pp. 101–2 for other instances of the stage direction *go in*, and p. 24 for *come out*.

12 list listen.

13 left-hand side traditionally unfortunate ('sinister'): cf. 1.1.68–71, 'The left-hand path … to the deepest hell.'

15–29 forest … innocents A vision of hell reminiscent of medieval wall-paintings.

21 hugy huge.

32 passing extremely.

4.6

0 SD *poniard … rope* a dagger and a noose, the conventional property of a would-be suicide on the Elizabethan stage. The instances cited by Dessen and Thomson (p. 168) may suggest that Kyd was the first dramatist to link the two.

1–24 Kyd uses rhyme to give this soliloquy an intermittent structure. Lines 1–18 rhyme *ababcdcd*. Line 9 is unrhymed, as are 12 and 14. The remaining lines include two couplets (10–11, 16–17), ending with a quatrain and a couplet. The effect is to portray Hieronimo's intermittent coherence.

1 sir Hieronimo is addressing an imagined interlocutor, as if preparing for a conversation.

4 toys … mute Bevington glosses **toys** as 'trifles, the vain petitions of court *standers-by*'. But perhaps they are the same toys that Isabella saw in her demented state (4.2.10–12). Hieronimo imagines himself losing the thread of his discourse. The next twenty lines show him in a manic state.

6 trudge walk slowly or for long distances.

16 this way Schick (1898, p. 142) observed that 'the sequence of ideas is exactly the same' as in Hieronimo's Latin dirge for Horatio (2.5.132 ff.).

21 have a fling attack; like 'be with thee to bring', incoherent threats.

31 go by walk past without attracting attention. This became a frequently ridiculed saying in Elizabethan drama.

31.0 SD *Withdraws* (Calvo–Tronch).

45 inexecrable Q2 altered Q1's reading to 'inexplicable'; other editors substitute 'inextricable'. In his 1951 edition C. T. Prouty accepted it as meaning 'not to be execrated; sacred', but the anonymous reader of this edition objects that the word 'really ought to mean "curseworthy"', pointing out that all nineteen instances of it in *EEBO* are 'very negative'. This is the only use of *inexecrable* in Kyd's canon. He likely intended 'inexorable' (from the Latin *inexorabilis*) which the texts contained in *EEBO* sometimes spell 'inexerable', quite near the Q1 spelling.

55 bends directs.

57 that his son so that his son may (the ransom frees Balthazar as a prisoner of war to the Spaniards).

61 see it given to Horatio The King is apparently unaware of Horatio's death, as again at line 81. But Calvo–Tronch point out that 'Hieronimo promised not to *entomb* his son until he had revenge (2.5.54) and decided to *dissemble* his mourning (2.5.66).' Kyd evidently wants to hold back general recognition of the murder until the closing scene.

69 ransom release.

72 deadly wounds 'For the first time Hieronimo publicly reveals that his son is dead' (Calvo–Tronch).

77 avengèd 'Hieronimo's first clear declaration of revenge' (Calvo–Tronch).

82 demean behave, carry himself.

86 covetous Lorenzo's allegation that Hieronimo is greedy for the ransom reveals his malice, as does his proposal that Hieronimo should be removed from office.

99 not exempt Q reads 'exempt', but Edwards added 'not', arguing that 'an elliptical construction must be supposed here', glossing: 'I will not debar [Hieronimo] from the position.'

103 prefix settle beforehand.

4.7

1 'Vindicta mihi!' Cf. Romans 12:19 '"Vengeance is mine: I will repay", saith the Lord.' Kyd shows Hieronimo rationally reviewing possible courses of action, beginning with the Bible, which he sets aside, shifting to classical *sententiae* as keynotes that ultimately influence his choice of revenge by direct action. There is no sign here of the madness alleged by some commentators.

2 ill evil act.

3 suffer leave, allow.

6 Per … iter 'for crimes the safest path is always through crimes' (Seneca, *Agamemnon* 115), from a soliloquy spoken by Clytemnestra.

9 death's … resolution i.e., 'resolute action can at worst end in death' (Boas).

10–11 patience … end The conclusion, 'his life shall easily end', is surely ironic.

12–13 Fata … sepulchrum 'If fate helps the wretched, you have a refuge; if fate denies you life, you have a tomb' (Seneca, *Troades* 510–12).

14, 16, 18 Kyd shows Hieronimo building a logical structure of choices and consequences. Three lines begin with 'For' (4, 6, 8), three with 'If', followed by 'Then' or 'Yet'.

19 Heaven … burial from Lucan's *Pharsalia*, 7.119 (not 8.118, as in Calvo-Tronch); '*Caelo tegitur, qui non habet urnam*.'

20 to conclude Hieronimo sums up one stage of his argument before beginning the next, which is also structured logically, with objections to one point ('But', 27) leading to deductions ('And therefore', 27; 'Thus therefore', 28). He follows with a negation ('Not', 31), another deduction ('For', 34) and a negation ('Nor', 36).

22 open, but inevitable ills 'easily recognized but unavoidable crimes'.

26 Closely secretly.

32 simplicity feigned naivety.

33 let … slip revealing secrets.

35 Remedium … est 'Ignorance is a feeble remedy for troubles' (Seneca, *Oedipus* 515).

38 nobility 'the power of their status as nobles' (Calvo-Tronch).

41 affords yields naturally.

44 when, where, and how three of the seven 'circumstances' that were taught as an aid to composition in the Elizabethan grammar school. Thomas Wilson, in his *Arte of Rhetorique* (1553, 1560), supplied this list: '1. Who did the deed? 2. What was done? 3. Where was it done? 4. What help had he to do it? 5. Wherefore did he do it? 6. How did he do it? 7. At what time did he do it?' These questions were originally formulated in Roman legal rhetoric for use in criminal proceedings.

45 coil fuss, noise.

49 several separate, particular.

54 equity fairness, impartiality.

58 Corregidor Spanish magistrate; **causes** legal cases.

60 action … battery violent attack.

62 ejectione firmae the ejection of a tenant before the lease has expired.
65 declaration statement of claim.
67 silly frail, defenceless.
71 Myrmidons tribe of warriors led by Achilles.
72 Corsic Corsican.
76 bewray reveal; **blood** blood-spilling.
80 Oh my son … Horatio Cf. David's exclamation: 'O my son Absalom, my son, my son Absalom!', 2 Samuel 18:33.
91 as one the same; **extremities** extreme sufferings.
99 meaner wits of inferior ability, education.
101–4 whenas … deep Hieronimo imagines himself as a ship being 'overturned' by adversity at his higher level of society ('upper billows') while the Old Man, at a lower point ('lesser waters'), is able to maintain his course in life by expressing love for his son.
108 passion Hieronimo describes his extreme emotional state.
109 Pluto god of the underworld. Kyd returns to the 'slimy strand' of Andrea's visit to hell (1.1), where Hieronimo imagines meeting Alcides (Hercules), the 'triple-headed porter' (Cerberus), 'the Thracian poet' (Orpheus) and Proserpine (1.1.78–9).
118 burden refrain, theme.
122 shivering splintering, tearing up.
135–9 Aeacus … Rhadamanth judges in the underworld: cf. 1.1.33.
143 changed transformed.
146 blasted blighted, turned pale.
148 favour appearance (changed by fate).
159 lively vivid, lifelike.
168 stay support.
170 framed composed; **discords … cords** Hieronimo puns on 'ropes', 'cords', 'chords' and 'discords'. In Renaissance rhetoric a speaker using such wordplay in painful circumstances was seen as subjecting language to pressure in order to express strong feelings.

4.8

0 SD *Enter* [*at one door the Spanish contingent*] *King of Spain … and Bel-Imperia* [*with servants; enter at another door the Portuguese*] *Viceroy and Don Pedro* The Spanish and Portuguese parties, opposed in the dialogue, should enter from different sides (Calvo–Tronch).
7 western Indies Portuguese Brazil (Freeman).
9 train accompanying officials and servants.
12 note take note of, celebrate; **troth** loyalty.
17 condescent consent, agreement.

23 thou The Spanish King addressed the Portuguese viceroy as 'you', but he replies in the second person form, perhaps to express affection. The King shifts to 'thy' at line 37, in sympathetic response to Castile's emotional upset.

24 doubtful followers uncommitted, undecided.

28 marriage Trisyllabic.

30 sith ... see since I see him living.

34 strangely surprisingly (*OED*), unexpectedly.

35 nature natural human feeling.

37 extremities sufferings, extreme feelings.

41 Seest thou The Duke of Castile asks his son a series of five searching questions, like the circumstances Hieronimo had used: 'what, why, who ...'

50 intercept disturb.

56 cross his suit block his requests.

61 common general.

66 health well-being; **passions** suffering.

68 exclaim complain.

74 vulgar common people.

75 advantage opportunity; **water-breach** leak.

77 keep back Cf. 4.6.28, 65–6.

79 passions Trisyllabic.

87 silly helpless, deserving pity; **distract** disturbed.

92 misconster misunderstand.

99–104 Balthazar and Bel-Imperia exchange banter in couplets as if they were alone. She forces him to request a 'truce'.

107 pledge 'guarantee of peace between Spain and Portugal, and of my own happiness' (Bevington).

109 sadly seriously.

117 device ... trow? 'do you think?' Hieronimo addresses himself, wondering what new subterfuge he should expect from Castile and Lorenzo.

118 Pocas palabras '[speak] few words': part of Hieronimo's defensive plot to disguise his wish for revenge. It became a widely used catchphrase in Elizabethan drama.

146 prevent forestall.

160 fit suitable, appropriate

170–1 Chi mi ... mi vuole 'Look at that! He who gives me more caresses than usual has betrayed me or wants to betray (me)' (Calvo-Tronch).

4.9

1 Erichtho ... Charon In his angry impatience for revenge Andrea's ghost calls on Greek mythological figures in the underworld. Erichtho is 'the Thessalian sorceress, well known from Lucan, Ovid, Dante and Goethe's *Faust*' (Schick, 1898); Erebus is the god of darkness; the remaining deities were invoked in 1.1.

10 warned to watch Cf. the phrase 'watch and ward'.

15 intercepts interrupts. The ghost is not fully aware of Hieronimo's plot.

17 worldlings ground mortals 'found their beliefs on what is a mere dream or fancy' (Edwards).

19 soliciting attempting to persuade.

24 wile trick.

25 instance example.

28 reveal ... mystery explain the meaning.

31 Hymen the Greek goddess of marriage; **hie** hurry.

32 sable ... saffron black and orange-yellow.

34 discontent angry: the blood prefigures the play's ending.

38 Rest ... rest An instance of the figure *epanalepsis*, the same word (with a change of meaning) used at the beginning and end of a phrase or sentence, to express coherence.

5.1

4 passions Trisyllabic; passionate utterances.

6 wont accustomed.

7 unkind unnatural.

9–10 Some editors assume that the repetition is a printer's [compositorial] error, but it is in fact a rhetorical figure. See Brian Vickers, '*Epistrophe* and the "lost line" in *The Spanish Tragedy*', *Notes and Queries* 268 (2023): 160–4.

20 tendered looked after.

21 in respect of by comparison with.

24 bear it out 'both "endure" and "pretend"' (Calvo-Tronch).

32 applies prepares, supports; **drift** plan, scheme.

39 care carefulness.

40 thoughtless unmindful; **mean** way.

44 determine decide the time of.

50 grace ... practices favour my plots.

57 cause motive.

61 show entertainment, dumbshow.

63 passing conducting (Bevington).

65 motion proposal, plan.

68 fit you fit you out with what is needed.

70 fruitless bringing no earnings; a common complaint by Elizabethan poets.
82 strange surprising.
83 plausible pleasing, deserving of applause.
85 Nero The emperor encouraged drama and acted in plays.
91 make one take part.
94 woman Aristocratic women like Bel-Imperia were allowed to take part in private masques.
96 needs be must take part if there's a woman's role.
102 scholars those with a knowledge of Latin. Cf. Hieronimo's explanation that he had intended the play to be performed 'in unknown languages' (165–71), and the later correction that it had been decided '*to be set down in English*' (5.4.9.2–3).
104 argument plot, summary.
105 roundly plainly.
110 Soliman Suleiman I (1494–1566), the most powerful sultan of the Ottoman empire.
113 break reveal, open.
115 bashaws Turkish officers of high rank.
116 solicited tried to persuade.
120 therefor for that reason.
131 conceited conceived, formed a conception of.
134 resolute determined. In Elizabethan drama the word is often used to describe male courage.
135 several abstracts separate summaries.
139 falchion a broad, curved sword, like the scimitar.
140 cross ... Rhodes a tunic embroidered with a distinctive cross, like that worn by the knights of Malta.
142 Phoebe ... Huntress Greek and Roman goddesses associated with hunting.
144 look to take care of.
146 furnish kit out.
148 liberal generous.
151 Kingly troop royal spectators.
153 Tragedia cothurnata In Athenian tragedy the actors wore *cothurni*, thick-soled boots reaching to the middle of the leg.
154 matter substantial material.
157 Italian tragedians performers of the *Commedia dell'arte*, usually comedies based on stock situations and characters.
158 meditation reflection, perhaps involving rehearsal.
162 Mass 'by the Mass'.

166 unknown languages Kyd did not follow up on this plan; perhaps it was intended to puzzle the actors taking part in his revenge plot and make them await his 'oration' and 'wondrous show ... behind a curtain', when he will reveal Horatio's corpse.

181 concluded in one scene Another hint that will not be understood until the climactic revenge.

184 soothe ... up humour his whim.

186 ply ... gear apply yourself to this business.

187 fall of Babylon either that of the capital city of the Babylonian empire, which Old Testament prophets saw as preceding the coming of the Messiah, or the tower of Babel, with its mixture of 'unknown languages'.

188 confusion chaos, destruction.

5.2

0 SD *Isabella with a weapon* to destroy the arbour in which Horatio was hanged. Isabella is deranged, but coherent.

7 unfortunate bringing misfortune.

12–13 Kyd has Isabella pun on two related words, the garden *plot* of land and a *complot* or conspiracy.

16 not ... unmanured The double negative conveys a prohibition.

17 noisome harmful.

18 blast blight.

24 solicits appeals.

25 Revenge ... death Isabella accuses herself of not having taken revenge on Horatio's murderers, although she was never in a position to do so.

28 Rhadamanth a judge in the underworld, who 'brings to light crimes done in life which the perpetrator vainly thought impenetrably hid': cf. H. Coursen, 'The Unity of *The Spanish Tragedy*', SP 65 (1968): 768–82 (771); **hold excused** apologize for.

30 Thy negligence Isabella adds her own reproach to those made by Bel-Imperia and Hieronimo himself, urging him to act.

5.3

0 SD *knocks up* fixes hastily. Editors have suggested various places where this curtain can be hung, so as to conceal the bodies of Horatio and perhaps Isabella, for whom no exit was specified in the previous scene.

1 fellows fellow actors.

6–7 copy ... argument either a book or a document containing the summary.

12 train the royal party and their attendants, retinue; **gallery** the 'long gallery' of an Elizabethan mansion, sometimes used for masques and spectacles; also the theatrical gallery overlooking the stage.

13 vouchsafe kindly agree.
16 title a board shown to spectators giving the title or the location. They were used in private indoor theatres, not in the large open-air public theatres. Sidney mentions them in his *Apology for Poetry* (1595).
19 dispatch make haste.
26 Behoves requires.
29 wants is lacking.

5.4
3 of pleasure 'with gracious consent' (Bevington).
8 bookkeeper the employee in public theatres who held the 'booke' or play manuscript during performances, in case an actor needed prompting; he also looked after the stage.
15 reserving preserving alive.
17 adamant 'the lodestone or magnet' (*OED*).
18 wait attend on (her).
24 betide happen, befall. Q prints a full-stop both to conclude this sentence by Hieronimo and Balthazar's reply. But the context suggests that Balthazar interrupts Hieronimo and is interrupted by him, two instances of the figure *aposiopesis*, when a speaker breaks off an utterance incomplete.
28 lights eyes.
32 plot summary or argument.
38–48 An extended passage of dialogue between Balthazar and Hieronimo.
43 remove withdraw, cancel.
50 wit know.
54 favour your ability to love me.
58 vain suits pointless requests.
67 Well said 'Well done!'; **bravely** splendidly, excellently.
68 plays acts.
74 vulgar vernacular.
75 Haply by chance; **bootless** in vain, pointless.
76 fabulously counterfeit fictitiously represented.
78 fashioning … scene adapting to the action onstage.
79 Ajax … Roman suicidal deaths.
80 starting up again standing up after the play is over.
84 latest tale last story (before dying).
86 instance proof, evidence.
95 wounds … life '*my* life-breath left me when these wounds were made in my son's body' (Mulryne).
101 pitchy pitch-black; **harms** evil deeds.
102 sorted chosen; **leisure** opportunity (*OED*).
111 Through-girt pierced.

117 Marched in a net 'considered himself free from suspicion when actually exposed to view all the time' (Tydeman); cf. note to 5.1.9–10.
118 rated berated, scolded.
120 brook digest, accept.
124 propitious of favourable omen; **reserved** kept.
126 Soliciting urging.
142 determine of decided.
144 resolution Cf. 'resolve', courage, bravery.
146 SD ***holding ... hand*** from Calvo-Tronch.
148 latest last, final.
151 SD ***he runs to hang himself.*** Introducing his play, when Bel-Imperia asked what became of the pasha, Hieronimo had seemingly planned his death: 'moved with remorse of his misdeed, | Ran to a mountain top and hung himself' (126–7). This suggests that a rope was visibly placed on stage for this purpose.
150 gentles persons of higher social rank.
160 stayest prevent, block.
163 undeserving unmerited.
169 by by the deaths of.
177 lesser liberty smaller freedom.
188 SD '*He bites out his tongue.*' Frustrated by Hieronimo's refusal to disclose his 'confederates', the Spanish King orders: 'Fetch forth the tortures! | ... I'll make thee tell' (180–1). Refusing to 'reveal | The thing which I have vowed inviolate', Hieronimo defies the King: 'First take my tongue, and afterwards my heart!' In 'Biting one's tongue: autoglossotomy and agency in *The Spanish Tragedy*' (*Renaissance Studies* 36 (2022): 278–94), Alanna Skuse has shown that Kyd has reproduced the exact situation of the most famous classical instance of such self-mutilation: when Zeno the Stoic was being tortured by the tyrant Nearchus he bit out his tongue and spat it in the tyrant's face. The same reaction was attributed to other philosophers and orators facing torture, including Anaxarchus and Hyperides. Kyd places Hieronimo alongside these exemplars of integrity and constancy.
194 As G. K. Hunter pointed out ('Tacitus and Kyd's *The Spanish Tragedy*', *Notes and Queries* 47 (2000): 424–5), here Kyd drew on the *Annals* of Tacitus VI.v.8, describing the suicide of Publius Vitellius. In the first English translation, by Richard Grenewey (1598), the passage reads: 'Vitellius through many delayes betwixt hope and fear wearied out, under colour of using it in his study, asking for a penknife, lightly pricked a vein and ended his life with grief and anguish of mind' (p. 117 in the 1640 reprint, *STC* 23748).
199 succeeding hope of favourable succession to the throne.

210 Scylla's ... gulf In Greek mythology a narrow sea passage between Italy and Sicily; on the other side was the rock Charybdis.

212 want for suffering for the lack of (*OED*).

5.5

5 quaint ingenious, cunning.

6 misdone destroyed, killed.

10 Dido Queen of Carthage, who committed suicide after Aeneas abandoned her.

13 Proserpine see 1.1.76 ff.

14 doom judgment.

18 inured practised.

19 train way of life (Calvo-Tronch).

27 hale haul, drag.

28 Furies avenging infernal spirits (cf. 1.1.65n); **bugs** objects of terror.

31 Tityus In Greek mythology the giant Tityus attempted to rape Lato, mother of Apollo and Diana, and was punished by being chained to a rock in Hades. Every day a vulture would rip out his liver, the seat of lust; every night the liver would grow back, for the torment to be repeated the next day, for all eternity.

33–4 Ixion's ... lover's In Greek mythology, a king who boasted of having seduced Zeus's wife. He was condemned to be bound to an endlessly revolving fiery wheel (cf. 1.1.66) (Calvo-Tronch).

36 Chimera In Greek mythology, a composite creature (lion, goat, snake) who snorted fire.

40 Sisyphus punished in the underworld by having to roll up hill a huge marble block, which always rolled down again.

42 boiling Acheron a river of fire in the underworld (cf. 1.1.19n).

43 still always.

45 friends and foes To place one group 'in ease', the other 'in woes', was common practice in antiquity (and since): cf. Mary Whitlock Blundell, *Helping Friends and Harming Enemies: A Study in Sophocles and Greek Ethics* (Cambridge, 1989).

THE HOUSEHOLDER'S PHILOSOPHY

Edited by Domenico Lovascio

INTRODUCTION

CIRCUMSTANCES OF PUBLICATION

The Householder's Philosophy, the first complete English translation of a work by Torquato Tasso, was entered in the Stationers' Register on 6 February 1588 as 'the Philosophicall Discourse of the householder'.[1] It was printed by John Charlewood for Thomas Hacket in the same year (*STC* 23702.5). As Kirk Melnikoff points out, Hacket had a 'career-long penchant for publishing translations', which 'would have distinguished him from many other Elizabethan publishers'.[2] 'As a distributor of translated material', Melnikoff adds, 'Hacket was able to capitalize not only on the extensive resources of continental, scholastic, and classical material but also on the ever-growing numbers of middle-class readers.'[3] Hacket's desire to cater to this segment of readership is evident in his repeatedly issuing 'books oriented towards the concern of the middling classes with self-improvement', books that all 'present thinly-veiled conduct guides for a bourgeois audience'.[4] From 1583 onwards, Hacket worked almost exclusively with Charlewood, who, as Jason Lawrence observes, was 'responsible at this time for the most significant body of Italian books to be printed in London which do not originate from [John] Wolfe', the foremost London specialist in the publication of Italian books, who had also published in 1584 an incomplete translation of Tasso's epic poem *Gerusalemme liberata* (1581) by Scipione Gentili in three separate volumes.[5] Kyd's book was therefore placed at the perfect juncture of the printer's and the publisher's interests; in addition, as Erne remarks,

1 Edward Arber, *A Transcript of the Registers of the Company of Stationers of London, 1554–1640*, 5 vols (London, 1875–94), 2:484.

2 Kirk Melnikoff, 'Thomas Hacket and the Ventures of an Elizabethan Publisher', *Library* 10 (2009): 257–71 (260, 268).

3 Ibid., 268.

4 Ibid., 265.

5 Ibid., 263; Jason Lawrence, *'Who the Devil Taught thee so much Italian?': Italian Language Learning and Literary Imitation in Early Modern England* (Manchester, 2005), p. 190. The three volumes published by Wolfe in 1584 are: *Torquati Tassi Solymeidos liber primus Latinis numeris expressus a Scipio Gentili*, with a dedication to Queen Elizabeth I; *Scipii Gentilis Solymeidos libri duo priores de Torquati Tassi Italicis expressi*; and *Plutonis Concilium; ex initio quarti libri Solymeidos*, which was dedicated to Sir Philip Sidney.

> Texts dealing with home and estate management were far from unusual in the sixteenth century. Anthony Fitzherbert's *Book of Husbandry* …, first printed in 1523, went through twenty editions by 1600; Thomas Tusser's *A Hundreth Good Pointes of Husbandrie* (1557) … was reprinted twice, then enlarged to *Five Hundreth Points of Good Husbandry* (1573) …, and reprinted eleven times before the end of the century. Barnabe Googe's translation of the work of Conrad Heresback of Cleves appeared as *Four Bookes of Husbandrie* in 1577 … and was reprinted four times until the turn of the century. H. S. Bennett explains that 'many a London merchant, having made his money in trade and invested in a country place, was buying books which described methods of leading successfully a rural life'.[6]

The Householder's Philosophy, then, would have carried an interesting commercial potential; yet it appears not to have sold well, and Erne is probably right in pointing out that, 'Mixing instruction and entertainment, it does not seem to have been instructive enough for esquires, nor entertaining enough for the *literati*.'[7] The book's commercial failure seems in line with what Melnikoff describes as Hacket's lack of an 'exceptional market acumen. Not only were few of his publications reprinted during his lifetime, but they failed to attract much interest from other investors.'[8] As a result, Hacket reissued *The Householder's Philosophy* later that year bound together with Bartholomew Dowe's *A dairie Booke for all good huswives*, which has its own title page and was entered separately in the Stationers' Register on 9 July 1588 (*STC* 23703). Arthur Freeman observes that 'what Hacket had done, simply, was to take the unsold sheets of his two 1588 pamphlets and reissue them, with a new title page, as a small "nonce collection"'; however, in doing so, Hacket was simultaneously combining Tasso's tract 'with a more practical dialogue directed at "all good huswiues"', in a likely attempt, as Melnikoff suggests, to hedge his bets and target 'a broader swathe of the domestic sphere'.[9]

6 Lukas Erne, *Beyond* The Spanish Tragedy: *A Study of the Works of Thomas Kyd* (Manchester, 2001), p. 219; H. S. Bennett, *English Books and Readers 1558 to 1603* (Cambridge, 1965), p. 165. See also Wendy Wall, *Staging Domesticity: Household Work and English Identity in Early Modern Drama* (Cambridge, 2002); Viviana Comensoli, *'Household Business': Domestic Plays of Early Modern England* (Toronto, 1996), esp. pp. 65–109.

7 Erne, *Beyond*, p. 220.

8 Melnikoff, 'Thomas Hacket', 263.

9 Arthur Freeman, *Thomas Kyd: Facts and Problems* (Oxford, 1967), p. 171; Kirk Melnikoff, *Elizabethan Publishing and the Makings of Literary Culture* (Toronto, 2018), p. 59.

THE SOURCE TEXT OF KYD'S TRANSLATION

The 'Catalogue or Index of those things worth the memory contained in this book', which occupies seven pages between the dedication and the main text, is modelled upon Tasso's 'Tavola delle cose notabili che nel *Padre di famiglia* si contengono', as Erne first pointed out.[10] It is, however, not a straightforward translation. Tasso's 'Tavola' has 180 headings; Kyd's 'Catalogue or Index' has 125. In most cases, Kyd does translate Tasso's headings. Yet Kyd often conflates two headings into one or divides one into two; at times, he completely ignores Tasso's headings and creates new ones.[11] At all events, the presence of the 'Catalogue or Index' is crucial to determine upon which edition of *Il padre di famiglia* Kyd relied for his translation.

Tasso completed *Il padre di famiglia* in 1580 and entrusted a gentleman from Mantua with the manuscript in the hope that it would soon reach his friend Cardinal Scipione Gonzaga, to whom he had dedicated it. The dialogue was first published in 1582 – and not in 1583 as commentators on Kyd's translation appear to think – in *Delle Rime del Signor Torquato Tasso. Parte seconda. Insieme con altri componimenti del medesimo* (Venice: Aldo Manuzio, 1582), a printing that Tasso could not check and in fact explicitly disapproved of.[12] This edition of *Il padre di famiglia* featured no 'Tavola' and no separate title page. However, both appeared the following year in *Delle Rime et Prose Del S. Torquato Tasso, Di nuovo con diligenza rivedute, corrette, et di vaghe Figure adornate, Parte Seconda* (Venice: Aldo Manuzio, 1583). The presence of the title page is relevant, inasmuch as Kyd clearly translated bits of it while preparing his own. Tasso's title page reads 'IL PADRE | DI FAMIGLIA | DIALOGO | Del S. Torquato Tasso. | Nel quale brevemente trattando la vera Econo- | mia, s'insegna, non meno con facilità, che dot- | tamente, il Governo non pur della Casa, tanto | di Città, quanto di Contado; ma ancora il vero | modo di accrescere, & conservar le ricchezze. | *Con la Tavola delle cose notabili.*'. Kyd's title page reads 'The Housholders | Philosophie. | Wherein is perfectly and profitably described, | the true *Oeconomia* and forme of | Housekeeping. | With a Table added thereunto of all the notable | thinges therein contained. | *First written in Italian by that excellent Orator and Poet | Signior Torquato Tasso, and now translated | by* T. K.'. As is evident at a glance, 'vera economia' becomes 'true *Oeconomia*';

[10] Erne, *Beyond*, p. 218.

[11] As it seemed to me to be of very little utility to the reader, I have not attempted to provide any detailed comparison between Kyd's 'Catalogue or Index' and Tasso's 'Tavola' in the commentary as I did with the text proper.

[12] Ezio Raimondi, 'Introduzione' to *Dialoghi* by Torquato Tasso, 2 vols (Florence, 1958), 1:3–313 (30). For a full account of the textual history of *Il padre di famiglia* in the sixteenth century, see ibid., pp. 111–19.

'il governo … della casa' becomes 'forme of housekeeping'; and 'la Tavola delle cose notabili' becomes 'a table … of all notable thinges', in spite of its being called 'Catalogue or Index' (and not 'Table') inside the book. In 1583, Manuzio also published the dialogue as an independent volume. There was yet another edition of *Il padre di famiglia* with the separate title page and the 'Tavola' before 1588, contained in the volume *Delle Rime, et Prose del Sig. Torquato Tasso. Parte Seconda, Di nuovo ristampate, con diligenza rivedute, e corrette* (Ferrara: Simon Vasalini, 1585).

Aside from the absence of the 'Catalogue or Index' and of a separate title page, a careful comparison of the English translation with the three editions of the Italian text that Kyd may have consulted reveals other elements that lead to the conclusion that he used the 1583 edition. First, one of Tasso's quotations from Petrarch that Kyd reproduces (l. 890) features the word 'armi' (1583 and 1585) rather than 'arme' (1582). Second, Kyd uses the word 'fashions' (l. 939), probably in the sense of 'manners and customs (of nations)', which would seem to translate the incorrect reading 'nazioni' (1583 and 1585) rather than 'azioni' (1582).[13] Third, Kyd apparently fails to understand a sentence because of the lack of the verb 'essendo' (being) in the 1583 and 1585 editions (ll. 565–7). Finally – and this is the variant that provides the decisive clue to discriminate between the 1583 and the 1585 editions and conclusively to ascertain that Kyd used the former – Kyd writes 'stirrers up' (l. 1346) because the text before him reads 'incitatrici' (1582 and 1583) rather than the correct reading 'imitatrici' (imitators), which is introduced in the 1585 edition. As it is the only one that includes all the variants followed by Kyd, the 1583 edition must be identified as the one Kyd used. On balance, it seems likely that Kyd may have used the standalone-volume issue, since it was cheaper and easier to work with on a practical level given its reduced size. Accordingly, the 1583 edition is my reference point in comparing Tasso's Italian and Kyd's translation. When previous commentators did so, they sometimes decided to use Ezio Raimondi's edition; however, despite being the most authoritative critical edition of Tasso's text to date, Raimondi's edition is based on Tasso's manuscript, which at times differs significantly from the editions available to Kyd. A comparison between the text of *Il padre di famiglia* as edited by Raimondi and Kyd's translation is bound to be misleading.

AUTHORSHIP

There is no contention as to the fact that 'T. K.' must be identified with Thomas Kyd. Boas persuasively argues for similarities between *Cornelia* (which is indisputably by Kyd) and *The Householder's Philosophy* both

13 *OED n.* 8b.

in the dedication and the main text; Freeman observes that 'T. K.' is 'an uncommon set of initials; and the only appropriately named writer of similar pretensions they might also fit is Timothy Kendall, whose *Epigrams* appeared in 1576. But Kendall's literary style is altogether different from Kyd's, and far from compatible with the translation in question.'[14] Probably, Kyd translated *Il padre di famiglia* on commission. It seems, however, impossible to identify the 'Thomas Reade' to whom the work is dedicated.[15] In the absence of more precise evidence as to the identity of the dedicatee, one must remain by necessity sceptical of speculative assertions such as Boas's that Kyd's translation of Tasso 'not improbably helped him to secure a position which improved his fortunes'.[16]

IL PADRE DI FAMIGLIA AND ITS SOURCES

Il padre di famiglia is one among the twenty-six *Dialoghi* that Tasso penned roughly between 1578 and 1594. Although Tasso wrote these treatises (which deal with philosophical, moral, and literary issues) as different but related experiments in the same literary vein and conceived of them as making up – as it were – a virtual unity, they never reached actual unity in a single volume.[17] As Raimondi argues, the *Dialoghi* were not written following a general plan: they were the result of cumulative additions, responding instead to the chain of occasions, meetings, readings, requests, needs, and drives animating Tasso's life, which accounts for their failure to display any clear univocal intellectual evolution; at the same time, however, the *Dialoghi* share a common stylistic design and are invariably characterized by a lucid and elegant writing style.[18] *Il padre di famiglia* contains the greatest amount of narrative among the *Dialoghi*, and it is possibly the one

14 Frederick S. Boas, 'Introduction' to *The Works of Thomas Kyd* (Oxford, 1901), pp. xiii–cvii (lxii–lxiii); Freeman, *Thomas Kyd*, p. 171 n. 1. The potential references to Kyd in Thomas Nashe's preface 'To the Gentlemen Students' in Robert Greene's *Menaphon* (London, 1589) are often taken as confirmations of Kyd's identity as the translator of Tasso's prose treatise (see Erne, *Beyond*, pp. 156–60). That being said, the passage 'and these men renowncing all possibilities of credit or estimation, to intermeddle with Italian translations' (Nashe, 'To the Gentlemen Students', **3r–v) could hardly be taken on its own as firm and specific evidence of Kyd's authorship of *The Householder's Philosophy*. Yet the presence of the initials is decisive, as are the several links between *The Householder's Philosophy* and the rest of Kyd's writings.

15 Freeman, *Thomas Kyd*, p. 172.

16 Boas, 'Introduction', p. lxiv.

17 Ezio Raimondi, 'Introduzione' to *Dialoghi* di Torquato Tasso, a cura di Giovanni Baffetti, 2 vols (Milan, 1998) 1:9–56 (9).

18 Ibid.

having the most perfectly calculated structure.[19] It is unknown precisely when Tasso wrote it, despite its composition being clearly linked to precise events of his biography, namely his sojourn at the house of a noble family in Vercelli (which is perhaps to be identified with the castle of the Bolgaro family) during his 1578 flight from Ferrara to Turin, where Tasso hoped to find shelter under the protection of the House of Savoy. Other memories take the reader back to a previous journey of Tasso's to France with Cardinal Luigi d'Este in 1570–1.[20]

The philosophical texture of *Il padre di famiglia* draws upon the model provided by the pseudo-Aristotelian *Oeconomicus*, as Tasso makes plain by mentioning 'un libretto, che ad Aristotile è attribuito', that is, a small book attributed to Aristotle – which Kyd mysteriously translates as 'a pamphlet that is *dedicated* to Aristotle' (l. 1474, my emphasis).[21] Tasso read Jacques-Louis d'Estrebay's translation of the pseudo-Aristotelian *Oeconomicus* in a Paris edition that also contained Xenophon's *Oeconomicus* and had been first printed in 1543. Tasso's text is also indebted to Aristotle's *Politics* and to Renaissance treatises on family and human relationships. Tasso explicitly mentions Giovanni Della Casa's *Trattato de gli uffici comuni*, which he read in a 1559 Milan edition, and the influence of Sperone Speroni's *Dialogo della cura famigliare* (Venice, 1542) is evident in several passages, while Tasso may or may not have been influenced by Francesco Tommasi's similarly titled *Reggimento del padre di famiglia* (Florence, 1580). A few examples cited in the text are taken from Giovanni Stobeo's *Anthologium*, which Tasso read in the 1551 Zurich edition by Konrad Gesner, whereas the convivial conversation between the householder and the narrator owes considerably to Athenaeus of Naucratis's *Deipnosophistarum sive coenae sapientium libri XV*, which Tasso perused in Natale Conti's 1556 Latin version published in Lyons. Other sources are detailed in the commentary.

THE QUALITY OF KYD'S TRANSLATION: A REASSESSMENT

Regrettably, the quality of Kyd's translation has been virtually the only topic of sustained interest in critical discussions of *The Householder's Philosophy*. Despite Boas's acknowledgement that Kyd's prose is 'spirited and vigorous', the translation has been generally judged negatively, with commentators repeatedly focusing on its being 'crowded with blunders'.[22] Though by no

19 Ibid., p. 41; Bruno Basile, 'Nota introduttiva', in Torquato Tasso, *Dialoghi. Il Messaggiero, Il Padre di famiglia, Il Malpiglio, La Cavaletta, La Molza* (Milan, 1991), pp. 107–8 (107).

20 Basile, 'Nota introduttiva', p. 107.

21 The sources of Tasso's treatise are further detailed ibid., p. 108.

22 Boas, 'Introduction', pp. lxiii, xx.

means entirely unfounded, this seems excessively severe. A fairer reappraisal of Kyd's translation therefore seems necessary in introducing the first critical edition of the text in over 120 years.

Kyd's translation is generally in line with Renaissance practices. As Massimiliano Morini argues regarding the strategies deployed by authors such as John Florio, Philemon Holland, and James Mabbe, Tudor and Stuart translators generally 'do not alter the *inventio* and *dispositio* of their sources, but feel free to adapt the *elocutio*, the style, to their and their audience's taste'.[23] More importantly, 'their adaptations are usually amplifications, in accordance with a common Renaissance idea that identifies elegance with abundance'; as a matter of fact, Morini remarks, 'as the sixteenth century wore on, amplification exercised more and more attraction on writers and translators' especially as concerns descriptions: for Tudor and early Stuart translators, 'a concise description is no description at all'.[24]

As a careful comparison between *Il padre di famiglia* and *The Householder's Philosophy* reveals, the number of Kyd's amplifications and additions is roughly five times that of his omissions or condensations, none of which appear sizeable. In particular, Kyd's most frequent translation strategy is the augmentation of Tasso's text by means of what may be termed synonymic amplification. In other words, Kyd takes a single word, phrase, or even clause in Tasso's text and turns it into two roughly synonymous words, phrases, or clauses – sometimes even three, as with 'worth, weight, and fineness' (l. 1371) for 'finezza', and 'mason, carpenter, or architect' (ll. 1455–6) for 'architetto'. In fact, Kyd's translation offers over 200 examples of such a strategy, which are too many to list in their entirety, either here or in the commentary. Often he pairs off words to produce alliteration – e.g., 'deposed and discharged' (l. 414) for 'ha deposto'; 'companions and consorts' (l. 442) for 'consorti'; 'base slaves or servants' (ll. 611–12) for 'servi'; 'entertainment and embracings' (l. 622) for 'abbracciamenti'; 'servitors and subjects' (l. 714) for 'servitori'; 'purveyed or provided' (l. 858) for 'comprate'; 'devised and divided' (l. 959) for 'fu … posta'; 'despised and dispraised' (l. 1489) for 'disprezzate', etc. Kyd also frequently couples an Anglo-Saxon word with a Latinate equivalent – e.g., 'of reasoning and talk' (l. 163) for 'del ragionare'; 'unpleasant or hurtful' (l. 262) for 'spiacevol'; 'greatness and magnificence' (l. 407) for 'grandezza'; 'infirmity or weakness' (l. 447) for 'infermità'; 'consort or fellow' (l. 452) for 'consorte'; 'indurate and harden' (l. 676) for 'indurargli'; 'ponderous and heavy' (l. 1289) for 'grande', etc. While this might be superficially dismissed as Kyd's way of displaying

23 Massimiliano Morini, *Tudor Translation in Theory and Practice* (Aldershot, 2006), p. 66.

24 Ibid., pp. 66, 77.

the amplitude of his own vocabulary, such doubling is in fact a mark of sixteenth-century prose, possibly reflecting the linguistic consciousness of writers who were producing the first coherent English prose discussing serious topics. In addition, as this practice was frequent in the writing of English legal documents as a means to avoid misunderstandings, it might reflect the fact that Kyd may have learned the trade of his father, who was a scribe, and therefore daily engaged in transcribing legal documents and contracts. Occasionally, Kyd even amplifies entire phrases or clauses, as when he translates 'nella notte riservate' as 'are enclosed with darkness and reserved to the night' (ll. 302–3).

Kyd's assiduous reliance on synonymic amplification seems to call into question Freeman's assertion that in Kyd's translation 'There is no euphuism or related rhetorical trickery, and the choice among synonyms nearly always seems to be for the simpler words … Kyd is closer to the chroniclers' direct narrative style than to the exfoliate belletristic style of Lily or Sidney or Greene's prose romances.'[25] To be sure, Kyd's translation never reaches the virtuosity of a prose romance, but its reiterated use of doublings and alliteration emerges as evidence of Kyd's conscious attempt at providing Tasso's text with additional rhetorical ornamentation.

Yet not all instances of Kyd's amplification can be classified as merely serving a stylistic function. In fact, while most of them do seem primarily aimed to display *copia*, others appear to be motivated by Kyd's desire for clarity and explicitness. Some of the additions clearly serve the purpose of helping readers understand Tasso's text, which seems to confirm the assumption that the book was especially addressed, on the English market, to the less well-educated readers of the burgeoning middle class. This is the case, for instance, of Kyd's more specific phrase 'according to the cosmographical description of some' (ll. 377–8), which translates Tasso's vaguer 'secondo alcuni', in the discussion over the season in which the world began, and it also occurs with mythological and geographical references, as Kyd apparently feels the need to specify that a certain Latin quotation is taken from 'the book of Virgil's *Aeneid*' (l. 467), that Penelope was 'the wife of Ulysses' (l. 1126), that Alcinous was the 'King of Phaeacians' (l. 1137), and that Praeneste and Nola are 'little towns in Italy' (ll. 1298–9).

Other translation choices seem aimed at anglicizing points of detail in the text in order to erase obscure foreign cultural elements in favour of others more familiar to English readers. For example, Kyd twice decides to avoid translating 'vigne' (ll. 992–3, 1017) in Tasso's text, since vineyards in Britain were certainly not as widespread as they were in Italy at the time. He shows a tendency to tone down superlatives – 'dolcissimo' becomes 'sweet'

[25] Freeman, *Thomas Kyd*, p. 173.

(l. 153); 'gli antichissimi secoli' becomes 'the old time' (l. 1218); 'nobilissime' becomes 'famous' (l. 1365). He translates the Italian concept of 'provincia' with the triplet 'province, shire, or country' (l. 1257), 'cavalieri' with 'gentlemen' (l. 53), and Tasso's 'manicaretti' with 'minced meat' (l. 207) in an attempt to domesticate Italian cookery. Finally, probably afraid that the obscure reference to one of Giovanni Boccaccio's *novelle* might be lost on most readers, Kyd renders the name Catelda (a character from *Decameron*, 3.6, who slept with her lover believing it was her husband) as 'Bell'Ingannus' (l. 625), thus devising a sort of *sprechender Name* joining the idea of beauty and deceit, as with the name of Bel-Imperia in *The Spanish Tragedy* mixing together the notions of beauty and rank, while simultaneously coining the word 'ingannus' by giving a Latin ending to an Italian word (*inganno*).

In broad terms, Freeman is right to argue that, despite the frequent use of Latinate words in parallel construction with Anglo-Saxon synonyms, 'in general Kyd heeds Sir John Cheke's adjuration to keep one's English clear of continental or classical coinages, or make it obvious, by italics or quotation, when such intrusions are being introduced.'[26] Borrowings from either Italian or French are indeed very infrequent, and Kyd appears to have made a point of enabling his readers to identify at a glance continental words, poetic quotations, and classical allusions through italicization.

As to syntax, Kyd follows Tasso's Italian quite closely, which causes what Freeman correctly identifies as 'a certain involution …, which … derives mainly from a somewhat legalistic overuse of periphrasis and qualifying clauses'; yet overall, Freeman continues, '*The Householder's Philosophy* is not difficult to read, and the translator has had the good sense for the most part to avoid passive constructions, sometimes employed in the original, in primary clauses.'[27]

At times, Kyd makes even more substantial additions to Tasso's Italian than the ones listed above; such additions might be interpreted as spelling out Kyd's stance on a number of issues, but Erne sensibly alerts that 'Whether any inferences about Kyd himself can be drawn from these writings is … no more than guesswork.'[28] The most sizable and interesting addition Kyd makes to Tasso's text is a vehement and protracted attack on the evils of usury, which is not to be found in *Il padre di famiglia*. Park Honan confidently speculates that Kyd 'adds *his own* diatribes to Tasso's work, in order to show that usury is "never to be cured"', thus also implying 'that moneylenders are the arch-enemies of society', and Christopher Crosbie argues

[26] Ibid., p. 174.

[27] Ibid., p. 173.

[28] Erne, *Beyond*, p. 219.

that 'The railings against usury … stem entirely from Kyd's own additions and seem to reflect his distaste for oppressive economies.'[29]

However, as I have recently demonstrated, the largest share of Kyd's additional remarks about usury (including his marginal heading) are in fact an almost verbatim translation of the Italian humanist Cristoforo Landino's commentary on the same passage of Dante's *Inferno* quoted by Tasso.[30] This not only sheds new light on Kyd's intellectual life but also exemplifies yet again the fact that amplifying a text through interpolation was considered a legitimate translation strategy in Tudor England, and apparently it was not felt necessary to acknowledge these kinds of debts. In this case, it seems to acquire supplementary significance, insofar as Kyd's decision to insert elements from such an encyclopedically comprehensive humanist text of literary criticism as Landino's *Comento sopra la Comedia di Dante* into a philosophical tract imbued with humanist notions concerning society, the family, astrology, philosophy, and cosmography also seems further to connect him with the continental intellectual *milieu*. The latter thus appears to have caught Kyd's interest even beyond his well-known penchant for neo-Senecan drama and French Renaissance literature.

Yet another dimension of Kyd's translation that has attracted virtually no commentary at all is his translations of the lines of Latin and Italian poetry quoted by Tasso: Virgil, Catullus, Petrarch, Dante, and Pietro Bembo. Freeman is the only one to have made a few remarks about them, pointing out that 'the verse-translations in *The Householder's Philosophy* are mostly into "fourteeners", … of which we have no other instance in Kyd's undoubted work (although the verse interspersed in prose writings and translations of the period is nearly always in this perhaps already quaint and outmoded form)'.[31] Apart from fourteeners, however, Kyd also uses iambic tetrameter, pentameter, and hexameter, and no one seems to have noticed that Kyd is especially interested in making all his verse translations rhyme. He deploys various rhyme schemes (AABB, ABAB, AABBB, ABABB), even making use of macaronic rhymes, thereby engaging in a playful metrical experimentation of which he would provide fuller scope in *Cornelia*.[32]

29 Park Honan, *Christopher Marlowe: Poet & Spy* (Oxford, 2005), p. 245 (my emphasis); Christopher Crosbie, '*Oeconomia* and the Vegetative Soul: Rethinking Revenge in *The Spanish Tragedy*', *English Literary Renaissance* 38 (2008): 1–33 (7).

30 Domenico Lovascio, 'Thomas Kyd's *The Householder's Philosophy* and Cristoforo Landino's *Comento sopra la Comedia di Dante*', *Ben Jonson Journal* 27 (2020): 84–104.

31 Freeman, *Thomas Kyd*, p. 174.

32 See Marie-Alice Belle and Line Cottegnies, 'Introduction', in *Robert Garnier in Elizabethan England: Mary Sidney Herbert's* Antonius *and Thomas Kyd's* Cornelia (Cambridge, 2017), pp. 1–84 (64–6).

Kyd's decision to have all his verse translations rhyme may in fact help to account for some of the translation 'blunders' with which he has been repeatedly taxed. One example is Kyd's translation of a passage from Book 9 of Virgil's *Aeneid* (ll. 697–702), which according to Boas 'he mistranslates badly'.[33] Kyd's translation is made up of three couplets of fourteeners rhyming AABBCC. According to Boas, '"purple buds" does not represent *murex*', '"your high priests' hats are made like hoods" is an incorrect rendering of *habent redimicula mitrae* … and "scale you high Ida hill" is an inaccurate version of *ite per alta Dindyma*.' Yet Boas fails to recognize a number of things. First, Kyd probably chose the words 'buds' and 'hoods' to build a rhyme; second, 'buds' is to be seen as an addition rather than a mistake; third, 'hood' could actually mean 'A separate article of apparel for the head worn by *women*', which would very effectively convey the fundamental idea of Virgil's Latin passage, namely the fear of feminization.[34] Finally, as regards '*ite per alta Dindyma*', it in fact means exactly what Kyd took it to be.[35] It should also be noted that Kyd actually understood the passage so well that he made explicit that '*Matris | Idaeae*' was Cybele.

On closer inspection, further alleged 'blunders' turn out not to be mistakes. An important instance is Kyd's translation of the Latin phrase '*ad lumina*' as 'by candlelight' (l. 1120). The translation is perfectly correct, as any decent Latin dictionary will confirm; for example, Theodore C. Williams rendered it as 'by the torch-light' in his twentieth-century translation of the *Aeneid*.[36] Yet Boas was adamant that the correct translation would have been "till dawn', and his judgment has been unquestioningly followed by all successive commentators, including Erne, who goes as far as to suggest that such a mistranslation may have prompted Nashe's sneer at Kyd that 'yet English Seneca read *by candle light* yeeldes manie good sentences' in the preface to Greene's *Menaphon*.[37] A further instance of Boas's biased perspective is his assessment of Kyd's rendering of 'uomini liberi' as 'manumitted and enfranchised' (l. 740). Boas dismisses this as a 'mistranslation'; in fact, Kyd seems in this case to be trying to be more specific and historically accurate than Tasso by using the Latinate verb 'to manumit', i.e., 'To release (a person) from slavery, bondage, or servitude; to set free.'[38]

33 Boas, 'Introduction', p. xvii.

34 *OED n.* 1b, my emphasis.

35 As can be gathered for example from *L'Eneide di Virgilio mantuano commentata in lingua volgare toscana da Giovanni Fabrini da Fighine, & Filippo Venuti da Cortona* (Venice, 1581), Kkr–v.

36 Virgil, *Aeneid*, tr. Theodore C. Williams (Boston, 1910).

37 Erne, *Beyond*, 149–50; Nashe, 'To the Gentlemen Students', **3r (my emphasis).

38 *OED v.* 1a.

One of the arguments more frequently deployed against the quality of Kyd's translation is its dedication. Freeman typically argues that 'both the modest brevity of the dedicatory poem and the choice of an uncelebrated dedicatee suggest that Kyd knew how little he had done and valued his work accordingly.'[39] Yet Kyd's description of his translation as an 'imperfection' and as so 'Plain and unpolished' as to have made 'waste' of Tasso's 'highly graced' treatise is not necessarily to be taken at face value; it may very well be an instantiation of the modesty topos that was so widespread in dedications of literary works of the period. In light of what has been shown above, it is probably more expedient to adopt the notion of 'amendment' put forward by Josephine A. Roberts and James F. Gaines in their discussion of *Cornelia* to evaluate Kyd's translation of *Il padre di famiglia* too: 'We propose the term *amendment* for two reasons: first, it implies two texts where one proceeds from the other, and second, it can involve omission, addition, or any degree of substitution or restructuring.'[40] Admittedly, *The Householder's Philosophy* can hardly 'be considered independently' of the source text, as is the case with *Cornelia*.[41] Yet, *si tertium datur*, a third alternative is therefore available between correct translation and 'blunder', so that some of Kyd's alleged errors can come to be seen in a different light. In fact, it is not always so easy to determine whether Kyd's choices stem from misunderstanding or deliberate substitution. Especially in the context of his verse translations, the very fact of having the Latin or Italian source text directly above the English translation would have allowed Kyd to focus on what he felt was the best possible rendition in English verse without having to worry excessively about any notion of 'faithfulness' to the source text. Readers who knew Latin or Italian would relish Kyd's creativity and poetic skills by comparing the source and target texts; those who did not know Latin or Italian would just not care.

Kyd's translation, however, is hardly flawless. In fact, it displays a number of evident misunderstandings, though not as many as is commonly believed. Some of his failures to understand the source text are simply inexplicable. As Boas aptly remarks:

> Kyd did not understand the significance of the term 'hero' in Greek mythology [ll. 216–17, 226, 228–9, 243, 709]. He twice shows his ignorance of important episodes in the story of Ulysses [ll. 221–2, 1136–7]. He confuses the Roman Servile War with one of the Civil Wars [l. 822],

[39] Freeman, *Thomas Kyd*, p. 172.

[40] Josephine A. Roberts and James F. Gaines, 'Kyd and Garnier: The Art of Amendment', *Comparative Literature* 31 (1979): 124–33 (125).

[41] Ibid., 133.

> and speaks of the Republican worthies as rising to be 'mightie men in Princes Courts [l. 1318]'.[42]

In addition, among other things, Kyd assigns a passage to the wrong book of the *Aeneid* in one of his marginal notes – though this could have just been a typo or a slip of the pen – while in another he chooses the English adjective '*Unkempt*' (l. 591) as a heading for the Italian '*non tosato o comato*', when a solution such as 'long-haired' would have been more appropriate. Also, when translating Tasso's allusion to the story of the Roman matron Lucrece, he fails to understand that 'se n'innamorò' refers only to Tarquin and not to Brutus as well (l. 1143), which is particularly odd given the importance and currency that Lucrece's story had in the early modern English imagination. All in all, it is hard to draw a firm conclusion based on Kyd's mistakes and amendments, but the impression is that on the one hand his classical learning may have been patchy and partly inaccurate. On the other hand, Kyd seems to have approached some sections of the translation too hurriedly, which resulted in some avoidable mistakes such as his confusing 'ghiande' (acorns) with 'ghiandaie' (jays, i.e., the birds, l. 125). At times, he just seems to have got lost in Tasso's complex syntactic acrobatics. Occasionally, he may have been led astray by misplaced punctuation or textual flaws in the 1583 edition.[43]

THE PLACE OF *THE HOUSEHOLDER'S PHILOSOPHY* WITHIN KYD'S CANON

Since the primary aim of the present edition of *The Collected Works of Thomas Kyd* is the re-definition of Kyd's canon, it seems appropriate to offer some remarks regarding the unity of *The Householder's Philosophy* within Kyd's oeuvre. While *The Householder's Philosophy* is unique within Kyd's canon by being both a translation and written in prose, it does simultaneously exhibit a few interesting connections to other works by the playwright.

First, as noted above, Boas points out several passages in which the phraseology used by Kyd in his translation of Tasso is close to *Cornelia* as well as to the *Letter to Sir John Puckering*. In particular, Boas suggests that Kyd's memory of a passage in *The Householder's Philosophy* in which the narrator concludes 'that autumn is the most noble and best season of the year and that which is indeed most acceptable to the housekeeper' (ll. 331–2) was probably behind his decision to describe autumn as the sweetest season

42 Boas, 'Introduction', p. xix. As for Homer, in one case Kyd may have been misled by a misplaced comma in Tasso's text; see commentary to ll. 221–2. Also see Commentary, ll. 216–17.

43 See the Commentary, ll. 25–6, 565–7, 807–9, 939.

in *Cornelia*, 2.132–5, a passage that significantly departs from the corresponding one in the source text by Garnier. The same is true, in Boas's view, of the phrase 'from the plough and cart' (ll. 1317–18), which seems to have suggested the phraseology of *Cornelia*, 1.133, which again deviates from the source text. Besides, the dedication to Thomas Reade in *The Householder's Philosophy* bears interesting similarities to that to the Countess of Sussex prefacing *Cornelia*. Kyd apologizes in both for his hasty execution of the translation, referring to his own work as 'Plain and unpolishèd' (l. 6) in the one case, and as 'rough unpolished' in the other. In addition, as Boas observes, 'in either case he asks his patron to make allowance for the loss of "grace" which the original has suffered under his hands. In both instances, too, he hints at detractors of the work, who will either "carpe" at it, or wonder at his undertaking it without the necessary qualifications.' Boas also remarks upon a few unusual lexical choices in *The Householder's Philosophy*, namely Kyd's use of the adjective 'regardant' (l. 109, cf. *Cornelia*, 5.207) and the verbs 'to signorize' (l. 745, cf. *Cornelia*, 1.55; 3.2.72) and 'to quader' (l. 995, cf. *Letter to Sir John Puckering*).[44] To these, the use of the adjective 'champaign' should be added (l. 1025, cf. *Cornelia*, 5.176), together with the decision to conclude both translations with a Latin *sententia* (cf. '*Me mea sic tua te | Cetera mortis erunt*' and '*Non prosunt Domino quae prosunt omnibus | Artes*').

In addition, it is possible to identify in *The Householder's Philosophy* the use of specific lexical items that recur in several other works of the canon. This is the case, for instance, of the noun 'thrall' (l. 793), which seems to be a favourite word of Kyd's, appearing in all his plays of uncontested attribution (*Cornelia*, 2.403; *Soliman and Perseda*, 5.Prol.6; *The Spanish Tragedy*, 2.1.27), while *Fair Em* has the participle 'thralled' (1.26, 34, 2.34). The same occurs with the unusual noun 'epithetons' (ll. 590, 1168), which Kyd also deploys in *Soliman and Perseda* (1.2.75).

Moreover, based on the results of Brian Vickers's systematic search of *The Householder's Philosophy* for phraseological matches with the three canonical plays and the newly attributed ones by means of antiplagiarism software (which automatically picks out every instance in which three consecutive words appear in two texts), it is possible to make some further considerations. As it is not possible to discuss here all the matches identified by Vickers, I will limit myself to mentioning a few that seem to carry special significance. One is the use of the phrase 'princely lion' (l. 578) in both *The Householder's Philosophy* and *King Leir* (7.60). While this phrase was not exclusive to writings by Kyd, it is interesting to note that in choosing the adjective 'princely' Kyd was making a deliberate addition to Tasso's text.

44 Boas, 'Introduction', pp. lxii–lxiii.

Then, in the sentence 'it **giveth** us **to understand that** married women are not forbid' (ll. 643–4), Kyd deploys the same syntactic construction that can be found in *King Leir* ('there **shall be given to understand that** my father hath detracted her', 12.87–8) and in *Fair Em* ('It **is given** us **to understand that** your daughter is suddenly become both blind and deaf', 11.22–3). In this case, the similarity is even more impressive in light of the fact that the same syntactic construction is used each and every time to talk about people in the family ('married women', 'my father', 'your daughter').

As regards *Arden of Faversham*, it seems worth pointing out that 'covered with a cloth' (1.237) is very similar to 'covered with a cloud' (l. 636) in *The Householder's Philosophy*, especially in the writer's making 'covered' alliterate with a noun starting with a /kl/ sound. Finally, Kyd's translation of Tasso argues that if a husband does 'not first **violate** the bands **by so defiling of the marriage bed**, he shall doubtless much confirm **the woman's chastity**' (ll. 542–4). *Arden of Faversham* features a passage that displays striking phraseological similarities with this one:

> I am by birth a gentle man of blood,
> And that injurious ribald that attempts
> **To violate my dear wife's chastity** –
> For dear I hold her love, as dear as heaven –
> **Shall on the bed which he thinks to defile,**
> See his dissevered joints and sinews torn,
> Whilst on the planchers pants his weary body,
> Smeared in the channels of his lustful blood. (1.35–42)

The closeness between the two passages is unmistakable and seems all the more significant given that in *The Householder's Philosophy* Kyd is actually expanding Tasso's text by introducing the phrase 'by so defiling of the marriage bed', possibly in order to make the accusation against adulterous husbands sharper than it is in the source text. While each of these parallels, analogies, and similarities would not appear to suggest much when considered in isolation, the cumulative evidence does in fact seem to place *The Householder's Philosophy* rather firmly within Kyd's accepted and newly proposed canon.

TEXT: COLLATION AND SURVIVING COPIES

The Housholders Philosophie (*STC* 23702.5) collates: 4°, ¶2, *4, A–G4; 34 leaves; foll. 1–27; $4 signed (–*4, G3, G4). Its contents run: ¶1r, title (verso blank); ¶2r, dedicatory epistle to 'Maister Thomas Reade Esquier' signed 'T.K.' (verso blank); *1r–*4r, index headed '*The Table.*' (*4v blank); A1r–G3v, text headed '*The Housholders* [left] *Philosophie.* [right]' signed 'T.K.' at the end. Engraved upper-case initials appear at the start of the index on sig. *1r (A) and the start of the text on A1r (I); a large but undecorated initial starts the dedicatory epistle on ¶2r (W). The same arrangement of the printer's flower heads ¶2r, *1r, and A1r. Ornaments appear on ¶2r and *4r. The dedicatory epistle is in roman type with incidental use of italic; the index is in roman type with headings in roman and italic; the text is in black letter with incidental use of roman type and italic. Marginal notes are in Latin and English, both in roman type with incidental use of italic. The text proper occupies 36 lines per page. The printed marginal notes, which consist of explanations regarding geography and natural history, identifications of classical allusions, and a gloss on an Italian phrase, are Kyd's addition.

STC 23702.5 copies are held at the Bodleian Library (Antiq.e.E.1588.3) and the Shakespeare Birthplace Trust (CLASS SR – 99.3/; Accession n. 81048246). *STC* 23703 copies are held at the British Library (003583171), the Bodleian Library (Antiq.e.E.1588.5), the Huntington Library (Rare Books 31925, which is the copy available in *EEBO*), the Beinecke Rare Book and Manuscript Library (BEIN 2013 479), and the Massachusetts Historical Society Library (Winthrop Lib. Pamphlets). There is therefore a total of seven known extant copies.[45] *STC* 23703 has a cancel title page, on which the words 'Whereunto is anexed a dairie Booke for | all good huswives' appear in minute letters. The reissue was reprinted (from Antiq.e.E.1588.5) in 'The English Experience, Its Record in Early Printed Books Published in Facsimile' series (Amsterdam: Theatrum Orbis Terrarum, 1975). Only one copy preserves the title page in its original state (Bodleian, Antiq.e.E.1588.3, which is the control text chosen for the present edition), while five others have the extended title page. The Shakespeare Birthplace Trust copy only has the text proper: it starts from A1r, the previous leaves having been removed, and ends at G3v, due to the removal of G4. Together with the Huntington copy and one of the Bodleian copies (Antiq.e.E.1588.3), it has discontinuous folio numbers after fol. 12: the numbering is 15, 14, 13, 16 instead of 13, 14, 15, 16. It also exhibits a few markings on G3v. The Beinecke copy exhibits a significant amount of underlinings from A1v to F4v, with no discernible rationale behind them. This copy also displays a few marginal comments on A4r, B3v, C4r, D4r, and E3v. One of the Bodleian copies (Antiq.e.E.1588.3) has a few markings on A4r and G4v. Overall, the markings and comments appear scarce across the seven copies, which would seem to hint at readers' lack of engagement with the text.

[45] I am grateful to the Malone Society for a research grant that enabled me to acquire digital reproductions of five of these exemplars.

The only critical edition of *The Householder's Philosophy* to date is that by Frederick S. Boas in *The Works of Thomas Kyd* (Oxford: Clarendon Press, 1901).

BIBLIOGRAPHY

Arber, Edward, *A Transcript of the Registers of the Company of Stationers of London, 1554–1640*, 5 vols (London, 1875–94).

Basile, Bruno, 'Nota introduttiva', in *Dialoghi. Il Messaggiero, Il Padre di famiglia, Il Malpiglio, La Cavaletta, La Molza* by Torquato Tasso (Milan, 1991), 107–8.

Belle, Marie-Alice and Line Cottegnies, 'Introduction', in *Robert Garnier in Elizabethan England: Mary Sidney Herbert's* Antonius *and Thomas Kyd's* Cornelia (Cambridge, 2017), 1–84.

Bennett, H. S., *English Books and Readers 1558 to 1603* (Cambridge, 1965).

Boas, Frederick S., 'Introduction' to *The Works of Thomas Kyd* (Oxford, 1901), xiii–cvii.

Comensoli, Viviana, *'Household Business': Domestic Plays of Early Modern England* (Toronto, 1996).

Crosbie, Christopher, '*Oeconomia* and the Vegetative Soul: Rethinking Revenge in *The Spanish Tragedy*', *ELR* 38 (2008): 1–33.

Erne, Lukas, *Beyond* The Spanish Tragedy*: A Study of the Works of Thomas Kyd* (Manchester, 2001).

Freeman, Arthur, *Thomas Kyd: Facts and Problems* (Oxford, 1967).

Honan, Park, *Christopher Marlowe: Poet & Spy* (Oxford, 2005).

Lawrence, Jason, *'Who the Devil Taught thee so much Italian?': Italian Language Learning and Literary Imitation in Early Modern England* (Manchester, 2005).

Lovascio, Domenico, 'Thomas Kyd's *The Householder's Philosophy* and Cristoforo Landino's *Comento sopra la Comedia di Dante*', *BJJ* 27 (2020): 84–104.

Melnikoff, Kirk, 'Thomas Hacket and the Ventures of an Elizabethan Publisher', *Library* 10 (2009): 257–71.

—— *Elizabethan Publishing and the Makings of Literary Culture* (Toronto, 2018).

Morini, Massimiliano, *Tudor Translation in Theory and Practice* (Aldershot, 2006).

Nashe, Thomas, 'To the Gentlemen Students', in *Menaphon* by Robert Greene (London, 1589), **–A3r.

Raimondi, Ezio, 'Introduzione' to *Dialoghi* by Torquato Tasso, 2 vols (Florence, 1958), 1:3–313.

—— 'Introduzione' to *Dialoghi* by Torquato Tasso, edited by Giovanni Baffetti, 2 vols (Milan, 1998), 1:9–56.

Roberts, Josephine A. and James F. Gaines, 'Kyd and Garnier: The Art of Amendment', *Comparative Literature* 31 (1979): 124–33.

Virgil, *L'Eneide di Virgilio mantuano commentata in lingua volgare toscana da Giovanni Fabrini da Fighine, & Filippo Venuti da Cortona* (Venice, 1581).

Wall, Wendy, *Staging Domesticity: Household Work and English Identity in Early Modern Drama* (Cambridge, 2002).

The only critical edition of [illegible] to date is that by [illegible] (1911).

[illegible]

The Householder's Philosophy.

Wherein is perfectly and profitably described the true *Oeconomia* and form of housekeeping.

With a table added thereunto of all the notable things therein contained.

First written in Italian by that excellent orator and poet Signor Torquato Tasso and now translated by T. K.

AT LONDON

Printed by J. C. for Thomas Hacket,

and are to be sold at his shop in Lombard Street, under the sign of the Pope's head.

M.D.LXXXVIII.

To the worshipful and virtuous gentleman Master Thomas Read, Esquire, health and all happiness

Worth more than this, digested thus in haste,
    Yet truly set according to the sense,
    Plain and unpolishèd for making waste
Of that which Tasso's pen so highly graced,
This work I dedicate to your defence.
    Let others carp; 'tis your discretion
    That must relieve mine imperfection.

Your worship's most affectionate

T. K.

A Catalogue or Index of those things worth the memory contained in this book

A

page

Achilles is not to be imitated of a noble man 283
Aid amongst servants for the help and ease of one another necessary 288
Action distinguished 288
Art of weaving honourable 292
Artificers defined 288
Autumn more copious of fruits than the springtime 273
Autumn wherefore judged the best of other seasons 274
Age in marriage to be looked unto 278
Apparel for women 280
Artificial riches, what 290

B

Beauty more regarded in a woman than a man 280
Beauty forced by painting insupportable in a woman 279
Beef at feasts more used for fashion than food 271
Beef sought for and desired by Ulysses' servants in their travel *eodem*
Body wedded to the soul 276

C

Catullus, why he called wine bitter 272
Colour of wine, and what it ought to be *eodem*
Circe given to weaving 293
Commodities of the spring and of autumn 273
Complexion of servants and what it should be 286
Conditions in servants *eodem*
Consideration in conditions of possessions 289
Clerks or secretaries, who and what they ought to be *eodem*
Conjunction of man and wife like that of the body and the soul 276
Conservation of things, how it should be used by a good housewife 291
Customs in bringing up of children 283

Care of housekeeping of divers sorts, and whether they vary in form only or in gettings 301
Care of children, how it is to be divided 'twixt father and the mother 282
Care of the housewife concerning things that are brought into the house 291
Cares necessary for a housekeeper desirous to preserve his wealth 289
Care of household is divided into two parts 276
Care of housekeeping as great to the fathers and masters thereof as is the care of a kingdom to a king 275
Cleanliness in housekeeping 287
Care of servants in their sickness 288
Chastisement towards servants, what 284
Country provision unbought serving for the table 269
Conserves necessary in houses 291

D

Desire of riches and how far it doth concern a housekeeper 297
Difference betwixt exchange and usury 298
Difference of servant and sovereign or master founded first by nature 284
Delights of the spring and of autumn 273
Division of land quadripartite 269
Difference betwixt the instruction of servants and of beasts 285
Discommodities of summer and winter 273
Disobedience of wives, whence it riseth 278
Distinction of nobility betwixt man and wife, how great 277
Difference in merchandise 296

E

Earth universal nurse of all things 295
Education of children as well appertains to the mother as the father 282
Education of children and what it ought to be 283
Exercise of housekeepers for health 298
Equality in marriage to be respected 277
Equality in marriage, wherein it doth consist *eodem*
Exercise, a husbandman's physic 298

F

Families or households, of what sort of servants to be made 286
Factors and surveyors and overseers *eodem*

Feasts not forbidden to women 280
Fortune maketh many men servile 286
Fruits preserved in vinegar 292
Fruits of the earth are natural gains 295
Fear not commendable in a man 281
Form of getting, what 295

G

Gain in war natural 295
Gain unnatural, how it is distinguished 298
Gain purchased with sweat or sweet *eodem*
Gain honestly made by the mistress of the house 292
Grapes gathered out of season 272
Grapes growing in Greece, of what colour, and what wine is made of them *eodem*
Grapes gathered in autumn 271

H

Homer, why he called wine sweet and why bitter 272
Homer, what properties he gave to wine *eodem*
Housewifery consisting much in spinning 292
Hair a great ornament of nature 280
Hair cut from women's heads and why *eodem*
Honest recreation not to be withheld from women *eodem*
Harts not bred in Africa 271

I

Idleness and ease make some servants evil 286
Instruments of household to be kept clean 287
Imitation of nature 284

L

Love figured without a beard 280
Lovers' wanton embracings different from those of married folk 281
Love of children 282
Linen and woollen weaving necessary in housekeeping 292

M

Money, why and how found out and used 290
Matrimony maketh equal many differences 278
Marriage, at what years to be solemnized 270
Meat wanting upon sudden entertainment of guests, how to be supplied 292
Mothers ought to give their own children suck 281
Mothers ought not to be too tender to their children 282

N

Nature changed by nurse's milk 281
Nurses commonly ordinary persons 282
Natural gain, how to be raised 295
Natural riches, what 290

O

Offices, how and when to be distinguished 286
Oxen placed by Hesiod instead of servants 285
Opinions of some concerning the soul 276
Orders in household business 286
Order of publicans 296

P

Practises of mind and body, how to be used 283
People regard appearances 284
Petrarch's opinion of the people *eodem*

Q

Quality of substance, what 290
Quality of servants, what 286

R

Revenues 290
Rents *eodem*
Regard of householders 291
Reason necessary in servants 285
Riches, how to be considered 297

S

Servants working 286
Servants' care in maintaining of their working tools 287
Salary or wages fit for servants 284
Shamefastness not improper to a married man 279
Situation of lands 269
Servants a defence to their master 285
Servants different from slaves 283
Servants, what and who they be 286
Servants, how to be used *eodem*
Servile wars begun by servants 285

T

Thales, one of the seven wise men of Greece, how he became rich 291
Times of the year to be considered of a householder and good husbands *eodem*

V

Virtues proper to men, what 279
Virtues proper to women *eodem*
Usury, how pernicious a thing it is 299

W

Wealth, how to be used 289
Weaving, how first found out 292
Women, how to be chosen in wedlock 277
Women married rather young than old 278

FINIS

The Householder's Philosophy

It was then about that time of the year that the grape-gatherers were wont to press their wines and that the trees were seen in some place despoiled of their fruit when I, in the habit of an unknown pilgrim, rode betwixt Novara and Vercelli, where, seeing the air wax black, and environed on every side with clouds ready to rain, I began to set spurs to my horse, but the whilst I heard a confused cry of dogs and turning me about I beheld a little kid surcharged, pursued, and anon overtaken by two swift greyhounds, insomuch as it there died at my feet. The unexpected pleasure of which game stayed me till a youth of eighteen or twenty years of age, tall of stature, of a good aspect, well-proportioned, tough-sinewed, and of a strong constitution, beating and crying out upon the dogs, took the poor kid from forth their mouths and gave it to a peasant attending on him, that laid it on his shoulders and at a beck of the youth gat him swiftly on before, whereupon the young man, turning towards me, said: 'Tell me, sir, of courtesy, whither is your journey?' 'I would to Vercelli', quoth I, 'this evening if the time would give me leave.' 'You might haply get thither', quoth he, 'were it not that the river that runneth before the city and that divideth the confines of Piedmont from those of Milan is so overflown that you can hardly pass it, so that I would advise you, if it please you, to lodge with me this evening, for not far hence near that river I have a little cottage, where you may repose yourself with less disease than in any other place nigh thereabouts.' Whilst he thus spake, I steadfastly beheld him, and methought I perceived in his very countenance a kind of gentility and grace, so that (judging him to be of no base or mean condition), seeing him afoot, giving my horse to a hireling that came with me, I dismounted. 'Thereupon', quoth he, 'you shall advise yourself yonder on the riverside whether you were better to pass on or stay, and thither will I go before, not to arrogate any superiority, but as your guide, because perhaps you are not well acquainted with the way.' 'Fortune', quoth I, 'doth favour me with too noble a conduct. God grant in other things she show herself as prosperous.' Here I became silent, and I followed him, but he regarded oft and often overlooked and looked on me as if he were desirous – it seemed – to understand of whence I was, so that I prevented his desire and in some sort to satisfy him said: 'I was never till now in this country, but heretofore going into France I passed by Piedmont, howbeit I repent me not that I came this way, for the country is very pleasant and inhabited of people passing courteous.' Here, perceiving that I ministered occasion of speech, he could no longer hide what he desired but said:

'Tell me, I pray you, what are you, what countryman, and what good fortune led you into these parts?' 'I was born', quoth I, 'in Naples, a famous city of Italy, my mother a Neapolitan, my father of Bergamo, a city situate in Lombardy; my name and surname I conceal, for they are so obscure as, if I should report them, yet you could not be the more informed of my state. The wrath of Fortune and of mighty men I shun, howbeit I am eftsoons shrouded under the estate of Savoy.' 'Under a magnanimous, just, and gracious prince you sojourn then', quoth he, but, modestly remembering that I desired to conceal some part of mine estate, he enquired no further of me. We had now walked little more than half a mile but we arrived on the side of the river, swifter than which never ran arrow fro forth the strongest bow of Parthia, and it was swollen so high as it far surpassed the wonted limits, neither could it be contained in the compass whereunto it was accustomed. And it was told me by the countrymen commorants there that the *passador* would not put off from the other side, but that (upon what occasion they knew not) he had refused to waft over some French gentlemen that would have given more than ordinary for their passage. Whereupon, turning to the youth that was my guide, I said that necessity now bound me to accept his courtesy, which notwithstanding I had not yet determined to refuse. 'Albeit', quoth he, 'I had rather acknowledge this favour proceeding from your own disposition than from fortune, it pleaseth me notwithstanding that she hath wrought it in such sort as we shall have no need to doubt of your abode.'

Thus more and more he confirmed mine opinion that he was neither of ignoble birth nor mean capacity, whereupon, content to be consorted with so well accomplished a host, 'The sooner', quoth I, 'you shall please that I receive the favour to be lodged, the more shall I accept of it', and therewithal he led me to his house, that was not far situate from the riverside, and it was as high as on the outside we might easily perceive it comprehended divers rooms and stories one above another. Before the house there was a little court environed with trees, and there they ascended by double stairs which were without the gate, either of them containing five and twenty large and most commodious steps. On the top of the stairs we entered into a fair hall, four-square and of convenient greatness, for it had two portals on the right and two on the left side, and as many in the upper end. Directly against the gate whereby we entered was there another gate, and thereby we descended by as many other steps into a little court about the which were pretty lodgings for servants and houses for corn, and thence we passed into a garden large enough and filled with fruitful trees, very orderly and artificially disposed. The hall was furnished with hangings and every other ornament beseeming the lodging of a gentleman. In the midst thereof was the table covered and the cupboard charged with curious plates of Candy, furnished with all sorts of dainty fruits. 'Fair and passing well-placed', quoth I, 'is this goodly house, and it cannot be possessed but of some noble gentleman, who, though amongst the woods and in a country town, lets not yet to imitate the delicacy and neatness of the city; but are you the lord thereof?' 'Not I', quoth he, 'my father is, whom God grant a long life, neither deny I him to be a gentleman of the city or unexperienced in court or on the world's conditions (albeit he hath spent the greater part of his time in the country), having a brother that hath long been a courtier in Rome and that yet abideth there, highly favoured of the good Cardinal Vercelli, whose valour and authority in these quarters highly are accounted of.' 'And in what part of Europe and of Italy', quoth I, 'is that good cardinal known and not accounted of?'

Thus as we were reasoning, there met us another youth of less years, but no less gentle spirit, that brought word of his father's coming, who eftsoons was returned from surveying his possessions. And anon there came the father on horseback, attended with a footman and another servitor that rode before, who, dismounted, immediately came up the stairs. He was a man of middle age, yet nearer threescore than fifty, of countenance very pleasant, mixed with comely gravity, and by the whiteness of his hair and beard, that only made him seem old, his dignity was much augmented. I, framing my passage towards the good man and master of the house, saluted him with that reverence which I thought fitting both his years and such as he should seem. And he, turning to his elder son with a pleasant countenance, asked him whence I was, 'For I have never seen him hereabouts or elsewhere', quoth he, 'to my remembrance.' To whom his son made answer thus: 'He cometh from Novara and travels towards Turin'; but, making nearer to his father, he whispered to him in such sort that he would enquire no further of my state but said: 'Whencesoever he be, he is welcome here ashore, for he is happened on a place where, to our power, honour and service always hath been used to strangers.' I, thanking him for his courtesy, prayed that, as I willingly received this favour of him, so in other things I might show myself mindful and regardant.

These things thus discoursed, the servants had provided water for our hands, and, having washed, we sat as it pleased the good old gentleman, who desired to do me honour, being a stranger. Forthwith was the table furnished with fruits, as melons, citrons, and such like, which at the end of supper were at a wink of his reserved and set up, and then he began thus: 'The good old man Corycius, the gardener of whom I remember I have read in Virgil,

Nocte domum dapibus mensas onerabat inemptis
(Hied home at night and filled his board with delicates unbought),

and in imitation whereof Petrarch speaketh, reasoning of his ploughman:

E poi la mensa ingombra
Di povere vivande
Simili a quelle ghiande
Le quai fuggendo tutto il mondo onora
(And then he decks his board about
With meats of mean esteem
Like to those jays whose flight contents
The world, 'cause fair they seem),

so that you need not marvel if I after their fashion fill your table with unbought viands, which though they be not such as you are used to taste elsewhere, remember you are in a country town and lodged in the house of a poor host.' 'I hold it', quoth I, 'a happy thing to have no need to send for necessaries to the city for the supply of good manners, I mean not of good meat, for thereof, sir, meseems here wants no store.' 'It lightly happeneth not', quoth he, 'that I send to the city for anything necessary or fit for the life of a poor gentleman, for – God be praised – I have abundance of everything ministered unto me upon mine own ground, the which I have divided into four parts or forms, call them what you will. The first and greatest part I plough and sow with wheat and all kind of grain. The second part I leave for trees and plants, which are also necessary either for fire, the use of architecture, and other instruments of household, as also in those places that are sown are many rews of trees, whereupon the vines after the manner of our *petit* countries are laid and fastened. The third is meadow ground, whereon the herds and little flocks I have are wont to graze. The fourth I have reserved for herbs, flowers, and roots, where also are some store of hives for bees, because beyond this orchard, wherein you see that I have grafted so many fruitful plants and which you see is somewhat separate from my possessions, there is another garden full of all sorts of salad-herbs and other roots.'

'You have well divided your lands', quoth I, 'and it is well seen that you are studious of Varro, not of Virgil only. But these melons here that are so sweet, are they also growing upon your own ground?' 'Yea', quoth he, 'and, if they please you, eat of them and tarry not for me, for if I have eaten but a little, it hath not been for sparing them, but because I deem them scarce wholesome, for, albeit they be sweet of savour and pleasant to the taste, nevertheless, hanging always on the earth and not discovered on all sides to the sun, it must needs be that there they soak up the superfluous humours of the earth, which most commonly (being impossible to be well or equally ripened by the virtue of the sun, which cannot enter into every part) it happeneth that there are few good melons to be found, but that many of them taste like gourds and cucumbers, which also hang upon the earth unripened.'

Here he became silent, and I, to show that I allowed of that he spake, said little, knowing that old men or they that grow in years were ever more desirous of reasoning and talk than any other thing, for we cannot please them better than to hearken to their speeches with attention. But he then, almost at a stay, said, because his wife was wanting: 'Sir, my wife, being withdrawn from your presence, haply looks to be invited; therefore, if it please you, I will cause her to be called, for, albeit I know that modest strangers are more abashed with the company of women than of men, yet not only the town but the custom of our country carrieth a certain privilege, whereof it will be well that you begin to advise yourself.'

The wife, being called, came and sat her down at the upper end of the table in that place that was purposely left empty for her, and the good man of the house began again: 'Now have you seen', quoth he, 'all my dearest things, for heaven hath not granted me a maiden child, for which I were to thank them much, were it not but that my wife lamententh oft for want of one to bear her company, for my sons are for the most part absent and employed otherwise, wherefore I thought good to have married mine eldest son, had he not much disliked and entreated to the contrary.' 'I cannot', quoth I, 'in any sort commend this custom of marrying young men so soon, for it standeth not with reason that they should first be getting children before themselves were come unto their growth, whereunto methinks your son here hath attained; besides, the fathers ought to exceed their children always eight and twenty or thirty years at the least, for otherwise they are in the vigour of their years when the youth of their sons begins to flourish, insomuch as their desires are yet unaccomplished, which if by none other means yet by example of their children they might moderate, and oft it is the cause that such regard is scarcely had or used to them by their children as is due to parents, for many times they are companions and brothers in their conversation; nay, now and then (which is most abominable) they are rivals and competitors in love, where, if they exceeded more in years, their fathers could not match them in their young desires, but, being decrepit, should solely expect and approve that aid and comfort at their hands which is their due and nature bindeth children unto. And herein I remember that apt form of speech used by Lucretius: *natis munire senectam*, for by nature children are the fortress and defences of their parents, neither could they be such, were they not of able and sufficient years when their parents are arrived and come unto their age, whereunto yourself being eftsoons nigh, methinks you ought to hold yourself no less satisfied of the help you have than of the good conditions of your son, who, though he cannot yet find in his heart to be married, shall happily conform himself thereunto ten or twelve years hence and time enough.' Whilst I spake thus, I remembered that my argument was more acceptable to the son than the father, and he, according to my remembrance, said: 'I hunted not all in vain today, for I have not only killed, but, more than I looked for, I have happened on an honest advocate to plead my cause', and thereupon he carved me of the daintiest morsels of the kid and laid it on my trencher, whereof some was roast, some was baked after the manner of minced meat. With the kid was served in several dishes some part of a wild boar, dressed after our country fashion with lard, and in two other dishes two pair of pigeons, the one roasted, the other boiled. 'This wild boar', quoth the good man, 'was taken by a gentleman, a friend and neighbour of ours, who oftentime participates the profit of his sports with my son; the pigeons, them I have from my own dovehouse, and with these few have we furnished a poor supper; as for beef and such like, I hold it rather a trouble to the stomach and the table than a necessary meat for this contagious weather.' 'It sufficeth me,' quoth I, 'if it be not more than needs, to eat of two kinds of wild flesh, and methinks I have supped with noble men tonight, in whose time we read there was none other flesh eaten than beef, pork, and venison, and such like, for the banquets of Agamemnon, as we read in Homer (although, by the opinion of Lucian, they might deserve to have old Nestor at them almost as a parasite), were not furnished with other viands; and the companions of Ulysses bore not so many mishaps and heats of the sun for the desire of pheasants or partridge but to feed upon beef; Virgil likewise induceth Aeneas, that in Africa slew seven harts, where, after the judgement of some, it should have been some other thing, for in Africa are no harts bred, but, in having regard to the convenience and custom of noble men's diet, he feigned or forgat that which properly is used and eaten in that province.'

'And wherefore', quoth the old man, 'did the poets feign that noble men of their time did eat such kind of flesh?' 'Because', quoth I, 'they are of great nourishment, and they, as those that exercise themselves with much labour, had need of great nourishment, which birds cannot yield that are so easily digested, but the flesh of wild beasts, although they be of great nourishment, yet are they wholesome because they be much exercised and stirring, and their fat is far more natural than that of swine or other beasts that fatteneth by the hand, for it is not so soon puffed up and fattened as those beasts that commonly are stalled and foddered; therefore, it was aptly said of Virgil, speaking of Aeneas's soldiers,

> *Implentur veteris Bacchi pinguisque ferinae*
> (And they are filled every one
> With old wine and fat venison),

for they fed thereof at will without any noisome or superfluous fullness. Herewithal I held my peace, and the old man began thus: 'The discourse that you have made of wine and of the ancient times of noble men makes me remember that which I have heard observed of Homer, who evermore in praising wine called it *nigrum et dulce*, which two conditions methinks are not very commendable, and so much the more it seemeth strange unto me that he should give wine commendations of that sort the more I have observed that the wines of Levant which are brought over here to us are white of colour, as are the malmseys and the Roman wine, which I have tasted of in Venice;[1] without that the wines which in the kingdom of Naples are called Grecian wines because they were made of the grapes that grow in Greece be white or, rather, gold-coloured, as that above all the rest is whereof we have spoken. And those wines are more properly white that are of the Rhine of Germany and those others that grow in cold countries, where the sun hath not so much force as it can ripen grapes before the time of grape-gathering, albeit haply the manner of their making may also be the cause of their whiteness.'

Here I answered that the wines were termed sweet of Homer with that kind of metaphor wherewith all things, either pleasing to the senses or acceptable to the mind, are required to be sweet. 'Howbeit,' quoth I, 'I deny not that perhaps he loved sweet wines himself, which also most contenteth me; neither is this sweetness of wine unpleasant or hurtful but at some seasons, and the malmsey, and Greek and Roman wines, whereof we have made mention, all of them have some kind of sweetness, which is nevertheless lost the older the wine is; whereupon we read:

Inger mi calices amariores
(Pray fill with bitter wine
These chalices of mine).

This was not because the poet desired bitter wine (for there is none to whom bitterness is not unpleasant), but because old wine, losing the sweetness, yieldeth that sharp and heady taste which he calleth bitter, and I would so wish you to understand that it is called sweet of Homer as it was called bitter by Catullus; afterwards, Homer calleth it black, having reference to some particular wine that was then in price as is now our lacrima, which, though it be pressed from one selfsame grape as the wine of Greece is, hath yet a vermilion colour.'[2] Having answered thus, I tasted of a cup of delicate white wine with my melons and afterwards, being begun to by him, I pledged him of a cup of neat claret wine, and upon interposition of some words we ended our merry supper, for, the meat taken away, there was set on the table all sorts of fruit in great abundance, whereof, when the old man had only tasted, he began thus to reason:

1 Wines of the eastern parts.
2 Which we call red wine.

'I have many times heard much questioning of the noblesse and variety of seasons, and I have seen two letters that are extant to be read, of Mutius the one, and the other of Tasso, wherein they contend of the worthiness betwixt winter and summer, but methinks no time may be compared to autumn, for the summer with extreme heat and the winter with extreme cold are otherwhile so intolerable as we can neither temperate the one with fruits nor the other with pastimes, and they are not only a hindrance to the mariner, who in the winter is enforced to keep the haven; to the traveller, soldier, and huntsman, who in summer are constrained to retire them from the heat, rains, and tempests under the shade of a tree or shroud of a church, whether they first find; but to the housekeeper also, who without many inconveniences cannot have the time so much as to survey his grounds. The one season, then, is full of labour and of sweat, neither enjoyeth it the third part of the fruit it bringeth forth for spoil of weather, worms, and winds. The other, slothful and sleepy, betwixt idleness and eating unjustly consumeth that which the labour of another time hath yielded, which injustice is indifferently to be noted by the difference betwixt the day and night, for in winter the day, which is most worthy, yieldeth to the night, whereof it is unreasonable that it should be overcome, and, being short, cold, and cloudy, it giveth not men convenient time to work or to contemplate, so that our operations and contemplations are enclosed with darkness and reserved to the night, a time nothing necessary for the one nor other, for the senses, that are ministers of understanding, cannot so entirely exercise their office in the night. In the summer the day becomes victor and reigneth not like a lord but like an extreme tyrant that usurpeth more than needs, leaving the night not so much time as that therein we may sufficiently restore our bodies resolved with the exceeding heat and contagions of the day, of whose shortness not only the lovers, that would have it long, were wont to lament, but the goodwife of the house also, who even then that she would nestle in the arms of her husband is by him forsaken and awaked', and therewithal he laughed so heartily looking upon his wife, that she, blushing, held down her head, and he proceeded: 'These, if I be not beguiled, are the inconveniences and discommodities of the winter and summer, whereof the spring and autumn are not to be touched, for they are fraught with millions of delights, and in their times the sun, like a most indifferent governor, formeth the day and night of such equality as the one hath little cause to complain of the other. But if we will compare autumn and the spring together, we shall soon find the spring so far inferior to autumn as hope is to effects and flowers to fruits, whereof autumn most aboundeth of all other seasons. Besides that, whatsoever fruit summer hath brought forth endureth even until then, and many other hath autumn only proper to his season, whereof as one especial is grape-gathering for the wine-press, which is, or ought to be, one of the chiefest cares the housekeeper should have, for, if he be deceived by his servants in gathering of his corn, he thereof only feels some loss and discommodity, but, if in making of his wines they practise never so little falsehood, he doth not only suffer the loss but shame, when it happeneth that, having honourable guests, he cannot commend his supper with good wines, without which *non solum frigescit Venus*, but all his meats are marred that might be dressed by the most excellent cook the Duke hath. Therefore, I conclude that autumn is the most noble and best season of the year and that which is indeed most acceptable to the housekeeper; and I remember I have heard my father say (who, if the troth reported of him may but be believed, was for natural and moral philosophy, and eloquent device, more than meanly learned) that in this season the world began, as indeed we may assuredly believe it did.'

'That', quoth I, 'hath been the opinion of some doctors of the Hebrews and Christians of great account, which notwithstanding being no article of our belief every man may credit as he list; I, for my part, am one of them that hold the contrary, and it seemeth to me more likely that, the world beginning as it is supposed, it then began about the spring, which I will thus constrain myself to prove.

You shall understand that heaven is round and hath all his parts so uniform as in it there can be perceived neither beginning nor end, right nor left, under nor over, before nor behind, which are the six positions of place, unless it haply be in respect only of the motion, because that is the right side whereof the motion hath his beginning; but, because the motion of the sun goes against the *primum mobile*, it may be doubted whether these six differences of place ought chiefly to be taken according to the motion of the *primum mobile* or according to the motion of the sun. Nevertheless, forasmuch as all things contained in this our variable and corruptible world chiefly depend upon the motion of the sun, which is the cause of generation and of corruption and is indeed the father of all living things, it is requisite that the motion of the sun determine the differences of the place. According, therefore, to the motions of the sun, our pole is the higher, which, according to the motion of the *primum mobile*, should be the lower. This being thus, if we will seek in what season it is like the world began, we shall see it is most reasonable that it then began when the sun, removing, foregoes not but approacheth us. Besides, it beginneth with generation, not with corruption, for, according to the custom of nature, things are first engendered and afterward corrupted, but the sun, removing out of Aries, it approacheth unto us and there giveth beginning to the generation and engendering of things. It is likely, then, that, when the world began, the sun was in Aries, which without doubt he shall see is so that diligently considereth what was said in Plato's *Timaeus* of God the Father to those inferior gods. True it is that who so taketh the positions of place from the motion of the *primum mobile*, it must follow that the Pole Antarctic is the higher by nature and that the world began in that season wherein the sun, removing, approacheth nearer unto our antipodes and beginneth generation in those parts of the other world that are opposite to these, which who so granteth, it would seem more likely that the world began in the autumnal equinoctial, when the sun was in Libra, and yet it would follow that it began in the spring, because this that is autumn to us is their springtime, in respect whereof the beginning of the motion should be taken. But the first opinion, as by natural reason it is most likely, so also may it be most commodiously consorted with persuasions, for our world was dignified with the presence of the true Son of GOD, who made choice to die in Jerusalem, which, according to the cosmographical description of some, is in the midst of our hemisphere. Moreover, it was his will to die in the spring of purpose to redeem our human generation in that time wherein at first he had created it.' And here I ceased, when the old man, moved with my speeches, began earnestly to look upon me and said:

'I have entertained a greater guest than I expected, and you', quoth he, 'are peradventure one of those of whom the cry is come into our country, who upon some common fault are fallen into misfortunes, whereof you are as worthy to be pardoned, considering your offence, as to be praised and admired for your speeches.' 'Report', quoth I, 'that could not haply blazon mine estimation or sufficiency, whereof you are too courteous a commender, is now derived from my misfortunes. But what or whosoever I may be, I am one that speaks more for truth's sake than of hatred, dispraise of others, or superfluous conceit of mine opinions.' 'If you be such a one,' quoth he, 'for I will not search or pry into your state, you cannot but be an indifferent and fit judge of a matter which my father, loaden both with age and with experience, participated unto me a few years before his death, giving up the government of his house and care of his family to me.' And whilst he thus spake, the servants took away, and the ancient gentlewoman, giving thanks, arose and was attended by her sons, who after a while returning, I began: 'Sir, it shall be very acceptable unto me to hear the discourse your father made unto you as you were in purpose to have told me, but, because it would be grievous unto me to hearken thereunto with the disease of those that are about us, I beseech you command your sons to sit', who obeying the gentle commands of their father, the good old man began thus:

'About that time that Charles the Fifth deposed his monarchy and withdrew himself from the world as from a tempest to contemplation and a quiet life, my good father, being then threescore and ten years old, myself somewhat more than thirty, called me to him and began to reason with me thus: "The deeds of greatest kings that turn the eyes of all the world upon their actions, albeit that for their greatness and magnificence it seems they can have no proportion of comparison with private men, nevertheless they move us now and then with the authority of their examples to imitate them in such sort as we behold the providence of our almighty God followed by nature not only in man, a reasonable creature whose dignity doth come so near the angels, but also in the industry of other little creatures, whereby it should not seem so strange to us if, now that Charles the Fifth, that thrice-renowned emperor, hath thus deposed and discharged him of the weight of his so famous monarchy, I also think by his example to disgrade me of this *petit* government of household, which to my private person is no less than is his empire to his majesty. But first, before I shall surrender this, that rather appertains to thee than to thy brother, as well in that thou art his elder as also more inclined to husbandry, a thing most needful and appropriate to housekeeping, I will so instruct thee, touching things belonging to good government, as I was taught not long since of my father, who, sprung of simple parentage and heir of a small patrimony, with industry, sparing, and good husbandry did much augment it, which hath not been deteriorated since by me, but twice as much increased since my father left it. Howbeit, if I have not looked to my husbandry with so great care nor lived so sparingly as he prescribed, nevertheless – let me boldly say thus much to thee, my son – the knowledge that I had touching the nature of things and fellowship of the world more than he hath been the cause that I with little more expense have easily accomplished what he, being unlettered and not experimented in the world, did hardly compass with much sparing and with exceeding toil even of his own person.

Now, to begin, I say thus, that the care of a good householder is divided into two things, that is, his body and his goods. In his person he is to exercise three offices, viz. of a father, a husband, and a master. In his goods two purposes are proposed, conservation and increase, touching every of which I will particularly reason, and first of his body rather than his goods, because the care of reasonable things is more worth than that of things unreasonable.

The good housekeeper, then, ought principally to have care in choosing of his wife, with whom he must sustain the person of a husband, which haply is termed by a title more effectual, consort, for the husband and the wife ought indeed to be companions and consorts of one self fortune; all the good and all the evil incident to life ought by them to be common and indifferently sustained. In such sort as the soul communicates her operations with the body, and the body with the soul, so that, when any part of the body grieveth us, the mind can hardly be content, and upon the malcontentment of the mind follows the infirmity or weakness of the body, so should the husband lament the sorrows of the wife, and the wife the troubles of the husband, and the like community should be in all offices and all operations.

And so much is that conjunction that the man hath with the wife like to that which the body hath with the soul, as not without reason the name of consort or fellow is to be attributed to the husband and the wife as to the soul it hath been heretofore attributed, forasmuch as Petrarch, reasoning of the soul, sayth,

L'errante mia consorte
(My wandering companion),

in imitation perhaps of Dante, who in his *Canzonet of Noblesse* said that the soul was espoused to the body, albeit for some other respect it ought rather to be resembled to the husband than the wife. And even as after that the band that ties the body and the soul together is dissevered it seemeth not that the soul can be conjoined with any other body, wherefore foolish is that opinion of some that imagined the soul did pass from one unto another as doth the pilgrim passing from one lodging to another, so should it seem convenient that that woman or man that have been divorced by death from that first band of matrimony ought not to be knit unto a second; nor without great admiration should Dido have continued her unwillingness of having a second husband, who speaketh thus in the book of Virgil's *Aeneid*:

Sed mihi vel tellus optem prius ima dehiscat,
Vel pater omnipotens adigat me fulmine ad umbras,
Ante, Pudor, quam te violem, aut tua iura resolvam.
Ille meos primus qui me sibi iunxit amores
Abstulit; ille habeat secum servetque sepulcro
(First would I that the parchèd earth did rive and raught me in
Or that th'almighty would with lightning drive me to the deep
Ere I to lose or violate my chastity begin.
He hath my love that first had me; interred he his shall keep).

Notwithstanding, forasmuch as custom and the laws dispense with them in this, the woman as well as the man may without shame undertake the second marriage, especially if they do it for desire of succession (a desire most natural in all reasonable creatures), but happier are they that have but once in all their life been tied with that band.

How much the greater, then, and straighter the conjunction is of the husband and the wife, so much the more ought every one provide to be indifferently matched, and truly this equality of marriage is in two special things to be considered: estate and age, for, as two palfreys or two oxen of unequal stature cannot be coupled under one self yoke, so a noble woman matching with a man of base estate or, contrarily, a gentleman with a beggar cannot be consorted well under the bands of wedlock. But, when it happeneth yet that by some accident of fortune a man marrieth a woman of so high a birth, he ought (not forgetting that he is her husband) more honour and esteem of her than of his equal or of one of meaner parentage, and not only to account her his companion in love and in his life, but in divers actions of public appearance hold her his superior, which honour is not yet accompanied with reverence as is that which for manner's sake we are wont to do to others. And she ought to consider that no distinction of nobility can be so great but that the league which nature hath ordained betwixt men and women far exceedeth it, for by nature woman was made man's subject, but, if a man shall take to wife an inferior or mean woman, he also ought to weigh that matrimony maketh equal many differences and, further, that he hath not taken her for a slave or servant, but for a fellow and companion of his life. And thus touching the estate of man and wife, let this suffice.

Now, passing to the age, I say that the husband should provide to choose his wife rather young than old, not only because a woman is more apt to childbearing in youth than otherwise, but because, according to the testimony of Hesiod, she can better receive and retain all forms of customs and conditions wherewith it shall content her husband to commend her, and for this – that the life of a woman is conscribed and ordinarily concluded in lesser time than man's and sooner waxeth old, as one in whom natural heat is not apportioned unto superfluous moisture – the man ought to exceed the woman so many years as the beginning of the one's age match not with the other's, so that one of them before the other become unable and unfit for generation. Now, if it happen that the husband take a wife with these conditions, he shall furthermore easily exercise in her that superiority that hath been granted unto man by nature, where otherwise it often cometh to pass that he shall find her so exceeding wayward, crabbed, and disobedient that, where he thought he made his choice of a companion that should help to lighten and exonerate that ponderous and heavy load which our humanity affordeth, he finds he is now matched and fallen into the hands of a perpetual enemy, who evermore none otherwise impugneth and resisteth him than our immoderate desires that in our minds so much oppose themselves to reason, for such is woman in respect of man as is desire in comparison of understanding, and even as desire, which of itself is unreasonable, is by obeying to understanding formed and beautified with many fair and necessary virtues, so a woman that conforms herself unto her husband is adorned with those virtues whereof by being obstinate she continueth unfurnished. It is, then, a virtue in a woman to know how to honour and obey her husband, not as a servant doth his master, or the body the mind, but civilly and in such sort as we see the citizens in well-governed cities obey the laws and reverence their magistrates, or so as in our souls, wherein as well the well-disposed powers as the orders of the citizens within their cities compel affections to be subject unto reason. And herein it hath been conveniently ordained of nature, for, being needful that in the fellowship of man and wife the offices and duties should be divers and the operations of the one varying from the other's, it is convenient also that their virtues should be divers.

The virtues proper to man are wisdom, fortitude, and liberality; to woman, modesty and chastity, wherewith both the one and the other of them may very well perform those operations that are requisite; but, albeit chastity or shamefastness be not properly the virtues of a man, yet ought a good husband to offend the league of matrimony as little as he possibly may and not to be so incontinent as, being absent for a season from his wife, he cannot abstain from pleasures of the flesh, for, if he himself do not first violate the bands by so defiling of the marriage bed, he shall doubtless much confirm the woman's chastity, who by nature libidinous and no less inclined to venery than man only by shame, love, and fear may not be withdrawn from breaking of her faith unto her husband, amongst which three affections fear is as worthy of praise as blame, where the other two are indeed most commendable. And, therefore, not without great reason was it said of Aristotle that shamefastness, which merits no praise in a man, is most praiseworthy in a woman, and his daughter very excellently approves that no colour better graceth or adorns a woman's cheeks than that which shamefastness depainteth, which increaseth and draweth as earnest love and desire of others to them as haply those other artificial oils and daubings which they use decreaseth and withdraweth from them, being indeed fitter for vizards, pageants, and puppets than wholesome, handsome, or toothsome.[3] And truly, as a woman of discretion will in no wise mar her natural complexion to recover it with slime or artificial coloured trash, so ought the husband in no sort to be consenting to such follies, but – because it behoveth the rule and authority of the husband to be moderate in those things chiefly which appertain to women, which, for that they are received and kept of custom, cannot be condemned as arguments of much unshamefastness – he can practise no way better to dissuade her from such muddy making fair her face than with showing himself a hater, contemner, and careless of those that are fair with that filthy sponging, pruning, painting, and polishing themselves. As for women desirous to seem fair to please others, I cannot say; but of honest women desirous to content their husbands, I may boldly speak that at such time as they shall see their tricking up their selves with lye and such like filth pleaseth not their husband's eyes, they – I know – of modesty and love will suddenly forbear it. Much more easy to be entreated should the husband be in granting her those things whereof her body with convenient ornaments should be sufficiently

3 Ovid, *De medicamine faciei: Certus amor morum est; formam populabitur aetas.*

apparelled, for, albeit superfluous pomp be fitter for a stage or theatre than the person of an honest matron, notwithstanding herein much may be attributed to use, neither should a woman's fantasy so sharply be offended, considering that by nature she is so desirous to adorn and beautify her body, for, albeit we see that nature in other creatures hath effected that the bodies of the male be more adorned than the female's, as the hart with his fair and bushy-branched horns, the princely lion with his proud and feltered locks (which the females never have), and hath embroidered the peacock's tail with more variety of colours than those of their hens, nevertheless we may perceive that in the shape of man she hath had more regard to the beauty of the female than the male, for the flesh of women, as it is more soft and dainty, so are they ordinarily more desired to be gazed on, neither are their faces shadowed with beards, which, albeit they become men, being proper unto us, yet can we not deny but that the countenances of youths, upon whose faces hair never came, are fairer and far more lovely than those of bearded men. And Love by the judicial figures of antiquity hath been portrayed like a boy; so Bacchus, so Apollo, who of all the other gods were most fair, were deciphered without beards but with long curled locks trussed up in tresses, whereupon the poets call him Phoebus with these epithetons almost continually: *non tosato o comato*.[4] But hair, which is a great ornament of nature, groweth not so hastily upon a man, nor so soft and fine as upon women, who delight in their hair as trees do in their leaves and, therefore, at the death of their husbands spoiling and disrobing themselves of all their other ornaments, they use yet in some place of Italy to cut away their hair, which also was an ancient custom, as we read of Helen in Euripides. How much the more regard, then, nature hath had to the beauty of women, so much the more convenient it is that they account of it and maintain the same with comely ornaments.

Wherefore, when thou shalt take a wife – such a one as I desire thou mayst have, fair, young, equal in estate with thee, modest, discreet, courteous, and brought up in good discipline under the education of a grave matron and wise mother – how much the more she shall content thee, so much the more thou shouldst contend not to discontent her. Wherein thou oughtst not only give consent that she may go apparelled as others of her calling do – not restraining her from going to feasts and other public shows where other honest women and those of credit do assemble, nor on the other side to give her the bridle of liberty so much that she be forward with the first at all dancings, comedies, and other such assemblies – but also not to forbid her those honest recreations and desires which are as incident to youth as flowers to the springtime, lest she hate or fear thee with the dread wherewith base

[4] Unkempt.

slaves or servants are kept under by their masters, nor yet to be so easily induced to watch or follow her as she thereby become so bold and hardy that she lay aside honest shame, a decent thing in honest women, which also is a kind of fear distinguished from servile, base fear and is as easily accompanied with love as servile fear with hate, and of this fear, which more properly is termed shamefastness or reverence, spake Homer, saying:

> *O da me ognor temuto e paventato*
> *Suocero caro*
> (O my beloved father-in-law, whom I have hourly feared).

Neither should he only cause or procure shamefastness in all her actions and business of her life, but also in her entertainment and embracings, for the husband cometh not with those profane and superstitious clippings as the delicate and wanton lover doth, which maketh me the less to marvel that the kisses of Bell'ingannus' paramour seemed sweeter to her than her husband's, albeit I believe that there was never greater sweet in love than that which moderately springs of honest matrimony. And I could compare the embracings of the husband and the wife to the temperate suppers of well-dieted men, wherein they taste no less commodity of the meats than the most incontinent and surfeiting companion, but haply so much the more by how much more their senses, ruled by reason, are upright judges of their opposites and indigested contraries. Neither will I yet desist in this mine enterprise, for, when Homer feigned that Juno, taking away Venus' garter, went to seek her husband on the Mount of Ida and, having enticed him with love and lovely terms and amorous games,

> Lay down with him upon the grass all covered with a cloud,

he meant none otherwise but this, that she, taking upon her the person of a lover and deposing the habit of a wife, went to seek Jupiter, for the fair words, pleasing fashions, and dainty whispering speech that she had taken with the garter from Venus were things more beseeming a lover than a wife; wherefore it was convenient that, being ashamed of herself, a cloud should be sent to hide her. And, where he sayth Jove had not then so much desire towards her as before when he first took her to his wife, it giveth us to understand that married women are not forbid for a little while to represent the person of young lovers, which notwithstanding she must speedily reform, because it is most unseemly in them that, as a father or mother, master or mistress of a house, desire to rule their family with honest and interchangeable love, which ought to be 'twixt man and wife, who are also to live under the laws of matrimony, for, if a man, having a vicious or unchaste wife, should presently kill her or in some other sort but punish her according to the laws, he may be haply employed better in some other action, which to eschew, taking a wife of our deciphering, he shall never need to be advertised by us.

Now, proceeding to the education of children, the care of them should be divided so between the father and the mother as she may nurse and he may teach them, for the mother ought not to deny her milk to her own children unless she be prevented or forbidden by infirmity, forasmuch as that first and tender age of infancy, apt to be moulded of any fashion, oftentimes with the milk sucketh the conditions of the nurse; besides, if the milk altered not the bodies and, consequently, the manners of young sucklings, the nurses should not be so narrowly forbid the often use of wines, but, the nurses being ordinary base persons, it follows that the first nourishment which the little ones receive of them cannot be so gentle or so delicate as the mother's, so that who so denieth the nursing of her child in some sort denies to be the mother of it, because the mother is chiefly known and commended by the bringing of her children up.

But that first age passed over that is nourished with milk, the little ones do yet continue in their mothers' custody, who are used to be so kind and tender over them as oftentimes they bring them up too delicately, for which the father is commanded to provide this remedy that, forasmuch as that first age aboundeth in natural heat, he accustom them to cold for restraining the natural heat within and, causing that which the philosophers call antiperistasis, the complexion of the child becometh strong and lusty.[5] And it was the manner of some nations, and especially those of Aquitaine and thereabouts, as we read in Aristotle, to wash their new-born children in the rivers to indurate and harden them against the cold, which custom is by Virgil attributed to the Latins, as it is to be noted in these verses:

Durum a stirpe genus natos ad flumina primum
Deferimus saevoque gelu duramus et undis:
Venatu invigilant pueri silvamque fatigant,
Flectere ludis equos et spicula tendere cornu
(A painful people by our birth, for first our babes we bring
Like us to be inured to cold and plunge them in the spring;
But bigger grown they tend the chase and tire the woods to frame
Their horses fit for service and their archery for aim),

which custom as I commend not, because to us that have not used it it seems extreme, so yet I think good to advise thee that, if it shall please God to give thee children, thou do not bring them up under so soft and easy discipline as

[5] Antiperistasis, where heat expels cold or cold expulseth heat; it is applied to well water, which is therefore cold in winter, because the high parts being cold, the heat withdraweth to the lower parts.

they become such milksops as were those Phrygians, of whom the same poet in that same book of his *Aeneid* maketh mention:

Vobis picta croco et fulgenti murice vestis,
Et tunica manicas et habent redimicula mitrae.
O vere Phrygiae, neque enim Phryges, ite per alta
Dindyma, ubi adsuetis biforem dat tibia cantum!
Tympana vos buxusque vocat berecyntia Matris
Idaeae: sinite arma viris et cedite ferro
(Your robes are dyed with saffron and with glistering purple buds,
Your coat hath mittens, and your high priests' hats are made like hoods.
O Phrygia indeed, nor Phrygians yet, scale you high Ida hill,
Where trumpets' echo clangs to those that of the custom skill!
Cybele's Berecyntian pipes and timbrels, you see,
Do call you thence: leave armour then to such as soldiers be),

whom – methinks – at this day they of some cities in Lombardy are like, for, if any there be valiant, many of the Phrygians also were courageous. Nor would I yet that thou shouldst bring them up so hardly or severely as the Lacedaemonians were accustomed or as Achilles of Chiron was. I would not – I say – that you shouldst bring them up so fiercely, for such an education makes them rather wild and savage, which though the Lacedaemonians reputed fitting for a noble man, yet was not Achilles such a one in his conditions as others of our time need to propose him or his behaviour for their example.

Thy private estate requires that so thou teach and bring up thy children as they may become good members of the city where thyself inhabitest or they shall dwell, good servitors and subjects to their prince, which in their trades if they be merchants, in good letters if they be learned, and in wars if they be able they may show themselves. Neither shall thy children be unfurnished of all or one of these professions if thou see that they become not wearish and of a womanish, effeminate complexion, but of a strong and manly constitution, and that they exercise themselves in practice of the mind and body, all alike or both together. But because all this part of education and bringing up of children is, or ought to be, in a manner the care of a father and good housekeeper – because it is wholly politic that should prescribe an order to the father how he is to educate and bring up his children to the end that the city's discipline may conform and be agreeable therewith – I will lay apart this argument or at least disjoin it from the rest which I will speak of housekeeping, and it shall suffice me solely to advise and counsel that thou bring them up in the fear and love of God, honour of their parents, and in their prince's service and obedience, and that they be continually exercised in those most commendable practices of mind and body as become them and may better their estate with praise and honesty.

We have now spoken so much as hath been convenient for thee to do in the person of a husband and a father, eftsoons it remaineth that we come to the consideration of the third person, I mean that of a governor or master, term it as you list, which solely hath relation to the servant. And if we shall give credit to antiquities written of housekeeping and government of families, the master ought to hold them satisfied with labour, victual, and chastisement, and to keep them exercised in obedience. But, forasmuch as their servants in old time were slaves taken in wars and afterward called servants *a servando* (for that they were preserved from death) and are at this day for the most part manumitted and enfranchised, methinks this latter part of chastisement might well be left as nothing requisite for our times or customs (except percase in those parts where slaves yet serve) and instead thereof the master to give them admonition, which should not be such neither as is used by the father to the son, but complete and uttered with more austerity and signorizing terms, and, if that will not serve, to suffer the disobedient, stiff-necked, and unprofitable servant to depart, and to provide himself of one that better may content him. And yet one thing hath been forgotten of those men of elder times which was not convenient for slaves, but not only fitting, but most needful, for freemen, and this is salary or wages. With wages, meat, work, and admonition, then, the housekeeper shall so govern his family as they shall rest content of him, and he be satisfied of their labour, but, because, albeit the laws and usages of men are variable and divers (as we see particularly in this of servants, who for the greater number are at this day freemen), yet forasmuch as the laws and differences of nature are not changed either by alteration of time or variety of customs – whatsoever others say – thou art thus to understand that this distinction of sovereign, ruler, governor, or master is first founded upon nature, for some are naturally born to command and others to obey, and he that is born to obey, were he of the king's blood, is nevertheless a servant, though he be not so reputed, because the people, that only have regard to exterior things, judge none otherwise of the conditions of men than they do in tragedies of him they call the King, who, apparelled in purple and glistering all in gold and precious stones, represents the person of Agamemnon, Atreus, or Eteocles, where, if he chance to fail in action, comeliness, or utterance, they do not yet derogate from his old title, but they say: «The King hath not played his part well.» Likewise, he that represents the person of a noble man or gentleman that in this life, which is a theatre of the world, hath been deposed or bereft of his dignity, he shall nevertheless be called the noble or the gentleman still, though he be haply Davus, Syrus, or Geta. But, when it happeneth that someone is found not only servile in condition and of fortune but base of mind, gross of understanding, and, as Petrarch sayth, *nudo di giudizio e povero d'argomento* (naked of judgement and poor of argument), as the greater number are, he may be properly termed a servant, and of him and such like the good housekeeper that would have such persons serve him as he might command with reason may well furnish his house, seeking no further virtue in them than that they may be capable of his commandments and execute them willingly, wherein they differ from horses, mules, and other beasts, whom nature hath also framed apt to learn and to be ruled, tamed, and guided by man, for they in the absence of their masters record the things commanded, which these no longer know than they are learned or scarce perform even when they are commanded, so that a servant may be called *animal rationale* (a reasonable creature) by participation, even as the moon and the stars receive light by participation with the sun or as men's appetites by participation with the light of understanding become reasonable, for as our appetites receive within themselves the form of that virtue which reason hath imprinted in them, so doth the servant reserve the form of those impressions whatsoever commanded or required in him by his master; and of them and of their master sometimes may be said, as Petrarch, speaking of himself and Laura, reasoneth,

Sì che son fatto uom ligio
Di lei ch'alto vestigio
M'impresse al core e fece'l suo simile
(So that I see I am become her liegeman and her thrall,
That made impressions in my heart and printed hers withal).

And, because the authority of Hesiod, that ancient poet, shall not beguile thee, who, reckoning up the properties of housekeeping, placed the ox instead of the servant, I will thou understand more properly that the manner wherewith servants are governed differeth much from that wherewith we govern beasts, for that instruction or kind of teaching beasts is not discipline but a use and custom, dissonant and segregate from reason, not unlike as the right hand holdeth and disposeth any sort of weapon better than the left, albeit there is no more reason in it than in the other. But the mind also of servants is accompanied with reason and may become discipline, as is that of children, wherefore they speak without sense and conjecture unreasonably that rob and reave their servants of the use of reason, considering it is no less needful for them than children but more peradventure, they having already so much temperance and strength as not only serveth to defend themselves, but to rescue many times and assist their masters in the peril of some civil broil or other troubles that may oftentimes betide them. And, therefore, was it well said of that Tuscan poet,

Ch'innanzi a buon signor fa servo forte
(Before his master whom he likes,
The sturdy servant stoutly strikes),

and not without cause were Milo's servants commended so by Cicero in his oration *pro Milone* and all those others of whom we read some memorable matters in Valerius Maximus, with many more, whose examples if I should but practise to recount, I should soon forget my purpose, that servants are properly those that are born to obey, who, therefore, are not capable of any office within the city because they want virtue, whereof they taste but barely so much as only makes them apt and ready to obey. But if thou hast perused histories and read of that most perilous conflict amongst the Romans which they called servile war, because it was begun and stirred up by servants, and likewise in our time of the armies which the Soldan gathered of slaves, and at this day of those fearful hosts which the great Turk mustereth and for the most part maketh of the like, thou shalt then record and bring to mind our plain distinction, that absolutely will resolve thee and discharge the greatest doubt thou canst imagine: many are servants by fortune that are free by nature. And it is not to be marvelled at that many cruel conflicts and dangerous wars are caused and continued by such as these, howbeit it is a great argument of baseness that servile fortune can engender servile evils in a gentle mind; and yet, for instance, I remember an example of the Scythians worthwhile the noting, who, having assembled an army of men against their servants that had then rebelled, knowing none other mean or policy to pacify or put them down, they advised to carry with them to the field, besides their weapons, many whips and bastinadoes, which, making them remember the stripes and strokes that in their servitude they had received, put them presently to flight.

But, returning to those servants whereof a house or family indeed should be composed or furnished, I cannot commend those that are neither fit for war, in mind nor body, but such as are of strong complexion, fit for labour, country business, and household exercise. These would I divide into two forms, the one under the other, as the one of superintendents, surveyors, or work-masters, the other of workmen: the first shall be the steward, to whom by the master of the house should the household care be commended; the next, to whom the business of the stable and of horses should be given, as in great houses it hath been accustomed; the third, the bailiff, to whom the town affairs belong and are committed. The others shall be such inferiors as shall be controlled and at commandment of those higher officers.

But, forasmuch as our fortune hath not given us that wealth whereby we should expect to have our houses so distinguished and multiplied with officers, it shall suffice thee to provide one for all that may be steward, horse-keeper, and bailiff, and him command the rest, that are thy hinds and meaner servants, to obey, giving every one his salary or day wages, more or less as in their labours they deserve, ordaining victual for them so as they may rather have too much than want. Howbeit, yet thou art to feed thy servants with some other meat than such as shall be set upon thine own board, where disdain not now and then to see such gross or homely kind of fare as according to the season shall be happily purveyed or provided for thy servants, to the end that they, seeing thyself sometimes vouchsafe to taste thereof, may the more willingly be satisfied therewith, amongst which those relicts and fragments of that finer fare that shall be taken from thy table may be served, still having some respect to the estate and desert of every one. But, because a family well fed and truly paid may with idleness and ease become pestilent, breeding evil thoughts and bringing forth worse works – not unlike those pools and standing waters, which, having no recourse, putrefy the good and engender naughty fish – thy chief care and the duty of thy steward shall be this, to keep everyone particularly exercised in his particular office and generally all in such business as thou canst not severally set them to, for everything that belongs to the keeping of a house cannot necessarily be done by him that hath another charge: the steward, he must purvey thy meats; the chamberlain, make the beds and brush; the horse-keeper, rub the horses and cleanse the stable; and, consequently, every other, otherwise be occupied. The careful steward or surveyor of the house should therefore with discretion dispose the works that are or cannot be divided or distributed now to one, now to another, but above the rest to have a special care that in the house courts, tables, or coffers be no uncleans, filth, or rubbish, but that the very walls and pavements, lofts and cellars, harness and implements of household may be polished and kept so clean that – as we term it – it may shine like silver or look as bright as crystal, for cleanliness is not only pleasing or delightful to behold but adjoineth worth and bettereth things by nature base and filthy, as continually beastliness and filth corrupt, disgrace, and spoil things otherwise of value and account; besides, cleanliness increaseth and preserveth the health as much as sluttishness annoyeth and impaireth it. Nay, what more is, every servant should particularly have such care of scouring and keeping clean those tools and instruments he works withal and that belong unto his office as the soldier hath to see his weapons to be bright, for such are, is, or should be every tool to him that hath the exercise thereof as are the weapons which the soldier useth, whereupon Petrarch, speaking of the ploughman, writeth thus:

> *L'avaro zappator l'armi riprende*
> (The ploughman takes his weapons once again),

after the imitation of Virgil, who, before he had called those instruments weapons which the countrymen did use, wrote thus:

> *Dicendum et quae sint duris agrestibus arma*
> (And tell the weapons wherewithal the sturdy clowns can work),

and where also he terms the baker's instruments weapons:

Tum Cererem corruptam undis, cerealiaque arma
Expediunt fessi rerum
(Then run the weary forth to fetch the watery rotten corn
And baking weapons etc.).[6]

But because it sometime happeneth that one is too much charged with labour and another hath more day than work, one should so help another as we see by use in our own bodies: when the one leg is weary, we can rest it on the other, or when the right hand is over laboured, we can ease it with the left; and when intercourse of love and courtesy entreats not thus amongst them, then should the master himself command the negligent and unprofitable servant to help and ease the weary and the well-employed.

But above all methinks the charity of masters and love of servants to their fellows in their sickness is especially to be used and shown, at which time the sick are to be severally lodged from the whole and nourished with more choice and dainty meat; nor should the master of the house disdain or show himself so scornful or unkind as not to visit them, for if brute beasts rejoice to see their masters cherish them, as we may daily see in dogs, how much more may we believe that men and reasonable creatures are comforted therewith? Whereupon it comes to pass that good servants liking and affecting of their masters understand them at a beck and obey them at a wink of the eye or bent of the brow, not as a water spaniel, but, as the hand is stirred to obey the mind, so prompt and ready is the servant to obey his master, for as the hand is said to be the instrument of instruments, being it, indeed, that serves to feed, apparel, and keep clean the rest of the limbs, which are also called instruments, so is the servant said to be an instrument of instruments, because he keepeth all the instruments of household occupied not only to live, but to live well, wherein he differeth from all the other instruments, for where they are *inanima* (things without soul), he is *animatus* and divinely is enriched with a soul, and herein differeth from the hand, for that the hand is fastened and united to the body, but he separate and disjoined from his master, and is also different from artificers, for artificers are instruments of those things which properly they call workmanship, but the servant is instrument of the action, which also is distinguished from workmanship, so that the servant, if you will rightly understand him, is *animatum actionis et instrumentum separabile* (a lively and several instrument of action). But, forasmuch as of actions some are placed in care of families and household business, some stretch further and extend to civil administration, there are some gentlemen – amongst whom I wish

6 *Aeneid*, Lib. 2.

thee to be numbered – that use to keep a youth who in their civil government doth serve to write and manage some of their affairs, and him they call their clerk, but these do far differ from the other, considering that for the most part they are, or ought to be, not of servile or material wit, but capable of fashions or apt to study or contemplate, and betwixt them and their masters can be properly no servitude or signory, but rather that kind of friendship which by Aristotle is applied in the highest, albeit in those good worlds of the Roman commonwealth these were taken from that number of other servants, and such a one was Terence, the writer of comedies, who was so familiar with Lelius and Scipio as it is thought there is somewhat of their doings in his works. The like was Tiro (of whom are many letters extant that were written by Tully), who, being an excellent grammarian, was also a most diligent observer of some little things whereof Cicero was rather a dispraiser than ignorant. But, because that use of service as we talked of is at this day utterly extinguished betwixt the masters and their servants of such singularity, those laws of friendship ought to be observed and maintained in more high degree, and hereupon was that treatise of under officers especially written by *Signor* Giovanni Della Casa, which – for that thou art desirous to peruse his works – I know must many times be read and read again by thee; I will therefore particularize none but refer thee to the book.

And now, because we have sufficiently spoken – though not so much as you desire – touching the regard of the person, for that our speech hath reference as well to maidens as menservants and because there hath been nothing left out that belongeth to a husband, a master, or a housekeeper, I think it requisite to come to that which we devised and divided for the second part of our discourse, that is, of wealth or substance, wherein we will effectually make mention of the duty of a housewife and of women's business. The care of wealth or substance, as we said before, is employed to conservation and increase, and is divided betwixt the master and mistress, because the increase is as proper to the master as the keeping to the mistress, howbeit to him that particularly considereth the care of the increase it is proper to the master, and the other common, whatsoever others heretofore have spoken to this purpose. But, forasmuch as nothing can be increased that is not first and wholly kept together, the housekeeper that is desirous to preserve his wealth should particularly know the quality and quantity of his revenues and expenses wherewith he is to keep his house and to maintain his family with credit and, measuring the manner of his revenues with the issue of his charges, so to live as his expense may prove the least, making that proportion with his comings in as four to eight (or six at least), for he that spends as much as he receives of his possessions cannot recover those losses which by chance or fortune may betide him, as by fires, tempests, inundations, and other such, nor supply the necessity of some expense which, being accidental, cannot be provided for. Furthermore, to be certified of his substance and the value of his riches, it behoves that he himself have seen and measured his possessions, even with those compasses which gave beginning to geometry in Egypt, which, though they be divers according to the variety of countries, is notwithstanding no occasion of substantial difference; it also behoveth that he know that what he reaps be answerable unto that he sowed and with what proportion the earth restoreth that which it receiveth; and as requisite it is that he take the like notice of all whatsoever else belongeth to husbandry or grazing and no less to hearken after the prices that are set by public magistrates or by consent of market folks within the country where he dwelleth than to be informed how they buy or sell in Turin, Milan, Lyons, or Venice, whereof being well advertised and instructed he cannot be deceived by his bailiff, being a husbandman, or abused by his factor, being a merchant. But, forasmuch as I have said that he ought to be advised both of the quantity and quality of that which he possesseth, I call not only that quantity which is measured by geometry, as are fields, meadows, woods, or that which is accustomed to be numbered by algorism, as flocks and herds, but that which is accounted as gold or silver coined, for in the quadering and making even of the entries with the expenses no quantity is more to be considered than that of money which may be gathered and received of rent and such like revenues, which is often changing and incertain, for lands are not always let at one rate, their price and profits rise and fall as other mean things or things of more account, in which incertainty and variable state of things a good husband's judgement, experience, and diligence so much prevails as not only is sufficient to preserve but to increase his substance, which being in the manurance and handling of an ignorant or overweener doth not only decrease, but perisheth.

That call I quality of substance, then, that is artificial or natural, of living things or things without life: artificial are movables or household implements, and haply the house itself and money, which was first found out by man's appointment, because we may live without it, as they did in the old time, wherein exchange of things was made without return of money; afterward, by the law of man was money invented, whereupon it was called *numus* of *νομός*, which by the Greek interpretation signifieth law, which, commodiously fitting and making equal things exchanged, hath made the intercourse of buying and selling very easy and more certain than when they only used exchange.

Artificial riches may all those things be called wherein the workmanship of the master is rather sold and more esteemed than the matter or the thing made; natural are those that are produced by nature, whereof also some are without life, as lands, meadows, metals, and some with life, as flocks and herds, whereof the good housekeeper oftentime receiveth profit.

Further it cometh into the consideration of quality to know whether the lands or possessions lie near or far from any city; if they join to any standing lake or pool, by the exhalation of whose evil vapours the air becometh filthy and infected; or whether any springs or rivers be adjacent, which by oft recourse and refluence may gather virtue to refine and purge the air; and whether they be girt or environed with hills or lie open to the winds; whether upon the banks to any navigable water or in a champaign country, whereby the commodities raised thereupon may be transported easily in cars or other carriages unto the city; or whether it lie steepward down the hills, uneasy and painful to be passed, so that he must needs be charged with sumpter men; whether it be near to any highway or common street through which the travellers, Italian merchants, or those of Germany or France, are used to pass; or far from frequence or resort of passengers or such as use to barter or exchange; if aloft, where it lies in prospect, or below, in some valley where it may be overflown; all which conditions, as they much increase and diminish the price and value of the things possessed, so may they be occasion of sparing in expenses and teach thee to conserve and multiply thy revenues if like a good husband thou advise thee and consider it.

But, to come somewhat more particularly to the care and regard that is indeed required, he should so provide that whatsoever is necessary for the use of his house in the city be brought from his farm or manor in the country and to leave his house there furnished of so much as may suffice him and his family when he shall be disposed to sojourn there, and to sell the rest at such convenient time as things are dearest, and with the money that ariseth thereof to buy those things which his own possessions yield not and yet are necessary for a gentleman now and then when they are better cheap. All which he may easily do if in sparing that expense he used at first he reserve some money overplus; again, he may keep his money by him many times when by his own conjecture, opinion of prognostications, or speech of other men's experience he hears or feareth any dearth or scarcity, and then to lay it out when he perceives the great abundance of the year and fruitfulness of seasons, remembering that example of Thales,[7] who through his knowledge of natural things suddenly became rich with a bargain that he made for oil. This shall be the husband's care. But such things whatsoever as are brought into the house either from the country or bought about in markets shall be wholly recommended to the wife's charge, who is to keep and set them up in several places according to their natures, for some would be kept moist and cold, and some dry, othersome would be one while set in the sun, another while in the wind, some will be long kept, othersome a little while, all which a good housewife, well considering, should cause those that

[7] Thales, one of the seven wise men of Greece.

will not keep to be first eaten and make store of the rest, howbeit those also that will not keep without corruption may be helped many ways and made to keep long, for salt and vinegar do not only keep flesh long time sweet and seasoned, but fish and fowl, which will be suddenly corrupt. Besides, many sorts of fruit that will quickly putrefy and perish, if they be sharp or tart (otherwise not) will be long maintained in vinegar. Likewise, the hanging up in smoke or baking of some kinds of flesh or fish and divers sorts of fruits draws away their moisture, that is cause of their corruption, and maketh that they may be kept the longer.

Again, there are some things which, being dried, would become both hard and naught to eat without some kind of liquor or conserves, whereof a good housewife making store for her provision (if it happen that by some mischance or hindrance whatsoever there cannot come sufficient store of meat from the market for her husband's table or that they suddenly are driven to entertain a stranger) she may in a minute furnish her mess with those junkets, and that in such good sort as there shall be no miss of any other meats. She must also have regard that all her household corn be some ground for bread and othersome made fit for drink, and so distribute it indifferently with equal measure both to the men and maidservants used for those purposes, amongst whom she shall have one above the rest, as the master hath his steward or cashier, that shall keep one key, and she another, that, though the master or mistress be abroad, there may be one to deliver out such things as shall be needful and to bid a stranger drink, which custom is not geason in some houses, where the steward or butler bears the keys as well of household necessaries as all things else pleasing the master and not unpleasant to the appetites of those he entertaineth. Therefore, a good housewife should so provide that all things whatsoever (if occasion of resort of strangers be not to the contrary) may be sparingly disposed, for thrift or liberality is as needful in a woman as a man. Besides, she should busy herself in viewing and surveying such things as she charged to be kept, measuring things to be measured and keeping just account of things that are to be accounted; neither ought her care only extend to the spending of them or unto other things rehearsed but also to the wines, which the older they are and the longer they are kept become so much the better – I speak of choice wines, which get strength with age, for the small wines and those of little spirit that quickly lose their strength should be first drunk or sold if thou have any quantity – but her principal care should be of linen or of woollen weaving, wherewith she may not only make provision necessary and fit for the ability and credit of her house but honestly gain, which is as requisite in her as is her husband's profit gathered by the buying, selling, or exchanging other things. Neither ought a good housewife to disdain or scorn to set her hand now and then to some work; I mean not in the kitchen or other soiled places, which may spoil or ray her garments, because such business are not to be managed and handled by noble matrons (yet to be seen unto by such whose state may tolerate such thrift), but in those only that without noisomeness or filthiness she may be bold to touch, and such are properly the wheels, looms, and other instruments that appertain to weaving, wherewith a good housewife may furnish any sufficient house or dwelling either for her eldest son or daughter. And not without reason was this art first attributed to Minerva, goddess of wisdom, insomuch as it was derived first from her, as appeareth by these verses in the book of Virgil:

Inde, ubi prima quies medio iam noctis abactae
Curriculo expulerat somnum, cum femina primum,
Cui tolerare colo vitam tenuique Minerva
Inpositum, cinerem et sopitos suscitat ignes,
Noctem addens operi famulasque ad lumina longo
Exercet penso castum ut servare cubile
Coniugis et possit parvos educere natos
(The first sleep ended, after midnight did the woman wake
That lived by spinning, and she 'gins the embers up to rake,
And adding so unto her labours some part of the night,
Hard at their distaff doth she hold her maids by candlelight
To keep her chaste, and that her children well maintain she might),

in which verses it appeareth that he spake not of base women, but of a mistress of a house which had been accustomed to be attended on by many servants; and so much worth it seemeth that this art hath in it as it hath not only been ascribed or attributed to private housewives, but to princely ladies, as appeareth by these verses of Penelope, the wife of wise Ulysses:

Come la nobil Greca ch'a le tele sue
Scemò la notte quanto il giorno accrebbe
(As did that noble Grecian dame that bated in the night
As much as she had woven by day to blear her suitors' sight),

and Virgil of Circe, which was not only a woman and a queen, but a goddess, wrote thus:

Arguto coniux percurrit pectine telas
(Upon a well-divided loom thy wife doth weave apace),

in which example he followed Homer, who not only brought Penelope and Circe in the number of women weavers but placed the daughter of Alcinous, the King of Phaeacians, amongst them;[8] and, albeit the Greeks observed

8 Homer in his *Odyssey*.

not so much *decorum* as was necessary, the Romans yet, that were both greater and more curious observers of such things, forbad the mistress of the house all other works, the kitchen cookery, and such like, but granted they might weave, and that not without great commendation; and in this kind of work was Lucrece often found by Collatine, by Brutus, and Tarquinius when they were enamoured of her.

But to return to the mistress of the house or housewife, who, being a fortunate mother of children, the further off she is from noblesse or estate, so much the less she may disdain to busy herself in such things as carry meaner worth in show and less workmanship than weaving, and herein seemeth it that in some sort she shall advance herself and come into comparison with her good man, for she not only gathereth but increaseth with the profit of those labours. Nevertheless, considering that those benefits are small and but of slender reckoning, we shall do well to say that it belongeth to the wife to keep and to the husband to increase. But, forasmuch as things preserved may the better be disposed if they be carefully provided for and ordered, the good housewife ought above all things to be diligent herein, for if she reserve not things confusedly but separate and placed in sunder according to their quality and the opportunity of using them, she shall always have them ready and at hand and evermore know what she hath and what she wants. And if there can be no similitude inferred to this purpose worthy of consideration, most notable is that of memory, which, laying up, preserving, and imprinting in itself all the images and forms of visible and intelligible things, could not utter them in time convenient and dispose them to the tongue and pen unless it had so ordered and oftentimes recounted them as without that the memory itself could scarce contain them;[9] of so great efficacy and force is order, but it hath also no less grace and comeliness in beautifying and adorning things as he that doth acquaint his study with the use of poetry very easily perceiveth, for poesy hath never more spirit added to it with the greatest art and industry than when it is set forth with well-disposed epithetons and significant terms, that the one ordered with the other may altogether consent or musically answer cross, as hath artificially been used by orators, which, though it be pleasant to the ear, is painful to the memory;[10] and be it so, as some philosophers have said, that the form or fashion of the world is none other than an order, comparing little things with great we may well report that the form of a house is the order, and the reformation of the house or family none other than a second setting it in order, wherein I purpose to speak somewhat, which, albeit of itself it bear no great semblance of credit, yet for the order and cleanliness it deserves so

9 *Ars memorativa.*

10 As by repetition or maintaining of a point, as musicians term it.

much as, having seen it without disdain and diversely admiring it, may without impeach – I hope – be profitably recounted.

Returning from Paris and coming by Beaune, I entered the hospital, wherein, though every room I saw methought was worthy commendations, yet was the kitchen to be wondered at, which as it was not used continually, so did I find it passing neat and quaintly tricked up, as if it were the chamber of a new married bride; therein saw I such a quantity of necessary implements, not only for the use of the kitchen but service of the table, so discreetly ordered and with such proportion, the pewter so set up, the brass and iron works so bright as when the sun shined on the windows thereupon cast such a delicate reflection as it might – methought – be well resembled to the armoury of Venice and of other places meeter to be spoken of than shown to strangers; and if Gnato, that disposed the household of his glorious *Signor Capitano* in manner of an army, had but had a sight of this, I am well assured he would have compared it to some higher matter than an armoury.

But, returning now from keeping to increasing, it may be doubted whether this art of increasing be housekeeping wholly or but a member, part, or minister thereof. If a minister, because it ministereth the instruments, as the armorer doth the cuirass and the helmet to the soldier, and that ministereth the subject or the matter, as the shipwright that receives the timber of him that fells and seasoneth the wood. It is very manifest that the art of housekeeping and getting is not all one, for the one it behoveth to provide, the other to put in use the things provided; now, it rests to be considered whether to get be a form or part of housekeeping or utterly disjoined and estranged from it. The faculty of getting may be natural and not natural: natural I call that which getteth the living out of those things that hath been brought forth by nature for man's use and service, and, forasmuch as nothing is more natural than nourishment which the mother giveth to her child, most natural above the rest must that gain needs be that is had and raised of the fruits of the earth, considering that the earth is the natural and universal mother of us all; natural also are the nourishments and food that we receive of beasts and of the gain that may be made of them, which is distinguished according to that destination of beasts; for of beasts some are tame and companable, othersome, solitary and untamed; of those are flocks, herds, and droves compact, of which no less profit may be raised; these they make their gain to hunt, and many of them serve for sustentation and succour of the life. It also seems that nature hath engendered not only brute beasts for the service of man but hath framed men that are apt to obey to serve those whom also she hath framed to command, so that whatsoever is gotten or obtained in the wars being just, the same may also be termed natural gain; and herein will I not conceal what Thucydides hath observed in the proem of his *History*, that in the old time preying or robbery was not to be blamed, whereupon we read that one asked another whether he were a pirate or a rover, as though it were no injury to ask him such a question, to which use or reason Virgil having regard brought in Numa boasting thus:

Canitiem galea premimus semperque recentes
Convectare iuvat praedas et vivere rapto
(We hide our grey hairs with our helmets, liking evermore
To live upon the spoil, and waste our preys from shore to shore).

And that may well be called natural gain which the Knights of Malta have against the barbarians and Turks. Every of which natural gains it seemeth necessary that housekeepers have knowledge of, but especial of husbandry, and he that mingleth and exchangeth the profit of all those things together which he gathereth should haply therein do nothing unworthy or against the title of good husbandry, for that trade or science is at this day commonly called merchandise, which is of many sorts and to be taken many ways, but that is the most just which taketh thence where things superfluously abound and transporteth them thither where is want and scarcity of those commodities, and in their stead returneth other things whereof there is some dearth, because it grows not otherwhere so plenteously; and hereof speaketh Tully in his book of *Offices* that merchandise, if they were small, were base and but of vile account, if great, not much to be disliked, but his words in that place are to be taken as the saying of a Stoic that too severely speaketh of those matters, for in other places, where he argueth like a citizen, he commendeth and defendeth merchants and the manner of their trade, and calleth that order of the publicans most honest, who had the whole revenues of the commonwealth in their possessions besides those things whereof they exercised traffic and the trade of merchandise. But as that form of merchandise is just and honest which traffics their commodities to countries where they want and thereof makes their best, so most unjust is that which, having bargained for the commodities of a country, retaileth them or selleth them again in the same place, watching the opportunity and time when they may utter them unto their most advantage, howbeit the care of opportunity to sell what is a man's own and what he gathereth of his own revenues and possessions and of his flocks, herds, and such like seem not either inconvenient or dishonest in a husbandman.

And so much touching natural gain, necessary for a housekeeper, wherein he shall much advantage him and his if he be but indifferently instructed not only of the nature, goodness, and value of all things that are used to be exchanged and are from place to place transported, but also in what province, shire, or country grow the better and in which the worse, and where in most abundance, where in less, where they are held dearest, and where best cheap. So should he also be informed of the fashions, sleights, and difficulties of transporting them, and of the times and seasons wherein they be carried or recarried most conveniently, and of the league and traffic that one city hath with another, one province or country with another, and of the times wherein such merchandise are sold, which for the most part are called fairs or marts.

Notwithstanding, the housekeeper ought to handle these things like a husbandman and not like a merchant, for where the merchant preposeth for his principal intent the increase and multiplying of his stock, which is done by traffic and exchange, by means whereof he many times forgets his house, his children, and his wife, and travels into foreign countries, leaving the care of them to factors, friends, and servants, the care of the husbandman or housekeeper doth reap his profit of exchange by a second object directed unto household government, and so much time and labour only he bestoweth as his chief and principal care may not thereby be annoyed or hindered. Moreover, even as every art doth infinitely seek the end it purposeth, as the honest physician will heal as much as he can, the architect erect and build with as much excellency and perfection as he can, so the merchant seems to make his benefit of things unto their uttermost. But the housekeeper hath his desires of riches certain and determinate, for riches are none other than a multitude of instruments that appertain unto familiar or public cares, but the instruments of some arts are not infinite either in number or in greatness, for, if they were infinite in number, the artificer could not know them, forasmuch as this word infinite (as touching the infinitive) is not comprehended in our understanding unless it be in things that cannot well be handled, managed, or lifted for their greatness.

And as in every art the instruments should be proportioned and fit as well for him that worketh as the thing that shall be wrought withal (for in a ship the rudder ought to be no less than may suffice to direct his course nor greater than the mariner can guide, and in graving or cutting the chisel should not be so ponderous and heavy as the mason may not lift nor so light as he cannot with much ado pierce the outside of the marble), even so should riches be proportioned and limited unto the housekeeper and the family that he is charged withal, that he may inherit and possess so much and no more than shall suffice not only for his living but his living well, according to his estate, condition of time, and customs of the city where he liveth and inhabiteth. And, where Crassus said he was not rich that was not able to maintain an army, he haply had reference unto those riches which are needful for a prince or ruler within the city of Rome, which were too too much and immoderate for any one in Praeneste or in Nola, little towns in Italy, and haply superfluous for many men in Rome, for to muster and maintain armies becometh kings, tyrants, and other absolute princes, and is not necessary or fitting for a citizen inhabiting a place of liberty, who indeed ought not to exceed the rest in any such condition as may interrupt or spoil that good proportion that is requisite and meet in the uniting of free men, for, as the nose upon some man's face, growing by disorder or disdiet more than nature made it, may become so gross and large in time as it may be no more resembled or reputed for a nose, so a citizen of any city whatsoever exceeding others in his riches either miserably gotten or increased by wrong is no more a citizen, be he what or who he will, for riches are to be considered always in respect of him that doth possess them. Nor can we well prescribe how much they ought to be, but this we may solely and safely say, that they ought to be apportioned to him that hath them, who ought so much and no more to increase them than may be afterwards divided and bequeathed amongst his children to live well and civilly withal. Neither resteth anymore for me to say concerning this natural gain convenient for a housekeeper, which may as properly be taken and derived from the earth, herds, and flocks as by the trade of merchandise, war, or hunting; wherefore we may call to mind that there were many Romans called from the plough and cart to be magistrates and mighty men in princes' courts, and afterwards, disrobed of their purple, returned to the plough. But, because the husbandman and careful housekeeper should have regard unto his health not as a physician but as a father of a family, he ought most willingly to apply himself unto that kind of gain which most preserveth health, wherein he shall also exercise himself and see his family and servants busied in those exercises of the body which not defiling or defacing him are great helps to health, whereunto idleness and superfluous ease are enemies professed. Let him therefore love to hunt and to make more reckoning of those gains which are got and followed with pain and sweat than those that through deceit and unconsorted with some labour have been and yet are used to be gotten.

But, sithence we have reasoned of that manner of gain that is natural, it shall not be unnecessary that we somewhat manifest the other, which is unnatural, although it be impertinent to husbandry and housekeeping. This we divide into two forms or kinds. The one is called exchange, the other usury, and it is not natural because it doth pervert the proper use, forasmuch as money was found out and used a while to make equal the inequality of things exchanged and to estimate and measure prices, not for that it ought to be exchanged, for of money (as touching the metal) we have no need, neither receive we any benefit thereof in our private or our civil life, but in respect of making even inequalities and justly measuring the worth and value of each thing it is thought both necessary and commodious. When money, then, is changed into money, not directed and employed to some other use, it is used beyond the proper use, and so abused; in which exchange nature is not imitated, for as well may exchange that doth multiply or accumulate infinite and excessive profits be said to have no end or absolute determination as usury, but nature always worketh to a certain set and determinate end, and to a certain end do all those means and members work that are ordained to be stirrers up of nature.

I have told you then that exchange may multiply in profits infinitely, because number (as touching number), not applied to material things, groweth to be infinite and in exchange is not considered to be otherwise applied. But for thy better understanding what we say, know that number is reputed either according to the formal or material being. Formal number is a collection of a sum, not applied to things numbered. Material number is a summary collection of things numbered. Formal number may infinitely increase, but the material cannot multiply so much: for, albeit in respect of the partition or division it seem that it may multiply in effect, notwithstanding, since division hath no place in that we speak of, we may say it cannot infinitely increase, because things of all kinds that cannot be divided are of number certain. This division being thus considered, much more may riches multiply that consist in bare money than that which consisteth in things measured and numbered from money: for, albeit the number of money be not formal as that which is applied to gold and silver, more easily may a great quantity of money be heaped up and gathered together than any other thing, and so by covetous desire to become infinite. Yet betwixt exchange and usury there is some difference. Exchange may be retained not only for the custom it hath taken and obtained in many famous cities, but for the force of reason that it seems to bear, for exchange is used instead of our transporting and conveying coin from place to place, which being hardly to be done without great discommodity and peril, it is reason that the party that exchangeth may have some sufficient gain allowed. Besides, the value of money of some country coin being variable and often to be changed as well by the laws and institutions as for the sundry worth, weight, and fineness of the gold and silver, the real exchange of money might be in some sort reduced unto natural industry, wherewith usury can never be acquainted, being an artificial gain, a corrupter of a commonwealth, a disobeyer of the laws of God, a rebel and resister of all human orders, injurious to many, the spoil of those that most uphold it, only profitable to itself, more infectious than the pestilence and consorted with so many perilous evils as are hard or never to be cured.[11] Every or either of which, having not only been condemned by Aristotle but utterly inhibited by the old and new law, who so considereth not let him read what verdict Dante hath given of it in these verses, who, to prove usury a sin, citeth a sentence put by Aristotle in his book *De Phisicis*:

11 *Leviticus: Pecuniam tuam non dabis fratri tuo ad vsuram et frugum superabundantiam non exiges. David: Qui habitabit, etc. qui pecuniam non dederit ad usuram. Luke: Date mutuum nec inde sperantes.*

E se tu ben la tua Fisica *note,*
Tu troverai, non dopo molte carte,
Che l'arte vostra quella, quanto pote,
Segue, come 'l maestro fa il discente;
Sì che vostr'arte a Dio quasi è nipote.
Da queste due, se tu ti rechi a mente
Lo Genesi *dal principio, convene*
Prender sua vita e avanzar la gente;
E perché l'usuriere altra via tene
Per sé natura e per la sua seguace
Dispregia, poi ch'in altro pon la spene
(If Aristotle's *Physics* thou peruse,
Not turning many leaves thou there shalt find
That art doth nature imitate and use
As pupils pleasing of their tutor's mind,
So that our art is niece to God by kind.
Of this and that, if thou remember it,
In *Genesis* even God himself doth say:
Quod ab initio oportuit
Humanum genus vitam sumere
Et unum alium excedere
Per artem et naturam. Now, because
The usurers do wander otherwise
Without regard of God or godly laws,
Nature and art, her follower, they despise,
For in their gold their hope beguilèd lies).

It is also said by Aristotle that God is *animal sempiternum et optimum*, of whom both heaven and nature do depend, which nature is imitated of our art as much as may be, for, art depending upon nature, she is as it were her child, and per consequence God's niece, so that offending nature we immediately offend God, and he that offendeth art offendeth God touching the hurt or annoyance of nature, but the usurer offendeth nature, for it is not natural that money should beget or bring forth money without corruption, since nature willeth that the corruption of one be the generation of another, and it offendeth God because it doth not exercise the art according as God commanded the first man when he said: «In the sweat of thy face thou shalt eat thy bread», and it is not artificial that money should bring forth money, as the usurers would have it, which putteth the use in the thing. With those verses, therefore, methinks not only our discourse of natural and not natural gain may be concluded and determined, but whatsoever else we purposed at first concerning husbandry and keeping of a house, which you have now seen how it turneth and returneth to the wife, how to the children, how to the servants and how to the converting and employing, as also the increase of whatsoever substance or possession, which were indeed those five especial points whereof we promised to speak and to entreat particularly.

But, for it is my chief desire that thou record effectually those things whereof I have advised thee, and that in so precise a sort as thou hereafter not forget them, I will bestow them and bequeath thee them in writing, that by often reading and perusing them thou mayst not only learn them but thoroughly resolve to imitate and practise them, for practice is the end imposed to all instructions of human life."

This was my father's discourse, gathered by him into a little book which I so often read and studiously observed as you need not marvel that I have so perfectly reported and repeated them. Now would I be silent, to the end that my discourse should not be made in vain, for if anything be said that in your opinion may be bettered, let it not – I pray – seem troublesome unto you thereof to certify me and amend it.'

'Sir,' quoth I, 'for anything that I can see, your father hath not only well and learnedly instructed you in all his institutions, but you – it seems – have exercised them as industriously. This only could I wish, that somewhat more might be annexed to that which he hath uttered, and that particularly is this: whether household care or household government be all one; if more than one, then, being more than one, whether, then, they be the knowledge and the labour of one or more'. 'You say true,' quoth he, 'and herein only failed his discourse, for the government of private houses and of princes' courts are different, but I can tell you why he spake not of it, because the care of princes' halls belongeth not to private men.'

'Trust me, sir,' quoth I, 'you are of swifter understanding and more eloquent device than I expected. But, since we found that there is difference in household governments, it rests that we consider whether they be discrepant in form or greatness, forasmuch as if they only differ in the greatness, then, even as the consideration of the form of a prince's palace and a poor man's cottage appertains to one and the selfsame mason, carpenter, or architect, so should the care of either housekeeping be one.' But thereunto he answered thus: 'Though I were swift of conceit at first, yet now I doubt I shall not be so prompt to find or so judicial as to censure that which you propose. Howbeit, I can tell you this, that if my heart or hap would give me leave to keep a great yet private house – I mean not a little court – I believe that private house of mine should far surpass that palace for a prince, which only differeth from the other in the pomp and greatness.'

'You are in the right,' quoth I, 'for as a prince is still to be distinguished from a private man by form, and as the form of their commandments is distinguished, so are the governments of princes and of private men distinguished, for when it happeneth that in comparison of number the household of a poor prince is as little as a rich man's family, yet are they to be governed diversely; nevertheless, if that be true which is approved by Socrates to Aristophanes in *Convivio Platonis*, that to compose or write a tragedy and comedy be both the work of one, albeit they only differ not in form but are opposite and contrary, it should consequently be as true that a good steward knoweth as well how to govern a prince's household as a private family, for the manner and faculty of either is alike, and I have read in a pamphlet that is dedicated to Aristotle that their governments or dispensations of a house are divided into four parts, kingly, lordly, civil, and private (*regia, satrapica, civilis, et privata*), which distinction I reprove not, for, albeit we differ far from those of elder times, yet I see the governments of those houses of the viceroys of Naples, Sicily, and the governor of Milan are as correspondent for proportion to those royal houses as were of old that custom of the dukes and other noble men, which proportion also may be found amongst the houses of the Dukes of Savoy, Ferrara, and Mantua, and those governors of Asti, Vercelli, Modena, Reggio, and Montferrat.[12] But I cannot see yet how the governments of a civil and a private house do differ unless he call his government civil that is busied and employed in office for the honours of a commonwealth, and that man's private that is segregate and not called to office, so that wholly he applies him to his household care. And that this is his distinction may we gather by the words that he hath written, that private government is the least, and yet raiseth profit of those things which are despised and dispraised of the others, which others are to be intended those civil governors or officers that, being used and exercised in affairs of more estate, dislike of many things which nevertheless are entertained and praised of private men. But, for it may percase come so to pass that some of your sons following the example of their uncle may endeavour and apply themselves to serve in court, I could wish that somewhat might be said concerning that so necessary care of governing a prince's house, but now it is so late, and we have sat so long that time and good manners will hardly give us leave, albeit some things unspoken of might be revived and produced, whereof he shall have time and ease to learn and to collect enough, part out of Aristotle's books and the rest by his own experience in court.'

Therewithal the gentleman, seeming to be satisfied with my speeches, arose and accompanied me, unworthy, to the chamber that the while had been provided for me, and there in a very soft bed I bequeathed my bones to rest.

Me mea sic tua te
Cetera mortis erunt.

T. K.

[12] Reggio, a city in Lombardy. There is Modone and Modena: Modone, a city in Greece; Modena, a city in Italy.

TEXTUAL NOTES

CATALOGUE OR INDEX

113 Order] this edition; *Orders* Q
137 Servile] this edition; *Ciuill* Q

MAIN TEXT

16 haply] this edition; *happily* Q; cf. *forse* TASSO
44 the] BOAS; *the the* Q
57 quoth he] BOAS; not in Q
62 'The sooner', quoth I, 'you] BOAS (*subst*); *(quoth I) the sooner you* Q
122 *tutto il mondo*] this edition; *tutto'l mondo* Q
166 haply] this edition; *happily* Q; cf. *forse* TASSO
238 *ferinae*] BOAS; *ferina* Q
256 haply] this edition; *happilie* Q; cf. *forse* TASSO
260 quoth I] this edition; not in Q
263 and Greek] BOAS; *Greeke* Q
308 with the] BOAS; *with* Q
334 natural and moral philosophy] BOAS; *natural moral philosophy* Q; cf. *natural e moral filosofia* TASSO
346 haply] this edition; *happilie* Q; cf. *forse* TASSO
386 haply] this edition; *happily* Q; cf. *per aventura* TASSO
389 speaks] this edition; *speake* Q
441 haply] this edition; *happily* Q; cf. *forse* TASSO
468 *dehiscat*] BOAS; *dehiscens* Q
470 *resolvam*] BOAS; *resolvem* Q
553 haply] this edition; *happily* Q; cf. *per aventura* TASSO
556n *Ovid, De medicamine faciei:*] this edition; *Ovid de | med: faciei* Q
565–6 to please others, I cannot say] BOAS (*subst*); *I cannot say to please other* Q
618–19 *O da me ognor temuto e paventato | Suocero caro*] this edition, based on TASSO; not in Q
630 haply] this edition; *hapely* Q; cf. *per aventura* TASSO
651 haply] this edition; *happily* Q; cf. *per aventura* TASSO
678 *stirpe*] BOAS; *stripe* Q
680 *silvamque*] Q; *silvasque* BOAS

692 *tunica*] Q; *tunicae* BOAS
694 *adsuetis*] this edition; *assuetis* Q
701 Cybele's] this edition; Cebiles Q
767–8 bereft of] BOAS; *bereft* Q
769 haply] this edition; *happily* Q
771 *giudizio*] this edition; *iudicio* Q
790 uom] BOAS; *huomo* Q
822 servile] this edition; *Cyuill* Q; cf. *servile* TASSO
869 to the keeping] BOAS; *to keeping* Q
890 *zappator*] BOAS; *Zappatore* Q
890 *riprende*] BOAS; *reprende* Q
931 *separabile*] this edition; *seperabile* Q
1006 haply] this edition; *hapely* Q; cf. *forse* TASSO
1115 *Exercet*] this edition; *Excercet* Q
1128 *Scemò*] BOAS; *Scenio* Q
1180 methought] BOAS; *my thought* Q
1190 *Signor*] this edition; *Sig.* Q.
1230 haply] this edition; *happilie* Q; cf. *forse* TASSO
1245 traffics] this edition; *traffique* Q
1246 makes] this edition; *make* Q
1296 haply] this edition; *happely* Q; cf. *per aventura* TASSO
1299 haply] this edition; *happely* Q; cf. *fors'anco* TASSO
1367 coin] BOAS; *Corne* Q; cf. *del danaro* TASSO
1378n *Leviticus*] BOAS; *Levit.* Q
1378n *Luke*] this edition; *Luk* Q
1383 *se tu ben*] BOAS; *setuben* Q
1387 *vostr'arte*] BOAS; *vostra arte* Q
1388 *queste*] this edition; *questi* Q
1389 *Lo*] BOAS; *Le* Q
1391 *usuriere*] BOAS; *usurier* Q
1393 *poi ch'in*] this edition; *poich'in* Q
1476 *satrapica*] this edition; *satrapicia* Q
1482 Modena] this edition; *Madona* Q
1483n Modena] this edition; *Modona* Q
1483n Modena] this edition; *Modona* Q

COMMENTARY

The following annotations are indebted to previous work on the text by Frederick S. Boas, *The Works of Thomas Kyd* (Oxford, 1901); Carnes Lord and Dain A. Trafton, *Tasso's Dialogues: A Selection, with the Discourse on the Art of Dialogue* (Berkeley, 1982); Bruno Basile, *Dialoghi. Il Messaggiero, Il Padre di famiglia, Il Malpiglio, La Cavaletta, La Molza* (Milano, 1991); Giovanni Baffetti, *Dialoghi* di Torquato Tasso, 2 vols (Milan, 1998). Quotations from Tasso are from the standalone edition of *Il padre di famiglia* (Venice, 1583). For the present-day English translations of bits of Tasso's text quoted in the notes, I have sometimes resorted to Lord and Trafton's translation.

Title page
3 perfectly completely.

Dedication
4–10 This dedication in iambic pentameter with a concluding rhyming couplet bears interesting similarities to that to the Countess of Sussex prefacing *Cornelia*. For further discussion, see my 'Introduction', p. 254.
9 discretion tetrasyllabic.
10 imperfection pentasyllabic.

A Catalogue or Index
32 gettings gains, earnings.
37 great weighty.
61 physic 'Healthy practice or habit' (*OED n.* 2a).
64 Factors farmers; **overseers** superintendents.
66 servile proper of slaves.
70 getting gain.
74 sweet 'That which is pleasant to the mind or feelings; something that affords enjoyment or gratifies desire; (a) pleasure, (a) delight; the pleasant part *of* something', often 'Contrasted with *sweat*' (*OED n.* 3a, 3b).
82 spinning 'The action or operation of converting fibres into thread or yarn by hand-labour or by machinery' (*OED n.* 1a).
87 Harts stags.
92 figured portrayed.

100 wanting lacking.
101 give … suck breastfeed.
104 Nature physical constitution.
109 Offices duties, tasks.
110 placed put.
113 Order of publicans the tax collectors of ancient Rome.
119 substance wealth.
124 Regard care.
131 Shamefastness modesty, sobriety of behaviour.
133 defence to protection for.
140 husbands husbandmen.

Main Text

3–4 betwixt … Vercelli In September 1578, Tasso fled from Ferrara to Turin, where he hoped he would find shelter under the protection of the House of Savoy. Novara and Vercelli are both in present-day Piedmont.

13 beck 'A mute signal or significant gesture' (*OED n.* 2 1); **gat** got; **gat … before** started walking at a rapid pace before his master.

15 would to would like to reach.

17 river the river Sesia, which flows in present-day Piedmont. At the time, it marked the border between the House of Savoy and the Spanish part of Lombardy.

20 a little cottage Basile suggests that the house may perhaps be identified with the castle of the Bolgaro family. The father and his sons may be identified either as Giovan Giacomo Bolgaro and his sons Nicolò and Cesare or as Scipione Bolgaro and his sons Nicolao and Alonso.

21 disease discomfort.

23 countenance appearance.

25–6 Thereupon … stay As Boas points out, Kyd 'has transferred these words to the "giovinetto"', while Tasso puts them into his own mouth: 'e gli dissi, che su la ripa del fiume prenderei consiglio, secondo il suo parere, di passar oltre, o di fermarmi' ('and I told him that I would decide on the bank of the river, as he advised, whether to cross or stop'). It may be that Kyd read 'e gli' ('and to him') as 'egli' ('he'), which led him to misinterpret the entire passage.

27 arrogate claim without justification.

29 conduct guide.

31 overlooked scrutinized, examined.

32 prevented anticipated.

34 heretofore … Piedmont in 1570–1 with Cardinal Luigi d'Este (1538–86). As Boas notes, Kyd mistranslates Tasso, 'who states that he passed through "Piemonte" before, but by a different road': 'percioché altra fiata, che, andando in Francia, passai per lo Piemonte, non feci questo camino' ('because on another occasion when I was going to France I passed though Piedmont but I did not take this route').

36–7 ministered occasion offered the opportunity.

40 my mother Porzia de' Rossi (1515–56); **my … Bergamo** Tasso's father, Bernardo (1493–1569), was born in Venice, but his family was from Bergamo.

43 mighty men Tasso has the more specific 'di principe' (of a prince). As Baffetti suggests, the reference was to Alfonso II d'Este (1533–97), who had grown to be suspicious of the unpredictable behaviour of Tasso, who had gone as far as to accuse himself of heresy before the Inquisitor of Bologna.

43–4 eftsoons shrouded already sheltered.

44–5 magnanimous … prince Filippo d'Este (1537–92), son-in-law to Emanuele Filiberto of Savoy (1528–80).

49 Parthia a kingdom south-east of the Caspian Sea (roughly present-day Iran), whose cavalry was especially celebrated and feared because the Parthian horsemen advanced flinging darts at the enemy and then swung away to avoid close combat, shooting arrows behind them as they retreated or appeared to retreat.

51 commorants 'dweller[s], sojourner[s], resident[s]' (*OED n.* B.); **passador** ferryman. Cf. Tasso: 'passatore'.

53 waft over carry across the river.

61 consorted with accompanied by.

65 high tall; **comprehended** contained.

66 stories floors.

67 environed surrounded.

68 without outside.

70 four-square of a square shape. Cf. Tasso: 'di forma quasi quadrata'; **portals** doorways.

71 against opposite.

75 artificially skilfully.

76 hangings curtains.

78 charged loaded; **curious** beautifully wrought; **plates of Candy** Tasso: 'piatti di creta' (clay plates). Kyd takes 'creta' literally as the name of the Greek island. The noun Candy (a domestication of the Arab name of the capital of the island) could refer to the island of Crete as a whole as well as to the city alone.

81 lets omits.

87 Cardinal Vercelli Guido Ferrero (1537–85), who had been cardinal since 1565. Basile remarks that Tasso met the cardinal that same year at the wedding between Alfonso II d'Este (1533–97) and Barbara of Austria (1539–72).

88 accounted of admired.

91 spirit liveliness.

92 eftsoons Boas points out that it 'Apparently means here "just then", though this is unusual.'

96 comely gravity pleasing seriousness of demeanour.

98 framing … towards approaching; **the good … house** Tasso's 'buon padre di famiglia' (good father of the family) refers back to the title, unlike Kyd's choice.

103 making moving.

106 to our power as much as it is possible for us.

109 regardant 'observant, watchful, attentive' (*OED adj.* 4); Boas remarks that it is 'Rarely used, as here, without reference to sight.' Cf. *Cornelia*, 5.207.

112 desired … honour i.e., in place at table; **being** because I was.

114 at … up at a sign of his put by and stored up.

115 Corycius born in the city of Corycus, in Cilicia.

116 Virgil, *Georgics*, 4.133.

117 A fourteener.

119–22 E … onora Petrarch, *Rerum Vulgarium Fragmenta* (*RVF*), 50.21–4.

123–6 Kyd uses a pair of rhyming fourteeners ('esteem' – 'seem'). By being broken by hemistichs to form a quatrain of lines with a 4-3-4-3 beat, they not only mirror the Italian quotation but also resemble the 'eight-and-six' form of ballad meter called 'common meter' or 'common measure'.

125 jays Kyd here mistakes *ghiande* (acorns) with *ghiandaie* (jays, common European birds of the crow family); hence, he mistranslates the last two lines of the quotation.

127 fill load.

128 unbought viands food that has not been purchased.

130–2 to send … meat a confused rendering of Tasso's 'di mandare alle città per cose necessarie al ben vivere, non che al vivere' (to send to the city for things necessary to a good life, as well as to mere subsistence).

132 lightly often, commonly.

140 rews rows.

141 petit countries little villages. Kyd adds a French touch to Tasso's 'piccioli paesi'.

149 of Varro … only by recalling both the threefold division of agricultural activities in Varro's *Res rusticae* together with Virgil's fourfold division in the *Georgics*, Tasso seeks to underline that the householder is not only a keen reader of poetry but also an expert agronomist (Baffetti; Lord and Trafton).

151 tarry not do not wait.
152 sparing hoarding.
154 discovered exposed.
156 humours dampness.
157 virtue force, power.
155–60 there … unripened cf. Atheneus, *Deipnosophistae*, 3.2. As Basile points out, Tasso read the chapter *De cucumeribus* in Natale Conti's Latin version, *Athenaei Dipnosophistarum sive coenae sapientum libri xv* (Lyons, 1556).
159 cucumbers The spelling in Q is 'Cowgomers', a unique variant of 'cucumbers' clearly modelled on Tasso's 'cogomeri'.
161 allowed … spake agreed with what he said.
165 almost … stay Kyd's unclear rendering of Tasso's 'quasi pur allora avveduto' (almost as if he had just realized); **wanting** missing.
166 withdrawn … presence kept away by your presence. Cf. Tasso: 'dalla vostra presenza ritenuta'; **haply looks** is perhaps waiting. Cf. Tasso: 'aspetta forse'.
169 carrieth … privilege permits a certain liberty.
170 advise accustom.
177 wherefore which is why.
177–8 married mine eldest son found a wife for my eldest son.
181 growth adulthood.
182 hath attained Tasso says the exact opposite; Kyd's translation is confusing.
185 their the fathers'.
185–6 which … moderate Tasso: 'le quali, se non per altro, almeno per esempio de' figliuoli, debbono moderare' ('which, if for no other reason, at least for the sake of example to be given to their children they have to restrain'). Kyd's mistranslation of 'per esempio' as 'by example' mars the correct understanding of the sentence.
187 regard respect.
189 conversation relationship.
190–3 where … unto As Boas notes, this is 'Completely mistranslated'. Tasso: 'ma, se di molto maggiore numero d'anni eccedessero, non potrebbono i padri ammaestrare i figliuoli, e sarebbon vicini alla decrepità, quando i figliuoli fossero ancor nella infanzia, o nella prima fanciullezza, né da lor potrebbono quell'aiuto attendere, e quella gratitudine, che tanto dalla natura è desiderata' ('but, if the fathers were much older than their children, they would not be able to discipline them and would be close to decrepitude when their children were still in their infancy or early young age, nor could the fathers expect from their children that help and gratitude that nature so desires').

194 natis ... senectam Lucretius, *De Rerum Natura*, 4.1256: 'To defend against old age by means of children.' As Basile remarks, Tasso read *De rerum natura* in the 1515 edition published in Venice by Aldo Manuzio.

197 eftsoons already.

200 conform himself adapt, show compliance.

205 carved me cut up for me; **kid** the young of a goat.

206–7 baked ... meat Kyd seems to be domesticating Italian cookery here. Tasso: 'condito in una maniera di manicaretti assai piacevole al gusto' ('dressed in a way of delicacies very pleasing to the taste'); **after ... of** in a similar fashion as.

208 wild ... lard As Basile points out, this recipe is to be found in Martino da Como, *Libro de arte coquinaria*, par. *Per fare brodo lardieri de salvaticina*, in *L'arte della cucina in Italia*, ed. Emilio Faccioli (Turin, 1987), p. 134; **dressed** prepared.

211 participates shares.

215 contagious pernicious, noxious.

216–17 noble men Kyd seemingly fails to understand that, when Tasso uses 'eroi', he means the heroes of Greek mythology and not men of noble birth in general. See also 226, 228–9, 243, 709. Heroes were a class of beings worshipped by the Greeks, generally conceived as the powerful dead, and often as forming a class intermediate between gods and men. Heracles was the most famous, sharing the characteristics of a hero (he was mortal, and like many other heroes, born to a human mother and a god) but also those of a god, being adopted by individuals and states as a protective deity. See Simon Hornblower and Antony Spawforth (eds), *The Oxford Classical Dictionary* (Oxford, 2003, third edition revised), pp. 684–5, 693–4.

218–21 the banquets ... viands Baffetti points out that, as Lucian (*De parasito*, 44–5) tells, the banquets of Agamemnon and the Greek heroes were so sumptuous that the role of the parasite was taken by Nestor himself. Yet those banquets were also sober as regards the viands served. See Homer, *Iliad*, 2.402 or 7.313.

220 parasite 'A person who lives at the expense of another, or of society in general' (*OED n.* 1a).

221–2 and the ... beef Boas contends that this is 'A mistranslation, showing that Kyd was ignorant of the Homeric story of Odysseus and the horses [*sic*] of the Sun'. While it is indisputable that Kyd mistranslated the passage – which refers to the episode in which Ulysses's hungry comrades killed the oxen of Sicily sacred to the sun-god Hyperion, thus enraging the gods (Homer, *Odyssey*, 12.325–88) – it is also true that he was probably at least partly misled by a misplaced comma in Tasso's text: 'i compagni d'Ulisse non per cupidità di fagiani o di pernici, ma per mangiare i buoi, del sole sopportarono tante sciagure' ('Ulysses' companions, not out of greed for pheasants or partridges, but in order to eat the oxen, suffered many curses of the sun'). The comma after 'buoi' disrupts the sense of the sentence, which should in fact read: 'i compagni di Ulisse non per cupidità di fagiani o di pernici, ma per mangiare i buoi del sole sopportarono tante sciagure' ('Ulysses' companions endured many misfortunes not out of greed for pheasants or partridges, but in order to eat the oxen of the sun).

223 Virgil … harts Cf. Virgil, *Aeneid*, 1.180–93; **induceth** introduces; **harts** stags.

224 it … thing meaning that Virgil erred.

225 convenience decorum.

226 feigned fashioned fictitiously; **forgat** forgot.

233–4 exercised and stirring active and always moving.

236 stalled and foddered put in stalls to be fattened.

238 Virgil, *Aeneid*, 1.215.

239–40 A pair of iambic tetrameters rhyming AA.

242 the old man Kyd again refrains from using Tasso's 'il buon padre di famiglia' ('the good father of the family').

244–5 I have … dulce Kyd mistranslates Tasso's 'da alcuni osservatori d'Omero' ('from some commentators of Homer'). As Baffetti argues, Tasso probably refers to Atheneus, *Deipnosophistae*, 1.26, who, however – possibly following Homer, *Odyssey*, 9.346 and 360 – records 'μέλας' (black) and 'αἶθοψ' (ardent), adjectives translated with 'niger' and 'ignitus' in the Latin version by Conti available to Tasso (see above, ll. 159–61). At any rate, an example of the two epithets quoted by Tasso ('nero e dolce') are to be found in Homer, *Odyssey*, 9.196–7. Boas contends that 'the use of the Latin epithets here is curious'; yet it probably made more sense to Kyd to quote Homer for an English audience in Latin rather than in Italian; besides, Kyd possibly wanted to avoid Greek as much as possible, thus using it only once, for *νομός* (l. 1011).

245 nigrum et dulce black and sweet.

248 wines of Levant wines coming from the East; **brought … us** imported.

249 malmseys 'A strong sweet wine, originally the product of the district of Monemvasia (Napoli di Malvasia) in the Peloponnese, Greece, later also from other parts of the Mediterranean, the Azores, the Canaries, Madeira, and elsewhere' (*OED n.* 1).

250 without that with the addition of the fact that.

255 as that.

266 Catullus, 27.2.

267–8 Kyd's translation is an alexandrine, or iambic hexameter, split over two lines at the central caesura.

268 chalices goblets.
271 heady intoxicating, potent.
274 lacrima 'a wine from Campania in southern Italy' (*OED n.*).
276 delicate the opposite of Tasso's 'assai generoso' (very strong).
277 begun to invited to drink; **pledged him** accepted his invitation to drink.
278 neat delicate.
282 noblesse nobility.
283–4 two ... Tasso As Baffetti points out, the reference is to an epistolary dispute between Girolamo Muzio and Bernardo Tasso concerning the nobility of the seasons: winter (defended by Mutius) vs. summer (defended by Tasso). The letters can be found in Bruno Tasso, *Lettere*, ed. Anton Federigo Seghezzi, 2 vols (Padua, 1733), 2:5, 15.
287 otherwhile at one time or other.
291 them themselves; **shroud** shelter.
292 whether ... find As Boas remarks, this is a mistranslation of Tasso's 'che sopragiungono all'improvviso' ('that hit unexpectedly'), which refers to 'procelle' ('tempests'); **whether** either of which.
296 worms parasites that attack plants, garden pests.
303 nothing necessary little appropriate.
308 resolved with weakened by; **contagions** infecting influences. Tasso has 'fatiche' ('labours').
319 so ... effects Tasso's 'cedano le speranze agli effetti' ('yield hopes to effects') is a self-quotation from Tasso's *Gerusalemme liberata*, 4.24.6 ('seguiteran gli effetti alle speranze'), which Kyd does not seem to identify.
326–7 if ... falsehood As Boas remarks, this is an 'inaccurate rendering' of Tasso's 's'egli nel fare i vini usa trascuraggine alcuna' ('if in making wine he neglects anything').
329 non ... Venus Tasso: 'non sol Venere è fredda' ('not only is Venus cold'). This is an allusion to Terence, *Eunuch*, 4.5.732: 'Sine Cerere et Libero friget Venus', which, as Boas points out, 'Kyd partly quotes, though inaccurately', in Latin. It may be that Kyd had no intention of making an accurate quotation, but simply wanted the reader to recognize the reference (the only actual mistake is *frigescit* for *friget*); **marred** insipid.
330 the Duke Emanuele Filiberto of Savoy. See ll. 44–5.
334 natural ... philosophy i.e., physics and ethics; **device** ingenuity.
337–8 some ... account As Basile points out, the reference is to such men of learning as Cosmas Indicopleustes, Ephrem the Syrian, George Syncellus, and Anastasius Sinaita. Tasso also had in mind the *auctoritates* reported in Philo of Alexandria, *De opificio mundi*.
339 article ... belief Cf. Tasso: 'articol di fede' ('article of faith'); **list** wishes.

343–52 You … sun As Basile remarks, Tasso follows Plato, *Timaeus*, 7.33b, 34a, 43b, through the comments in Marsilio Ficino, *Opera*, 2 vols (Basel, 1561), 2:1442 ff.

348 primum mobile the outermost moving sphere in the Ptolemaic model of the universe. Yet, as Basile remarks, here Tasso is thinking specifically of Girolamo Fracastoro, *Homocentricorum sive de stellis liber unus* (1535), rather than Claudius Ptolemy's *Almagest*.

350–4 Nevertheless … place Cf. Plato, *Timaeus*, 11.39b–c, 7.33c–d; *Republic*, 509b (Lord and Trafton).

353 requisite appropriate, necessary.

358 removing moving; **foregoes** goes away from.

359 Besides … corruption Tasso: 'e comincia [i.e., il sole] la generazione, e non la corruzione' ('and it [i.e., the sun] starts generation, and not corruption').

361 Aries the first constellation of the zodiac, which the sun enters on the spring equinox (Baffetti).

363 likely plausible. Cf. Tasso: 'ragionevole' ('reasonable'). Also at 371, 376.

365 Timaeus See Plato, *Timaeus*, 11.39bff (Baffetti).

371 Libra the seventh constellation of the zodiac, corresponding to the autumnal equinox.

373 their of the inhabitants of the austral hemisphere.

374 the first opinion i.e., the one that takes as its reference point the movement of the sun.

375 commodiously … persuasions easily accompanied by belief.

377–8 Jerusalem … hemisphere This was the medieval geographers' and cosmographers' theory: cf., for instance, Rabanus Maurus, *De universo* (IX c.), 15.2. Basile points out that Tasso was probably thinking of Dante, *Inferno*, 34.112–17 and *Purgatorio*, 2.1–3.

380 the old man Kyd again refrains from using Tasso's 'il buon padre di famiglia' ('the good father of the family').

386–7 Report … sufficiency Kyd mistranslates Tasso's 'quella fama, che per aventura non poteva derivar dal mio valore' ('that fame, which perhaps could not derive from my own worth').

386 blazon 'To describe fitly, set forth honourably in words' (*OED* v. 4).

388–89 I am … others The sentence is adapted from Petrarch, *RVF*, 128.63–4: 'I' parlo per ver dire, | non per odio altrui, né per disprezzo' (Baffetti).

390 conceit excessive pride.

393 participated unto shared with.

398 in purpose about. Kyd seems to misunderstand Tasso's 'in questo proposito' ('regarding this matter').

399 disease discomfort.

402 About … monarchy around 1556.

414 deposed freed; **him** himself.

415 disgrade As Boas points out, 'Very rarely used, as here, to mean "deprive, unburden", without a punitive sense.'

416 petit Kyd's addition. See also l. 141.

419 husbandry agriculture.

420 housekeeping 'The action or activity of running a household with regard to performing or directing the everyday domestic tasks involved, such as cleaning, cooking, etc.; management of resources to provide for a household' (*OED n.* 1b).

421 government management of household matters.

422 sparing frugality.

427 fellowship 'Communication, dealings, social interaction' (*OED n.* 3c); cf. Tasso's 'commerci'.

429 unlettered i.e., without a humanistic education, centred on the study of Greek and Latin. As Basile points out, Tasso's 'uomo senza lettere' is almost a technical expression, profoundly different from its present-day equivalent; **experimented** experienced.

432–6 Now … reason As Basile argues, this treatise-like section depends on the *partitiones* of the economic theme as established in the classical tradition, especially by Aristotle and Xenophon. Tasso owned their *Oeconomica* in the Latin version by Jacobus Ludovicus Strebaeus (Paris, 1543).

432 householder curiously the only instance in the main text of Kyd's using the noun he uses in the title of this translation. The only other instances are in the title page and twice in the 'Catalogue or Index'.

433 his body Kyd mistranslates Tasso's 'persone' ('people'). Also at l. 437; **In his person** Kyd mistranslates Tasso's 'con le persone' ('with people').

434 offices duties.

435 every each.

437 reasonable rational.

440 person role.

441 effectual accurate.

444 indifferently without distinction.

452–3 to … attributed Basile points out that this is a *sententia* by the Pythagorean philosopher Callicratidas, which Tasso takes from *Sermo LXVII, Laus pulchritudinis* in Johannes Stobaeus, *Sententiae ex thesauris Graecorum delectae*, ed. Conrad Gesner (Antwerp, 1551), C39v.

455 Petrarch, *RVF*, 214.35.

456 An iambic tetrameter.

457–8 Dante … body Cf. Dante, *Convivio*, 4.3.121–4.

458–9 albeit … wife Cf. St Augustine, *De Trinitate*, 12.3.3.

462–3 the soul ... another The reference is to the Pythagorean doctrine of the transmigration of souls, or metempsychosis.

464 convenient fitting.

468–72 Virgil, *Aeneid*, 4.24–5, 27–9. In Q, Kyd misquotes 'dehiscat' as 'dehiscens' and 'resolvam' as 'resolvem'. Tasso's quotation is correct.

473–6 Kyd translates Virgil's lines with four fourteeners traditionally rhyming ABAB.

473 would wish; **rive** cleave, crack; **raught** 'M. E. pret[eritum] of "reach", here used with "in" in the unusual sense of "swallow up"' (Boas).

485 palfreys horses.

493–5 which ... others Kyd mistranslates Tasso's 'i quali [atti] da niuna esistenza sono accompagnati quali sono quegli onori, che per buona creanza si sogliono fare altrui' ('which gestures are not accompanied by any concreteness as are those honours that are customarily made to others out of good breeding').

496 league distance.

499 weigh consider.

499–501 he ... life As Basile notes, this is a common theme in several Renaissance treatises with which Tasso may have been acquainted, such as Sperone Speroni, *Dialogo della cura famigliare*, in *I Dialogi* (Venice, 1542), and Francesco Tommasi, *Reggimento del padre di famiglia* (Florence, 1580).

504–6 according ... her Cf. Hesiod, *Opera et dies*, 695–705, but also see Xenophon, *Oeconomicus*, 7.5.

505 receive and retain learn and adopt.

505–6 customs and conditions habits and modes of behaviour.

506 commend impart to.

508–9 natural ... moisture According to the theory of humours, the early moderns assumed that the human body contained four fluids: blood, yellow bile, black bile, and phlegm. These humours were believed to correspond to the four elements – air, fire, earth, and water – and to the qualities of cold, hot, dry, and wet. These fluids were thought to be mixed in different amounts in each individual, thus determining their personality, but they were also related to sex: men were said to have a propensity to be hot and dry; women were assumed to have a tendency to be cold and moist. Women were believed to be characterized by a shamefully excessive production of fluids that made them to be regarded as 'leaky vessels'; the shame derived from the belief that women were unable to control their own body.

510 age old age.

510–11 as the beginning ... other's Cf. Aristotle, *Politics*, 5.16.1335a20.

515 crabbed 'Of disagreeably froward or wayward disposition, cross-grained, ill-conditioned, perverse, contrarious, fractious' (*OED adj.* 1a.).
517 exonerate The verb, as Boas remarks, 'Usually has as object the person or thing relieved, not, as here, the load.'
519 impugneth opposes.
526 unfurnished devoid, unprovided.
529–31 or so as ... reason Kyd's confused rendering of Tasso's 'o nell'anima nostra, nella quale, così ordinate le potenze come nella città gli ordini dei cittadini, la parte affettuosa suole alla ragionevole ubbidire' ('or in our soul, in which – being the powers arranged like the ranks of citizens in a city – the passions usually obey reason').
531 affections emotions, passions.
536–8 The ... requisite Cf. Aristotle, *Politics*, 1.5.1254b10 ff.
539 shamefastness modesty, sobriety of behaviour.
540 league union.
544 confirm strengthen.
547 is as ... blame Kyd misinterprets Tasso's 'anzi di lode che di biasmo è degno' ('is worthy of praise rather than blame').
548–52 of Aristotle ... depainteth Cf. *Sermo XXXI, De verecundia et pudore* in Stobaeus, *Sententiae*, C162r; Aristotle's daughter's name was Pythias. See also Aristotle, *Politics*, 1260a30 and 1277b23 (Lord and Trafton).
552–6 which ... toothsome Kyd alters and expands Tasso's 'il qual tanto alle donne accresce di vaghezza, quanto lor per aventura ne tolgono quei colori artificiali, de' quali quasi maschere, o scene si soglion colorare' ('which increases women's beauty as much as those artificial colours with which they usually paint themselves like masks or painted sceneries perhaps decrease it').
552 depainteth paints; **draweth** attracts.
556n Ovid, *De Medicamine formae foeminae*, 45.
553 daubings 'Material with which anything is daubed; esp. mortar or clay used in daubing walls; rough-cast' (*OED n.* 2a.).
554 withdraweth sends away.
555–6 toothsome agreeable.
556–7 will ... trash A free rendering of Tasso's 'a niun modo dovrebbe le bellezze naturali con gli artificiali imbellettamenti guastare, e ricoprire' ('in no way should [she] impair and cover up her natural beauties with cosmetics').
557 to recover by covering up.
563 muddy 'sinful; morally impure or corrupt' (*OED adj.* 7); **making fair** embellishing; **contemner** scornful.
564 pruning primping.

565–7 As … husbands Kyd seems to have misunderstood Tasso's 'percioché tutte le donne vaghe di parer belle, e di piacere altrui, e l'oneste donne particolarmente di piacer al marito desiderose' ('because all women [being] eager to look beautiful and to please others, and honest women [being] particularly desirous of being liked by their husbands'). Kyd was perhaps unable to understand the sentence because the verb 'essendo' ('being') was missing after 'percioché' in both the 1583 and the 1585 editions of the Italian text.

567 as such time as as soon as.

568 lye 'A cosmetic for the hair' (*OED n.*1 1c).

573 person body.

578 proud … locks splendid and tangled manes.

581 shape species. Cf. Tasso: 'specie'.

583 dainty delicate; **desired** desirous.

584 become accord with; **proper** natural.

587 judicial judicious.

589 deciphered represented.

590 epithetons Greek for 'epithets', adjectives 'indicating some quality or attribute which the speaker or writer regards as characteristic of the person or thing described' (*OED n.* 1a). Cf. *Soliman and Perseda*, 1.2.75.

591n '*Unkempt*' does not seem a particularly felicitous marginal heading here. Something like 'long-haired' would have been more appropriate.

596 Helen in Euripides Cf. Euripides, *Helen*, 1187–8. Helen cut her hair as a sign of mourning because she believed Menelaus had died.

599 comely decent.

601–4 fair … her Cf. Xenophon, *Oeconomicus*, 10.10–13.

604 contend try.

605 calling rank.

608 be … first Kyd seems not to have understood exactly Tasso's 'sia fra le prime veduta e vagheggiata' ('be one of the most looked at and courted').

614 decent fitting.

615 servile proper of slaves; **base** ignoble.

618–19 Cf. Homer, *Iliad*, 3.172. I have inserted Tasso's own Italian version of the line from the *Iliad*, absent in Kyd's Q, in line with Kyd's procedure in the rest of the translation.

623 profane … clippings unholy embracings not based in religion.

624–5 the kisses … husband's Tasso: 'a Catelda parvero più saporiti i baci dell'amante, che quei del marito fossero paruti' ('her lover's kisses tasted sweeter to Catelda than her husband's had been'). The reference is to Boccaccio's *Decameron*. See my 'Introduction', p. 249.

629 commodity benefit.

632 opposites … contraries chaotic urges and drives.

633–4 Homer … Ida Cf. Homer, *Iliad*, 14.153–351.

636 As Boas remarks, this is 'A verse-rendering of Tasso's prose': 'con lui si corca nell'erba ricoperta da una nuvola maravigliosa' ('lies with him in the grass, covered by a wonderful cloud'). It is another fourteener.

637 person disguise.

638 deposing the habit abandoning the role.

644 forbid forbidden.

644–5 represent the person adopt the role.

647–8 honest and interchangeable decent and reciprocal.

649 vicious wicked, immoral.

650 presently immediately.

651–3 he … us As Boas comments, this is a 'confused version' of Tasso's 'è considerazione che per aventura può più opportunamente in altro proposito esser avuta; e se tu tale la prenderai, qual figurata l'abbiamo, non dei temer che mai ti venga occasione per la quale d'esser da me stato intorno a ciò consigliato debba desiderare' ('it is a consideration that can perhaps be treated more fittingly elsewhere; and if you take the kind of wife that I have described, you need not fear that you will ever have occasion to wish that you had been counselled by me on this matter').

652 a wife … deciphering such a wife as I have described; **advertised** counselled.

659 conditions habits.

661 forbid forbidden.

671 aboundeth … heat is characterized by a higher bodily temperature.

673 antiperistasis the action of two opposite qualities, a technical philosophical term of Aristotelian ascendance; see Aristotle, *Physics*, 267a2–20; *On Sleep and Waking*, 457b1–3; *Meteorology*, 348b2 ff; **complexion** constitution.

675 in Aristotle Cf. Aristotle, *Politics*, 7.17.1336a17.

678–81 Virgil, *Aeneid*, 9.603–6. Kyd's Q misquotes 'silvasque' as 'silvamque' (like T) and 'ludus' as 'ludis' (unlike T) and translates accordingly.

682–5 Kyd's translation is made up of two couplets of fourteneers rhyming AABB.

689 milksops men who are 'indecisive, effeminate, or lacking in courage' (*OED n.* 1a).

691–6 Virgil, *Aeneid*, 9.614, 616–20. Kyd misquotes 'tunicae' as 'tunica' (like T) and translates accordingly. 'Dindyma' rather than 'Dyndima' (T) was a common alternative spelling in Renaissance commentaries of the *Aeneid*.

697–702 Kyd's translation is made up of three successive couplets of fourteeners rhyming AABBCC. For Kyd's alleged mistakes in the translation, see my 'Introduction', pp. 246–53.

701 timbrels trisyllabic.

705 hardly rigorously.

706 Lacedaemonians Spartans; **Chiron** the centaur and demi-god who trained heroes such as Achilles, Hercules, and Jason.

710 conditions habits.

714 servitors servants.

718 wearish puny; **effeminate complexion** weak bodily constitution.

722–3 because … father As Boas remarks, this is a 'confused version' of Tasso's 'ch'ella è insieme del politico, il quale dovrebbe prescrivere a' padri' ('which also concerns the political man, who should prescribe to fathers').

722 politic politics.

732 eftsoons likewise.

734 list wish; **hath relation** is connected.

735–6 antiquities … families the ancient works of Aristotle and Xenophon; cf. esp. Aristotle, *Oeconomicus*, 1.5.1344a–b.

736 hold keep.

739 a servando As Basile remarks, this etymology can be traced back to Isidore of Seville, *Etymologiae*, 9.4.43, and was often quoted by Renaissance writers; cf. Tommasi, *Reggimento*, 195.

740 manumitted and enfranchised Tasso: 'uomini liberi' ('free men'). For Kyd's alleged mistake in the translation, see my 'Introduction', p. 251.

742 percase perhaps.

745 signorizing Cf. *Cornelia*, 1.55; 3.2.72.

746 stiff-necked stubborn; **unprofitable** unhelpful.

763 Agamemnon … Eteocles The first two were Kings of Mycenae; the latter was King of Thebes. Here they are recalled as main characters of Greek tragedies.

764 action acting.

766–8 he that … dignity an incorrect rendering of Tasso's 'chi non ben sostiene la persona di principe o di gentiluomo che in questa vita, che è quasi teatro del mondo, dalla fortuna l'è stata imposta' ('whoever fails to perform well the role of prince or gentleman that fortune has imposed on him in this life, which is almost a theatre of the world').

769 Davus … Geta examples of servants in Latin comedies.

771–3 and … are Kyd's addition. Jackson Campbell Boswell and Gordon McMurry Braden, *Petrarch's English Laurels, 1475–1700: A Compendium of Printed References and Allusions* (Farnham, 2012), argue that this 'spurious quotation … appears to derive from a line ("povero d'argomento e di consiglio") that appears in a sonnet of Tasso's ("alma leggiadra il cui splendor traluce") and in Remigio Nannini's translation of Ovid, *Heroides* 12'. Yet the line rather seems to be an incorrect quotation from Petrarch's *Triumphus Eternitatis*, 52–3 ('O veramente sordi, ignudi e frali, | Poveri d'argomento e di consiglio'), which also features the word 'ignudi' ('naked') as quoted by Kyd.

776 capable of able to understand.

779 record remember.

782 animal rationale rational animal. Kyd introduces the Latin, not used by Tasso, in order to recall the classical definition of humanity associated with Aristotelianism; **by participation** through his relationship with his master.

786 reserve retain; **impressions** notions.

790–2 Petrarch, *RVF*, 360.126–8. Kyd follows Tasso's incorrect quotation. The actual text by Petrarch reads: 'poi che fatt'era uom ligio | di lei, ch'alto vestigio | l'impresse al core, e fecel suo simile.'

793–4 Kyd translates Tasso's quotation from Petrarch with a pair of rhyming fourteeners. Kyd's customary strategy of synonymic amplification is at work here too, with '*uom ligio*' becoming 'her liegeman and her thrall'. On Kyd's use of 'Thrall', see my Introduction, p. 254.

795–7 because … servant Cf. Hesiod, *Opera et dies*, 405–7; see also Aristotle, *Politics*, 1.2.1252b10.

800 dissonant … from discordant with and unconnected to.

803 become turn into.

805 reave plunder.

807–9 as … them Kyd needs to expand Tasso's 'quanto lor basti [per non abbandonare l'opere commandate da' padroni o per ubbrachiezza o per altro piacere,] o pure i padroni medesimi ne' pericoli delle brighe civili, e negli altri che possono avenire' ('as much as is enough for them [not to neglect – either because of drunkenness or some other pleasure – the tasks that their master has appointed, or abandon] their masters themselves amidst the dangers of a civil or other kind of upheaval that might occur'), because the sentence in square brackets is missing in the edition of Tasso's text Kyd consulted.

811 Dante, *Inferno*, 17.90.

812–3 Kyd's free translation of Dante's line is done through a couple of rhyming iambic tetrameters, the second of which features conspicuous alliteration.

814–5 in … Milone The reference is to Cicero, *Pro Milone*, 10.29.

815–6 some … Maximus Cf. Valerius Maximus, *Factorum ac dictorum memorabilium libri IX*, 8.6.

819 want lack; **virtue** fortitude, power; **taste** have.

822 servile by the slaves. Q reads 'Cyuill', but I emend the text because Tasso is not talking about civil war in general but specifically about the Roman 'servile' war, and the adjective 'civil' makes little sense in this context. Even though historians today identify at least three servile wars (139–33 BCE, 103–100 BCE, 73–71 BCE), Tasso's allusion is probably to the latter, led by Spartacus.

823 Soldan … slaves the Ottoman janissaries, elite infantry units made up of Christian prisoners converted to Islam, which composed the Sultan's household troops.

824 hosts armies.

825 maketh … like likewise makes up of slaves; **record** remember.

826 resolve 'To free (a person) from doubt or perplexity' (*OED v.* 20a).

831 gentle noble.

831–7 the Scythians … flight The Scythians were a group of tribes of nomadic warriors who originally lived in what is now southern Siberia. The reference is here to Herodotus, *Histories*, 4.3–4.

835 bastinadoes sticks.

837 presently instantly.

840 complexion physical constitution.

842–3 the one … workmen Cf. Aristotle, *Oeconomicus*, 1.5.1344a25.

843 the first Tasso: 'nella prima' (i.e., in the first of the two classes just mentioned).

844 commended entrusted.

845 the next Tasso: 'e quel' (Tasso is in fact continuing his enumeration of the people in the first class).

846 the third Tasso: 'ed' (Tasso is in fact continuing his enumeration of the people in the first class).

851 one for all a single man.

852 hinds domestics.

853 meaner inferior.

861 relicts remains.

864 pestilent corrupt.

865 standing waters ponds, bodies of water that do not move; **recourse** movement, flow.

866 naughty bad, worthless.

868 severally individually.

870 steward cashier. Cf. Tasso: 'spenditore'.

871 purvey provide, supply; **brush** 'To pass a brush briskly across (a surface), so as to sweep off dirt, dust, or light particles, or to smooth the surface' (*OED v.*2 1a).

876 courts courtyards; **uncleans** dirt.

880 adjoineth adds.

883 sluttishness dirtiness, gross untidiness; **annoyeth** harms.

886 office job.

890 Petrarch, *RVF*, 50.18.

891 Kyd translates the quotation from Petrarch with a line of iambic pentameter, leaving out 'avaro'.

892–3 who … use a confused rendering of 'il quale prima aveva chiamate armi quegl'instrumenti, che adoperano i contadini' ('who had earlier called weapons those instruments the peasants use').

894 Virgil, *Georgics*, 1.160.

895 A fourteener.

897–8 Virgil, *Aeneid*, 1.177–8. As Boas notes, 'The marginal reference to "*Aeneid*, Lib[er] 2", which is not given by Tasso, is wrong.'

899–900 Kyd uses fourteeners again here; the second line is interrupted, as is the Latin quotation.

901 charged burdened.

905 intercourse mutual exchange; **entreats** invites.

910 severally separately.

916 beck 'A mute signal or significant gesture' (*OED n.*2 1).

917 bent … brow frown.

919–30 as … workmanship As Basile points out, the archetypes of this section are to be found in Aristotle, *Politics*, 1.2.1252b.

923 well honestly.

924 inanima Tasso: 'inanimati'. Kyd again provides a Latin version of Tasso's Italian.

925 animatus Tasso: 'animato'. Kyd again provides a Latin version of Tasso's Italian.

928 artificers craftsmen.

931 animatum … separabile Tasso: 'instrumento delle azioni animato e separato' ('instrument of actions, animate and separate'). Kyd again provides a Latin version of Tasso's Italian.

938 servile … wit slavish or coarse intelligence.

939 capable … contemplate Kyd's 'fashions' probably depends on the text he was using, insofar as the 1583 edition incorrectly reads 'nazioni' ('nations') rather than 'azioni', which is the correct reading. Yet, even if one accepts that here Kyd might have used **fashions** with the meaning of 'Manners and customs (of nations)' (*OED n.* 8b), it is hard to justify his failure to understand that Tasso was referring to the traditional Renaissance opposition between *vita activa* and *vita contemplativa*.

940 signory lordship.

941 by Aristotle Cf. Aristotle, *Nicomachean Ethics*, 8.3.1156a–b; **is … highest** is praised as excellent. Cf. Tasso: 'è detta in eccellenza'.

942 worlds Tasso: 'secoli' ('centuries'). Kyd uses the word in its obsolete meaning of 'The state of human affairs, the state of things; (hence) season or time as marked by the state of affairs' (*OED n.* 3b).

943–5 Terence … works As Basile remarks, Terence had been a slave to Terentius Lucanus. As for the accusation that he had become, as a playwright, a figurehead for the members of the Scipionic circle, cf. Aelius Donatus, *Vita Terentii*, 4.

945 Tiro Tullius Tiro, the freedman of Cicero, was also one of his chief correspondents; book 16 of *Ad familiares* is addressed to him entirely. Besides, Tiro was an accomplished grammarian (*De usu atque ratione linguae latinae*) and invented a system of shorthand, also known as *notae tironianae*.

945–6 of … Tully a confused translation of Tasso's 'al quale sono scritte molte lettere di Marco Tullio' ('to whom many of Marcus Tully's letters are written').

947 dispraiser denigrator.

951 under officers people employed in minor duties.

952 Signor … Casa the famous author of the *Galateo*, here mentioned, as Basile observes, for his *Trattato degli uffici comuni tra gli amici superiori e inferiori* (1559).

955–7 though … menservants a confused translation of Tasso's 'se non forse, quanto tu potessi desiderare, che così delle fantesche si parlasse, come de' servitori s'è favellato' ('although perhaps you would have liked to hear as much about maidservants as you have heard about menservants').

956 the … person the care of the people.

961 effectually 'So as adequately to answer the purpose' (*OED adv.* 1a).

966 common proper to both.

966–7 whatsoever … purpose The allusion is to Plato, *Republic*, 5.4.452e ff., who granted men and women an identical role in his ideal State.

971–2 the … charges the reasons of his expenses.

972 prove the least be inferior to his revenues.

972–3 making … least) making sure that his expenses are related proportionally to his revenues as four is to eight or, at the most, as six is to eight.

974 recover those losses repair those damages.

977 be certified have a clear awareness.

979 compasses measurements.

979–80 which … Egypt As Basile and Baffetti point out, the measuring of the fields fertilized by the inundations of the Nile gave rise to geometry according to Strabo, *Geography*, 16.2.24.

985 husbandry or grazing agriculture or animal farming.

990 factor farmer.

993 by algorism Algorism is 'The Arabic (decimal) system of numbering (characterized by a zero, 0); arithmetic in which Arabic numerals are used rather than Roman numerals or the abacus' (*OED n.* 1).

995 quadering ... even The verb **to quader** used intransitively means 'To conform; to agree or be in harmony *with*' (*OED v.* 2). Cf. *Letter to Sir John Puckering*.

998 let ... rate sold at the same price.

1002 manurance management; **handling** control.

1003 overweener 'an arrogant, conceited, or presumptuous person' (*OED n.*).

1004 substance property; **artificial** man-made.

1010 numus the Latin word for 'coin'; **νομός** Kyd uses the Greek alphabet where Tasso simply writes 'Nomos'.

1012 certain precise.

1023 recourse and refluence flow and reflow; **virtue** power, faculty.

1025 champaign 'level and open' (*OED* B. *adj*. 2). Cf. *Cornelia*, 5.176.

1026 cars carts.

1027 uneasy rough, difficult.

1028 charged provided; **sumpter men** men employed to drive a packhorse.

1029–31 any ... pass As Boas argues, this is 'An inaccurate rendering' of Tasso's 'strade correnti per le quali i peregrini e i mercanti d'Italia in Germania o in Francia soglion trapassare' ('highways by which travellers and merchants are accustomed to pass from Italy into Germany or France').

1031 frequence or resort significant traffic or a large number.

1032 in prospect with an open and extensive view.

1040 furnished provided.

1044 better cheap cheaper.

1047 opinion of prognostications judgement regarding predictions.

1050–2 Thales ... oil Cf. Aristotle, *Politics*, 1.11.1259a13–23; Plutarch, *Solon*, 2. Thales (c. 624/3–c. 548/5 BCE) was a Greek philosopher, mathematician, and astronomer from Miletus (present-day Milet in Turkey). He was one of the Seven Sages of Greece and is widely regarded as the first philosopher in the Greek tradition.

1051 bargain deal.

1053 about in various places.

1062 suddenly soon.

1068 Again on the other hand. Cf. Tasso: 'all'incontra'.

1069 naught to eat inedible.

1073 furnish her mess provide the table.

1074 junkets delicacies.

1077 indifferently without distinction.

1079 cashier The spelling '*Cashur*' in Q is unusual and unrecorded in *OED*; at all events, Kyd is here probably thinking of Tasso's 'spenditore' a few lines earlier (l. 871), which translates 'cashier' in English.

1081–2 which custom … houses Kyd seems to misunderstand Tasso's 'che strana usanza è certo quella d'alcune case' ('which is certainly a strange custom in some houses'). **Geason** means 'rare', 'uncommon'.

1084 Therefore Tasso: 'nondimeno' ('nonetheless'). As Boas notes, 'the change destroys the logical connexion.'

1086–7 for … man As Boas remarks, Kyd changes the meaning of Tasso's 'perché la parsimonia è virtù così propria di lei, come dell'uomo la liberalità' ('because parsimony is her proper virtue, just as liberality is a man's').

1088 charged … kept ordered to be stored.

1091 rehearsed described.

1092 choice select.

1094 spirit liveliness.

1097 honestly gain make some honest profit.

1101 ray 'To smear, bespatter, soil *with* blood, dirt, etc.; to dirty, defile' (*OED v.* 4b).

1104 noisomeness unwholesomeness.

1110–16 Virgil, *Aeneid*, 8.407–13.

1117–21 Kyd's translation extends over a quintain of fourteeners rhyming AABBB. For Kyd's alleged mistranslation of '*ad lumina*', see 'Introduction', p. 251.

1127–8 Pietro Bembo, *Stanze*, 37.5–6. Kyd adds 'nobil' to Tasso's quotation of Bembo.

1129–30 A pair of rhyming fourteeners. Kyd interestingly uses the same rhymes as the latter three lines of the previous verse translation, perhaps to create a sense of continuity between them.

1129 bated subtracted, took away.

1130 blear dim.

1133 Virgil, *Aeneid*, 7.14.

1134 A fourteener.

1136–7 but … them Tasso: 'ma la figliola del Re Alcinoo pone fra le lavatrici' ('but places King Alcinous's daughter among a group of ladies doing laundry'). Cf. Homer, *Odyssey*, 6. According to Boas, 'Kyd's mistranslation shows that he had not read the story of Nausicaa', which seems plausible.

1139 more … observers more carefully observant.

1142–3 they … her Kyd mistranslates Tasso's 'se n'innamorò' ('he [i.e., Tarquin] fell in love with her'), though this is odd given the importance and currency of Lucrece's story in early modern English culture. Livy, 1.57.9, narrates that Lucrece's husband Collatine had boasted of her virtue to Tarquin and other men. Hence, they all made a wager on the honesty of their wives, and Lucrece was the only one found in her room weaving, while the Etruscan ladies were feasting with friends.

1145 noblesse or estate nobility or exalted social rank.

1154 diligent industrious.

1155 reserve ... confusedly arranges things so as to avoid confusion.

1161 in time convenient at the appropriate time.

1162 recounted enumerated.

1167–8 well-disposed epithetons pleasingly arranged expressions.

1168 significant terms highly expressive words.

1169 answer cross act as counterpoint; **artificially** skilfully.

1170–1 though ... memory Kyd completely changes Tasso's 'come che sia di molto ornamento agevola ancora molto la fatica di coloro, che imparano le prose, e i versi a mente' ('even as it provides much ornamentation, it greatly facilitates the labour of memorizing either prose or verse').

1171 some philosophers i.e., the Platonists.

1174 reformation rearranging.

1178 impeach 'Injury, damage, detriment' (*OED n.* 2).

1179 Beaune where Tasso was in 1571; **the hospital** The Hôtel-Dieu, built between 1443 and 1451 by Jean Rateau for Philippe le Bon, Duke of Burgundy.

1182 passing neat extremely clean; **quaintly ... up** artfully adorned.

1185 discreetly ordered neatly arranged; **pewter** pewterware; **set up** arranged.

1188 the armoury of Venice the renowned, splendid armoury of the Palazzo Ducale, formerly the Doge's residence and the seat of government, in Venice; **meeter** fitter.

1189 Gnato Cf. Terence, *Eunuch*, 4.7.771 ff. With an army of slaves, Gnato wanted to free the beautiful Panfila from the house of the courtesan Thais for his master Thraso.

1191 matter subject.

1192 increasing As Basile points out, Tasso depends on Aristotle, *Politics*, 1.3–4.1253b–1254a for the meaning of increase in economics.

1194 minister attendant, subordinate.

1197 fells and seasoneth cuts down and dries so as to harden.

1200 get gain.

1203 hath As N. F. Blake, *A Grammar of Shakespeare's Language* (Basingstoke, 2002), p. 90, points out, verbs in the 'plural could also end in <-(e)s> or <(e)th>, and examples are not infrequent'.

1209 destination Tasso: 'distinzion' ('distinction').

1210 companable companionable; **untamed** Tasso: 'erranti' ('wandering').

1211 droves compact groups of beasts closely packed together; **no less profit** Tasso: 'non picciola utilità' ('no little use'). As Boas observes, 'The use of the comparative is confusing.'

1216 the … just provided the war is just. Cf. Tasso: 'quando la guerra sia giusta.'

1217–8 Thucydides … History Cf. Thucydides, *Histories*, 1.5.

1218 preying pillage.

1219–20 a pirate … a rover a marauder or a raider.

1220 injury insult.

1221 having regard paying attention; **Numa** As Boas remarks, 'Virgil is referring to Ufens and his people, not to Numanus, wrongly called Numa by Kyd' (but not by Tasso).

1222–3 Virgil, *Aeneid*, 9.612–13.

1224–5 A pair of rhyming fourteeners.

1227 barbarians i.e., Berbers.

1228 especial especially.

1229 mingleth and exchangeth blends and markets.

1230 haply perhaps.

1231 science craft.

1236–7 hereof … Offices Cf. Cicero, *De officiis*, 1.42.151.

1240–4 in … merchandise Cf. Cicero, *In Verrem*, 2.2.3.7; *Pro Plancio*, 26, 64; *Pro lege Manilia*, 17.

1244 traffic commerce.

1249 utter sell.

1252 inconvenient inappropriate.

1254 indifferently alike.

1258 held dearest most expensive.

1259 best cheap cheapest; **fashions** ways, means; **sleights** precise methods or tricks.

1261 recarried carried back.

1264 marts markets.

1266 preposeth places before other things.

1270–2 the care … government As Boas argues, this is 'A confused rendering' of Tasso's 'il padre di famiglia ha l'acquisto della trasmutazione per obietto secondo, e dirizzato al governo della casa' ('the father of the family considers acquisition through trade only secondary and subordinates it to running the house').

1271 object goal.

1278 determinate limited.

1280 of some arts Tasso: 'in alcun'arte' ('in any art'). Kyd's mistranslation compromises the argument.

1283–4 that ... greatness Kyd mistranslates Tasso's 'se di grandezza non potrebbono esser maneggiati, oltre che non si concede corpo d'infinita grandezza' ('[if they were infinite] in size, they would be unusable, not to mention the fact that a body of infinite size is considered an impossibility').

1288 graving or cutting engraving and sculpting.

1295 Crassus Cf. Cicero, *De officiis*, 1.8.25. Marcus Licinius Crassus (115–52 BCE), a member of the so-called first triumvirate with Gaius Julius Caesar and Gnaeus Pompeius Magnus, was especially renowned for his wealth.

1297–8 too too much While Boas argues that 'Perhaps the repetition of "too" is a misprint, but "too much" may be treated as equivalent to a single epithet qualified by "too"', this may in fact be a case in which repetition, as Blake, *Grammar*, p. 230, suggests, 'appears to have a light emotional emphasis'.

1298 any ... Nola i.e., a provincial man.

1304 disorder disease; **disdiet** 'Improper or irregular diet or regimen of food' (*OED n.*).

1313 civilly 'In a manner befitting or appropriate to a citizen (*OED adv.* 1).

1317 many Romans an allusion to Lucius Quinctius Cincinnatus, an impoverished aristocrat who had been consul of Rome in 460 BCE. In 458 the Romans decided to appoint him as dictator to solve a severe military crisis in which Rome was embroiled. The messengers who oversaw informing him found him ploughing his fields. After ending the crisis, he returned to the fields. Cf. Valerius Maximus, *Factorum*, 4.7.

1317–18 from ... cart cf. *Cornelia*, 1.133.

1318 and mighty ... courts As Boas notes, 'Added by Kyd, and curiously inapplicable to Roman Republicans.'

1324 defiling or defacing degrading or demeaning.

1325 professed openly declared.

1328 unconsorted with unaccompanied by (the lemma **unconsorted** is not in *OED*).

1329 sithence because.

1331 impertinent not belonging; **to husbandry and housekeeping** Tasso: 'al padre di famiglia'. Kyd again refrains from mentioning the title of the treatise.

1332 exchange As Lord and Trafton (pp. 252–3) point out, 'Money changing in the sixteenth century involved two kinds of related activities: exchanging coins of one origin for those of another and dealing in bills of exchange – devices for making payments at a great distance without incurring the risk of shipping gold and silver. While both activities met an important economic need, both could be, and apparently frequently were, performed in a manner that at least bordered on fraud. The money-changer was open to the often justified suspicion that through the use of debased, sweated, or clipped coins he was cheating his clients. And because he purchased bills of exchange at a discount that was in fact a thinly disguised form of interest, he also acquired some of the odium of the usurer.'

1336–9 of … commodious Cf. Aristotle, *Politics*, 1.9.1257a-b.

1343 no … determination no termination or definite conclusion.

1346 stirrers up instigators. Kyd follows the 1583 edn of Tasso, which reads 'incitatrici', but the correct reading is 'imitatrici' ('imitators'). The 1585 edn features the correct reading, so that the 1583 edn can be identified as the one Kyd used.

1348 number … things number in its essence, when not used to count material objects.

1351–3 Formal … numbered A formal number is a group of units that have no reference to objects. A material number is a group of objects that have been enumerated. Cf. Aristotle, *Metaphysics*, 13.9.1085a1 ff.

1355 partition sectioning.

1358 of number certain finite in number.

1359 in bare money in money considered as money.

1363 and so … infinite Kyd alters Tasso's 'e par che co'l desiderio s'aspiri all'infinito' ('and it seems that one desires to reach infinity').

1369 allowed granted.

1378n Cf. Lev. 25:37; Psalm 14:5; Lk 6:35. The marginal reference is taken almost verbatim from Cristoforo Landino's *Comento sopra la Comedia di Dante* (Florence, 1481), I4r. For a fuller discussion, see Domenico Lovascio, 'Thomas Kyd's *The Householder's Philosophy* and Cristoforo Landino's *Comento sopra la Comedia di Dante*', *BJJ* 27 (2020): 84–104.

1373 reduced unto traced back to.

1373–8 wherewith … cured Kyd amplifies and modifies Tasso's 'alla quale l'usura non si può ridurre, come quella, che è scompagnata da ogni pericolo' ('to which usury cannot be reduced, insofar as it is devoid of any risk'), especially adding harsh words against usury.

1378–82 Every … Phisicis Kyd continues the amplification and changes the sense of Tasso's sentence: 'e che niuna di queste cose considera; la qual non sol fu dannata da Aristotle, ma proibita ancora nella nuova legge, e nella vecchia, e di lei ragionando Dante disse' ('and that takes no account of these things, which was not only condemned by Aristotle, but also prohibited by both the new and the old laws, and Dante said this about it'). The last bit, 'to prove … *De Phisicis*' is again interpolated from Landino's *Comento*, I3v.

1379 inhibited prohibited; **the … law** the Old Testament and the New Testament, as referenced by Kyd in the margin.

1381 Aristotle Cf. Aristotle, *Politics*, 1.10.1258b 2–4.

1383–93 Dante, *Inferno*, 11.101–11. At 1389–94 Dante has in mind Gen 2:15 and 3:17–19. Kyd adds to Tasso's quotation the personal pronoun 'tu' (l. 1384), which he found in Landino's edition of Dante's *Inferno*.

1394–1408 This is not a straightforward translation of Dante's lines as quoted by Tasso, because Kyd interpolates them with a passage in Latin drawn from Landino's commentary: 'Oportuit ab initio seculi humanum genus sumere vitam, excedere unum alium per naturam, & artes' (I4r). Here Kyd avoids the use of fourteeners, his translation being made up of fifteen lines of iambic pentameter. It can be seen as a succession of three English quintains with the rhyme scheme ABABB CDCDD EFEFF. The second quintain features macaronic rhymes ('remember it – *oportuit*' and 'say – *sumere* – *excedere*'), with the Latin following the metrical rules of English rather than Latin poetry.

1398 niece … kind 'grandchild to God by relationship' (Boas).

1400 Genesis the Book of Genesis, the first book of the Hebrew Bible and the Old Testament, an account of the creation of the world and the origins of the Jewish people.

1405 wander otherwise proceed on a different path.

1408 beguilèd deceived, mistaken.

1409–20 It … thing This passage, added by Kyd, is an almost verbatim translation of another passage from Landino's *Comento*, I3v. For a fuller discussion, see Lovascio, 'Thomas Kyd's *The Householder's Philosophy* and Cristoforo Landino's *Comento sopra la Comedia di Dante*'. The Aristotelian reference in this passage is to *Physics*, 2.194a; the biblical quotation is from Gen 3:19.

1413 art 'Human workmanship or agency; human skill as an agent' (*OED n.* 12a).

1419 artificial 'Of an argument: relying on sound rational principles' (*OED adj.* 11).

1420 putteth … thing considers the essence of the object and its use as they were one and the same thing.

1424 turneth and returneth pays particularly close attention.

1436 Now … silent Kyd radically alters Tasso's 'Or rimarrebbe solo' ('It would only remain').

1441 institutions principles.

1444 all one one and the same thing.

1449 halls palaces.

1451 device ingenuity.

1458 so … censure so discerning as to pass judgement.

1459 hap luck, chance.

1461–2 I believe … greatness As Boas remarks, this is a 'mistranslation' of Tasso's 'posso creder, che la casa del privato da quella del principe per altro, che per grandezza sola sia differente' ('I can believe that private households differ from those of princes in other ways besides size').

1469 approved demonstrated; **in Convivio Platonis** Cf. Plato, *Symposium*, 29.223d ff.

1469–70 to … one the same writer should be able to compose both tragedies and comedies.

1473–6 in … privata) Cf. Aristotle, *Oeconomicus*, 2.1.1345b15 ff. As Basile points out, Tasso regards the *Oeconomicus* as a work attributable to Aristotle but not certainly by him.

1474 dedicated Tasso: 'attribuito' ('attributed').

1476 satrapica i.e., ruled by a satrap, the governor of a province under the ancient Persian monarchy; **reprove not** do not disagree with.

1479–80 that … men Tasso: 'come anticamente quello de' satrapi' ('as that of the satraps in ancient times').

1482 Reggio Reggio nell'Emilia, formerly known as Reggio di Lombardia.

1485–6 segregate … office withdrawn from public life.

1488–92 that … men Cf. Aristotle, *Oeconomicus*, 2.1.1346a10.

1497 unspoken Tasso: 'oltre le dette' ('apart from those we have said').

1498 revived and produced recalled for consideration.

1499 collect pick up.

1502 unworthy that was undeserving of such an honour.

1505–6 An English translation would be 'I like mine like you like yours. | The rest belongs to Death.' Kyd here merges two sayings that in early modern culture circulated autonomously as *sententiae*. The first part almost certainly derives from Cicero, *Tusculanae Disputationes*, 5.22.63 (Loeb edn). Here Cicero (with reference to the story of Damon and Dionysius I, tyrant of Siracuse) alludes to the fact that every poet likes his own poetry: the full quotation is 'sic se res habet: te tua, me delectant mea'. In this case, Kyd seems to have left the verb implicit as a way to convey a higher level of sententiousness. The second part can be traced back to the pseudo-Virgilian *Elegiae in Maecenatem*, 1.38 ('vivitur ingenio, cetera mortis erunt'). Between the sixteenth and the seventeenth centuries the line circulated autonomously as a motto, especially in books of medicine and anatomy. In its originary context, however, it alludes to the topos of the superiority of literary works (Maecenas', in this specific case) as compared to marble ones. I am indebted to Sergio Audano for this explanation.

SOLIMAN AND PERSEDA

Edited by Matthew Dimmock

INTRODUCTION

The Tragedye of Solyman and Perseda is an enigmatic play. Appearing first in an undated, anonymous, and rather untidy quarto that gives no hint of playing company or initial performance contexts, the play closely follows a single primary source and yet is innovative and experimental. Before a recent flurry of interest in its dramatization of Christian-Islamic conflict it was largely neglected by nineteenth- and twentieth-century directors and scholars, with no recorded performances and only a small number of editions since that first quarto, which probably dates to late 1592 or early 1593.[1]

Although its title page offers scant information in most other respects, the colophon of the first quarto does indicate that it had been printed by Edward Allde for Edward White and was to be sold from his shop 'at the little North doore of Paules Church, at the signe of the Gun'.[2] The play, then titled *Salamon and Perceda*, had been entered into the Stationers' Register to Edward White on 20 November 1592, and was licenced for publication by John Aylmer, the Bishop of London. The same partnership of Allde and White subsequently produced a second quarto – now *Solimon and Perseda* – that was dated to 1599, the second issue of which was stamped on the title page as 'Newly corrected and amended'.[3] Here are the first potential connections to Thomas Kyd: his celebrated play *The Spanish Tragedy* had been entered into the Stationers' Register not long before, on 6 October 1592, and a similarly undated quarto of that play printed by Edward Allde and published by Edward White appeared around the same time. Another play associated with Kyd, *Arden of Faversham*, was also entered earlier in the same year to White (on 3 April 1592) and was published that year by

1 Martin Wiggins dates the first quarto to c. 1592, *British Drama 1533–1642: A Catalogue*, Vol. II: 1567–1589 (Oxford, 2012), p. 406; Lukas Erne makes the persuasive point that the lateness in the year of the Stationers' Register entry may suggest that the quarto did not appear until early 1593. Thomas Kyd, *Soliman and Perseda* [1592/3], ed. Lukas Erne (Manchester, 2014), p. xiii. The bibliographical data in this section is taken from Erne.

2 Thomas Kyd, *The Tragedye of Solyman and Perseda. Wherein is laide open, Loues constancy, Fortunes inconstancy, and Deaths Triumphs* (London, n.d.), colophon.

3 W. W. Greg suggests that this line was hand-stamped after printing: *A Bibliography of the English Printed Drama to the Restoration*, 4 vols (London, 1939–59), I. 187.

the same partnership of the two Edwards. This may suggest a selling off of manuscripts by Kyd to White (who would produce second editions of all three) at this point and, as Lukas Erne notes, although 'it is impossible to recover what events or processes' led to the near simultaneous appearance in print of these three plays, it is nonetheless 'intriguing'.[4]

Kyd's authorship of *Soliman and Perseda* (as the play is now commonly titled, following its most frequent spelling of the Ottoman Sultan Suleyman I's name) is further suggested on the level of content. It was Thomas Hawkins in the second volume of his 1773 compendium *The Origin of the English Drama* who, in the context of reprinting the play, first suggested Thomas Kyd as its author. Hawkins wrote that 'might the editor be allowed to indulge a conjecture, he would ascribe it to *Kyd*, as it carries with it many internal marks of that author's manner of composition' and that 'in *The Spanish Tragedy* the story of *Erastus* and *Perseda* is introduced by *Hieronimo*' as the basis for his climactic play-within-the-play.[5] This narrative is drawn from the English translation of Jacques Yver's *Printemps d'Yver* (1572); Henry Wotton's *A Courtlie Controversy of Cupids Cautels* (1578). The 'firste Historie' of that collection comes apparently from the 'Grecian Chroniclers' and relates the virtuous life and lamentable tragedy of the Rhodian 'damoysell' Persida, her youthful love for Erastus, and its thwarting by the intervention of cruel Fortune.[6] Arthur Freeman recognized that its use in both *The Spanish Tragedy* and *Soliman and Perseda* might imply the same author because neither Wotton nor Yver's texts are used as a source by any other playwright in this period.[7] The shift of emphasis away from Perseda and Erastus and onto the 'Great Turk' Soliman is one that begins in *The Spanish Tragedy*, where a story supposedly drawn from 'the Chronicles of Spain' concerning a 'Knight of Rhodes' and 'an Italian dame' is transmuted into 'the Tragedy / Of Soliman the Turkish Emperor', reflecting the dramatic preoccupations of early modern London in the late 1580s and early 1590s (on which more below).

The play's main plot follows the first history of Wotton's *A Courtlie Controversy* closely. Erastus and Perseda have loved each other from their infancy. During a victorious performance at a tournament held to celebrate the wedding of the Prince of Cyprus to Cornelia, the daughter of Philippo, the Governor of Rhodes, Erastus loses a precious chain given to him by Perseda. It is found by Ferdinando, a kinsman of Philippo, who presents

4 Kyd, *Soliman and Perseda*, ed. Erne, p. xvi.

5 Thomas Hawkins (ed.), *The Origin of the English Drama* (Oxford, 1773), 2. 197.

6 Henry Wotton's *A Courtlie Controversy of Cupids Cautels* (London, 1578), pp. 42–3. The original source has been traced to Fontaine's *De Bello Rhodio* (1540): see Arthur Freeman, *Thomas Kyd: Facts and Problems* (Oxford, 1967), p. 146.

7 Freeman, *Thomas Kyd*, p. 140.

it as a token of love to Lucina. Perseda sees Lucina wearing it, presumes infidelity, and rejects Erastus. He wins back the chain but violently encounters Ferdinando, who is slain. Expecting death in punishment, Erastus flees to Ottoman Turkey. Meanwhile, one of the tournament competitors, a Turkish knight named Brusor, has been spying on the defences of Rhodes to inform an Ottoman attack (Brusor's role is considerably expanded from the source). He returns to the Ottoman court with this information, closely followed by Erastus, who is enthusiastically welcomed and employed by the Emperor, Soliman, in his wars, but declines to participate in the invasion of Rhodes, which is brutally prosecuted by Brusor. He returns with prisoners, including Perseda and Lucina, to Soliman, who is immediately besotted with Perseda but allows her reconciliation with Erastus once he realizes their love. The couple return to Rhodes with Erastus installed as Governor. Soliman soon regrets his actions and, encouraged by Brusor, recalls Erastus to his execution on fabricated charges. In response, Perseda resists Ottoman possession of Rhodes and Soliman mounts a second invasion, in which – in another notable departure from the source – Perseda, disguised as a man, fights and is killed by Soliman but in turn kills him with poison daubed on her lips. Beyond this central plot from Wotton is added an allegorical superstructure reminiscent of *The Spanish Tragedy* in which Love, Fortune, and Death compete to see who is the most influential and thus the more appropriate Chorus – Death claims the victory – and a comic subplot involving the misadventures of the braggart knight Basilisco, another suitor to Perseda.[8]

Following the initial proposal by Thomas Hawkins, the decisive scholarly study in modern times was Gregor Sarrazin's 1892 book on Kyd.[9] Sarrazin identified many verbal details that the author of *Soliman and Perseda* had borrowed from Wotton, but also showed that several close parallels existed between the novella and *The Spanish Tragedy*, strong evidence that Kyd had written both plays.[10] His attribution was endorsed by F. S. Boas in 1901, who looked to a more detailed consideration of the plays' internal evidence to connect them to each other and to Kyd. Boas pointed to common dramatic dynamics between *The Spanish Tragedy* and *Soliman and Perseda* in the similar shift of a group of characters from one locale to another (Spain to Portugal; Rhodes to Constantinople); the linguistic similarity of exchanges

8 The interrelation of play and source is considered in further detail in Lukas Erne, *Beyond* The Spanish Tragedy: *A Study of the Works of Thomas Kyd* (Manchester, 2001), pp. 170–82.

9 See G. Sarrazin, *Thomas Kyd und sein Kreis. Eine Litterarhistorische Untersuchung* (Berlin, 1892), pp. 1–48, including a partial reprint (2–40) of the source, Wotton's *Courtlie Controversie of Cupids Cautels* (1578).

10 Ibid., pp. 42–4.

between Horatio and Bel-Imperia and Ferdinando and Lucina, and those between Balthazar and Bel-Imperia and Erastus and Perseda; the equivalent trial/arraignment of Alexandro and Erastus; and the late reprieve of both Alexandro and Perseda.[11] Boas also identified a common metrical stamp across three plays now attributed to Kyd – *The Spanish Tragedy*, *Soliman and Perseda*, and *Cornelia* – in the use of rhyme schemes (*aca*, *abab*, and *aaa*), a recognition confirmed in further detail by James Routh.[12] Boas and subsequent scholars have further noted parallels in specific lines. There are many examples (highlighted in the notes to the present edition) but the most striking are clustered in *Soliman and Perseda*'s final act: for instance, *The Spanish Tragedy*'s lines 'Ay, ay, my nightly dreams have told me this' (1.3.76), 'What boots complaint when there's no remedy?' (1.4.92), and 'Sweet lovely rose, ill-plucked before thy time' (2.4.108) are closely mirrored in *Soliman and Perseda*'s 'Ah no, my nightly dreams foretold me this' (5.3.23), 'What boots complaining where's no remedy' (5.2.86), and 'Fair springing rose, ill-plucked before thy time' (5.4.81). Arthur Freeman moved beyond what he called 'parallelisms in dramatic construction' to identify shared characteristics 'of melodrama and dramatic irony' and allegorical superstructures as well as 'some coincidences in language, style, versification, and terminology' and 'verbal parallelism'.[13]

A parallel development in authorship studies, largely ignored by literary scholars, produced incontrovertible evidence for Kyd's authorship of the play. In 1903 Charles Crawford published an essay in a German journal on 'The Authorship of *Arden of Faversham*', reprinted in his collected essays a few years later.[14] In it he drew attention to many passages in *Arden of Faversham* matching *The Spanish Tragedy*, but it was in *Soliman and Perseda* that he found 'evidence of complete identity with *Arden of Faversham* as regards words, expressions, figures of speech, and general style'.[15] Having quoted several striking longer parallels between the two plays, Crawford felt sufficiently confident of his case to 'string together for comparison' other evidence, amassing in four pages over fifty instances of identical

11 Thomas Kyd, *The Works of Thomas Kyd*, ed. Frederick S. Boas (Oxford, 1901), pp. lvi–lix.

12 Kyd, *The Works*, ed. Boas, p. lvii; James E. Routh Jr, 'Thomas Kyd's Rime Schemes and the Authorship of *Soliman and Perseda* and *The First Part of Jeronimo*', *MLN* 20:2 (1905): 49–51.

13 Freeman, *Thomas Kyd*, p. 142.

14 Crawford, 'The Authorship of *Arden of Faversham*', *Jahrbuch der Deutschen Shakespeare Gesellschaft* 39 (1903): 74–86, reprinted in Crawford, *Collectanea*, First Series (Stratford-on-Avon, 1906), pp. 101–30; quotations from the later version.

15 Ibid., p. 123.

phrasing between the two plays.[16] Crawford's use of *Soliman and Perseda* as a reference point for Kyd's authentic style was evidently based on his own research in preparing his 1906 *Concordance to Kyd*, which included *Soliman and Perseda* in the canon.[17] The subsequent authorship studies of *Arden* by Miksch (1907), Dugdale Sykes (1919), and Rubow (1948) all accepted Kyd's authorship of *Soliman and Perseda*.[18]

In her survey of scholarship between the 1930s and the 1960s Jill Levinson found that Kyd was 'the only serious candidate' for the authorship of *Soliman and Perseda*: 'Almost every scholar who discusses either the play or the playwright acknowledges the connection that has been made between them. Many simply assume that Kyd wrote *Soliman and Perseda*, while others explain why the attribution seems plausible.'[19] Levinson included some writers who disputed the attribution, but Lukas Erne's study has decisively established Kyd's authorship. His substantial case was supplemented by a reference to *Soliman and Perseda* and to Kyd in John Donne's poem 'The Bracelet: Upon the Losse of his Mistresses Chaine, for Which he Made Satisfaction' identified by Helen Gardner in 1965.[20] Indeed, the likely sequence of brief play-within-the-play followed by its elaboration into a full drama affirmed by Boas, Freeman, Erne, and the play's most recent editor, Ladan Niayesh, suggests that Kyd wrote the later play in 'an attempt to capitalise on the prior success of *The Spanish Tragedy*'; as a kind of sequel.[21]

Whilst the dating of the printed text of *Soliman and Perseda* is relatively straightforward, pinpointing the date of composition, the location(s) of its initial performances, and the identity of the company that performed it, is considerably more challenging. It is clear that Kyd cannot have written the play any earlier than its source, Wotton's *A Courtlie Controversy*, which appeared in 1578, or later than the play's appearance in the Stationers' Register in November 1592. It is also, as noted above, almost certainly later in date than *The Spanish Tragedy*, the composition of which is usually dated to 1587.[22] Only T. W. Baldwin advocates the earlier part of this range with

16 Ibid., pp. 125–9.

17 *A Concordance to the Works of Thomas Kyd*, 3 vols (Louvain, 1906–10; Materialien zur Kunde des älteren englischen Dramas, herausgegeben von W. Bang).

18 See Brian Vickers, 'Recognizing Kyd', pp. 39–40 above.

19 Levinson, '*Soliman and Perseda*', in Terence P. Logan and Denzell S. Smith (eds), *The Predecessors of Shakespeare. A Survey and Bibliography of Recent Studies in English Renaissance Drama* (Lincoln, NE, 1973), pp. 230–9 (233). See also Darren Freebury-Jones, *Shakespeare's Tutor: The Influence of Thomas Kyd* (Manchester, 2022), pp. 4–7.

20 See Erne, pp. 161–2 and John Donne, *The Poems of John Donne*, ed. Helen Gardner, 2 vols (Oxford, 1965), 2. 78.

21 Ladan Niayesh (ed.), *Three Romances of Eastern Conquest* (Manchester, 2018), p. 26.

22 Wiggins, *British Drama 1533–1642*, Vol. II, 369.

the rationale that a fairly neutral depiction of the Spanish Knight in the opening tournament would not have been possible in England after the defeat of the Spanish Armada in the summer of 1588.[23] His argument has been persuasively challenged by Niayesh, who finds it hardly conceivable that the play could stage a tournament in Rhodes 'with its representatives of the prominent nations of the West without the presence of a single Spaniard in it'.[24] For further nuance we need to look to the theatrical phenomenon in which *Soliman and Perseda* is unquestionably embedded: the 'Turk play', which emerged in the aftermath of the popular success of Christopher Marlowe's two *Tamburlaine the Great* plays (1587–8), dramas that 'changed the theatrical landscape' and exerted a 'complex' influence on the Elizabethan repertory, a repertory in which Kyd's was now a prominent voice.[25]

Many dramatists responded to *Tamburlaine*, including Marlowe himself in a second part and in the near-contemporary *The Jew of Malta*; it is further echoed through ballads, pamphlets, and libels. The complex sources of its popularity can be charted through the nature of these responses: they include the play's hierarchy-defying conqueror and his unbounded ambition; the expansive reach of its geographies; the railing against organized religion by 'that Atheist *Tamburlan*', as Robert Greene called him; and the compelling nature of what is often called Marlowe's 'mighty line'.[26] Later, Ben Jonson would ridicule this style – also associated with those 'Turk plays' that followed – as '*scenicall* strutting, and furious vociferation' fit only for 'ignorant gapers'.[27] If the succeeding plays were in part motivated by a desire to emulate *Tamburlaine*'s financial rewards, they were also responding to Marlowe's provocation, and each took on that challenge in a different way. Mark Hutchings has eloquently argued that this phenomenon also needs to be understood repertorially: that it represents a competitive rivalry between playing companies who, perhaps for a decade or more, competed to 'out-Turk' one another.[28] So where does *Soliman and Perseda* fit?

23 T. W. Baldwin, 'On the Chronology of Thomas Kyd's Plays', *MLN* 40:6 (1925): 343–9, and 'The Chronology of Thomas Kyd's Plays', in Baldwin, *On the Literary Genetics of Shakspere's Plays 1592–1594* (Urbana, IL, 1958), pp. 177–99.

24 Niayesh (ed.), *Three Romances*, p. 28.

25 Mark Hutchings, 'The "Turk Phenomenon" and the Repertory of the late Elizabethan Playhouse', *EMLS* Special Issue 16 (2007): 1–39: http://purl.oclc.org/emls/si-16/hutcturk.htm.

26 Robert Greene, *Perimedes the Blacksmith* (London, 1588), 3.

27 Ben Jonson, 'Timber, or Discoveries', in *The Workes of Beniamin Ionson* [the second part] (London, 1641), 100.

28 Elaborated throughout Mark Hutchings, *Turks, Repertories, and the Early Modern English Stage* (Basingstoke, 2017).

Initial advantage lay with the Admiral's Men, who staged both parts of *Tamburlaine* with the stentorian Edward Alleyn in the lead role. First to produce a dramatic riposte was Greene, with the bombastic Christian triumphalism of *Alphonsus of Aragon*, probably as early as 1587–8. Greene returned repeatedly to the same themes in search of a winning formula, first with the Ottoman dynastic drama *Selimus* (1591?) for the Queen's Men. The sequel *Friar Bacon and John of Bordeaux* (1592?) was possibly written for Lord Strange's Men, the company associated with *The Spanish Tragedy*.[29] Simultaneously George Peele produced first *The Turkish Mahomet and Hiren the Fair Greek* (1588) and then the North Africa-set *The Battle of Alcazar* (1588–9), the former of which is no longer extant but was a notable success (alongside *Tamburlaine* and *Alcazar* it is comically parodied by Pistol in Shakespeare's *2 Henry IV*, (2.4.142–56)). Both of Peele's plays were likely written for the Admiral's Men, who also performed *The Jew of Malta* and the two parts of the now lost *Tamar Cham*.[30] A web of elaborate cross-reference is characteristic of this body of 'Turk plays' and the rivalry that generated them, as Pistol's pointed ridiculing suggests. *Soliman and Perseda* is similarly imbricated: Freeman and Erne note a Pistol-like parodic take on Tamburlaine's reference to the 'murdering dart' of 'the ugly monster Death' who 'when I look away, comes stealing on' (*2 Tamburlaine*, 5.3.67–71) in Piston's pricking of the absurd Basilisco's backside:

> [...] sawst thou not how Cupid, god of love,
> Not daring look me in the martial face,
> Came like a coward stealing after me,
> And with his pointed dart pricked my posteriors? (4.2.45–8)[31]

This kind of playful mocking of Marlowe's hero and his language indicates a date after 1588 (when the second part of *Tamburlaine* was likely staged) for the composition of *Soliman and Perseda* and might imply it appeared after the initial wave of imitators, which tend to be less irreverent. This is confirmed by an apparent echo of Peele's *The Battle of Alcazar* noted by Niayesh, in which the description of the villainous Moor Muly Mahamet mounted 'on a hot Barbarian horse' (*Alcazar*, 5.1.239) is repeated in Erastus's reference to 'The Moor upon his hot barbarian horse' (*Soliman and Perseda*, 1.1.56).[32] Following Peele's play would suggest a date of around

29 On the complex text of *John of Bordeaux*, see Darren Freebury-Jones, *Reading Robert Greene: Recovering Shakespeare's Rival* (London, 2022), pp. 96–101.

30 The dates and playing companies associated with different 'Turk plays' are to some extent conjectural, and are taken from the appendix to Hutchings, 'The "Turk Phenomenon"'.

31 Freeman, *Thomas Kyd*, p. 142; Lukas Erne, *Beyond* The Spanish Tragedy, p. 158.

32 Niayesh (ed.), *Three Romances*, p. 27.

1589 or later. Erne's suggestion that the reference to the Ottoman conquest of Rhodes early in Marlowe's *The Jew of Malta* (c. 1589) may have followed Kyd's account of the siege rather than the accepted historical narrative offers a potential end-date for composition and is also entirely in keeping with the self-referential 'Turk play' genre.[33] The brutality with which Soliman exhorts his soldiers to capture Rhodes at the conclusion of the play – 'assault the town on every side, | Spoil all, kill all, let none escape your fury!' (5.4.121–2) – would therefore explain the Vice Admiral of Spain, Martin Del Bosco's report of Rhodes that 'not a man survived | To bring the hapless news to Christendom' (*The Jew of Malta*, 2.2.50–1), whereas historically the Knights of St John were allowed to leave the island and would find further fame in their defence of Malta against the Ottomans in 1565 (another of a sequence of island sieges that are often referenced on the stage – as well as *The Jew of Malta*, see *Othello* 1.3.1–49, for instance – and offer further context for this play). Placing *Soliman and Perseda* back into this milieu therefore strongly implies it was written in or around 1589, a date which is broadly accepted in recent scholarship on the play.

Although *Soliman and Perseda* is in many respects fairly typical of this flurry of 'Turk plays', it is also something of an outlier. It better fits with the more innovative nature of the output of the Admiral's Men than that of the Queen's Men, which seems to have been dominated by Greene, but Philip Henslowe never mentions the play in his diary as part of the Rose theatre's repertoire.[34] The play's interest in boundary crossing, in conversion, and in the Ottoman harem mark it out as something different, pointing to the later Jacobean preoccupations of plays such as Robert Daborne's *A Christian Turn'd Turk* (c. 1611) and Philip Massinger's *The Renegado* (c. 1623). The contemporary play with which *Soliman and Perseda* is most closely connected is Peele's lost *The Turkish Mahomet and Hiren the Fair Greek* which – although no text remains – certainly dramatized the famous 'Irene myth'.[35] In this well-known tale an Ottoman Sultan, most often Mehmed II, 'The Conqueror', is smitten with a Greek maiden, Irene/Hiren, to the extent that he is politically and militarily incapacitated. His counsellors intervene and the Sultan, realizing his folly and martial responsibilities, beheads Irene/Hiren and leads his armies to the momentous conquest of Constantinople.[36] The tale is a useful example of the process through which actual

33 Erne, *Beyond* The Spanish Tragedy, p. 158.

34 As pointed out by Erne, Kyd, *Soliman and Perseda*, ed. Erne, p. xi.

35 See Samuel Chew, *The Crescent and the Rose* (Oxford, 1937), pp. 484–5; and the entry on Peele's play in the LPD: https://lostplays.folger.edu/Turkish_Mahomet_and_Hiren_the_Fair_Greek,_The (accessed 5 January 2023).

36 The tale would have been most familiar in English in the version reproduced from Bandello as the tale of 'Hyrenee the faier Greeke' ['the xl novelle'] in William Painter,

historical events and figures – Ottoman westward expansion and the fall of Constantinople in 1453; the figure of Mehmed II; and Sultan Suleyman I's Christian chief consort, Hurrem Sultan, known in Christian Europe as Roxelana – could be mingled and transmuted into popular drama.[37] Its narrative is clearly paralleled in Soliman's ruinous, all-encompassing infatuation with the Greek Perseda. The appearance of both plays in London in the same year, in or around 1589, is certainly feasible, but it may be more likely that Peele's success prompted Kyd to revisit the source he had earlier used for Hieronimo's playlet in *The Spanish Tragedy* and expand it to feed a popular appetite for such material.

If the Admiral's Men's likely staging of *The Turkish Mahomet* makes them improbable candidates for also staging *Soliman and Perseda* (despite Baldwin's claims to the contrary), and the Queen's Men are similarly unlikely, one viable alternative is Lord Strange's Men, for whom Kyd had perhaps written *The Spanish Tragedy*. They do not seem to have had an original 'Turk play' in their repertoire at this stage and were certainly engaged in staging geopolitically relevant material.[38] In this new era of sequels this may have been an appealing proposition.[39] Yet the one company to which it can be connected is the Earl of Pembroke's Men (formed around 1591). Alfred Hart and subsequently Lukas Erne have affirmed the likelihood that it belonged to that company on the basis of a series of what Hart called 'interplay borrowings' between *Soliman and Perseda* and a play that unequivocally belongs in that repertory: the *True Tragedy of Richard Duke of York*, the 'bad' quarto of Shakespeare's *3 Henry VI*.[40] The lines 'Ah stay, no more, for I can hear no more!' (2.2.25), 'Their horse, I deem them fifty thousand strong' (3.1.48), and 'Ay, sayst thou so? Why then, it shall be so' (4.1.241)

The palace of pleasure (London, 1566), 107v–112v, and is the likely source for Peele's play.

37 On Hurrem/Roxelana in Christian European culture see the essays in Galina I. Yermolenko (ed.), *Roxolana in European Literature, History and Culture* (London, 2010).

38 See Lawrence Manley and Sally Beth MacLean, *Lord Strange's Men and Their Plays* (New Haven, 2014), pp. 166–71.

39 Baldwin, 'On the Chronology', pp. 347–8. The prospect of Lord Strange's Men, although endorsed in his earlier *Beyond* The Spanish Tragedy (p. 163), has recently been deemed unlikely by Erne, who finds the absence of reference to the play in Henslowe's diary a major obstacle. Strange's Men were, however, fairly peripatetic at this point. Erne, Kyd, *Soliman and Perseda*, ed. Erne, p. xvi.

40 Alfred Hart, *Stolne and Surreptitious Copies: A Comparative Study of Shakespeare's Bad Quartos* (Melbourne, 1942), pp. 352–90. On the indebtedness of Shakespeare's early plays to Kyd, and specifically to *Soliman and Perseda*, see Darren Freebury-Jones, *Shakespeare's Tutor: The Influence of Thomas Kyd*, especially chapter 3 (pp. 89–108).

from *Soliman and Perseda* correspond to the lines 'O speake no more, for I can heare no more' (B3v), 'Their power I gesse them fifty thousand strong' (B5v), and 'I, saist thou so boie? why then it shall be so' (A7r) from the *True Tragedy*. This indicates that 'whoever prepared the manuscript from which the *True Tragedy* was set up' had recourse to *Soliman and Perseda*.[41] Since the 1591–2 composition of Pembroke's Men included material and actors from Lord Strange's company, the movement of the play between the two (or, indeed, from another company) is certainly feasible.[42]

Such a complicated theatrical genesis makes definitively identifying a first performance impossible. There are, however, tantalizing clues to a possible performance history for the play. In his triumphal speech Death promises to 'ride in triumph through the wicked world' and spare no one,

> [...] but sacred Cynthia's friend,
> Whom Death did fear before her life began.
> For holy fates have graven it in their tables,
> That Death shall die before he attempt her end,
> Whose life is heaven's delight and Cynthia's friend. (5.Epilogue.36–41)

The decision to make this slightly clumsy and rather uncharacteristic address from Death the play's final lines is suggestive of a court performance before the Queen, in whose personal mythology Cynthia was a prominent figure. Erne posits that this may have taken place during the 1592–3 Christmas festivities, on either 26 December or 6 January, when Pembroke's Men were engaged at court. This date also ingeniously explains why such a prestige performance was not mentioned on the title page of the first quarto, because it had already been entered in the Stationers' Register by that point.[43] The opening act of the play, with its elaborate tournament in which 'Brave knights, of Christendom and Turkish both' assemble in Rhodes 'in thirsty honour's cause' (1.2.1–2) and ritually proclaim their national allegiances might also fit a royal performance. Quasi-dramatic, pseudo-chivalric tournaments in which knights from all over the world come together in honour of a particular sovereign were common at Christian courts and civic spectacles throughout this period. Scottish performances featuring Ethiopian, Persian, and Far Northern knights appeared in spring 1563 and 1581, for example, and in autumn

41 Erne, *Beyond* The Spanish Tragedy, pp. 162–3.

42 See E. K. Chambers, *The Elizabethan Stage*, 4 vols (Oxford, 1923), 2. 118–27.

43 Erne, *Beyond* The Spanish Tragedy, p. 163. Baldwin also suggests a court performance, but earlier, in Christmas 1585–6, in keeping with his pre-Armada thesis: Baldwin, 'On the Chronology', pp. 347–8.

1565 the English court staged a notable tournament featuring a sequence of 'foreign knights' and Amazons.[44]

A later reference in Thomas Dekker's *Satiromastix* (1601) to a performance of a play named 'Zulziman' at Paris Garden may, if its title is a comic exaggeration of 'Soliman', refer to the public staging of *Soliman and Perseda* at the Swan theatre where Pembroke's Men were based from 1597.[45] Finally, the diary of Zdenek Brtnicky z Valdstejna, Baron Waldstein, references the Baron seeing a play performed by Thomas Sackville's touring company in Strasbourg on 8 August 1597 which he names *De Erasto* or *The Play of Erastus*.[46] If this is a version of *Soliman and Perseda* then it indicates a popular currency for the play that is also confirmed in contemporary reference. Most famously, Shakespeare's *King John* (c. 1596) contains the line 'Knight, knight, good mother, Basilisco-like!' answered with 'Knave, good fellow, knave, knave' (1.1.244–5), but Kyd's play also seems to appear in good company in Simon Eyre's claim in Dekker's *The Shoemaker's Holiday* (1599) to know 'how to speak to a Pope, to Sultan Soliman, to Tamburlaine, an he were here' (5.4.90–1). Thomas Nashe's attack on Gabriel Harvey in *Have With You to Saffron Walden* (1596) characterizes Harvey as 'such a vaine *Basilisco* and *Captain Crackstone* in all his actions and conversations', linking Kyd's braggart knight to a similar figure in Anthony Munday's earlier play *Fidele and Fortunio* (1584).[47] Although lacking specificity these lines confirm at least a late Elizabethan flourishing and suggest a rich early performance history that is otherwise blank until a well-received recent revival of the play by Trifle Productions at the Rose Theatre, Bankside, in spring 2010.[48]

Soliman and Perseda's relative success when compared to many of its fellow 'Turk plays' is a likely consequence of Kyd's willingness to innovate. This is affirmed in the evident popularity of the memorable braggart Basilisco, a character who does not appear in his source, Wotton's *A Courtlie Controversy*, and has been described as 'Kyd's most important addition to his narrative source'.[49] Marlowe's *Tamburlaine* plays had established a template for masculine martial heroism based upon a commanding, declamatory rhetoric and relentless, unrepentant destruction. Greene and

44 See entries 368, 411, and 696 in Wiggins, *British Drama 1533–1642* Vols I and II, 390, 430–1, 261.

45 Niayesh (ed.), *Three Romances*, p. 28.

46 Wiggins, *British Drama 1533–1642* Vol. II, 406 [entry n. 800].

47 These references are collected in Freeman, *Thomas Kyd*, p. 158.

48 See for instance Kevin Quarmby's review of the production for the *British Theatre Guide*: https://www.britishtheatreguide.info/reviews/tragsoliman-rev (accessed 10 February 2023).

49 Erne, *Beyond* The Spanish Tragedy, p. 193.

Peele's early responses, in plays which Peter Berek memorably described as '*Tamburlaine*'s weak sons', largely reproduced that template, often exaggerating a specific element and/or grafting the original onto a more Manichean vision of Christian-Islamic conflict.[50] With a name that aptly invoked a particularly noisy cannon, Basilisco is not exactly the antithesis of the Tamburlaine type, but rather a bombastic puncturing of it, and the first time a dramatist was able to identify and take advantage 'of the comic richness latent in the Marlovian prototype'.[51] His character certainly draws upon earlier dramatic figures such as the swaggering *Il Capitano* in the *Commedia del arte* tradition and his English manifestations (such as the already mentioned Captain Crack-stone), and also has an element of the Elizabethan renegade Thomas Stukeley about him, a figure who had briefly appeared in Peele's *Battle of Alcazar* and later gained his own play.[52] Basilisco is something different, however, loudly proclaiming his valour and martial/sexual potency in grandiloquent terms even as he is revealed to be a serial liar and an amoral coward. Other dramatists would do something similar: Marlowe's own Barabas has nothing but disdain for the hypocrisy latent in the posturing of either of his Christian or Muslim antagonists. However, it is probably in Shakespeare's absurd Pistol that the parodic trajectory initiated with Basilisco reaches its fullest expression, although both James Shapiro and Robert Logan have argued that the Prince of Morocco in *The Merchant of Venice* (c. 1596) is a similar, but perhaps more nuanced, burlesquing of Marlowe's 'aggressive over-reachers'. Basilisco's bombast acts as a persistent (and largely unintentional) commentary on Erastus's heroism and on the world through which he moves; in contrast, Morocco finds himself lost in a comic world where his 'heroic visions' are entirely 'misplaced' – he should belong in an entirely different and, by the later 1590s, unfashionable play of the *Tamburlaine* type. Where Basilisco pokes fun at a genre from within, both Morocco and Pistol mercilessly expose its redundancy.[53]

Basilisco is also the primary means through which another novel theme is introduced in *Soliman and Perseda*: conversion from Christianity to Islam. Accepting conversion rather than death after the first fall of Rhodes, Basilisco is converted off-stage in Turkey and in an extraordinary address to the audience relates his experience. Nothing like this had appeared in

50 Peter Berek, '*Tamburlaine*'s Weak Sons: Imitation as Interpretation Before 1593', *RD* 13 (1982): 55–82.

51 Robert Logan, *Shakespeare's Marlowe: The Influence of Christopher Marlowe on Shakespeare's Artistry* (Aldershot, 2007), p. 157.

52 The anonymous *The Famous History of the Life and Death of Captain Thomas Stukeley*, probably written around 1595 and printed by Thomas Pavier in 1605.

53 James Shapiro, 'Which is *The Merchant* here, and which *The Jew*?', *SS* 20 (1988): 269–79, 273; Logan, *Shakespeare's Marlowe*, p. 156.

any previous English play and there was little source material available through which the ritual of Islamic conversion might be constructed. Kyd again adopts the parodic mode, but the gulf between what Basilisco claims and what an audience knows is made even more stark, and perhaps more ripe for ridicule, because he stands alone on the stage, animated and transformed, in his Ottoman turban and robes. It also again has a peculiar puncturing effect. Greene's earlier characterization of Islam as idolatry and its Prophet an idol in *Alphonsus* here prompts Basilisco to imagine that the Turks who carried him to the Church as 'a second Mahomet' intended 'to adore me for a God' (4.2.10–11).[54] He then assumes that the act of circumcision, in which they 'lopped a collop off my tenderest member' (4.2.15), was a Herculean trial of his valour; once he had passed he was carried on a 'milk white ass' to sit 'in Pompey's chair' to view 'the Capitol, and was Rome's greatest glory' (4.2.19–20). Yet an audience are primed to realize that this narrative is a self-aggrandizing fiction, and in the process recognize the fallacy of the medieval vision of Islam pedalled by some of the more regressive contemporary 'Turk plays'. There is nevertheless much of Kyd's own imagination in this episode: Basilisco's vague description of the ritual he is subjected to draws upon classical contexts with the exception of the ass, which may reflect the Old Testament address to those 'which ride on milk white asses' in Judges 5:10, a passage which was assumed to refer to Syria, a region that had become associated with Islam and the Ottomans.[55] In these terms Basilisco's assertion that Istanbul was a second Rome and the Ottoman Sultan implicitly a kind of Caesar also interestingly mirrors claims being made by the Ottoman court, claims which were vigorously contested by the Habsburg Holy Roman Emperor, who insisted the same title was his.[56]

Soliman and Perseda's different stage version of Islam and Islamic culture is further reflected in the play's depiction of its two most prominent Ottoman characters, Soliman and Brusor. The latter receives a greater and more coherent prominence than in Wotton's *A Courtlie Controversy* or in *The Spanish Tragedy*'s playlet, his rise unwittingly thwarted by Erastus's favour at Soliman's hands. Lucina too plays a greater role than in the source, and of the four Christian characters that move from Rhodes to Turkey, she makes the smoothest transition to Ottoman subjecthood (a transition that

54 Greene's erroneous depiction of Islam as a kind of idolatry is discussed in detail in Matthew Dimmock, *Mythologies of the Prophet Muhammad in Early Modern English Culture* (Cambridge, 2013), pp. 101–31.

55 See the interpretation offered by Pietro Martire Vermigli [Peter Martyr] in *Most fruitfull [and] learned co[m]mentaries* (London, 1564), 106r.

56 A contest discussed in Einar Wigen, 'Ottoman Concepts of Empire', *Contributions to the History of Concepts* 8:1 (2013): 44–66.

would have been marked for most characters in a change of costume that is not signalled in the stage directions, but which is hinted in the text) to become Brusor's partner and accomplice. For his depiction of Soliman, Kyd drew what emotional complexity he could from Wotton's translation, but that text figures the 'Emperour of the Turkes' as a one-dimensional ruler whose 'flintie Turkishe breaste' never felt compassion until he encountered Perseda, and thereafter was unable 'to master his rebellious passions' before he was undone by love.[57] In *Soliman and Perseda*, in contrast, Soliman's dangerous unpredictability is present from his first appearance in 1.6. In that scene – another of Kyd's inventions – he undergoes a series of transformations. First, he is implacably hostile to Christianity – determined to prick 'the heart of Christendom' (1.6.16). Then he engages in a highly topical (for the late 1580s) and statesmanlike consultation concerning spheres of Ottoman military engagement with his brothers. This is followed by murderous vengefulness once Amurath kills Haleb. Finally, he falls to tearful self-recrimination and lamentation – and all of this in the space of just over one hundred lines.[58] This is quite unlike those earlier 'Grand Turks' who had strutted London's stages, with the possible exception of Mahomet in Peele's lost *The Turkish Mahomet and Hiren the Fair Greek* (who, on the basis of the likely source material, may have been closer to the Soliman of Kyd's source). Bajazeth in *1 Tamburlaine* is disdainful and bombastic until rendered pathetic by captivity; Amurack and Selimus in Greene's plays *Alphonsus* and *Selimus* are both relentlessly hostile and dogged in their pursuit of victory, whether over Christians or rival claimants. Soliman's instability, further evidenced in his initial reaction to Perseda and his rapid resolution to destroy Erastus, therefore introduced a new type of 'Turk' to the stage that would reappear in a number of subsequent dramas, including Fulke Greville's *Mustapha* (1596), Thomas Goffe's *The Raging Turk* (c. 1613), and Massinger's *The Renegado* (c. 1623).

One further innovation comes in the depiction of the Ottoman court harem. Later this space would be endlessly dramatized and scrutinized as 'the obligatory topos' of the Orient, but it barely features at all in the early 'Turk plays'.[59] The one earlier definitive reference comes when Bajazeth

57 Wotton, *A Courtlie Controversy*, pp. 56, 62.

58 This episode does not seem intended to reflect directly upon the well-known Ottoman practice of accessional fratricide, but rather on the murderous dynamics of the Ottoman dynasty: Sultan Suleyman, for instance, was understood to have ordered the murder of his eldest son Şehzade Mustapha in 1553 (the subject of Greville's later closet drama). This event was first reported in Johannes Sleidanus, *A famous cronicle of our time* (London, 1560), 429v.

59 Alain Grosrichard, *The Sultan's Court: European Fantasies of the East*, tr. Liz Heron (London, 1998 ed.), p. 125.

threatens to make Tamburlaine 'a chaste and lustless eunuch' who 'in my sarell' will 'tend my concubines' (*1 Tamburlaine*, 3.3.77–8) and the Ottoman Sultan's concubines make a brief entry in *2 Tamburlaine* as Tamburlaine contemptuously divides them between his followers (4.3.64–73). The serail/saray or harem (a term which did not appear until the mid-seventeenth century) may have appeared in some form in *The Turkish Mahomet*, but in those plays that remain extant there is no suggestion of the sensuous delights with which the space is later, often pruriently, associated. In the absence of dramatic precedent, Wotton's translation of Yver offered a means of access. In that narrative Perseda is taken from a Rhodian religious house and brought to Turkey as a gift for the Ottoman Emperor: she 'was lodged among yong Damoysels, nourished, maintained, and taught by olde cunning *Eunuchs*, to sing, daunce, playe an instrumente, and to speake the *Arabian* tongue' with the intention of making her 'a principall threasure to delyghte the Emperoure'.[60] In the play Perseda has no such education before being reunited with Erastus, but this description seems to have been the basis for a different kind of engagement.

The harem is mentioned twice in *Soliman and Perseda*, however, and may even have been dramatized in some fashion. Both references are similar: in the first Soliman attempts to cheer the melancholy Erastus by asking him to follow, 'Where thou shalt see what pleasures and what sports | My minions and my eunuchs can devise' (3.1.151–2). The second comes whilst Soliman awaits Brusor luring Erastus back to Turkey and his death; he resolves that, 'now to ease my troubled thoughts at last | I will go sit among my learned eunuchs, | And hear them play, and see my minions dance' (4.1.257–9). The association of the Ottoman harem with concubines and eunuchs was still relatively recent – aside from references like those in Wotton's *A Courtlie Controversy*, the first substantial description only appeared with Nicolas de Nicolay's *The navigations, peregrinations and voyages* (1585) – and in *Soliman and Perseda* it is clearly depicted as a space of pleasure and eroticism.[61] The spectacle may have been heightened in performance, for the sole surviving first quarto of the play, now British Library C.34.b.44, features only two handwritten marginal directions, which intriguingly appear alongside these two harem references. Soliman's invitation to Erastus is accompanied by the lines 'the daunc | before Piston | enters' (E4v); his later retreat to his eunuchs and minions features 'the songe to | be sunge before | Basilisco enters' (G2r). Although it is necessarily conjectural, these may suggest supplementary dramatic elements of dance and music that were for

60 Wotton, *A Courtlie Controversy*, p. 55.

61 Nicolas de Nicolay, *The nauigations, peregrinations and voyages, made into Turkie by Nicholas Nicholay Daulphinois, Lord of Arfeuile* (London, 1585), 53r–54r.

the first time designed to give a sense of the Ottoman harem, a space that came to so preoccupy later readers and audiences.

Such elements reaffirm the centrality of Soliman and his court as the pivot on which the plot of *Soliman and Perseda* turns and as the source of its innovation. Soliman's death in the climactic moment is not remotely historically accurate – he died on campaign in Hungary in 1566, forty-four years after the Ottoman conquest of Rhodes – but it is another example of Kyd's willingness to diverge from Wotton in order to create dramatic tension and tragedy. The final triumph of Death over Love and Fortune is emphatically affirmed as the Emperor becomes another of the many bodies that litter the stage as Rhodes falls to the Ottomans for the second time in the play. It is a spectacular conclusion, one of many set-pieces throughout the drama that argue for Kyd's keen sense of the workings of theatrical spectacle, which overrides all other considerations and requires that history and source material are reimagined in order to shock and disorient an audience, at least some of whom may have had a grasp of what had happened at Rhodes in 1522. This creation of spectacle is also an attempt to respond to, nuance, and supersede those 'Turk plays' that had gone before. *Soliman and Perseda* can therefore only be fully appreciated as part of a web of dramatic reference; its vision of the Ottoman Sultan and his court only understood in relation to those preceding it; its depiction of Islam coherent only in relation to earlier stagings of idolatry; even the play's curiously anachronistic portrayal of Mediterranean geopolitics makes sense only in relation to an English dramatic preoccupation with the subject. In all of these respects *Soliman and Perseda* was generated by a relatively brief flourishing of a theatrical phenomenon and is a striking demonstration of how the English stage could engage imaginatively with Christian-Islamic conflict as it moved beyond the confines of *Tamburlaine*'s example.

BIBLIOGRAPHY

Baldwin, T. W., 'On the Chronology of Thomas Kyd's Plays', *MLN* 40:6 (1925): 343–9.

—— *On the Literary Genetics of Shakespeare's Plays 1592–1594* (Urbana, 1958).

Berek, Peter, '*Tamburlaine*'s Weak Sons: Imitation as Interpretation Before 1593', *RD* 13 (1982): 55–82.

Burton, Jonathan, *Traffic and Turning: Islam and English Drama, 1579–1624* (Cranbury, 2005).

Carrère, Félix, *Le Théâtre de Thomas Kyd: Contribution à l'étude du drama élizabéthain* (Toulouse, 1951).

Chambers, E. K., *The Elizabethan Stage*, 4 vols (Oxford, 1923).

Chew, Samuel, *The Crescent and the Rose: Islam and England During the Renaissance* (Oxford, 1937).

Crawford, Charles, 'The Authorship of *Arden of Faversham*', *Jahrbuch der Deutschen Shakespeare Gesellschaft* 39 (1903): 74–86.

—— *A Concordance to the Works of Thomas Kyd*, 3 vols (Louvain: A. Uystpruyst [Materialien zur Kunde des älteren englischen Dramas, herausgegeben von W. Bang], 1906–10).

Dagenhardt, Jane Hwang, *Islamic Conversion and Christian Resistance on the Early Modern Stage* (Edinburgh, 2010).

Dimmock, Matthew, *New Turkes: Dramatizing Islam and the Ottomans on the Early Modern English Stage* (Aldershot, 2005).

—— *Mythologies of the Prophet Muhammad in Early Modern English Culture* (Cambridge, 2013).

Donne, John, *The Poems of John Donne*, ed. Helen Gardner, 2 vols (Oxford, 1965).

Erne, Lukas, *Beyond* The Spanish Tragedy*: A Study of the Works of Thomas Kyd* (Manchester, 2001).

Freebury-Jones, Darren, *Shakespeare's Tutor: The Influence of Thomas Kyd* (Manchester, 2022).

—— *Reading Robert Greene: Recovering Shakespeare's Rival* (London, 2022).

Freeman, Arthur, *Thomas Kyd: Facts and Problems* (Oxford, 1967).

Greg, W. W., *Bibliography of the English Printed Drama to the Restoration*, 4 vols (London, 1939–59).

Grosrichard, Alain, *The Sultan's Court: European Fantasies of the East*, tr. Liz Heron (London, 1998 ed).

Hart, Alfred, *Stolne and Surreptitious Copies: A Comparative Study of Shakespeare's Bad Quartos* (Melbourne, 1942).

Hawkins, Thomas (ed.), *The Origin of the English Drama* (Oxford, 1773).

Hutchings, Mark, 'The "Turk Phenomenon" and the Repertory of the late Elizabethan Playhouse', *EMLS* Special Issue 16 (2007): 1–39, http://purl.oclc.org/emls/si-16/hutcturk.htm.

Hutchings, Mark, *Turks, Repertories, and the Early Modern English Stage* (Basingstoke, 2017).

Kyd, Thomas, *The Works of Thomas Kyd*, ed. Frederick S. Boas (Oxford, 1901).

—— *The Tragedye of Solyman and Perseda*, ed. John J. Murray (New York and London, 1991).

—— *Soliman and Perseda* [1592/3], ed. Lukas Erne (Manchester, 2014).

Levinson, Jill, '*Soliman and Perseda*', in Terence P. Logan and Denzell S. Smith (eds), *The Predecessors of Shakespeare. A Survey and Bibliography of Recent Studies in English Renaissance Drama* (Lincoln, NE, 1973), pp. 230–9.

McMillin, Scott, and Sally-Beth MacLean, *The Queen's Men and Their Plays: William Shakespeare's Early Career and the Acting Companies, 1577–1594* (Cambridge, 1998).

Manley, Lawrence, and Sally-Beth MacLean, *Lord Strange's Men and Their Plays* (New Haven, CT, 2014).

Merriam, Thomas, 'Possible Light on a Kyd Canon', *Notes & Queries* 240:42 (1995): 340–1.

Niayesh, Ladan (ed.), *Three Romances of Eastern Conquest* (Manchester, 2018).

Routh Jr, James E., 'Thomas Kyd's Rime Schemes and the Authorship of *Soliman and Perseda* and *The First Part of Jeronimo*', *MLN* 20:2 (1905): 49–51.

Sarrazin, Gregor, *Thomas Kyd und sein Kreis: Eine Litterarhistorische Untersuchung* (Berlin, 1892).

Vitkus, Daniel (ed.), *Three Turk Plays from Early Modern England* (New York, 2000).

Wiggins, Martin, *British Drama 1533–1642: A Catalogue*, Vol. I: 1533–66 (Oxford, 2011).

—— *British Drama 1533–1642: A Catalogue*, Vol. II: 1567–89 (Oxford, 2012).

Yermolenko, Galina I. (ed.), *Roxolana in European Literature, History and Culture* (London, 2010).

THE

TRAGEDY OF *SOLIMAN* AND *PERSEDA*

Wherein is laid open Love's
constancy, Fortune's incon-
stancy, and Death's
Triumphs.

AT LONDON
Printed by *Edward Allde* for
Edward White, and are to be sold at
the little North door of Paul's
Church, at the sign of
the Gun.

THE PERSONS IN THE PLAY

The Chorus:
LOVE
FORTUNE
DEATH
Of the Court of Rhodes:
PHILIPPO, Governor of Rhodes
Prince of CYPRUS, his son-in-law
ERASTUS, knight of Rhodes and partnered with Perseda
PERSEDA, lady of Rhodes
FERDINANDO, close ally of Philippo and partnered with Lucina
LUCINA, lady of Rhodes
GUELPIO, friend of Erastus
JULIO, friend of Erastus
PISTON, servant to Erastus
Knights attending the Tournament:
BASILISCO, a boastful knight
ENGLISHMAN, an English knight
FRENCHMAN, a French knight
SPANIARD, a Spanish knight
BRUSOR, a Turkish knight
Of the Turkish Court:
SOLIMAN, Emperor of the Turks
HALEB, Soliman's brother
AMURATH, Soliman's brother
Lord MARSHAL of Turkey
Two Witnesses
Messenger, Knights, a Page, a Crier, two Drummers, Soldiers, a Captain, Janissaries

[1. Prologue]

Enter Love, Fortune, [*and*] *Death.*

LOVE
What, Death and Fortune cross the way of Love?

FORTUNE
Why, what is Love, but Fortune's tennis-ball?

DEATH
Nay, what are you both, but subjects unto Death?
And I command you to forbear this place:
For here the mouth of sad Melpomene
Is wholly bent to tragedy's discourse,
And what are tragedies but acts of death?
Here means the wrathful muse, in seas of tears
And loud laments, to tell a dismal tale,
A tale wherein she lately hath bestowed
The husky humour of her bloody quill,
And now for tables takes her to her tongue.

LOVE
Why, thinks Death Love knows not the history
Of brave Erastus and his Rhodian dame?
'Twas I that made their hearts consent to love,
And therefore come I now as fittest person
To serve for chorus to this tragedy.
Had not I been, they had not died so soon.

DEATH
Had I not been, they had not died so soon.

FORTUNE
Nay then it seems you both do miss the mark.
Did not I change long love to sudden hate,
And then rechange their hatred into love,
And then from love deliver them to death?
Fortune is chorus. Love and Death be gone.

DEATH
I tell thee Fortune, and thee wanton Love,
I will not down to everlasting night

Till I have moralised this tragedy,
Whose chiefest actor was my sable dart.

LOVE
Nor will I up into the brightsome sphere
From whence I sprung, till in the chorus' place
I make it known to you and to the world
What interest Love hath in tragedies.

FORTUNE
Nay then, though Fortune have delight in change,
I'll stay my flight and cease to turn my wheel,
Till I have shown by demonstration
What interest I have in a tragedy.
Tush, Fortune can do more than Love or Death.

LOVE
Why stay we then? Let's give the actors leave
And, as occasion serves, make our return.

Exeunt.

[1.1]

Enter Erastus and Perseda.

ERASTUS
Why when, Perseda, wilt thou not assure me,
But shall I like a mastless ship at sea
Go every way and not the way I would?
My love hath lasted from mine infancy,
And still increasèd as I grew myself.
When did Perseda pastime in the streets,
But her Erastus over-eyed her sport?
When didst thou, with thy sampler in the sun,
Sit sowing with thy feres, but I was by,
Marking thy lily hand's dexterity,
Comparing it to twenty gracious things?
When didst thou sing a note that I could hear,
But I have framed a ditty to the tune,
Figuring Perseda twenty kind of ways?
When didst thou go to church on holy days,
But I have waited on thee to and fro,
Marking my times as falcons watch their flight?
When I have missed thee, how have I lamented,
As if my thoughts had been assurèd true?

Thus in my youth; now since I grew a man,
I have persevered to let thee know
The meaning of my true heart's constancy.
Then be not nice, Perseda, as women wont
To hasty lovers whose fancy soon is fled.
My love is of a long continuance,
And merits not a stranger's recompence.

PERSEDA
Enough, Erastus, thy Perseda knows.
She whom thou wouldst have thine, Erastus knows.

ERASTUS
Nay, my Perseda knows, and then 'tis well.

PERSEDA
Ay, watch you vantages? Thine be it then.
I have forgot the rest, but that's the effect;
Which to effect, accept this carcanet.
My grandam on her deathbed gave it me,
And there, even there, I vowed unto myself
To keep the same until my wandering eye
Should find a harbour for my heart to dwell.
Even in thy breast do I elect my rest.
Let in my heart, to keep thine company.

ERASTUS
And sweet Perseda accept this ring
To equal it; receive my heart to boot.
It is no boot, for that was thine before,
And far more welcome is this change to me
Than sunny days to naked savages,
Or news of pardon to a wretch condemned
That waiteth for the fearful stroke of death.
As careful will I be to keep this chain
As doth the mother keep her children
From waterpits, or falling in the fire.
Over mine armour will I hang this chain,
And when long combat makes my body faint,
The sight of this shall show Perseda's name,
And add fresh courage to my fainting limbs.
This day the eager Turk of Tripolis,
The Knight of Malta, honoured for his worth,
And he that's titled by the golden spur,

The Moor upon his hot barbarian horse,
The fiery Spaniard bearing in his face
The impress of a noble warrior,
The sudden Frenchman, and the big-boned Dane,
And English Archers, hardy men at arms,
Yclept lions of the western world:
Each one of these approvèd combatants,
Assembled from several corners of the world,
Are hither come to try their force in arms
In honour of the Prince of Cyprus' nuptials.
Amongst these worthies will Erastus troop,
Though like a gnat amongst a hive of bees.
Know me by this, thy precious carcanet,
And if I thrive in valour, as the glass
That takes the sun-beams burning with his force,
I'll be the glass, and thou that heavenly sun,
From whence I'll borrow what I do achieve.
And sweet Perseda, unnoted though I be,
Thy beauty yet shall make me known ere night.

PERSEDA
Young slips are never graft in windy days,
Young scholars never entered with the rod.
Ah, my Erastus, there are Europe's knights,
That carry honour graven in their helms,
And they must win it dear that win it thence.
Let not my beauty prick thee to thy bane,
Better sit still than rise and overta'en.

ERASTUS
Counsel me not, for my intent is sworn,
And be my fortune as my love deserves.

PERSEDA
So be thy fortune as thy features serve,
And then Erastus lives without compare.

Enter a messenger.

Here comes a messenger to haste me hence.
I know your message: hath the Princess sent for me?

MESSENGER
She hath, and desires you to consort her to the triumphs.

Enter Piston.

PISTON Who saw my master? O sir, are you here? The Prince and all the outlandish gentlemen are ready to go to the triumphs; they stay for you.

ERASTUS Go sirrah, bid my men bring my horse, and a dozen staves.

PISTON You shall have your horses and two dozen of staves.

Exit.

ERASTUS
Wish me good hap Perseda, and I'll win
Such glory as no time shall ere raze out,
Or end the period of my youth in blood.

PERSEDA
Such fortune as the good Andromache
Wished valiant Hector wounded with the Greeks,
I wish Erastus in his maiden wars.
Ore'come with valour these high-minded knights,
As with thy virtue thou hast conquered me.
Heavens hear my hearty prayer and it effect!

Exeunt.

[1.2]

Enter Philippo, the Prince of Cyprus, Basilisco, and all the Knights.

PHILIPPO
Brave knights, of Christendom and Turkish both,
Assembled here in thirsty honour's cause,
To be enrollèd in the brass-leaved book
Of never-wasting perpetuity:
Put lamb-like mildness to your lion's strength,
And be our tilting like two brothers' sports,
That exercise their war with friendly blows.
Brave Prince of Cyprus, and our son-in-law,
Welcome these worthies by their several countries,
For in thy honour hither are they come,
To grace thy nuptials with their deeds at arms.

CYPRUS
First welcome, thrice renownèd Englishman,

Graced by thy country, but ten times more
By thy approvèd valour in the field.
Upon the onset of the enemy,
What is thy motto when thou spurs thy horse?

ENGLISHMAN
In Scotland was I made a knight at arms,
Where for my country's cause I charged my lance.
In France I took the standard from the King,
And give the flower of Gallia in my crest.
Against the light-foot Irish have I served,
And in my skin bear tokens of their skenes.
Our word of courage all the world hath heard:
Saint George for England, and Saint George for me!

CYPRUS
Like welcome unto thee, fair knight of France:
Well famed thou art for discipline in war.
Upon the encounter of thine enemy,
What is thy mot, renownèd knight of France?

FRENCHMAN
In Italy I put my knighthood on,
Where in my shirt but with my single rapier,
I combated a Roman much renowned,
His weapon's point empoisoned for my bane,
And yet my stars did bode my victory.
Saint Denis is for France, and that for me!

CYPRUS
Welcome Castilian too amongst the rest,
For fame doth sound thy valour with the rest.
Upon thy first encounter of thy foe,
What is thy word of courage, brave man of Spain?

SPANIARD
At fourteen years of age was I made knight,
When twenty thousand Spaniards were in field,
What time a daring rutter made a challenge
To change a bullet with our swift-flight shot,
And I, with single heed and level, hit
The haughty challenger and struck him dead.
The Golden Fleece is that we cry upon,
And Jaques, Jaques is the Spaniards' choice!

CYPRUS
Next, welcome unto thee, renownèd Turk,
Not for thy lay, but for thy worth in arms.
Upon the first brave of thine enemy,
What is thy noted word of charge, brave Turk?

BRUSOR
Against the Sophy in three pitchèd fields,
Under the conduct of great Soliman,
Have I been chief commander of an host,
And put the flint-heart Persians to the sword.
The desert plains of Afric have I stained
With blood of Moors, and there in three set battles fought,
Marched conqueror through Asia
Along the coasts held by the Portuguese.
Even to the verge of gold, aboarding Spain
Hath Brusor led a valiant troop of Turks,
And made some Christians kneel to Mahomet.
Him we adore, and in his name I cry,
Mahomet for me and Solyman!

CYPRUS
Now, signor Basilisco, you we know,
And therefore give not you a stranger's welcome.
You are a rutter born in Germany.
Upon the first encounter of your foe,
What is your brave upon the enemy?

BASILISCO
I fight not with my tongue: this is my oratrix.
Laying his hand upon his sword.

CYPRUS
Why, signor Basilisco, is it a she-sword?

BASILISCO
Ay, and so are all blades with me. Behold my instance: pardie, each female is the weaker vessel, and the vigour of this arm infringeth the temper of any blade. Quoth my assertion, and thereby gather that this blade being approved weaker than this limb, may very well bear a feminine epitheton.

CYPRUS
'Tis well proved. But what's the word that glories your country?

BASILISCO
Sooth to say, the earth is my country, as the air to the fowl, or the marine moisture to the red-gilled fish. I repute myself no coward, for humility shall mount. I keep no table to character my fore-passed conflicts. As I remember, there happened a sore drought in some part of Belgia, that the juicy grass was seared with the Sun God's element. I held it policy to put the men-children of that climate to the sword, that the mothers' tears might relieve the parched earth. The men died, the women wept, and the grass grew. Else had my Friesland horse perished, whose loss would have more grieved me than the ruin of that whole country. Upon a time in Ireland I fought on horseback with an hundred kerns, from Titan's eastern uprise to his western downfall, insomuch that my steed began to faint. I, conjecturing the cause to be want of water, dismounted in which place there was no such element; enraged therefore, with this scimitar, all on foot, like an Herculean offspring, endured some three or four hours' combat, in which process, my body distilled such dewy showers of sweat that from the warlike wrinkles of my front my palfrey cooled his thirst. My mercy in conquest is equal with my manhood in fight. The tear of an infant hath been the ransom of a conquered city, whereby I purchased the surname of 'Pity's Adamant'. Rough words blow my choler, as the wind doth Mulciber's workhouse. I have no word, because no country; each place is my habitation, therefore each country's word mine to pronounce. Princes, what would you? I have seen much, heard more, but done most. To be brief, he that will try me, let him waft me with his arm; I am his, for some five lances. Although it go against my stars to jest, yet to gratulate this benign prince, I will suppress my condition.

PHILIPPO
He is beholding to you greatly, sir.
Mount, ye brave lordings. Forwards to the tilt!
Myself will censure of your chivalry,
And with impartial eyes behold your deeds.
Forward, brave ladies, place you to behold
The fair demeanour of these warlike knights.

Exeunt [*all but Basilisco*].

[1.3]

BASILISCO
I am melancholy: an humour of Venus beleagereth me. I have rejected with contemptible frowns the sweet glances of many amorous girls, or rather ladies. But certes, I am now captivated with the reflecting eye of that admirable comet, Perseda. I will place her to behold my triumphs and do wonders in her sight. O heavens, she comes, accompanied with a child whose chin bears no impression of manhood, not an hair, not an excrement.

Enter Erastus, Perseda, and Piston.

ERASTUS
My sweet Perseda –

Exeunt Erastus and Perseda.

BASILISCO
Peace, infant, thou blasphemest.

PISTON
You are deceived sir, he swore not.

BASILISCO
I tell thee, jester, he did worse; he called that lady his.

PISTON
Jester? *O extempore, o flores*!

BASILISCO
O harsh uneducate, illiterate peasant! Thou abusest the phrase of the Latin.

PISTON
By God's fish, friend, take you the Latins' part, I'll abuse you too!

BASILISCO
What, sans dread of our indignation?

PISTON
'Sans'? What language is that? I think thou art a word-maker by thine occupation.

BASILISCO
Ay, term'st thou me of an occupation? Nay then this fiery humour of choler is suppressed by the thought of love. Fair Lady –

PISTON
Now, by my troth, she is gone.

BASILISCO
Ay, hath the infant transported her hence? He saw my anger figured in my brow, and at his best advantage stole away. But I will follow for revenge.

PISTON
Nay, but hear you, sir, I must talk with you before you go.

Then Piston gets on his back and pulls him down.

BASILISCO
Oh, if thou beest magnanimous, come before me!

PISTON
Nay, if thou beest a right warrior, get from under me!

BASILISCO
What, wouldst thou have me a Typhon, to bear up Pelion or Ossa?

PISTON
Typhon me no Typhons, but swear upon my dudgeon dagger not to go till I give thee leave, but stay with me, and look upon the tilters.

BASILISCO
Oh, thou seekst thereby to dim my glory!

PISTON
I care not for that; wilt thou not swear?

BASILISCO
Oh, I swear, I swear!

He sweareth him on his dagger.

PISTON
By the contents of this blade –

BASILISCO
By the contents of this blade –

PISTON
I, the aforesaid Basilisco –

BASILISCO
I, the aforesaid Basilisco – Knight, good fellow, knight, knight!

PISTON
Knave, good fellow, knave, knave! – Will not offer to go from the side of Piston –

BASILISCO
Will not offer to go from the side of Piston –

PISTON
Without the leave of the said Piston obtained.

BASILISCO
Without the leave of the said Piston, licensed, obtained, and granted.

PISTON
Enjoy thy life and live: I give it thee.

BASILISCO
I enjoy my life at thy hands, I confess it. I am up, but that I am religious in mine oath.

PISTON
What would you do, sir, what would you do? Will you up the ladder, sir, and see the tilting?

Then they go up the ladders, and they sound within to the first course.

BASILISCO
Better a dog fawn on me than bark.

PISTON
Now, sir, how likes thou this course?

BASILISCO
Their lances were couched too high, and their steeds ill borne.

PISTON
It may be so, it may be so.

Sound to the second course.

Now, sir, how like you this course?

BASILISCO
Pretty, pretty, but not famous. Well for a learner, but not for a warrior.

PISTON
By my faith, methought it was excellent.

BASILISCO
Ay, in the eye of an infant, a peacock's tail is glorious.
Sound to the third course.

PISTON
Oh, well run! The bay horse with the blue tail and the silver knight are both down! By cock and pie and mouse foot, the Englishman is a fine knight!

BASILISCO
Now, by the marble face of the welkin, he is a brave warrior.

PISTON What an oath is there? Fie upon thee, extortioner!
Sound to the fourth course.

BASILISCO
Now comes in the infant that courts my mistress. Oh, that my lance were in my rest, and my beaver closed for this encounter!

PISTON
Oh, well ran! My master hath overthrown the Turk!

BASILISCO
Now fie upon the Turk! To be dismounted by a child, it vexeth me!
Sound to the fifth course.

PISTON
Oh, well run, master! He hath overthrown the Frenchman!

BASILISCO
It is the fury of his horse, not the strength of his arm. I would thou wouldst remit my oath, that I might assail thy master.

PISTON
I give thee leave, go to thy destruction. But sirrah, where's thy horse?

BASILISCO
Why, my page stands holding him by the bridle.

PISTON
Well, go mount thee, go.

BASILISCO
I go, and Fortune guide my lance!

Exit.

PISTON
Take the braggingest knave in Christendom with thee! Truly, I am sorry for him. He joust like a knight? He'll jostle like a jade! It is a world to hear the fool prate and brag! He will jet as if it were a goose on a green! He goes many times supperless to bed, and yet he takes physic to make him lean. Last night he was bidden to a gentlewoman's to supper, and because he would not be put to carve, he wore his hand in a scarf and said he was wounded. He wears a coloured lath in his scabbard, and when 'twas found upon him, he said he was wrathful, he might not wear no iron. He wears civet, and when it was asked him, where he had that musk, he said all his kindred smelt so. Is not this a counterfeit fool? Well, I'll up and see how he speeds.

Sound the sixth course.

Now, by the faith of a squire, he is a very faint knight. Why, my master hath overthrown him and his curtal, both to the ground! I shall have old laughing: it will be better than the fox in the hole for me.

[1.4]

Sound: Enter Philippo, [the Prince of Cyprus], Erastus, Ferdinando, Lucina, and all the knights.

CYPRUS
Brave gentlemen, by all your free consents,
This knight unknown hath best demeaned himself.
According to the proclamation made,
The prize and honour of the day is his.
But now unmask thyself, that we may see
What warlike wrinkles time hath charactered
With age's print upon thy warlike face.

ENGLISHMAN
Accord to his request, brave man at arms,
And let me see the face that vanquished me.

FRENCHMAN
Unmask thyself, thou well approvèd knight.

BRUSOR
I long to see thy face, brave warrior.

LUCINA
Nay, valiant sir, we may not be denied.
Fair ladies should be coy to show their faces,
Lest that the sun should tan them with his beams.
I'll be your page this once, for to disarm you.

PISTON
[*aside*] That's the reason, that he shall help your husband to arm his head. Oh, the policy of this age is wonderful!

PHILIPPO
What, young Erastus, is it possible?

CYPRUS
Erastus, be thou honoured for this deed.

ENGLISHMAN
So young, and of such good accomplishment!
Thrive, fair beginner, as this time doth promise,
In virtue, valour, and all worthiness.
Give me thy hand: I vow myself thy friend.

ERASTUS
Thanks, worthy sir, whose favourable hand
Hath entered such a youngling in the war;
And thanks unto you all, brave worthy sirs.
Impose me task, how I may do you good:
Erastus will be dutiful in all.

PHILIPPO
Leave protestations now, and let us hie
To tread lavolta, that is women's walk.
There spend we the remainder of the day.

Exeunt [*all but*] *Ferdinando.*

FERDINANDO
Though overborne and foilèd in my course,
Yet have I partners in mine infamy.
'Tis wondrous, that so young a toward warrior
Should bide the shock of such approvèd knights
As he this day hath matched and mated too.
But virtue should not envy good desert:
Therefore Erastus happy, laud thy fortune.
But my Lucina, how she changed her colour
When at the encounter I did loose a stirrup,
Hanging her head as partner of my shame.
Therefore will I now go visit her,
And please her with this carcanet of worth
Which by good fortune I have found today.
When valour fails, then gold must make the way.

Exit.

[1.5]

Enter Basilisco riding a mule.

BASILISCO
O cursèd Fortune, enemy to Fame,
Thus to disgrace thy honoured name,
By overthrowing him that far hath spread thy praise,
Beyond the course of Titan's burning rays!

Enter Piston.

Page, set aside the jester of my enemy. Give him a fiddler's fee and send him packing.

PISTON
Ho, God save you, sir. Have you burst your shin?

BASILISCO
Ay, villain, I have broke my shin bone, my back bone, my channel bone, and my thigh bone, beside two dozen small inferior bones.

PISTON
A shrewd loss, by my faith, sir. But where's your courser's tail?

BASILISCO
He lost the same in service.

PISTON
There was a hot piece of service, where he lost his tail. But how chance his nose is slit?

BASILISCO
For presumption, for covering the Emperor's mare.

PISTON
Marry, a foul fault! But why are his ears cut?

BASILISCO
For neighing in the Emperor's court.

PISTON
Why then thy horse hath been a colt in his time!

BASILISCO
True, thou hast said. Oh, touch not the cheek of my palfrey, lest he dismount me while my wounds are green. Page, run,

bid the surgeon bring his incision. – Yet stay, I'll ride along with thee myself.

Exit.

PISTON
And I'll bear you company.

Piston gets up on his ass and rides with him to the door and meets the Crier.

Enter the Crier.

PISTON
Come, sirrah, let me see how finely you'll cry this chain.

CRIER
Why, what was it worth?

PISTON
It was worth more than thou and all thy kin are worth.

CRIER
It may be so, but what must he have that finds it?

PISTON
Why, a hundred crowns.

CRIER
Why then, I'll have ten for the crying of it.

PISTON
Ten crowns? And had but six pence for crying a little wench of thirty years old and upwards that had lost herself betwixt a tavern and a bawdy house?

CRIER
Ay, that was a wench, but this is gold. She was poor, but this is rich.

PISTON
Why then, by this reckoning, a hackneyman should have ten shillings for horsing a gentlewoman, where he hath but ten pence of a beggar.

CRIER
Why, and reason good: let them pay that best may, as the lawyers use their rich clients, when they let the poor go under *forma pauperis.*

PISTON
Why then, I pray thee, cry the chain for me, *sub forma pauperis*, for money goes very low with me at this time.

CRIER
Ay sir, but your master is, though you be not.

PISTON
Ay, but he must not know that thou cryest the chain for me. I do but use thee to save me a labour, that am to make enquiry after it.

CRIER
Well, sir, you'll see me considered, will you not?

PISTON
Ay, marry will I. Why, what lighter payment can there be than consideration?

CRIER Oyez!

Enter Erastus.

ERASTUS
How now, sirrah, what are you crying?

CRIER
A chain, sir, a chain, that your man bad me cry.

ERASTUS
Get you away, sirrah, I advise you meddle with no chains of mine! [*Exit Crier.*] You paltry knave, how durst thou be so bold to cry the chain, when I bid thou shouldst not? Did I not bid thee only underhand make privy enquiry for it through the town, lest public rumour might advertise her, whose knowledge were to me a second death?

PISTON
Why, would you have me run up and down the town, and my shoes are done?

ERASTUS
What you want in shoes, I'll give you in blows!

PISTON
I pray you, sir, hold your hands, and as I am an honest man, I'll do the best I can to find your chain.

Exit.

ERASTUS
Ah, treacherous Fortune, enemy to Love,
Didst thou advance me for my greater fall?
In dallying war, I lost my chiefest peace;
In hunting after praise, I lost my love;
And in love's shipwreck will my life miscarry.
Take thou the honour, and give me the chain,
Wherein was linked the sum of my delight.
When she delivered me the carcanet,
'Keep it,' quoth she, 'as thou wouldst keep myself.'
I kept it not, and therefore she is lost,
And lost with her is all my happiness,
And loss of happiness is worse than death.
Come therefore, gentle Death, and ease my grief;
Cut short what malice Fortune misintends.
But stay a while, good Death, and let me live:
Time may restore what Fortune took from me.
Ah no, great losses seldom are restored.
What if my chain shall never be restored?
My innocence shall clear my negligence.
Ah, but my love is ceremonious,
And looks for justice at her lover's hand.
Within forced furrows of her clouding brow,
As storms that fall amid a sunshine day,
I read her just desires, and my decay!

Exit.

[1.6]

Enter Soliman, Haleb, Amurath, and Janissaries.

SOLIMAN
I long till Brusor be returned from Rhodes,
To know how he hath borne him 'gainst the Christians
That are assembled there to try their valour;
But more to be well assured by him
How Rhodes is fenced, and how I best may lay
My never failing siege to win that plot.
For by the holy Alcaron I swear,
I'll call my soldiers home from Persia
And let the Sophy breathe, and from the Russian broils
Call home my hardy, dauntless Janissaries,
And from the other skirts of Christendom
Call home my Bassoes and my men of war,

And so beleaguer Rhodes by sea and land.
That key will serve to open all the gates
Through which our passage cannot find a stop
Till it have pricked the heart of Christendom,
Which now that paltry island keeps from scathe.
Say, brother Amurath, and Haleb, say:
What think you of our resolution?

AMURATH
Great Soliman, heaven's only substitute,
And earth's commander under Mahomet,
So counsel I, as thou thyself hast said.

HALEB
Pardon me, dread sovereign, I hold it not
Good policy, to call your forces home
From Persia and Polonia, bending them
Upon a paltry isle of small defence.
A common press of base superfluous Turks
May soon be levied for so slight a task.
Ah Soliman, whose name hath shaked thy foes,
As withered leaves with autumn throwen down,
Fog not thy glory with so foul eclipse!
Let not thy soldiers sound a base retire
Till Persia stoop, and thou be conqueror.
What scandal were it to thy mightiness,
After so many valiant Bassoes slain,
Whose blood hath been manured to their earth,
Whose bones hath made their deep ways passable,
To sound a homeward, dull, and harsh retreat
Without a conquest or a mean revenge?
Strive not for Rhodes by letting Persia slip:
The one's a lion almost brought to death,
Whose skin will countervail the hunter's toil;
The other is a wasp with threatening sting,
Whose honey is not worth the taking up.

AMURATH
Why, Haleb, didst thou not hear our brother swear
Upon the Alcaron religiously
That he would make an universal camp
Of all his scattered legions? And darest thou
Infer a reason why it is not meet,
After his highness swears it shall be so?

Were it not thou art my father's son,
And striving kindness wrestled not with ire,
I would not hence, till I had let thee know
What 'twere to thwart a monarch's holy oath!

HALEB
Why, his highness gave me leave to speak my will,
And far from flattery I spoke my mind,
And did discharge a faithful subject's love.
Thou Aristippus-like didst flatter him,
Not like my brother or a man of worth.
And for his highness' vow I crossed it not,
But gave my censure, as his highness bade.
Now for thy chastisment, know Amurath,
I scorn them as a reckless lion scorns
The humming of a gnat in summer's night!

AMURATH
I take it, Haleb, thou art friend to Rhodes?

HALEB
Not half so much am I a friend to Rhodes,
As thou art enemy to thy sovereign!

AMURATH
I charge thee say wherein, or else by Mahomet,
I'll hazard duty in my sovereign's presence!

HALEB
Not for thy threats, but for myself I say,
It is not meet that one so base as thou
Shouldst come about the person of a king!

SOLIMAN
Must I give aim to this presumption?

AMURATH
Your highness knows I speak in duteous love.

HALEB
Your highness knows I spake at your command
And to the purpose, far from flattery.

AMURATH
Thinks thou I flatter? Now I flatter not!

Then he kills Haleb.

SOLIMAN
What dismal planets guide this fatal hour?
Villain, thy brother's groans do call for thee –
Then Soliman kills Amurath.
To wander with them through eternal night!

AMURATH
O Soliman, for loving thee I die!

SOLIMAN
No, Amurath, for murdering him thou diest!
O Haleb, how shall I begin to mourn,
Or how shall I begin to shed salt tears,
For whom no words nor tears can well suffice?
Ah, that my rich imperial diadem
Could satisfy thy cruel destiny!
Or that a thousand of our Turkish souls,
Or twenty thousand millions of our foes'
Could ransom thee from fell Death's tyranny!
To win thy life would Soliman be poor,
And live in servile bondage all my days!
Accursed Amurath, that for a worthless cause,
In blood hath shortened our sweet Haleb's days!
Ah, what is dearer bond than brotherhood?
Yet Amurath, thou wert my brother too,
If wilful folly did not blind mine eyes!
Ay, ay, and thou as virtuous as Haleb,
And I as dear to thee as unto Haleb,
And thou as near to me as Haleb was!
Ah Amurath, why wert thou so unkind to him
For uttering but a thwarting word?
And Haleb, why did not thy heart's counsel
Bridle the fond intemperance of thy tongue?
Nay, wretched Soliman, why didst not thou
Withhold thy hand, from heaping blood on blood?
Might I not better spare one joy than both?
If love of Haleb forced me on to wrath,
Cursed be that wrath that is the way to death!
If justice forced me on, cursed be that justice
That makes the brother, butcher of his brother!
Come, Janissaries, and help me to lament,
And bear my joys on either side of me –
Ay, late my joys, but now my lasting sorrow.

Thus, thus, let Soliman pass on his way,
Bearing in either hand his heart's decay.

Exeunt.

* * * * *

[2. Prologue]

Enter Chorus.

LOVE
Now, Death and Fortune, which of all us three
Hath in the actors shown the greatest power?
Have not I taught Erastus and Perseda
By mutual tokens to seal up their loves?

FORTUNE
Ay, but those tokens, the ring and carcanet,
Were Fortune's gifts: Love gives no gold or jewels.

LOVE
Why, what is jewels, or what is gold but earth,
An humour knit together by compression,
And by the world's bright eye, first brought to light,
Only to feed men's eyes with vain delight?
Love's works are more than of a mortal temper:
I couple minds together by consent.
Who gave Rhodes' Princess to the Cyprian Prince, but Love?

FORTUNE
Fortune that first by chance brought them together;
For till by Fortune persons meet each other,
Thou canst not teach their eyes to wound their hearts.

LOVE
I made those knights of several sects and countries
Each one by arms to honour his beloved.

FORTUNE
Nay one alone to honour his beloved.
The rest by turning of my tickle wheel,
Came short in reaching of fair honours mark.
I gave Erastus only that day's prize;
A sweet renown, but mixed with bitter sorrow,
For in conclusion of his happiness,
I made him lose the precious carcanet
Whereon depended all his hope and joy.

DEATH
And more than so: for he that found the chain,
Even for that chain shall be deprived of life.

LOVE
Besides, Love hath enforced a fool,
The fond braggardo to presume to arms.

FORTUNE
Ay, but thou seest how he was overthrown
By Fortune's high displeasure.

DEATH
Ay, and by Death had been surprised,
If Fates had given me leave.
But what I missed in him and in the rest,
I did accomplish on Haleb and Amurath,
The worthy brethren of great Soliman.
But wherefore stay we? Let the sequel prove
Who is greatest: Fortune, Death, or Love.

Exeunt.

[2.1]

Enter Ferdinando and Lucina.

FERDINANDO
As fits the time, so now well fits the place
To cool affection with our words and looks,
If in our thoughts be semblance sympathy.

LUCINA
My words, my looks, my thoughts are all on thee:
Ferdinando is Lucina's only joy.

FERDINANDO
What pledge thereof?

LUCINA
An oath, a hand, a kiss.

FERDINANDO
Oh, holy oath, fair hand, and sugared kiss!
Oh, never may Fernando lack such bliss.
But say, my dear, when shall the gates of heaven
Stand all wide open for celestial gods

With gladsome looks to gaze at Hymen's robes?
When shall the Graces, or Lucina's hand,
With rosy chaplets deck thy golden tresses,
And Cupid bring me to thy nuptial bed,
Where thou in joy and pleasure must attend
A blissful war with me thy chiefest friend?

LUCINA
Full fraught with love and burning with desire,
I long have longed for light of Hymen's lights.

FERDINANDO
Then that same day, whose warm and pleasant sight
Brings in the spring with many gladsome flowers,
Be our first day of joy and perfect peace;
Till when, receive this precious carcanet,
In sign that, as these links are interlaced,
So both our hearts are still combined in one,
Which never can be parted but by death.

Enter Basilisco and Perseda.

LUCINA
And if I live this shall not be forgot:
But see, Ferdinando, where Perseda comes,
Whom women love for virtue, men for beauty,
All the world loves, none hates but Envy.

BASILISCO
All hail, brave cavalier! Good morrow, madam!
The fairest shine that shall this day be seen,
Except Perseda's beauteous excellence,
Shame to Love's queen, and empress of my thoughts.

FERDINANDO
Marry, thrice happy is Perseda's chance,
To have so brave a champion to her squire!

BASILISCO
Her squire? Her knight! And who so else denies,
Shall feel the rigour of my sword and lance!

FERDINANDO
O sir, not I!

LUCINA
Here's none but friends, yet let me challenge you,
For gracing me with a malignant style
That I was fairest, and yet Perseda fairer.
We ladies stand upon our beauties much.

PERSEDA
Herein, Lucina, let me buckler him!

BASILISCO
Not Mars himself had ere so fair a buckler!

PERSEDA
Love makes him blind,
And blind can judge no colours.

LUCINA
Why then the mends is made, and we still friends.

PERSEDA
[*aside*] Still friends? Still foes: she wears my carcanet!
Ah, false Erastus, how am I betrayed!

LUCINA
What ails you, madam, that your colour changes?

PERSEDA
A sudden qualm. I therefore take my leave.

LUCINA
We'll bring you home.

PERSEDA
No, I shall soon get home.

LUCINA
Why then, farewell. Fernando, let's away.

Exeunt Ferdinando and Lucina.

BASILISCO
Say, world's bright star,
Whence springs this sudden change?
Is it unkindness at the little praise
I gave Lucina with my glozing style?

PERSEDA
No, no, her beauty far surpasseth mine,
And from my neck, her neck hath won the praise.

BASILISCO
What is it then, if love of this my person,
By favour and by justice of the heavens,
At last have pierced through thy tralucent breast,
And thou misdoubtst, perhaps, that I'll prove coy?
Oh, be assured 'tis far from noble thoughts,
To tyrannise over a yielding foe.
Therefore be blithe, sweet love, abandon fear.
I will forget thy former cruelty.

PERSEDA
Ah, false Erastus full of treachery!

BASILISCO
I always told you that such coward knights
Were faithless swains and worthy no respect.
But tell me, sweet love, what is his offence,
That I with words and stripes may chastise him,
And bring him bound for thee to tread upon?

PERSEDA
[*aside*] Now must I find the means to rid him hence!
– Go thou forthwith, arm thee from top to toe,
And come an hour hence unto my lodging,
Then will I tell thee this offence at large,
And thou in my behalf shalt work revenge.

BASILISCO
Ay, thus should men of valour be employed.
This is good argument of thy true love.
I go, make reckoning that Erastus dies,
Unless forewarned, the weakling coward flies!

Exit.

PERSEDA
Thou foolish coward! 'Flies'? Erastus lives,
The fairest-shaped, but foulest-minded man,
That ere sun saw within our hemisphere!
My tongue to tell my woes is all too weak.
I must unclasp me, or my heart will break!
But inward cares are most pent in with grief,
Unclasping therefore yields me no relief.
Ah, that my moist and cloud-compacted brain
Could spend my cares in showers of weeping rain.

But scalding sighs like blasts of boisterous winds,
Hinder my tears from falling on the ground,
And I must die by closure of my wound.
Ah, false Erastus, how had I misdone,
That thou shouldst quit my love with such a scorn?

Enter Erastus.

Here comes the Sinon to my simple heart!
I'll frame myself to his dissembling art.

ERASTUS
[*aside*] Desire persuades me on, fear pulls me back.
Tush I will to her: innocence is bold!
– How fares Perseda, my sweet second self?

PERSEDA
Well now, Erastus, my heart's only joy,
Is come to join both hearts in union.

ERASTUS
And till I came whereas my love did dwell,
My pleasure was but pain, my solace woe.

PERSEDA
What love means my Erastus? Pray thee, tell?

ERASTUS
Matchless Perseda, she that gave me strength
To win late conquest from many victors' hands.
Thy name was conqueror, not my chivalry;
Thy looks did arm me, not my coat of steel;
Thy beauty did defend me, not my force;
Thy favours bore me, not my light-foot steed;
Therefore to thee I owe both love and life.
But wherefore makes Perseda such a doubt,
As if Erastus could forget himself?
Which if I do, all vengeance light on me!

PERSEDA
Ay me, how graceless are these wicked men?
I can no longer hold my patience!
Ah, how thine eyes can forge alluring looks,
And feign deep oaths to wound poor silly maids!
Are there no honest drops in all thy cheeks,
To check thy fraudful count'nance with a blush?

Callest thou me love, and lovest another better?
If heavens were just, thy teeth would tear thy tongue
For this thy perjured false disloyalty!
If heavens were just, men should have open breasts
That we therein might read their guileful thoughts!
If heavens were just, that power that forceth love
Would never couple wolves and lambs together!
Yes, heavens are just, but thou art so corrupt
That in thee all their influence doth change,
As in the spider good things turn to poison.
Ah, false Erastus, how had I misdone,
That thou shouldst pawn my true affection's pledge,
To her whose worth will never equal mine?
What, is Lucina's wealth exceeding mine?
Yet mine sufficient to encounter thine.
Is she more fair than I? That's not my fault,
Nor her desert. What's beauty but a blast,
Soon cropped with age, or with infirmities?
Is she more wise? Her years are more than mine.
What ere she be, my love was more than hers.
And for her chastity, let others judge.
But what talk I of her? The fault is thine!
If I were so disgracious in thine eye
That she must needs enjoy my interest,
Why didst thou deck her with my ornament?
Could nothing serve her but the carcanet,
Which as my life I gave to thee in charge?
Couldst thou abuse my true simplicity,
Whose greatest fault was overloving thee?
I'll keep no tokens of thy perjury.
Here, give her this [*she returns the ring*]; Perseda now is free,
And all my former love is turned to hate.

ERASTUS
Ah stay, my sweet Perseda, hear me speak.

PERSEDA
What are thy words but Sirens' guileful songs,
That please the ear, but seek to spoil the heart?

ERASTUS
Then view my tears, that plead for innocence.

PERSEDA
What are thy tears, but Circe's magic seas,
Where none 'scape wrack, but blindfold mariners?

ERASTUS
If words and tears displease, then view my looks,
That plead for mercy at thy rigorous hands.

PERSEDA
What are thy looks but like the cockatrice,
That seeks to wound poor silly passengers?

ERASTUS
If words, nor tears, nor looks may win remorse,
What then remains? For my perplexèd heart
Hath no interpreters but words, or tears, or looks.

PERSEDA
And they are all as false as thou thyself!

Exit.

ERASTUS
Hard doom of death, before my case be known!
My judge unjust, and yet I cannot blame her,
Since love and jealousy mislead her thus.
Myself in fault, and yet not worthy blame,
Because that Fortune made the fault, not Love.
The ground of her unkindness grows because I lost
The precious carcanet she gave to me.
Lucina hath it, as her words import,
But how she got it, heaven knows, not I.
Yet this is some alledgement to my sorrow,
That if I can but get the chain again,
I boldly then shall let Perseda know
That she hath wrongd Erastus and her friend.
Ah Love, and if thou be'st of heavenly power,
Inspire me with some present stratagem!
It must be so: Lucina's a frank gamester,
And like it is, in play she'll hazard it.
For if report but blazon her aright,
She's a frank gamester, and inclined to play. Ho, Piston?

Enter Piston.

PISTON Here sir, what would you with me?

ERASTUS Desire Guelpio and Signior Julio come speak with me, and bid them bring some store of crowns with them. And sirrah, provide me four vizards, four gowns, a box, and a drum. For I intend to go in mummery.

PISTON I will sir.

Exit.

ERASTUS
Ah virtuous lamps of ever turning heavens,
Incline her mind to play, and mine to win.
Nor do I covet but what is mine own.
Then shall I let Perseda understand
How jealousy had armed her tongue with malice.
Ah, were she not Perseda, whom my heart
No more can fly than iron can adamant,
Her late unkindness would have changed my mind!

Enter Guelpio and Julio and Piston [*and Drummer*].

GUELPIO
How now, Erastus, wherein may we pleasure thee?

ERASTUS
Sirs, thus it is: we must in mummery
Unto Lucina, neither for love nor hate,
But if we can, to win the chain she wears;
For though I have some interest therein,
Fortune may make me master of mine own,
Rather than I'll seek justice 'gainst the dame.
But this assure yourselves: it must be mine
By game or change, by one device or other.
The rest I'll tell you when our sport is done.

JULIO
Why then, let's make us ready and about it.

ERASTUS
What store of crowns have you brought?

GUELPIO
Fear not for money, man, I'll bear the box.

JULIO
I have some little reply, if need require.

PISTON
Ay, but hear you master, was not he a fool that went to shoot, and left his arrows behind him?

ERASTUS
Yes, but what of that?

PISTON
Marry, that you may lose your money, and go without the chain, unless you carry false dice.

GUELPIO
Mass, the fool says true, let's have some got.

PISTON
Nay, I use not to go without a pair of false dice: here are tall men and little men.

JULIO
High men and low men, thou wouldst say.

ERASTUS
Come sirs, let's go. Drumsler, play for me and I'll reward thee; and, sirrah Piston, mar not our sport with your foolery.

PISTON
I warrant you, sir, they get not one wise word of me.
Sound up the drum to Lucina's door.

Enter Lucina

LUCINA Ay, marry, this shows that Charlemagne is come! What, shall we play here? Content, since Signor Ferdinand will have it so.
Then they play, and when she had lost her gold, Erastus pointed to her chain, and then she said:
Ay, were it Cleopatra's union!
Then Erastus wins the chain and loses his gold. And Lucina says:
Signor Fernando, I am sure 'tis you,
And gentlemen, unmask ere you depart,
That I may know to whom my thanks is due
For this so courteous and unlooked for sport.
No? Will't not be? Then sup with me tomorrow?
Well then, I'll look for you. 'Till then, farewell.

Exit.

ERASTUS
Gentlemen, each thing hath sorted to our wish.
She took me for Fernando, marked you that?
Your gold shall be repaired with double thanks;
And, fellow drumsler, I'll reward you well.

PISTON
But is there no reward for my false dice?

ERASTUS
Yes sir, a garded suit from top to toe!

Enter Ferdinando.

FERDINANDO
Dazzle mine eyes, or is't Lucina's chain?
False treacher, lay down the chain that thou hast stole!

ERASTUS
He lewdly lies that calls me treacherous!

FERDINANDO
That lie my weapon shall put down thy throat!
Then Erastus slays Ferdinando.

JULIO
Fly, Erastus, ere the Governor have any news,
Whose near ally he was, and chief delight!

ERASTUS
Nay gentlemen, fly you and save yourselves,
Lest you partake the hardness of my fortune!

Exeunt Guelpio and Julio.

Ah, fickle and blind guideress of the world,
What pleasure hast thou in my misery?
Was't not enough when I had lost the chain,
Thou didst bereave me of my dearest love?
But now, when I should repossess the same,
To cross me with this hapless accident?
Ah, if but time and place would give me leave,
Great ease it were for me to purge myself,
And to accuse fell Fortune, Love, and Death,
For all these three conspire my tragedy.
But danger waits upon my words and steps.
I dare not stay, for if the Governor
Surprise me here, I die by martial law.

Therefore I go. But whither shall I go?
If into any stay adjoining Rhodes,
They will betray me to Philippo's hands,
For love, or gain, or flattery.
To Turkey must I go: the passage short,
The people warlike, and the king renowned
For all heroical and kingly virtues.
Ah hard attempt, to tempt a foe for aid!
Necessity yet says it must be so,
Or suffer death for Ferdinando's death,
Whom honour's title forced me to misdo,
By checking his outrageous insolence.
Piston, here, take this chain, and give it to Perseda,
And let her know what hath befallen me.
When thou hast delivered it, take ship and follow me.
I will be in Constantinople.
Farewell my country, dearer than my life;
Farewell sweet friends, dearer than country soil;
Farewell Perseda, dearest of them all,
Dearer to me than all the world besides.

Exit.

PISTON
Now am I growing into a doubtful agony what I were best to do: to run away with this chain, or deliver it, and follow my master? If I deliver it and follow my master, I shall have thanks, but they will make me never the fatter. If I run away with it, I may live upon credit all the while I wear this chain, or domineer with the money when I have sold it. Hitherto all goes well, but if I be taken, ay, marry sir, then the case is altered, aye, and haltered too! Of all things I do not love to preach with a halter about my neck! Therefore, for this once, I'll be honest against my will: Perseda shall have it. But before I go, I'll be so bold as to dive into this gentleman's pocket, for good luck's sake, if he deny me not. How say you sir? Are you content? A plain case: *Quit tacet consitiri videtur.*

Enter Philippo and Julio.

JULIO
See where his body lies.

PHILIPPO
Ay, ay, I see his body all too soon.
What barbarous villain is't that rifles him?

Ah Ferdinand, the stay of my old age,
And chief remainder of our progeny!
Ah loving cousin, how art thou misdone
By false Erastus? Ah no, by treachery,
For well thy valour hath been often tried!
But whilst I stand and weep, and spend the time
In fruitless plaints, the murderer will escape
Without revenge, sole salve for such a sore!
Say, villain, wherefore didst thou rifle him?

PISTON
Faith, sir, for pure good will. Seeing he was going towards heaven, I thought to see if he had a passport to Saint Nicholas or no.

PHILIPPO
Some sot he seems to be, 'twere pity to hurt him. Sirrah, canst thou tell who slew this man?

PISTON
Ay sir, very well, it was my master Erastus.

PHILIPPO
Thy master? And whither is he gone now?

PISTON
To fetch the sexton to bury him, I think.

PHILIPPO
'Twere pity to imprison such a sot.

PISTON
[*aside*] Now it fits my wisdom to counterfeit the fool.

PHILIPPO
Come hither, sirrah. Thou knowest me for the Governor of the city, dost thou not?

PISTON
Ay, forsooth, sir.

PHILIPPO
Thou art a bondman, and wouldst fain be free?

PISTON
Ay, forsooth, sir.

PHILIPPO
Then do but this, and I will make thee free, and rich

withal: learn where Erastus is and bring me word, and I'll reward thee well.

PISTON
That I will, sir. I shall find you at the castle, shall I not?

PHILIPPO
Yes.

PISTON Why, I'll be here, as soon as ever I come again.

Exit.

PHILIPPO
But for assurance that he may not 'scape,
We'll lay the ports and havens round about,
And let a proclamation straight be made,
That he that can bring forth the murderer
Shall have three thousand ducats for his pains.
Myself will see the body borne from hence,
And honourèd with balm and funeral.

Exit.

[2.2]

Enter Piston.

PISTON
God sends fortune to fools! Did you ever see wise man escape as I have done? I must betray my master, ay, but when? Can you tell?

Enter Perseda.

See where Perseda comes, to save me a labour. After my most hearty commendations, this is to let you understand that my master was in good health at the sending hereof. Yours for ever and ever and ever. In most humble wise, Piston.

Then he delivered her the chain.

PERSEDA
This makes me think that I have been too cruel.
How got he this from off Lucina's arm?

PISTON
Faith, in a mummery, and a pair of false dice. I was one of the mummers myself, simple as I stand here.

PERSEDA
I rather think it cost him very dear.

PISTON
Ay, so it did, for it cost Ferdinando his life.

PERSEDA
How so?

PISTON
After we had got the chain in mummery, and lost our box in counter-cambio, my master wore the chain about his neck. Then Ferdinando met us on the way, and reviled my master, saying he stole the chain; with that they drew, and there Ferdinando had the prickado.

PERSEDA
And whither fled my poor Erastus then?

PISTON
To Constantinople, whither I must follow him. But ere he went, with many sighs and tears, he delivered me the chain, and bade me give it you, for perfect argument that he was true, and you too credulous.

PERSEDA
Ah stay, no more, for I can hear no more!

PISTON
And I can sing no more.

PERSEDA
My heart had armed my tongue with injury,
To wrong my friend, whose thoughts were ever true.
Ah, poor Erastus, how thy stars malign!
Thou great commander of the swift-winged winds,
And dreadful Neptune, bring him back again!
But Eolus and Neptune, let him go,
For here is nothing but revenge and death!
Then let him go, I'll shortly follow him,
Not with slow sails, but with love's golden wings!
My ship shall be borne with tears, and blown with sighs!
So will I soar about the Turkish land,
Until I meet Erastus my sweet friend;
And then and there, fall down amid his arms,
And in his bosom there pour forth my soul,

For satisfaction of my trespass past.

Enter Basilisco, armed.

BASILISCO
Fair love, according unto thy command,
I seek Erastus and will combat him.

PERSEDA
Ay, seek him, find him, bring him to my sight,
For till we meet, my heart shall want delight!

Exit.

BASILISCO
My petty fellow, where hast thou hid thy master?

PISTON
Marry, sir, in an armourer's shop, where you had not best go to him.

BASILISCO
Why so? I am in honour bound to combat him.

PISTON
Ay sir, but he, knowing your fierce conditions, hath planted a double cannon in the door, ready to discharge it upon you, when you go by: I tell you for pure good will.

BASILISCO
In knightly courtesy, I thank thee. But hopes the coistrel to escape me so? Thinks he bare cannon shot can keep me back? Why, wherefore serves my targe of proof, but for the bullet? That, once put by, I roughly come upon him, like to the wings of lightning from above. I with a martial look astonish him. Then falls he down, poor wretch, upon his knee, and all too late, repents his surquidry. Then do I take him on my finger's point, and thus I bear him through every street, to be a laughingstock to all the town. That done, I lay him at my mistress' feet, for her to give him doom of life or death.

PISTON
Ay, but hear you, sir, I am bound, in pain of my master's displeasure, to have a bout at cuffs, afore you and I part.

BASILISCO
Ha, ha, ha! Eagles are challenged by paltry flies!
Thy folly gives thee privilege; be gone, be gone!

PISTON
No, no, sir, I must have a bout with you, sir, that's flat; lest my master turn me out of service.

BASILISCO
Why, art thou weary of thy life?

PISTON
No, by my faith, sir.

BASILISCO
Then fetch thy weapons, and with my single fist I'll combat thee, my body all unarmed.

PISTON
Why, lend me thine, and save me a labour.

BASILISCO
I tell thee, if Alcides lived this day, he could not wield my weapons.

PISTON
Why, wilt thou stay till I come again?

BASILISCO
Ay, upon my honour.

PISTON That shall be when I come from Turkey.

Exit.

BASILISCO Is this little desperate fellow gone? Doubtless he is a very tall fellow, and yet it were disgrace to all my chivalry to combat one so base. I'll send some crane to combat with the pygmy, not that I fear, but that I scorn to fight.

Exit.

* * * * *

[3. Prologue]

Enter Chorus.

LOVE
Fortune, thou mad'st Fernando find the chain,
But yet by Love's instruction he was taught
To make a present of it to his mistress.

FORTUNE
But Fortune would not let her keep it long.

LOVE
Nay, rather Love, by whose suggested power
Erastus used such dice, as being false,
Ran not by Fortune, but necessity.

FORTUNE
Meantime I brought Fernando on the way,
To see and challenge what Lucina lost.

DEATH
And by that challenge I abridged his life,
And forced Erastus into banishment,
Parting him from his love, in spite of Love.

LOVE
But with my golden wings I'll follow him,
And give him aid and succour in distress.

FORTUNE
And doubt not too, but Fortune will be there,
And cross him too, and sometimes flatter him
And lift him up, and throw him down again.

DEATH
And here and there in ambush Death will stand,
To mar what Love or Fortune takes in hand.

Exeunt.

[3.1]

Enter Soliman and Brusor, with Janissaries.

SOLIMAN
How long shall Soliman spend his time
And waste his days in fruitless obsequies?
Perhaps my grief and long continual moan,
Adds but a trouble to my brothers' ghosts,
Which but for me would now have took their rest.
Then farewell sorrow, and now revenge draw near.
In controversy touching the isle of Rhodes,
My brothers' died; on Rhodes I'll be revenged.
Now tell me, Brusor, what's the news at Rhodes?
Hath the young prince of Cyprus married
Cornelia, daughter to the Governor?

BRUSOR
He hath my lord, with the greatest pomp,
That ere I saw at such a festival.

SOLIMAN
What, greater than at our coronation?

BRUSOR
Inferior to that only.

SOLIMAN
At tilt, who won the honour of the day?

BRUSOR
A worthy knight of Rhodes, a matchless man;
His name Erastus, not twenty years of age,
Not tall, but well proportioned in his limbs.
I never saw, except your excellence,
A man whose presence more delighted me;
And had he worshipped Mahomet for Christ,
He might have borne me throughout all the world,
So well I loved and honourèd the man.

SOLIMAN
These praises, Brusor, touch me to the heart,
And makes me wish that I had been at Rhodes,
Under the habit of some errant knight,
Both to have seen and tried his valour.

BRUSOR
You should have seen him foil and overthrow
All the knights that there encountered him.

SOLIMAN
What'er he be, even for his virtues' sake,
I wish that fortune of our holy wars
Would yield him prisoner unto Soliman;
That for retaining one so virtuous,
We may our selves be famed for virtuous.
But let him pass, and Brusor, tell me now,
How did the Christians use our knights?

BRUSOR
As if that we and they had been one sect.

SOLIMAN
What thinkst thou of their valour and demeanour?

BRUSOR
Brave men at arms, and friendly out of arms;
Courteous in peace, in battle dangerous;
Kind to their foes, and liberal to their friends;
And all in all, their deeds heroical.

SOLIMAN
Then tell me, Brusor, how is Rhodes fenced?
For either Rhodes shall be brave Soliman's,
Or cost me more brave soldiers
Than all that isle will bear.

BRUSOR
Their fleet is weak;
Their horse, I deem them fifty thousand strong;
Their footmen more, well exercised in war;
And as it seems, they want no needful victual.

SOLIMAN
How ever Rhodes be fenced by sea or land,
It either shall be mine, or bury me!

Enter Erastus.

What's he that thus boldly enters in?
His habit argues him a Christian.

ERASTUS
Ay, worthy lord, a forlorn Christian.

SOLIMAN
Tell me, man, what madness brought thee hither?

ERASTUS
Thy virtuous fame, and mine own misery.

SOLIMAN
What misery? Speak, for though you Christians
Account our Turkish race but barbarous,
Yet have we ears to hear a just complaint,
And justice to defend the innocent,
And pity to such as are in poverty,
And liberal hands to such as merit bounty.

BRUSOR
My gracious sovereign, as this knight
Seems by grief tied to silence,

So his desert binds me to speak for him:
This is Erastus the Rhodian worthy,
The flower of chivalry and courtesy.

SOLIMAN
Is this the man that thou hast so described?
Stand up, fair knight, that what my heart desires,
Mine eyes may view with pleasure and delight!
This face of thine should harbour no deceit.
Erastus, I'll not yet urge to know the cause
That brought thee hither,
Lest with the discourse thou shouldst afflict thyself,
And cross the fullness of my joyful passion.
But that we are assured:
Heavens brought thee hither for our benefit.
Know thou that Rhodes, nor all that Rhodes contains,
Shall win thee from the side of Soliman,
If we but find thee well inclined to us.

ERASTUS
If any ignoble or dishonourable thoughts
Should dare attempt, or but creep near my heart,
Honour should force disdain to root it out;
As air-bred eagles, if they once perceive
That any of their brood but close their sight
When they should gaze against the glorious sun,
They straightway seize upon him with their talons,
That on the earth it may untimely die,
For looking but askew at heaven's bright eye.

SOLIMAN
Erastus, to make thee well assured
How well thy speech and presence liketh us,
Ask what thou wilt: it shall be granted thee.

ERASTUS
Then this, my gracious lord, is all I crave,
That being banished from my native soil,
I may have liberty to live a Christian.

SOLIMAN
Ay, that, or anything thou shalt desire!
Thou shalt be Captain of our Janissaries,
And in our council shalt thou sit with us,
And be great Soliman's adopted friend.

ERASTUS
The least of these surpass my best desert,
Unless true loyalty may seem desert.

SOLIMAN
Erastus, now thou hast obtained thy boon,
Deny not Soliman this one request:
A virtuous envy pricks me with desire
To try thy valour. Say, art thou content?

ERASTUS
Ay, if my sovereign say content, I yield.

SOLIMAN
Then give us swords and targets.
And now Erastus think me thine enemy,
But ever after thy continual friend,
And spare me not, for then thou wrongst my honour.

Then they fight, and Erastus overcomes Soliman.

Nay, nay Erastus, throw not down thy weapons,
As if thy force did fail! It is enough
That thou hast conquered Soliman by strength;
By courtesy let Soliman conquer thee!
And now from arms to counsel sit thee down.
Before thy coming I vowed to conquer Rhodes.
Say, wilt thou be our lieutenant there,
And further us in manage of these wars?

ERASTUS
My gracious sovereign, without presumption,
If poor Erastus may once more entreat,
Let not great Soliman's command,
To whose behest I vow obedience,
Enforce me sheath my slaughtering blade
In the dear bowels of my countrymen.
And were it not that Soliman hath sworn,
My tears should plead for pardon to that place.
I speak not this to shrink away for fear,
Or hide my head in time of dangerous storms.
Employ me elsewhere in thy foreign wars:
Against the Persians or the barbarous Moor,
Erastus will be foremost in the battle.

SOLIMAN
Why favourst thou thy countrymen so much,

By whose cruelty thou art exiled?

ERASTUS
'Tis not my country, but Philippo's wrath,
It must be told, for Ferdinando's death,
Whom I in honour's cause have reft of life.

SOLIMAN
Nor suffer this or that to trouble thee.
Thou shalt not need Philippo nor his isle,
Nor shalt thou war against thy countrymen.
I like thy virtue in refusing it.
But that our oath may have his current course,
Brusor, go levy men,
Prepare a fleet to assault and conquer Rhodes.
Meantime, Erastus and I will strive
By mutual kindness to excel each other.
Brusor, be gone, and see not Soliman
Till thou hast brought Rhodes in subjection.

Exit Brusor.

And now, Erastus, come and follow me
Where thou shalt see what pleasures and what sports
My minions and my eunuchs can devise,
To drive away this melancholy mood.

Exit Soliman [*as Erastus is leaving, Piston intercepts him*].
Enter Piston.

PISTON
O master, see where I am!

ERASTUS
Say, Piston, what's the news at Rhodes?

PISTON
Cold and comfortless for you. Will you have them all at once?

ERASTUS
Ay.

PISTON
Why, the Governor will hang you and he catch you;
Ferdinando is buried; your friends commend them to you;
Perseda hath the chain, and is like to die for sorrow.

ERASTUS
Ay, that's the grief, that we are parted thus.
Come, follow me and I will hear the rest,
For now I must attend the Emperor.

Exeunt.

[3.2]

Enter Perseda, Lucina, and Basilisco.

PERSEDA
Accursèd chain! Unfortunate Perseda!

LUCINA
Accursèd chain! Unfortunate Lucina!
My friend is gone, and I am desolate.

PERSEDA
My friend is gone, and I am desolate.
Return him back, fair stars, or let me die.

LUCINA
Return him back fair heavens, or let me die,
For what was he, but comfort of my life?

PERSEDA
For what was he, but comfort of my life?
But why was I so careful of the chain?

LUCINA
But why was I so careless of the chain?
Had I not lost it, my friend had not been slain!

PERSEDA
Had I not asked it, my friend had not departed.
His parting is my death.

LUCINA
His death's my life's departing!
And here my tongue doth stay with swollen heart's grief.

PERSEDA
And here my swollen heart's grief doth stay my tongue.

BASILISCO
For whom weep you?

LUCINA
Ah, for Fernando's dying.

BASILISCO
For whom mourn you?

PERSEDA
Ah, for Erastus flying.

BASILISCO
Why lady, is not Basilisco here?
Why lady, doth not Basilisco live?
Am not I worth both these for whom you mourn?
Then take one half of me, and cease to weep,
Or if you gladly would enjoy me both,
I'll serve the one by day, the other by night,
And I will pay you both your sound delight.

LUCINA
Ah, how unpleasant is mirth to melancholy.

PERSEDA
My heart is full, I cannot laugh at folly.

Exeunt Ladies.

BASILISCO
See, see, Lucina hates me like a toad,
Because that when Erastus spake my name,
Her love Fernando dièd at the same:
So dreadful is our name to cowardice!
On the other side, Perseda takes it unkindly
That ere he went I brought not bound unto her
Erastus that faint hearted runaway.
Alas, how could I? For his man no sooner
Informed him, that I sought him up and down,
But he was gone in twinkling of an eye.
But I will after my delicious love,
For well I wot, though she disemble thus,
And cloak affection with her modesty,
With love of me her thoughts are overgone,
More than was Phyllis with her Demophon.

Exit.

[3.3]

Enter Philippo, the Prince of Cyprus, with other Soldiers.

PHILIPPO
Brave Prince of Cyprus, and our son-in-law,
Now there is little time to stand and talk:
The Turks have past our galleys and are landed.
You with some men at arms shall take the tower,
I with the rest will down unto the strand.
If we be beaten back, we'll come to you,
And here in spite of damnèd Turks we'll gain
A glorious death or famous victory!

CYPRUS
About it, then!

Exeunt.

[3.4]

Enter Brusor, and his soldiers.

BRUSOR
Drum, sound a parley to the citizens!
The Prince of Cyprus on the walls.

CYPRUS
What parley craves the Turkish at our hands?

BRUSOR
We come with mighty Soliman's command,
Monarch and mighty emperor of the world,
From East to West, from South to Septentrion.
If you resist, expect what war affords:
Mischief, murder, blood, and extremity!
What, wilt thou yield and try our clemency?
Say ay, or no, for we are peremptory.

CYPRUS
Your lord usurps in all that he posesseth,
And that great God which we do truly worship
Shall strengthen us against your insolence.

BRUSOR
Now if thou plead for mercy, 'tis too late.
Come, fellow soldiers, let us to the breach

That's made already on the other side!

Exeunt, to the battle.

Philippo and Cyprus are both slain.

Enter Brusor, with soldiers, having [taken] Guelpio, Julio, and Basilisco, with Perseda and Lucina, prisoners.

BRUSOR
Now Rhodes is yoked, and stoops to Soliman.
There lies the Governor, and there his son.
Now let their souls tell sorry tidings to their ancestors,
What millions of men oppressed with ruin and scathe,
The Turkish armies did in Christendom!
What say these prisoners? Will they turn Turk, or no?

JULIO
First Julio will die ten thousand deaths!

GUELPIO
And Guelpio, rather than deny his Christ!

BRUSOR
Then stab the slaves, and send their souls to hell!

They stab Julio and Guelpio.

BASILISCO
I turn, I turn! Oh, save my life, I turn!

BRUSOR
Forbear to hurt him. When we land in Turkey,
He shall be circumcised and have his rites.

BASILISCO
Think you I turn Turk for fear of servile death?
That's but a sport! I'faith sir, no!
'Tis for Perseda whom I love so well
That I would follow her, though she went to hell!

BRUSOR
Now for these ladies: their lives' privilege
Hangs on their beauty. They shall be preserved
To be presented to great Soliman,
The greatest honour fortune could afford.

PERSEDA
The most dishonour that could ere befall!

Exeunt.

[4. Prologue]

Enter Chorus.

LOVE
Now, Fortune, what hast thou done in this latter passage?

FORTUNE
I placed Erastus in the favour
Of Soliman, the Turkish emperor.

LOVE
Nay, that was Love, for I couched myself
In poor Erastus' eyes, and with a look
O'erspread with tears, bewitchèd Soliman.
Beside I sat on valiant Brusor's tongue,
To guide the praises of the Rhodian knight.
Then in the ladies' passions, I showed my power,
And lastly Love made Basilisco's tongue
To countercheck his heart by turning Turk,
And save his life, in spite of Death's despite.

DEATH
How chance it then, that Love and Fortune's power
Could neither save Philippo nor his son,
Nor Guelpio, nor Signor Julio,
Nor rescue Rhodes from out the hands of Death?

FORTUNE
Why, Brusor's victory was Fortune's gift.

DEATH
But had I slept, his conquest had been small.

LOVE
Wherefore stay we? There's more behind, which proves
That though Love wink, Love's not stark blind!

Exeunt.

[4.1]

Enter Erastus and Piston.

PISTON
Faith, master, methinks you are unwise that you wear not the high sugarloaf hat, and the gilded gown the Emperor gave you.

ERASTUS
Peace, fool, a sable weed fits discontent. Away, be gone.

PISTON
I'll go provide your supper: a shoulder of mutton, and never a salad.

Exit.

ERASTUS
I must confess that Soliman is kind
Past all compare, and more than my desert.
But what helps gay garments when the mind's oppressed?
What pleaseth the eye when the sense is altered?
My heart is overwhelmed with thousand woes,
And Melancholy leads my soul in triumph.
No marvel then if I have little mind,
Of rich embroidery or costly ornaments,
Of honour's titles, or of wealth, or gain,
Of music, viands, or of dainty dames.
No, no, my hope full long ago was lost,
And Rhodes itself is lost, or else destroyed;
If not destroyed, yet bound and captivate;
If captivate, then forced from holy faith;
If forced from faith, forever miserable.
For what is misery, but want of God?
And God is lost, if faith be overthrown.

Enter Soliman.

SOLIMAN
Why, how now Erastus, always in thy dumps?
Still in black habit fitting funeral?
Cannot my love persuade thee from this mood,
Nor all my fair entreats and blandishments?
Wert thou my friend, thy mind would jump with mine,
For what are friends, but one mind in two bodies?
Perhaps thou doubtst my friendship's constancy?
Then dost thou wrong the measure of my love,
Which hath no measure, and shall never end.
Come, Erastus, sit thee down by me,
And I'll impart to thee our Brusor's news;
News to our honour, and to thy content:
The Governor is slain that sought thy death.

ERASTUS
A worthy man, though not Erastus' friend.

SOLIMAN
The Prince of Cyprus too is likewise slain.

ERASTUS
Fair blossom, likely to have proved good fruit.

SOLIMAN
Rhodes is taken, and all the men are slain,
Except some few that turn to Mahomet.

ERASTUS
Ay, there it is! Now all my friends are slain,
And fair Perseda murdered or deflowered!
Ah, gracious Soliman, now show thy love
In not denying thy poor suppliant.
Suffer me not to stay here in thy presence,
But by myself lament me once for all.
Here if I stay, I must suppress my tears,
And tears suppressed will but increase my sorrow.

SOLIMAN
Go then, go spend thy mournings all at once,
That in thy presence Soliman may joy –

Exit Erastus.

For hitherto have I reaped little pleasure.
Well, well, Erastus, Rhodes may bless thy birth.
For his sake only will I spare them more
From spoil, pillage, and oppression
Than Alexander spared warlike Thebes
For Pindarus, or than Augustus
Spared rich Alexandria for Arius's sake.

Enter Brusor, Perseda, and Lucina.

BRUSOR
My gracious lord, rejoice in happiness:
All Rhodes is yoked, and stoops to Soliman!

SOLIMAN
First thanks to heaven, and next to Brusor's valour,
Which I'll not guerdon with large promises,
But straight reward thee with a bounteous largesse.

But what two Christian virgins have we here?

BRUSOR
Part of the spoil of Rhodes, which were preserved
To be presented to your mightiness.

SOLIMAN
This present pleaseth more than all the rest.
And were their garments turned from black to white,
I should have deemed them Juno's goodly swans,
Or Venus' milk-white doves, so mild they are,
And so adorned with beauty's miracle.
Here, Brusor, this kind turtle shall be thine:
Take her and use her at thy pleasure.
But this kind turtle is for Soliman,
That her captivity may turn to bliss.
Fair locks resembling Phoebus' radiant beams,
Smooth forehead like the table of high Jove,
Small pencilled eyebrows like to glorious rainbows,
Quick lamp-like eyes, like heaven's two brightest orbs,
Lips of pure coral breathing ambrosy,
Cheeks where the rose and lily are in combat,
Neck whiter than the snowy Apennines,
Breasts like two overflowing fountains,
'Twixt which a vale leads to the Elysian shades,
Where under covert lies the fount of pleasure,
Which thoughts may guess, but tongue must not prophane.
A sweeter creature nature never made;
Love neuer tainted Soliman till now.
Now, fair virgin, let me hear thee speak.

PERSEDA
What can my tongue utter but grief and death?

SOLIMAN
The sound is honey, but the sense is gall.
Then, sweeting, bless me with a cheerful look.

PERSEDA
How can mine eyes dart forth a pleasant look,
When they are stopped with floods of flowing tears?

SOLIMAN
If tongue with grief and eyes with tears be filled,
Say, virgin, how doth thy heart admit

The pure affection of great Soliman?

PERSEDA
My thoughts are like pillars of adamant,
Too hard to take a new impression.

SOLIMAN
[*aside*] Nay then, I see my stooping makes her proud;
She is my vassal, and I will command.
– Coy virgin, knowst thou what offence it is
To thwart the will and pleasure of a king?
Why, thy life is done, if I but say the word.

PERSEDA
Why, that's the period that my heart desires.

SOLIMAN
And die thou shalt, unless thou change thy mind.

PERSEDA
Nay then, Perseda groweth resolute.
Soliman's thoughts and mine resemble
Lines parallel that never can be joined.

SOLIMAN
Then kneel thou down,
And at my hands receive the stroke of death,
Doomed to thyself by thine own wilfulness!

PERSEDA
Strike, strike, thy words pierce deeper than thy blows.

SOLIMAN
Brusor, hide her, for her looks withhold me.

Then Brusor hides her with a lawn.

O Brusor, thou hast not hid her lips,
For there sits Venus with Cupid on her knee,
And all the Graces smiling round about her,
So craving pardon that I cannot strike.

BRUSOR
Her face is covered over quite, my lord.

SOLIMAN
Why, so!
O Brusor, seest thou not her milk-white neck,
That alabaster tower?

'Twill break the edge of my keen scimitar,
And pieces flying back will wound myself.

BRUSOR
Now she is all covered, my lord.

SOLIMAN
Why now at last she dies.

PERSEDA
O Christ, receive my soul!

SOLIMAN
Hark, Brusor, she calls on Christ.
I will not send her to him,
Her words are music,
The self-same music that in ancient days
Brought Alexander from war to banqueting,
And made him fall from skirmishing to kissing.
No, my dear, Love would not let me kill thee,
Though majesty would turn desire to wrath.
[*Soliman sets down his sword.*]
There lies my sword, humbled at thy feet,
And I myself, that govern many kings,
Entreat a pardon for my rash misdeed.

PERSEDA
Now Soliman wrongs his imperial state.
But if thou love me and have hope to win,
Grant one boon that I shall crave of thee.

SOLIMAN
Whate're it be, Perseda, I grant it thee.

PERSEDA
Then let me live a Christian virgin still,
Unless my state shall alter by my will.

SOLIMAN
My word is past, and I recall my passions.
What should he do with crown and empery,
That cannot govern private fond affections?
Yet give me leave in honest sort to court thee,
To ease, though not to cure, my malady.
Come, sit thee down upon my right hand here,
This seat I keep void for another friend.

Go, Janissaries, call in your governor!
So shall I joy between two captive friends,
And yet myself be captive to them both,
If friendship's yoke were not at liberty.
See where he comes, my other best beloved.

Enter Erastus.

PERSEDA
My sweet and best beloved!

ERASTUS
My sweet and best beloved!

PERSEDA
For thee, my dear Erastus, have I lived.

ERASTUS
And I for thee, or else I had not lived.

SOLIMAN
What words in [this] affection do I see?

ERASTUS
Ah, pardon me great Soliman, for this is she
For whom I mourned more than for all Rhodes,
And from whose absence I derived my sorrow.

PERSEDA
And pardon me, my lord, for this is he
For whom I thwarted Soliman's entreats,
And for whose exile I lamented thus.

ERASTUS
Even from my childhood have I tendered thee,
Witness the heavens of my unfeigned love.

SOLIMAN
[*aside*] By this one accident I well perceive
That heavens and heavenly powers do manage love.
I love them both, I know not which the better.
They love each other best. What then should follow
But that I conquer both by my deserts,
And join their hands whose hearts are knit already.
– Erastus and Perseda, come you hither,
And both give me your hands.
Erastus, none but thou couldst win Perseda;

Perseda, none but thou couldst win Erastus
From great Soliman, so well I love you both.
And now to turn late promises to good effect,
Be thou, Erastus, governor of Rhodes;
By this thou shalt dismiss my garrison.

BRUSOR
[*aside*] Must he reap that for which I took the toil?
Come, Envy, then, and sit in friendship's seat!
How can I love him that enjoys my right?

SOLIMAN
Give me a crown, to crown the bride withal.
Then he crowns Perseda.
Perseda, for my sake wear this crown.
[*aside*] Now is she fairer then she was before.
This title so augments her beauty, as the fire
That lay with honour's hand raked up in ashes,
Revives again to flames; the force is such;
Remove the cause, and then the effect will die.
They must depart, or I shall not be quiet.
– Erastus and Perseda, marvel not,
That all in haste I wish you to depart.
There is an urgent cause, but privy to myself.
Command my shipping for to waft you over.

ERASTUS
My gracious lord, when Erastus doth forget this favour,
Then let him live abandond and forlorn.

PERSEDA
Nor will Perseda slack even in her prayers,
And still solicit God for Soliman,
Whose mind hath proved so good and gracious.

SOLIMAN
Farewell, Erastus; Perseda, farewell too.

Exeunt [*Perseda and Erastus*].

Methinks I should not part with two such friends,
The one so renowned for arms and courtesy,
The other so adorned with grace and modesty.
Yet of the two Perseda moves me most,
Ay, and so moves me, that I now repent
That e'er I gave away my heart's desire.

What was it but abuse of Fortune's gift?
And therefore Fortune now will be revenged.
What was it but abuse of Love's command?
And therefore mighty Love will be revenged.
What was it but abuse of heavens that gave her me?
And therefore angry heavens will be revenged.
Heavens, Love, and Fortune, all three have decree
That I shall love her still, and lack her still,
Like ever-thirsting wretched Tantalus.
Foolish Soliman! Why did I strive
To do him kindness, and undo myself?
Well governed friends do first regard themselves.

BRUSOR
[*aside*] Ay, now occasion serves to stumble him
That thrust his sickle in my harvest corn!
– Pleaseth your majesty to hear Brusor speak?

SOLIMAN
To one past cure, good counsel comes too late.
Yet say thy mind.

BRUSOR
With secret letters woo her, and with gifts.

SOLIMAN
My lines and gifts will but return my shame.

LUCINA
Hear me, my lord, let me go over to Rhodes,
That I may plead in your affection's cause.
One woman may do much to win another.

SOLIMAN
Indeed, Lucina, were her husband from her,
She happily might be won by thy persuades.
But whilst he lives, there is no hope in her.

BRUSOR
Why lives he then to grieve great Soliman?
This only remains, that you consider:
In two extremes the least is to be chosen.
If so your life depend upon her love,
And that her love depends upon his life,
Is it not better that Erastus die
Ten thousand deaths, than Soliman should perish?

SOLIMAN
Ay, sayst thou so? Why then, it shall be so.
But by what means shall poor Erastus die?

BRUSOR
This shall be the means:
I'll fetch him back again,
Under colour of great consequence.
No sooner shall he land upon our shore,
But witnesses shall be ready to accuse him
Of treason done against your mightiness,
And then he shall be doomed by martial law.

SOLIMAN
Oh, fine device! Brusor, get thee gone.
Come thou again, but let the lady stay,
To win Perseda to my will. Meanwhile
Will I prepare the judge and witnesses,
And if this take effect, thou shalt be Viceroy,
And fair Lucina Queen of Tripoli.
Brusor, be gone, for till thou come I languish!

Exeunt Brusor and Lucina.

And now to ease my troubled thoughts at last,
I will go sit among my learned eunuchs,
And hear them play, and see my minions dance;
For till that Brusor bring me my desire,
I may assuage, but never quench love's fire.

Exit.

[4.2]

Enter Basilisco.

BASILISCO
Since the expugnation of the Rhodian isle, methinks a thousand years are overpast, more for the lack of my Perseda's presence than for the loss of Rhodes, that paltry isle, or for my friends that there were murdered. My valour everywhere shall purchase friends, and where a man lives well, there is his country. Alas, the Christians are but very shallow in giving judgement of a man at arms: a man of my desert and excellence! The Turks, whom they account for barbarous, having foreheard of Basilisco's worth, a number underprop me with their shoulders, and in procession

bare me to the church, as I had been a second Mahomet. I, fearing they would adore me for a god, wisely informed them that I was but man, although in time perhaps I might aspire to purchase godhead, as did Hercules; I mean by doing wonders in the world. Amidst their church they bound me to a pillar, and to make trial of my valiancy, they lopped a collop off my tenderest member. But think you Basilisco squitched for that? Even as a cow for tickling in the horn! That done, they set me on a milk white ass, compassing me with goodly ceremonies. That day, methought, I sat in Pompey's chair and viewed the Capitol, and was Rome's greatest glory.

Enter Piston.

PISTON
I would my master had left some other to be his agent here. Faith, I am weary of the office already. What, Signor Tremomundo, that rode a pilgrimage to beg cake-bread!

BASILISCO
Oh, take me not unprovided, let me fetch my weapons.

PISTON
Why, I meant nothing but a *basolus manus.*

BASILISCO
No, didst thou not mean to give me the privy stab?

PISTON
No, by my troth, sir.

BASILISCO
Nay, if thou hadst, I had not feared thee, I. I tell thee, my skin holds out pistol proof.

PISTON
Pistol proof? I'll try if it will hold out pin proof.

Then he pricks him with a pin.

BASILISCO Oh, shoot no more! Great god, I yield to thee!

PISTON
I see his skin is but pistol proof from the girdle upward. What sudden agony was that?

BASILISCO
Why, sawst thou not how Cupid, god of love,
Not daring look me in the martial face,
Came like a coward stealing after me,

And with his pointed dart
Pricked my posteriors?

PISTON
Then hear my opinion concerning that point: the ladies of Rhodes, hearing that you have lost a capital part of your lady ware, have made their petition to Cupid, to plague you above all other, as one prejudicial to their muliebrity. Now sir, Cupid, seeing you already hurt before, thinks it a greater punishment to hurt you behind; therefore I would wish you to have an eye to the back door.

BASILISCO
Sooth, thou sayest, I must be fenced behind? I'll hang my target there.

PISTON
Indeed, that will serve to bear off some blows, when you run away in a fray.

BASILISCO
Sirrah, sirrah, what art thou that thus encroaches upon my familiarity without special admittance?

PISTON
Why do you not know me? I am Erastus' man.

BASILISCO
What, art thou that petty pigmy, that challenged me at Rhodes, whom I refused to combat for his minority? Where is Erastus? I owe him chastisement in Perseda's quarrel.

PISTON
Do not you know that they are all friends, and Erastus married to Perseda, and Erastus made governor of Rhodes, and I left here to be their agent?

BASILISCO
O coelum, O terra, O maria Neptune! Did I turn Turk to follow her so far?

PISTON
The more shame for you.

BASILISCO
And is she linked in liking with my foe?

PISTON
That's because you were out of the way.

BASILISCO
O wicked Turk, for to steal her hence.

PISTON
O wicked turncoat that would have her stay.

BASILISCO
The truth is, I'll be a Turk no more.

PISTON
And I fear thou wilt never prove good Christian.

BASILISCO
I will after, to take revenge.

PISTON
And I'll stay here about my master's business.

BASILISCO
Farewell Constantinople, I will to Rhodes. *Exit.*

PISTON
Farewell, counterfeit fool! God send him good shipping. 'Tis noised about that Brusor is sent to fetch my master back again. I cannot be well till I hear the rest of the news, therefore I'll about it straight.

Exit.

* * * * *

[5. Prologue]

Enter Chorus.

LOVE
Now, Fortune, what hast thou done in this latter act?

FORTUNE
I brought Perseda to the presence
Of Soliman the Turkish emperor,
And gave Lucina into Brusor's hands.

LOVE
And first I stung them with consenting love,
And made great Soliman, sweet beauty's thrall,
Humble himself at fair Perseda's feet,

And made him praise love and captives' beauty.
Again I made him to recall his passions,
And give Perseda to Erastus' hands,
And after make repentance of the deed.

FORTUNE
Meantime I filled Erastus' sails with wind,
And brought him home unto his native land.

DEATH
And I suborned Brusor with envious rage,
To counsel Soliman to slay his friend.
Brusor is sent to fetch him back again:
Mark well what follows, for the history
Proves me chief actor in this tragedy.

Exeunt.

[5.1]

Enter Erastus and Perseda.

ERASTUS
Perseda, these days are our days of joy.
What could I more desire than thee to wife,
And that I have; or than to govern Rhodes,
And that I do, thanks to great Soliman?

PERSEDA
And thanks to gracious heavens, that so
Brought Soliman from worse to better;
For though I never told it thee till now,
His heart was purposed once to do thee wrong.

ERASTUS
Ay, that was before he knew thee to be mine.
But now, Perseda, let's forget old griefs,
And let our studies wholly be employed
To work each other's bliss and heart's delight.

PERSEDA
Our present joys will be so much the greater
When as we call to mind forepassèd griefs.
So sings the mariner upon the shore,
When he hath past the dangerous time of storms.
But if my love will have old griefs forgot,

They shall lie buried in Perseda's breast.

Enter Brusor and Lucina.

ERASTUS
Welcome, lord Brusor.

PERSEDA
And Lucina too.

BRUSOR
Thanks, Lord Governor.

LUCINA
And thanks to you, madam.

ERASTUS
What hasty news brings you so soon to Rhodes,
Although to me you never come too soon?

BRUSOR
So it is my lord, that upon great affairs,
Importuning health and wealth of Soliman,
His highness by me entreateth you,
As ever you respect his future love,
Or have regard unto his courtesy,
To come yourself in person and visit him,
Without enquiry what should be the cause.

ERASTUS
Were there no ships to cross the seas withal,
My arms should frame mine oars to cross the seas,
And should the seas turn tide to force me back,
Desire should frame me wings to fly to him.
I go; Perseda thou must give me leave.

PERSEDA
Though loth, yet Soliman's command prevails.

LUCINA
And sweet Perseda, I will stay with you,
From Brusor my beloved, and I'll want him
Till he bring back Erastus unto you.

ERASTUS
Lord Brusor come, 'tis time that we were gone.

BRUSOR
Perseda, farewell, be not angry
For that I carry thy beloved from thee;
We will return with all speed possible.
And thou, Lucina, use Perseda so,
That for my carrying of Erastus hence,
She curse me not, and so farewell to both.

PERSEDA
Come, Lucina, let's in, my heart is full.

Exeunt.

[5.2]

Enter Soliman, Lord Marshal, the two witnesses, and Janissaries.

SOLIMAN
Lord Marshal, see you handle it cunningly,
And when Erastus comes, our perjured friend,
See he be condemned by martial law.
Here will I stand to see and not be seen.

MARSHAL
Come fellows, see when this matter comes in question, you stagger not; and Janissaries, see that your strangling cords be ready.

SOLIMAN
Ah, that Perseda were not half so fair,
Or that Soliman were not so fond;
Or that Perseda had some other love,
Whose death might save my poor Erastus' life.

Enter Brusor and Erastus.

See where he comes, whom though I dearly love,
Yet must his blood be spilt for my behoof,
Such is the force of marrow-burning love!

MARSHAL
Erastus, Lord Governor of Rhodes, I arrest you in the King's name.

ERASTUS
What thinks Lord Brusor of this strange arrest?
Hast thou entrapped me to this treachery,
Intended, well I wot, without the leave

Or licence of my lord, great Soliman?

BRUSOR
Why then appeal to him, where thou shalt know
And be assured that I betray thee not.

SOLIMAN
[*aside*] Yes, thou and I and all of us betray him.

MARSHAL
No, no, in this case no appeal shall serve.

ERASTUS
Why then, to thee, or unto any else,
I here protest by heavens unto you all
That never was there man more true or just,
Or in his deeds more loyal and upright,
Or more loving, or more innocent
Than I have been to gracious Soliman,
Since first I set my feet on Turkish land.

SOLIMAN
[*aside*] Myself would be his witness if I durst,
But bright Perseda's beauty stops my tongue.

MARSHAL
Why sirs, why face to face express you not the treasons you revealed to Soliman?

FIRST WITNESS
That very day Erastus went from hence, he sent for me into his cabinet, and for that man that is of my profession.

ERASTUS
I never saw them, ay, until this day!

FIRST WITNESS
His cabin door fast shut, he first began to question us of all sorts of fireworks, wherein, when we had fully resolved him what might be done, he, spreading on the board a huge heap of our imperial coin: 'All this is yours,' quoth he, 'if you consent to leave great Soliman and serve in Rhodes.'

MARSHAL
Why, that was treason. But onwards with the rest.

Enter Piston.

PISTON
[*aside*] What have we here? My master before the Marshal?

FIRST WITNESS
We said not aye, nor durst we say him nay, because we were already in his galleys, but seemed content to fly with him to Rhodes. With that he pursed the gold, and gave it us. The rest I dare not speak, it is so bad!

ERASTUS
Heavens, hear you this, and drops not vengeance on them?

SECOND WITNESS
The rest, and worst, will I discourse in brief: 'Will you consent,' quoth he, 'to fire the fleet that lies hard by us here in Bosphoron? For be it spoke in secret here,' quoth he, 'Rhodes must no longer bear the Turkish yoke.' We said the task might easily be performed, but that we lacked such drugs to mix with powder, as were not in his galleys to be got. At this he leapt for joy, swearing and promising that our reward should be redoubled. We came aland, not minding for to return, and as our duty and allegiance bound us, we made all known unto great Soliman. But ere we could summon him aland, his ships were past a kenning from the shore; belike he thought we had bewrayed his treasons.

MARSHAL
That all is true that here you have declared,
Both lay your hands upon the Alcaron.

FIRST WITNESS
Foul death betide me if I swear not true!

SECOND WITNESS
And mischief light on me, if I swear false!

SOLIMAN
[*aside*] Mischief and death shall light upon you both.

MARSHAL Erastus, thou seest what witness hath produced against thee. What answerest thou unto their accusations?

ERASTUS
That these are Sinons and myself, poor Troy!

MARSHAL
Now it resteth. I appoint thy death,

Wherein thou shalt confess I'll favour thee:
For that thou wert beloved of Soliman,
Thou shalt forthwith be bound unto that post
And strangled, as our Turkish order is.

PISTON
[*aside*] Such favour send all Turks, I pray God.

ERASTUS
I see this train was plotted ere I came.
What boots complaining where's no remedy?
Yet give me leave before my life shall end
To moan Perseda, and accuse my friend.

SOLIMAN
[*aside*] O unjust Soliman, O wicked time,
Where filthy lust must murder honest love!

MARSHAL
Dispatch, for our time limited is past.

ERASTUS
Alas, how can he but be short, whose tongue
Is fast tied with galling sorrow?
Farewell, Perseda, no more but that for her;
Inconstant Soliman, no more but that for him;
Unfortunate Erastus, no more but that for me.
Lo, this is all, and thus I leave to speak.

Then they strangle him.

PISTON
[*aside*] Marry sir, this is a fair warning for me to get me gone.

Exit.

SOLIMAN
Oh, save his life, if it be possible!
I will not lose him for my kingdom's worth.
Ah, poor Erastus, art thou dead already?
What bold presumer durst be so resolved
For to bereave Erastus's life from him,
Whose life to me was dearer than mine own?
Wast thou, and thou? Lord Marshal, bring them hither,
And at Erastus' hand let them receive
The stroke of death, whom they have spoiled of life.
What is thy hand too weak? Then mine shall help

To send them down to everlasting night,
To wait upon thee through eternal shade.
Thy soul shall not go mourning hence alone:
Thus die, and thus, for thus you murdered him.

Then he kills the two Janissaries that killed Erastus.

But soft, methinks he is not satisfied.
The breath doth murmur softly from his lips,
And bids me kill those bloody witnesses,
By whose treachery Erastus died.
Lord Marshal, hale them to the tower's top,
And throw them headlong down into the valley.
So let their treasons with their lives have end!

FIRST WITNESS
Yourself procured us!

SECOND WTINESS
Is this our hire?

Then the Marshal bears them to the tower top.

SOLIMAN
Speak not a word, lest in my wrathful fury
I doom you to ten thousand direful torments!
And Brusor, see Erastus be interred
With honour in a kingly sepulchre.
Why, when Lord Marshal? Great Hector's son,
Although his age did plead for innocence,
Was sooner tumbled from the fatal tower
Than are those perjured wicked witnesses!

Then they are both tumbled down.

Why, now Erastus' ghost is satisfied.
Ay, but yet the wicked judge survives
By whom Erastus was condemned to die.
Brusor, as thou lovest me, stab in the Marshal,
Lest he detect us unto the world
By making known our bloody practices,
And then will thou and I hoist sail to Rhodes,
Where thy Lucina and my Perseda lives.

BRUSOR
I will, my lord. Lord Marshal, it is his highness' pleasure that you commend him to Erastus' soul.

Then he kills the Marshal.

SOLIMAN
Here ends my dear Erastus' tragedy,

And now begins my pleasant comedy.
But if Perseda understand these news,
Our scene will prove but tragicomical.

BRUSOR
Fear not, my lord, Lucina plays her part,
And woos apace in Soliman's behalf.

SOLIMAN
Then Brusor come, and with some few men,
Let's sail to Rhodes with all convenient speed.
For till I fold Perseda in mine arms,
My troubled ears are deaf with Love's alarms. *Exeunt.*

[5.3]

Enter Perseda, Lucina, and Basilisco.

PERSEDA
Now, Signor Basilisco, which like you,
The Turkish or our nation best?

BASILISCO
That which your ladyship will have me like.

LUCINA
I am deceived, but you were circumcised?

BASILISCO
Indeed, I was a little cut in the purpose.

PERSEDA
What means made you to steal back to Rhodes?

BASILISCO
The mighty pinken-eyed brand-bearing god,
To whom I am so long true servitor,
When he espied my weeping floods of tears
For your depart, he bade me follow him.
I followed him, he with his firebrand
Parted the seas, and we came o'er dry shod.

LUCINA
A matter not unlikely. But how chance
Your Turkish bonnet is not on your head?

BASILISCO
Because I now am Christian again, and that by

natural means, for as the old canon says very prettily: *Nihil est tam naturali, quod eo modo colligatum est* and so forth. So I became a Turk to follow her; to follow her, am now returned a Christian.

Enter Piston.

PISTON
O lady and mistress, weep and lament and wring your hands, for my master is condemned and executed.

LUCINA
Be patient, sweet Perseda, the fool but jests.

PERSEDA
Ah no! My nightly dreams foretold me this,
Which, foolish woman, fondly I neglected.
But say, what death died my poor Erastus?

PISTON
Nay, God be praised, his death was reasonable: he was but strangled.

PERSEDA
But strangled, ah double death to me.
But say, wherefore was he condemned to die?

PISTON
For nothing but high treason.

PERSEDA
What treason, or by whom was he condemned?

PISTON
Faith two great knights of the post swore upon the Alcaron, that he would have fired the Turk's fleet.

PERSEDA
Was Brusor by?

PISTON
Ay.

PERSEDA
And Soliman?

PISTON
No, but I saw where he stood to hear and see the matter well conveyed.

PERSEDA
Accursed Soliman, prophane Alcaron!
Lucina, came thy husband to this end,
To lead a lamb unto the slaughterhouse?
Hast thou for this, in Soliman's behalf
With cunning words tempted my chastity?
Thou shalt abye for both your treacheries,
It must be so. Basilisco, dost thou love me? Speak!

BASILISCO
Ay, more than I love either life or soul. What, shall I stab the Emperor for thy sake?

PERSEDA
No, but Lucina. If thou lovest me, kill her.

Then Basilisco takes a dagger and feels upon the point of it.

BASILISCO
The point will mar her skin.

PERSEDA
What, darest thou not? Give me the dagger then.
There's a reward for all thy treasons past.

Then Perseda kills Lucina.

BASILISCO
Yet dare I bear her hence, to do thee good.

PERSEDA
No, let her lie, a prey to ravening birds.
Nor shall her death alone suffice for his:
Rhodes now shall be no longer Soliman's.
We'll fortify our walls, and keep the town,
In spite of proud, insulting Soliman.
I know the lecher hopes to have my love,
And first Perseda shall with this hand die,
Then yield to him and live in infamy.

Exeunt [*all but Basilisco*].

BASILISCO
I will ruminate. Death, which the poets feign to be pale and meagre, hath deprived Erastus' trunk from breathing vitality; a brave cavalier, but my approved foeman. Let me see. Where is that Alcides, surnamed Hercules, the only club man of his time? Dead. Where is the eldest son of Priam, that Abraham-coloured Trojan? Dead. Where is the leader of the Myrmidons, that

well-knit Achil? Dead. Where is that furious Ajax, the son of Telamon; or that fraudful squire of Ithaca, yclept Ulysses? Dead. Where is tipsy Alexander, that great cup conqueror; or Pompey, that brave warrior? Dead. I am myself strong, but I confess Death to be stronger; I am valiant, but mortal; I am adorned with Nature's gifts, a giddy goddess, that now giveth and anon taketh. I am wise, but quiddits will not answer Death. To conclude: in a word, to be captious, virtuous, ingenious, or to be nothing when it pleaseth Death to be envious. The Great Turk, whose seat is Constantinople, hath beleaguered Rhodes, whose chieftain is a woman. I could take the rule upon me, but the shrub is safe when the cedar shaketh. I love Perseda as one worthy, but I love Basilisco as one I hold more worthy, my father's son, my mother's solace, my proper self. Faith, he can do little that cannot speak, and he can do less that cannot run away. Then, sith man's life is as a glass, and a fillip may crack it, mine is no more and a bullet may pierce it. Therefore I will play least in sight.

Exit.

[5.4]

Enter Soliman, Brusor, with Janissaries.

SOLIMAN
The gates are shut, which proves that Rhodes revolts,
And that Perseda is not Soliman's.
Ah, Brusor, see where thy Lucina lies,
Butchered despitefully without the walls.

BRUSOR
Unkind Perseda, couldst thou use her so?
And yet we used Perseda little better.

SOLIMAN
Nay, gentle Brusor, stay thy tears a while,
Lest with thy woes thou spoil my comedy,
And all too soon be turned to tragedies.
Go Brusor, bear her to thy private tent,
Where we at leisure will lament her death,
And with our tears bewail her obsequies.
For yet Perseda lives for Soliman.
Drum, sound a parley! Were it not for her,
I would sack the town ere I would sound a parley.

The drum sounds a parley.
Perseda comes upon the walls in man's apparel.

[*Enter*] *Basilisco and Piston upon the walls.*

PERSEDA
At whose entreaty is this parley sounded?

SOLIMAN
At our entreaty. Therefore yield the town.

PERSEDA
Why, what art thou that boldly bids us yield?

SOLIMAN
Great Soliman, lord of all the world.

PERSEDA
Thou art not lord of all: Rhodes is not thine.

SOLIMAN
It was, and shall be, maugre who says no.

PERSEDA
I that say no will never see it thine.

SOLIMAN
Why, what art thou that dares resist my force?

PERSEDA
A gentleman and thy mortal enemy,
And one that dares thee to the single combat.

SOLIMAN
First tell me, doth Perseda live or no?

PERSEDA
She lives to see the wreck of Soliman.

SOLIMAN
Then I'll combat thee what ere thou art.

PERSEDA
And in Erastus' name I'll combat thee,
And here I promise thee on my Christian faith,
That if thy strength shall overmatch my right,
Then will I yield Perseda to thy hands
To use, as to thy liking shall seem best.
But ere I come to enter single fight,

First let my tongue utter my heart's despite.
And thus my tale begins: thou wicked tyrant,
Thou murderer, accursèd homicide,
For whom hell gapes, and all the ugly fiends
Do wait for to receive thee in their jaws!
Ah, perjured and inhuman Soliman,
How could thy heart harbour a wicked thought
Against the spotless life of poor Erastus?
Was he not true? Would thou hadst been as just.
Was he not valiant? Would thou hadst been as virtuous.
Was he not loyal? Would thou hadst been as loving.
Ah, wicked tyrant, in that one man's death
Thou hast betrayed the flower of Christendom.
Died he because his worth obscurèd thine,
In slaughtering him thy virtues are defamed.
Didst thou misdo him, in hope to win Perseda?
Ah, foolish man, therein thou art deceived,
For though she live, yet will she ne'er live thine,
Which to approve, I'll come to combat thee.

SOLIMAN
Injurious foul-mouthed knight! My wrathful arm
Shall chastise and rebuke these injuries.

Then Perseda comes down to Soliman,
[*together with*] *Basilisco and Piston.*

PISTON
Ay, but hear you, are you so foolish to fight with him?

BASILISCO
Ay, sirrah, why not, as long as I stand by?

SOLIMAN
I'll not defend Erastus' innocence,
But die maintaining of Perseda's beauty.

Then they fight, Soliman kills Perseda.

PERSEDA
Ay, now I lay Perseda at thy feet,
But with thy hand first wounded to the death.
Now shall the world report that Soliman
Slew Erastus in hope to win Perseda,
And murdered her for loving of her husband.

SOLIMAN
What, my Perseda, ah what have I done!

Yet kiss me, gentle love, before thou die.

PERSEDA
A kiss I grant thee, though I hate thee deadly.

SOLIMAN
I loved thee dearly and accept thy kiss.
Why didst thou love Erastus more than me,
Or why didst not give Soliman a kiss
Ere this unhappy time? Then hadst thou lived!

BASILISCO
Ah, let me kiss thee too before I die.

Then Soliman kills Basilisco.

SOLIMAN
Nay, die thou shalt for thy presumption,
For kissing her whom I do hold so dear.

PISTON
I will not kiss her, sir, but give me leave to weep over her, for while she lived, she loved me dearly, and I loved her.

SOLIMAN
If thou didst love her, villain, as thou saidst,
Then wait on her thorough eternal night.

Then Soliman kills Piston.

Ah, Perseda, how shall I mourn for thee?
Fair springing rose, ill-plucked before thy time.
Ah, heavens that hitherto have smiled on me,
Why do you unkindly lour on Soliman?
The loss of half my realms, nay crown's decay,
Could not have pricked so near unto my heart
As doth the loss of my Perseda's life.
And with her life, I likewise lose my love,
And with her love my heart's felicity.
Even for Erastus' death, the heavens have plagued me.
Ah no, the heavens did never more accurse me,
Than when they made me butcher of my love.
Yet justly, how can I condemn myself,
When Brusor lives that was the cause of all?
Come Brusor, help to lift her body up.
Is she not fair?

BRUSOR
Even in the hour of death.

SOLIMAN
Was she not constant?

BRUSOR
As firm as are the poles whereon heaven lies.

SOLIMAN
Was she not chaste?

BRUSOR
As is Pandora or Diana's thoughts.

SOLIMAN
Then tell me: his treasons set aside,
What was Erastus in thy opinion?

BRUSOR
Fair spoken, wise, courteous, and liberal;
Kind, even to his foes; gentle and affable;
And all in all, his deeds heroical.

SOLIMAN
Ah, was he so?
How durst thou then, ungracious counsellor,
First cause me murder such a worthy man,
And after tempt so virtuous a woman?
Be this therefore the last that ere thou speak.
Janissaries, take him straight unto the block,
Off with his head, and suffer him not to speak!

Exit Brusor.

And now, Perseda, here I lay me down,
And on thy beauty still contemplate,
Until mine eyes shall surfeit by my gazing.
But stay, let me see: what paper is this?
Then he takes up a paper, and reads in it as followeth.
'Tyrant, my lips were sauced with deadly poison,
To plague thy heart that is so full of poison.'
What, am I poisoned? Then Janissaries,
Let me see Rhodes recovered ere I die.
Soldiers, assault the town on every side.
Spoil all, kill all! Let none escape your fury!
Sound an alarum to the fight.

[*Enter Captain and Janissaries*].

Say Captain, is Rhodes recovered again?

CAPTAIN
It is, my lord, and stoops to Soliman.

SOLIMAN
Yet that allays the fury of my pain
Before I die, for doubtless die I must,
Ay fates, injurious fates, have so decreed.
For now I feel the poison 'gins to work,
And I am weak even to the very death.
Yet something more contentedly I die,
For that my death was wrought by her device,
Who living was my joy, whose death my woe.
Ah, Janissaries, now dies your emperor,
Before his age hath seen his mellowed years,
And if you ever loved your emperor,
Affright me not with sorrows and laments,
And when my soul from body shall depart,
Trouble me not but let me pass in peace
And in your silence let your love be shown.
My last request, for I command no more,
Is that my body with Perseda's be
Interred, where my Erastus lies entombed,
And let one epitaph contain us all.
Ah, now I feel the paper told me true:
The poison is dispersed through every vein,
And boils like Etna in my frying guts.
Forgive me, dear Erastus, my unkindness;
I have revenged thy death with many deaths.
And, sweet Perseda, fly not Soliman,
Whenas my gliding ghost shall follow thee,
With eager mood, through eternal night.
And now pale Death sits on my panting soul,
And with revenging ire doth tyrannise.
And says for Soliman's too much amiss,
This day shall be the period of my bliss.
Then Soliman dies, and they carry him forth with silence.

Exeunt.

[5. Epilogue]

Enter Chorus.

FORTUNE
I gave Erastus woe and misery,
Amidst his greatest joy and jollity.

LOVE
But I that have power in earth and heaven above,
Stung them both with never failing love.

DEATH
But I bereft them both of love and life.

LOVE
Of life, but not of love, for even in death
Their souls are knit, though bodies be disjoined.
Thou didst but wound their flesh, their minds are free,
Their bodies buried, yet they honour me.

DEATH
Hence, foolish Fortune, and thou, wanton Love!
Your deeds are trifles, mine of consequence.

FORTUNE
I give world's happiness and woes increase.

LOVE
By joining persons, I increase the world.

DEATH
By wastening all, I conquer all the world.
And now to end our difference at last:
In this last act, note but the deeds of death.
Where is Erastus now, but in my triumph?
Where are the murderers, but in my triumph?
Where's judge and witness, but in my triumph?
Where's false Lucina, but in my triumph?
Where's fair Perseda, but in my triumph?
Where's Basilisco, but in my triumph?
Where's faithful Piston, but in my triumph?
Where's valiant Brusor, but in my triumph?
And where's great Soliman, but in my triumph?
Their loves and fortunes ended with their lives
And they must wait upon the car of death.
Pack, Love and Fortune, play in comedies,

For powerful Death best fitteth tragedies!

LOVE
I go, yet Love shall never yield to Death.

Exit.

DEATH
But Fortune shall, for when I waste the world,
Then time's and kingdom's fortunes shall decay.

FORTUNE
Meantime will Fortune govern as she may.

Exit.

DEATH
Ay, now will Death in his most haughty pride,
Fetch his imperial car from deepest hell,
And ride in triumph through the wicked world,
Sparing none but sacred Cynthia's friend,
Whom Death did fear before her life began.
For holy fates have graven it in their tables,
That Death shall die if he attempt her end,
Whose life is heaven's delight and Cynthia's friend.

FINIS.

TEXTUAL NOTES

Act 1

1.Prologue] this edition; *Actus primus* Q1

1.1.15 holy days] NIAYESH; *hollidaies* Q1

1.1.30 Ay … vantages] NIAYESH; *I watch you vauntages* Q1; *I watch you vantages* Q2

1.1.59 big-boned] NIAYESH; bigbound Q1; bigbon'd Q2

1.1.60 Archers, hardy men] Q2; *Arthers hardy men* Q1

1.1.84 thy features serve] Q2; *thy features serues* Q1

1.1.87–95 I … staves] set as prose this edition; set as verse Q1

1.2.70–110 Why … condition] set as prose this edition; set as verse (aside from 73–5 and 100–2 set as prose) Q1

1.2.120 It is] Q2; *It it* Q1

1.3.1–7 I … excrement] set as prose this edition; set as verse Q1

1.3.9–97 Peace … me] set as prose this edition; largely set as verse Q1

1.3.69SD *Sound … course*] this edition; placed between 70–1 Q1

1.4.16–17 That's … wonderful] set as prose this edition; set as verse Q1

1.5.5–63 Page … chain] set as prose this edition; largely set as verse Q1

1.5.29 crying of it] Q2; *crying it* Q1

1.5.61 you] Q2; *ye* Q1

1.6.78 guide] NIAYESH; *guides* Q1

Act 2

2.Prologue] this edition; not in Q1

2.1.3 sympathy] Q2; *siuipathy* Q1

2.1.8 Fernando] Q1; *Ferdinando* Q2

2.1.82 weakling] Q2; *weakoning* Q1

2.1.160 wrack] NIAYESH; *wrackt* Q1

2.1.188–93 Here … sir] set as prose this edition; set as verse Q1

2.1.212–28 Why … so] set as prose this edition; largely set as verse Q1

2.1.224 play] BOAS; *pray* Q1

2.1.283–94 Now … *videtur*] set as prose this edition; set as verse Q1

2.1.293 good luck's sake] NIAYESH; *good luck sake* Q1

2.1.307–25 Faith … again] set as prose this edition; set as verse Q1

2.1.321 withal] Q2; *wiihall* Q1

2.2.1–7 God … Piston] set as prose this edition; set as verse Q1

2.2.10–11 Faith … here] set as prose this edition; set as verse Q1
2.2.15–19 After … prickado] set as prose this edition; set as verse Q1
2.2.21–4 To … credulous] set as prose this edition; set as verse Q1
2.2.9 off] NIAYESH; *of* Q1
2.2.29 malign] BOAS; *maling* Q1
2.2.46–82 My … fight] set as prose this edition; set as verse Q1
2.2.64 a bout] BOAS; *about* Q1
2.2.67–8 line removed] Q2; *That, for retaining one so virtuous* Q1. See note.

Act 3

3.Prologue] this edition; not in Q1
3.1.3–4 Perhaps … ghosts] Q2; lines reversed in Q1
3.1.4 ghosts] NIAYESH; *ghost* Q1; *ghoast* Q2
3.1.34 That … virtuous] Q2; line not in Q1 but appears earlier in error between 2.2.67–8. See note.
3.1.66 desert] Q2; *deserts* Q1
3.1.88 talons] NIAYESH; *talents* Q1
3.1.92 presence] NIAYESH; *presents* Q1
3.1.104 one] NIAYESH; *owne* Q1
3.1.155–6 Cold … once] set as prose this edition; set as verse Q1
3.2.2 Unfortunate] Q2; *unforrunate* Q1
3.3.5 strand] BOAS; *strane* Q1
3.4.28–30 Think … no!] this edition; *Thinke you I turne Turque, | For feare of seruile death thats but a sport, | I saith sir no* Q1

Act 4

4.Prologue] this edition; not in Q1
4.Prol.8 Rhodian] BOAS; *Herodian* Q1
4.Prol.10 tongue] BOAS; *tougue* Q1, *tongne* Q2
4.1.1–5 Faith … salad] set as prose this edition; mostly set as verse Q1
4.1.75 locks] BOAS; *looks* Q1
4.1.98 a new] NIAYESH; *an new* Q1
4.1.108 Lines parallel] BOAS; *Liues paralise* Q1
4.1.110 at] Q2; *ar* Q1
4.1.190 Revives] BOAS; *reuies* Q1
4.2.1–31 Since … that] set as prose this edition; set as verse Q1
4.2.38–73 Then … straight] set as prose this edition; mostly set as verse Q1

Act 5

5.Prologue] this edition; not in Q1
5.2.5–7 Come … ready] set as prose this edition; set as verse Q1
5.2.14 marrow-burning] BOAS; morrow burning Q1
5.2.15–16 Erastus … name] set as prose this edition; set as verse Q1

5.2.34–8 Why … profession] set as prose this edition; mostly set as verse Q1
5.2.36SH First Witness] this edition; *Witnesses* Q1
5.2.40SH First Witness] this edition; *Witnesse* Q1; *Witnesses* Q2
5.2.40–50 His … bad] set as prose this edition; set as verse Q1
5.2.47SH First Witness] this edition; *Witn.* Q1; *Wit.* Q2
5.2.52SH Second Witness] this edition; *The other wit.* Q1
5.2.52–63 The … treasons] set as prose this edition; set as verse Q1
5.2.62 aland] BOAS; *a land* Q1
5.2.69–70 Erastus … accusations?] set as prose this edition; set as verse Q1
5.2.143 deaf] This edition; *deft* Q1; *deafed* NIAYESH; *deft* BOAS
5.3.5 purpose] NIAYESH; *porpose* Q1
5.3.7 pinken-eyed] NIAYESH; *pinckanied* Q1; *pinckanyed* Q2
5.3.15–21 Because … executed] set as prose this edition; set as verse Q1
5.3.26–7 Nay … strangled] set as prose this edition; set as verse Q1
5.3.32–8 Faith … conveyed] set as prose this edition; set as verse Q1
5.3.46–7 Ay … sake] set as prose this edition; set as verse Q1
5.3.47 Emperor] Q2; *Emperout* Q1
5.3.61–84 I … sight] set as prose this edition; set as verse Q1
5.3.67 Achil] NIAYESH; *Accill* Q1
5.3.72 gifts] Q2; *gifs* Q1
5.4.31–2 That … hands] NIAYESH; lines reversed in Q1
5.4.52 ne'er] *nere* Q2; *neare* Q1
5.4.59 die] BOAS; *thee* Q1
5.4.59 maintaining] Q2; *maintianing* Q1
5.4.75–7 I … her] set as prose this edition; set as verse Q1
5.4.91 Than] NIAYESH; *Then* Q1
5.4.117 sauced] NIAYESH; *sawst* Q1
5.4.148 death] BOAS; *deaths* Q1
5.Epilogue] this edition; not in Q1

COMMENTARY

NOTES ON PERSONS

Love, Fortune, Death the choral and allegorical function of these characters links them to the role of Revenge in *The Spanish Tragedy*; they do not interact directly with any of the characters in the play. Lukas Erne suggests that they may have been inspired by a similar chorus in an earlier play, the anonymous *Rare Triumphs of Love and Fortune* (c. 1582).

Philippo as Christian Governor of Rhodes he represents the role of Grand Master of the Knights of St John, a Roman Catholic military order which occupied the island between 1309 and 1522 (although not mentioned directly in the play). Philippo is presumably loosely based on the figure of Phillipe Villiers de L'Isle-Adam (1464–1534), Grand Master of the order during the six-month siege and defeat to the Ottomans that led to their withdrawal from the island, fictionalized in this play.

Prince of Cyprus remains unnamed throughout and the tournament with which the play begins celebrates his marriage to Cornelia, Philippo's daughter. Lucius Sergius Paulus, a 'Prince of Cyprus', was converted to Christianity by St Paul (Acts 13:6–12), but later princes of the island were also renowned for their resistance of Ottoman expansion into the Mediterranean (see Renniger, *A treatise* (1587), sig. D5r). The most immediate association for Kyd's audience would have been the fate of the final Christian governor, Marco Antonio Bragadin, described in English accounts as the 'Prince of Cyprus' who was mutilated and skinned alive upon the Ottoman conquest of the island in 1571 (see Anon., *An oration militarie* (1588), sig. B1r).

Erastus described as less than twenty and beardless, Erastus later becomes Captain of the Ottoman Janissaries and Governor of Rhodes. His most celebrated precursor is probably the steward or treasurer of Corinth mentioned as a Christian follower of St Paul in Acts 19:22, Romans 16:23 and 2 Timothy 4:20.

Perseda characterized in *The Spanish Tragedy* as 'an Italian dame. | Whose beauty ravished all that her beheld' (5.1.108–9) and as 'chaste and resolute' (5.1.134), her name is not common in the period.

Ferdinando a knight, described as an ally and kinsman of Philippo. Depending on the requirements of the verse, his name also appears in the play as Ferdinand and Fernando. For English audiences that name was most readily associated with the Holy Roman Emperor Ferdinand I (regularly spelled 'Ferdinando' in English accounts; 1503–64), known for his conflicts with the Ottomans. See for instance Curione, *A notable Historie of the Saracens* (1575).

Lucina a name etymologically connected to light and perhaps chosen for its mythical associations with the Roman goddess of childbirth, whose name was also linked to Diana and Juno and hence to the Moon. In 1581 John Maplet wrote of how Luna 'is with the Poets called *Lucina* the Governour or Goddesse of the nyghte' (*The diall of destiny*, 6v).

Piston (also Pystan) a name which does not gain the modern sense of the word until the eighteenth century. Its proximity to postern, meaning both the backdoor and the backside (*OED n.* and *adj.*), is perhaps a useful context.

Guelpio a highly unusual Italianate name of which I can identify no earlier examples in English writing.

Julio a very common Italianate name of the period.

Basilisco a German knight and a figure of bombast (he is also jestingly called Bragardo and Signor Tremomundo). Kyd's choice of name is particularly appropriate, for although a basilisco carried associations with the mythical basilisk, the 'king of serpents' (*Batman upon Batholome* (1582, 350v)), it was most immediately recognized as a 'great gunne'; a cannon of considerable scale and volume (Anon., *All the famous battels* (1578), 192).

Englishman; Frenchman; Spaniard all unnamed knights associated with their respective nations' patron saints or knightly orders. The inclusion of a Spanish knight has led to the suggestion that the play must be pre-Armada, but as Niayesh points out, the Spanish knight enters after both the English and French knights, and his feat of arms 'is much less impressive than the others' achievements' (28).

Brusor a prominent Ottoman military leader, who has been sent to the opening tournament to spy on the fortifications of Rhodes. A name with no Turkish provenance, it may be related to *brusere*, an uncommon Latin term for burning or scorching. A later epigram by Thomas Freeman describes a Brusor who has 'growne to be a man of wealth / Onely by knavery, cozenage, and stealth' (*Rubbe, and a great cast* (1614), sig. H4v).

Soliman (also Solyman) based on the historical Suleiman 'the Magnificent' (1496–1566; reigned 1520–66), tenth Ottoman sultan and the most widely known of all the 'Grand Turks' that appeared on early modern English stages and in printed texts in the later sixteenth century. It was early in his rule that Suleiman commanded the attack on Rhodes that forms the subject of the play.

Haleb an Ottoman prince but a name with no relevant Turkish provenance. It has been speculated by Freeman that it is connected to the figure of Hali Bassa in Greene's near-contemporary play *Selimus*, but it appears most often in English writing as an alternative name for Aleppo ('*Heleb, Halep*, is that famous city or marttowne, which we commonly call *Hallepo*, or Allepo', Bedwell, *Mohammedis imposturæ* (1615), sig. M3v). If this is the source, it may have been suggested to Kyd because 'Halep' was identified as the location where Suleiman 'commanded his eldest son Mustapha to bee put to death' (Carr, *Mahumetane or Turkish Historie* (1600), 45v).

Amurath an Anglicized version of the Ottoman name Murad, and widely known in England because of the reign of Sultan Murad III (1546–95; reigned 1574–95), contemporary to Kyd's play. As a result, Amurath (or Amurack) appears in a number of contemporary 'Turk plays', including Greene's *Alphonsus, King of Aragon* (c. 1587).

Lord Marshal or Earl Marshal was not an Ottoman office but a Christian European one, which in England entailed jurisdiction over the Court of Chivalry; the Ottoman near-equivalent would be the *Kazasker*, although Kyd may have intended to represent the better-known role of Grand Vizier. When this play was performed, the English Earl Marshal was George Talbot, 6th Earl of Shrewsbury, who held the office until his death in 1590.

NOTES ON THE PLAY

Act 1, Prologue

0 Setting: the heavens (perhaps in the gallery space looking down on the action).

5 Melpomene Greek Muse of Tragedy, often depicted holding a tragic mask.

10–11 A … quill likely a reference to Kyd's print source, which appears in Wotton's 1578 translation of Yver's *A Courtlie Controuersie*, as Boas notes.

11 husky humour melancholic; in Hippocratic theory a dry (husky), cold humour was associated with black bile and generated melancholy.

12 for tables to make a lasting record: cf. 2 Corinthians 3:3.

17 To … tragedy Boas notes the similarity to 'And serve for Chorus in this tragedy' from *Sp. T.* 1.1.91.

26 everlasting night the Greek underworld, a place of darkness. Boas notes that the same phrase appears in *AF* 5.9 and 'eternal night' in *Sp. T.* 2.2.57.

28 sable dart black spear, one of Death's key accoutrements: the 'inevitable Dart of Death' is referenced twice in *Corn.* (2.237 and 2.281).

34 my wheel Fortune is regularly depicted in the medieval and early modern period turning a wheel as a symbol of the mutability of fortune. See Tilley, F617.

35 demonstration establishing the truth of a proposition; in logic, an argument or sequence of propositions showing that a conclusion is a necessary consequence of previously accepted statements (*OED n.* 1).

36 interest share or entitlement.

1.1

0 Setting: the Isle of Rhodes.

2-3 But … would Boas suggests that a more elaborate version of the same simile appears in *Corn.* 1.79–87.

6 pastime play.

7 over-eyed observed; watched over.

8 sampler beginner's exercise in embroidery (*OED n.* 3b).

9 feres companions.

10 marking observing.

13 framed … ditty created a (love) song.

14 figuring poetically representing.

23 nice shy; coy (*OED adj.* 6a); **wont** are accustomed to be.

24 fancy love.

30 watch … vantages? do you look for opportunities?

32 carcanet ornamental necklace, often gold and given as tokens of love; see Henry Chettle's *Piers Plainnes seauen yeres prentiship* (1595), sig. D3v.

33 grandam grandmother.

36 Should … dwell Boas finds the same metaphor elaborated in *Sp. T.* 2.2.7–9.

37 elect choose to take.

40 to boot as well.

43 naked savages nakedness amongst indigenous people was considered a sure sign of savagery; amongst those of the equatorial Americas (as is probably implied here) as with the Irish. For a near-contemporary reference to the 'sauage people, which goe all naked' in the West Indies from Walter Raleigh's voyage, see Bigges, *A summarie and true discourse* (1589), 20.

48 waterpits wells or storage pools.

53 Tripolis capital of present-day Libya, the strategically crucial port of Tripoli had been in the possession of the Knights of St John between 1530 and 1551 after the Ottomans had expelled them from Rhodes. Philip II, King of Spain, attempted unsuccessfully to reclaim it from the Ottoman corsair Dragut Reis in 1560 and was comprehensively defeated at the Battle of Djerba.

54 Knight … Malta having resisted the famous Ottoman siege of 1565, the Knights of St John, by that point based on Malta, became celebrated across Christendom for their valour, epitomized in the figure of their Grand Master, Jean Parisot de Valette.

55 golden spur order of papal knighthood (referring to the Knights of Malta).

56 hot … horse North African horses were highly prized in this period. Thomas Blundeville notes that 'those horses which we commonly call Barbarians' are mostly 'little horses, but therewith verye swifte and able to make a verye long Cariere, which is the cause why we esteme theym so much' (*The fower chiefyst offices belongyng to horsemanshippe* (1566), sig. 7r–7v). As noted by Niayesh, the same phrase appears in Peele's *The Battle of Alcazar* 5.1.239.

58 impress distinctive characteristics of (*OED n.* 1 2a.) but also carries connotations of blazon or emblem (*OED n.* 3).

59 sudden swift and sharp; but also hasty and impetuous.

61 Yclept called.

67 gnat … bees gnats were proverbially worthless (Tilley, G149) whilst bees were associated with industriousness and thick swarms (Tilley, B210). Erastus is being depreciating.

69 glass mirror.

75 slips plants; **graft** planted (*OED v.* 1 4.).

76 entered admitted to school.

78 graven engraved; carved.

80 prick drive; impel; **bane** death.

81 Better … overta'en rather remain static than rise and be caught. Niayesh suggests a connection with Tilley, S493: 'He sits not sure that sits too high.'

88 consort accompany.

91 outlandish foreign; alien.

94 staves staffs or quarterstaffs; long wooden poles used as weapons.

96 hap fortune; luck.

98 period time or phase.

99–100 Andromache … Greeks in fact, Andromache unsuccessfully attempted to dissuade the Trojan Hector from fighting the Greeks in Homer's *Iliad* (6.433–9).

101 maiden wars first battle.

1.2

0 Setting: the Rhodian tilts.

3 brass-leaved with pages made of brass; this book of eternal memory was a classical commonplace.

4 never-wasting never-decaying; eternal.

9 several separate.

15 onset approach.

17 Scotland the most recent Anglo-Scottish conflict had taken place in the final years of the reign of Henry VIII and culminated in an English victory at the Battle of Solway Moss, in November 1542.

19 France although English troops were engaged in the French wars of religion in the 1560s, the last victorious English campaign in France had been Henry VIII's siege of Boulogne in 1544; **standard** flag or figure that was the distinctive sign of a monarch (commander, city, or nation) displayed in battle (*OED n.* A.I.1.a).

20 give display (*OED v.* 24); **flower ... Gallia** the royal lily of France.

21 light-foot swift.

22 skenes knives or daggers, 'one of the chief weapons of the Irish kerns' (*OED n.* 1).

24 Saint George patron saint of England, adopted by Edward III in 1348. Fourth-century CE Coptic and Ethiopian accounts suggest origins in Cappadocia, and he has been widely adopted as an emblem of righteous iconoclasm in Christian as well as Islamic contexts: see Jerry Brotton, 'St George between East and West' pp. 50-65 in Gerald MacLean ed., *Re-Orienting the Renaissance: Cultural Exchanges with the East* (Basingstoke: Palgrave Macmillan, 2005), 54–6.

28 mot motto.

29 Italy the French campaigned in Italy throughout the first half of the sixteenth century as Francois I sparred with the Holy Roman Emperor Charles V over competing territorial claims.

30 shirt undergarment; without armour and unprepared to fight; **single rapier** one light sword.

34 Saint Denis patron saint of France, Denis was a martyred third-century CE bishop of Paris.

41 What time at which time (*OED pron* I.a.); **rutter** a cavalry soldier, often a German mercenary (*OED n.* 1).

42 change ... shot compete a shot from a gun against a Spanish arrow: presumably the archer won because his reloading was faster.

43 single ... level one sighting opportunity.

45 Golden Fleece the highest chivalric order in the Habsburg Spanish empire in the late sixteenth century, established by Philip III, Duke of Burgundy, in 1430.

46 Jaques Saint James (Iago), patron saint of Spain and one of the twelve apostles, whose remains are traditionally understood to be housed in the Cathedral of Santiago de Compostela.

48 lay religion.

49 brave bravado; challenge (*OED n.* 2).

50 word ... charge battle motto.

51 Sophy ruler of Persia; in the late sixteenth century this was Shah Abbas I 'the Great' (reigned 1587–1629), who was depicted on the English stage in Day, Rowley, and Wilkins' *The Travels of the Three English Brothers* (1607). Compare the Prince of Morocco's similar speech in *The Merchant of Venice* 2.2.24–6. The specific meaning of Sophy in an English context is further explored in Jane Grogan, *The Persian Empire in English Renaissance Writing*, 1549–1622 (Basingstoke: Palgrave Macmillan, 2014), 26–7; **pitched** planned; organized (*OED adj.* 2.2). The same meaning is conveyed by 'set' at l. 57.

55–6 Afric ... fought likely a reference to the three pivotal battles (Marj Dabiq, Yaunis Khan, and Ridanieh) won by Ottoman sultan Selim I in his victorious campaign against the Mamluks in 1516–18. Subsequent Ottoman campaigns in Africa were largely naval-based.

57–9 Marched ... Spain an oddly compressed reference that led Boas to assume that the text is corrupt here. It may, as Niayesh contends, refer to Portuguese colonial possessions on the Gold Coast of modern-day Ghana; alternatively, its Asian frame of reference may be intended to signal Ottoman-Portuguese conflicts in the Red and Arabian Seas in the first half of the sixteenth century, with the 'verge of gold' referencing Spanish colonial possession of the Philippines: the Peninsular of Malaysia was after all referred to as 'the Golden Chersonese [peninsular]' by the Portuguese and Spanish in this period (see Fernando Cervantes, *Conquistadores: A New History* (London, 2020), p. 51).

61 Mahomet the common Christian misrepresentation of the Prophet Muhammad.

63 Solyman an alternative spelling of Soliman.

69 oratrix female orator.

71 instance a case adduced in objection to a universal assertion (*OED n.* 3.5.), another example of Basilisco's pompous invocation of scholastic logic.

71 Pardie 'par Dieu' in French; by God.

73–5 Quoth ... epitheton Basilisco is speaking in a parody of educated, legal language: quoth is say or speak; epitheton is Greek for epithet.

74 approved proven.

76 proved demonstrated.

78–9 Sooth ... fowl as noted by Peyré and Niayesh, a quotation from Ovid's *Fasti*, 'Omne solum forti patria est, ut piscibus aequor, | Ut volucri vacuo quicquid in orbe patet' ('The whole universe is a homeland to the brave, as water is to fish, or air to birds': 1.494–5).

79 red-gilled fish a reference that may precede *OED*'s presumed original, from Marlowe and Nashe's *Dido* (perhaps written c. 1590): 'A silver stream, | Where thou shalt see the red-gill'd fishes leap' (4.5.10); **table ...**

character tablet to record (with connotations of the stone tablets/tables on which the ten commandments were carved).

83 policy an expedient course of action.

86 Friesland Northern Dutch.

88 kerns light-armed Irish foot-soldier (*OED n.* 1.1a.)

88–9 Titan's ... downfall the rising and setting of the sun.

92 scimitar short sword with a curved blade; **Herculean offspring** child of Hercules, thus inheriting his prodigious strength, endurance, and virility.

95 palfrey standard riding horse.

98 Pity's adamant i.e., hard-hearted (adamant was a proverbially hard rock).

99 Mulciber's workhouse Vulcan's forge; Vulcan/Mulciber was the Roman god of fire and metalworking.

102 waft signal or wave (*OED v.* 2.1.b.).

103 five lances five courses on the jousting field. A fresh lance was needed for each course.

104 gratulate ... prince celebrate this kindly prince.

105 condition state; i.e., choleric.

108 censure judge (*OED v.* 3).

1.3

0 Setting: outside the Rhodian tiltyard.

1 humour ... Venus melancholy was the lover's humour.

3 certes certainly.

4 reflecting bright; reflecting light; **admirable comet** brilliant phenomenon.

7 excrement outgrowth (*OED n.* 2.1a).

9 infant baby, addressed to Erastus (again at l. 70), whom Basilisco also describes as 'child' at ll. 6 and 74.

12 O ... flores! a mangling of a Ciceronian lament characteristic of Basilisco: the original 'O tempora! O mores!' ('O the times! O the customs!') is from *Catiline Orations*, 1.

14 God's fish an oath, likely derived from 'God's flesh' (*OED* 'god' P3.b).

16 sans without (borrowed from French).

18–19 occupation that of a working man. Basilisco takes offence at this slight on his assumed knightly status.

27 SD Piston jumps on Basilisco from behind, knocking him forwards and onto the ground, with Piston on top of him.

28 magnanimous noble; generous. Basilisco is pleading for Piston to stand in front of him.

30–1 Typhon … Ossa another muddled allusion, mingling the Greek myth of the serpent-giant Typhon and his unsuccessful revolt against Zeus (Ovid, *Metamorphosis*, 5.445–7) with that of the twin giants Otus and Ephialtes, who stacked the mountains Pelion and Ossa on top of each other in an attempt to attack Olympus (Homer, *Odyssey*, 11.313–18).

33–4 dudgeon dagger knife with a wooden hilt (*OED n.* 1.2).

41–2 Knight … knight a line, as Boas notes, referenced in Shakespeare's *King John*: 'Knight, knight, good mother, Basilisco-like!' (1.1.244).

43 knave villain.

47 licensed … granted terms associated with royal permission (*OED* 'license' *v.* 3a).

50 enjoy only have the use of.

51 religious scrupulous (*OED n.* 4a.).

53 ladder enabling them to see over the wall of the tiltyard. Presumably the ladder would lead up the back of the stage towards the gallery.

54 fawn show affection.

55 course one charge through the lists by opponents on horseback at each other. The *OED* lists Spenser's usage in the second part of *The Faerie Queene* (1596) as apparently the sole example. The direction that follows indicates that trumpets announce the first joust.

56–7 their … borne their lances were positioned too high in attack, and their horses poorly ridden.

63 in … glorious a reference to the proverb 'The peacock has fair feathers but foul feet' (Tilley, P158); Basilisco is implying that Piston has been dazzled by style over substance.

64 bay reddish-brown.

65 cock … foot a comic composite oath, with 'cock' originally deriving from 'god' (*OED n.* 6 2a.).

67 marble … welkin marbled heavens.

69 extortioner wrester of meaning; contradictor; Basilisco has just completely changed his mind about Erastus's knightly valour.

71 beaver visor.

84 braggingest most bragging.

85–6 jostle … jade meaning that he will bump into his opponent like an ill-tempered, inferior horse, but also with sexual connotations.

86 prate chatter; prattle.

86–7 jet … green strut and waddle like a proverbially pompous goose.

87 physic medicine.

89 carve standard invitation to a male guest; Basilisco takes offence at a task he sees as beneath him.

91 lath wooden sword.

92 civet also known as musk, the substance extracted from the glands of the African civet cat and often used in perfume.
96 curtal horse with a docked or cut tail (*OED n.* A.I.1); **old** much (*OED adj.* a.15).
97 fox ... hole as Boas points out, this was a game played by boys, who hopped on one leg whilst beating each other with pieces of leather.

1.4
0 Setting: the Rhodian tiltyard.
0 SD *Sound* i.e., trumpets.
2 knight unknown Erastus, who had implied his intention to fight in the tournament in disguise to Perseda in 1.1.68 and 74; **demeaned** conducted.
13 coy reticent; modest.
17 arm ... head grow cuckolds' horns; implying Lucina seeks a sexual encounter.
24 favourable conveying favour.
25 youngling youngster.
29 hie go quickly.
30 lavolta a lively Italian dance involving lifts.
32 overborne ... course this line indicates that Ferdinando fought in the tilt (as does 1.4.39–40 below) and may have been the Spanish knight.
34 toward promising.
35 bide ... shock withstand the force.
36 mated defeated.
40 loose unfasten.

1.5
0 Setting: in the city of Rhodes.
5 fiddler's fee a proverbial sum: see Tilley, F204, 'Fiddler's fare, meat, drink, and money' and F205, 'To give one a fiddler's fee.'
9 channel bone or cannel-bone; the collarbone.
11 courser's a substantial battle horse.
13–15 But ... mare further sexual innuendo, with punning on service and the reference to covering – having intercourse with – the Emperor's stallion.
14 nose ... slit the cutting or removal of the nose was a punishment for sexual transgression.
18 colt both a young horse and a lascivious individual.
20 green new; raw.
24 cry proclaim; publicize.

28 crowns probably gold coins, after the medieval French crown, rather than the English silver crown, worth five shillings.

35 hackneyman someone who hires out horses for general use (*OED n.*).

36 horsing potentially both providing a horse to, and having sex with.

39–40 forma pauperis in the name of a pauper, a legal formula justifying lower payment. Piston then follows by suggesting he be considered *sub* or beneath the status of a pauper.

47 considered advanced; given advantageous treatment.

48 lighter less substantial.

50 Oyez the standard crier's call, meaning 'listen and hear ye' deriving from the Middle French 'to hear'.

52 bad bade; instructed.

56 underhand secretly; **privy** private.

60 done worn out.

64 Fortune … Love a reference that draws attention to the personified forces driving the action; Death is also mentioned at ll. 81 and 83.

66 dallying playing.

72 quoth said.

78 ceremonious predisposed to ceremony and formality (*OED adj.* 5.).

85 forced furrows wrinkles.

87 just rightful.

1.6

0 Setting: the Ottoman Turkish court in Istanbul.

5 fenced fortified.

7 holy Alcaron the usual English term for the Qur'an, which had been polemically translated into Latin first in 1143, and then printed by Theodore Bibliander in 1543, thereafter circulating across Christian Europe.

8 Persia the Sunni Ottomans had been engaged in military campaigns against the Shia Persians intermittently through the sixteenth century, in particular the long conflict orchestrated by Suleiman I between 1532 and 1555, but more recently by Murad III between 1578 and 1590, news of which was widely reported in Christian Europe.

9 Russian broils the Ottomans had sought to check Russian expansionist campaigns against the Tatars around Astrakhan in a campaign of 1568–70 but were ultimately unsuccessful.

10 Janissaries the elite soldiers ('new troop') of the Ottoman army and a preoccupation of Christian writers, who lamented their often Christian origins and the *devshirme* (or 'child levy') that supplied them, in which soldiers were recruited from newly conquered provinces. See Daniel Goffman, *The Ottoman Empire and Early Modern Europe* (Cambridge: Cambridge University Press, 2002), 47–50.

12 Bassoes bashaws or pashas; Ottoman military leaders.

16 heart … Christendom control of Rhodes and ultimately of the central Mediterranean was seen as a prelude for an Ottoman attack on Italy, as had happened when Mehmed II took Otranto in 1480–1.

17 scathe harm.

25 Polonia Poland; throughout much of the sixteenth century the Ottomans had negotiated a series of favourable peace treaties with the Jagiellonian kings of Poland. However, this arrangement began to unravel in the early 1590s, a consequence of Polish manoeuvrings during Ottoman campaigns in Hungary in which the English were controversially involved, making this a highly topical reference.

33 retire retreat.

39 mean tolerable (*OED adj.* 2.7c.).

42 countervail reciprocate; counterbalance.

52 striving battling.

58 Aristippus-like Aristippus was a Greek hedonistic philosopher and pupil of Socrates. That he gained a posthumous reputation as an excessive flatterer is demonstrated by his appearance in that role in Richard Edwards's play *Damon and Pythias*, written around 1564.

69 hazard risk.

113 my joys my dead brothers.

Act 2, Prologue

0 Setting: the heavens.

8 humour … compression earth was associated with one of the four Hippocratic humours, black bile, but the usage here suggests a more general material element (*OED n.* 4.).

9 world's … eye the sun.

11 mortal temper human character.

17 sects religions.

20 tickle changeable; inconstant.

30 fond braggardo foolish boaster.

2.1

0 Setting: the streets of Rhodes.

2–3 To … sympathy Boas suggests a parallel with *Sp. T.* 2.2.3–4.

3 semblance similar; the same.

11 Hymen's robes Hymen was the Greek god of marriage.

12 Graces the three Greek Graces symbolized art, beauty, and joy; **Lucina** the Roman goddess of light and childbirth.

13 chaplets wreaths or garlands worn on the head.

18 long ... lights the lighting of Hymen's torches as part of a marriage ceremony; as Niayesh notes, an example of double *antanaclasis* – long/longed, light/lights.
30 cavalier knight, but also increasingly in this period signifying a courtly gallant (*OED n.* A1. and 2a.).
31 fairest shine addressing Lucina.
33 Shame ... queen i.e., Perseda's beauty puts Venus to shame.
43 buckler protect; a buckler was a small round shield.
44 Mars the Roman god of war.
47 mends amends; recompense.
57 glozing flattering or fawning.
62 tralucent translucent (the first recorded use of this spelling in the *OED*). Kyd uses the standard spelling in a similar context in *Sp. T.* 1.4.97: 'In whose translucent breast my heart is lodged.'
63 misdoubtst fear; mistrust.
66 blithe friendly; gentle.
70 swains shepherds/lovers; often a feature of pastoral poetry in this period.
72 stripes lashes (from a whip).
87 unclasp me literally 'unfasten myself', but here meaning make this situation known to others.
88 inward ... grief a reference to the common Renaissance theory that emotional distress needed to be released if a healthy, balanced body was to be maintained.
90 moist ... brain dominant medical theories, based on the Greek Hippocratic corpus, stipulated that women's bodies were troublingly moist when compared to the balance of the male body.
97 Sinon a byword for treachery; Sinon was the captive who encouraged the Greeks to accept the Trojan horse in Book 2 of the *Aeneid.*
101 my ... self Boas finds the same line echoed in *Sp. T.* 2.4.9.
132 spider ... poison a widespread belief that spiders turned the nectar of flowers to poison.
139 blast a decayed bud or blossom (*OED n.* 1.7.).
140 cropped cut off by; eaten by.
156 Sirens monstrous Greek figures who allured sailors onto rocks with their singing, most famously early in the *Odyssey.*
159 Circe's ... seas a muddled recollection of episodes from the *Odyssey* in which Circe's magic – which turned men to swine – is mixed up with the Sirens' enchanting songs. In neither case was Odysseus or any of his crew blindfolded.
163 cockatrice mythical creature, a combination of cockerel and serpent, with a proverbially lethal gaze (see Tilley, C495).
164 passengers passers by.

178 alledgement relief; alleviation.
183 present sudden; immediate.
184 frank gamester liberal gambler.
186 blazon proclaim (*OED v.* 6a.).
191 vizards masks.
192 in mummery in disguise, often in extravagant costume. Mummers' plays were associated with popular festivities and with mime or dumb shows.
200 fly escape; **iron … adamant** adamant or the lodestone was understood to be magnetic, and thus a useful metaphor for amorous attraction. See Shakespeare's *A Midsummer Night's Dream*, 'You draw me, you hard hearted Adamant' (2.1.195).
201 late unkindness i.e., her recent accusations of infidelity and professions of hatred.
206 interest personal stake.
210 change exchange.
214 bear … box carry the money. In contemporary usage, box could refer to both the receptacle – a money box (*OED n.* 2.4a.) – or to the money in such a box (*OED n.* 2.4b.).
215 reply supply. The first recorded use in the *OED*.
219 false dice dice weighted in order to give advantage in games of chance to the owner.
220 Mass a mild oath: 'By the Mass'.
221–2 tall … men 'high men' and 'low men' were dice weighted in order to roll either high numbers or low numbers.
224 Drumsler drummer.
227 Charlemagne the king of hearts in a pack of cards, named after the celebrated eighth-century Frankish king.
229 union a substantial pearl; this is the first of a series of references in early modern English texts to Cleopatra's union, referencing her dissolving and drinking of a pearl, as related by Pliny (9.98).
241 garded suit decorated with livery; a servant's uniform.
243 treacher cheat; deceiver.
244 lewdly wrongly; foolishly.
249 partake share in.
250 guideress conductress, referring to Fortune.
255 cross confront; confound.
264 stay hide-out; a place offering succour.
267 passage sea-crossing.
273 honour's title Erastus's reputation as an honourable man.
287 domineer tyrannize.

289 haltered a pun on alter (change – see Tilley, C111) and halter (noose); if he is caught, Piston is likely to be executed.
292–4 dive … pocket Piston is robbing Ferdinand's corpse.
294 Quit … videtur another misquotation, here of the proverbial Latin phrase 'qui tacet consentire videtur' ('Silence equals consent'). See Tilley, S446.
297 rifles loots; plunders.
304 plaints grievances.
305 sole … sore the only relief for such a wound.
308 passport a warrant or permission to travel; **Saint Nicholas** the devil. Rather than the early Christian bishop, the context suggests (as Niayesh recognizes) a humorous reference to 'Old Nick', or the devil; Piston claims to be checking whether Ferdinando is destined for hell.
309 sot foolish or stupid person; **Sirrah** a term of address to a social inferior.
313 sexton parish church officer with responsibilities for church buildings, bell-ringing, and grave-digging.
319 bondman a man in bondage; a slave or indentured servant; **fain** gladly.
328 lay set watch in.
333 balm embalmment, the preparation of the dead body.

2.2
0 Setting: the streets of Rhodes.
4–7 After … Piston Piston imitates the conventional salutations of an Elizabethan letter.
16 counter-cambio exchange. The first and only recorded usage in the *OED*, from the Italian *contracambio*.
19 prickado sword-stab. Another coinage and sole usage, according to the *OED*, likely to be related to the Italian *passata* (a forward thrust) and the later cognate use of passado in English (which first appears in 1595).
24 credulous willing to believe.
29 malign speak ill; do wrong (*OED v.* 1.a and 2.a).
32 Eolus or Aeolus, Greek god of the winds; **Neptune** Roman god of the sea.
41 For satisfaction in compensation for.
47 armourer's shop a place where weapons and armour are made and repaired.
51 double cannon likely a doubly charged cannon, containing two projectiles to inflict maximum damage.
53 coistrel worthless coward.
55 targe … bullet what is the point of my trusted shield (targe) if not to protect me from bullets; comical, because the size and composition of a targe would offer little protection.

56 once ... by having been discarded or ignored.

59 surquidry arrogance.

64 cuffs bare-knuckle boxing.

67–8 between these lines in Q1 is another line – 'That, for retaining one so virtuous' – which appears at the very top of sig. E2r in the original printed text. It is clearly an error, as the catchwords demonstrate, and should appear at the top of sig. E3r, as it does in Q2, at line 3.1.34 in this edition. An early reader has even added a manicule to the top of sig. E2r in Q1 (the British Library copy) to indicate this error. Both can be argued to make some sense (see for instance Niayesh), but it is clearly an easily explained printer's error.

74 Alcides Hercules.

81–2 crane ... pygmy the apparently longstanding enmity of 'pygmies' (a legendary race of small people often located in Ethiopia) for cranes (large, long-necked birds) was detailed by Pliny (7.51). A *Play of the Pygmies* featuring this conflict may have been performed in London in 1579 – see Wiggins n. 661.

Act 3, Prologue

0 Setting: the heavens.

5 suggested furnished; supplied. The first and only example of this use in the *OED* (*adj.* 1).

19 mar damage or destroy.

3.1

0 Setting: the Ottoman court in Istanbul.

2 obsequies funeral rites.

22 worshipped ... Christ revealing the common Christian misconception that 'Mahomet' – the Prophet Muhammad – was an infernal double of Christ. He in fact claimed no divinity. See Dimmock, *Mythologies*, esp. pp. xi–xiv.

27 habit clothing; **errant knight** a knight who travelled in pursuit of adventure or quest, from the French *chevalier errant*.

34 retaining maintaining in service as a follower (*OED v.* 4a).

50 victual food; supplies.

59 barbarous although there were many different perspectives in circulation, the dominant popular characteristic of the 'terrible Turk' across Christendom was indeed violent barbarity. Compare this brief section to Shylock's celebrated 'Hath not a Jew eyes?' speech in Shakespeare's *The Merchant of Venice* (3.1.58–68).

63 bounty reward; liberality.

67 desert excellence; worthiness.

72 should shall.

76 cross counteract; deflate.

85 air-bred eagles, proverbially the noblest birds, were thought to breed on the wing and to be able to stare into the sun (see Tilley, E3). Kyd reuses the analogy in *KL* 6.45–7.

103 boon requested gift.

108 targets small round shields.

123 behest authority.

137 reft deprived; bereft.

148 in subjection under my authority; to submission. Four syllables.

151 minions … eunuchs a reference to the sensual pleasures of Soliman's harem, in which the minion – routinely gendered male in Marlowe's *Edward II* or *The Massacre at Paris*, for instance – is likely to be female. This is the first description of the harem in the English 'Turk play', signalling a new direction in the portrayal of the Ottomans, a shift away from martial belligerence towards erotic self-indulgence that would dominate later depictions. In near-contemporary writings the harem is most famously described by Thomas Dallam, an English organ-maker who travelled with an English diplomatic mission to Istanbul to deliver a clockwork organ to Sultan Mehmed III in 1599. See Gerald MacLean, *The Rise of Oriental Travel: English Visitors to the Ottoman Empire*, 1580–1720 (Basingstoke: Palgrave Macmillan, 2004), 3–47.

152 at this point in the margin of the BL copy of Q1 an early hand has written 'the dance before Piston enters', suggesting the spectacle of the harem may have been further magnified.

158 and if.

3.2

0 Setting: Rhodes.

1–19 Kyd balances the speeches of Perseda and Lucina, with variations in the structure, like an operatic duet, perhaps with some irony at the similarity of lovers' complaints.

15 stay cease.

28 hates … toad toads were proverbially loathsome (see Tilley, T361).

31 our Basilisco is using the 'royal plural'.

37 twinkling … eye again, proverbial (Tilley, T635).

39 wot know.

42 Phyllis … Demophon Phyllis married Demphon, a noble Athenian warrior, in Thrace as he returned from the Trojan war. He left the day after their wedding, promising to come back, and when he did not (having settled in Cyprus) she killed herself (Ovid, *Heroides*, 2.1).

3.3

0 Setting: upon the walls of Rhodes.

3 past moved beyond the range/reach of (*OED prep.* and *adv.* 3.a); **galleys** oared warships largely crewed by captive slaves that dominated Mediterranean sea-borne and coastal conflicts throughout this period.

5 strand beach; coast. Q1's spelling of 'strane' is likely a compositor's error.

3.4

0 Setting: outside the walls of Rhodes.

1 parley a signal for the two sides to discuss terms.

1 SD *walls* the Prince of Cyprus presumably appears in the gallery space above the stage, as with Perseda's appearance on the walls of Rhodes at 5.4.15.

5 Septentrion north.

7 extremity brutal violence.

9 peremptory resolved.

10 usurps is illegitimate, by implication because of his Islamic faith.

14 breach break (in the defensive walls).

16 yoked subjected. Rhodes fell to the Ottoman forces of Suleiman I in late 1522.

19 scathe destruction.

21 turn Turk convert to Islam. For a discussion of this idea in early modern English drama, see Burton, *Traffic and Turning*, 93–101.

27 circumcised ... rites forcibly converted to Islam through the ritual of circumcision. For further details see the notes to 4.2 below.

29 servile abject but also death in captivity.

33 lives' privilege immunity from death (*OED n.* 2.a).

Act 4, Prologue

0 Setting: the heavens.

4 couched hid; concealed (*OED v.* 1.13).

8 Rhodian Q1 and Q2 both have 'Herodian' here, but Boas's emendation to Rhodian (referring to Erastus) makes better sense.

11 countercheck counteract; also used by Kyd in *Sp. T.* 2.2.37: 'I'll countercheck thy kiss.'

12 despite contemptuous treatment.

20 wink closes her eyes; **Love ... blind** a coyly self-referential allusion to the proverb 'Love is blind' (Tilley, L506).

4.1

0 Setting: the Ottoman court in Istanbul.

2 sugarloaf hat the turban, a key dramatic signifier of Ottoman Turkish identity and of Islam on the stage and later in the play described as a 'Turkish bonnet' (5.3.14). Piston may be identifying it in terms of a conical hat already current in early modern London (*OED* 'sugar-loaf' *n.* 2a) as there was little agreement about what the Ottoman turban was called at this point: in *Sp. T.* it is 'a Turkish cap' (5.1.138) and in the earlier play *John of Bordeaux* it is ridiculed as a pile of 'cloute' or bandages (2.145). Indeed, the term 'turbant' probably first appears in English in the second edition of Richard Hakluyt's collection of travel texts, *The Principal Navigations* (1598–1600), 207. See also Matthew Dimmock, 'Materialising Islam on the Early Modern English Stage' pp. 115–32 in Sabine Schulting, Sabine Lucia Muller and Ralf Hertel eds, *Early Modern Encounters with the Islamic East: Performing Cultures* (Farnham: Ashgate, 2012), 120–30; **gilded gown** the gifted gown, or *hil'at*, was central to the way Ottoman court politics operated, with these luxurious and expensive items bestowed by the sultan and worn as a sign of prestige. See Matthew Dimmock, *Elizabethan Globalism: England, China and the Rainbow Portrait* (London: Yale University Press for the Paul Mellon Centre, 2019), 224–6.

3 sable weed black gown, associated with melancholic sobriety.

5 salad as Murray recognizes, a raw salad was understood to bring on melancholy.

8 gay colourful and ostentatious.

15 viands foodstuffs; **dainty dames** delicate, beautiful women.

18 captivate captured.

23 dumps distractedness; fits of melancholy or depression (*OED n.* 2).

24 fitting befitting.

26 blandishments flattering words.

28 friends ... bodies a common Renaissance conceit, referencing male friendship. See Laurens J. Mills, *"One Soul in Bodies Twain": Friendship in Tudor Literature and Stuart Drama* (Bloomington, IN, 1937).

42 deflowered raped; deprived of her virginity.

54 pillage looting.

55–7 Alexander ... Arius's Arrian reports that Alexander the Great spared the house and family of the poet Pindarus (*Anabasis Alexandri*, 1.9.9–10), and in Dio Cassius's account the Emperor Augustus spared the preceptor Arius in Alexandria (*Roman History*, 51.16). Their connection seems to have been well known, and appears (as noted by Boas) in Wotton's *Cupid's Cautels*: 'Euen as Alexander the greate pardoned Thebes for the loue of Prindarus, and Stagiris for the good will he bare to Aristotle: or as the fortunate Augustus entreated rebellious Alexandria at the request of Arrius' (55).

61 guerdon reward.

62 largesse generous gift of money.

68 Juno's … swans as the Roman goddess of marriage, Juno was associated with swans, which were understood to mate for life, as mentioned in Shakespeare's *As You Like It* 1.3.74.

69 Venus's … doves the dove was the emblem of Venus, the Roman goddess of love, who rode in a chariot pulled by doves.

71 turtle turtledove, often used as an emblem of affection. Here Soliman gives Lucina to Brusor.

75 Phoebus's … beams Phoebus was the Greek god of the sun.

76–85 An example of the blazon, popular in Renaissance love poetry, in which the beloved's physical beauty is itemized from the forehead downwards.

79 ambrosy divine foodstuff of the gods.

80 rose … lily the emblematic colours of an idealized English woman's complexion: red cheeks and white skin.

81 Apennines Italian mountain range.

83 Elysian the paradisiacal space of the blessed in Greek myth.

84 covert concealed.

87 tainted corrupted.

90 gall bitter; a proverbial pairing: see Tilley, H556 and H557.

91 sweeting darling; sweetheart.

93 stopped blocked.

97 adamant legendarily hard rock.

99 stooping self-humbling (*OED v.* 1.2a).

104 period end.

113 withhold restrain (*OED v.* 1a).

113 SD *lawn* a piece of fine linen.

115 Venus … knee Venus, the Roman goddess of love, was the mother of Cupid.

120 alabaster a gypsum-based stone often used for statuary famed for its smoothness and whiteness.

129–31 self-same … kissing Niayesh suggests a reference to the celebrated Theban musician Timotheus, who could supposedly influence Alexander the Great's emotions through his music (although the direction of influence was from feasting to battle, not the other way around [see Dio Chrysostom's *On Kingship*, 1.1–2]).

142 Unless … will i.e., unless I choose to lose my virginity.

146 court woo.

149 void empty.

167 unfeigned sincere; genuine.

168 accident incident.

195 privy … myself known only to me; private.
196 waft carry across water. The *OED* (*v.* 2a) cites Shakespeare's *3 Henry 6*: 'Away with her, and waft her hence to France' (5.7.41).
201 gracious kindness, gentleness; a characteristic associated with true nobility (*OED adj.* 2c). Trisyllabic.
217 Tantalus for his transgressions (stealing from the gods; brutally sacrificing his son) Tantalus was forced to stand in a pool of water that receded when he sought to drink, beneath a tree of fruit that he could not grasp. An emblem of frustrated desire, he is the origin of the verb 'tantalize'.
220 well … themselves thus rejecting the Renaissance ideal of male friendship introduced earlier, at 4.1.28.
222 thrust … corn spoiled or robbed my harvest – Brusor sees an opportunity for revenge on Erastus for taking the governorship of Rhodes which he deemed rightfully his.
232 persuades persuasions.
245 colour … consequence i.e., pretending of a matter of great importance.
261 assuage allay; **love's fire** as at 3.1.152, in the margin of the BL Q1 the same hand has written 'the songe to be sunge before Basilisco enters'.

4.2
0 Setting: Istanbul.
1 expugnation conquest.
7 and … country as noted by Niayesh, this line is quoted by Tilley to illustrate proverb M468, 'A man's country is where he does well.'
7–19 Basilisco's unwittingly comic relation of his circumcision ritual (anticipated by Brusor's earlier remark at 3.4.27) is probably the earliest such description on the English stage. The role of circumcision in Islam was well known and, as in descriptions of Jewish religious practice, was often derided by English writers as an antiquated bodily mark of faith that was superseded by the 'new covenant' of Christian baptism, imagined as a circumcision of the heart. The Islamic rituals are most fully detailed in chapters titled 'The Turkish rites and ceremonies' and 'The maner of the turkishe circumcision' in Hugh Goughe's translation of Bartolomej Georgijevic's celebrated history, *The ofspring of the house of Ottomano* (1553). There was certainly popular curiosity about these religious practices, and following Kyd they would be comically dramatized in a similar fashion by Robert Daborne in his play *A Christian Turn'd Turk* (1612).
9 underprop held upright; supported.
12–13 purchase … Hercules a gift from his father Zeus upon his death, Hercules gained godly status thanks to his deeds in life.

14–15 to … valiancy to test his bravery: Basilisco completely misunderstands what is happening, imagining it as a martial, Herculean test of his masculinity.

15 lopped … member cut a piece of flesh (collop) from his penis.

16 squitched flinched.

17 ass often an accompaniment to Christian dramatic imaginings of Islamic conversion, perhaps as a parodic reference to Christ's entry into Jerusalem; an ass similarly appears in Robert Daborne's later *A Christian Turn'd Turk* (1612), 8.1 SD.

18–19 Pompey's … glory Gnaeus Pompeius Magnus, or Pompey the Great, was a celebrated Roman general and three times Roman consul.

21–2 Tremomundo a comedic version, as Boas suggests, of the Spanish word *tremebundo*, meaning either terrifying or ear-splittingly loud.

22 pilgrimage … cake-bread Piston is ridiculing Basilisco for undertaking a trip to Turkey in the hope of riches and Perseda's love, but gaining nothing but metaphorical crusty bread (cake-bread).

23 unprovided unprepared (*OED adj.* 1).

24 Basolus Manus a comic corruption of the Spanish greeting 'Beso las manos' ('I kiss your hands') which, as Boas notes, appears often in English writing of this period: see Puttenham, *Arte of English Poesie*, 292; Harvey, *Letters*, 136; Munday, *Fidele and Fortunio*, 1.1.50.

25 privy stab a sly stabbing, but also potentially a stab in the private parts.

26 troth truth; faith: a pledge of honesty.

31 girdle belt.

33–7 Cupid … posteriors Basilisco, having internalized his alliance with Venus in 2.1, now imagines that Cupid has shot an arrow into his backside.

39–40 capital … ware prominent part of your penis; again eliding circumcision with castration, as in 4.1.15.

41 muliebrity womanliness. The *OED* records this as the first usage.

44 eye … door an implication that, following his circumcision/castration, Basilisco is vulnerable to sodomy.

53 minority youth.

58 O … Neptune! 'O heaven, O earth, O Neptune's seas!' quoted from Terence, *The Brothers* (l. 790), ed. and tr. John Barsby, Loeb Terence (Cambridge, MA and London, 2001), p. 342.

64 turncoat renegade, referencing his conversion.

67 after pursue (Erastus).

Act 5, Prologue

0 Setting: the heavens.

5 stung shot with love's arrow (*OED v.* 1.1).

6. thrall slave.
17 history i.e., these preceding events; but also, with the following reference to tragedy, a knowing reflection on the generic constitution of the play.

5.1
0 Setting: Rhodes.
39 forepassèd previous; earlier.
15–16 So … storms lines reminiscent, as Boas notes, of a passage from *Sp. T.* 2.2.7–11: 'My heart (sweet friend) is like a ship at sea: | She wishes port, where riding all at ease, | She may repair what stormy times have worn, | And leaning on the shore may sing with joy | That pleasure follows pain, and bliss annoy.'
33 frame become; form.
39 want be without; miss (*OED v.* 4a and 4c).

5.2
0 Setting: outside the Ottoman fortress in Istanbul.
2 perjured oath-breaking; false.
4 Here … seen Soliman conceals himself and remains hidden from all but Piston until after Erastus's execution.
6 stagger waver (*OED v.* 2a).
7 strangling cords strangling was known to be the common mode of execution for the Ottoman elite. In English writing it is particularly associated with the practice of fratricide, as first referenced in Geuffroy's *The order of the greate Turckes court* (1542) when Selim I resolved to 'dyspatch his brethren' by having them strangled 'with a bowe string' (sig. I4r).
13 behoof benefit.
14 marrow-burning both sexually thrilling and essence consuming.
17 strange unnatural.
19 wot know.
37 cabinet Erastus's private room or chamber on the ship, with the implication that something illicit took place.
38 that … profession i.e., the other witness.
41 fireworks explosives for use in war.
42 resolved him explained to him (*OED v.* 17b).
43 imperial coin the silver *akçe* was the standard imperial currency in the Ottoman empire in this period.
46 What … here Piston arrives but remains unseen to the rest. As Boas recognizes, this leads to 'an unusually complicated grouping', with Piston to one side of the stage, Soliman to the other, and Erastus, the Marshal, and the two witnesses in the centre.
53 fire set alight; destroy.

54 Bosphoron Bosphorus, the strategically significant strait that connects the Black Sea to the Marmara Sea and passes through the city of Istanbul/ Constantinople.
57 drugs chemical ingredients (*OED n.* 1 1a).
59 aland ashore.
59–60 minding intending.
62 a kenning sight.
63 bewrayed exposed.
65 Alcaron the Qur'an.
66 betide befall.
67 light … me descend upon me (*OED v.* 1 9b).
71 Sinons … Troy Sinon was identified as the betrayer of Troy: see note to 2.1.97.
76 strangled … is strangling was associated with the execution of Ottoman nobility: see note to 5.2.7. In Wotton, Kyd's source, Erastus is beheaded for his treason.
78 train plan.
79 What … remedy? A similar line appears in Kyd's *Sp. T.*: 'What boots [is the value in] complaint, when there's no remedy?' (1.4.92).
80 moan lament; grieve.
86 galling vexatious.
101 spoiled robbed.
111 hale compel; force. The tower's top was probably represented by the theatre's gallery space above the stage.
115 hire reward.
119 sepulchre tomb.
120 Hector's son Astyanax was cast from the walls of Troy as the city fell, as his mother Andromache had predicted; see *Iliad*, 24.
128 detect reveal.
134–7 tragedy … tragicomical in this, one of several metatheatrical references in the play, Soliman appears to be writing and directing his own drama, in which he intends the happy resolution of a comedy to follow Erastus's necessarily tragic demise but worries that his rejection by Perseda might result in a tragicomedy, a mix of the two. Soliman picks this theme up again at 5.4.8–9.
136 understand learns about.
143 alarms call to arms (*OED n.* B.I.a).

5.3
0 Setting: the Governor's palace in Rhodes.
5 purpose a pun on prepuce (foreskin) highlighted by Q1 and Q2's spelling: 'porpuse'.

7 pinken-eyed … god Cupid; to be 'pinken-eyed' was to have squinting or half-closed eyes and, as Niayesh notes, Cupid was the blind god of love, regularly depicted holding a wedding torch (or 'brand'). See a similar reference to the blindness of Love at 4.Pro.20.

8 servitor devoted lover, reaffirming his claimed link to Cupid (*OED n.* 2b).

12 dry shod without getting our boots wet.

14 Turkish bonnet turban, a key signifier of Ottoman Turkish identity on stage; see note to 4.1.2.

16 canon Church law; the body of ecclesiastical rules laid down by the papacy was known as canon law.

17–18 Nihil … forth 'Nothing is so natural as to be connected in that way', a nonsensical mangling of a legal formula (not an example of canon law), '*Nihil tam naturale est, quam eo genere quidque dissolvere, quo colligatum est*' ('Nothing is so natural as that an obligation should be dissolved by the same principles with which it was contracted').

23 My … this an almost identical line appears in *Sp. T.*: 'my nightly dreams have told me this' (1.3.76).

32 knights … post notorious perjurers who made their living from giving false evidence (*OED n.* 'post'). Thomas Nashe in *Pierce Penilesse* (1592) refers to such an individual as 'a fellow that will sweare you any thing for twelue pence' (sig. B4r).

44 abye pay the price.

49 mar damage.

52 dare … good Basilisco offers to take on the demeaning role of disposing of the corpse.

53 ravening hungry; compare Barabas's fate in Marlowe's *The Jew of Malta*, who is thrown from the city walls 'To be a prey for vultures and wild beasts' (5.1.59).

58 lecher a grossly lascivious man.

61 meagre emaciated; skeletal.

63 approved well-established; **foeman** enemy.

64 Alcides … time in text and image Hercules was regularly depicted wielding a club.

65–6 Priam … Trojan Paris, whose auburn ('Abraham-coloured') hair is often remarked upon, and whose abduction of Helen triggered the events of the Trojan War.

67 Achil Achilles, legendary Greek warrior of the Trojan War and leader of the Myrmidons; **Ajax** another prominent Greek warrior in the Trojan War and cousin of Achilles.

68 yclept named; **Ulysses** Greek king of Ithaca and another prominent protagonist in the Trojan War, his return home from Troy was also the central narrative of Homer's *Odyssey*.

69 tipsy … conqueror Alexander the Great had a (largely posthumous) reputation for excessive drinking, particularly towards the end of his life: see in particular Arrian, *Anabasis of Alexander*, 2.14.
70 Pompey great Roman general and consul: see note to 4.2.18–19.
73 quiddits quibbles, especially in a legal context.
74 captious cunning; subtle.
78 shrub … shaketh a proverb: 'High cedars fall when low shrubs remain' (Tilley, C208).
82 sith since; **glass** mirror; **fillip** a blow or strike (*OED n.* 2).
83 play … sight a likely reference to a popular hide-and-seek-style game. John Lyly refers to Martin Marprelate playing 'least in sight now, yet we hope to see him stride from Aldgate to Ludgate' in *Pappe with an hatchet* (1589), D3r.

5.4
0 Setting: outside the walls of Rhodes.
3 Lucina lies Lucina's body has presumably remained onstage from the previous scene.
4 despitefully cruelly.
10 bear … tent Boas finds a parallel between this line and *Sp. T.* 1.4.35.
15 sack plunder.
15 SD *walls* Perseda, Basilisco, and Piston likely appear on the gallery above the stage.
21 maugre in spite of.
27 wreck ruin; destruction.
35 despite defiance (*OED n.* 2b).
38 hell … fiends compare the infernal end of Faustus in Marlowe's *Doctor Faustus*, who is told that 'the jaws of hell are open to receive thee' (5.2.125).
50 misdo wrong.
59 SD in the Wotton source Perseda is killed by a volley from the muskets of the Ottoman soldiers.
79 thorough throughout.
81 Fair … time see a similar line in Kyd's *Sp. T.* 2.4.108: 'Sweet lovely rose, ill-plucked before thy time.'
83 lour frown.
88 felicity bliss; delight.
98 poles … lies the two points in the celestial sphere around which the heavens were understood to revolve.
100 Pandora the original woman in Greek mythology, as first related by Hesiod in his *Theogony* (560–612) and later developed in Hesiod, *Works*

and Days (953–105); **Diana** Greek and Roman goddess of childbirth and the hunt, associated with virginity and the moon.

107 durst dare.

115 surfeit fill to excess.

143 contain include.

146 Etna long-active volcano on the east coast of Sicily, also referenced by Kyd in *Sp. T.* 4.4.79.

152 panting breathless.

153 ire fury.

154 amiss error; fault; evil deed (*OED* C. *n.*).

155 SD in the Wotton source, Soliman survives the conquest of Rhodes and buries Erastus and Perseda together in a glorious tomb.

5.Epilogue

0 Setting: the heavens.

7 **disjoined** separated.

14 **wastening** devastating.

15 **difference** disagreement.

17 **triumph** victory; traditionally the celebration accorded a victorious Roman commander and their troops as they entered Rome.

27 **car** chariot.

28 **Pack** leave; be dismissed (*OED v.* 11b).

37 **Cynthia's friend** Queen Elizabeth I, who was regularly associated with Cynthia and Diana (as well as a host of other female deities) in the literature and entertainments of her court. Lukas Erne suggests that this reference indicates a likely performance at court (see Introduction).

39 **graven … tables** carved it into their stone tablets (implying an absolute, unchanging truth).

KING LEIR

Edited by Eugene Giddens

INTRODUCTION

It is difficult to imagine *King Leir* outside of the context of Shakespeare's *King Lear*, and for most of their critical history the plays have been inextricably linked.[1] Grace Ioppolo argued recently, and with good reason, that *King Leir* 'has not been properly evaluated on its own merit' owing to the looming presence of Shakespeare's version.[2] Yet the fifteen or so years that separate *Leir* and *Lear* is a very long time in the context of late Elizabethan and early Jacobean drama. Stage conventions underwent radical changes that make for very different plays, not just in terms of language, as one might expect when comparing any play to a work of Shakespeare, but also in terms of genre, characterization, and staging. More importantly, *King Leir*'s qualities can be hidden by too much reference to Shakespeare's better-known adaptation, and therefore this introduction will largely focus on the earlier play itself, including its innovations and potentials for modern interpretation by students, playgoers, and actors, without drowning by Shakespeare.[3]

The play opens upon the death of the queen, with King Leir determined to divide his kingdom amongst his three daughters, as long as they marry as he sees fit. In keeping with contemporary warnings about the miseries of forced marriage, Leir's wise councillor, Perillus, argues against the decision: 'Do not force love where fancy cannot dwell' (1.73), while the scheming courtier, Scaliger, goes off to warn Gonorill and Ragan about Leir's intentions. Perillus will prove Leir's most loyal companion, remaining at his side for the remainder of the play. We meet the elder sisters in the next scene, where they express a profound, seemingly motiveless, hatred for Cordella,

1 Michie goes so far to say that 'After its few performances, the play would probably have faded into obscurity if Shakespeare had not used it as one of the major sources for his tragedy *King Lear*. Shakespeare's indebtness [*sic*] to *The True Chronicle History* and the fame of his *King Lear* have assured the old play a place of importance in literary study' (Donald M. Michie, ed., *A Critical Edition of The true chronicle history of King Leir and his three daughters, Gonorill, Ragan, and Cordella* [New York, 1991], p. 3).

2 Grace Ioppolo, '"A Jointure more or less": Re-measuring "The True Chronicle History of King Leir and his three daughters"', *Medieval and Renaissance Drama in England* 17 (2005): 165–79, here at 165.

3 For Shakespeare's uses of *King Leir*, see Martin Mueller, 'From *Leir* to *Lear*', *Philological Quarterly* 73 (1994): 195–217.

and plot to 'flatter' Leir, knowing that he wishes to marry them to men they fancy, while Cordella is allotted to the 'Irish King', whom she clearly does not wish to marry (2.79, 96). Once Cordella offers a moderate answer to the love test, 'look what love the child doth owe the father, | The same to you I bear, my gracious lord', Gonorill and Ragan pounce and magnify the sense of disrespect (3.80–1). In a rage, Leir decides to 'dispossess myself' in favour of the elder sisters, while disinheriting Cordella altogether (3.124). Scene four introduces the King of Gallia, who plans to travel from France to Leir's Britain 'in some disguise' to observe the beauty of Leir's daughters (4.3). His clown-warrior-servant Mumford, a crucial role combining comic relief (usually of a sexual nature) with military skill, begs to accompany him. Scene five stages the meeting of Cornwall and Cambria on their way to Leir's court to marry Gonorill and Ragan. These characters largely serve as foils for their future wives, and have relatively little to do in the course of the play, but are apparently innocent of Gonorill and Ragan's various schemes. Accelerating these marriages, scene six brings together the two couples with Leir's blessing, while Perillus begs Leir to reconsider the banishment of Cordella. A much more romantic marriage emerges in scene seven, when Gallia and Mumford, freshly arrived in Britain disguised as pilgrims to a holy shrine, observe Cordella lamenting her fate, and planning to work as a seamstress. Gallia immediately falls in love – proven to be 'true love' and not a dynastic match as their royal identities are at first occluded – and Cordella agrees to marry him that very day. We next see an amplification of the loyalty of Perillus, who is given a monologue about the ill treatment Leir is suffering from Gonorill, with whom he now lives in Cornwall. Scene nine shows the return of Scaliger, who counsels Gonorill to reduce Leir's allowance by half to put him in his place. Scaliger's final lines reveal his reluctance to deal with a 'viperous woman' that makes him 'a villain' and a flatterer, at which point he disappears from the play altogether (9.38, 40). The next scene puts Gonorill's plan into action, with an enraged Leir counselled to travel to Ragan by Perillus, who accompanies him. Scene 11 offers Ragan a monologue in which she celebrates her new life, where 'I rule the King of Cambria as I please' (5), and notes that if her father stayed with her, she would 'send him packing' (16). Scene 12 discloses Cornwall's worries about the disappearance of Leir, and his plan to write to Cambria about it. Gonorill intercepts the letters and replaces them with her own to Ragan, enlisting the Messenger, a comically self-serving character, to murder Leir if Ragan asks him to, as her letter recommends.

Cordella, now in France as queen to Gallia, is given an extended monologue in scene 13, in which she laments her separation from her father and prays for reconciliation. Leir and Perillus then arrive in Cambria, where they are welcomed by the king, but Ragan in an aside promises his experience will go 'from bad to worse' (14.57). When the Messenger delivers Gonorill's letters, Ragan pays him to 'give a stab or two' to her father and Perillus (15.52). At the same time Cordella and Gallia send an Ambassador to Cornwall to effect a reconciliation with Leir. Gonorill receives the Ambassador badly, comically mishearing his messages, but Cornwall promises to 'be a mediator' for Cordella (18.53). Meanwhile, Ragan has set up a meeting with Leir and Perillus in a remote location, where the Messenger is sent to kill them. In this extended scene, Leir and Perillus sleep while the Messenger watches them. Leir dreams that Gonorill and Ragan kill him, while the Messenger comically revels in their plight by playing cat-and-mouse with them over his intention to stab them, but ultimately is dissuaded from murder through the lengthy appeals of Leir and Perillus, especially surrounding the punishments of hell, which are accompanied by '*Thunder*' as a stage effect (19.191, 291). These kinds of comic assassin scenes, whether resulting in murder or preventing it, were staples of the drama of the period. The Messenger proves to Leir, with Gonorill and Ragan's letters, that they have sought to have him murdered. Leir and Perillus resolve to travel to Cordella in France, and the Messenger flees. In scene 21 the French Ambassador, fed up with waiting for Leir in Cornwall, travels to Cambria to seek him there, where he is rudely treated by Ragan. Meanwhile, Gallia, Cordella, and Mumford decide to travel to Britain to see Leir, once again adopting a disguise so as to remain unknown, while Leir and Perillus have to exchange their clothes with sailors to pay for their passage to France. These elements of disguise crucially heighten the reconciliation in scene 24, where Cordella saves her father and Perillus from starving in the French countryside, and both repeatedly kneel to one another, seeking forgiveness. Gallia then vows vengeance against Gonorill and Ragan and raises an army to attack Britain. In a comic pair of scenes, two British watchmen become drunk and do not raise the alarm when Gallia's army lands. Mumford proves his skill as a soldier with set fight scenes, ultimately chasing away both Cambria and Cornwall in battle. After this victory, Leir admits that he took Cordella's response to the love test wrongly, gives his kingdom to Gallia and Cordella, and praises Perillus for his 'true love' and Mumford for his 'lion-like' fighting (33.24, 27). The scenic form of the play is deft, balancing the competing desires of Leir and his daughters against a wider cast of ancillary characters, comic and loyal, and encompassing four kingdoms (Britain, Cornwall, Cambria, and France) with swift action and tight character development.

DATE

King Leir was probably written by 1589, and possibly earlier, although evidence for precise dating is uncertain. Martin Wiggins and Catherine Richardson give a potential range of 1586–94.[4] Scholars have long noted the parallels to *The Spanish Tragedy* in the treatment of the murderous Messenger, suggesting that *King Leir* 'must be' a subsequent play,[5] although it is difficult to determine an order on the basis of plot and characterization alone. The first mention of *King Leir* appears in the diary of Philip Henslowe, manager of the Rose theatre, London, who recorded door receipts of £1.18s and £1.6s for performances of 'kinge leare' and 'Kinge leare' on 6 and 8 April 1594.[6] Henslowe's notes almost certainly refer to Kyd's *King Leir*. At this date the Queen's Men and Lord Sussex's Men, two separate companies, were staging alternating performances at the Rose. E. K. Chambers points out that *King Leir* does not appear on Henslowe's list of Sussex's Men plays, so it is generally taken to be the work of the Queen's Men.[7] Interestingly, as was often his habit for new plays, Henslowe did not label the play as 'ne', so it might have been on another stage or stages prior to 1594. The Queen's Men did not perform at Henslowe's Rose before then. Any more precise date for its composition between 1588 and 1594, and for any subsequent performance, must be open to conjecture.

The printing and publishing history of the play is more secure. The first Stationers' Register entry protects the ownership rights of Edward White, publisher, on 14 May 1594: 'Edward White. /. Entred alsoe for his Copie vnder th[e h]andes of bothe the wardens a booke entituled / The moste famous Chronicle historye of Leire kinge of England and his Three Daughters'.[8] White's name replaced and erased Adam Islip's, who might have initially owned the rights and transferred them to White, or perhaps had been recorded in error. Registration in 1594 would suggest that a manuscript copy of the play was owned by the publisher in order to claim his rights at Stationers' Hall. The proximity of this registration to the recent performances at the Rose theatre implies that the publisher might have been hoping to capitalize on recent audience interest. Ioppolo notes, however,

4 Martin Wiggins and Catherine Richardson, *British Drama 1533–1642: A Catalogue: Volume II: 1567–1589* (Oxford, 2012), #838.

5 Ibid.

6 R. A. Foakes and R. T. Rickert, *Henslowe's Diary*, second edition (Cambridge, 2002), p. 21.

7 E. K. Chambers, *The Elizabethan Stage*, 4 vols (Oxford, 1923), 4:25.

8 *Stationers' Register Online* SRO3604.

that the Queen's Men disbanded and sold 'a number of playbooks in 1594',[9] which suggests that the playbook could have come directly from them.

To prepare for the 1605 printing, the rights to the play were transferred in the register from Simon Stafford to John Wright, to be printed by Stafford (8 May 1605): 'Simon Stafford Entred for his Copie vnder th[e h]andes of the Wardens A booke called the Tragecall historie of kinge Leir and his Three Daughters &c. As it was latelie Acted'.[10] It is not known how Stafford obtained the rights, if indeed he did, from Edward White. Rights and their transference were not always recorded in the *Register* and sometimes a play or other text might have competing claims of ownership. The play appears again in the *Register* on 29 June 1624, when Alice White, widow of Edward White's son, who presumably inherited the rights to the play from the 1594 entry, ignoring the 1605 one, transferred them to Edward Allde.[11] Further transfers are recorded in 1640 and 1665, but again do not seem to have led to editions. It is not fully possible to trace the hows and whys of these transfers, or even whether the 1594 manuscript was the same as that which led to the printed edition of 1605.

The full title of the 1605 first printing is:

> THE | True Chronicle Hi- | story of King LEIR, and his three | *daughters, Gonorill, Ragan,* | and *Cordella.* | As it hath bene diuers and sundry | times lately acted. | [ornament] | LONDON, | Printed by Simon Stafford for Iohn | Wright, and are to bee sold at his shop at | Christes Church dore, next Newgate- | Market. 1605.

No prior sixteenth-century or subsequent seventeenth-century printings are known, making this the copytext for all subsequent editions.

SOURCES

The sources of *King Leir* retell the history of the legendary king himself, one of the mythical first rulers of Britain. They tend to offer a bare-bones plot of the elderly monarch wishing to divide his kingdom amongst his three daughters at his death, putting them to a love test to determine who might be most deserving, disinheriting his youngest daughter, regretting his choice, and then, with the help of his youngest daughter and her husband, regaining the throne. The story was in wide circulation from medieval times, as Wilfrid Perrett's *The Story of King Lear from Geoffrey of Monmouth to Shakespeare* covers in detail. Hopkinson argues that the primary source is Raphael Holinshed's *Chronicles of England, Scotlande,*

9 Ioppolo, '"A Jointure more or less"', 166.

10 *Stationers' Register Online* SRO4976.

11 Ibid., SRO7965.

and Ireland (1577).[12] Wiggins and Richardson list sources as William Warner, *Albion's England* (1586); John Higgins, *The First Part of the Mirror for Magistrates* (1587); Edmund Spenser, *The Faerie Queene* (1590) – noting that *The Faerie Queene* was known in manuscript before publication – and Thomas Lodge's *Rosalind* (1590) and *Euphues' Shadow* (1592) for certain dramatic moments. Given that Holinshed, Warner, and Higgins tell fairly short versions of the Leir story, deriving from Geoffrey of Monmouth's Latin *Historia Regum Britanniae* of the twelfth century, there is little reason to support the selection of one historian over another as the primary source, except, as James H. Forse argues, Holinshed mistakenly makes Gonorill's husband the Duke of Cornwall, which is followed by the play.[13] (He is Albany in other sources, and subsequently in Shakespeare.) Holinshed's *Chronicles* requires only two folio pages to tell the stories of Leir and his daughters, including Cordella's reign after his death. Thomas Kyd in fact had very little material upon which to build a play. He crafted something much more than a chronicle – or a step-by-step historical procession of statecraft and rule – by introducing an element of romance and the independent machinations of several major and minor figures: '... Skalliger, Perillus, Mumford, the Messenger, and the two bumbling watchmen who fail to capture Mumford are not found in any source material'.[14] Seen in this light, as Ioppolo argues, the play 'stands out as cleverly structured and well-plotted drama' with several original elements.[15]

The play does choose to concentrate on the quasi-historical final days of Leir, and not on what might have been better known to contemporary audiences, the subsequent rule of Cordella. Some of the sources, such as *The Mirror for Magistrates*, focus more heavily on the famous warrior queen, and even Holinshed has two (as opposed to his usual one) woodcut illustrations of her five-year reign, usurpation by nephews, and ultimate suicide. In focusing on Leir, Kyd was given the model of a good leader, with Holinshed calling him 'a prince of right noble demeanour, governing his land and subjects in great wealth' (19), with the dramatic conflict focusing on succession. When Leir became 'unwieldy through age' he sought to 'prefer her whom he best loved' (19). Cordella's answer to this love test in Holinshed is more elaborate than in the play:

12 A. F. Hopkinson (ed.), *The True Chronicle History of King Leir*, Old English Plays (London, 1895), p. xiii.

13 James H. Forse, 'To Die or Not to Die, that is the Question: Borrowing and Adapting the King Lear Legend in the Anonymous *The True Chronicle History of King Leir* and Shakespeare's *King Lear*', *Ben Jonson Journal* 21:1 (2014): 53–72, here at 55.

14 Ioppolo, '"A Jointure more or less"', 177.

15 Ibid., 166.

> I have loved you ever, and shall continually while I live, love you as my natural father, and if you would more understand of the love that I bear you, ascertain yourself, that so much as you have, so much you are worth, and so much I love you, and no more (19).

King Leir's Cordella offers a much less fulsome – and less petulant – response of four lines, making her father seem to overreact: 'Why how now, minion, are you grown so proud? | Doth our dear love make you thus peremptory?' (3.86–7). Kyd's innovation here is to have Gonorill and Ragan spur on their father's anger, as Cordelia Caroline Sherman notes.[16] Leir's slow repentance and Cordella's repeated demonstrations of demure piety, alongside the invented machinations of Gonorill and Ragan, build upon only a few hints from source material. In that sense even the chronical history elements of *King Leir* dramatize a largely original take on a bare-bones account from British mythology. Add to that the entirely invented comic episodes, including a well-crafted warrior-clown in Mumford, and the courtship of Cordella and Gallia, which make much of the action independent of the source material.

AUTHORSHIP

The general editors of this edition have provided an 'Authorship Commentary as Footnotes to the Text' to guide readers passage-by-passage through the associations of *King Leir* with Kyd and his works. Edmond Malone first proposed the possibility of Kyd as author, and Brian Vickers traces the full history of the attribution in 'Kyd's Authorship of *King Leir*' (2018), which provides, alongside the work of Darren Freebury-Jones, the most important account to date.

GENRE AND CHARACTERIZATION

King Leir tells an almost fairytale-like story of an old man giving up his kingdom to two of his seemingly loving daughters while disinheriting a third.[17] The play mixes three genres popular in the period: pastoral romance, with chance encounters and rescues in the countryside, connecting to the work of John Lyly, Thomas Lodge, and Robert Greene; the tragedy of court

16 Cordelia Caroline Sherman (ed.), 'A Critical Edition of "King Leir"', PhD thesis, Brown University, 1981, p. 24.

17 Alan R. Young, 'The Written and Oral Sources of *King Lear* and the Problem of Justice in the Play', *Studies in English Literature, 1500–1900* (1975): 309–19, traces the variations of the Cinderella story, especially 'Cap O'Rushes', in England and how they influenced the development of the Leir story.

intrigue, recalling *The Spanish Tragedy*; and chronicle history, concerned with rightful rule redressed through war, aligning with plays by Thomas Nashe and Shakespeare, including the collaborative *1 Henry VI*. This medley of genres might explain why the *Stationers' Register* first entry is for a 'Chronicle historye' and the second entry, just before printing, is for a 'Tragecall historie' (although there is an equal possibility that the second entry is an attempt to allude to Shakespeare's play, one that was second-thought at the point of publication, when the 'Chronicle' was restored to the title page).

The play's three strong and individuated female parts have provoked some interest in its representation of gender. They also map onto plot conventions about arranged versus romantic marriages, with Cornwall and Cambria coming to bad ends on the basis of their poor dynastic choices, although, as Ioppolo points out, the betrothal of Gonorill and Ragan 'reflects the two women's own desires'.[18] The play deliberately contrasts the arranged marriages against the pastoral romance of Cordella and Gallia, where their chance countryside meeting in disguise prompts love at first sight. Set against this romantic notion of love is a more puerile, humorous set of concerns. Cambria and Cornwall pun on the 'two holes' of their intended brides (5.52); Gonorill jokes about marrying with 'nothing' (i.e., vagina) in a metatheatrical joke on the male actor, perhaps (6.23); and most of Mumford's dialogue about women is highly sexualized – even Cordella exchanges bawdy puns with him (21.36). Ragan is willing to be forthright about gender when she asks of men 'Why should they have preeminence over us | Since we are creatures of more brave resolve?' (25.19–20). The play gives plenty of room (and spoken lines, including soliloquies and asides) to the three female parts, who have distinctive roles, as Donald M. Michie points out, with 'Ragan … more subtle and quiet than her forthright sister'.[19] Both characters are also playful in their uses of language, with each other and most especially in attempting to convince the Messenger to do their bidding. At the same time, the play emphasizes male comradery – Leir and Perillus's deep bond through catastrophic trouble, recalling Sydney's *Arcadia*, and Mumford and Gallia's banter – providing two different models of friendship, both eschewing strict social hierarchies. The rustic humour of the mariners and watchmen also partakes of the pastoral comedic traditions of the 1580s, where the witty bumpkin is a stock clown role. (Interestingly, when Cordella speaks of being 'Amongst the merry crew of country folk' (24.7), the lines suggest the textual remnant of a missing masque or dancing scene also typical of the genre.) The play's combination of 'homosocial

[18] Ioppolo, '"A Jointure more or less"', 172.

[19] Michie, *A Critical Edition*, p. 48.

friendship and female agency',[20] alongside finding love and comedy in the countryside, then, is typical of the bucolic romance of the 1580s.

The final reconciliation of Cordella and Leir steers the play fully away from family tragedy to comedy, and further emphasizes the more romantic elements of love and reunion, but family machination and misunderstanding remains a parallel generic strand until the close. This political context is significant to shaping the play away from the domestic and romantic and towards a more traditional chronicle history play, particularly in the rapid final scenes. The play focuses on models of statecraft through a stagecraft of public, court-based scenes (including the embarrassing love tests) alongside private reflections and machinations. Such conflicts also affect the thematic contrast of political goodwill and rampant individualism in the play, 'juxtaposing scenes of compassion and openness with those of jealousy and deception. Words, images, and actions are mirrored in every set of two scenes for the first part of the play, creating dramatically effective binary opposition.'[21] The Queen's Men are by royal decree concerned with justifying the Elizabethan political circumstance, and a fear about duplicitous counsel is very much in keeping with court culture of the 1580s and 1590s. Sir Richard Barckley complains in 1598 about the sometimes unrecognized differences between virtuous and malicious courtiers: 'For men given to virtue, take it as a great offence and disgrace, when there is no respect had of their merits; and when vicious men, or they that have little or nothing in them, shall be made equal, or preferred before them in favour.'[22] *King Leir* represents several tests of this dialectic. Scaliger seeks preferment through the new generation of rulers in Gonorill and Ragan (although his disappearance from the play makes that attempt unresolved). The Messenger is direct in his quest for status and money, and Gonorill promises 'a highway of preferment' (12.97). These are stock characters in tragedies of court intrigue, like the Queen's Men play and Shakespearean source *The True Tragedy of Richard III*. Perillus, in contrast, is opposed to these Machiavellian characters as a virtuous courtier, on a model of sage and loyal counsel, opposing 'vain, flatt'ring words' (3.136), and refusing advancement (10.70–1), even in the face of Leir telling him: 'Go learn to flatter, where thou mayst in time | Get favour 'mongst the mighty and so climb' (10.58–9). Finally, Mumford represents the apogee of the

20 Andy Kesson, 'John Lyly and Shakespeare's Early Career', in R. Loughnane and A. Power (eds), *Early Shakespeare, 1588–1594* (Cambridge, 2020), pp. 167–79, here at p. 177.

21 Ioppolo, '"A Jointure more or less"', 172.

22 Richard Barckley, *A Discovrse of the Felicitie of Man: Or His Summum Bonum* (London, 1598), p. 519.

plain-spoken hero, often an integral part of the chronicle history play, as Thomas Nashe points out:

> … the subject of them (for the most part) it is borrowed out of our English Chronicles, wherein our forefathers valiant acts (that have line long buried in rusty brass and worm-eaten books) are revived, and they themselves raised from the Grave of Oblivion … than which, what can be a sharper reproof, to these degenerate effeminate days of ours?[23]

Towards the end the play participates in this vogue for patriotic militarism through chronicle history (even if that is represented by a French character), through the rapid excursions and mini-battles that bring a triumphal and rightful king back to his rule, to '*sound victory*' (33.0 SD). This generic context gives sense to how Mumford's heroism seems to come from nowhere, especially given his principal early focus is on finding a 'wench' (7.144).

This mixture of genres is ambitious, with two of them – tragedy and romance – being distinct from the source material. The innovative blending of generic modes might also explain some of the play's weaknesses. Many critics agree that the language is somewhat leaden, but that derives in part from the need to reconcile so many competing genres and plot strands, and explain all of them to the audience. Michie describes the writing as 'far too often wooden and ponderous'.[24] Scott McMillin and Sally-Beth MacLean frame this limitation through the tradition of 'a Protestant drive for substantial truth and plain speech … *King Leir* is virtually an exercise in plain speaking', and judge the language ultimately as 'stilted and self-conscious'.[25] Andrew Griffin instead recognizes how the generic constraints – most particularly of Queen's Men chronicle history – impose themselves on more fluid verse, and defends a need for unadventurous clarity in speech because of the 'generic obligations and didactic ends which compel the play's dialogue in certain, perhaps boring, wooden, or baffling directions'.[26] Yet beyond the moralizing of the history genre, the play makes creative use of the tragic-intrigue conventions of eavesdropping (7.14ff, 24.15ff), aside (from 1.90 and throughout), (deliberate) mishearing (18.41ff), and soliloquy, by a host of characters including Perillus (scene 8), Ragan (scenes 11, 25), Cordella (scene 13), the Messenger (scenes 15, 17), and the Gallian ambassador (scene 20). Although the principal character, King Leir, is

23 Thomas Nashe, *Pierce Penniless his Supplication to the Devil* (London, 1592), H2.

24 Michie, *A Critical Edition*, p. 39.

25 Scott McMillin and Sally-Beth MacLean, *The Queen's Men and Their Plays* (Cambridge, 1998), pp. 33, 146.

26 Andrew Griffin (ed.), King Leir (Modern), Queen's Men Editions (University of Victoria, 2012).

prone to speaking somewhat formally and, at times, woodenly, his daughters and the wider cast are given their own ways of talking that delimit fully articulated characterization across a variety of generic character types.

PERFORMANCE

The context of the first recorded performance in 1594 has received substantial attention from McMillin and MacLean in their book *The Queen's Men and Their Plays* (1998). They argue that the play takes complete advantage of the available acting resources of the company, in requiring 14 actors at a minimum, across 26 speaking roles.[27] Moreover, only 'the "disappearance" of characters from scenes where they would normally be expected enables the doubling',[28] so that the play is tightly crafted to benefit from the maximum available acting talent. This situation is consistent in all Queen's Men plays of 1594 (which is where McMillin and MacLean place *King Leir*, as a known performance year), suggesting that the author of the play was deeply familiar with the company, and that the play was crafted in collaboration with them. Thomas Kyd might have had a longstanding connection with the Queen's Men. The *Oxford Dictionary of National Biography* points out that 'According to Thomas Dekker's pamphlet *A Knight's Conjuring* (1607) Kyd was a playwright for the Queen's Men between 1583 and 1585' (Mulryne), an intriguing possibility that might suggest that the play was an even earlier part of their back catalogue when it was put on in 1594, or, if written later in the 1580s, that Kyd had maintained a close connection with the company. The three daughters of Leir match well to the company's three skilled boy actors, with well-drawn and roughly equal parts. The Queen's Men were also known for their clowning roles – even after the death of their famous comic actor Richard Tarlton in 1588. *King Leir* has several roles that partake of Tarlton's tradition of combining wit and downrightness, including the Messenger, mariners, and watchmen. Such lightness and humour across multiple roles is characteristic of the Queen's Men.[29] It is also possible, if the play is earlier than 1594, that Mumford, in his combination of speaking comic truth to power and being an excellent soldier, was written for Tarlton, who was an expert swordsman, a likely requirement for the actor in the final scenes.

27 McMillin and MacLean, *The Queen's Men*, pp. 100–1.

28 Ibid., p. 107.

29 Helen M. Ostovich, Holger Schott Syme, and Andrew R. Griffin (eds), *Locating the Queen's Men, 1583–1603: Material Practices and Conditions of Playing* (Farnham, 2009), pp. 16–23.

Given this care in construction, alongside the 'better than average'[30] takings during two performances at the Rose in 1594, it is difficult to imagine that the play was put on *only* twice. As noted above, Henslowe does not call it 'ne', or new, and the play might have been performed elsewhere in London or more probably, given the Queen's Men's usual practice, in touring. The company performed at the Rose for only one week, and were by 1594 travelling players without a secure venue. The play is particularly portable. For the most part only hand properties – letters, swords, bags of money – are required, and the costuming is bifurcated into either the elite robes of kings and courtiers (generic requirements from most plays of this period) or the garb of beggars and the poor (such as the mariners' garments or the disguise of the King of Gallia). The one large property that seems to be required – the table of scene 24 – might of course be found in situ in touring venues such as inns or the halls of country houses. Intriguingly, on 10 March 1598, Henslowe also lists as theatrical properties for the Rose: 2 steeples, 1 chime of bells, and 1 beacon;[31] these items are mentioned in the watchmen scenes of *King Leir*, but in no other known play. The steeples might enhance the spectacle of the scene, but are not directly required by the action. The chimes and beacon might be fairly portable, and presumably the steeples were scaled down, too. The acquisition of or investment in these particular props would suggest a history of prior performance or an intention to stage the play more regularly than is recorded.

The title page of the 1605 quarto claims that the play 'hath bene diuers and sundry times lately acted'. Griffin takes this literally: 'they continued to perform Leir throughout the next decade of their existence, a fact that implies its general success over a fairly long span of time'; Ioppolo more tentatively agrees that this claim '... may in fact be legitimate rather than a publisher's exaggeration'.[32] The force of the implication that the play has been 'diuers' (separately), 'sundry' (many times), and 'lately' (recently) put on stage does seem to protest too much, however. Play text title pages, in their attempts to market a book, are notoriously unreliable; 'their assertions cannot be taken at face value',[33] and as Chambers argues, 'It seems a little improbable that *Leire* should have been revived as late as 1605 ...'[34] The dual facts of the text of the play being sold off for publication almost immediately after the Rose theatre performances and Henslowe's retention of significant stage properties – that presumably would be useful for further

30 Ioppolo, '"A Jointure more or less"', 169.

31 Foakes and Rickert, *Henslowe's Diary*, p. 319.

32 Ioppolo, '"A Jointure more or less"', 71.

33 Eugene Giddens, *How to Read a Shakespearean Play Text* (Cambridge, 2011), p. 63.

34 Chambers, *The Elizabethan Stage*, 4:25.

performances – suggest that the play might not have been performed at all by the Queen's Men after 1594.

Once the play was printed in 1605, it could of course be staged by any amateur or professional group, not just by a company holding the licensed manuscript copy. The Queen's Men were, in keeping with their established position as Queen Elizabeth's troupe of actors, known to voice royal interests, and particularly Protestant ones.[35] There is therefore some contention over the next possible performance of the play in 1610, in the context of a staging for a Catholic audience. Testimonies from the legal trial of Sir John Yorke from Yorkshire make extensive mention of a touring group of actors who performed a 'Kinge Lere' on 2 February 1610. There has been much debate about which *Leir/Lear* this might be, but Douglas H. Arrell convincingly argues that the tastes of this recusant audience would be more inclined to the original, especially with its narrative of redemption and many allusions to Catholic practices such as 'prayer beads', 'Purgatory', 'nuns', and 'blessing one-self'.[36] At the very least *King Leir* can be as readily seen as a Catholic play as Shakespeare's *King Lear*, and it is certain that one of them was staged in Yorkshire in 1610. A version of an English *Lear* play was also performed in Dresden at the Court of Saxony on 26 September 1626, but, as Wiggins and Richardson note, it 'might have been either this one or Shakespeare's'.[37]

King Leir has no other performance history known to me until 2006, when the play was part of a tryptic of Queen's Men performance-as-research productions (with *The Famous Victories of Henry V* and *Friar Bacon and Friar Bungay*) by Poculi Ludique Societas, directed by Peter Cockett, at Convocation Hall, McMaster University and University College West Hall, University of Toronto, 24 and 27 October 2006. The staging was filmed in a two-camera set-up (https://qme.uvic.ca/Theater/kingleir/index.html), and Griffin's edition is intertwined with the production. The performance discloses how tightly crafted the scenes are, permitting rapid costume changes and doubling, and also a fluid navigation of limited playing space, with members of the audience flanking the performers and three 'dignitaries' (as King calls them) permanently on stage in a way that might mimic the 'lord's room' of early modern public theatres.[38] Two exits were made through the audience and one through the rear of the stage, dealing

35 McMillin and MacLean, *The Queen's Men*, p. 33.

36 Douglas H. Arrell, '"King Leir" at Gowthwaite Hall', *Medieval and Renaissance Drama in England* 25 (2012): 83–93, here at 88.

37 Wiggins and Richardson, *British Drama 1533–1642*, #838.

38 Pamela King, 'Review of *King Leir*, *The Famous Victories of Henry V* and *Friar Bacon and Friar Bungay*', *Early Modern Literary Studies* 13:3 (2008), https://extra.shu.ac.uk/emls/13-3/revsqm.htm.

effectively with the limited space (and number of doors). The production also disclosed that the play is funny – which might remain hidden at a first reading but came through readily in this staging – and that the rhythm of comedy 'punctuates the moralistic seriousness that critics have found so troubling, even if it refuses to undermine the seriousness entirely' (Griffin). The adult male actors effectively represented the nuances of the three sisters, although it would have been more interesting to see boys in the roles, as almost certainly was the case for the original Queen's Men. Despite being staged with good pace and no interval, the play ran for two hours and forty minutes, creating 'quite an ordeal for the on-stage audience' (King). Original-practices rehearsal – with actors given parts to learn quickly – might have contributed to a sense that the language of the play had a 'lack of affective power' (King), but the actors sustained the story very well in the light of these constraints, and demonstrated the elasticity of a play almost certainly originally designed for touring.

Perhaps inspired by the Toronto project, more recent attempts have tested the staging potential of the play. A '"King Leir": Play Reading and Symposium' in conjunction with the Malone Society included a staged reading on 16 May 2015 at Somerville College, Oxford. Another staged reading appeared at the Adobe Rose Theatre in Santa Fe, New Mexico, on 1 September 2018. The Madison Shakespeare Company performed the play in Milwaukee's Peck Pavilion, 8–19 July 2018, in association with a production of Shakespeare's *King Lear*. An understanding of even the most basic issues of character, language, and stagecraft will be realized only through further staging, and the increased interest of recent years points to the potential of this play to test performers and engage audiences.

TEXT

The 1605 quarto printing is the only version of the play with any authority, and it provides the copytext for this edition. Stafford was an experienced printer of plays, having produced seven by 1605, including Ben Jonson's *Every Man In His Humour* (1601) and John Lyly's *Love's Metamorphosis* (1601). *King Leir* is well printed for the play-text standards of the time, with few cruces or corruptions. Greg and Bond record forty-seven 'Irregular and Doubtful Readings', and these are for the most part minor or easy to correct, e.g., 'Palerno' for Palermo (12.81) or 'Se' for She (19.325). Although forty-seven might seem like a large number of errors, the nature of play-text printing, effectively a quick job that generated little potential profit, means that this level of corruption is relatively low.

A comparison of surviving copies of the play discloses no evidence of correction during printing. Sherman's PhD edition of the play collated the surviving quartos to discover sixteen variants across twelve formes. Closer examination shows that each of these variants is unlikely to be a deliberate correction. Some occur because of type slippage of the kind frequently found in the course of presswork in this period (like the Folger copy's printing of 'goodi n' instead of 'good in', likely to be a shift of loose type and possibly reflecting a pulled blank space), or blurred or indistinct inking of the sort that makes a comma look like a full-stop. I can find no evidence of textual changes where presswork was stopped during proofreading to make corrections, but that does not necessarily mean that none took place, as few copies survive.

King Leir has garnered competing views as to what kind of manuscript Stafford received in order to print the play. The crucial question is whether the text derives (perhaps at some remove) from the theatre or from some copy of the author's original manuscript. Michie asserts that 'the author's manuscript, most likely his fair copy, formed the basis for the 1605 text'.[39] Ioppolo points instead to theatrical origins, largely because of '... the presence of absolutely regular exit directions'.[40] Almost every necessary entrance and exit is recorded (two are missing for scenes 15 and 16), and this consistency is fairly unusual in manuscript and printed plays from the period. Andrew Griffin, on the other hand, engages with Ioppolo's points to, like Michie, take the opposite view on the basis of non-entry or exit directions: 'Missing stage directions in the 1605 Leir ... suggest – perhaps more compellingly – that it was printed from an authorial copy.' He notes that sometimes minor hand properties go unmentioned, such as Ragan's purses (17.7 SD), and once a major property – the table – is not signalled until it is needed in the dialogue (24.0 SD). These missing directions are few in number, and Paul Werstine has shown convincingly that early modern playhouses did not bother systematically to correct all minor or major lacunae in stage directions.[41] I agree with Ioppolo that '... it is reasonable to conclude that the copy was a transcript of the 1594 or later company "book", possibly made especially for use as a printer's copy'.[42] A transcription is more plausible than a licensed copy or promptbook, because theatrical companies were unlikely to release the only copies of these significant documents. The underlying manuscript for the printed text of *King Leir* therefore is probably a scribal copy of a theatrical document, which therefore might have been corrupted, or regularized and tidied up, in places. Looking for absolute consistency in such a copy would be a frustrating enterprise.

39 Michie, *A Critical Edition*, p. 17.

40 Ioppolo, '"A Jointure more or less"', 168.

41 Paul Werstine, *Early Modern Playhouse Manuscripts and the Editing of Shakespeare* (Cambridge, 2012), pp. 107–47.

42 Ioppolo, '"A Jointure more or less"', 169.

The play apparently presented few complications to Stafford. The catchwords have 'no anomalies',[43] and the text regularly prints thirty-eight lines per page until gatherings H and I, when extra lines were added to save the need to print a new gathering 'K'.[44] That the play fits neatly onto nine full quarto sheets suggests both a tidy underlying manuscript and experienced printers. To 'cast off' – or estimate the printed space taken up by a manuscript – can be a messy business in this period, especially if the manuscript is unclear in some way.[45] The few confusions over verse and prose in *King Leir* are spread throughout and not concentrated in any one sheet, suggesting that local difficulties in the otherwise clear printer's copy are the likely cause for them (i.e., that a handful of manuscript lines might have been run together or otherwise muddled). The play was set by formes, as suggested tentatively by Michie – 'evidence for this inference is not overwhelming'[46] – but his inference is correct. Michie worked from photocopies and found eight headlines being deployed across all skeleton formes in the quarto. In fact, there are only four. His headline I is the same as II, III is the same as IV, V is the same as VII, and VI is the same as VIII. These headlines experienced minor alteration over the course of presswork, as early modern type did under repeated impressions from the powerful press, but with the aid of high magnification of digital photographs it is possible to discern that there are only four recurring headlines, with the minimum of two verso settings of '*The History of King Leir*' and two recto ones for '*and his three daughters*' required for a quarto edition (that printed four pages per forme). These headlines were reused from forme to forme eighteen times, with the exception of A inner and outer, which lacks three headlines on the title page, half title, and a blank page. The play therefore must have been printed by formes and not seriatim. Spelling evidence and spacing habits are inconclusive as to the potential number of compositors working on the play. Michie suggests three hands, largely on the basis of spelling variations (i.e., the speech-heading *Kin./King.*), but the available evidence is slight and somewhat inconsistent. I agree on the basis of his evidence that at least two compositors worked on the play. That might explain why Britain is rendered 'Brittany' at the beginning of the play (from A3) and 'Britayne' later (from E2v) and several other spelling variations (like 'Fraunce' and 'France' or 'eche' and 'each'). Since spelling does not tend to be retained

43 Michie, *A Critical Edition*, p. 6.

44 Ibid., p. 7.

45 See, for instance, the varying line lengths caused by the difficult casting off of the first quarto of *Romeo and Juliet* (1597) or the need to completely reset parts of James Shirley's *Bird in a Cage* (1633) because of such confusion (Giddens, *How to Read a Shakespearean Play Text*, pp. 40–1).

46 Michie, *A Critical Edition*, p. 57, n. 16.

by compositors from the underlying manuscript, these look like distinct compositorial habits.

Deploying two or more compositors is not an unusual practice for a printer in this period, even for a short book like a play. This and other evidence points to a fairly straightforward printing job for Stafford, one that subsequently presents little difficulty to a modernizing editor. The biggest challenges are some adjustments of the verse, where it has obviously been misprinted, including where prose has been printed as verse. Although the play has been edited many times, from John Nichols's 1779 edition to Griffin's 2012 one, it has rarely appeared in modernized spelling or had its lineation adjusted. There are several reprint editions connected to an interest in Shakespeare's sources, but which do not significantly improve stage directions, modernize, or offer substantive commentary. Many of the editors of *King Leir* in fact disclose reluctance to do the job at all. Hopkinson complains: 'The play I think suffers chiefly from a want of dramatic action, a defect that must always be considered a grave fault in a play intended for theatrical representation,'[47] while a century later Michie finds that 'Leir is a shallow creation, lacking any kind of complexity of personality'.[48] But even the unmodernized and reluctant edition has proven helpful in editing this play in local moments, and I have recorded in collation any decisions I have adopted from previous editors. Of special note in the editorial history are the following editions: Bond and Greg introduced scene divisions; Hopkinson added many of the needed stage directions; and the further iteration of effort by Michie, Tiffany Stern, and Griffin have provided almost any other ones required by the action. Hopkinson was also particularly adept at navigating the quarto's erroneous settings of prose as verse, or vice versa, and its mislineations. It is fair to say that Hopkinson has been the most influential editor for subsequent modernization (although other editors have not always credited his original emendations). Minor corrections from other editors have been adopted and acknowledged in this edition from across the play's editorial history, including those by Nichols, William Hazlitt, and Sidney Lee.

47 Hopkinson, *True Chronicle*, p. xii.

48 Michie, *A Critical Edition*, p. 48.

BIBLIOGRAPHY

Arrell, Douglas H., '"King Leir" at Gowthwaite Hall', *Medieval and Renaissance Drama in England* 25 (2012): 83–93.

Barckley, Richard, *A Discovrse of the Felicitie of Man: Or His Summum Bonum* (London, 1598).

Bond, R. Warwick and W. W. Greg (eds), *The History of King Leir, 1605* (Oxford, 1907 [1908]).

Chambers, E. K., *The Elizabethan Stage*, 4 vols (Oxford, 1923).

Cunliffe, John W., 'Early English Tragedy', in *The Cambridge History of English Literature*, vol. 5, part 1 (Cambridge, 1910), pp. 61–88.

Foakes, R. A. and R. T. Rickert, *Henslowe's Diary*, second edition (Cambridge, 2002).

Forse, James H., 'To Die or Not to Die, that is the Question: Borrowing and Adapting the King Lear Legend in the Anonymous *The True Chronicle History of King Leir* and Shakespeare's *King Lear*', *Ben Jonson Journal* 21:1 (2014): 53–72.

Freebury-Jones, Darren, '"Fearful Dreams" in Thomas Kyd's Restored Canon', *Digital Studies/Le champ numérique* 9:1 (2019): 3.1–25.

—— *Shakespeare's Tutor: The Influence of Thomas Kyd* (Manchester, 2022).

Furness, Horace H. (ed.), Variorum *King Lear* (Modern Language Association, 1880; 1963).

Giddens, Eugene, *How to Read a Shakespearean Play Text* (Cambridge, 2011).

Griffin, Andrew (ed.), King Leir (Modern), Queen's Men Editions (University of Victoria, 2012), http://qme.uvic.ca/edition/Leir/.

Hazlitt, William (ed.), *Shakespeare's library: a collection of the plays, romances, novels, poems and histories employed by Shakespeare in the composition of his works, with introduction and notes*, second edition (London, 1875).

Holinshed, Raphael, *The firste volume of the chronicles of England, Scotlande, and Irelande* (London, 1577).

Hopkinson, A. F. (ed.), *The True Chronicle History of King Leir*, Old English Plays (London, 1895).

Ioppolo, Grace, '"A Jointure more or less": Re-measuring "The True Chronicle History of King Leir and his three daughters"', *Medieval and Renaissance Drama in England* 17 (2005): 165–79.

Kermode, Lloyd Edward, '"King Leir" within the Thicket: Gender, Place, and Power', *Renaissance and Reformation/Renaissance et Réforme* 35 (2012): 65–84.

Kesson, Andy, 'John Lyly and Shakespeare's Early Career', in R. Loughnane and A. Power (eds), *Early Shakespeare, 1588–1594* (Cambridge, 2020), pp. 167–79.

King, Pamela, 'Review of *King Leir, The Famous Victories of Henry V* and *Friar Bacon and Friar Bungay*', *Early Modern Literary Studies* 13.3 (2008), https://extra.shu.ac.uk/emls/13-3/revsqm.htm.

Lee, Sidney (ed.), *The Chronicle History of King Leir: The Original of Shakespeare's 'King Lear'* (London, 1909).

McMillin, Scott and Sally-Beth MacLean, *The Queen's Men and Their Plays* (Cambridge, 1998).

Michie, Donald M. (ed.), *A Critical edition of The true chronicle history of King Leir and his three daughters, Gonorill, Ragan, and Cordella* (New York, 1991).

Mueller, Martin, 'From *Leir* to *Lear*', *Philological Quarterly* 73 (1994): 195–217.

Mulryne, J. R., 'Kyd, Thomas (bap. 1558, d. 1594), playwright and translator', *Oxford Dictionary of National Biography* (Oxford, 2004), <https://www.oxforddnb.com>.

Nashe, Thomas, *Pierce Penniless his Supplication to the Devil* (London, 1592).

Nichols, John (ed.), *Six Old Plays, on which Shakespeare founded his Measure for Measure, Comedy of Errors, Taming the Shrew, King John, K. Henry IV, and K. Henry V., King Lear* (London, 1779).

Ostovich, Helen M., Holger Schott Syme, and Andrew R. Griffin (eds), *Locating the Queen's Men, 1583–1603: Material Practices and Conditions of Playing* (Farnham, 2009).

Perrett, Wilfrid, *The Story of King Lear from Geoffrey of Monmouth to Shakespeare* (Berlin, 1904).

Rubow, Paul, *Shakespeare og hans samtidige* (Copenhagen, 1948).

Satin, Joseph Henry (ed.), *Shakespeare and His Sources* (Boston, 1966).

Shakespeare, William, *The New Oxford Shakespeare: The Complete Works Modern Critical Edition*, ed. Gary Taylor *et al.* (Oxford, 2016). All references to Shakespeare cite this edition.

Sherman, Cordelia Caroline (ed.), 'A Critical Edition of "King Leir"', PhD thesis, Brown University, 1981.

Stationers' Register Online, ed. Giles Bergel and Ian Gadd, CREATe, University of Glasgow, http://stationersregister.online.

Stern, Tiffany (ed.), *King Leir*, Globe Quartos (London, 2002).

Vickers, Brian, 'Kyd's Authorship of *King Leir*', *Studies in Philology* 115 (2018): 433–71.

Werstine, Paul, *Early Modern Playhouse Manuscripts and the Editing of Shakespeare* (Cambridge, 2012).

Wiggins, Martin and Catherine Richardson, *British Drama 1533–1642: A Catalogue: Volume II: 1567–1589* (Oxford, 2012).

Young, Alan R., 'The Written and Oral Sources of *King Lear* and the Problem of Justice in the Play', *Studies in English Literature, 1500–1900* (1975): 309–19.

THE

True Chronicle History
of King LEIR, and his three
*daughters, Gonorill, Ragan,
and Cordella.*

As it hath been divers and sundry
times lately acted.

LONDON,
Printed by Simon Stafford for John
Wright and are to be sold at his shop at
Christ Church door, next Newgate-
Market. 1605.

THE PERSONS IN THE PLAY

King LEIR
SCALIGER, a courtier
PERILLUS, a courtier
GONORILL, RAGAN, CORDELLA — Leir's daughters
NOBLES to the court of King Leir
King of GALLIA
MUMFORD, a Gallian lord
Gallian NOBLES
AMBASSADOR from Gallia
King of CORNWALL
SERVANT to the King of Cornwall
MESSENGER from Cornwall
Morgan, King of CAMBRIA
SERVANT to the King of Cambria
FIRST MARINER
SECOND MARINER
FIRST CAPTAIN of the watch
SECOND CAPTAIN of the watch
FIRST WATCHMAN
SECOND WATCHMAN
French NOBLES
British NOBLE
Soldiers
Townsmen and townswomen

[Scene 1]

Enter King Leir, [Scaliger, Perillus,] and nobles.

LEIR
Thus to our grief, the obsequies performed[1]
Of our too late deceased and dearest queen,
Whose soul, I hope, possessed of heavenly joys
Doth ride in triumph 'mongst the cherubins,
Let us request your grave advice, my lords,
For the disposing of our princely daughters,
For whom our care is specially employed,
As nature bindeth, to advance their states
In royal marriage with some princely mates.[2]
For wanting now their mother's good advice,
Under whose government they have received
A perfect pattern of virtuous life,
Left as it were a ship without a stern
Or silly sheep without a pastor's care,
Although ourselves do dearly tender them,
Yet are we ignorant of their affairs.
For fathers best do know to govern sons,
But daughters' steps the mother's counsel turns.
A son we want for to succeed our crown,
And course of time hath cancellèd the date
Of further issue from our withered loins.
One foot already hangeth in the grave,
And age hath made deep furrows in my face.
The world of me, I of the world am weary,
And I would fain resign these earthly cares
And think upon the welfare of my soul,
Which by no better means may be effected[3]
Than by resigning up the crown from me
In equal dowry to my daughters three.

SCALIGER
A worthy care, my liege, which well declares

1 Cf. *Corn.* 3.3.12: 'And did **perform** his **obsequies**'.
2 Cf. *Sp. T.* 4.6.38: 'First, for the **marriage** of his **princely** son'.
3 Cf. *Corn.* 2.1.70: 'And all your hopes with hap **may be effected**'.

The zeal you bare unto our quondam queen.
And since your grace hath licensed me to speak,
I censure thus: your majesty knowing well
What several suitors your princely daughters have,
To make them each a jointure, more or less
As is their worth, to them that love profess.

LEIR
No more, nor less, but even all alike.
My zeal is fixed, all fashioned in one mould.
Wherefore, unpartial shall my censure be;
Both old and young shall have alike for me.

NOBLE
My gracious lord, I heartily do wish
That God had lent you an heir indubitate,
Which might have sat upon your royal throne
When fates should loose the prison of your life,
By whose succession all this doubt might cease,
And, as by you, by him we might have peace.
But after-wishes ever come too late,
And nothing can revoke the course of fate.
Wherefore, my liege, my censure deems it best
To match them with some of your neighbour kings
Bord'ring within the bounds of Albion,[4]
By whose united friendship this our state
May be protected 'gainst all foreign hate.

LEIR
Herein, my lords, your wishes sort with mine,
And mine, I hope, do sort with heavenly powers.[5]
For at this instant two near-neighbouring kings –
Of Cornwall and of Cambria – motion love
To my two daughters, Gonorill and Ragan.
My youngest daughter, fair Cordella, vows
No liking to a monarch, unless love allows.
She is solicited by diverse peers,

4 Cf. *Sp. T.* 1.2.51: 'And gapes to swallow **neighbour-bounding** lands'; *Corn.* 1.1.138: '**Within the bounds of** further Brittany'.

5 Cf. *SP* 2.1.182: 'Ah Love, and if thou be'st of **heavenly power**'; 4.1.169: 'That heavens and **heavenly powers do** manage love'. Cf. also *KL* 1.93: 'When **heavenly powers do** frustrate their intent'.

But none of them her partial fancy hears.[6]
Yet, if my policy may her beguile,
I'll match her to some king within this isle
And so establish such a perfect peace
As Fortune's force shall ne'er prevail to cease.

PERILLUS
Of us and ours, your gracious care, my lord,
Deserves an everlasting memory
To be enrolled in chronicles of fame[7]
By never-dying perpetuity.
Yet, to become so provident a prince,
Lose not the title of a loving father.[8]
Do not force love where fancy cannot dwell,
Lest streams, being stopped, above the banks do swell.

LEIR
I am resolved, and even now my mind
Doth meditate a sudden stratagem
To try which of my daughters loves me best,
Which, till I know, I cannot be in rest.
This granted, when they jointly shall contend
Each to exceed the other in their love,
Then at the vantage will I take Cordella,
Even as she doth protest she loves me best,
I'll say 'Then, daughter, grant me one request:
To show thou lovest me as thy sisters do,
Accept a husband whom myself will woo.'
This said, she cannot well deny my suit,
Although, poor soul, her senses will be mute.
Then will I triumph in my policy
And match her with a king of Brittany.

SCALIGER
[*aside*] I'll to them before and bewray your secrecy.

PERILLUS
[*aside*] Thus fathers think their children to beguile,
And oftentimes themselves do first repent,

6 Cf. *Sp. T.* 4.2.3: 'Ah, but **none of them** will purge the heart.'

7 William Wells compares this line to *SP* 1.2.3: '**To be enrolled in** the brass-leaved book.' 'The Authorship of *King Leir*', *N&Q* 25 (1939): 434–8 (434).

8 Cf. *Sp. T.* 4.7.95: '**a loving father** to his son.'

When heavenly powers do frustrate their intent.

Exeunt.

* * * * *

[Scene 2]

Enter Gonorill and Ragan.

GONORILL
I marvel, Ragan, how you can endure
To see that proud pert peat, our youngest sister,
So slightly to account of us, her elders,
As if we were no better than herself!
We cannot have a quaint device so soon,
Or new-made fashion of our choice invention,
But if she like it, she will have the same,
Or study newer to exceed us both.
Besides, she is so nice and so demure,
So sober, courteous, modest, and precise,
That all the court hath work enough to do
To talk how she exceedeth me and you.

RAGAN
What should I do? Would it were in my power
To find a cure for this contagious ill.[9]
Some desperate medicine must be soon applied
To dim the glory of her mounting fame,
Else, ere't be long, she'll have both prick and praise,
And we must be set by for working days.
Do you not see what several choice of suitors
She daily hath, and of the best degree?
Say, amongst all, she hap to fancy one,[10]
And have a husband when as we have none.
Why then, by right, to her we must give place,
Though it be ne'er so much to our disgrace.[11]

GONORILL
By my virginity, rather than she
Shall have a husband before me,

[9] Cf. *HP* ll. 214–15: 'a necessary meat **for this contagious** weather'.

[10] Cf. *Sp. T.* 4.4.20: '**she hap to** stand on terms with us'.

[11] Cf. *Corn.* 4.2.167: 'Than th'evil itself, **though it be ne'er so** sore'.

I'll marry one or other in his shirt –
And yet I have made half a grant already
Of my good will unto the King of Cornwall.

RAGAN
Swear not so deeply, sister. Here cometh
My Lord Scaliger.
Something his hasty coming doth import.

Enter Scaliger.

SCALIGER
Sweet princesses,
I am glad I meet you here so luckily,
Having good news which doth concern you both
And craveth speedy expedition.

RAGAN
For God's sake tell us what it is, my lord;
I am with child until you utter it.

SCALIGER
Madam, to save your longing, this it is:
Your father in great secrecy today
Told me he means to marry you out of hand
Unto the noble Prince of Cambria –
[*To Gonorill*] You, madam, to the King of Cornwall's grace.
Your younger sister he would fain bestow
Upon the rich King of Hibernia,
But that he doubts she hardly will consent,
For hitherto she ne'er could fancy him.
If she do yield, why then, between you three,
He will divide his kingdom for your dowries.
But yet there is a further mystery,
Which, so you will conceal, I will disclose.

GONORILL
Whate'er thou speak'st to us, kind Scaliger,
Think that thou speak'st it only to thyself.

SCALIGER
He earnestly desireth for to know,
Which of you three do bear most love to him,
And on your loves he so extremely dotes,
As never any did, I think, before.
He presently doth mean to send for you,

To be resolved of this tormenting doubt –
And look, whose answer pleaseth him the best,
They shall have most unto their marriages.

RAGAN
Oh, that I had some pleasing mermaid's voice
For to enchant his senseless senses with!

SCALIGER
For he supposeth that Cordella will,
Striving to go beyond you in her love,
Promise to do whatever he desires.
Then he will straight enjoin her for his sake
The Hibernian King in marriage for to take.
This is the sum of all I have to say,
Which being done, I humbly take my leave,
Not doubting but your wisdoms will foresee
What course will best unto your good agree.

GONORILL
Thanks, gentle Scaliger, thy kindness undeserved
Shall not be unrequited, if we live.

Exit Scaliger.

RAGAN
Now have we fit occasion offered us
To be revenged upon her unperceived.

GONORILL
Nay, our revenge we will inflict on her,
Shall be accounted piety in us.
I will so flatter with my doting father,
As he was ne'er so flattered in his life.
Nay, I will say that if it be his pleasure,
To match me to a beggar, I will yield.
For why, I know whatever I do say,
He means to match me with the Cornwall King.

RAGAN
I'll say the like, for I am well assured,
Whate'er I say to please the old man's mind,
Who dotes, as if he were a child again,
I shall enjoy the noble Cambrian Prince.
Only to feed his humour will suffice
To say I am content with anyone

Whom he'll appoint me. This will please him more
Than e'er Apollo's music pleasèd Jove.

GONORILL
I smile to think in what a woeful plight
Cordella will be, when we answer thus.
For she will rather die than give consent
To join in marriage with the Irish King.
So will our father think she loveth him not,
Because she will not grant to his desire,
Which we will aggravate in such bitter terms,
That he will soon convert his love to hate –
For he, you know, is always in extremes.

RAGAN
Not all the world could lay a better plot;
I long till it be put in practice.

Exeunt.

* * * * *

[Scene 3]

Enter Leir and Perillus.

LEIR
Perillus, go seek my daughters. Will them
Immediately come and speak with me.

PERILLUS
I will, my gracious lord.

Exit.

LEIR
Oh, what a combat feels my panting heart,
'Twixt children's love and care of common weal!
How dear my daughters are unto my soul,
None knows but He that knows my thoughts and secret deeds.
Ah, little do they know the dear regard,
Wherein I hold their future state to come.
When they securely sleep on beds of down,
These agèd eyes do watch for their behalf;
While they like wantons sport in youthful toys,

This throbbing heart is pierced with dire annoys.[12]
As doth the sun exceed the smallest star,
So much the father's love exceeds the child's.
Yet my complaints are causeless, for the world
Affords not children more conformable.
And yet, methinks,[13] my mind presageth still –
I know not what, and yet I fear some ill.[14]

Enter Perillus, with the three daughters [Gonorill, Ragan, and Cordella].

Well, here my daughters come. I have found out
A present means to rid me of this doubt.[15]

GONORILL
Our royal lord and father, in all duty,
We come to know the tenor of your will,
Why you so hastily have sent for us.

LEIR
Dear Gonorill, kind Ragan, sweet Cordella,
Ye flourishing branches of a kingly stock,
Sprung from a tree that once did flourish green,
Whose blossoms now are nipped with winter's frost,[16]
And pale, grim death doth wait upon my steps,[17]
And summons me unto his next assizes.
Therefore, dear daughters, as ye tender the safety
Of him that was the cause of your first being,[18]
Resolve a doubt which much molests my mind:
Which of you three to me would prove most kind?
Which loves me most, and which, at my request,
Will soonest yield unto their father's hest?

12 Cf. *Sp. T.* 2.4.64: 'And chill my **throbbing heart with** trembling fear'.

13 Cf. *Sp. T.* 4.1.75: '**And yet methinks** you are'; 5.4.107: '**and yet methinks** I hear'. Cf. also *KL* 19.272–3: '**and yet methinks** the strength of their persuasions stirs me a little'.

14 Cf. *Sp. T.* 2.4.14–15: '**I know not what** myself: | **And yet my** heart foretells me **some** mischance'.

15 Cf. *SP* 2.1.74: 'Now must **I find** the **means to rid** him hence'.

16 Paul V. Rubow compares this line to *Sp. T.* 1.1.13: 'Death's **winter nipped** the **blossoms** of my bliss'. *Shakespeare og hans samtidige* (Copenhagen, 1948).

17 Cf. *Sp. T.* 1.4.39: 'Could win **pale death**'; 5.4.106: 'In black, dark night, to **pale**, dim, cruel **death**'; *SP* 5.4.152: 'And now **pale Death** sits **on my** panting soul'. (Rubow)

18 Cf. *Sp. T.* 5.1.125: '**Of him that was the** bashaw'; *SP* 5.4.93: 'When Brusor lives **that was the cause of** all'.

GONORILL
I hope, my gracious father makes no doubt
Of any of his daughters' love to him.
Yet, for my part, to show my zeal to you,
Which cannot be in windy words rehearsed,
I prize my love to you at such a rate,
I think my life inferior to my love.
Should you enjoin me for to tie a millstone
About my neck and leap into the sea,
At your command I willingly would do it.
Yea, for to do you good, I would ascend
The highest turret in all Brittany,
And from the top leap headlong to the ground.
Nay, more, should you appoint me for to marry
The meanest vassal in the spacious world,
Without reply I would accomplish it.
In brief, command whatever you desire,
And if I fail, no favour I require.

LEIR
Oh, how thy words revive my dying soul!

CORDELLA
[*aside*] Oh, how I do abhor this flattery!

LEIR
But what saith Ragan to her father's will?

RAGAN
Oh, that my simple utterance could suffice
To tell the true intention of my heart,
Which burns in zeal of duty to your grace,
And never can be quenched, but by desire[19]
To show the same in outward forwardness.
Oh, that there were some other maid that durst
But make a challenge of her love with me,
I'd make her soon confess she never loved
Her father half so well as I do you.
Ay, then, my deeds should prove in plainer case,
How much my zeal aboundeth to your grace.
But for them all, let this one mean suffice,

[19] Cf. *SP* 2.1.25: 'Which **never can be** parted **but by** death'; *Corn.* 1.1.58: 'Could **never** have **been** curbed, **but by** itself'.

To ratify my love before your eyes:
I have right noble suitors to my love,
No worse than kings, and haply I love one.
Yet, would you have me make my choice anew,
I'd bridle fancy and be ruled by you.

LEIR
Did never Philomel sing so sweet a note!

CORDELLA
[*aside*] Did never flatterer tell so false a tale!

LEIR
Speak now, Cordella, make my joys at full,
And drop down nectar from thy honey lips.

CORDELLA
I cannot paint my duty forth in words;
I hope my deeds shall make report for me.
But look what love the child doth owe the father,
The same to you I bear, my gracious lord.

GONORILL
Here is an answer answerless indeed.
Were you my daughter, I should scarcely brook it.

RAGAN [*to Cordella*]
Dost thou not blush, proud peacock as thou art,
To make our father such a slight reply?

LEIR [*to Cordella*]
Why how now, minion, are you grown so proud?
Doth our dear love make you thus peremptory?
What, is your love become so small to us,
As that you scorn to tell us what it is?
Do you love us as every child doth love
Their father? True indeed, as some,
Who by disobedience short their father's days,
And so would you. Some are so father-sick,
That they make means to rid them from the world,
And so would you. Some are indifferent,
Whether their agèd parents live or die,
And so are you. But, didst thou know, proud girl,
What care I had to foster thee to this,
Ah, then thou wouldst say as thy sisters do:
'Our life is less than love we owe to you.'

CORDELLA
Dear father, do not so mistake my words,
Nor my plain meaning be misconstrued.
My tongue was never used to flattery.

GONORILL
You were not best say I flatter. If you do,
My deeds shall show, I flatter not with you.[20]
I love my father better than thou canst.

CORDELLA
The praise were great, spoke from another's mouth,
But it should seem your neighbours dwell far off.

RAGAN
Nay, here is one, that will confirm as much
As she hath said, both for myself and her.
I say, thou dost not wish my father's good.

CORDELLA
Dear father –

LEIR
Peace, bastard imp, no issue of King Leir!
I will not hear thee speak one tittle more.
Call not me 'father', if thou love thy life,
Nor these thy sisters once presume to name.
Look for no help henceforth from me nor mine –
Shift as thou wilt, and trust unto thyself.
My kingdom will I equally divide
'Twixt thy two sisters to their royal dower,
And will bestow them worthy their deserts.
This done, because thou shalt not have the hope
To have a child's part in the time to come,
I presently will dispossess myself
And set up these upon my princely throne.

GONORILL
I ever thought that pride would have a fall.

RAGAN [*to Cordella*]
Plain-dealing sister, your beauty is so sheen,
You need no dowry to make you be a queen.

[20] Cf. *SP* 1.6.76–7: 'And to the purpose, far from **flattery**. | Thinks **thou I flatter?** Now **I flatter not!**'. (Rubow)

Exeunt Leir, Gonorill, [and] Ragan.

CORDELLA
Now whither, poor forsaken, shall I go,
When mine own sisters triumph in my woe,
But unto Him which doth protect the just?
In Him will poor Cordella put her trust.
These hands shall labour for to get my spending,
And so I'll live until my days have ending.

[Exit.]

PERILLUS
Oh, how I grieve to see my lord thus fond,
To dote so much upon vain, flatt'ring words.[21]
Ah, if he but with good advice had weighed,
The hidden tenor of her humble speech,
Reason to rage should not have given place,
Nor poor Cordella suffer such disgrace.

Exit.

* * * * *

[Scene 4]

Enter the King of Gallia with Mumford, and three nobles more.

GALLIA Dissuade me not, my lords. I am resolved
This next fair wind to sail for Brittany
In some disguise to see if flying fame
Be not too prodigal in the wonderous praise
Of these three nymphs, the daughters of King Leir.
If present view do answer absent praise,
And eyes allow of what our ears have heard,
And Venus stand auspicious to my vows,
And Fortune favour what I take in hand,
I will return seized of as rich a prize
As Jason when he won the golden fleece.

MUMFORD
Heavens grant you may. The match were full of honour
And well beseeming the young Gallian King.
I would your grace would favour me so much

[21] Cf. *Sp. T.* 3.2.75: 'As fear or **flattering words** may make him false'.

As make me partner of your pilgrimage.[22]
I long to see the gallant British dames
And feed mine eyes upon their rare perfections.
For, till I know the contrary, I'll say
Our dames in France are far more fair than they.

GALLIA
Lord Mumford, you have saved me a labour
In offering that which I did mean to ask,
And I most willingly accept your company.
Yet first I will enjoin you to observe
Some few conditions which I shall propose.

MUMFORD
So that you do not tie mine eyes for looking
After the amorous glances of fair dames,
So that you do not tie my tongue from speaking,
My lips from kissing when occasion serves,
My hands from congees, and my knees to bow
To gallant girls, which were a task more hard
Than flesh and blood is able to endure,
Command what else you please, I rest content.

GALLIA
To bind thee from a thing thou canst not leave
Were but a mean to make thee seek it more,
And therefore speak, look, kiss, salute for me.
In these myself am like to second thee.
Now hear thy task: I charge thee from the time
That first we set sail for the British shore
To use no words of dignity to me,
But in the friendliest manner that thou canst
Make use of me as thy companion.
For we will go disguised in palmers' weeds
That no man shall mistrust us what we are.

MUMFORD
If that be all, I'll fit your turn, I warrant you.
I am some kin to the Blunts and I think the bluntest of all my kindred.
Therefore if I be too blunt with you, thank yourself for praying me to be so.

22 Cf. *Sp. T.* 5.1.79–80: 'Now **would your** lordships **favour me so much | As** but to **grace** me with your acting it'.

GALLIA
Thy pleasant company will make the way seem short.
[*To nobles*] It resteth now that in my absence hence
I do commit the government to you,
My trusty lords and faithful counsellors.
Time cutteth off the rest I have to say.
The wind blows fair, and I must needs away.

NOBLES
Heavens send your voyage to as good effect
As we your land do purpose to protect.

Exeunt.

* * * * *

[Scene 5]

Enter the King of Cornwall and [Cornwall's Servant] booted and spurred, a riding wand and a letter in his hand.

CORNWALL
But how far distant are we from the court?

CORNWALL'S SERVANT
Some twenty miles, my lord, or thereabouts.

CORNWALL
It seemeth to me twenty-thousand miles,
Yet hope I to be there within this hour.

CORNWALL'S SERVANT
(*To himself*) Then are you like to ride alone for me.
I think my lord is weary of his life.[23]

CORNWALL
Sweet Gonorill, I long to see thy face,[24]
Which hast so kindly gratified my love.

Enter [from another door] the King of Cambria booted and spurred, and [Cambria's servant] with a wand and a letter.

[23] Cf. *SP* 2.2.70: 'Why, art thou **weary of** thy **life**?'.

[24] Cf. *SP* 1.4.11: '**I long to see thy face,** brave warrior'.

CAMBRIA
Get a fresh horse – (*He looks on the letter.*) For by my soul I swear
I am past patience longer to forebear
The wishèd sight of my beloved mistress,
Dear Ragan, stay and comfort of my life.

CAMBRIA'S SERVANT
(*To himself*) Now what in God's name doth my lord intend?
He thinks he ne'er shall come at's journey's end.
I would he had old Daedalus' waxen wings
That he might fly, so I might stay behind.
For e'er we get to Troy Novant, I see,
He quite will tire himself, his horse, and me.

Cornwall and Cambria look one upon another and start to see each other there.

CORNWALL
Brother of Cambria, we greet you well,
As one whom here we little did expect.

CAMBRIA
Brother of Cornwall, met in happy time.[25]
I thought as much to have met with the Sultan of Persia
As to have met you in this place, my lord.
No doubt it is about some great affairs
That makes you here so slenderly accompanied.

CORNWALL
To say the truth, my lord, it is no less.
And for your part some hasty wind of chance
Hath blown you hither thus upon the sudden.

CAMBRIA
My lord, to break off further circumstances,
For at this time I cannot brook delays,
Tell you your reason, I will tell you mine.

CORNWALL
In faith, content, and therefore to be brief,
For I am sure my haste's as great as yours:
I am sent for to come unto King Leir,
Who by these present letters promiseth
His eldest daughter, lovely Gonorill,

[25] Cf. *Sp. T.* 1.4.102: 'stooped **in happy time**'. Cf. also *KL* 14.22: 'And, lo, **in happy time** the Cambrian prince'.

To me in marriage, and for present dowry
The moiety of half his regiment.[26]
The lady's love I long ago possessed,
But until now I never had the father's.[27]

CAMBRIA
You tell me wonders! Yet I will relate
Strange news, and henceforth we must brothers call.
[*Showing letters*] Witness these lines: his honourable age,
Being weary of the troubles of his crown,
His princely daughter Ragan will bestow
On me in marriage with half his seigniories,
Whom I would gladly have accepted of
With the third part, her complements are such.

CORNWALL
If I have one half and you have the other,
Then between us we must needs have the whole.

CAMBRIA
The hole! How mean you that? 'Sblood, I hope,
We shall have two holes between us.

CORNWALL
Why, the whole kingdom.

CAMBRIA
Ay, that's very true.

CORNWALL
What then is left for his third daughter's dowry,
Lovely Cordella, whom the world admires?

CAMBRIA
'Tis very strange. I know not what to think,
Unless they mean to make a nun of her.

CORNWALL
'Twere pity such rare beauty should be hid
Within the compass of a cloister's wall.
But howsoe'er, if Leir's words prove true,
It will be good, my lord, for me and you.

[26] Cf. *Sp. T.* 2.3.16–17: 'And shall enjoy **the moiety of his** land. | I'll grace her **marriage**'.
[27] Cf. *Corn.* 4.2.93: '**I never had the** thought to injure them'.

CAMBRIA
Then let us haste all danger to prevent,
For fear delays do alter his intent.

Exeunt.

* * * * *

[Scene 6]

Enter Gonorill and Ragan.

GONORILL
Sister, when did you see Cordella last,
That pretty piece that thinks none good enough
To speak to her, because, sir-reverence,
She hath a little beauty extraordinary?

RAGAN
Since time my father warned her from his presence
I never saw her that I can remember.
God give her joy of her surpassing beauty.
I think her dowry will be small enough.

GONORILL
I have incensed my father so against her,
As he will never be reclaimed again.

RAGAN
I was not much behind to do the like.

GONORILL
Faith, sister, what moves you to bear her such good will?

RAGAN
In truth, I think the same that moveth you:
Because she doth surpass us both in beauty.

GONORILL
Beshrew your fingers, how right you can guess.
I tell you true, it cuts me to the heart.

RAGAN
But we will keep her low enough, I warrant,
And clip her wings for mounting up too high.

GONORILL
Whoever hath her shall have a rich marriage of her.

RAGAN
She were right fit to make a parson's wife.
For they, men say, do love fair women well
And many times do marry them with nothing.

GONORILL
With nothing! Marry, God forbid. Why, are there any such?

RAGAN
I mean, no money.

GONORILL
I cry you mercy, I mistook you much.
And she is far too stately for the church.
She'll lay her husband's benefice on her back,
Even in one gown, if she may have her will.

RAGAN
In faith, poor soul, I pity her a little.
Would she were less fair or more fortunate.
Well, I think long until I see my Morgan,
The gallant Prince of Cambria, here arrive.

GONORILL
And so do I until the Cornwall King
Present himself to consummate my joys.
Peace, here cometh my father.

Enter Leir, Perillus, and [*nobles*].

LEIR
Cease, good my lords, and sue not to reverse
Our censure, which is now irrevocable.
We have dispatchèd letters of contract
Unto the Kings of Cambria and of Cornwall.
Our hand and seal will justify no less.
Then do not so dishonour me, my lords,
As to make shipwreck of our kingly word.
I am as kind as is the pelican
That kills itself to save her young ones' lives
And yet as jealous as the princely eagle
That kills her young ones if they do but dazzle
Upon the radiant splendour of the sun.[28]

[28] Cf. *SP* 3.1.85–7: 'As air bred **eagles**, if they once perceive | That any of their **brood** but close their sight | When they should **gaze against the glorious sun**'. (Wells)

Within this two days I expect their coming.

Enter Kings of Cornwall and Cambria.

But in good time they are arrived already.
This haste of yours, my lords, doth testify
The fervent love you bear unto my daughters.
And think yourselves as welcome to King Leir
As ever Priam's children were to him.

CORNWALL
My gracious lord, and father too, I hope,
Pardon, for that I made no greater haste,
But were my horse as swift as was my will,
I long ere this had seen your majesty.

CAMBRIA
No other 'scuse of absence can I frame
Than what my brother hath informed your grace.
For our undeservèd welcome we do vow
Perpetually to rest at your command.

CORNWALL
But you, sweet love, illustrious Gonorill,
The regent and the sovereign of my soul,[29]
Is Cornwall welcome to your excellency?

GONORILL
As welcome as Leander was to Hero,
Or brave Aeneas to the Carthage Queen,
So and more welcome is your grace to me.

CAMBRIA
Oh, may my fortune prove no worse than his,
Since heavens do know my fancy is as much.
Dear Ragan, say if welcome unto thee.
All welcomes else will little comfort me.

RAGAN
As gold is welcome to the covetous eye,
As sleep is welcome to the traveller,
As is fresh water to sea-beaten men,
Or moistened showers unto the parchèd ground,

[29] Cf. *Sp. T.* 4.8.96: 'My sorrow's ease **and sovereign of my** bliss'; 5.4.39: 'And fair Perseda, **sovereign of my soul**'.

Or anything more welcome than this,
So and more welcome lovely Morgan is.

LEIR
What resteth then, but that we consummate
The celebration of these nuptial rites?
My kingdom I do equally divide.
Princes, draw lots and take your chance as falls.

Then [*Cambria and Cornwall*] *draw lots.*

These I resign as freely unto you
As erst by true succession they were mine.
And here I do freely dispossess myself
And make you two my true adopted heirs.
Myself will sojourn with my son of Cornwall
And take me to my prayers and my beads.
I know my daughter Ragan will be sorry
Because I do not spend my days with her.
Would I were able to be with both at once!
They are the kindest girls in Christendom.

PERILLUS
I have been silent all this while, my lord,
To see if any worthier than myself
Would once have spoke in poor Cordella's cause.
But love or fear ties silence to their tongues.
Oh, hear me speak for her, my gracious lord,
Whose deeds have not deserved this ruthless doom
As thus to disinherit her of all.

LEIR
Urge this no more, an if thou love thy life.[30]
I say, she is no daughter that doth scorn
To tell her father how she loveth him.
Whoever speaketh hereof to me again
I will esteem him for my mortal foe.
Come, let us in to celebrate with joy
The happy nuptials of these lovely pairs.

Exeunt [*all but*] *Perillus.*

PERILLUS
Ah, who so blind as they that will not see
The near approach of their own misery?

[30] Cf. *Sp. T.* 3.4.69: '**an if thou lovest thy life**'.

Poor lady! I extremely pity her,
And whilst I live each drop of my heart blood
Will I strain forth to do her any good.

Exit.

* * * * *

[Scene 7]

Enter the [King of Gallia] and Mumford, disguised like pilgrims.

MUMFORD
My lord, how do you brook this British air?

GALLIA
'My lord'? I told you of this foolish humour
And bound you to the contrary, you know.

MUMFORD
Pardon me for once, my lord. I did forget.

GALLIA
'My lord' again? Then let's have nothing else
And so be ta'en for spies, and then 'tis well.[31]

MUMFORD
Zounds! I could bite my tongue in two for anger.
For God's sake name yourself some proper name.

GALLIA
Call me Tresillus. I'll call thee Denapoll.

MUMFORD
Might I be made the monarch of the world,
I could not hit upon these names, I swear.

GALLIA
Then call me Will; I'll call thee Jack.

MUMFORD
Well, be it so,
For I have well deserved to be called Jack.

Enter Cordella.

[31] Cf. *SP* 1.1.29: 'Nay, my Perseda knows**, and then 'tis well**'.

GALLIA
[*Standing apart*] Stand close, for here a British lady cometh.
A fairer creature ne'er mine eyes beheld.

CORDELLA
This is a day of joy unto my sisters,
Wherein they both are married unto kings,
And I, by birth as worthy as themselves,
Am turned into the world to seek my fortune.
How may I blame the fickle Queen of Chance
That maketh[32] me a pattern of her power?
Ah, poor weak maid, whose imbecility
Is far unable to endure these brunts!
Oh, father Leir, how dost thou wrong thy child,
Who always was obedient to thy will!
But why accuse I Fortune and my father?
No, no, it is the pleasure of my God,
And I do willingly embrace the rod.

GALLIA
It is no goddess, for she doth complain
On Fortune and th'unkindness of her father.

CORDELLA
These costly robes ill-fitting my estate
I will exchange for other, meaner habit.

MUMFORD
Now if I had a kingdom in my hands,
I would exchange it for a milkmaid's smock and petticoat
That she and I might shift our clothes together.

CORDELLA
I will betake me to my thread and needle
And earn my living with my fingers' ends.

MUMFORD
Oh, brave! God willing, thou shalt have my custom.
By sweet St Denis, here I sadly swear,
For all the shirts and night-gear that I wear.

CORDELLA
I will profess and vow a maiden's life.

32 Cf. *Corn.* 1.1.124: '**A** *note* **of Chance that** *may the proud control*'.

MUMFORD
Then I protest thou shalt not have my custom.

GALLIA
I can forbear no longer for to speak,
For if I do, I think my heart will break.[33]

MUMFORD
'Sblood, Will, I hope you are not in love with my sempster.

GALLIA
I am in such a labyrinth of love
As that I know not which way to get out.

MUMFORD
You'll ne'er get out, unless you first get in.

GALLIA
I prithee, Jack, cross not my passions.

MUMFORD
Prithee, Will, to her, and try her patience.

GALLIA
[*Coming forward*] Thou fairest creature, whatsoe'er thou art,
That ever any mortal eyes beheld,
Vouchsafe to me, who have o'erheard thy woes,
To show the cause of these thy sad laments.[34]

CORDELLA
Ah, pilgrims, what avails to show the cause[35]
When there's no means to find a remedy?

GALLIA
To utter grief doth ease a heart o'ercharged.[36]

CORDELLA
To touch a sore doth aggravate the pain.

GALLIA
The silly mouse, by virtue of her teeth,

33 Cf. *SP* 2.1.87: '**I** must unclasp me, or **my heart will break**'.
34 Cf. *Sp. T.* 4.1.61: 'Woe to **the cause of these** constrainèd wars'.
35 Cf. *Sp. T.* 1.4.60: 'Yet **what avails to** wail Andrea's death'.
36 Cf. *Sp. T.* 2.4.102–3: 'To know the author were some **ease** of **grief**, | For in revenge my **heart** would find relief'.

Released the princely lion from the net.[37]

CORDELLA
Kind palmer, which so much desir'st to hear
The tragic tale of my unhappy youth,
Know this in brief: I am the hapless daughter
Of Leir, sometimes King of Brittany.

GALLIA
Why, who debars his honourable age
From being still the King of Brittany?

CORDELLA
None but himself hath dispossessed himself
And given all his kingdom to the Kings
Of Cornwall and of Cambria, with my sisters.

GALLIA
Hath he given nothing to your lovely self?

CORDELLA
He loved me not, and therefore gave me nothing,
Only because I could not flatter him.
And in this day of triumph to my sisters
Doth Fortune triumph in my overthrow.

GALLIA
Sweet lady, say there should come a king
As good as either of your sisters' husbands
To crave your love – would you accept of him?

CORDELLA
Oh, do not mock with those in misery,
Nor do not think, though Fortune have the power[38]
To spoil mine honour and debase my state,
That she hath any interest in my mind.
For if the greatest monarch on the earth
Should sue to me in this extremity,
Except my heart could love and heart could like
Better than any that I ever saw,
His great estate no more should move my mind

[37] Cf. *HP* l. 578: '**the princely lion** with his proud and feltered locks'.

[38] Cf. *SP* 1 Prologue 33: 'Nay then, **though Fortune have** delight in change'; *Corn.* 1.1.98–9: 'And so much more we think our **misery**, | The more that **Fortune hath** with others stood'.

Than mountains move by blast of every wind.

GALLIA
Think not, sweet nymph, 'tis holy palmer's guise
To grievèd souls fresh torments to devise.
Therefore in witness of my true intent
Let heaven and earth bear record of my words:
There is a young and lusty Gallian king,
So like to me as I am to myself,
That earnestly doth crave to have thy love
And join with thee in Hymen's sacred bonds.

CORDELLA
The like to thee did ne'er these eyes behold.
Oh, live to add new torments to my grief!
Why didst thou thus entrap me unawares?
Ah, palmer, my estate doth not befit
A kingly marriage as the case now stands.
Whilom whenas I lived in honour's height
A prince perhaps might postulate my love.
Now misery, dishonour, and disgrace
Hath light on me and quite reversed the case.
Thy king will hold thee wise, if thou surcease
The suit whereas no dowry will ensue.
Then be advisèd, palmer, what to do:
Cease for the king, seek for thyself to woo.

GALLIA
Your birth's too high for any but a king.

CORDELLA
My mind is low enough to love a palmer
Rather than any king upon the earth.

GALLIA
Oh, but you never can endure their life,
Which is so straight and full of penury.

CORDELLA
Oh, yes I can, and happy if I might.
I'll hold thy palmer's staff within my hand
And think it is the sceptre of a queen.
Sometime I'll set thy bonnet on my head[39]

[39] Cf. *SP* 5.3.13–14: 'your Turkish **bonnet** is not **on your head?**'.

And think I wear a rich imperial crown.[40]
Sometime I'll help thee in thy holy prayers
And think I am with thee in paradise.
Thus I'll mock Fortune as she mocketh me
And never will my lovely choice repent.
For having thee, I shall have all content.

GALLIA
[*aside*] 'Twere sin to hold her longer in suspense,
Since that my soul hath vowed she shall be mine. –
Ah, dear Cordella, cordial to my heart,
I am no palmer, as I seem to be,
But hither come in this unknown disguise
To view th'admired beauty of those eyes.
I am the King of Gallia, gentle maid,
Although thus slenderly accompanied,
And yet thy vassal by imperious love,
And sworn to serve thee everlastingly.

CORDELLA
Whate'er you be, of high or low descent,
All's one to me. I do request but this:
That as I am you will accept of me,
And I will have you whatsoe'er you be.
Yet well I know you come of royal race;
I see such sparks of honour in your face.

MUMFORD
Have palmer's weeds such power to win fair ladies?[41]
Faith, then I hope the next that falls is mine.
Upon condition I no worse might speed,
I would forever wear a palmer's weed.
I like an honest and plain-dealing wench
That swears, without exceptions, 'I will have you'.
These foppets that know not whether to love a man or no, except they first go ask their mother's leave – by this hand, I hate them ten times worse than poison.

GALLIA
What resteth then our happiness to procure?

[40] Cf. *SP* 1.6.86: 'Ah, that my **rich imperial** diadem'.

[41] Cf. *Sp. T.* 2.3.42: '**To win fair** Bel-Imperia from her will'.

MUMFORD
Faith, go to church to make the matter sure.

GALLIA
It shall be so, because the world shall say[42]
King Leir's three daughters were wedded in one day.
The celebration of this happy chance
We will defer until we come to France.

MUMFORD
I like the wooing that's not long a-doing.
Well, for her sake, I know what I know. I'll never marry whilst I live, except I have one of these British ladies. My humour is alienated from the maids of France.

Exeunt.

* * * * *

[Scene 8]

Enter Perillus [*alone*].

PERILLUS
The king hath dispossessed himself of all,
Those to advance which scarce will give him thanks.
His youngest daughter he hath turned away,
And no man knows what is become of her.[43]
He sojourns now in Cornwall with the eldest,
Who flattered him until she did obtain
That at his hands which now she doth possess,
And now she sees he hath no more to give,
It grieves her heart to see her father live.
Oh, whom should man trust in this wicked age,
When children thus against their parents rage?
But he, the mirror of mild patience,
Puts up all wrongs and never gives reply.
Yet shames she not in most opprobrious sort
To call him fool and dotard to his face
And sets her parasites of purpose oft
In scoffing-wise to offer him disgrace.
O iron age! O times! Oh, monstrous, vild

[42] Cf. *Sp. T.* 5.1.147: 'As all **the world shall say**'.
[43] Cf. *Sp. T.* 3.4.46: '**And no man knows** it'.

When parents are contemnèd of a child!
His pension she hath half restrained from him
And will, e'er long, the other half, I fear.
For she thinks nothing is bestowed in vain
But that which doth her father's life maintain.
Trust not alliance, but trust strangers rather,
Since daughters prove disloyal to the father.
Well, I will counsel him the best I can.[44]
Would I were able to redress his wrong,
Yet what I can, unto my utmost power,
He shall be sure of to the latest hour.

Exit.

* * * * *

[Scene 9]

Enter Gonorill and Scaliger.

GONORILL
Ay, prithee, Scaliger, tell me what thou thinkst.
Could any woman of our dignity
Endure such quips and peremptory taunts
As I do daily from my doting father?
Doth't not suffice that I him keep of alms,
Who is not able for to keep himself?
But as if he were our better, he should think
To check and snap me up at every word.
I cannot make me a new-fashioned gown
And set it forth with more than common cost,
But his old doting doltish withered wit
Is sure to give a senseless check for it.
I cannot make a banquet extraordinary
To grace myself and spread my name abroad,
But he, old fool, is captious by and by
And saith the cost would well suffice for twice.
Judge then, I pray, what reason is't that I[45]
Should stand alone charged with his vain expense,
And that my sister Ragan should go free,

[44] Cf. *SP* 1.5.62–3: '**I'll do the best I can** to find your chain'. Cf. also *KL* 3.22: 'Thee to requite, **the best I can, I'll do**'.

[45] *Sp. T.* 4.4.38: 'Or wherein **is't that I** offended thee'.

To whom he gave as much as unto me?
Ay, prithee, Scaliger, tell me, if thou know
By any means to rid me of this woe.

SCALIGER
Your many favours still bestowed on me
Bind me in duty to advise your grace
How you may soonest remedy this ill:
The large allowance which he hath from you
Is that which makes him so forget himself.
Therefore abridge it half, and you shall see
That, having less, he will more thankful be.
For why, abundance maketh us forget
The fountains whence the benefits do spring.

GONORILL
Well, Scaliger, for thy kind advice herein
I will not be ungrateful, if I live.
I have restrained half his portion already,
And I will presently restrain the other,
That having no means to relieve himself
He may go seek elsewhere for better help.

Exit.

SCALIGER
Go, viperous woman, shame to all thy sex.
The heavens, no doubt, will punish thee for this,
And me, a villain that to curry favour
Have given the daughter counsel 'gainst the father.
But us the world doth this experience give:
That he that cannot flatter, cannot live.[46]

Exit.

* * * * *

[Scene 10]

Enter King of Cornwall, Leir, Perillus, and nobles.

CORNWALL
Father, what aileth you to be so sad?
Methinks you frolic not as you were wont.

46 Cf. *SP* 2.1.329: '**That he that can** bring forth the murderer'.

LEIR
The nearer we do grow unto our graves,
The less we do delight in worldly joys.

CORNWALL
But if a man can frame himself to mirth,
It is a mean for to prolong his life.

LEIR
Then welcome sorrow, Leir's only friend,
Who doth desire his troubled days had end.

CORNWALL
Comfort yourself, father. Here comes your daughter,
Who much will grieve, I know, to see you sad.

Enter Gonorill.

LEIR
[*aside*] But more doth grieve, I fear, to see me live.

CORNWALL
My Gonorill, you come in wishèd time
To put your father from these pensive dumps.
In faith, I fear that all things go not well.[47]

GONORILL
What do you fear, that I have angered him?
Hath he complained of me unto my lord?
I'll provide him a piece of bread and cheese,
For in a time he'll practice nothing else
Than carry tales from one unto another.[48]
'Tis all his practice for to kindle strife
'Twixt you, my lord, and me your loving wife.
But I will take an order, if I can,
To cease th'effect where first the cause began.

CORNWALL
Sweet, be not angry in a partial cause.
He ne'er complained of thee in all his life.
Father, you must not weigh a woman's words.

47 Cf. *Sp. T.* 5.3.4: 'To look **that all things** may **go well**'.
48 Cf. *HP* l. 462: 'did pass **from one unto another**'.

LEIR
Alas, not I. Poor soul, she breeds young bones,
And that it is makes her so touchy, sure.

GONORILL
What, breeds young bones already! You will make
An honest woman of me then, belike.
Oh, vild old wretch! Whoever heard the like,
That seeketh thus his own child to defame?

CORNWALL
I cannot stay to hear this discord sound.

Exit.

GONORILL
For anyone that loves your company
You may go pack and seek some other place
To sow the seed of discord and disgrace.

Exit.

LEIR
Thus, say or do the best that e'er I can,
'Tis wrested straight into another sense.
This punishment my heavy sins deserve,
And more than this ten-thousand-thousand times,
Else agèd Leir them could never find
Cruel to him to whom he hath been kind.
Why do I over-live myself to see
The course of nature quite reversed in me?
Ah, gentle death, if ever any wight
Did wish thy presence with a perfect zeal,
Then come, I pray thee, even with all my heart,
And end my sorrows with thy fatal dart.

He weeps.

PERILLUS
Ah, do not so disconsolate yourself,
Nor dew your agèd cheeks with wasting tears.

LEIR
What man art thou that takest any pity
Upon the worthless state of old Leir?

PERILLUS
One who doth bear as great a share of grief
As if it were my dearest father's case.

LEIR
Ah, good my friend, how ill art thou advised
For to consort with miserable men.
Go learn to flatter, where thou mayst in time
Get favour 'mongst the mighty and so climb.
For now I am so poor and full of want
As that I ne'er can recompense thy love.

PERILLUS
What's got by flattery doth not long endure,
And men in favour live not most secure.
My conscience tells me, if I should forsake you,
I were the hatefullest excrement on the earth,
Which well do know, in course of former time,
How good my lord hath been to me and mine.

LEIR
Did I ere raise thee higher than the rest
Of all thy ancestors which were before?

PERILLUS
I ne'er did seek it, but by your good grace,
I still enjoyed my own with quietness.

LEIR
Did I e'er give thee living to increase
The due revenues which thy father left?

PERILLUS
I had enough, my lord, and having that,
What should you need to give me any more?

LEIR
Oh, did I ever dispossess myself
And give thee half my kingdom in good will?

PERILLUS
Alas, my lord, there were no reason why
You should have such a thought to give it me.

LEIR
Nay, if thou talk of reason, then be mute,
For with good reason I can thee confute.
If they, which first by nature's sacred law,
Do owe to me the tribute of their lives;
If they to whom I always have been kind

And bountiful beyond comparison;
If they for whom I have undone myself
And brought my age unto this extreme want
Do now reject, contemn, despise, abhor me,
What reason moveth thee to sorrow for me?

PERILLUS
[*He weeps*] Where reason fails, let tears confirm my love
And speak how much your passions do me move.
Ah, good my lord, condemn not all for one.
You have two daughters left, to whom I know
You shall be welcome, if you please to go.

LEIR
Oh, how thy words add sorrow to my soul[49]
To think of my unkindness to Cordella,
Whom causeless I did dispossess of all
Upon th'unkind suggestions of her sisters.
And for her sake I think this heavy doom
Is fallen on me, and not without desert.
Yet unto Ragan was I always kind
And gave to her the half of all I had.
It may be, if I should to her repair,
She would be kinder and entreat me fair.

PERILLUS
No doubt she would and practice, ere't be long,
By force of arms for to redress your wrong.

LEIR
Well, since thou dost advise me for to go,
I am resolved to try the worst of woe.

Exeunt.

* * * * *

[Scene 11]

Enter Ragan [*alone*].

RAGAN
How may I bless the hour of my nativity,
Which bodeth unto me such happy stars!

[49] Cf. *Sp. T.* 1.5.3: 'These pleasant sights are **sorrow to my soul**'.

How may I thank kind Fortune that vouchsafes
To all my actions such desired event!
I rule the King of Cambria as I please.
The states are all obedient to my will,
And look whate'er I say it shall be so.
Not anyone, that dareth, answers 'no'.
My eldest sister lives in royal state
And wanteth nothing fitting her degrees.
Yet hath she such a cooling card withal,
As that her honey savoureth much of gall.
My father with her is quartermaster still
And many times restrains her of her will.
But if he were with me and served me so,[50]
I'd send him packing somewhere else to go.
I'd entertain him with such slender cost
That he should quickly wish to change his host.

Exit.

* * * * *

[Scene 12]

Enter Cornwall, Gonorill, and attendants.

CORNWALL
Ah, Gonorill, what dire, unhappy chance
Hath sequestered thy father from our presence
That no report can yet be heard of him?
Some great unkindness hath been offered him,
Exceeding far the bounds of patience.
Else all the world shall never me persuade[51]
He would forsake us without notice made.

GONORILL
Alas, my lord, whom doth it touch so near,
Or who hath interest in this grief, but I,
Whom sorrow had brought to her longest home,
But that I know his qualities so well?[52]
I know he is but stolen upon my sister
At unawares to see her how she fares

[50] Cf. *Sp. T.* 4.6.96: '**But if he be** thus'; 5.4.47: '**But if he be** your rival'.
[51] Cf. *Sp. T.* 5.1.147: 'As **all the world shall** say'.
[52] Cf. *Sp. T.* 1.2.166: '**But that I know** your grace for just and wise'.

And spend a little time with her to note
How all things go and how she likes her choice.
And when occasion serves he'll steal from her
And unawares return to us again.[53]
Therefore, my lord, be frolic, and resolve
To see my father here again ere long.

CORNWALL
I hope so, too, but yet to be more sure,
I'll send a post immediately to know
Whether he be arrivèd there or no.

Exit.

GONORILL
But I will intercept the messenger
And temper him before he doth depart
With sweet persuasions and with sound rewards
That his report shall ratify my speech
And make my lord cease further to inquire.
If he be not gone to my sister's court,
As sure my mind presageth that he is,
He haply may, by travelling unknown ways,
Fall sick and as a common passenger
Be dead and buried. Would God it were so well.
For then there were no more to-do but this:[54]
He went away, and none knows where he is.
But say he be in Cambria with the king
And there exclaim against me, as he will?
I know he is as welcome to my sister
As water is into a broken ship.
Well, after him I'll send such thunderclaps
Of slander, scandal, and invented tales
That all the blame shall be removed from me
And unperceived rebound upon himself.
Thus with one nail another I'll expel
And make the world judge that I used him well.[55]

Enter the Messenger *that should go to Cambria, with a letter in his hand.*

53 Cf. *SP* 1 Prologue 39: '**And**, as **occasion serves**, make our **return**'.
54 Cf. *SP* 2.1.321: '**Then do but this**, and I will make thee free'.
55 Cf. *Sp. T.* 3.2.77: '**I used him** in this enterprise'.

My honest friend, whither away so fast?

MESSENGER
To Cambria, madam, with letters from the king.

GONORILL
To whom?

MESSENGER
Unto your father, if he be there.

GONORILL
Let me see them.[56]

She opens them.

MESSENGER
Madam, I hope your grace will stand between me and my neck-verse, if I be called in question for opening the king's letters.[57]

GONORILL
'Twas I that opened them. It was not thou.

MESSENGER
Ay, but you need not care, and so must I, a handsome man, be quickly trussed up. And when a man's hanged, all the world cannot save him.

GONORILL
He that hangs thee were better hang his father,
Or that but hurts thee in the least degree.
I tell thee, we make a great account of thee.

MESSENGER
I am o'erjoyed; I surfeit of sweet words.
Kind queen, had I a hundred lives, I would
Spend ninety nine of them for you, for that word.

GONORILL
Ay, but thou wouldst keep one life still,
And that's as many as thou art like to have.

MESSENGER
That one life is not too dear for my good queen. This

[56] Cf. *Sp. T.* 4.7.50: '**let me see them**'.

[57] Cf. *Sp. T.* 3.3.14: '**Will stand between me and** ensuing harms'; 4.1.26: 'You **will stand between** the gallows **and me**?'.

sword, this buckler, this head, this heart, these hands, arms, legs, tripes, bowels, and all the members else whatsoever are at your dispose. Use me, trust me, command me. If I fail in anything, tie me to a dung-cart and make a scavenger's horse of me and whip me, so long as I have any skin on my back.

GONORILL
In token of further employment, take that.

Flings him a purse.

MESSENGER
A strong bond, a firm obligation, good in law, good in law. If I keep not the condition, let my neck be the forfeiture of my negligence.

GONORILL
I like thee well. Thou hast a good tongue.

MESSENGER
And as bad a tongue, if it be set on it, as any oyster-wife at Billingsgate hath. Why, I have made many of my neighbours forsake their houses with railing upon them, and go dwell elsewhere, and so by my means houses have been good cheap in our parish. My tongue being well whetted with choler is more sharp than a razor of Palermo.

GONORILL
Oh, thou art a fit man for my purpose.

MESSENGER
Commend me not, sweet queen, before you try me.
As my deserts are, so do think of me.

GONORILL
Well said. Then this is thy trial. [*Producing letters*] Instead of carrying the king's letters to my father, carry thou these letters to my sister, which, containing matter[58] quite contrary to the other, there shall she be given to understand that my father hath detracted her, given out slanderous speeches against her, and that he hath most intolerably abused me, set my lord and me at variance, and made mutinies amongst the commons.
These things, although it be not so,
Yet thou must affirm them to be true,
With oaths and protestations as will serve

[58] Cf. *Sp. T.* 5.1.154: '**Containing matter**, and not common things'.

To drive my sister out of love with him
And cause my will accomplishèd to be.
This do, thou winst my favour forever
And makest a highway of preferment to thee
And all thy friends.

MESSENGER
It sufficeth. Conceit it is already done.[59] I will so tongue-whip him that I will leave him as bare of credit as a poulter leaves a cony when she pulls off his skin.

GONORILL
Yet there is a further matter.

MESSENGER
I thirst to hear it.

GONORILL
If my sister thinketh convenient, as my letters importeth, to make him away, hast thou the heart to effect it?

MESSENGER
Few words are best in so small a matter.
These are but trifles. By this book I will.

Kiss the paper.

GONORILL
About it presently. I long till it be done.

MESSENGER
I fly; I fly.

Exeunt.

* * * * *

[Scene 13]

Enter Cordella [*alone*].

CORDELLA
I have been over-negligent today
In going to the temple of my God
To render thanks for all His benefits,
Which He miraculously hath bestowed on me
In raising me out of my mean estate,

[59] Cf. *Sp. T.* 5.1.131: 'For I **already** have **conceited** that'.

Whenas I was devoid of worldly friends,
And placing me in such a sweet content
As far exceeds the reach of my deserts.
My kingly husband, mirror of his time
For zeal, for justice, kindness, and for care
To God, his subjects, me, and commonweal,
By His appointment was ordained for me.
I cannot wish the thing that I do want;
I cannot want the thing but I may have,
Save only this which I shall ne'er obtain:
My father's love. Oh, this I ne'er shall gain.
I would abstain from any nutriment
And pine my body to the very bones.
Barefoot I would on pilgrimage set forth
Unto the furthest quarters of the earth,
And all[60] my lifetime would I sackcloth wear,
And mourning-wise pour dust upon my head,
So he but to forgive me once would please
That his grey hairs might go to heaven in peace.
And yet I know not how I him offended
Or wherein justly I have deserved blame.
Oh, sisters! You are much to blame in this.
It was not he, but you that did me wrong.
Yet God forgive both him and you and me,
Even as I do in perfect charity.
I will to church and pray unto my saviour
That ere I die, I may obtain his favour.

Exit.

[Scene 14]

Enter Leir and Perillus faintly.

PERILLUS
Rest on me, my lord, and stay yourself.
The way seems tedious to your agèd limbs.

LEIR
Nay, rest on me, kind friend, and stay thyself.
Thou art as old as I, but more kind.

[60] Cf. *Corn.* 4.2.25: 'The sea, **the earth, and all** is almost ours'.

PERILLUS
Ah, good my lord, it ill befits that I
Should lean upon the person of a king.[61]

LEIR
But it fits worse that I should bring thee forth
That had no cause to come along with me
Through these uncouth paths and tireful ways
And never ease thy fainting limbs a whit.
Thou hast left all, ay, all to come with me,
And I, for all, have naught to guerdon thee.

PERILLUS
Cease, good my lord, to aggravate my woes
With these kind words, which cuts my heart in two
To think your will should want the power to do.[62]

LEIR
Cease, good Perillus, for to call me lord,
And think me but the shadow of myself.

PERILLUS
That honourable title will I give
Unto my lord so long as I do live.
Oh, be of comfort, for I see the place
Whereas your daughter keeps her residence.
And, lo, in happy time the Cambrian prince
Is here arrived to gratify our coming.

Enter Prince of Cambria, Ragan, and nobles.
[*Leir and Perillus*] *look upon them and whisper together.*

LEIR
Were I best speak or sit me down and die?
I am ashamed to tell this heavy tale.

PERILLUS
Then let me tell it, if you please, my lord.
'Tis shame for them that were the cause thereof.

CAMBRIA
What two old men are those that seem so sad?
Methinks I should remember well their looks.[63]

[61] Cf. *SP* 1.6.72: '**Shouldst** come about **the person of a king**'.
[62] Cf. *Corn.* 3.3.132: 'That have **the power to do** what pleaseth them'.
[63] Cf. *SP* 4.1.203: '**Methinks I should** not part with two such friends'.

RAGAN
No, I mistake not – sure it is my father!
[*Aside*] I must dissemble kindness now of force.
She runs to him and kneels down, saying:
Father, I bid you welcome full of grief
To see your grace used thus unworthily
And ill-befitting your reverend age,
To come on foot a journey so indurable.
Oh, what disaster chance hath been the cause
To make your cheeks so hollow, spare, and lean?
He cannot speak for weeping. – For God's love, come!
Let us refresh him with some needful things,
And at more leisure we may better know
Whence springs the ground of this unlooked-for woe.[64]

CAMBRIA
Come, father, e'er we any further talk,
You shall refresh you after this weary walk.

Exeunt [*all but*] *Ragan.*

RAGAN
Comes he to me with finger in the eye
To tell a tale against my sister here,
Whom I do know he greatly hath abused?
And now like a contentious, crafty wretch
He first begins for to complain himself[65]
Whenas himself is in the greatest fault.
I'll not be partial in my sister's cause,
Nor yet believe his doting, vain reports,
Who for a trifle, safely I dare say
Upon a spleen, is stolen thence away.
And here, forsooth, he hopeth to have harbour
And to be moaned and made on like a child.
But ere't be long, his coming shall curse
And truly say he came from bad to worse.
Yet will I make fair weather to procure
Convenient means, and then I'll strike it sure.

Exit.

* * * * *

64 Cf. *Sp. T.* 4.8.72: '**Whence** grows **the ground of this** report'.
65 Cf. *SP* 5.2.40: '**he first began to** question us'.

[Scene 15]

Enter Messenger [alone with letters].

MESSENGER
Now happily I am arrivèd here
Before the stately palace of the Cambrian king.
If Leir be here safe-seated and in rest,
To rouse him from it I will do my best.

Enter Ragan

[*Aside*] Now bags of gold, your virtue is, no doubt,
To make me in my message bold and stout.
[*To Ragan*] The King of Heaven preserve your majesty
And send your highness everlasting reign.

RAGAN
Thanks, good my friend, but what imports thy message?

MESSENGER
Kind greetings from the Cornwall Queen.
[*Giving letters*] The residue these letters will declare.
She opens the letters.

RAGAN
How fares our royal sister?

MESSENGER
I did leave her at my parting in good health.
She reads the letter, frowns, and stamps.
[*Aside*] See how her colour comes and goes again,
Now red as scarlet, now as pale as ash.
See how she knits her brow and bites her lips
And stamps and makes a dumb show of disdain,
Mixed with revenge and violent extremes.
Here will be more work and more crowns for me.

RAGAN
Alas, poor soul, and hath he used her thus?
And is he now come hither with intent
To set divorce betwixt my lord and me?[66]
Doth he give out that he doth hear report
That I do rule my husband as I list
And therefore means to alter so the case

[66] Cf. *Sp. T.* 1.1.14: 'Forcing **divorce betwixt my** love **and me**'.

That I shall know my lord to be my head?
Well, it were best for him to take good heed,
Or I will make him hop without a head
For his presumption, dotard that he is.
In Cornwall he hath made such mutinies –
First, setting of the king against the queen,
Then stirring up the commons 'gainst the king –
That had he there continued any longer,
He had been called in question for his fact.
So upon that occasion thence he fled
And comes thus slyly stealing unto us,
And now already since his coming hither,
My lord and he are grown in such a league
That I can have no conference with his grace.
I fear he doth already intimate
Some forgèd cavillations 'gainst my state.
'Tis therefore best to cut him off in time,
Lest slanderous rumours,[67] once abroad dispersed,
It is too late for them to be reversed. –
Friend, as the tenor of these letters shows,
My sister puts great confidence in thee.

MESSENGER
She never yet committed trust to me
But that, I hope, she found me always faithful.
So will I be to any friend of hers[68]
That hath occasion to employ my help.

RAGAN
Hast thou the heart to act a stratagem
And give a stab or two, if need require?[69]

MESSENGER
I have a heart compact of adamant,
Which never knew what melting pity meant.[70]
I weigh no more the murdering of a man
Than I respect the cracking of a flea
When I do catch her biting on my skin.
If you will have your husband or your father

[67] Cf. *SP* 1.5.56–7: '**Lest** public **rumour** might advertise her'.

[68] Cf. *SP* 1.1.46: 'As careful **will I be to** keep this chain'.

[69] Cf. *SP* 2.1.215: 'I have some little reply, **if need require**'.

[70] Cf. *SP* 1.2.97–8: 'Whereby **I** purchased the surname of "**Pity's adamant**"'.

Or both of them sent to another world,
Do but command me do't. It shall be done.

RAGAN
It is enough. We make no doubt of thee.[71]
Meet us tomorrow here at nine o'clock.
Meanwhile farewell, [*giving money*] and drink that for my sake.

Exit.

MESSENGER
Ay, this is it will make me do the deed.[72]
Oh, had I every day such customers,
This were the gainfulest trade in Christendom!
A purse of gold given for a paltry stab.
Why, here's a wench that longs to have a stab.
Well, I could give it her and ne'er hurt her neither.[73]

[*Exit.*]

* * * * *

[Scene 16]

Enter the King of Gallia and Cordella.

GALLIA
When will these clouds of sorrow once disperse,
And smiling joy triumph upon thy brow?
When will this scene of sadness have an end
And pleasant acts ensue to move delight?
When will my lovely queen cease to lament
And take some comfort to her grievèd thoughts?
If of thyself thou deign'st to have no care,
Yet pity me, whom thy grief makes despair.

CORDELLA
Oh, grieve not you, my lord. You have no cause.[74]
Let not my passions move your mind a whit,
For I am bound by nature to lament
For his ill will that life to me first lent.

[71] Cf. *Sp. T.* 5.1.129: '**make no doubt of** it'.
[72] Cf. *Sp. T.* 1.3.86: '**Ay, this was it**'.
[73] Cf. *Sp. T.* 4.8.31: 'I **give it her and** thee'.
[74] Cf. *Sp. T.* 4.8.136: 'I hope **you have no cause**'.

If so the stock be drièd with disdain,
Withered and sere the branch must needs remain.

GALLIA
But thou art now graft in another stock.
I am the stock and thou the lovely branch,
And from my root continual sap shall flow
To make thee flourish with perpetual spring.
Forget thy father and thy kindred now
Since they forsake thee like inhuman beasts.
Think they are dead, since all their kindness dies,
And bury them where black oblivion lies.
Think not thou art the daughter of old Leir
Who did unkindly disinherit thee,
But think thou art the noble Gallian queen
And wife to him that dearly loveth thee.
Embrace the joys that present with thee dwell;
Let sorrow pack and hide herself in hell.

CORDELLA
Not that I miss my country or my kin –
My old acquaintance or my ancient friends
Doth any whit distemperate my mind,
Knowing you, which are more dear to me
Than country, kin, and all things else can be.
Yet pardon me, my gracious lord, in this:
For what can stop the course of nature's power?
As easy is it for four-footed beasts[75]
To stay themselves upon the liquid air
And mount aloft into the element
And overstrip the feathered fowls in flight,
As easy is it for the slimy fish
To live and thrive without the help of water,
As easy is it for the blackamoor
To wash the tawny colour from his skin,
Which all oppose against the course of nature,
As I am able to forget my father.

GALLIA
Mirror of virtue, phoenix of our age,

[75] Cf. *Sp. T.* 4.8.89: 'how **easy is it for** him to err'. Cf. also *KL* 16.40: '**As easy is it for** the slimy fish'; 16.42: '**As easy is it for** the blackamoor'.

Too kind a daughter for an unkind father![76]
Be of good comfort, for I will dispatch
Ambassadors immediately for Britain
Unto the King of Cornwall's court, whereas
Your father keepeth now his residence,
And in the kindest manner him entreat,
That setting former grievances apart,
He will be pleased to come and visit us.
If no entreaty will suffice the turn,
I'll offer him the half of all my crown.
If that moves not, we'll furnish out a fleet
And sail to Cornwall for to visit him,
And there you shall be firmly reconciled
In perfect love, as erst you were before.

CORDELLA
Where tongue cannot sufficient thanks afford,
The King of Heaven remunerate my lord.

GALLIA
Only be blithe and frolic, sweet, with me.
This and much more I'll do to comfort thee.

[*Exeunt.*]

* * * * *

[Scene 17]

Enter Messenger [*alone*].

MESSENGER
It is a world to see, now I am flush,
How many friends I purchase everywhere,[77]
How many seeks to creep into my favour
And kiss their hands and bend their knees to me![78]
No more.
Here comes the queen. Now shall I know her mind
And hope for to derive more crowns from her.

Enter Ragan [*with two purses*].

[76] Cf. *Sp. T.* 5.1.7: '**unkind father**'.
[77] Cf. *SP* 4.2.4–5: 'My valour **everywhere** shall **purchase friends**'.
[78] Cf. *Sp. T.* 1.4.171: '**And** made **them bow their knees to** Albion'.

RAGAN
My friend, I see thou mind'st thy promise well
And art before me here, methinks, today.

MESSENGER
I am a poor man, an it like your grace,
But yet I always love to keep my word.

RAGAN
Well, keep thy word with me, and thou shalt see
That of a poor man I will make thee rich.

MESSENGER
I long to hear it. It might have been dispatched,
If you had told me of it yesternight.

RAGAN
It is a thing of right strange consequence
And well I cannot utter it in words.

MESSENGER
It is more strange that I am not by this
Beside myself with longing for to hear it.
Were it to meet the devil in his den
And try a bout with him for a scratched face,
I'd undertake it, if you would but bid me.

RAGAN
Ah, good my friend, that I should have thee do
Is such a thing as I do shame to speak –
Yet it must needs be done.

MESSENGER
I'll speak it for thee, queen. Shall I kill thy father?
I know 'tis that, and if it be so, say.

RAGAN

Ay.

MESSENGER
Why, that's enough.

RAGAN
And yet that is not all.

MESSENGER
What else?

RAGAN
Thou must kill that old man that came with him.

MESSENGER
Here are two hands; for each of them is one.

RAGAN
And for each hand here is a recompence.

Gives him two purses.

MESSENGER
Oh, that I had ten hands by miracle!
I could tear ten in pieces with my teeth,[79]
So in my mouth you'd put a purse of gold.
But in what manner must it be effected?

RAGAN
Tomorrow morning ere the break of day
I by a wile will send them to the thicket
That is about some two miles from the court
And promise them to meet them there myself,
Because I must have private conference
About some news I have received from Cornwall.
This is enough; I know they will not fail.
And then be ready for to play thy part.
Which done, thou mayst right easily escape
And no man once mistrust thee for the fact.
But yet, before thou prosecute the act,
Show him the letter which my sister sent.
There let him read his own indictment first,
And then proceed to execution.
But see thou faint not, for they will speak fair.

MESSENGER
Could he speak words as pleasing as the pipe
Of Mercury, which charmed the hundred eyes
Of watchful Argus and enforced him sleep,
(*To the purse*) Yet here are words so pleasing to my thoughts,
As quite shall take away the sound of his.

Exit.

RAGAN
About it then, and when thou hast dispatched,

[79] Cf. *Sp. T.* 4.7.122: 'Shivering their limbs **in pieces with my teeth**.'

I'll find a means to send thee after him.

Exit.

* * * * *

[Scene 18]

Enter Cornwall and Gonorill.

CORNWALL
I wonder that the messenger doth stay
Whom we dispatched for Cambria so long since.
If that his answer do not please us well,
And he do show good reason for delay,
I'll teach him how to dally with his king,
And to detain us in such long suspense.

GONORILL
My lord, I think the reason may be this:
My father means to come along with him,
And therefore 'tis his pleasure he shall stay
For to attend upon him on the way.

CORNWALL
It may be so, and therefore till I know
The truth thereof, I will suspend my judgement.

Enter Servant.

SERVANT
An't like your grace, there is an ambassador arrived from Gallia and craves admittance to your majesty.

CORNWALL
From Gallia? What should his message
Hither import? Is not your father haply
Gone thither? Well, whatsoe'er it be,
Bid him come in. He shall have audience.

Enter Ambassador.

What news from Gallia? Speak, ambassador.

AMBASSADOR
The noble King and Queen of Gallia first salutes,
By me, their honourable father, my lord Leir.
Next, they commend them kindly to your graces,

As those whose welfare they entirely wish.
Letters I have to deliver to my lord Leir,
And presents, too, if I might speak with him.

GONORILL
If you might speak with him? Why, do you think
We are afraid that you should speak with him?

AMBASSADOR
Pardon me, madam, for I think not so,
But say so only 'cause he is not here.

CORNWALL
Indeed, my friend, upon some urgent cause
He is at this time absent from the court.
But if a day or two you here repose,
'Tis very likely you shall have him here
Or else have certain notice where he is.

GONORILL
Are not we worthy to receive your message?

AMBASSADOR
I had in charge to do it to himself.

GONORILL
[*To herself*] It may be then 'twill not be done in haste. –
How doth my sister brook the air of France?

AMBASSADOR
Exceeding well, and never sick one hour
Since first she set her foot upon the shore.[80]

GONORILL
I am the more sorry.

AMBASSADOR
I hope not so, madam.

GONORILL
Didst thou not say that she was ever sick
Since the first hour that she arrivèd there?

AMBASSADOR
No, madam, I said quite contrary.

[80] Cf. *Corn.* 3.3.183: '**Upon the shore**'.

GONORILL
Then I mistook thee.

CORNWALL
Then she is merry, if she have her health?

AMBASSADOR
Oh, no, her grief exceeds, until the time
That she be reconciled unto her father.

GONORILL
God continue it.

AMBASSADOR
What, madam?

GONORILL
Why, her health.

AMBASSADOR
Amen to that. But God release her grief
And send her father in a better mind
Than to continue always so unkind.

CORNWALL
I'll be a mediator in her cause
And seek all means to expiate his wrath.

AMBASSADOR
Madam, I hope your grace will do the like.

GONORILL
Should I be a mean to exasperate his wrath
Against my sister,[81] whom I love so dear?[82] No, no.

AMBASSADOR
To expiate or mitigate his wrath,
For he hath misconceived without a cause.

GONORILL
Oh, ay, what else?

AMBASSADOR
'Tis pity it should be so.
Would it were otherwise.

81 Cf. *Sp. T.* 4.4.70: 'My father's old **wrath** hath **exasperate**'; *Corn.* 3.3.128: '**His wrath against** you 'twill **exasperate**'. (Rubow)

82 Cf. *SP* 3.5.31: ''Tis for Perseda **whom I love so** well'.

GONORILL

It were great pity
It should be otherwise.

AMBASSADOR

Than how, madam?

GONORILL

Than that they should be reconciled again.

AMBASSADOR

It shows you bear an honourable mind.

GONORILL

[*Speaks to herself*] It shows thy understanding to be blind
And that thou hadst need of an interpreter.
Well, I will know thy message ere't be long
And find a mean to cross it, if I can.

CORNWALL

Come in, my friend, and frolic in our court
Till certain notice of my father come.

Exeunt.

* * * * *

[Scene 19]

Enter Leir and Perillus [*with books*].

PERILLUS

My lord, you are up today before your hours.
'Tis news to you to be abroad so rathe.

LEIR

'Tis news indeed. I am so extreme heavy
That I can scarcely keep my eyelids open.

PERILLUS

And so am I, but I impute the cause
To rising sooner than we use to do.

LEIR

Hither my daughter means to come disguised.
I'll sit me down and read until she come.

Pull out a book and sit down.

PERILLUS
She'll not be long, I warrant you, my lord.
But say a couple of these they call goodfellows
Should step out of a hedge and set upon us?
We were in good case for to answer them.

LEIR
'Twere not for us to stand upon our hands.

PERILLUS
I fear we scant should stand upon our legs,
But how should we do to defend ourselves?

LEIR
Even pray to God to bless us from their hands,
For fervent prayer much ill hap withstands.

PERILLUS
I'll sit and pray with you for company,
Yet was I ne'er so heavy in my life.

They fall both asleep.

Enter the Messenger or murderer with [a letter and] two daggers in his hands.

MESSENGER
Were it not a mad jest if two or three of my profession should meet me and lay me down in a ditch and play rob-thief with me and perforce take my gold away from me whilst I act this stratagem, and by this means the greybeards should escape? Faith, when I were at liberty again, I would make no more to-do but go to the next tree and there hang myself.

See them and start.

But stay, methinks my youths are here already
And with pure zeal have prayed themselves asleep.
I think they know to what intent they came
And are provided for another world.

He takes their books away.

Now could I stab them bravely while they sleep
And in a manner put them to no pain,[83]
And doing so, I showed them mighty friendship.
For fear of death is worse than death itself,[84]

[83] Cf. *Sp. T.* 4.6.87: '**and in a manner** lunatic'.
[84] Cf. *SP* 1.5.75: 'And loss of happiness **is worse than death**'.

But that my sweet queen willed me for to show
This letter to them ere I did the deed.
Mass, they begin to stir. I'll stand aside.
So shall I come upon them unawares.

They wake and rise.

LEIR
I marvel that my daughter stays so long.[85]

PERILLUS
I fear we did mistake the place, my lord.

LEIR
God grant we do not miscarry in the place.
I had a short nap, but so full of dread
As much amazeth me to think thereof.

PERILLUS
Fear not, my lord.[86] Dreams are but fantasies
And slight imaginations of the brain.

MESSENGER
[*aside*] Persuade him so, but I'll make him and you
Confess that dreams do often prove too true.

PERILLUS
I pray, my lord, what was the effect of it?
I may go near to guess what it pretends.

MESSENGER
[*aside*] Leave that to me. I will expound the dream.

LEIR
Methought my daughters, Gonorill and Ragan,
Stood both before me with such grim aspects,
Each brandishing a falchion in their hand[87]
Ready to lop a limb off where it fell,
And in their other hands a naked poniard
Wherewith they stabbed me in a hundred places
And to their thinking left me there for dead.
But then my youngest daughter, fair Cordella,
Came with a box of balsam in her hand

85 Cf. *Sp. T.* 3.3.30: '**I wonder that** his lordship **stays so long**'.

86 Cf. *SP* 5.2.138: '**Fear not, my lord,** Lucina plays her part'. Cf. also *KL* 23.75: '**Fear not, my lord**'.

87 Cf. *Corn.* 2.1.172: '**his falchion in his fist**'; 5.1.307: 'with their **falchions in their fists**'.

And poured it into my bleeding wounds,[88]
By whose good means I was recovered well,
In perfect health, as erst I was before.
And with the fear of this I did awake,
And yet for fear my feeble joints do quake.

MESSENGER
[*Coming forward*] I'll make you quake for something presently.
Stand, stand!

They reel.

LEIR
We do, my friend, although with much ado.

MESSENGER
Deliver, deliver!

PERILLUS
Deliver us, good Lord, from such as he.

MESSENGER
You should have prayed before while it was time,
And then perhaps you might have 'scaped my hands,
But you, like faithful watchmen, fell asleep
The whilst I came and took your halberds from you.
(*Show their books.*) And now you want your weapons of defence,
How have you any hope to be delivered?
This comes because you have no better stay
But fall asleep, when you should watch and pray.

LEIR
My friend, thou seem'st to be a proper man –

MESSENGER
'Sblood, how the old slave claws me by the elbow.
He thinks, belike, to 'scape by scraping thus.

PERILLUS
And it may be are in some need of money.

MESSENGER
That to be false, behold my evidence.

Shows his purses.

[88] Cf. *Sp. T.* 5.4.123: 'Within the river of his **bleeding wounds**'; *Corn.* 4.1.24: '**And** launched his **bleeding wound into** the sea'.

LEIR
[*Offers gold.*] If that I have will do thee any good,
I give it thee,[89] even with a right good will.

[Messenger] takes it.

PERILLUS
Here, take mine, too, and wish with all my heart
To do thee pleasure it were twice as much.

Take his and weigh them in both his hands.

MESSENGER
I'll none of them. They are too light for me.

Puts them in his pocket.

LEIR
Why, then farewell. And if thou have occasion
In anything to use me to the queen,
'Tis like enough that I can pleasure thee.

[Leir and Perillus] proffer to go.

MESSENGER
Do you hear, do you hear, sir?
If I had occasion to use you to the queen,
Would you do one thing for me I should ask?

LEIR
Ay, anything that lies within my power.
Here is my hand upon it, so farewell.

Proffer to go.

MESSENGER
Hear you, sir, hear you? Pray, a word with you.
Methinks a comely, honest, ancient man
Should not dissemble with one for a vantage.
I know when I shall come to try this gear[90]
You will recant from all that you have said.

PERILLUS
Mistrust not him, but try him when thou wilt.
He is her father, therefore may do much.

MESSENGER
I know he is and therefore mean to try him.
You are his friend, too. I must try you both.

[89] Cf. *SP* 1.3.49: 'Enjoy thy life and live: **I give it thee**.'
[90] Cf. *SP* 1.1.64: 'Are hither **come to try** their force in arms.'

LEIR *and* PERILLUS
Prithee do, prithee do.

Proffer to go out.

MESSENGER
Stay, greybeards, then, and prove men of your words.
The queen hath tied me by a solemn oath
Here in this place to see you both dispatched.
Now for the safeguard of my conscience
Do me the pleasure for to kill yourselves.
So shall you save me labour for to do it[91]
And prove yourselves true old men of your words.
And here I vow in sight of all the world[92]
I ne'er will trouble you, whilst I live, again.

LEIR
Affright us not with terror, good my friend,
Nor strike such fear into our agèd hearts.
Play not the cat, which dallieth with the mouse,
And on a sudden maketh her a prey.
But if thou art marked for the man of death
To me and to my Damon, tell me plain,
That we may be preparèd for the stroke
And make ourselves fit for the world to come.

MESSENGER
I am the last of any mortal race
That ere your eyes are likely to behold
And hither sent of purpose to this place
To give a final period to your days,
Which are so wicked and have lived so long
That your own children seek to short your life.

LEIR
Camest thou from France of purpose to do this?

MESSENGER
From France? Zounds, do I look like a Frenchman?
Sure I have not mine own face on; somebody hath changed faces with me, and I know not of it. But I am sure my apparel is all English. Sirrah, what meanest thou to ask that question? I could spoil the fashion of this face for anger. A French face!

[91] Cf. *SP* 1.5.45: 'I do but use thee to **save me a labour**'; 2.2.4: 'See where Perseda comes, to **save me a labour**'; 2.2.73: 'Why, lend me thine, and **save me a labour**'.

[92] Cf. *Sp. T.* 5.1.42: '**And here I vow**'.

LEIR
Because my daughter, whom I have offended
And at whose hands I have deserved as ill
As ever any father did of child,
Is Queen of France, no thanks at all to me,
But unto God, who my injustice see.
If it be so that she doth seek revenge,
As with good reason she may justly do,
I will most willingly resign my life,
A sacrifice to mitigate her ire.[93]
I never will entreat thee to forgive,
Because I am unworthy for to live.
Therefore speak soon, and I will soon make speed,
Whether Cordella willed thee do this deed?

MESSENGER
As I am a perfect gentlemen, thou speakst French to me.
I never heard Cordella's name before,
Nor never was in France in all my life.
I never knew thou hadst a daughter there
To whom thou didst prove so unkind a churl,
But thy own tongue declares that thou hast been
A vile old wretch and full of heinous sin.

LEIR
Ah no, my friend, thou art deceivèd much,
For her except, whom I confess I wronged,
Through doting frenzy and o'er-jealous love,
There lives not any under heaven's bright eye[94]
That can convict me of impiety.
And therefore sure thou dost mistake the mark,
For I am in true peace with all the world.

MESSENGER
You are the fitter for the King of Heaven,
And therefore, for to rid thee of suspense,
Know thou the Queens of Cambria and Cornwall,
Thy own two daughters Gonorill and Ragan,
Appointed me to massacre thee here.
Why wouldst thou then persuade me that thou art
In charity with all the world? But now

[93] Cf. *Corn.* 1.1.9: 'Oft hath such **sacrifice** appeased your **ires**.'

[94] Cf. *SP* 3.1.90: 'For looking but askew at **heaven's bright eye**.' (Wells)

When thy own issue hold thee in such hate
That they have hired me t'abridge thy fate –
Oh, fie upon such vile, dissembling breath
That would deceive even at the point of death.

PERILLUS
Am I awake, or is it but a dream?

MESSENGER
Fear nothing, man. Thou art but in a dream,
And thou shalt never wake until doomsday.
By then, I hope, thou wilt have slept enough.

LEIR
Yet, gentle friend, grant one thing ere I die.

MESSENGER
I'll grant you anything except your lives.

LEIR
Oh, but assure me by some certain token
That my two daughters hired thee to this deed.
If I were once resolved of that, then I
Would wish no longer life, but crave to die.

MESSENGER
That to be true, in sight of heaven I swear.[95]

LEIR
Swear not by heaven, for fear of punishment.
The heavens are guiltless of such heinous acts.

MESSENGER
I swear by earth, the mother of us all.

LEIR
Swear not by earth, for she abhors to bear
Such bastards[96] as are murderers of her sons.

MESSENGER
Why, then, by hell and all the devils I swear.

LEIR
Swear not by hell, for that stands gaping wide
To swallow thee an if thou do this deed.

95 Cf. *Sp. T.* 5.1.25: 'For here **I swear in sight of heaven** and earth'.
96 Cf. *Corn.* 3.2.74: 'Or think'st thou Romans **bear such bastard** hearts'.

Thunder and lightning.

MESSENGER
[*aside*] I would that word were in his belly again.
It hath frighted me even to the very heart.[97]
This old man is some strong magician.
His words have turned my mind from this exploit.
[*To them*] Then neither heaven, earth, nor hell be witness,
But let this paper witness for them all.

Shows Gonorill's letter. [*Leir and Perillus read it.*]

[*Aside*] Shall I relent, or shall I prosecute?
Shall I resolve, or were I best recant?
I will not crack my credit with two queens
To whom I have already passed my word.
Oh, but my conscience for this act doth tell
I get heaven's hate, earth's scorn, and pains of hell.

[*Leir and Perillus*] *bless themselves.*

PERILLUS
O just Jehovah, whose almighty power
Doth govern all things in this spacious world,
How canst Thou suffer such outrageous acts
To be committed without just revenge?
Oh, viperous generation and accursed,
To seek his blood whose blood did make them first!

LEIR
Ah, my true friend in all extremity,
Let us submit us to the will of God.
Things past all sense, let us not seek to know.
It is God's will and therefore must be so.
[*To Messenger*] My friend, I am preparèd for the stroke.
Strike when thou wilt, and I forgive thee here
Even from the very bottom of my heart.

MESSENGER
[*aside*] But I am not preparèd for to strike.

LEIR
Farewell, Perillus, even the truest friend
That ever livèd in adversity.
The latest kindness I'll request of thee
Is that thou go unto my daughter Cordella

[97] Cf. *SP* 5.4.129: 'And I am weak **even to the very** death'. Cf. also *KL* 24.160: 'And all I had, **even to the very** clothes'.

And carry her her father's latest blessing.
Withal desire her that she will forgive me,
For I have wronged her without any cause. –
Now, Lord, receive me, for I come to thee
And die, I hope, in perfect charity.
[*To Messenger*] Dispatch, I pray thee. I have lived too long.

MESSENGER
Ay, but you are unwise[98] to send an errand
By him that never meaneth to deliver it.
Why, he must go along with you to heaven.
It were not good you should go all alone.

LEIR
No doubt he shall, when by the course of nature
He must surrender up his due to death,
But that time shall not come till God permit.

MESSENGER
Nay, presently to bear you company.
I have a passport for him in my pocket[99]
Already sealed, and he must needs ride post.

Show a bag of money.

LEIR
The letter which I read imports not so.
It only toucheth me, no word of him.

MESSENGER
Ay, but the queen commands it must be so,
And I am paid for him as well as you.

PERILLUS
I, who have borne you company in life,
Most willingly will bear a share in death.
It skilleth not for me, my friend, a whit,
Nor for a hundred such as thou and I.

MESSENGER
Marry, but it doth, sir, by your leave. Your good days are past. Though it be no matter for you, 'tis a matter for me. Proper men are not so rife.

[98] Cf. *SP* 4.1.1: 'Faith, master, methinks **you are unwise**'.
[99] Cf. *Sp. T.* 1.1.35: 'To crave **a passport for** my wandering ghost'.

PERILLUS
Oh, but beware how thou dost lay thy hand
Upon the high anointed of the Lord.
Oh, be advisèd ere thou dost begin:
Dispatch me straight, but meddle not with him.

LEIR
Friend, thy commission is to deal with me,
And I am he that hath deservèd all.
The plot was laid to take away my life,[100]
And here it is: I do entreat thee take it.
Yet for my sake, and as thou art a man,
Spare this my friend that hither with me came.
I brought him forth, whereas he had not been,
But for goodwill to bear me company.
He left his friends, his country, and his goods
And came with me in most extremity.
Oh, if he should miscarry here and die,
Who is the cause of it, but only I?

MESSENGER
Why, that am I. Let that ne'er trouble thee.

LEIR
Oh no, 'tis I. Oh, had I now to give thee
The monarchy of all the spacious world
To save his life, I would bestow it on thee.
But I have nothing but these tears and prayers
And the submission of a bended knee. *Kneels.*
Oh, if all this to mercy move thy mind,
Spare him. In heaven thou shalt like mercy find.

MESSENGER
[*aside*] I am as hard to be moved as another, and yet methinks the strength of their persuasions stirs me a little.

PERILLUS
My friend, if fear of the almighty power
Have power to move thee, we have said enough,
But if thy mind be moveable with gold,
We have not presently to give it thee,
Yet to thyself thou mayst do greater good
To keep thy hands still undefiled from blood.

[100] Cf. *Sp. T.* 5.3.27: '**The plot is laid**'.

For do but well consider with thyself
When thou hast finished this outrageous act
What horror still will haunt thee for the deed.
Think this again: that they which would incense
Thee for to be the butcher of their father,
When it is done, for fear it should be known,
Would make a means to rid thee from the world.
Oh, then art thou forever tied in chains
Of everlasting torments to endure,
Even in the hottest hole of grisly hell,
Such pains as never mortal tongue can tell.[101]

It thunders. [The Messenger] quakes and lets fall the dagger next to Perillus.

LEIR
Oh, heavens be thanked! He will spare my friend.
Now when thou wilt come, make an end of me.[102]

[The Messenger] lets fall the other dagger.

PERILLUS
Oh, happy sight! He means to save my lord.
The King of Heaven continue this good mind.

LEIR
Why stayst thou to do execution?

MESSENGER
I am as willful as you for your life.
I will not do it, now you do entreat me.

PERILLUS
Ah, now I see thou hast some spark of grace.

MESSENGER
Beshrew you for it. You have put it in me,
The parlousest old men that e'er I heard.
Well, to be flat, I'll not meddle with you.
Here I found you, and here I'll leave you.
If any ask you why the case so stands,
Say that your tongues were better than your hands.

Exit Messenger.

[101] Cf. *Sp. T.* 1.1.57–8: 'I saw more sights than thousand **tongues can tell**, | Or pens can write, or **mortal** hearts can think.' (Rubow)

[102] Cf. *Corn.* 5.1.118: 'Which brightly shone shall **make an end of me**.'

PERILLUS
Farewell. If ever we together meet,
It shall go hard, but I will thee re-greet. –
Courage, my lord, the worst is overpassed.
Let us give thanks to God and hie us hence.

LEIR
Thou art deceived, for I am past the best[103]
And know not whither for to go from hence.
Death had been better welcome unto me
Than longer life to add more misery.

PERILLUS
It were not good to return from whence we came
Unto your daughter, Ragan, back again.
Now let us go to France unto Cordella,
Your youngest daughter. Doubtless she will succour you.

LEIR
Oh, how can I persuade myself of that,
Since the other two are quite devoid of love,
To whom I was so kind,[104] as that my gifts
Might make them love me, if 'twere nothing else?

PERILLUS
No worldly gifts, but grace from God on high
Doth nourish virtue and true charity.
Remember well what words Cordella spake,
What time you asked her, how she loved your grace.
She said her love unto you was as much
As ought a child to bear unto her father.

LEIR
But she did find my love was not to her[105]
As should a father bear unto a child.

PERILLUS
That makes not her love to be any less
If she do love you as a child should do.
You have tried two. Try one more for my sake.
I'll ne'er entreat you further trial make.

[103] Cf. *SP* 5.4.51–2: 'therein **thou art deceived, | For** though she live'.
[104] Cf. *SP* 5.3.8: '**To whom I am so** long true servitor'.
[105] Cf. *SP* 2.1.142: 'What ere she be, **my love was** more than **her**'.

Remember well the dream you had of late,
And think what comfort it foretells to us.

LEIR
Come, truest friend that ever man possessed,
I know thou counsellest all things for the best.
If this third daughter play a kinder part,
It comes of God and not of my desert.

Exeunt.

* * * * *

[Scene 20]

Enter the Gallian Ambassador [*alone*].

AMBASSADOR
There is of late news come unto the court
That old lord Leir remains in Cambria.
I'll hie me thither presently to impart
My letters and my message unto him.
I never was less welcome to a place
In all my lifetime than I have been hither,[106]
Especially unto the stately queen,
Who would not cast one gracious look on me,
But still with louring and suspicious eyes
Would take exceptions at each word I spake,
And fain she would have underminèd me
To know what my ambassage did import.
But she is like to hop without her hope
And in this matter for to want her will,
Though, by report, she'll have't in all things else.
Well, I will post away for Cambria.
Within these few days I hope to be there.

Exit.

* * * * *

[106] Cf. *SP* 5.2.30: '**Than I have been** to gracious Soliman'.

[Scene 21]

Enter the King [of Gallia, Cordella], and Mumford.

GALLIA
By this, our father understands our mind
And our kind greetings sent to him of late.
Therefore my mind presageth, ere't be long
We shall receive from Britain happy news.

CORDELLA
I fear my sister will dissuade his mind,
For she to me hath always been unkind.

GALLIA
Fear not, my love, since that we know the worst,
The last means helps, if that we miss the first.
If he'll not come to Gallia unto us,
Then we will sail to Britain unto him.

MUMFORD
Well, if I once see Britain again, I have sworn I'll ne'er come home without my wench, and I'll not be forsworn. I'll rather never come home while I live.

CORDELLA
Are you sure, Mumford, she is a maid still?

MUMFORD
Nay, I'll not swear she is a maid, but she goes for one. I'll take her at all adventures, if I can get her.

CORDELLA
Ay, that's well put in.

MUMFORD
Well put in? Nay, it was ill put in. For had it been as well put in as e'er I put in, in my days, I would have made her follow me to France.

CORDELLA
Nay, you'd have been so kind as take her with you.
Or else, were I as she, I would have been
So loving as I'd stay behind you.
Yet I must confess you are a very proper man
And able to make a wench do more than she would do.

MUMFORD
Well, I have a pair of slops for the nonce will hold all your mocks.

GALLIA
Nay, we see you have a handsome hose.

CORDELLA
Ay, and of the newest fashion.

MUMFORD
More bobs, more. Put them in still. They'll serve instead of bombast, yet put not in too many, lest the seams crack and they fly out amongst you again. You must not think to outface me so easily in my mistress' quarrel, who, if I see once again, ten team of horses shall not draw me away till I have full and whole possession.

GALLIA
Ay, but one team and a cart will serve the turn.

CORDELLA
Not only for him, but also for his wench.

MUMFORD
Well, you are two to one. I'll give you over. And since I see you are so pleasantly disposed, which indeed is but seldom seen, I'll claim a promise of you, which you shall not deny me. For promise is debt, and by this hand you promised it me. Therefore you owe it me, and you shall pay it me, or I'll sue you upon an action of unkindness.

GALLIA
Prithee, Lord Mumford, what promise did I make thee?

MUMFORD
Faith, nothing but this: that the next fair weather, which is very now, you would go in progress down to the seaside,[107] which is very near.

GALLIA
Faith, in this motion I will join with thee
And be a mediator to my queen.
[*To Cordella*] Prithee, my love, let this match go forward.
My mind foretells 'twill be a lucky voyage.

[107] Cf. *Corn.* 5.1.62: '**Down to the seaside**'.

CORDELLA
Entreaty needs not, where you may command.
So you be pleased, I am right well content.
Yet as the sea I much desire to see,
So am I most unwilling to be seen.

GALLIA
We'll go disguised, all unknown to any.

CORDELLA
Howsoever you make one, I'll make another.

MUMFORD
And I the third – oh, I am overjoyed!
See what love is, which getteth with a word
What all the world besides could ne'er obtain.[108]
But what disguises shall we have, my lord?

GALLIA
Faith, thus: my queen and I will be disguised
Like a plain country couple, and you shall be Roger
Our man and wait upon us. Or if you will,
You shall go first, and we will wait on you.

MUMFORD
'Twere more than time. This device is excellent.
Come, let us about it!

Exeunt.

* * * * *

[Scene 22]

Enter [King of] Cambria and Ragan, with nobles.

CAMBRIA
What strange mischance or unexpected hap
Hath thus deprived us of our father's presence?
Can no man tell us what's become of him,
With whom we did converse not two days since?
My lords, let everywhere light horse be sent
To scour about through all our regiment.[109]

[108] Cf. *SP* 2.1.282: 'Dearer to me than **all the world besides**'; *Corn.* 1.1.117: 'And almost yokèd **all the world beside**'.

[109] Cf. *Corn.* 5.1.296: 'Where th'adverse navy, **sent to scour** the seas'.

Dispatch a post immediately to Cornwall
To see if any news be of him there.
Myself will make a strict inquiry here
And all about our cities near at hand
Till certain news of his abode be brought.

RAGAN
All sorrow is but counterfeit to mine,
Whose lips are almost sealèd up with grief.
Mine is the substance, whilst they do but seem
To weep the less, which tears cannot redeem.
Oh, ne'er was heard so strange a misadventure,
A thing so far beyond the reach of sense,
Since no man's reason in the cause can enter.
What hath removed my father thus from hence?
Oh, I do fear some charm or invocation
Of wicked spirits or infernal fiends,
Stirred by Cordella, moves this innovation
And brings my father timeless to his end.
But might I know that the detested witch
Were certain cause of this uncertain ill,
Myself to France would go in some disguise
And with these nails scratch out her hateful eyes.
For since I am deprived of my father,
I loathe my life and wish my death the rather.

CAMBRIA
The heavens are just and hate impiety[110]
And will, no doubt, reveal such heinous crimes.
Censure not any till you know the right.
Let Him be judge that bringeth truth to light.[111]

RAGAN
Oh, but my grief, like to a swelling tide,[112]
Exceeds the bounds of common patience.
Nor can I moderate my tongue so much
To conceal them whom I hold in suspect.

[110] Cf. *Sp. T.* 2.4.124: '**The heavens are just**, murder cannot be hid'.

[111] Cf. *Sp. T.* 2.4.125–6: 'Time is the author both of truth and **right**, | And time will **bring this** treachery **to light**'.

[112] Cf. *Sp. T.* 1.2.49: 'When, roaring loud, and with **a swelling tide**'.

CAMBRIA
This matter shall be sifted. If it be she,
A thousand Frances shall not harbour her.

Enter the Gallian Ambassador.

AMBASSADOR
All happiness unto the Cambrian King.

CAMBRIA
Welcome, my friend. From whence is thy ambassage?

AMBASSADOR
I came from Gallia, unto Cornwall sent,
With letters to your honourable father,
Whom there not finding as I did expect,
I was directed hither to repair.

RAGAN
Frenchman, what is thy message to my father?

AMBASSADOR
My letters, madam, will import the same,
Which my commission is for to deliver.

RAGAN
In his absence you may trust us with your letters.

AMBASSADOR
I must perform my charge in such a manner
As I have strict commandment from the king.[113]

RAGAN
There is good packing 'twixt your king and you.[114]
You need not hither come to ask for him.
You know where he is better than ourselves.

AMBASSADOR
Madam, I hope not far off.

RAGAN
Hath the young murderess, your outrageous queen,
No means to colour her detested deeds[115]
In finishing my guiltless father's days,

[113] Cf. *Sp. T.* 3.2.102: 'Upon precise **commandment from the king**'.

[114] Cf. *Sp. T.* 1.4.148: 'That which may comfort both **your king and you**'.

[115] Cf. *Sp. T.* 4.1.46: 'That such a monstrous and **detested deed**'.

Because he gave her nothing to her dower,
But by the colour of a feigned ambassage[116]
To send him letters hither to our court?[117]
Go carry them to them that sent them hither,
And bid them keep their scrolls unto themselves.
They cannot blind us with such slight excuse
To smother up so monstrous vild abuse.[118]
And were it not it is 'gainst law of arms
To offer violence to a messenger,
We would inflict such torments on thyself
As should enforce thee to reveal the truth.[119]

AMBASSADOR
Madam, your threats no whit appal my mind.
I know my conscience guiltless of this act.
My king and queen, I dare be sworn, are free
From any thought of such impiety.
And therefore, madam, you have done them wrong
And ill beseeming with a sister's love,
Who in mere duty tender him as much
As ever you respected him for dower.[120]
The king your husband will not say as much.

CAMBRIA
I will suspend my judgement for a time
Till more appearance give us further light.
Yet, to be plain, your coming doth enforce
A great suspicion to our doubtful mind,
And that you do resemble, to be brief,
Him that first robs,[121] and then cries 'stop the thief'.

AMBASSADOR
Pray God some near you have not done the like.

[Ragan] strikes him.

RAGAN
Hence, saucy mate! Reply no more to us,

[116] Cf. *Sp. T.* 3.1.20: 'That **feignèd** love had **coloured** in his looks'.

[117] Cf. *Sp. T.* 2.1.84: 'She **sent him letters**'.

[118] Cf. *Sp. T.* 4.1.46–7: 'That such a **monstrous** and detested deed, | **So** closely **smothered,** and so long concealed'.

[119] Cf. *Sp. T.* 5.4.184–5: 'But never shalt thou **force me to reveal** | **The** thing'.

[120] Cf. *SP* 5.1.28: '**As ever you respect** his future love'.

[121] Cf. *SP* 1.1.102: '**To be brief, he that** will try me'.

For law of arms shall not protect thy tongue.[122]

AMBASSADOR
Ne'er was I offered such discourtesy.
God and my king, I trust, ere it be long,
Will find a mean to remedy this wrong.

Exit Ambassador.

RAGAN
How shall I live to suffer this disgrace
At every base and vulgar peasant's hands?
It ill befitteth my imperial state
To be thus used and no man take my part.

She weeps.

CAMBRIA
What should I do? Infringe the law of arms
Were to my everlasting obloquy.
But I will take revenge upon his master
Which sent him hither to delude us thus.

RAGAN
Nay, if you put up this, be sure ere long,
Now that my father thus is made away,
She'll come and claim a third part of your crown
As due unto her by inheritance.

CAMBRIA
But I will prove her title to be naught
But shame and the reward of parricide
And make her an example to the world
For after-ages to admire her penance.
This will I do, as I am Cambria's King,
Or lose my life to prosecute revenge.
Come, first let's learn what news is of our father
And then proceed as best occasion fits.

Exeunt.

* * * * *

[122] Cf. *Sp. T.* 1.2.168–9: 'Enforced by nature and by **law of arms**, | **My tongue** should plead'.

[Scene 23]

Enter Leir, Perillus, and two mariners in sea-gowns and sea-caps.

PERILLUS
My honest friends, we are ashamed to show
The great extremity of our present state,
In that at this time we are brought so low
That we want money for to pay our passage.
The truth is so: we met with some goodfellows
A little before we came aboard your ship,
Which stripped us quite of all the coin we had
And left us not a penny in our purses.
Yet, wanting money, we will use the mean
To see you satisfied to the uttermost.

[*The mariners*] *look on Leir.*

FIRST MARINER
Here's a good gown. 'Twould become me passing well. I should be fine in it.

[*The mariners*] *look on Perillus.*

SECOND MARINER
Here's a good cloak. I marvel how I should look in it.

LEIR
Faith, had we others to supply their room,
Though ne'er so mean, you willingly should have them.

FIRST MARINER
[*To Leir*] Do you hear, sir? You look like an honest man. I'll not stand to do you a pleasure.[123] Here's a good strong motley gaberdine, cost me fourteen good shillings at Billingsgate. Give me your gown for it, and your cap for mine, and I'll forgive your passage.

LEIR
With all my heart and twenty thanks.

Leir and he change.

SECOND MARINER
[*To Perillus*] Do you hear, sir? You shall have a better match than he, because you are my friend. Here is a good sheep's russet sea-gown, will bide more stress, I warrant you, than two of his. Yet, for you seem to be an honest gentleman, I am

[123] Cf. *SP* 1.5.62–3: 'and as I am **an honest man**, **I'll do** the best I can **to** find **your** chain'.

content to change it for your cloak and ask you nothing for your passage more.

Pulls off Perillus' cloak.

PERILLUS
[*To Second Mariner*] My own I willingly would change with thee
And think myself indebted to thy kindness.
[*To First Mariner*] But would my friend might keep his garment still,
My friend, I'll give thee this new doublet, if thou wilt
Restore his gown unto him back again.

FIRST MARINER
Nay, if I do, would I might ne'er eat powdered beef and mustard more, nor drink can of good liquor whilst I live. My friend, you have small reason to seek to hinder me of my bargain, but the best is: a bargain's a bargain.

LEIR
([*aside*] *to Perillus*) Kind friend, it is much better as it is,
For by this means we may escape unknown
Till time and opportunity do fit.

SECOND MARINER
[*aside to First Mariner*] Hark, hark. They are laying their heads together. They'll repent them of their bargain anon. 'Twere best for us to go while we are well.

FIRST MARINER
[*To Leir*] God be with you, sir, for your passage back again. I'll use you as unreasonable as another.

LEIR
I know thou wilt, but we hope to bring
Ready money with us, when we come back again.

Exeunt mariners.

Were ever men in this extremity,
In a strange country and devoid of friends,
And not a penny for to help ourselves?
Kind friend, what thinkst thou will become of us?

PERILLUS
Be of good cheer, my lord. I have a doublet
Will yield us money enough to serve our turns
Until we come unto your daughter's court,
And then, I hope, we shall find friends enough.

LEIR
Ah, kind Perillus, that is it I fear
And makes me faint or ever I come there.
Can kindness spring out of ingratitude,
Or love be reaped where hatred hath been sown?
Can henbane join in league with mithridate,
Or sugar grow in wormwood's bitter stalk?
It cannot be. They are too opposite,
And so am I to any kindness here.
I have thrown wormwood on the sugared youth
And like to henbane poisonèd the fount
Whence flowed the mithridate of a child's goodwill.
I, like an envious thorn, have pricked the heart[124]
And turned sweet grapes to sour, unrelished sloes.
The causeless ire of my respectless breast
Hath soured the sweet milk of dame Nature's paps.
My bitter words have galled her honey thoughts,
And weeds of rancour choked the flower of grace.
Then what remainder is of any hope
But all our fortunes will go quite aslope?

PERILLUS
Fear not, my lord, the perfect good indeed
Can never be corrupted by the bad.
A new fresh vessel still retains the taste
Of that which first is poured into the same,
And therefore, though you name yourself the thorn,
The weed, the gall, the henbane, and the wormwood,
Yet she'll continue in her former state
The honey, milk, grape, sugar, mithridate.

LEIR
Thou pleasing orator unto me in woe,
Cease to beguile me with thy hopeful speeches.
Oh, join with me and think of naught but crosses
And then we'll one lament another's losses.

PERILLUS
Why, say the worst. The worst can be but death,
And death is better than for to despair.
Then hazard death, which may convert to life.

[124] Cf. *SP* 1.6.16: 'Till it **have pricked the heart** of Christendom'; 5.4.85: 'Could not **have pricked** so near unto my **heart**'.

Banish despair, which brings a thousand deaths.

LEIR
O'ercome with thy strong arguments, I yield
To be directed by thee as thou wilt.
As thou yieldst comfort to my crazèd thoughts,
Would I could yield the like unto thy body,
Which is full weak, I know, and ill apaid
For want of fresh meat and due sustenance.

PERILLUS
Alack, my lord, my heart doth bleed to think
That you should be in such extremity.

LEIR
Come, let us go and see what God will send.
When all means fail, he is the surest friend.

Exeunt.

* * * * *

[Scene 24]

Enter the King [*of Gallia*] *and Queen* [*Cordella*] *and Mumford, with a basket, disguised like country folk,* [*to a table*].

GALLIA
This tedious journey all on foot, sweet love,
Cannot be pleasing to your tender joints,
Which ne'er were usèd to these toilsome walks.

CORDELLA
I never in my life took more delight
In any journey than I do in this.
It did me good, when as we happed to light
Amongst the merry crew of country folk
To see what industry and pains they took
To win them commendations 'mongst their friends.
Lord, how they labour to bestir themselves
And in their quirks to go beyond the moon
And so take on them with such antic fits
That one would think they were beside their wits!
Come away, Roger, with your basket.

Enter Leir and Perillus very faintly [*not seeing them.*]

MUMFORD
Soft, dame, here comes a couple of old youths. I must needs make myself fat with jesting at them.

CORDELLA
Nay, prithee do not. They do seem to be
Men much o'ergone with grief and misery.
Let's stand aside and harken what they say.

LEIR
Ah, my Perillus, now I see we both
Shall end our days in this unfruitful soil.
Oh, I do faint for want of sustenance,
And thou, I know, in little better case.
No gentle tree affords one taste of fruit
To comfort us until we meet with men.
No lucky path conducts our luckless steps
Unto a place where any comfort dwells.
Sweet rest betide unto our happy souls,
For here I see our bodies must have end.

PERILLUS
Ah, my dear lord, how doth my heart lament
To see you brought to this extremity!
Oh, if you love me, as you do profess
Or ever thought well of me in my life –

He strips up his arm.

Feed on this flesh, whose veins are not so dry
But there is virtue left to comfort you.
Oh, feed on this. If this will do you good,
I'll smile for joy to see you suck my blood.

LEIR
I am no cannibal that I should delight
To slake my hungry jaws with human flesh.
I am no devil, or ten times worse than so,
To suck the blood of such a peerless friend.
Oh, do not think that I respect my life
So dearly as I do thy loyal love.
Ah, Britain, I shall never see thee more
That has unkindly banishèd thy king.
And yet not thou dost make me to complain,
But they which were more near to me than thou.

CORDELLA
What do I hear? This lamentable voice,
Methinks, ere now I oftentimes have heard.

LEIR
Ah, Gonorill, was half my kingdom's gift
The cause that thou didst seek to have my life?
Ah, cruel Ragan, did I give thee all,
And all could not suffice without my blood?
Ah, poor Cordella, did I give thee naught,
Nor never shall be able for to give?
Oh, let me warn all ages that ensueth
How they trust flattery and reject the truth.
Well, unkind girls, I here forgive you both,
Yet the just heavens will hardly do the like,
And only crave forgiveness at the end
Of God, Cordella, and of thee, my friend –
Of God, whose majesty I have offended
By my transgression many thousand ways;
Of her, dear heart, whom I for no occasion
Turned out of all through flatterers' persuasion;
Of thee, kind friend, who but for me, I know,
Hadst never come unto this place of woe.

CORDELLA
Alack that ever I should live to see
My noble father in this misery!

GALLIA
Sweet love, reveal not what thou art as yet,
Until we know the ground of all this ill.

CORDELLA
Oh, but some meat, some meat! Do you not see
How near they are to death for want of food?

PERILLUS
Lord, which didst help thy servants at their need,
Or now or never send us help with speed.
[*Seeing them*] Oh, comfort, comfort! Yonder is a banquet
And men and women, my lord. Be of good cheer,
For I see comfort coming very near.
Oh, my lord, a banquet and men and women!

LEIR
Oh, let kind pity mollify their hearts
That they may help us in our great extremes.

PERILLUS
God save you, friends, and if this blessed banquet
Affordeth any food or sustenance,
Even for His sake that saved us all from death,
Vouchsafe to save us from the gripe of famine.
[*Cordella*] *brings him to the table.*

CORDELLA
Here, father, sit and eat. Here, sit and drink,
And would it were far better for your sakes.
Perillus takes Leir by the hand to the table.

PERILLUS
I'll give you thanks anon. My friend doth faint
And needeth present comfort.
Leir drinks.

MUMFORD
I warrant he ne'er stays to say grace. Oh, there's no sauce to a good stomach.

PERILLUS
The blessed God of heaven hath thought upon us.

LEIR
The thanks be His, and these kind courteous folk,
By whose humanity we are preserved.
They eat hungrily. Leir drinks.

CORDELLA
And may that draught be unto him as was
That which old Aeson drank, which did renew
His withered age and made him young again.
And may that meat be unto him as was
That which Elias ate, in strength whereof
He walkèd forty days and never fainted.
[*Aside to Gallia*] Shall I conceal me longer from my father?
Or shall I manifest myself to him?

GALLIA
Forbear a while until his strength return,
Lest being overjoyed with seeing thee
His poor weak senses should forsake their office
And so our cause of joy be turned to sorrow.

PERILLUS
What cheer, my lord? How do you feel yourself?

LEIR
Methinks I never ate such savoury meat.
It is as pleasant as the blessed manna,
That rained from heaven amongst the Israelites.
It hath recalled my spirits home again
And made me fresh as erst I was before.
But how shall we congratulate their kindness?

PERILLUS
In faith, I know not how sufficiently,
But the best mean that I can think on is this:
I'll offer them my doublet in requital,
For we have nothing else to spare.

LEIR
Nay, stay, Perillus, for they shall have mine.

PERILLUS
Pardon, my lord, I swear they shall have mine.

Perillus proffers his doublet. They will not take it.

LEIR
Ah, who would think such kindness should remain
Among such strange and unacquainted men,
And that such hate should harbour in the breast
Of those which have occasion to be best?

CORDELLA
Ah, good old father, tell to me thy grief.
I'll sorrow with thee, if not add relief.

LEIR
Ah, good young daughter, I may call thee so,
For thou art like a daughter I did owe.

CORDELLA
Do you not owe her still? What, is she dead?

LEIR
No, God forbid, but all my interest's gone
By showing myself too much unnatural.
So have I lost the title of a father
And may be called a stranger to her rather.

CORDELLA
Your title's good still, for 'tis always known
A man may do as him list with his own.
But have you but one daughter then in all?

LEIR
Yes, I have more by two than would I had.

CORDELLA
Oh, say not so, but rather see the end.
They that are bad may have the grace to mend.
But how have they offended you so much?

LEIR
If from the first I should relate the cause,
'Twould make a heart of adamant to weep.
And thou, poor soul, kind-hearted as thou art,
Dost weep already ere I do begin.

CORDELLA
For God's love, tell it, and when you have done
I'll tell the reason why I weep so soon.

LEIR
Then know this first: I am a Britain born
And had three daughters by one loving wife,
And though I say it, of beauty they were sped,
Especially the youngest of the three,
For her perfections hardly matched could be.
On these I doted with a jealous love
And thought to try which of them loved me best
By asking them which would do most for me.
The first and second flattered me with words
And[125] vowed they loved me better than their lives.
The youngest said she loved me as a child[126]
Might do. Her answer I esteemed most vild,
And presently in an outrageous mood
I turned her from me to go sink or swim.
And all I had, even to the very clothes,
I gave in dowry with the other two,
And she that best deserved the greatest share

[125] Cf. *SP* 2.1.72: 'That I **with words and** stripes'.

[126] Cf. *Sp. T.* 2.1.23: 'Yet might **she love me as** her brother's friend'; 2.1.27: 'Yet might **she love me as** her beauty's thrall'.

I gave her nothing but disgrace and care.
Now mark the sequel: when I had done thus
I sojourned in my eldest daughter's house,
Where for a time I was entreated well
And lived in state sufficing my content,
But every day her kindness did grow cold,
Which I with patience put up well enough
And seemed not to see the things I saw.
But at the last she grew so far incensed
With moody fury and with causeless hate
That in most vild and contumelious terms
She bade me pack and harbour somewhere else.
Then was I fain for refuge to repair
Unto my other daughter for relief,
Who gave me pleasing and most courteous words,[127]
But in her actions showed herself so sore
As never any daughter did before.
She prayed me in a morning out betime
To go to a thicket two miles from the court,
'Pointing that there she would come talk with me.
There she had set a shag-haired murdering wretch
To massacre my honest friend and me.
Then judge yourself, although my tale be brief,
If ever man had greater cause of grief.

GALLIA
Nor never like impiety was done
Since the creation of the world begun.

LEIR
And now I am constrained to seek relief
Of her to whom I have been so unkind,
Whose censure, if it do award me death,
I must confess she pays me but my due.
But if she show a loving daughter's part,
It comes of God and her, not my desert.

CORDELLA
No doubt she will. I dare be sworn she will.

LEIR
How know you that, not knowing what she is?

[127] Cf. *Sp. T.* 4.8.82: 'I held him thence with kind **and courteous words**.'

CORDELLA
Myself a father have a great way hence
Used me as ill as ever you did her.
Yet that his reverend age I once might see,
I'd creep along to meet him on my knee.

LEIR
Oh, no men's children are unkind but mine!

CORDELLA
Condemn not all because of others' crime.
But look, dear father. Look, behold, and see:
Thy loving daughter speaketh unto thee! *She kneels.*

LEIR
Oh, stand thou up. It is my part to kneel
And ask forgiveness for my former faults. *He kneels.*

CORDELLA
Oh, if you wish I should enjoy my breath,
Dear father, rise, or I receive my death.

LEIR
Then I will rise to satisfy your mind. *He rises.*
But kneel again till pardon be resigned. *He kneels.*

CORDELLA
I pardon you? The word beseems not me,
But I do say so, for to ease your knee.
You gave me life. You were the cause that I
Am what I am who else had never been.

LEIR
But you gave life to me and to my friend,
Whose days had else had an untimely end.

CORDELLA
You brought me up whenas I was but young
And far unable for to help myself.

LEIR
I cast thee forth whenas thou wast but young
And far unable for to help thyself.

CORDELLA
God, world, and nature say I do you wrong
That can endure to see you kneel so long.

GALLIA
Let me break off this loving controversy,
Which doth rejoice my very soul to see.
Good father, rise. ([*Leir*] *rises.*) She is your loving daughter
And honours you with as respective duty
As if you were the monarch of the world.

CORDELLA
But I will never rise from off my knee, *She kneels.*
Until I have your blessing and your pardon
Of all my faults committed any way
From my first birth unto this present day.

LEIR
The blessing, which the God of Abraham gave
Unto the tribe of Judah light on thee
And multiply thy days that thou mayst see
Thy[128] children's children prosper after thee.
Thy faults, which are just none that I do know,
God pardon on high, and I forgive below. *She rises.*

CORDELLA
Now is my heart at quiet and doth leap
Within my breast for joy of this good hap.
And now, dear father, welcome to our court,
And welcome, kind Perillus, unto me,
Mirror of virtue and true honesty.

LEIR
Oh, he hath been the kindest friend to me
That ever man had in adversity.

PERILLUS
My tongue doth fail to say what heart doth think,
I am so ravished with exceeding joy.

GALLIA
All you have spoke. Now let me speak my mind
And[129] in few words much matter here conclude. *He kneels.*
If e'er my heart do harbour any joy
Or true content repose within my breast

[128] Cf. *Sp. T.* 4.4.81–2: '**thou mayst see | Thy**'.

[129] Cf. *SP* 1.6.76–7: 'And far from flattery **I spoke my mind, | And** did discharge a faithful subject's love'.

Till I have rooted out this viperous sect[130]
And repossessed my father of his crown,
Let me be counted for the perjured'st man
That ever spake word since the world began. *Rises.*

MUMFORD
Let me pray, too, that never prayed before. *Mumford kneels.*
If e'er I resalute the British earth –
As ere't be long I do presume I shall –
And do return from thence without my wench,
Let me be gelded for my recompence. *Rises.*

GALLIA
Come, let's to arms for to redress this wrong.
Till I am there, methinks the time seems long.

Exeunt.

* * * * *

[Scene 25]

Enter Ragan [*alone*].

RAGAN
I feel a hell of conscience in my breast
Tormenting me with horror for my fact
And makes me in an agony of doubt
For fear the world should find my dealing out.[131]
The slave whom I appointed for the act,
I ne'er set eye upon the peasant since.
Oh, could I get him for to make him sure,
My doubts would cease, and I should rest secure.
But if the old men with persuasive words
Have saved their lives and made him to relent,
Then are they fled unto the court of France
And like a trumpet manifest my shame.
A shame on these white-livered slaves, say I,
That with fair words so soon are overcome.
O God, that I had been but made a man,

[130] Cf. *Sp. T.* 1.4.64–5: 'But how can love **find harbour in my breast, | Till I** revenge the death of my beloved?'.

[131] Cf. *Sp. T.* 3.4.80–1: '**For fear the** privy whispering of the wind | Convey our words amongst unfriendly ears'.

Or that my strength were equal with my will![132]
These foolish men are nothing but mere pity
And melt as butter doth against the sun.
Why should they have preeminence over us
Since we are creatures of more brave resolve?
I swear I am quite out of charity
With all the heartless men in Christendom.
A pox upon them when they are afraid
To give a stab or slit a paltry windpipe,
Which are so easy matters to be done.
Well, had I thought the slave would serve me so,
Myself would have been executioner.
'Tis now undone, and if that it be known,[133]
I'll make as good shift as I can for one.
He that repines at me, howe'er it stands,
'Twere best for him to keep him from my hands.

Exit.

* * * * *

[Scene 26]

Sound drums and trumpets. Enter the King [of Gallia], Leir, Mumford, and the army.

GALLIA
Thus have we brought our army to the sea,
Whereas our ships are ready to receive us.[134]
The wind stands fair, and we in four hours' sail
May easily arrive on British shore,
Where unexpected we may them surprise
And gain a glorious victory with ease.[135]
Wherefore, my loving countrymen, resolve,
Since truth and justice fighteth on our sides,
That we shall march with conquest where we go.
Myself will be as forward as the first
And step by step march with the hardiest wight.
And not the meanest soldier in our camp
Shall be in danger but I'll second him.

132 Cf. *SP* 1.2.95–6: '**My** mercy in conquest is **equal with my** manhood in fight'.
133 Cf. *Sp. T.* 4.8.15: '**now that it be known**'.
134 Cf. *Sp. T.* 1.3.56: 'Mine ear **is ready to receive** ill news'.
135 Cf. *SP* 3.4.7–8: 'we'll **gain | A glorious** death or famous **victory**'.

[*To Mumford*] To you, my lord, we give the whole command
Of all the army, next unto ourself,
Not doubting of you, but you will extend
Your wonted valour in this needful case,
Encouraging the rest to do the like
By your approvèd magnanimity.

MUMFORD
My liege, 'tis needless to spur a willing horse
That's apt enough to run himself to death.
For here I swear by that sweet saint's bright eyes,[136]
Which are the stars which guide me to good hap,[137]
Either to see my old lord crowned anew
Or in his cause to bid the world adieu.

LEIR
Thanks, good lord Mumford, 'tis more of your good will
Than any merit or desert in me.

MUMFORD
[*To the army*] And now to you, my worthy countrymen,
Ye valiant race of Genovestan Gauls,
Surnamèd Redshanks for your chivalry,
Because you fight up to the shanks in blood,
Show yourselves now to be right Gauls indeed,
And be so bitter on your enemies
That they may say you are as bitter as gall.
Gall them, brave shot, with your artillery.
Gall them, brave halberds, with your sharp-point bills.
Each in their 'pointed place, not one, but all.
Fight for the credit of yourselves and Gaul!

GALLIA
Then what should more persuasion need to those
That rather wish to deal than hear of blows?
Let's to our ships, and if that God permit,
In four hours' sail I hope we shall be there.

MUMFORD
And in five hours more, I make no doubt,
But we shall bring our wished desires about.

Exeunt.

[136] Cf. *Sp. T.* 5.1.25: '**For here I swear** in sight of heaven and earth'.
[137] Cf. *Corn.* 2.1.290: 'Can we be over-hasty **to good hap**?'.

[Scene 27]

Enter [First] Captain of the watch and two Watchmen.

FIRST CAPTAIN
My honest friends, it is your turn tonight
To watch in this place near about the beacon
And vigilantly have regard
If any fleet of ships pass hitherward.
Which, if you do, your office is to fire
The beacon presently and raise the town.

Exit.

FIRST WATCHMAN
Ay, ay, I fear nothing.[138] We know our charge, I warrant. I have been a watchman about this beacon this thirty year, and yet I ne'er see it stir, but stood as quietly as might be.

SECOND WATCHMAN
Faith, neighbour, an you'll follow my 'vice, instead of watching the beacon, we'll go to Goodman Jennings and watch a pot of ale and a rasher of bacon. An if we do not drink ourselves drunk, then so I warrant, the beacon will see us when we come out again.

FIRST WATCHMAN
Ay, but how if somebody excuse us to the captain?

SECOND WATCHMAN
'Tis no matter. I'll prove by good reason that we watch the beacon: as-s for example –

FIRST WATCHMAN
I hope you do not call me ass by craft, neighbour.

SECOND WATCHMAN
No, no, but for example. Say here stands the pot of ale. That's the beacon.

FIRST WATCHMAN
Ay, ay, 'tis a very good beacon.

SECOND WATCHMAN
Well, say here stands your nose. That's the fire.

[138] Cf. *SP* 2.1.296: '**Ay, ay, I** see his body all too soon'.

FIRST WATCHMAN
Indeed, I must confess, 'tis somewhat red.

SECOND WATCHMAN
I see come marching in a dish half-a-score pieces of salt bacon.

FIRST WATCHMAN
I understand your meaning. That's as much to say, half-a-score ships.

SECOND WATCHMAN
True, you conster right. Presently, like a faithful watchman,
I fire the beacon and call up the town.

FIRST WATCHMAN
Ay, that's as much as to say, you set your nose to the pot and drink up the drink.

SECOND WATCHMAN
You are in the right; come, let's go fire the beacon.

Exeunt.

* * * * *

[Scene 28]

Enter the King of Gallia with [the army marching quietly], Mumford, and soldiers.

GALLIA
Now march our ensigns on the British earth,
And we are near approaching to the town.
Then look about you, valiant countrymen,
And we shall finish this exploit with ease.
Th'inhabitants of this mistrustful place
Are dead asleep, as men that are secure.
Here shall we skirmish but with naked men,
Devoid of sense, new-wakèd from a dream,
That know not what our coming doth pretend
Till they do feel our meaning on their skins.
Therefore, assail! God and our right for us!

Exeunt.

* * * * *

[Scene 29]

Alarum, with men and women half-naked. Enter two Captains without doublets, with swords.

FIRST CAPTAIN
Where are these villains that were set to watch
And fire the beacon if occasion served,
That thus have suffered us to be surprised
And never given notice to the town?
We are betrayed and quite devoid of hope
By any means to fortify ourselves.

SECOND CAPTAIN
'Tis ten to one the peasants are o'ercome
With drink and sleep, and so neglect their charge.

FIRST CAPTAIN
A whirlwind carry them quick to a whirlpool
That there the slaves may drink their bellies full.

SECOND CAPTAIN
This 'tis to have the beacon so near the alehouse.

Enter the watchmen drunk, with each a pot.

FIRST CAPTAIN
Out on ye, villains! Whither run you now?

FIRST WATCHMAN
To fire the town and call up the beacon.

SECOND WATCHMAN
No, no, sir – to fire the beacon.

He drinks.

SECOND CAPTAIN
What, with a pot of ale, you drunken rogues?

FIRST CAPTAIN
You'll fire the beacon when the town is lost;
I'll teach you how to tend your office better!

Draws to stab them.

Enter Mumford. Captains run away.

MUMFORD
Yield, yield, yield!

He kicks down their pots.

FIRST WATCHMAN
Reel? No, we do not reel? You may lack a pot of ale ere you die.

MUMFORD
But in mean space I answer you want none.
Well, there's no dealing with you. You're tall men
And well weaponed.[139] I would there were no worse
Than you in the town.

Exit.

SECOND WATCHMAN
'A speaks like an honest man. My choler's past already. Come, neighbour, let's go.

FIRST WATCHMAN
Nay, first let's see an we can stand.

Exeunt.

* * * * *

[Scene 30]

Alarum, excursions [by soldiers]. Mumford [exits] after them and some [townsfolk] half-naked.

Enter the King [of Gallia], Leir, Mumford, Cordella, Perillus, and soldiers, with the chief of the town bound [and an English noble].

GALLIA
Fear not, my friends. You shall receive no hurt,
If you'll subscribe unto your lawful king
And quite revoke your fealty from Cambria
And from aspiring Cornwall, too, whose wives
Have practised treason 'gainst their father's life.
We come in justice of your wrongèd king
And do intend no harm at all to you,
So you submit unto your lawful king.

LEIR
Kind countrymen, it grieves me that perforce
I am constrained to use extremities.[140]

[139] Cf. *SP* 2.1.221–2: 'here are **tall men and** little men'.
[140] Cf. *Corn.* 3.1.24: '**It grieves me that I** know not why you grieve'.

NOBLE
Long have you been looked for, good my lord,
And wished for by a general consent.
And had we known your highness had arrived,
We had not made resistance to your grace.
And now, my gracious lord, you need not doubt
But all the country will yield presently,
Which since your absence have been greatly taxed
For to maintain their over-swelling pride.
We'll presently send word to all our friends;
When they have notice, they will come apace.

LEIR
Thanks, loving subjects, and thanks, worthy son.
Thanks, my kind daughter. Thanks to you, my lord,
Who willingly adventured have your blood,
Without desert, to do me so much good.

MUMFORD
Oh, say not so!
I have been much beholding to your grace.
I must confess, I have been in some skirmishes,
But I was never in the like to this.
For where I was wont to meet with armed men,
I was now encountered with naked women.

CORDELLA
We that are feeble and want use of arms
Will pray to God to shield you from all harms.

LEIR
The while your hands do manage ceaseless toil,
Our hearts shall pray the foes may have the foil.

PERILLUS
We'll fast and pray whilst you for us do fight,
That victory may prosecute the right.

GALLIA
Methinks your words do amplify, my friends,
And add fresh vigour to my willing limbs.[141]

Drum [*beats*].

[141] Cf. *SP* 1.1.52: '**And add fresh** courage **to my** fainting **limbs'** (Wells). Cf. also *KL* 14.10: 'And never ease thy **fainting limbs** a whit'.

But hark, I hear the adverse drum approach.
God and our right, Saint Denis and Saint George!

Enter Cornwall, Cambria, Gonorill, Ragan, and the army.

CORNWALL
Presumptuous King of Gauls, how darest thou
Presume to enter on our British shore?
And more than that to take our towns perforce
And draw our subjects' hearts from their true king?
Be sure to buy it at as dear a price
As e'er you bought presumption in your lives.

GALLIA
O'er-daring Cornwall, know we came in right
And just revengement of the wrongèd king,
Whose daughters there, fell vipers as they are,
Have sought to murder and deprive of life.
But God protected him from all their spite,
And we are come in justice of his right.

CAMBRIA
Nor he nor thou have any interest here
But what you win and purchase with the sword.
Thy slanders to our noble, virtuous queens
We'll in the battle thrust them down thy throat.
Except for fear of our revenging hands
Thou fly to sea, as not secure on lands.

MUMFORD
Welshman, I'll so ferret you ere night for that word that you shall have no mind to crake so well this twelvemonth.

GONORILL
They lie that say we sought our father's death.

RAGAN
'Tis merely forgèd for a colour's sake[142]
To set a gloss on your invasion.
Methinks an old man ready for to die
Should be ashamed to broach so foul a lie.

CORDELLA
Fie, shameless sister, so devoid of grace

[142] Cf. *Sp. T.* 4.4.64: 'You, gentle brother, **forged** this **for** my **sake**'.

To call our father liar to his face!

GONORILL
Peace, Puritan, dissembling hypocrite,
Which art so good that thou wilt prove stark naught!
Anon, when as I have you in my fingers,
I'll make you wish yourself in purgatory.

PERILLUS
Nay, peace thou monster, shame unto thy sex,
Thou fiend in likeness of a human creature!

RAGAN
I never heard a fouler-spoken man.

LEIR
Out on thee, viper, scum, filthy parricide,
More odious to my sight than is a toad!
[*Showing scrolls*] Knowest thou these letters?
[*Ragan*] *snatches them and tears them.*

RAGAN
Think you to outface me with your paltry scrolls?
You come to drive my husband from his right
Under the colour of a forgèd letter.[143]

LEIR
Whoever heard the like impiety?

PERILLUS
You are our debtor of more patience.
We were more patient when we stayed for you
Within the thicket two long hours and more.[144]

RAGAN
What hours? What thicket?

PERILLUS
There where you sent your servant with your letters,
Sealed with your hand, to send us both to heaven,[145]
Where, as I think, you never mean to come.

RAGAN
Alas, you are grown a child again with age,

[143] Cf. *Sp. T.* 1.3.66: '**Under the colour of a** duteous friend'.
[144] Cf. *Sp. T.* 1.2.63: 'In all this turmoil, three **long hours and more**'.
[145] Cf. *Sp. T.* 3.1.55: 'I'll lend a **hand to send thee to** the lake'.

Or else your senses dote for want of sleep.

PERILLUS
Indeed, you made us rise betimes, you know,
Yet had a care we should sleep where you bade us stay,
But never wake more till the latter day.

GONORILL
Peace, peace, old fellow. Thou art sleepy still.

MUMFORD
Faith, and if you reason till tomorrow,
You get no other answer at their hands.
'Tis pity two such good faces
Should have so little grace between them.
Well, let us see if their husbands with their hands
Can do as much as they do with their tongues.

CAMBRIA
Ay, with their swords they'll make your tongue unsay
What they have said, or else they'll cut them out.

GALLIA
To't gallants, to't. Let's not stand brawling thus.

Exeunt both armies.

* * * * *

[Scene 31]

Sound alarum. Excursions. Mumford must chase Cambria away, then cease [and exit].

Enter Cornwall.

CORNWALL
The day is lost. Our friends do all revolt
And join against us with the adverse part.
There is no means of safety but by flight,
And therefore I'll to Cornwall with my queen.

Exit.

* * * * *

[Scene 32]

Enter Cambria.

CAMBRIA
I think there is a devil in the camp
Hath haunted me today. He hath so tired me
That in a manner I can fight no more.

Enter Mumford.

Zounds, here he comes. I'll take me to my horse! *Exit.*
Mumford follows him to the door and returns.[146]

MUMFORD
Farewell, Welshman. Give thee but thy due,
Thou hast a light and nimble pair of legs.
Thou are more in debt to them than to thy hands.
But if I meet thee once again today,
I'll cut them off and set them to a better heart.

Exit.

* * * * *

[Scene 33]

Alarums and excursions. Then sound victory.

Enter Leir, Perillus, King [of Gallia], Cordella, and Mumford.

GALLIA
Thanks be to God, your foes are overcome,
And you again possessèd of your right.

LEIR
First to the heavens, next thanks to you, my son,[147]
By whose good means I repossess the same.[148]
Which if it please you to accept yourself,
With all my heart I will resign to you.
For it is yours by right and none of mine.
First have you raised at your own charge a power
Of valiant soldiers – this comes all from you –
Next have you ventured your own person's scathe.

[146] Cf. *SP* 1.5.23.1 SD: '*rides* **with him to the door, and** *meets*'.
[147] Cf. *SP* 4.1.60: '**First thanks to heaven**, and **next to** Brusor's valour'. (Wells)
[148] Cf. *SP* 2.1.254: 'But now, when **I** should **repossess the same**'.

And lastly, worthy Gallia never-stained,
My kingly title I by thee have gained.

GALLIA
Thank heavens, not me. My zeal to you is such,
Command my utmost, I will never grutch.

CORDELLA
He that with all kind love entreats his queen,
Will not be to her father unkind seen.

LEIR
Ah, my Cordella! Now I call to mind
The modest answer which I took unkind.
But now I see I am no whit beguiled.
Thou lov'st me dearly and as ought a child.[149]
And thou, Perillus, partner once in woe,
Thee to requite, the best I can, I'll do.
Yet all I can, ay, were it ne'er so much,
Were not sufficient, thy true love is such.
Thanks, worthy Mumford, to thee last of all,
Not greeted last 'cause thy desert was small.
No, thou hast lion-like laid on today,
Chasing the Cornwall king and Cambria,
Who with my daughters – 'daughters' did I say? –
To save their lives, the fugitives did play.
Come, son and daughter, who did me advance.
Repose with me awhile, and then for France.
Sound drums and trumpets.

Exeunt.

FINIS

[149] Cf. *SP* 5.4.76–7: 'She **loved me dearly**, **and** I loved her'.

TEXTUAL NOTES

Scene 1

Scene 1] BOND and GREG (*subst*); *ACTVS 1.* Q
0SD *Scaliger, Perillus,*] HOPKINSON; not in Q
1SH] HAZLITT; not in Q
35 jointure] Q (*Ioynter*)
40 for] Q; from STERN
43 sat] HOPKINSON; *set* Q
83–5] quotation marks HOPKINSON; not in Q
90SD] HOPKINSON; not in Q

Scene 2

Scene 2] BOND and GREG (*subst*); no scene division Q
25–6] lineation this edition; 'haue |' Q
30–1] lineation HOPKINSON; one line Q
33–4] lineation this edition; one line Q

Scene 3

Scene 3] BOND and GREG (*subst*); no scene division Q
1–2] line division STERN; 'daughters, |' Q
55SD] HOPKINSON; not in Q
75SD] HOPKINSON; not in Q
100] quotation marks STERN; not in Q
134SD] HOPKINSON; not in Q
136 flatt'ring] Q (*flattering*)

Scene 4

Scene 4] BOND and GREG (*subst*); no scene division Q
1SH] STERN (*subst*); *King. or Kin.* throughout Q
44] verse this edition; prose in Q

Scene 5

Scene 5] BOND and GREG (*subst*); no scene division Q
0SD.1 *Cornwall's Servant*] this edition; *his man* Q
2SH] *Ser.* throughout Q
5SD] in margin Q

8SD.2 *Cambria's servant*] this edition; *his man* Q
9SD] in margin Q
13SH] *Ser.* throughout Q
13SD] in margin Q
22 Sultan] Q (*Souldan*)
43SD] STERN (*subst*); not in Q

Scene 6
Scene 6] BOND and GREG (*subst*); no scene division Q
35SD *nobles*] STERN; *others* Q
48SD] in margin Q
81SD *Cambria and Cornwall*] STERN; *they* Q
105SD *all but*; Q (*omnes, manet*)

Scene 7
Scene 7] BOND and GREG (*subst*); no scene division Q
0SD *King of Gallia*] STERN; *Gallian King* Q
2, 5 'My lord'] quotation marks STERN; not in Q
12–13 Well ... Jack] lineation this edition; one line Q
51SD] MICHIE (*subst*); not in Q
146 foppets] Q; soppets CUNLIFFE *conj.*
156–8] prose STERN; verse 'know: | ...liue, | ...Ladyes |' Q

Scene 8
Scene 8] BOND and GREG (*subst*); no scene division Q
0SD *alone*] STERN; *solus* Q

Scene 9
Scene 9] BOND and GREG (*subst*); no scene division Q

Scene 10
Scene 10] BOND and GREG (*subst*); no scene division Q
12SD] STERN; not in Q
16 What] Q (*What,*)

Scene 11
Scene 11] BOND and GREG (*subst*); no scene division Q
0SD *alone*] STERN; *solus* Q

Scene 12
Scene 12] BOND and GREG (*subst*); no scene division Q
50–2] prose HOPKINSON; verse 'stand | ...be |' Q

54–6] prose HOPKINSON; verse 'I | …vp |' Q
65–70] prose HOPKINSON; verse 'this | …armes, | …at | …any | …of |' Q
72–4] prose HOPKINSON; verse 'good | …forfey- |' Q
76–81] prose HOPKINSON; verse 'Oysterwife | … neighbours | … else | … in | … more |' Q
81 Palermo] Q (*Palerno*)
100–2] prose HOPKINSON; verse 'done: | …will | …Poulter |' Q

Scene 13
Scene 13] BOND and GREG (*subst*); no scene division Q
0SD *alone*] STERN; *solus* Q
1SH] NICHOLS; not in Q

Scene 14
Scene 14] BOND and GREG (*subst*); no scene division Q
23.1SD *Leir and Perillus*] STERN (*subst*); not in Q
31.1SD *Aside*] HOPKINSON; not in Q
31.2SD *runs*] Q (*runneth*)
43SD *all but*] STERN; *manet* Q

Scene 15
Scene 15] BOND and GREG (*subst*); no scene division Q
0SD *alone with letters*] STERN (*subst*); *solus* Q
7SD] STERN; not in Q
14SD] HOPKINSON; not in Q
16 See] NICHOLS; *She* Q
63.1SD] MICHIE (*subst*); not in Q
69SD] HOPKINSON; not in Q

Scene 16
Scene 16] BOND and GREG (*subst*); no scene division Q
0SD *King of Gallia*] STERN; *Gallian King* Q
64SD] HAZLITT; not in Q

Scene 17
Scene 17] BOND and GREG (*subst*); no scene division Q
0SD *alone*] STERN; *solus* Q
5] lineation this edition; line combined with 6 Q
7SD] STERN; *Enter Ragā.* in margin Q

Scene 18
Scene 18] BOND and GREG (*subst*); no scene division Q

13–14] prose HOPKINSON; verse 'Ambassador |' Q
60–1 'Tis … otherwise] lineation this edition; one line Q
61–2 It … otherwise] lineation this edition; one line Q

Scene 19

Scene 19] BOND and GREG (*subst*); no scene division Q
0SD *with books*] MICHIE (*subst*); not in Q
19.2SD *a letter and*] STERN (*subst*); not in Q
45SD] HOPKINSON; not in Q
48 pretends] Q; *portends* STERN
49SD] HOPKINSON; not in Q
64SD] MICHIE; not in Q
83SD *Messenger takes*] STERN; *Take* Q
89SD *Leir and Perillus*] STERN (*subst*); *They* Q
104SH] STERN (*subst*); *Ambo.* Q
119 Damon] HOPKINSON; *Damion* Q
129 Zounds] Q (*zoones*)
191SD] HOPKINSON; not in Q
195SD] MICHIE; not in Q
202SD *Leir and Perillus*] STERN; not in Q
213SD] STERN; not in Q
272SD] HOPKINSON; not in Q
290SD *The Messenger*] STERN (*subst*); *He* Q
292SD *The Messenger*] STERN (*subst*); *He* Q
300 parlousest] Q (*parlosest*)
325 She] Q (*Se*)

Scene 20

Scene 20] BOND and GREG (*subst*); no scene division Q
0SD *alone*] HOPKINSON; *solus* Q

Scene 21

Scene 21] BOND and GREG (*subst*); no scene division Q
0SD *of Gallia, Cordella*] STERN (*subst*); *and Queene of Gallia* Q
11–13] prose HOPKINSON; verse 'agayne, | …wench, | …forsworne, |' Q
18–20] prose HOPKINSON; verse 'it | …dayes |' Q
22–3 been | So] HOPKINSON; line break 'she, |' Q
26–7] prose HOPKINSON; verse 'nonce |' Q
30–4] prose HOPKINSON; verse 'still, | …many, | …game: | …quarrel, | … shall |' Q
37–41] prose HOPKINSON; verse 'over: | …disposed, | …clayme | …me: | …me. | …me, |' Q

43–5] prose HOPKINSON; verse 'this, | …now, | …seaside |' Q
48SD] MICHIE; not in Q

Scene 22
Scene 22] BOND and GREG (*subst*); no scene division Q
0SD *King of*] the King of STERN; not in Q
85SD *Ragan*] this edition; *She* Q

Scene 23
Scene 23] BOND and GREG (*subst*); no scene division Q
22SD *change*] HOPKINSON; *changeth* Q
23SD] MICHIE; not in Q
28SD *Pulls*] HOPKINSON; *Pull* Q
38SD *aside*] STERN; *Leir* Q
41–3 prose STERN; verse 'together, | …anon, |' Q
46–7] line break this edition; 'money | With' Q

Scene 24
Scene 24] BOND and GREG (*subst*); no scene division Q
0.1SD *King of Gallia*] STERN; *Gallian King* Q
0.1SD *Cordella*] HOPKINSON (*subst*); not in Q
0.2SD *to a table*] GRIFFIN (*subst*); not in Q
15–16] prose this edition; verse 'youthes, |' Q
61 God] this edition; *good* Q
85SD *Cordella brings*] GRIFFIN (*subst*); *She bringeth* Q
90–1] prose STERN; verse 'grace: |' Q
101SD] GRIFFIN (*subst*); not in Q
225SD *Leir rises*] HOPKINSON; *He riseth* Q
237SD *rises*] HOPKINSON; *riseth* Q
254SD] Q (*rise.*)
259SD] Q (*rise.*)

Scene 25
Scene 25] BOND and GREG (*subst*); no scene division Q
0SD *alone*] HOPKINSON; *sola* Q

Scene 26
Scene 26] BOND and GREG (*subst*); no scene division Q
0.1SD *King of Gallia*] STERN; *Gallian King* Q
14SD] GRIFFIN; not in Q
22 eyes] LEE; *eye* Q
28SD] GRIFFIN (*subst*); not in Q

Scene 27

Scene 27] BOND and GREG (*subst*); no scene division Q
0SD *First*] STERN (*subst*); *a* Q
1SH FIRST] STERN (*subst*); not in Q
11 Jennings] NICHOLS (*subst*); *Genitings* Q

Scene 28

Scene 28] BOND and GREG (*subst*); no scene division Q
0.1SD *the army marching quietly*] this edition; *a stil march* Q

Scene 29

Scene 29] BOND and GREG (*subst*); no scene division Q
7–8] verse HOPKINSON; prose Q
19–20] prose HOPKINSON; verse 'reele: |' Q
22–4] verse this edition; prose Q

Scene 30

Scene 30] BOND and GREG (*subst*); no scene division Q
0.1SD *by soldiers*] this edition; not in Q
0.1SD *exits*] this edition; not in Q
0.2SD *townsfolk*] this edition; not in Q
0.3SD *King of Gallia*] STERN; *Gallian King* Q
0.4SD *and an English noble*] HOPKINSON (*subst*); not in Q
38SD *beats*] sounded HOPKINSON; not in Q
45 sure] NICHOLS; *sute* Q
77.1SD] HOPKINSON; not in Q
77.2SD *Ragan*] this edition; *She* Q

Scene 31

Scene 31] BOND and GREG (*subst*); no scene division Q

Scene 32

Scene 32] this edition; no scene division Q
1–3] verse HOPKINSON; prose Q

Scene 33

Scene 33] Sc. xxxii BOND and GREG; no scene division Q
0.2SD *of Gallia*] STERN (*subst*); not in Q

COMMENTARY

NOTES ON PERSONS

LEIR Mythical tenth King of Britain, from the eighth century BC. His story is first recounted by Geoffrey of Monmouth in the twelfth century. Raphael Holinshed's *The firste volume of the chronicles of England, Scotlande, and Irelande* (London, 1577) provides the probable source for the character and his story in the play.

SCALIGER A character not in the sources, perhaps with a name alluding to Joseph Justus Scaliger, a French scholar who produced editions of classical texts in this period. The character disappears after the early scenes, possibly to permit doubling with another, later character.

PERILLUS Another invented character, possibly suggesting 'perilous', which is the situation he finds himself in with King Leir throughout much of the play.

GONORILL Gonorilla in Holinshed, is Leir's eldest daughter and married to the Duke of Cornwall.

RAGAN middle sister, married to the Duke of Albania in Holinshed.

CORDELLA Cordilla/Cordeilla in Holinshed, ruled Britain for five years after the death of her father. When her husband, Gallia, died, Gonorill and Ragan's sons imprisoned her, where she, 'beeing a woman of a manly courage', took her life (20).

GALLIA i.e., France.

MUMFORD A common English surname, making for a nationally ambivalent 'French' lord.

CORNWALL Gonorill's husband in Holinshed, but not in other versions of the Lier story, or in Shakespeare, as James H. Forse notes: 'Perhaps all that this suggests [the author of *King Leir*] looked nowhere else but to Holinshed for his story line' ("To Die or Not to Die, that is the Question: Borrowing and Adapting the King Lear Legend in the Anonymous *The True Chronicle History of King Leir* and Shakespeare's *King Lear*', *Ben Jonson Journal* 21:1 (2014): 53–72, 55).

Morgan The first name is used only twice in the play. Ragan's husband is the Duke of Albania in Holinshed and called 'Maglanus'.

The Persons in the Play] HOPKINSON (*subst*); not in Q

NOTES ON THE PLAY

[Scene 1]

0 SD *nobles* Such plural indications of cast are permissive of any number from two or above. McMillin and MacLean's work on casting and doubling counts these instances as two actors to determine that a minimum of fourteen actors are required to perform the play (with doubling). If more than two appear, more actors would be required (Scott McMillin and Sally-Beth MacLean, *The Queen's Men and Their Plays* (Cambridge, 1998), pp. 100–7).

1 Thus … grief Leir underscores the recentness of the funeral and, possibly, that it is time to move on. He and the lords might enter as if directly from the funeral. Compare *Titus Andronicus,* also performed at the Rose theatre in 1594, which begins with an ongoing funeral, potentially including the onstage representation of a tomb; **obsequies** funeral rites.

2 late recently.

4 ride … cherubins Leir imagines a funeral procession led by a company of angels (*OED*, Cherubin *n.*2).

5 grave serious, but with a contextual association to the recent funeral.

8 states estates, fortunes.

15 tender love, care for.

16 affairs business, activities (*OED*, Affair *n.*2a); not 'romantic relationships', a meaning that emerges late in the seventeenth century (*OED*, *n.*3a).

17–18 Although this sounds like an aphorism, it is not. Leir expresses an ideology at odds with practices of child-rearing in the period, which did not generally advocate parents advising or caring for children only of the same sex. Fathers had plenty to say about daughters' lives in the drama of the period.

18 steps … turns i.e., daughters turn their steps towards their mothers for advice.

19 want lack (not desire, or wish for); **for to** i.e., to. The extra 'for' is common before infinitive forms in this period. It is also deployed often in this play for metrical purposes.

21 loins 'seat of … generative power' (*OED*, Loin *n.*2b). Leir effectively states that he is now impotent.

22 one … grave 'An old man has one foot in the grave' was proverbial (Tilley M346) for impending death (*OED*, foot *n.*P5a(b)).

25 fain like to.

25–8 The ruler who would give up power for a life of contemplation is a common literary trope (most famously in *The Tempest*), but not something endorsed by the political-religious philosophies of the early modern period. This plot point also touches upon the contemporary

succession question. By 1594 Queen Elizabeth was over sixty years old and had produced no heir. (For a discussion of the succession crisis in relation to the play, see Forse, pp. 58–60.)
31 quondam former.
32 licensed me given me the freedom.
33 censure give an opinion (*OED*, *v.*1).
34 several often means separate.
35–6 Scaliger ambiguously plants the idea of unequal dowries based upon a test of love.
38 fixed unchangeable; **mould** vessel, i.e., womb.
39 unpartial unbiased, fair (*OED*, *adj.*1a).
40 for me for my (part). Stern emends to 'from me', but the sense here is clear; no alteration is needed.
42 lent It was commonly held that life is only lent, as a debt to be repaid; **indubitate** undoubted (i.e., only one clear heir, with clarification at line 45 of it being a male heir) (*OED*, *adj.*).
50 them i.e., the three daughters.
55 sort with accord with.
57 motion propose (*OED*, *v.*2a).
60 allows gives approval, i.e., that both parties are in love.
61 diverse several.
62 partial sparing (*OED*, *adj.*A.I.†2c), picky.
63 policy proposed 'course of action' (*OED*, *n.*I.4) but with connotations of Machiavellian deception; **beguile** charm, divert (*OED*, *v.*4). The term also carries a sense of deception (*v.*1a).
73 fancy 'amorous inclination' (*OED*, *n.*A.8†b), attraction.
74 Perillus's implication is that a mismatch might lead to a passionate disaster (i.e., through infidelity).
77 try test.
79 contend compete.
81 vantage point of (my) advantage.
85 woo court, solicit (on your behalf).
87 senses … mute i.e., she will be unable to speak (owing to the moment of surprise).
90 them i.e., Gonorill and Ragan; **bewray** expose.

[Scene 2]
2 pert forward; **peat** This usage predates *OED*'s earliest example (1599) of peat as 'a term of obloquy for a woman' *OED*[2] 2.a; an earlier meaning is 'a term of endearment to a girl' *OED*[2] 1.a, so Gonorill could be ironically applying one of Leir's pet names for Cordella.
6 choice select.

17 prick and praise proverbial, 'success and its acknowledgement' *OED sb* VI.20, but 'prick' is also bawdy.
18 set … days set aside.
21 hap happen.
27 in … shirt i.e., in his underwear.
28–9 The scrambled metrics of the previous lines, and Ragan's belated 'Swear not so deeply …' (30), suggest that this may be a later addition; **grant** pledge.
30 deeply intensely.
36 expedition five syllables, i.e., ex-pe-di-ti-on.
38 with child expectant.
39 longing expectancy, but also, continuing the metaphor, 'cravings incident to women during pregnancy' *OED sb* 1.2.
42 Cambria Roughly equivalent to the modern Wales.
45 Hibernia Ireland. See 2.96.
46 doubts suspects.
51 so provided.
54 for to an old-fashioned form of the preposition to, used to make up a full line.
77 our … we our revenge (that) we.
92 Apollo's music Apollo played music for the gods on Olympus.
97 loveth extrametrical.

[Scene 3]
1 Will Direct, order.
5 common weal commonwealth, general good.
11 watch stay awake.
12 wantons neglectful, playing young people.
17 conformable compliant.
30 assizes judgement.
36 hest behest.
40 windy words proverbial: 'words are but wind', i.e., they can be meaningless (Tilley W833).
47 Brittany Britain.
51 accomplish perform.
68 mean means.
74 Philomel Mythological woman raped by Tereus and transformed into a nightingale.
78 paint portray; falsify, cover up.
80 look consider.

82 answer answerless i.e., containing no answer (*OED*, *adj.* 2a). The phrase was famously given by Elizabeth in response to whether she wished to have Mary, Queen of Scots executed in 1586.
83 brook tolerate.
86 minion like 'peat' 2.2, the word had both positive connotations, 'a favourite child' (*OED sb1* A.1.b), and pejorative, 'one who owes everything to his patron's favour' (*OED sb1* A.1.c).
92 short shorten.
94 them i.e., their fathers.
97 did'st ... know if you did know.
108 your ... off i.e., you over-praise yourself. The full proverb is 'He dwells far from neighbours ... that is fain to praise himself' (Tilley N117). The comment also suggests the private, familial nature of *Leir*'s division of the kingdom.
113 imp demon.
114 tittle 'a minute amount' (*OED sb* 2).
118 Shift Look after yourself.
120 to ... dower for their ... dowry.
125 these i.e., Gonorill and Ragan.
127 sheen bright.
128 queen both 'female ruler' and 'whore'.
131 But unto None other than to.
138 hidden tenor true meaning.

[Scene 4]

3 flying fame fast-travelling rumour. 'Flying Fame' is also the title of a contemporary tune, providing the music for many ballads, including 'A Lamentable Song of the Death of King Lear' (See *A Collection of Old Ballads* (London, 1723), vol. 2, pp. 8–17). This phrase might therefore allude to an existing popular ballad, although no copies from the sixteenth century are known.
4 prodigal lavish.
6 i.e., If they look in person as good as they are said to.
7 allow of approve of.
8 vows proclamations of love.
11 Jason ... fleece In Greek mythology Jason sailed with the Argonauts to steal the golden fleece, which was guarded by a dragon, hence offering a model for a difficult 'prize'. Jason's wife was Medea, however, who infamously killed their children over his infidelity, so the picture of courtship here is ironically mixed.
16 gallant fine-looking (*OED*, A. *adj.* †2).
23 observe i.e., continually obey.

29 congees bidding farewell (*OED*, *n.*2 I. †2b), or possibly giving 'hellos' (see line 35).

33 bind restrain; **leave** stop (doing).

39 words … dignity formal titles.

40 friendliest i.e., as equals.

42 palmers' weeds the clothing of (poor) religious pilgrims, from the practice of pilgrims carrying palm branches from their journey to the Holy Land.

43 mistrust suspect.

44 fit … turn serve your purpose; **warrant you** pledge, promise (to do it for) you.

45 bluntest Mumford's advocacy of plain speaking deftly shifts to prose. The play is notable for a skillful, if minimal, deployment of prose, including characters who are made to swap between prose and verse as the situation demands.

46 praying i.e., asking, entreating.

55 purpose intend.

[Scene 5]

0.1 SD *booted … wand* It is unclear in this direction, and in the parallel one for Cambria and his servant at line 8, whether both master and servant are so dressed. It seems clear that the kings hold the letters, which we later learn have invited them to King Leir's court.

2–6 Twenty miles per hour is an impossibly quick – and as the servant points out, dangerous – pace for a horse.

5 for me i.e., as far as I'm concerned.

8 gratified rewarded, requited (*OED*, gratify *v.*†1.a).

9 fresh horse again the implication is that the kings are racing to court, in their keenness to see their potential brides in person.

10 forbear await.

11 wishèd desired; **mistress** In this period the word signified a 'sweetheart' being openly courted by a man (*OED*, *n.*A.I†5a).

12 stay 'person that affords support' (*OED*, *n.*2 1b).

15 Daedalus' waxen wings Daedalus was an inventor in classical mythology who fashioned wings from willow branches and wax to escape imprisonment from King Minos's labyrinth, famously warning his son, Icarus, not to fly too close to the sun, or the wax would melt. In the *Chronicle* history, Leir's father, Baldud 'uppon a presumptuous pleasure which he had … he tooke upon him to flie in the ayre, but he fell upon the temple of Apollo, which stoode in the Citie of Troynouant' (Holinshed, 19).

17 Troy Novant i.e., new Troy, a common name for London, following Geoffrey of Monmouth's claim in the twelfth century that Brutus fled ancient Troy and founded London.

18 SD *start* i.e., are startled.

25 slenderly accompanied each king has only one servant, instead of the large retinue expected for typical royal travel.

27–8 These lines might be delivered as a question. Cornwall and Cambria are being wry with one another – probably because they suspect they are on the same business.

29 break … circumstances i.e., stop discussing the occasions (that bring us here).

30 brook tolerate, be patient with.

32 content i.e., agreed; (I) accept (your proposal).

37 present immediate.

38 moiety of half of. Possibly Q's 'of' is an error for 'or'.

42 call call (one another).

46 seigniories territories (*OED*, seigniory *n.* 3).

47–8 Whom … part I would have gladly taken up the offer for only one-third of his lands (as originally projected in the triple division of the kingdom).

48 complements perfections (*OED*, complement *n.* 3a).

51 hole i.e., vagina; **'Sblood** by Christ's blood, an oath.

59 compass confines.

62 danger … prevent risk to anticipate.

[Scene 6]

3 sir-reverence 1) with all due respect (ironic) (*OED n.* †1b); 2) 'human excrement' (*n.* 2).

10 reclaimed called back (to her) (*OED*, reclaim *v.* 1a).

11 I … behind I was just about.

12 Faith (By my) faith – a mild oath; **moves** motivates.

15 Beshrew … fingers i.e., Curse you. The phrase appears elsewhere in the drama of the period (e.g., 'beshrew his fingers' in Francis Beaumont's *Knight of the Burning Pestle* (London, 1613), D4v).

17 low humbled.

18 clip … wings alluding to overambitious flight, like Icarus (5.15n), trimming wing feathers prevents domesticated birds from being able to fly.

20 right fit entirely suitable; **parson's wife** Parsons were proverbially attracted to pretty women (Tilley P68).

23 nothing A typical early modern joke about women's thing (i.e., 'vagina'), which was also commonly aligned with 'nought', zero, or nothing (Gordon Williams, *A Dictionary of Sexual Language and Imagery in*

Shakespearean and Stuart Literature, 3 vols (London and Atlantic Highlands, NJ, 1994), 'nothing', pp. 960–1).

25 cry … mercy beg your pardon.

26 stately high-ranking, majestic (*OED*, *adj.* A.1a).

27 benefice pay; **on … back** i.e., wear it in fine clothing.

31 long i.e., (it's too) long.

35 consummate make the marriage complete by having sex.

36 sue not do not ask, entreat (me).

37 censure judgement.

40 hand … seal i.e., formal signature and royal seal; **justify** confirm (*OED*, *v.* 3a).

43–4 kind … lives Pelicans were held to puncture their own breasts to revive their dead young with blood. Shakespeare inverted this image in *King Lear* to describe the unnatural behaviour of Goneril and Regan: ''twas this flesh begot | Those pelican daughters' (3.4.60–1). Cf. *Edward III*, 8.111–14: 'A pelican, my lord, | Wounding her bosom with her crookèd beak | That so her nest of young ones might be fed | With drops of blood that issue from her heart'.

45–7 eagle … sun According to Pliny the Elder, a sea eagle 'beats its young ones while in an unfledged state, with its wings, and forces them from time to time to look steadily upon the rays of the sun; and if it sees either of them wink, or even its eye water, it throws it headlong out of the nest, as being spurious and degenerate, while, on the other hand, it rears the one whose gaze remains fixed and steady' (*Natural History*, tr. John Bostock, *Perseus Digital Library*, Book 10.3 <http://www.perseus.tufts.edu/hopper/text?doc=Perseus:text:1999.02.0137>).

50 testify demonstrate.

53 Priam's children Priam was King of Troy, famously ransacked by the Greeks, and his children, including Hector, Troilus, and Cassandra, had unhappy fates. This irony seems to escape Leir.

56 will inclination, desire.

58 frame construct, offer.

61 rest remain.

65 Leander … Hero In Greek myth, the ill-fated lovers met each night after Leander swam the Hellespont, until he drowned when Hero was unable to maintain the torch that showed his way across. Hero killed herself in despair when she discovered his body.

66 Aeneas … Queen The classical myth of Dido, Queen of Carthage, and Aeneas, Trojan War hero whom she loved, was told in Christopher Marlowe's play *Dido, Queen of Carthage* (published 1594). It is another story of tragic love, with Dido killing herself after Aeneas abandons her.

68 no … his Aeneas went on to found Rome and marry another woman, Lavinia, but Cambria ignores the tragic implications in favour of Aeneas's heroic story.
76 this i.e., these comparisons.
78 resteth remains.
81 as falls as (it) falls.
82 These The half-kingdoms.
83 erst formerly.
87 beads prayer beads, as used by those practising the Catholic faith.
94 in … cause i.e., on poor Cordella's behalf.
97 doom fate.
99 an if if.
103 esteem … for think him to be (*OED*, Esteem *v.* II).
109–10 each … forth i.e., I will put every drop of my blood to help her.

[Scene 7]
0 SD *pilgrims* travellers to religious sites in holy pilgrimage. Such travellers would often wear identifying badges and clothing, in part to signal 'a protection afforded to pilgrims upon pain of excommunication following a declaration by the 1123 Lateran Council' (Helena Guzik, 'Memory, Imagination, Identity: Pilgrimage and Portraiture in Medieval and Early Modern Europe', *International Journal of Religious Tourism and Pilgrimage* 9:2 (2021): 81–97, 83). Guzik identifies the typical garb as: 'a staff, a small cross-body satchel …, a cape or cloak, a simple tunic, a broad-brimmed hat or cowl …, worn shoes or bare feet, a flask or gourd, prayer beads, as well as scallop shells …, and pilgrim badges' (84). We later learn that Gallia carries a 'palmer's staff' (7.115), and the actor might be wearing other items from Guzik's list.
1 brook tolerate.
2 humour habit (*OED*, I.7a).
3 bound you made you promise.
6 ta'en … spies mistaken for being spies.
7 Zounds By Christ's wounds, an oath.
10 Might … made i.e., If I were made.
11 hit upon recall.
13 Jack 'An ordinary man … esp. a man of low social status' (*OED*, *n*.2 I.2a), possibly with the sense of being a ladies' man (*OED*, P3), which appears in later periods.
14 close nearby, hidden.
19 turned turned (out).
20 Queen of Chance Fortune.
21 pattern example.

22 **imbecility** 'feebleness' (*OED*, *n.* †1a).
23 **brunts** attacks (*OED*, *n.*1 I.†2).
28 **rod** 'stick or bundle of twigs used as an instrument of punishment, esp. for a child' (*OED*, *n.*1 I.1a).
31 **estate** i.e., her current, impoverished economic situation.
32 **meaner** poorer.
35 **shift** change. Mumford wants to get naked with her.
36 **betake ... to** take up (as an occupation).
38 **custom** trade (i.e., as a customer, with the implication of sexual transactions, too).
39 **St Denis** Patron saint of France – reminding the audience that Mumford is French.
40 **shirts ... night-gear** Shirts are undergarments in this period, typically worn by men to bed. Night-gear = nightclothes (*OED*, *n.* 1).
43 **forbear ... speak** bear no longer to be silent.
45 **'Sblood** By Christ's blood (an oath); **sempster** seamstress.
48 **get in** i.e., to the 'labyrinth of love'; with a bawdy double meaning.
49 **prithee** please, '(I) pray thee'; **cross ... passions** i.e., don't provoke my ire.
50 **patience** i.e., with a suitor.
53 **Vouchsafe** Bestow, give.
57 **to ... o'ercharged** i.e., too full (of sorrow).
59–60 **mouse ... net** Alluding to Aesop's fable, in which a mouse promises to help a lion in exchange for not being killed, and is later able to chew through a net that holds the lion captive.
63 **hapless** unlucky.
65 **debars** prevents.
77 **crave** 'ask earnestly ... beg for' (*OED*, *v.* 2a).
80 **spoil ... honour** i.e., sexually assault her. Cordella alludes to the risk of rape for a woman travelling alone.
81 **interest in** power over; **mind** here, inclination to love.
83 **sue to** entreat; **extremity** extreme situation, crisis.
86 **move** i.e., change.
89 i.e., To come up with ways to cause new suffering to those already in despair.
92 **lusty** several senses might apply in context: 1) 'cheerful, lively' (*OED*, *adj.* †1a); 2) 'pleasant' (†2a); 3) 'full of desire' (to court you) (†3); 4) 'full of lust or sexual desire' (†4); 5) 'vigorous' (5a).
93 **like** similar.
95 **Hymen** The Greek god of marriage.
97 **live** Cordella implies that she has lived long enough to be made even more miserable.

100 case … stands situation is at present.
101 Whilom whenas Once when.
102 postulate 'claim, request' (*OED*, *v.* †3a – first usage).
104 light lit.
105 surcease abandon (*OED*, *v.* 3a).
106 whereas 'considering that' (*OED*, *adv.* II.2).
110 mind wish, desire, expectations (*OED*, *n.*1 II.9); **low enough** i.e., sufficiently unambitious.
113 straight unwavering, steadfast (*OED*, *adj.* A.3a); **penury** poverty.
114 happy fortunate.
117 bonnet soft, brimless hat.
123 lovely choice i.e., choice of love.
128 unknown disguise i.e., disguise (designed to make me) unknown.
129 admired implying that the rumour of her beauty brought him to Britain.
131 slenderly accompanied i.e., lacking the normal retinue of servants.
133 vassal … love i.e., The god Cupid has made me your servant.
141 next … falls next (lady) we meet.
142 speed succeed.
146 foppets (presumably) mind-changing women. *OED* records no other usage of the term. John W. Cunliffe conjectures 'soppets', a diminutive of 'sop' or 'milksop', which fits the context of being considered weak-willed.
153 chance fortune.
156 I know … know i.e., 'my mind is made up: I'll marry only an honest and plain-dealing wench'.

[Scene 8]
2 advance promote; **which** who (i.e., Gonorill and Ragan).
12 he Leir.
14 opprobrious sort detestable ways.
15 dotard (pejorative term for) one mentally impaired by age (*OED*, *n.*1 A.1).
16 sets … oft orders her servants purposefully and often.
17 In scoffing-wise i.e., by scoffing, mocking.
18 iron age In the classical ages of man, the iron age was set against the golden, silver, bronze, and heroic ages as a time of baseness and misery; **vild** vile (archaic).
19 contemnèd treated with contempt.
20 pension regular allowance; **restrained from** kept away from.
22–3 nothing … maintain the only wasted expenditures are those keeping her father alive.
24 alliance established bonds of kinship.

[Scene 9]

2 dignity status.

3 quips sarcastic remarks.

5 alms charitable contributions (of food and shelter).

6 keep look after.

8 check correct, rebuke; **snap … up** snap back at me.

10 set … forth i.e., trim it with ornamentation (like lace, gold, or silver thread, etc.).

11 doltish foolish; **withered** i.e., shrunken, empty.

12 senseless 1) without reason; 2) without cause.

13 extraordinary i.e., unusually extravagant.

14 abroad broadly (*OED*, *adv.* A.1a). As a new queen, Gonorill wishes to gain a reputation for being a lavish host.

15 captious 'fault-finding' (*OED*, *adj.* 2).

23 favours gifts.

28 abridge it reduce it by.

36 relieve sustain (*OED*, *v.* I.3a).

38 viperous 'malignant, treacherous' (*OED*, *adj.* 3a). Vipers were thought in this period to eat their own mothers at birth. See Shakespeare's *Pericles* 1.2.65–6: 'I am no viper, yet I feed | On mother's flesh which did me breed'.

40 favour approval, goodwill.

43 A common maxim. See for instance James Shirley's *The Sisters*: 'you must be flatter'd, | Great Ladies cannot live els' (*Six New Plays* (London, 1656), p. 37).

[Scene 10]

1 aileth you causes; **sad** serious.

2 wont used (to do).

6 prolong … life It was commonly thought in this period that laughter either 'lengthens life' (Shakespeare, *Taming of the Shrew*, Ind.2.129) or shortens it (see Matthew Steggle, *Laughing and Weeping in Early Modern Theatres* (Aldershot, 2007), p. 23).

14 dumps 'fit of melancholy or depression' (*OED*, *n.* 2).

18 bread … cheese The association of bread and cheese with gossip is obscure. A one-sheet printed ballad from the end of the seventeenth century notes that 'Men of Wales | Leave Toasted *Cheese to feed upon Tales*', and there might have been earlier currency to the idea (*An Elegy on the Death of the Author of the Characters…* (London, 1699)).

19–20 In a while Leir will be constantly giving false reports of each daughter's behaviour.

23 take i.e., give.

25 partial cause argument favouring one side over another (*OED*, Cause *adj.* II).

27 not … words mistrusting women's words was a common misogynistic idea expressed variously in proverbs in the period, such as 'a woman's heart and her tongue are not relatives' (Tilley W672), 'a woman's weapon is her tongue (W675), and 'women are great talkers' (W701).

28 breeds … bones i.e., is pregnant.

30 already Gonorill implies that she has not been married long enough to be pregnant.

31 honest woman i.e., chaste woman (*OED*, honest *adj.* A.3b). Gonorill is being ironic.

35 For i.e., Towards.

45 reversed i.e., instead of a parent caring for a child, he must expect to be cared for by a child.

46 wight man.

47 perfect complete (wish for death).

51 wasting tears 'Both weeping, and laughter, can be dangerous, indeed fatal, in excess' in Renaissance thinking (Steggle, *Laughing and Weeping*, p. 15).

57 consort with associate with.

60 want 'lacking the necessities of life' (*OED*, *n.*2 B.2a).

63 in favour i.e., favoured by the powerful.

65 excrement dung.

66 Which Referring to his conscience.

71 my own i.e., what was mine.

73 due revenues revenues due as payment (to your estate).

81 confute defeat in argument.

83 tribute obligation. Leir's theories of filial loyalty are not relevant to the early modern context, where children did not owe their lives to parents, but relate back to longstanding tropes, such as the biblical sacrifice of Isaac by Abraham, or the ancient Roman right of the father to kill his child.

84 kind generous. Leir uses the word heavily in this scene, also implying the related sense of 'natural', in opposition to 'unkind', or 'unnatural' (as at 96, 98).

85 bountiful generous.

91 passions emotive pleas; **do … move** affect me.

92 all … one i.e., everyone for one (bad) example.

103 repair go (*OED*, *v.*1 2.a).

108 try … woe he will test how much unhappiness he can endure, with the foreboding implication that Ragan will make him no more welcome than Gonorill.

[Scene 11]

2 **stars** fortune. Early modern astrologers created nativity charts, supposedly with a prognosticating force, from the alignment of stars at the time and place of a person's birth.

4 **event** outcomes.

6 **states** people of rank (*OED*, *n.* II.†19); 'body politic' or people more generally (20); or 'the princes, dukes, nobles, etc., together with the delegates of the several classes, chief cities, etc., of a country, assembled in a parliament' (21). The specific meaning depends upon Cambria's (undisclosed) imaginary political system.

7 **look** ensure.

9 **state** estate, condition.

10 **degrees** titles, rank.

11 **cooling card** 'something which cools or lessens a person's passion or enthusiasm' (*OED*), i.e., the presence of Leir.

12 **honey ... gall** i.e., her apparent happiness tastes bitter, like gall, or oak-tree gall, used to make a medicine in this period.

13 **quartermaster** i.e., the person in charge, from the nautical role of 'petty or warrant officer aboard a warship responsible to the captain for stowing provisions and ensuring the correct trim of the ship, for care of navigational instruments and for steering, and (subsequently) for general discipline' (*OED*, *n.* I.1a).

14 **will** inclination, wishes.

16 **cost** expenditure.

[Scene 12]

1 **dire ... chance** dreadful, unfortunate event.

2 **sequestered** separated.

3 **report** information.

4 **offered** given (to).

5 **patience** three syllables.

6 **Else** Otherwise (*OED*, *adv.* B). The line means 'No one could convince me otherwise (that)'.

10 **longest home** i.e., death.

11 **But** Except; **qualities** habits, dispositions.

12 **stolen upon** snuck, crept to.

13 **At unawares** i.e., Without her foreknowledge.

16 **steal** sneak away.

18 **frolic** 'joyous, merry, mirthful' (*OED*, *adj.* 1a).

21 **post** messenger with a letter.

24 **temper** influence.

25 **sound** 'ample' (*OED*, *adj.* I.7a).

26 report account (of the situation); **ratify** support.
29 presageth predicts.
30 haply by chance; **ways** paths.
31 common passenger commoner person travelling (and therefore not given the funeral rites of a former king, but buried in an unmarked grave).
33 to-do hubbub, turmoil.
36 exclaim 'accuse loudly' (*OED*, *v.* 2a).
38 broken i.e., wrecked, breached.
42 unperceived 'undetected' (*OED*, *adj.*).
43 The idea is that one can remove a nail (e.g., from a piece of wood) by driving another into it (Tilley N17).
51 neck-verse 'A Latin verse printed in black letter (usually the beginning of Psalm 51 Miserere mei Deus, "Have mercy upon me, O God") formerly set before a person claiming benefit of clergy … by reading which he might prove his clerical status and hence save his neck' (*OED*, *n.*). One did not actually need to be in the clergy to receive this benefit (for instance, the dramatist Ben Jonson did in 1598). The ability to speak Latin was sufficient to claim it.
55 trussed up strung up, i.e., hanged.
57 were better had been better off to.
58 Or that Or (he, anyone) who; **we … thee** we value you highly.
60 surfeit of am stuffed with.
65–7 buckler … tripes To be a 'sword and buckler' man was to offer life in service, but the Messenger comically extends this list to include his very bowels.
67 members limbs (with bawdy innuendo).
69 scavenger's horse i.e., the lowest (and by implication most abused) role for a horse, to pull the cart used by street cleaners (i.e., those who collect the excrement that has been thrown out of houses).
72 good … law i.e., legally valid.
76–7 oyster-wife … Billingsgate oyster-wives (i.e., female oyster-sellers) of Billingsgate were considered notoriously loud and vulgar. Billingsgate was 'The principal of the old water-gates of London' – i.e., the largest wharf – known especially for boats bringing in fish and therefore its fish market, but also markets for other goods (Edward H. Sugden, *A Topographical Dictionary to the Works of Shakespeare and His Fellow Dramatists* (Manchester, 1925), p. 60).
80 choler bile, one of the four humours or fluids in the body, 'believed to determine, by their relative proportions and conditions, the state of health and the temperament of a person …' (*OED*, humour *n.* I.1a). An overabundance of choler was thought to induce a quick, angry temper.

81 Palermo Razors made in Palermo were prized for their quality in this period. The earlier play *Damon and Pythias* (c. 1564) has a character say: 'It is a razor and that a very good one, | It came lately from Palermo …' (*The Collected Works of Richard Edwards*, ed. Ros King (Manchester, 2001), 13.249–50).
84 my deserts things I deserve.
87 other other (letters from the king).
88 detracted disparaged, belittled (*OED*, detract *v.* I.3a).
89 given out made public.
90 at variance at odds, against one another.
91 mutinies … commons the common people uprise (against their king and queen).
95 out … him i.e., to stop loving her father.
98 preferment 'promotion or advancement' (*OED*, *n.* II).
100 sufficeth is enough; **Conceit** Imagine; **tongue-whip** i.e., tongue-lash, berate.
101 credit reputation; **poulter** seller of poultry, which in this period included rabbits.
102 cony rabbit.
105 importeth conveys (*OED*, import *v.* I.†4).
105–6 make … away kill him.
106 heart courage.
109 presently immediately; **long … done** 'have a yearning desire or strong wish for' the message to be delivered (*OED*, long *v.* II.6a).
110 fly go in haste.

[Scene 13]
1 over-negligent The implication is that Cordella traverses the stage as if heading to church.
7 content contentment, happiness.
9 mirror exemplar.
11 commonweal general well-being of a nation (*OED*, commonweal *n.* 2).
12 appointment 'decree' (*OED*, *n.* 6); **ordained** arranged.
17 nutriment food.
18 pine waste away.
20 sackcloth traditional dress of the penitent, made of extremely poor-quality cloth, used for sacks, that was uncomfortable to wear.
22 dust ashes. In the Bible to wear sackcloth and ashes is a sign of penance (Matthew 11:21; Luke 10:13).
23 he Leir.
29 both can refer to two or more things in this period.
30 perfect complete.

[Scene 14]

0 SD *faintly* i.e., as if ready to faint.

1 stay support.

6 person body.

7 bring … forth take you away.

9 uncouth 'unknown … uncertain' (*OED*, *adj.* A.†1). 'The open space of ancient Britain is wild, dangerous, and "uncouth" (4.2.9) only a few miles from civilized houses. The court and household hospitality together represent a major contrast with the "natural" world, which constitutes a "space" between the places of proper occupation and human activity' (Lloyd Edward Kermode, '"King Leir" within the Thicket: Gender, Place, and Power', *Renaissance and Reformation/Renaissance et Réforme* 35 (2012): 65–84, 74). The thicket, as Kermode points out, prefigures the heath in Shakespeare's *King Lear* as an embodiment of wild Britain; **tireful** tiresome, wearisome.

10 fainting increasingly feeble, weary; **a whit** one bit.

12 guerdon reward.

13 aggravate make worse.

14 cuts 'which' or 'that' often take a verb form with 's' in this period (Jonathan Hope, *Shakespeare's Grammar* (London, 2003), p. 162).

15 will desire.

18 that … title i.e., 'lord'.

20 of comfort comforted.

22 happy fortuitous.

23 gratify 'give welcome to' (*OED*, *v.* †3).

24 Were … best i.e., Would it be better for me to.

25 heavy grave.

27 i.e., It's Gonorill and Cornwall's shame (not ours in telling of it).

31 of force because I am forced to (keep up appearances).

35 indurable 'unbearable' (*OED*, *adj.*[2] – predating first instance).

36 disaster chance disastrous event.

37 spare 'having little flesh' (*OED*, *adj.* II.4a).

38 For … come! This line is probably directed to the attending nobles, or perhaps the king, and asks that they should rush to Leir's aid.

44 finger … eye i.e., to produce false tears.

46 abused harmed, deceived.

47 crafty wretch scheming (pretend) exile (*OED*, wretch *n.* A.†1).

48 complain himself complain (about) his treatment.

52 a trifle i.e., something insignificant.

53 spleen The spleen was considered to be the organ producing both melancholy and mirth in this period, so Ragan is saying either that this is a fit of (unprovoked) sadness or that this is all just a joke to Leir (see *OED*, *n.* 1†b and †c); **is … away** has snuck away from there.

54 harbour shelter.

55 moaned … on pitied (*OED*, moan *v.* 3) and 'treated with consideration' (*OED*, make I.29a).

56 shall curse (he) shall curse.

58 make … weather 'make a show of friendliness' (*OED*, weather *n.* 2†b).

59 i.e., To make space for a good time to enact my plan.

[Scene 15]

1 happily by good fortune.

3 safe-seated i.e., safely placed; **in rest** in a state of tranquility (*OED*, rest *n.* I.3a).

4 rouse wake.

5 virtue 'power' (*OED*, *n.* II.8), referring to the 'bags of gold' he has received from Gonorill.

6 stout courageous.

9 imports is the meaning of.

11 residue remainder (of the message); **declare** 'make clear' (*OED*, *v.* †1).

14 colour i.e., of her face.

15 Now … now Now … then.

16 knits … brow i.e., frowns.

17 dumb show 'a part of a play represented by action without speech' (*OED*, *n.* 1). The most famous of these is the scene in *Hamlet* in which the old king's murder is re-enacted.

18 extremes i.e., extreme emotions.

19 crowns five-shilling gold coins.

20–44 These lines might be delivered as an aside, as Stern has it, although that puts the Messenger in an awkward stage situation in having to occupy himself without listening for so long. Even if Ragan does not mind being overheard by the Messenger, she is largely speaking to herself.

20 used treated.

22 divorce separation.

23 report rumour.

24 list wish.

25 alter … case change the situation; proverbial (Tilley C111).

26 The 'head' of the household in this period would legally, religiously, and culturally be the husband, so Ragan advocates a reversal of marital hierarchy.

28 hop … head 'to hop headless' was a traditional expression for being beheaded (*OED*, hop *v.* †P1).

34 fact crime (*OED*, *n.* A.I.2).

39 conference conversation.
40 intimate 'communicate' (*OED*, *v.* 1a).
41 cavillations 'frivolous, quibbling, or unfair objections, arguments, or charges' (*OED*, cavillation *n.* 1†a).
47 trust to 'confidence or faith in' (*OED*, trust *n.* 1a).
51 act enact.
52 stab i.e., to a person.
53 compact … adamant made of 'a hard, strong rock or mineral' (*OED*, adamant *n.* A.1a).
54 melting pity A heart softened to pity was proverbially said to 'melt' (*OED*, melt *v.*[1] 3c).
55 weigh weigh up, value.
56 cracking … flea i.e., killing a flea – an insubstantial act of violence.
64 this i.e., the money.
66 gainfulest most profitable.
68 a stab i.e., sex.

[Scene 16]
1–2 clouds … brow To have a 'cloudy brow' was a common way to describe looking sad (see Shakespeare, *2 Henry VI*, 3.1.155). Cf. *SP* 1.6.85: 'Within forced furrows of her clouding brow'; *AF* 2.47: 'With mighty furrows in his stormy brows.'
4 move change to (*OED*, *v.* I.5a).
7 If you don't care about yourself.
10 move 'trouble, disquiet, perturb' (*OED*, *v.* II.25b).
12 his i.e., Leir's.
13 stock tree trunk; **dried … disdain** dried up with hatred.
14 sere 'dry, withered' (*OED*, *adj.*1 1a).
15 graft in grafted to – the practice of binding a branch to a different tree.
22 oblivion 'the state or condition of being forgotten' (*OED*, *n.* 2a).
27 present now.
28 pack leave (*OED*, *v.* II).
31 distemperate cause unease, distemper to.
35 nature's power filial gratitude.
37 stay support (i.e., fly) (*OED*, *v.*2 1a).
38 element i.e., element (of air), one of the four elements (earth, air, water, fire).
42 blackamoor black African. Moors are followers of Islam. It was a common misconception that all Africans were moors in this period. For discussions of these confusions see Nabil Matar, *Turks, Moors, and Englishmen in the Age of Discovery* (New York, 1999), and Margo Hendricks, 'Race:

A Renaissance Category?', in Michael Hattaway (ed.), *A Companion to English Renaissance Literature and Culture* (Oxford, 2001), pp. 690–8.

43 tawny brown. The impossibility of turning a 'blackamoor' white is the subject of one of Aesop's *Fables*.

46 phoenix in mythology only one phoenix at a time can be alive.

47 unkind unloving, unnatural.

56 crown i.e., rule, dominion.

61 Because my spoken thanks will never be enough.

63 blithe happy.

[Scene 17]

1 world 'great thing', 'marvel' (*OED*, *n.* †P14); **flush** 'plentifully supplied (*esp.* with money)' (*OED*, *adj.*[1] 3a).

4 kiss … knees signs of respect in this period.

7 derive 'draw, bring' (*OED*, *v.* I.†5).

8 mind'st remember.

10 an … like if it please.

14 dispatched i.e., already done.

15 yesternight last night.

16 right … consequence very unusual importance. In keeping with stage traditions of commissioning murderers, Ragan circumvents a direct request here.

18 this this (hesitation).

21 i.e., Have a fight with him.

22 bid ask.

34 ten i.e., ten victims.

36 i.e., How should I kill them?

38 wile trick.

43 fail fail (to show up).

46 mistrust … fact suspect you for the evil deed.

52–4 pipe … sleep In classical mythology Jupiter falls in love with Io, transforming her into a heifer while he became a bull. His wife, Hera, grew jealous and sought to guard Io with Argus, who with 100 eyes would not take all of them off her. Jupiter sent Mercury to retake Io, and he lulled Argus to sleep by playing his pipe.

56 of his i.e., of Leir's pleas.

58 send … him i.e., send you to your death, too.

[Scene 18]

1 stay remain (*OED*, *v.*1 I.4a).

6 detain 'to keep waiting' (*OED*, *v.* 4).

9 his … he i.e., Leir's pleasure to detain the messenger.

10 attend upon 'accompany as servant' (*OED*, attend *v.* II).
16 haply as it happens; possibly, 'fortunately' (*OED*, *adv.*).
21 By me i.e., Through my delivery of their message.
22 commend … kindly i.e., extend their kind regards.
23 entirely 'without exception or reservation' (*OED*, *adv.* B.2a).
30 cause matter.
34 notice information.
36 in charge i.e., according to my instructions.
37 'twill … haste it will take a little while (to determine exactly what the message says).
41–66 Gonorill consistently says the opposite of what politeness would expect, revealing her true feelings.
46 merry happy.
47 exceeds i.e., is intense.
53 mediator person bringing about reconciliation.
54 expiate 'extinguish (a person's rage) by suffering it to the full' (*OED*, *v.* †7 – earliest citation 1594).
56 exasperate aggravate.
68 cross work against.
69 frolic 'make merry', i.e., take full advantage of our hospitality (*OED*, *v.* 1 – earliest citation 1593).

[Scene 19]
0 SD *with books* Michie has the characters carrying the books in 'small bags'. Alternatively, they might have them in their pockets or elsewhere on their persons.
1 before … hours i.e., earlier than usual.
2 news … rathe new for you to be out of your chamber so quickly (*OED*, rathe *adv.* †1a).
3 heavy drowsy.
5 impute reckon (*OED*, *v.* †4).
6 use to are accustomed to.
10 But say i.e., What if; **goodfellows** thieves (*OED*, goodfellow *n.* A.†2).
11 set upon attack.
12 were … them we would be in a good situation to respond to them (ironic).
13 stand … hands rely upon our ability to fight.
15 how what.
17 ill hap misfortune.
18 for company i.e., for companionship.
19 heavy sleepy.

20 mad jest i.e., madcap, bizarre event (*OED*, jest *n.* †1); **my profession** i.e., that of murderer.
21 lay … down i.e., knock me unconscious; tie me up.
23 the greybeards Leir and Perillus.
24 at liberty free; **to-do** fuss.
25 SD *start* i.e., be startled.
26 stay wait; **methinks** I think; **my youths** i.e., the young people I seek (ironic).
27 pure 'guiltless' (*OED*, *adj.* III.4a).
28 intent end (*OED*, *n.* 6).
29 provided for prepared for (by conducting their final prayers).
30 bravely 1) fearlessly; 2) excellently (*OED*, *adv.* 1 and 3 – predates earliest usage in both instances).
34 willed instructed, ordered.
36 Mass By the mass (an oath); **stir** move, awaken.
37 unawares unnoticed.
38 marvel am surprised (*OED*, *v.*1 2a).
39 place (appointed meeting) place.
40 miscarry 'come to harm' (*OED*, *v.* †1a).
43 fantasies delusions (*OED*, fantasy *n.* 3a).
44 slight insubstantial.
47 effect 'purport' (*OED*, *n.* 3b).
48 pretends signifies (*OED*, *v.* †7).
49 expound interpret.
51 grim aspects 'fierce' looks, expressions (*OED*, grim *adj.* A.1a).
52 falchion broad, curved sword.
54 poniard sharp, narrow knife.
56 to … thinking in their belief.
58 balsam medicinal ointment.
63 yet still.
65–7 Stand … deliver The traditional shout of a thief, equivalent to 'don't move and hand over everything!'.
65 SD *reel* i.e., spin around as if dazed.
70 'scaped escaped.
71 faithful watchmen attentive lookouts (ironic).
72 halberds long spears with axe heads. The messenger is being metaphorical, referring to the protection offered by their religious books.
73 want lack.
74 delivered 1) saved (in the religious sense); 2) rescued (from a criminal).
77 proper 'admirable, excellent, fine' (*OED*, *adj.* III.7a).
78 claws Perillus is attempting to be friendly by taking the messenger by the arm.

79 scraping fawning, behaving obsequiously.
88 use ... queen make use of my access to the queen (in order to gain favour).
89 pleasure thee i.e., be of service to you.
89 SD *proffer* attempt (*OED*, *v.* †4a).
90 Do ... hear i.e., Pay attention.
96 comely handsome (*OED*, *adj.* A.1b).
97 a vantage an advantage.
100 try this gear check out your promises.
107 dispatched killed.
108 safeguard protection (i.e., in keeping his conscience clear by acting on his oath to the queen).
114 good ... friend i.e., my good friend.
117 dallieth plays.
119 Damon Damon and Pythias were classical models of friendship. Pythias was sentenced to death by Dionysius, ruler of Syracuse. Pythias asked to return to his home to put his estate in order, but Dionysius insisted that Damon stay in his stead to be executed if Pythias did not return at an appointed time. Pythias did return to liberate his friend, and Dionysius was so impressed by their friendship that he set them both free. The story was dramatized by Richard Edwards in the c. 1564 *Damon and Pythias*.
121 the ... come heaven.
125 period end.
132 Sirrah 'A term of address used to ... [social inferiors] expressing contempt, reprimand' (*OED*, *n.* 1a).
133 spoil ... fashion disfigure the handsomeness.
142 mitigate ... ire reduce her anger.
145 speed haste.
151 churl 'base fellow' (*OED*, *n.* 5).
155 except excepted.
156 doting frenzy foolish passion; **o'er-jealous** overly vehement, passionate.
158 impiety 'absence of natural piety, as of child to parent' (*OED*, *n.* 2).
159 mistake ... mark 'miss one's target', make this mistake (*OED*, mistake *v.* 3).
168 issue children.
169 t'abridge ... fate to shorten your life.
170 breath i.e., words.
172 but only.
178 certain unambiguous.
190 SD Thunder and lightning are traditional stage effects at ominous moments, often suggesting the direct intervention of heaven or fate.

191 word … again i.e., speech was unspoken.
194 turned changed.
197 prosecute 'continue with (a course of action)' (*OED*, *v.* 1a).
199 crack break, ruin; **credit** reputation, high standing.
200 passed given.
202 SD *bless* i.e., make the sign of the cross over. Following the *Book of Common Prayer* of 1559, the sign of the cross in the Anglican church was used only for baptism, and its use became controversial across the sixteenth and seventeenth centuries, so this instance points to a Catholic context. See Colin Buchanan, *Historical Dictionary of Anglicanism* (London, 2015), 'Sign of the Cross', pp. 533–4.
206 just righteous.
207 viperous generation See Matthew 3:7, 'O generation of vipers', John the Baptist's description of the Pharisees and Sadducees who attended his baptism. Christ repeats it at Matthew 12:34; **generation** = descendants (*OED*, *n.* I.†1a).
219 latest i.e., last, final.
228 him i.e., Perillus.
235 passport i.e., letter (granting him 'travel' to death). A favourite Kyd expression: *Sp. T.*, 1.1.35, 54, 77; *SP* 2.1.307.
236 sealèd stamped with authority (i.e., Ragan's royal seal or signature); **ride post** 'travel as a post or courier', i.e., go quickly (after you to heaven) (*OED*, post *n.*3 †P1 'to ride post').
238 toucheth concerns.
243 skilleth … for doesn't matter to; **a whit** at all.
244 Perillus seems to suggest that any great friendship such as theirs would not care about the fate of dying together.
245 Marry An interjection of surprise or contempt (derived from the Holy Virgin). The Messenger objects to Perillus's claim that no one would care about death, i.e., because he does.
247 rife common. The Messenger here remembers Perillus calling him a 'proper man' at line 77.
249 high anointed divinely appointed. Kings were thought to be selected by God in this period.
250 advisèd warned.
261 extremity danger.
271 like the same.
282 still continually.
294 mind i.e., way of thinking.
295 stayest wait, hesitate.
296 willful … you stubborn as you (are).

298 spark … grace trace of God-inspired virtue (*OED*, spark *n.* 2a; grace *n.* I.1b).
300 parlousest most talkative; cleverest (*OED*, parlous *adj.* A.1).
306 go hard be awkward (*OED*, hard *adj.* II.12a).
307 overpassed i.e., behind us.
308 hie us hurry ourselves.
309 past … best Leir contrasts his current state with Perillus's claim that they are past 'the worst' (307).
316 succour assist.
323 spake spoke.
331 tried tested.

[Scene 20]
7 stately 'haughty, arrogant' (*OED*, *adj.* A.3†a).
9 louring 'scowling' (*OED*, *adj.* 1).
13 like likely; **hop … hope** i.e., dance about without her expectations being met.
14 will desire.

[Scene 21]
1 By this By this (time), by now; **mind** intention.
3 presageth predicts.
5 mind inclination.
8 last means final solution.
12 forsworn 'perjured', found to be lying (*OED*, *adj.* 1).
14 maid virgin.
15 goes for i.e., seems as if she is.
16 all adventures 'whatever the consequences may be' (*OED*, adventure *n.* P.1b).
17 that's i.e., your condition (that you need to win her over) is.
18 put in i.e., through sex.
21–3 Rejecting Mumford's insistence that good sex would make his mistress chase him, Cordella says that he needs to be more courteous to keep her interested.
26 slops wide, baggy breeches; **for … nonce** for this purpose (*OED*, *n.*1 I.1).
28 hose stockings, worn by men in this period under their breeches (which will be exposed by implication when he uses his slops to take in their mockery).
29 newest fashion ironic, the implication being that Mumford is very out-of-fashion in his dress.
30 bobs tricks, mocks (*OED*, †bob, *n.*2 1); **still** continuously.

31 bombast stuffing, of the type used to line garments, here connecting to the clothing discussion at hand and the wider sense of 'nonsense'; **crack** i.e., come undone.
32 outface 'disconcert, silence, or defeat ... by face-to-face confrontation' (*OED*, *v.* 1a).
33 my ... quarrel dispute (about) my mistress.
34 possession legal term, compare 'possession is nine points of the law', and Mumford's use of legalisms at 39–41.
35 a cart The traditional punishment for prostitution and fornication was 'carting', to be exposed to humiliation while being driven in a cart through public.
37 give ... over i.e., leave you alone.
41 action of i.e., illegal act of.
44 progress the formal procession of a royal court.
46 motion proposal; journey.
47 mediator ... queen i.e., Gallia will make the same request, on both his and Mumford's behalf, to the queen.
48 match 'agreement or arrangement' (*OED*, *n.* II.†9).
50 needs not is not necessary.
51 So So (long as).
52 as as (much as).
62 man servant.
64 more ... time about time; **device** 'arrangement, plan, scheme' (*OED*, *n.* 6).
65 about it i.e., get going.

[Scene 22]
5 light horse i.e., men on fast horseback.
6 regiment kingdom (*OED*, *n.* †4).
9 strict 'stringent and rigorous' (*OED*, *adj.* II.11a).
14 substance 'essential part, essence' (of grief) (*OED*, *n.* I.6b).
14–29 Ragan's many uses of rhyme, two quatrains and three couplets, has the effect to make her seem insincere.
15 redeem help. Ragan implies that she is so desolate that she is beyond weeping.
18 i.e., No one is clever enough to determine the reason why (Leir has disappeared).
20 invocation 'action or an act of conjuring or summoning a devil or spirit by incantation' (*OED*, *n.* 2).
22 Stirred Instigated; **Cordella** Sherman sees Q as reading '*Cordelia*' here, but the 'i' is a poorly printed 'l'; **moves** causes; **innovation** new situation (often used in this period for unwelcome change).

23 timeless prematurely.
25 certain proven, doubtless; **uncertain** ambiguous (because they do not know what has happened to Leir).
32 the right i.e., the right (of it), what has actually happened.
38 sifted worked through carefully.
45 repair come.
52 packing plotting together, scheming (*OED*, *v.*2 †I.1a).
57 colour misrepresent (*OED*, *v.* II.6a).
64 slight insubstantial.
66 law … arms It was considered a grave offence to harm a messenger.
76 tender him love Leir.
80 light clarity.
82 doubtful 'apprehensive' (*OED*, *adj.*†5).
85 The ambassador implies that Ragan dissimulates, causing her to strike him.
86 saucy mate disrespectful fellow.
90 mean means.
93 imperial state royal status.
94 take … part act as my defender, advocate.
96 obloquy shame.
98 delude trick.
99 put up tolerate.
106 admire … penance wonder at her punishment.

[Scene 23]
0 SD *sea-gowns* i.e., the typical dress of sailors, here an outer garment protecting them from the elements. Leir and Perillus have just arrived in France by boat.
2 state i.e., finances.
4 passage i.e., transport on the ship.
5 good fellows thieves.
11 good gown Both Leir and Perillus are likely to be wearing expensive clothing, given their social standing, and the 'gown' is their top-most, loose-fitting layer.
13 marvel would be full of wonder (to see).
14 room place.
15 mean poor.
17 stand hesitate.
17–18 motley gaberdine multicoloured coarse smock.
18 fourteen … shillings a substantial sum of money (and likely to be an exaggeration).
19 forgive forgive (the debt for).

23–4 sheep's russet 'coarse woollen cloth of a reddish-brown or subdued colour, formerly used for clothing esp. by country people and the poor', here as worn by shepherds (*OED*, russet A.1a; see also sheep *n.* C3 †sheep's russet).

24 bide … stress i.e., endure more rough treatment.

26 change exchange.

30 my friend i.e., Leir.

31 doublet fitted man's jacket (*OED*, *n.* 1a), here worn under his gown.

33 powdered 'salted, pickled, or spiced for future use; preserved; cured' (*OED*, *adj.* 1a), of the kind used for long sea voyages.

34 can container, cup, or tankard.

36 bargain's … bargain proverbial reason for not reneging on an agreement (Tilley B76).

38 escape unknown i.e., escape notice.

44 use … another i.e., treat you as well as anyone ('unreasonable' is a malapropism).

45 hope plan.

48 strange foreign.

56 faint … ever lose courage before.

57–81 Leir's speech uses a rhetorical figure involving a division of a speech into separate topics; Perillus responds to it by 'collecting' or repeating them in sequence.

59 henbane poisonous plant; **mithridate** 'universal antidote to poison' (*OED*, *n.* 1a).

60 wormwood's astringent medicinal plant's.

67 unrelished 'unpalatable' (*OED*, *adj.* †1); **sloes** bitter fruit of the blackthorn.

69 paps breasts.

73 aslope 'athwart', awry (*OED*, *adj.*).

84 crosses disappointments.

85 one … another's i.e., lament one another's.

89 despair In Christian thought despair is a sin, because it denies the possibility of divine grace and forgiveness, and dooms the sinner to exclusion from heaven.

94 apaid 'rewarded' (*OED*, *adj.* †2).

[Scene 24]

0 SD *basket* carrying their food.

6 happed … light happened to come across.

8 industry … pains diligence and effort. Cordella goes on to describe some sort of country festival, where the people compete in games and sports. Such festivities would often be staged as a rough dance.

10 bestir 'move actively' (*OED*, *v.* 2a).
11 quirks idiosyncrasies. Cordella appears to have seen festive dancing or other activity.
12 antic fits mirthful sport, behaviour.
13 were … wits had lost their minds.
14 i.e., Bring your basket over here, Mumford (who had been dubbed 'Roger' as part of his disguise at 21.61).
16 fat i.e., rich, and by implication contented.
19 harken listen to.
21 unfruitful i.e., barren, because there is nothing for them to forage.
24 gentle kind; **affords** offers.
28 betide upon happen to.
33 SD *strips up* i.e., rolls back his sleeve.
39 slake satisfy.
48 lamentable extremely sad.
61 God The triple parallelism below this line would suggest that Q's 'good' is a misprint.
65 Turned out i.e., Stripped, deprived.
72 meat generic term for 'food' in this period.
75 Or Either.
77 men … women The imagined space, or literal staging, of the scene might include 'country folk' (line 7), but they are not included in the entry direction or as clear participants beyond this plural use of 'women'.
80 mollify reduce the hardness of.
90 stays waits.
90–1 no … stomach Proverbial for hunger making food taste better (Tilley S870).
96 Aeson In Greek mythology Aeson was killed by his daughter-in-law, Medea, who used magic to bring him back to life as a youth by boiling him in a pot.
99 Elias Another name for Elijah, who in the Bible escapes from Jezebel and is able to walk for forty days after being given food from an angel (Kings 19:8).
102 manifest disclose, make known (*OED*, *v.* 1b).
105 their office i.e., his duty, function.
107 What cheer How are you doing?
108 savoury that which savours, or tastes good; 'pleasing' (*OED*, *adj.* A.1a).
109–10 manna … Israelites In the Bible, God provided food to the Israelites during their forty years in the desert: 'the Lord said to Moses, "I will rain down bread from heaven for you"' (Exodus 16:4); 'The people of Israel called the bread manna' (Exodus 16:31).
113 congratulate 'express joy, pleasure, or satisfaction at' (*OED*, *v.* †2a).

121 strange i.e., as strangers.
124 father The word has a general sense of 'old man', but of course doubles here as 'biological father'.
127 owe own, possess, have. Leir uses the language of financial obligation here.
129 interest 'right or title to, a claim upon, or a share in' (*OED*, interest *n.* I.1a); influence over (I.6).
134 as … list as he likes.
137 see … end Latin saying, '*respice finem*', see how things turn out.
148 were sped were well provided.
152 try test.
158 outrageous 'excessively injurious or cruel' (*OED*, *adj.* A.1).
163 care sorrow.
164 mark … sequel i.e., pay attention to what follows.
166 entreated dealt with (*OED*, entreat *v.* †I).
167 content contentment, happiness.
173 contumelious 'reproachful and tending to convey disgrace and humiliation' (*OED*, *adj.* 1a).
175 harbour live.
178 sore severe (*OED*, *adj.* 4a).
182 'Pointing Appointing.
183 shag-haired with shaggy hair, in Elizabethan drama the sign of a villain; **wretch** poor fellow (*OED*, *n.* 2a).
210 resigned i.e., offered up.
211 beseems fits.
226 respective 'respectful' (*OED*, *adj.* 3a).
232–5 blessing … prosper The blessing God gave to Judah, a younger son of Jacob, included having authority, in his tribe of descendants, over all his brothers: 'Judah, your brothers will praise you; your hand will be on the neck of your enemies; your father's sons will bow down to you' (Genesis 49:8). God calls himself the 'God of Abraham' in Exodus (3:6) and promises Solomon to 'multiply thy days' (1 Kings 3:14). The phrase 'children's children' appears many times in the Bible (e.g., Proverbs 17:6; Psalm 128:6).
238 quiet peace.
251 viperous sect i.e., Gonorill and Ragan.

[Scene 25]
3 doubt fear.
7 make … sure i.e., kill him to keep him quiet.
12 manifest reveal.

13 white-livered i.e., lily-livered, cowardly. The liver was held to be 'the seat of cowardice' (*OED*, liver *n.* 4b).

17 mere pure (*OED*, *adj.*2 I.1†a).

21 charity affection, Christian love of one's fellow man (*OED*, *n.*).

23 pox … them The 'pox' was syphilis, and wishing it upon enemies was a common curse.

29 i.e., I'll look after myself as best I can.

30 repines expresses discontent (*OED*, repine *v.* 1†c).

31 keep … hands avoid my punishment.

[Scene 26]

0 SD *and … army* This force might be represented economically by two to three actors costumed as soldiers.

10 forward advanced (in the line of battle).

11 wight man.

12 meanest lowliest.

13 second back up, fight beside.

15 next unto just behind.

17 wonted 'customary' (*OED*, *adj.* II.3).

19 approvèd 'tried, tested' (*OED*, *adj.* 1a); **magnanimity** courage.

20 needless … horse proverbial phrase for something that is superfluous (Tilley H688).

22 sweet … eyes Mumford appears to be alluding to his mistress again.

23 hap fortune.

29 Genovestan Gauls Seemingly a way of expressing the Celtic origins of the Gauls, one that is passed down through Warner's *Albion's England* and its treatment of the Lear story: 'the *Cenousean Gawles*' (III.xvi) was misprinted in later editions as 'Genouesean Gawles'. A version of this phrase seems to have been misread by the author or the play's printer as 'Genouestan Gawles'. See Robert Adger Law, 'Tripartite Gaul in the Story of King Leir', *Studies in English* 4 (1924): 39–48.

31 shanks legs.

32 right Gauls Punning on 'gall', as a bitter experience for the enemy (see note 11.12 and the lines below).

35 shot archers or gunners.

36 halberds soldiers carrying long spears with sharp points and axe heads, also known as 'bills'.

39 (Rather than that) what more persuasion is needed to those.

[Scene 27]

2 beacon Watch beacons were lit to warn of invasion.

3 have regard pay attention.

5 office duty; **fire** set alight.

6 raise alert, wake up.
7 charge duty, instruction.
8 ne'er … it have never seen it.
10 'vice advice.
11 Goodman Jennings i.e., a public house or inn run by someone of that name. 'Goodman' is a title for a 'host of an inn' (*OED*, *n.* 2†b).
12 rasher … bacon Slices of hot bacon or other meats were served with alcohol, much as salty snacks are today (*OED*, rasher *n.* †2).
13–14 i.e., Their noses or faces will be so red from alcohol that no other light will be needed.
15 excuse malapropism for 'accuse'.
17 as-s The watchmen appear to be already drunk, as this word is slurred.
25 half-a-score ten.
29 conster another spelling for 'construe' (*OED*, *v.*); **Presently** Immediately.

[Scene 28]
1 ensigns troops (*OED*, ensign *n.* †6).
3 look … you i.e., be ready.
5 mistrustful suspicious.
7 naked men 1) men without armaments; 2) men in their nightclothes.
8 Devoid … sense i.e., Fuzzy-headed because half asleep; **new-waked** 'newly awakened' (*OED*, *adj.*); first usage in *OED*.
9 pretend portend, intend.
11 assail attack. The call to attack probably leads to a quick and loud exit.

[Scene 29]
0 SD *Alarum* i.e., Noise designed to awaken the town, such as shouts or the ringing of church bells.
3 suffered allowed.
11 This … have i.e., This is the effect of having.
17 tend … office keep your responsibilities.
19 Reel The First Watchman mishears Mumford's 'yield'; **You may** i.e., May you. The Watchman is upset to have his ale knocked over.
21 i.e., It doesn't take me long to say that you are not short of a drink.
22 tall brave (ironic).
23 weaponed i.e., loaded (with ale).

[Scene 30]
Michie argues that scene divisions are not needed here or in the remainder of the play, because 'The action beginning with scene 29 is a battle; and even though one set of characters replaces another several times, the locale does not change and the action is continuous' (53).

0 SD ***excursions*** i.e., a sally across the stage, here probably in one door and out another in haste. The word is associated with soldiers and usually, as here, coupled with the sound of an alarm (Charles Edelman, *Shakespeare's Military Language* (London, 2004), 'excursion'). There is a general hubbub of entry and exit by soldiers (on either or both sides), Mumford, and townsfolk (who we learn at line 30 are the people '*half-naked*').

2 subscribe unto express agreement to.

3 fealty 'obligation of fidelity on the part of a feudal tenant or vassal to his lord' (*OED*, *n.* 1).

4 aspiring (overly) ambitious.

9 perforce of necessity.

10 extremities extremes (by bringing an army to the town).

11 looked for waited for.

17 Which i.e., The country; **have … taxed** i.e., had to pay onerous taxes.

20 apace quickly.

34 foil defeat.

39 adverse opposing, adversary.

40 St George Patron saint of England.

43 perforce by force.

45 Be sure (You will) be sure.

49 fell 'deceitful, false' (*OED*, *adj.* 1 A.1†b).

53 interest concern.

56 down … throat It was common in this period to threaten to shove a lie back down an opponent's throat. For instance, in *Titus Andronicus* Demetrius warns he will 'Thrust those reproachful speeches down his throat, | That he hath breathed in my dishonour here' (2.1.53–6). To state that someone was lying was one of the gravest of offences – see 66–7 below.

57 Except for Unless.

58 Thou Thou (would).

59 ferret hunt down (*OED*, *v.* 3a).

60 crake call like a crow (traditionally a bird of cowardice).

62 forgèd … sake fabricated in order to misrepresent (and seem acceptable to others). See the similar use of 'colour' at 22.57 and line 80 below. Cf. *Sp. T.* 1.3.66: 'Under the colour of a duteous friend'.

63 gloss on better excuse for.

68 Puritan Member of a Protestant religious group that sought to remove formal elements, especially those seeming to align with Catholicism, from the Church of England, but more generally a 'person who practices or who is characterized by extreme strictness or austerity in religion, morals' (*OED*, *n.* A.2).

71 purgatory Space between heaven and hell for the dead to repent, a Catholic belief, and hence Gonorill accuses Cordella of opposite religious extremes in this speech.
76 toad Toads were proverbially loathsome in this period (Tilley T361).
82 You … of i.e., You owe us.
83 stayed waited.
91 betimes in good time, early.
92 bade asked.
103 gallants gentlemen (*OED*, gallant *n.* †2a); soldiers (†2b); **brawling** squabbling.
103 SD *both armies* The implication of this phrase is that the armies leave through different doors.

[Scene 31]
1 friends i.e., those on our side.
2 adverse part i.e., opposing army.

[Scene 32]
5 but only.

[Scene 33]
0 SD *sound victory* i.e., a triumphal flourish of trumpets.
10 scathe harm.
11 never-stained i.e., never tainted with dishonour.
14 grutch complain.
27 laid on fought, given blows.

THE COLLECTED WORKS OF THOMAS KYD VOLUME TWO

Arden of Faversham (1590) ed. Darren Freebury-Jones

Fair Em (1590) ed. Brian Vickers

I Henry VI (1592) ed. David Bevington and Brian Vickers

Edward III (1593) ed. David Bevington and Brian Vickers

Letters to Sir John Puckering (1593) ed. Rebekah Owens and Daniel Starza Smith

Cornelia (1594), ed. Adam Horsley and Lucy Rayfield

Studies in Renaissance Literature

ISSN 1465-6310

Studies in Renaissance Literature offers investigations of topics in English literature focussed in the sixteenth and seventeenth centuries; its scope extends from early Tudor writing, including works reflecting medieval concerns, to the Restoration period. Studies exploring the interplay between the literature of the English Renaissance and its cultural history are particularly welcomed.

Proposals or queries should be sent in the first instance to the editors, or to the publisher, at the addresses given below; all submissions receive prompt and informed consideration.

Professor Brooke Conti, Cleveland State University, English Department, Rhodes Tower, Cleveland, OH 44115, USA

Professor Jane Grogan, University College Dublin, School of English, Drama and Film, Newman Building, Belfield, Dublin 4, Ireland

Professor Ramona Wray, Queen's University Belfast, School of Arts, English and Languages, University Square, Belfast, BT7 1NN

Boydell & Brewer Limited, PO Box 9, Woodbridge, Suffolk, IP12 3DF

Previously published volumes in this series are listed below.

Studies in Renaissance Literature

Details of earlier volumes in the series can be found at
www.boydellandbrewer.com

Volume 20: *The Heroines of English Pastoral Romance*
Sue P. Starke

Volume 21: *Staging Islam in England: Drama and Culture, 1640–1685*
Matthew Birchwood

Volume 22: *Early Modern Tragicomedy*
edited by Subha Mukherji and Raphael Lyne

Volume 23: *Spenser's Legal Language: Law and Poetry in Early Modern England*
Andrew Zurcher

Volume 24: *George Gascoigne*
Gillian Austen

Volume 25: *Empire and Nation in Early English Renaissance Literature*
Stewart Mottram

Volume 26: *The English Clown Tradition from the Middle Ages to Shakespeare*
Robert Hornback

Volume 27: *Lord Henry Howard (1540–1614): an Elizabethan Life*
D. C. Andersson

Volume 28: *Marvell's Ambivalence: Religion and the Politics of Imagination in mid-seventeenth century England*
Takashi Yoshinaka

Volume 29: *Renaissance Historical Fiction: Sidney, Deloney, Nashe*
Alex Davis

Volume 30: *The Elizabethan Invention of Anglo-Saxon England*
Laurence Nowell, William Lambarde, and the Study of Old English
Rebecca Brackmann

Volume 31: *Pain and Compassion in Early Modern English Literature and Culture*
Jan Frans van Dijkhuizen

Volume 32: *Wyatt Abroad: Tudor Diplomacy and the Translation of Power*
William T. Rossiter

Volume 33: *Thomas Traherne and Seventeenth-Century Thought*
edited by Elizabeth S. Dodd and Cassandra Gorman

Volume 34: *The Poetry of Kissing in Early Modern Europe*
From the Catullan Revival to Secundus, Shakespeare and the English Cavaliers
Alex Wong

Volume 35: *George Lauder (1603–1670): Life and Writings*
Alasdair A. MacDonald

Volume 36: *Shakespeare's Ovid and the Spectre of the Medieval*
Lindsay Ann Reid

Volume 37: *Prodigality in Early Modern Drama*
Ezra Horbury

Volume 38: Poly-Olbion: *New Perspectives*
edited by Andrew McRae and Philip Schwyzer

Volume 39: *The Atom in Seventeenth-Century Poetry*
Cassandra Gorman

Volume 40: *Pity and Identity in the Age of Shakespeare*
Toria Johnson

Volume 41: *John Cruso of Norwich and Anglo-Dutch Literary Identity in the Seventeenth Century*
Christopher Joby

Volume 42: *Localizing Christopher Marlowe: His Life, Plays and Mythology, 1575–1593*
Arata Ide

Volume 43: *Picturing Divinity in John Donne's Writings*
Kirsten Stirling

Printed and bound by CPI Group (UK) Ltd, Croydon, CR0 4YY

28/03/2024

14476913-0001